S0-BZG-314

"The strength of the [Berlitz Travellers Guides] lies in remarks and recommendations by writers with a depth of knowledge about their subject."
—*Washington Times*

"The most readable of the current paperback lot."
—*New York Post*

"Highly recommended."
—*Library Journal*

"Very strong on atmosphere and insights into local culture for curious travellers."
—*Boston Herald*

"The [Berlitz Travellers Guides] eliminate cumbersome lists and provide reliable information about what is truly exciting and significant about a destination. . . . [They] also emphasize the spirit and underlying 'vibrations' of a region—historical, cultural, and social—that enhance a trip."
—*Retirement Life*

"Information without boredom. . . . Good clear maps and index."
—*The Sunday Sun* (Toronto)

CONTRIBUTORS

BARBARA COEYMAN HULTS, the author of a travel guide-book to Italy, has studied Italian civilization in Rome and has contributed articles to *Art & Antiques, Italy Italy,* and other magazines and newspapers. She has also written *Balloon,* a newsletter for travel fanatics, as well as a series of walking-tour tapes on several Italian cities. She travels in Italy five months a year and is the editorial consultant for this guide-book.

SIMON FINAZZI-WILLIAMS is a writer and poet. He lives on the shores of Lake Como and works as a translator and author for the Reader's Digest in Milan.

JOANNE HAHN has lived and studied in Italy and returns there regularly. A contributor to several magazines, she is coauthor of a travel guidebook to Italy.

LOUIS INTURRISI is a writer, journalist, and longtime resident of Rome. His articles on Italy appear regularly in the *New York Times,* the *International Herald Tribune,* and *Architectural Digest.*

PAOLO LANAPOPPI was born in Italy, studied in Venice and Padua, and currently lives in Venice. He frequently contributes articles to *Travel & Leisure* and other major magazines. For 12 years he was professor of Italian literature and civilization at Cornell, Vassar, and other universities in the United States. His biography of Mozart's librettist Lorenzo da Ponte was published in 1991.

BILL MARSANO travels regularly to Italy to study its wine and food and to visit his sprawling network of cousins. He has written two books and is the recipient of a Lowell Thomas Travel Writing Award for his article on the Columbus landfall controversy, which he wrote as a contributing editor of *Condé Nast Traveler* magazine.

MICHELE SCICOLONE contributes articles on travel and food to *Gourmet* magazine and to the *New York Times.* She is the author of *La Dolce Vita,* a book on Italian desserts, and of *The Antipasto Table.*

DAVID TABBAT lives in Milan, where he works as an Italian-language advertising copywriter. He is the author of various articles and translations dealing with the history of Italian art. A cellist with a graduate degree in music, he frequently performs as a chamber player.

ANNE MARSHALL ZWACK divides her time between Tuscany and Hungary. She has written extensively for magazines and for the travel section of the *New York Times,* and is now writing her first book, about her husband's family in Hungary.

THE BERLITZ
TRAVELLERS GUIDES

THE BERLITZ TRAVELLERS GUIDE TO NORTHERN ITALY
AND ROME

Second Edition

ALAN TUCKER
General Editor

BERLITZ PUBLISHING COMPANY, INC.
New York, New York

BERLITZ PUBLISHING COMPANY LTD.
Oxford, England

THE BERLITZ TRAVELLERS GUIDE
TO NORTHERN ITALY
Second Edition

First published as
The Berlitz Travellers Guide
to Northern Italy 1993

Berlitz Trademark Reg U.S. Patent and Trademark Office
and other countries—Marca Registrada

Published by Berlitz Publishing Company, Inc.
257 Park Avenue South, New York, New York 10010, U.S.A.

Distributed in the United States by
the Macmillan Publishing Group

Distributed elsewhere by Berlitz Publishing Company Ltd.
Berlitz House, Peterley Road, Horspath, Oxford OX4 2TX, England

ISBN 2-8315-1712-5
ISSN 1057-4654

Designed by Beth Tondreau Design
Cover design by Dan Miller Design
Cover photograph © Scott Barrow, Inc.
Maps by Nina Wallace
Illustrations by Bill Russell
Fact-checked in Italy by Iris Jones
Copyedited by Norma Frankel
Edited by Katherine Ness

Printed in the United States of America
1 3 5 7 9 10 8 6 4 2

THIS GUIDEBOOK

The Berlitz Travellers Guides are designed for experienced travellers in search of exceptional information that will enhance the enjoyment of the trips they take.

Where, for example, are the interesting, out-of-the-way, fun, charming, or romantic places to stay? The hotels described by our expert writers are some of the special places, in all price ranges except for the very lowest—not just the run-of-the-mill, heavily marketed places in advertised airline and travel-wholesaler packages.

We are *highly* selective in our choices of accommodations, concentrating on what our insider contributors think are the most interesting or rewarding places, and why. Readers who want to review exhaustive lists of hotel choices as well, and who feel they need detailed descriptions of each property, can supplement the *Berlitz Travellers Guide* with tourism industry publications or one of the many directory-type guidebooks on the market.

We indicate the approximate price level of each accommodation in our description of it (no indication means it is moderate in local, relative terms), and at the end of every chapter we supply more detailed hotel rates as well as contact information so that you can get precise, up-to-the-minute rates and make reservations.

The Berlitz Travellers Guide to Northern Italy and Rome highlights the more rewarding parts of Rome and northern Italy so that you can quickly and efficiently home in on a good itinerary.

Of course, this guidebook does far more than just help you choose a hotel and plan your trip. *The Berlitz Travellers Guide to Northern Italy and Rome* is designed for use *in* Italy. Our writers, each of whom is an experienced travel journalist who either lives in or regularly tours the city or region of northern Italy he or she covers, tell you what you really need to know, what you can't find out so easily on your own. They identify and describe the truly out-of-the-ordinary restaurants, shops, activities, and sights, and tell you the best way to "do" your destination.

Our writers are highly selective. They bring out the significance of the places they *do* cover, capturing the personality and the underlying cultural and historical resonances of a city or region—making clear its special appeal.

The second edition of *The Berlitz Travellers Guide to Northern Italy and Rome* is full of reliable information. We would like to know if you think we've left out some very special place. Although we make every effort to provide the most current information available about every destination described in this book, it is possible too that changes have occurred before you arrive. If you do have an experience that is contrary to what you were led to expect by our description, we would like to hear from you about it.

A guidebook is no substitute for common sense when you are travelling. Always pack the clothing, footwear, and other items appropriate for the destination, and make the necessary accommodation for such variables as altitude, weather, and local rules and customs. Of course, once on the scene you should avoid situations that are in your own judgment potentially hazardous, even if they have to do with something mentioned in a guidebook. Half the fun of travelling is exploring, but explore with care.

ALAN TUCKER
General Editor
Berlitz Travellers Guides

Root Publishing Company
350 West Hubbard Street
Suite 440
Chicago, Illinois 60610

CONTENTS

MAPS

THE
BERLITZ
TRAVELLERS
GUIDE TO
NORTHERN
ITALY

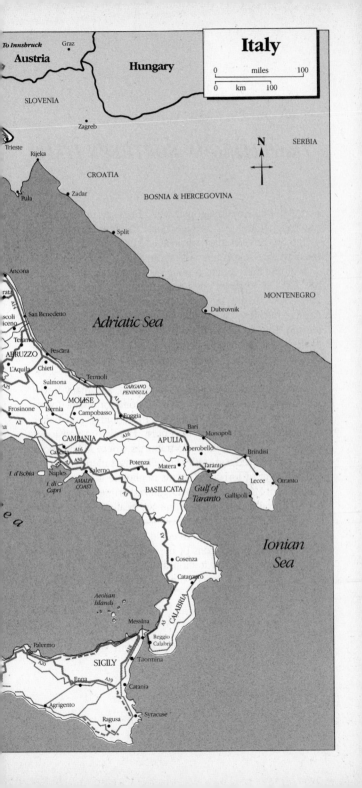

TRAVELLING IN NORTHERN ITALY

Reports of Italy's outrageously high prices are, unfortunately, not exaggerated. An average hotel room in a major city would be considered a bargain at US$125. A full-course meal in an average restaurant costs about $50.

Avoiding these prices is not easy, but neither is it impossible. Off-season travel costs less, of course. Remember that Italy's low season in major cities includes August, when regular business clients and European tourists are at the seaside. Tour operators list at reduced rates very good hotels in their off-season "independent packages." We have mentioned many lower-cost but charming hotels in each city section.

Staying outside the cities costs far less, and many towns are within a day-trip's distance from Rome or Milan. Towns provide a more personal view of the country, and better hospitality, and are usually less noisy. Family-run pensiones and hotels still abound, as do trattorias where Mama cooks while the beloved son smiles and dispenses menus.

The threat of terrorism seems negligible at present, despite recent Mafia bombings. Organized crime reaches tourists mostly through street criminals stealing for narcotics money, but rarely involves violence. Preventive measures usually work, as we've outlined in the "Safety" section of "Useful Facts" at the front of the book. Some attention to safety is necessary, but it should not ruin your enjoyment. Italy is still the country of the Renaissance. Thieves were abundant then too.

—*Barbara Coeyman Hults*

OVERVIEW

By Barbara Coeyman Hults

Barbara Coeyman Hults has lived, studied, and worked in Italy. Formerly the editor of Balloon, *a travel newsletter, she is the author of a travel guidebook on Italy and has written a series of walking-tour tapes on several Italian cities.*

Italy is an addiction.

The 19th-century English traveller was well aware of its power. Shelley, Keats, and Byron succumbed, and Browning cried, "Open my heart, and you will see graved inside of it, 'Italy.' " Perhaps there should be a sign at Rome's gates or Venice's lagoons advising visitors to abandon all hope of ever wanting to go anywhere else. Those who fall victim are condemned, like the ancient mariner, to collar other travellers who have known its pleasures: Are the azaleas in bloom on the Spanish Steps in Rome yet? Does the old man still cane chairs in the piazza every afternoon? Did you happen to see the dawn in Venice? Was it that blend of scarlet and shell pink? Were you in Tuscany when the grapes were being harvested?

But, you might ask, would these poets recognize Italy today? While it's true that this mobile century has provided its share of good things such as the automobile and the airplane, these same advantages have brought countless tourists (not just the elite of the poets' day) and clogged the new highways with polluting cars that sometimes pass unattractive recent housing developments and industries not mentioned in travel guides, including this one. There is far more than enough splendor to seek out; you'll easily avoid the rest.

Italy's problems are familiar to all modern countries, including a very unpoetic inflation rate and growing crime (theft). What the poets might notice with approval, however, is that the Italian economy now includes a sizable middle class, the ones who own first and second cars, unlike the semifeudal situation the poets observed, when low wages and class distinctions made travel a bargain for foreigners but kept goods out of the reach of most natives. Many of the privileges they enjoyed depended on an economy of wealthy landowners and poor peasants.

The tourist seeking a living Disneyland will be disappointed, but anyone who finds joy in fine art, cultural resonance in ancient stones, pleasure in delicious meals, and comfort in warm, responsive people will find a remarkable degree of all these things in 20th-century Italy.

The Geography of the North

Italy, we all know, is shaped like a delicate boot, with Sicily just off the toe. France, Switzerland, Austria, and Slovenia provide the northern political boundaries. The Alps turn into the Apennines, which follow the western part of the peninsula down its length. The eastern flatland ends in the marshy lagoons of Venice to the north, and beaches run down both coasts. Lakes dot the north above Milan: Como, Orta, Maggiore, Iseo, and Garda. The far northwest coast ends at the French border in an arc of Ligurian coast called the Italian Riviera.

Along their southwest boundaries, the industrialized north-central plains of Emilia and the farmlands of Romagna give over abruptly to the mountains of Tuscany, with Florence near its center. Umbria, between Tuscany and Rome's region of Lazio, follows ancient hills and valleys, and Abruzzo and Molise stretch from east of Rome to the Adriatic, rising at the center point to the Gran Sasso range, home to the highest peak of the Apennines. In the center of Lazio, on the west coast near the Tyrrhenian Sea, stands Rome, the Eternal City, to which all roads have led for 2,000 years—and which marks the southern boundary of our coverage of northern Italy.

Campania, south of Lazio, follows the beautiful rocky coast of Amalfi on the west side of Italy down to the toe of the boot, to Calabria's territory of mountains and lovely sea views. Eastward, the boot's instep is Basilicata, often neglected by travellers, partly because tourist facilities in its mountains and coastal villages are few. Its vineyards and olive groves, however, are beloved by those who take the time to know them. The high heel and spur of the boot are Apulia, the most industrially developed of the southern regions. Dramatic mountains cover its mystical northern

Gargano peninsula; in the south, the stunning rocky eastern coast continues around the tip to the lovely white-sand beaches and gentle harbors along the inner heel south of Taranto.

The island off the toe, Sicily, has a mountainous center yielding to plains, encircled with small cove beaches along the coast. The other major island, Sardinia, west of the mainland, is ruggedly mountainous at the center, while its coasts are rimmed with white-sand beaches.

The History of the North

Italy's geographical variety is only part of its interest, however. Add to that the different historical destinies of its regions and you have the beginning of the myriad permutations in the country. Italy's history is exceedingly complicated, for rare is the conqueror who did not see something of value here, whether in natural resources or in enticing plunder.

"Ancient Italy" traditionally begins about 20,000 B.C., although areas throughout the peninsula and Sicily were inhabited long before then. Among many central Italian tribes, the Etruscans—whose origins have not been determined—emerged victorious during the sixth century B.C., only to be defeated by Rome in 351 B.C.

From the eighth to the sixth century B.C., Greek and Phoenician traders were establishing trading ports in southern Italy, and soon they set up colonies as well. Tradition says that Rome was founded in 753 B.C. by Romulus and Remus, and this date, or at least that century, seems accurate, according to recent excavations.

The city's power grew, especially after kinship was abolished and Rome became a republic. Finally in 27 B.C., under Augustus, Rome became a full-fledged empire that ultimately stretched as far west as England, through North Africa, and east to Syria. Invasions of barbarians from the north began about the time of Marcus Aurelius, and by then the Roman empire was on the wane. When Constantine (whose Edict of Milan ended the persecution of the Christians) moved the capital to Constantinople, the handwriting on the wall was etched in stone.

During the Middle Ages the Germanic Ostrogoths ruled from Ravenna while the papacy grew in influence, laying the groundwork for the Papal States that would follow. This was largely the work of Pope Gregory the Great (590–604), whose strength of purpose helped the papacy emerge as a major power from the muddle of the Middle Ages. In the year 800 the pope crowned Charlemagne Holy Roman Emperor, after which papal power increased as its troubles multiplied. After Frederick Barbarossa was crowned emperor in 1155 war broke out between his supporters, the Ghibellines, and the pope's backers, the Guelphs. During this period the Normans established a successful kingdom in Sicily.

Renaissance princes and dukes struggled in the city-states that had evolved, but foreign domination soon grew and lasted for centuries as Spain, Austria, and France held the reins. The Spanish Hapsburgs were a dominating force in Italy in post-Renaissance years, until the War of Spanish Succession (1701–1713) ended with Austria in control. Napoléon briefly annexed large portions of Italy, breaking the Austrian hold and moving Italy forward as a modern state. After the Congress of Vienna in 1815 the years were filled with riots, protests, and finally revolution as Mazzini, the great political thinker, joined forces with the man of action, Garibaldi, and with the brilliant Cavour, who would forge the new republic to Verdi's accompaniment.

In 1860 the revolution began, and by 1870 Italy was an independent republic with a king. After the wars of the 20th century the king's popularity diminished, and the last king, Umberto II, died in Portugal in exile.

Italy, once Europe's whiz kid with an economy bulging with Made in Italy labels, has recently been seeing hard times. The prestigious label sells at an ever-increasing price, for residents as well as tourists. Public debt and labor costs have made Italy one of the most expensive countries in the world. Entering the Monetary System would mean that the old method of coping with debt—devaluing the lira—would no longer be possible. Revelations of countrywide embezzlement and protection rackets created a nervous backdrop for a weakening economy. The lira was devalued and Italy withdrew (at least temporarily) from dreams of entering the European Monetary System. National elections in 1992 brought a new coalition government without the Communist Party, once Europe's largest. No party, however, has been given a strong majority. Italians, like many Americans today, have little confidence in their government. The brutal car-bomb murder of the illustrious anti-Mafia judge Giuseppe Falcone, his wife, and their bodyguards in May 1992 plunged the country into despair.

Recent surprises include a low birth rate (the lowest in Europe) and a growing population over age 70, the result, many think, of the very healthy diet and active life Italians enjoy. TV and fast food have not overtaken their vitality—a permanent condition, one hopes.

The Traveller's Northern Italy

Rome, the seductive, infuriating colossus, smugly aware that everyone will go there sooner or later, makes few adjustments to visitors. The traffic is ghastly, its unmuffled noise and gassy fumes at horror-show proportions. But should you then avoid Rome? Of course not. (Just be careful crossing the street when you get there.) Here you participate in Roman life; you do as the Romans do and you find it exhilarating. Rome provides visitors with layer upon layer of history—turning a corner may call up a new age altogether. You'll find the ghosts of Roman emperors and Renaissance popes, lavish Baroque churches, prisons and palaces, piazzas unchanged from the Middle Ages, arbors to dine under, and the Tiber winding calmly past it all. Each age makes its presence known in Rome, bizarrely juxtaposed as in a Fellini circus. An unexpected bonus in recent years is the unveiling of the many handsomely restored monuments, the magnificent column of Trajan among them.

Lazio, the region surrounding Rome, is a place where Etruscan tombs, ancient Roman apartment houses, and Renaissance castles are silhouetted against the sea and the sky, and where shepherds still lead their flocks along the airport road. (The urban sprawl around Rome is best sped past—unless you're a Roman who finds the modern comforts in these often unattractive areas more livable than the dark and unheated palazzi so romantic to the visitor's eye.)

North of Lazio, **Umbria's** hills and frescoed monasteries evoke the region's mystical past. The town of Assisi is still enticing, despite the endless pilgrimages that march through its tiny, steep streets. Game and venison are the menu choices here, with wine from Orvieto, the town whose striped Duomo guards the mystery of Corpus Christi and looks out across those soft Umbrian hills. The **Marches** is a less-travelled region, giving it a special cachet, although Urbino and the Conero coast south of Ancona merit attention. Urbino's ducal palace of the Montefeltro family is one of the finest of Renaissance palaces, overlooking the gentle hills and fertile valleys.

Florence and its well-loved region, **Tuscany**, still represent the Renaissance, an age of inspired artists of indomitable spirit. Florence's incomparable wealth of aesthetic treasures is reassuringly unchanged, and now a car-free zone protects the visitor from the fumes of the traffic that has so plagued the city during recent years. Alas, the growing city that surrounds the historical center of Florence owes nothing to Renaissance planning and everything to an expansion caused by a diminishing agricultural economy and a growing number of foreign workers, as Italy, along with the rest of Europe, tries to accommodate the millions who want to immigrate. The most menial work is often done by foreigners, as it once was by emigrant Italians in other parts of the world.

Tuscany, lying northwest of Lazio, is at once golden fields and black-green cypresses defining hillside boundaries and the cities of Medieval and Renaissance Siena and even older Pisa, as well as ancient Etruscan sites. But there is also a Tuscan coastline 200 miles long, where the Argentario peninsula leads to Porto Ercole's expensive, glamorous coast and islands as well: Giannutri, whose sea depths reveal Roman galleons, and Elba ("Lucky Napoleon," wrote Dylan Thomas). Tuscany's Chianti is as pleasurable to see in the growing as it is to drink, and at Greve, for example, you'll taste the year's vintage accompanied by sausage cured on the ashes of a wood fire. You may want to stay on an estate and sample the land's bounty at close quarters.

The fertile plain of **Emilia-Romagna**, north across the Apennines from Tuscany, attracts lovers of food: truffles and porcini mushrooms, tortellini Bolognese, and *zampone* (pig's foot) *modenese*. Parma has French allure, with Parma ham and Parmigiano cheese thrown in for gastronomes and Verdi's various dwellings displayed for opera lovers. Bologna is a mixture of Medieval shadows and modern university life; Ferrara has splendid castles and Ravenna the soft gold of Byzantine mosaics.

Northeast of Emilia-Romagna is the **Veneto**, which claims the legendary **Venice** as one of its cities. The Veneto's plains are elegantly arrayed with Palladian villas, and the idyllic town of Asolo is a nice place to return to after a hard day's touring. Venice, the impossibly beautiful, is purely impossible when tourist crowds overrun its legendary canals. It's best to see this romantic city on breezy spring mornings when the wind whips the waves to whitecaps and jostles the gondolas at their moorings, but it is almost equally fascinating on winter days beneath a pearl-gray sky.

Is Venice sinking into the sea? Apparently. Is there sometimes an odor of aging algae in summer? Yes. Should you then snub the Queen of the Adriatic? That would be like avoiding spring because the earth is damp and earthworms might come out.

East of the Veneto, **Friuli–Venezia Giulia** rounds the top of the Adriatic Sea, stretching from the beaches at Lignano to **Trieste**, where James Joyce taught English and wrote in exile. North of the coastline, hills covered with vineyards (and farms producing the finest prosciutto) lead toward wooded, rocky mountains dotted with colorful, undiscovered villages—and the border with Austria.

North of the Veneto the Dolomite mountains and green pastures of **Trentino–Alto Adige** betray the nearness of Austria. The pristine towns and hamlets of this region offer facilities for hikers, skiers, and fishermen—an abundance of summer and winter pleasures in a dramatic landscape punctuated with medieval castles and churches.

The north-central region, **Lombardy**, is the richest in Italy, in finance, industry, and agriculture. Here you will find **Milan**, the sleek capital of Italian design and finance, proud of its accomplishments that have given the "Made in Italy" label precedence in the best of boutiques. The city's monuments to the arts—the Brera painting collections and the world-famous La Scala opera house in particular—keep the city high on artistic itineraries, and restaurants such as Gualtiero Marchesi keep gourmands stylishly thin with *ravioli aperti* (open-topped ravioli) and scallopine with sweet-and-sour sauce. Go to Milan in August, when everyone is gone and the vast city is quiet and pretty as a country town; many museums and restaurants stay open during the summer these days—for the convenience of visitors.

Lago di Como may be the lake best known for its beauty, but lesser-known **Lago d'Orta** and its town of San Giulio are so appealing that you may not want to move on to anywhere else at all. **Lago Maggiore** and its principal town of Stresa—from which the Isola Bella is an easy boat excursion away—and **Lago d'Iseo** and **Lago di Garda** farther east, are quiet places, provided you don't choose to travel here in the summer. You may want to stay at the lakes when visiting Milan, allowing yourself a city to explore by day and an expanse of blue to soften the night.

In the far northwest is the mountainous region of **Valle d'Aosta**, beloved of skiers and hikers. To its south, and to the west of Lombardy, is **Piedmont**, the region of the Nebbiolo grape, source of the Barolo and Barbaresco vintages—both of which have caused tasters to question France's primacy in wines. Piedmont's tables, laden with gnocchi, *fonduta* (fondue), *bollito misto* with *salsa verde* (boiled meat with a parsley-based sauce), and other passions of the gastronomic heart, lure many a hungry traveller. **Turin,** the often neglected capital of the region, is not industrialized at all at its center, as is often believed. Instead, this former capital of Italy stretches out in a handsome pattern of parks and palaces, arcades and notable museums—its Museo Egizio (Egyptian Museum) has few rivals. West of Turin, Sestriere and other resorts cater to skiers.

Liguria lies south of Piedmont along the Mediterranean, at the border of the French Riviera. Along the Italian Riviera we've singled out the Cinque Terre, where five little pastel-colored hamlets face the sea. Shelley lived nearby at Lerici, as did Byron (Shelley drowned offshore). At **Genoa** the summer of 1992 was festive, marking the 500th year since native son Christopher Columbus sailed west looking for India.

There is enough variety and pleasure in each of these regions to keep you coming back every year, as we think our descriptions will prove. Read on.

USEFUL FACTS

When to Go

Spring and fall (especially May, June, and October) are the ideal months—for climate, for flowers, and for lighter tourism and better prices. Summer is a cavalcade of tourists and winter is often drizzly. That said, both summer and winter have much to offer as well. Summer has the obvious advantages of beaches and water sports, and the unexpected discovery of cities when all the cars have gone. August is a wasteland, for all of Europe flees the cities, but that is when, ironically, they are at their most beautiful. Anna Magnani said she felt the old Rome only in August, when she could walk through the medievally dark streets that surround the Pantheon and hear the echo of her own footsteps. Trattorias are unrushed then, and life is slow. The downside of summer is the same as the upside: Everyone *has* left the cities, leaving many restaurants and shops closed, and those that remain open are filled with non-Italian faces for the most part. Museums, however, have recently realized that summer days are among their best attended, and they often stay open through August. Winter, too, has advantages, especially cultural: the opera, the theater, concert halls, and uncrowded museums. Because there are fewer tourists, there are fewer lines to wait in, restaurants are on their best behavior (in summer they sometimes think no one will know the difference if they take short cuts with the sauce), and the weather is often lovely—although showers and fog are common.

Entry Documents

Just a passport is necessary for travellers to Italy, or an identity card for citizens of the EC. Motorists need a driver's license and a civil-liability insurance policy if they rent a car (usually provided when the car is picked up; see "Renting a Car and Driving," below).

Arrival at Major Gateways by Air

Alitalia offers direct daily flights from New York to Rome and Milan. Alitalia also flies from Los Angeles, Chicago, Miami, and Boston direct to Milan, with a connection to Rome. If you will be going on to other destinations in Italy or elsewhere, Alitalia is the airline of choice at present, because of its excellent add-on plans. For example, with the "Visit Italy" program, those purchasing an Alitalia ticket from North America to Rome or Milan pay only $100 for a round-trip ticket to any additional Italian airport. (The cost would normally be double this or more.) The "Europlus" Plan offers a round-trip ticket to any city serviced by Alitalia in Europe or North Africa for $119 each way. Another package provides a railroad ticket to Florence for passengers arriving in Rome: nonstop rail service between the Alitalia terminal at Rome's Leonardo da Vinci Airport and Santa Maria Novella Station in Florence. Two trains daily in each direction are timed to meet Alitalia flights; travel time is about two and a half hours. The service is included in Alitalia's ticket price, which is comparable to or lower than other fares to Rome only. Passengers on other airlines can also use the airport train; the round-trip Rome–Florence fare is approximately $112.

All these special Alitalia tickets must be purchased in the United States or Canada when the transatlantic flight is booked.

As for North American carriers, new routes are added almost monthly, and only travel agents can stay up-to-the-minute. At present, TWA, Delta, American, Canadian Airlines International, and United have direct flights to Italy. Most flights from North America arrive in Italy during the morning, usually about 8:00 or 9:00. A good travel agent will work out the most convenient routing, by plane or train.

From London, Alitalia and some British carriers provide service to Rome, Milan, Bologna, Genoa, Pisa (for Florence), Turin, and Venice. Qantas and Alitalia fly from Sydney and Melbourne to Rome.

Rome's Leonardo da Vinci Airport at Fiumicino is an advantage to travellers who wish to continue on another flight. At Milan you frequently have to travel to Linate, the domestic airport, which entails several hours of in-transit time, although Malpensa, the international airport, now initiates more domestic flights than it used to.

Airport buses run to and from Milan at regular intervals; the terminus is at viale Luigi Sturzo near Stazione Porta Garibaldi. From there you can get a train, taxi, or public transportation—bus or Metropolitana (subway)—to your destination. The trip from the airport into Milan by taxi costs about 95,000 lire ($75).

Rome's principal airport, Leonardo da Vinci at Fiumicino, has undergone a transformation so glamorous that Clinique cosmetics has opened a boutique there, for a flying re-do. (Only a cosmetic surgeon in the wings is lacking.)

Added to this glamour is a shiny new train, ready to whiz you to the Eternal City. (The clumsy old airport bus to Stazione Termini of course has been banished. No style.)

Sounds celestial?

Not quite.

Unfortunately you can't get from the airport luggage carousel to the train (or vice versa) if you need a luggage cart, as many international, and certainly intercontinental, passengers do. An escalator between airport and train prohibits carts, and lines can be long at the single elevator.

Next, there are the two new station stops in Rome: The first incoming stop, Trastevere, is convenient only for those with room reservations at the Vatican; the second, Stazione Ostienze, was apparently chosen for those who wish to see Keats's grave immediately upon arrival. There is public transportation at these stops, but you must know which city bus to take, where it stops, and where to buy bus tickets before getting on. The Piramide Metro stop is within walking distance of Ostiense, for those without luggage. Taxis may be waiting at the station if it isn't raining.

Bureaucratic irascibility worthy of Tiberius is behind this state of transit—or is it the taxi union? In any case, at present the only way to enter the Eternal City with luggage is by taxi: about 60,000 lire ($50). However, many independent air and hotel packages offer transfers from airport to hotel. This is a decided advantage.

When you are making your plans, also consider charter flights. Many charter-flight organizations at present use regularly scheduled airlines, and reserved seats can be arranged in advance. You'll probably be the one in the center if the plane is crowded, however, because the higher-paying passengers will of course get the more desirable aisle or window seats. The Sunday editions of major city newspapers, including the *Los Angeles Times, New York Times,* and *Toronto Sun,* run ads regularly for special fares. In London, *Time Out* and the *Times* run similar ads.

Specialized travel agencies, such as Italy for Less (Tel: 800-794-8259 or 212-599-0577; Fax: 212-599-3288), will find the most economical fares. Summer and holiday fares are usually not discounted by the airlines. Other discounters are Access International (Tel: 212-465-0707) and TFI Tours International in New York (Tel: 212-736-1140), and Council Charter in New York (Tel: 212-254-2525) and Los Angeles (Tel: 213-208-3551).

Porters

A lack of porters is a chronic problem in Italy. Do not take more than you can carry unless you'll be renting a car at the airport or intend to rely on taxis. Most railway stations are cleverly designed with long stairways to the tracks, rendering even portable luggage carts useless.

Travelling Around by Air

Italy's domestic airlines are often attractively priced for weekend packages under the Nastro Verde (Green Ribbon) plan: You must leave and return on specific days and hours, which are different for each city but generally cover the weekend period. These can be purchased only in Italy, however, at any travel agent or Alitalia office. (All domestic airlines are owned by Alitalia.)

In Rome, call Skyreps for discounted European and worldwide fares: via Calabria 17, Tel: (06) 488-4208. Many travel agents sell these tickets as well.

If making plans for railroad or air travel, make sure no strike (*sciopero*) is planned for your day of departure. Strikes are announced in the newspaper, and your hotel *portiere* should be able to forewarn you if you explain your plans.

Travelling Around by Train

Italy's rail service is excellent, and improving. The Milan–Rome express flashes from point to point in four hours, and Florence to Rome requires only two hours, station to station. The glamorous ETR 450 first-class-only train connects Rome and Milan, via Bologna and Florence, in 5½ hours; Rome and Venice, via Florence, Bologna, and Padua, in 4 hours 10 minutes. Reservations are required. (See also Alitalia's plane/train ticket, under "Arrival at Major Gateways," above.)

Before leaving on the trip, check with your travel agent for the numerous train passes available, each with different advantages. For example, the Kilometric Ticket costs about

$238 first class and $140 second class. Valid for two months, it permits 20 trips or a total of 1,875 miles. As many as five people, even unrelated, may travel together on it. If you are travelling elsewhere in Europe, the Eurailpass is also available. Apart from these passes, which should be purchased before departure if possible (some *must* be bought in North America), youth, senior, and family passes are also sold at special rates.

Almost every city you will want to visit, large or small, has train service. For those that don't, bus connections are generally available though probably less frequent. If you are travelling any distance, ask about the InterCity trains, which are nonstop, at least between important cities on a given route. They run from Sicily to Venice or Genoa. Always reserve a seat if possible, especially on InterCity trains. They are heavily used by Italians as well as foreigners, midweek and midday as well as peak seasons. The four-hour Rome–Milan train, the InterCity "Nonstop," *must* be reserved, as must several others. It's worth the extra charge (no charge if you buy the special passes discussed above). Sleeping cars are available on long-distance trains and require supplements and reservations. For information, ask your travel agent.

Note: Italy's previously casual railroad officialdom has tightened up on its rules. Don't sit in first class without a first-class ticket; make sure the return portion of your round-trip ticket is stamped before you board; and don't assume you can buy a ticket on the train. All of these once-common practices (generally methods of avoiding lines and overcrowding) can incur a costly fine.

Travelling Around by Bus

Bus travel can best be arranged through travel agents. American Express, Italiatours, Central Holiday, and TWA offer good programs, catering to independent travellers as well as groups. Regional bus companies vary from very comfortable, and frequently faster than local trains, to the sardine-can variety. Travel agents and tourist offices in Italy are your best sources of information.

By Taxi

Metered yellow cabs (the only ones you want) usually line up at cab stands, to be picked up there or telephoned. In most cities they don't pick up en route. If you call a taxi, the meter starts when and where he does. If you can't find a cab, go into a hotel or bar and ask whether they will call one for you. It's worth a tip.

Renting a Car and Driving

Although you'll want a car in the countryside to follow your inclinations to turreted hill towns and sea resorts, driving in any of the major cities is far more pain than pleasure. Congestion, speedway-style driving (Rome), hard-to-find parking, and auto theft in some cities are a few of the reasons you will be happier parking at the hotel or a good lot and walking or taking taxis or public transport.

All you will need to drive in Italy is a valid license from your own country. Major car-rental companies in Italy are Maiellano, Hertz, Avis, Budget, National (called Europcar in Europe), and Dollar Rent a Car (affiliated with InterRent). The smallest compact will probably be too small, so opt for at least the next size up. You may request an automatic (usually more than double the price of a standard, as is air-conditioning), but learn a bit about shifting gears just in case. Car rentals are subject to an 18 percent tax, higher for luxury cars.

Before leaving on the trip, investigate with your travel agent the cost of fly-drive programs, which are often less expensive (don't ask for the smallest car unless you're under four feet tall), and also about special promotional offers and independent packages, such as those that TWA, Alitalia's Italiatours, and CIT offer, which include a choice of hotels without the disadvantages of group travel.

Insurance for all vehicles is compulsory in Italy. A Green Card (*Carta Verde*) or Frontier Insurance, valid for 15, 30, or 45 days, should be issued to cover your car at the Italian border or by the rental company. Access America provides a health and theft policy that includes collision damage. Many automobile and health insurance policies cover the same emergencies.

Telephoning

The international telephone country code for Italy is 39. When telephoning from outside Italy, omit the zero from the local area codes. (For example, to call Rome from the United States, dial 011-39-6 and then the number.)

Plastic is the answer if you'll be using the telephone frequently, for calls within the country or abroad. For overseas calls, use your telephone card number. You can now reach an American operator to call collect or to use your telephone credit card: For AT&T dial 172-1011, for MCI 172-1022, and for Sprint 172-1877. You need a coin (200 lire) to activate the number. For other international operator assistance, dial 170 for non-European countries and 15 for Europe and Mediterranean countries. To dial directly (hotels charge a huge tax for this): dial 00-1 for the United States and Canada, 44 for the U.K., 61 for Australia, 64 for New Zealand, and then the number. (New information is issued regularly from U.S. telephone companies; check with yours before you leave for the best way to phone home.)

To call within Italy, a SIP (Italian telephone company) card (*scheda*) is a great help, as Italian coins are heavy and phone calls require a lot of them. Buy SIP cards in denominations of 5,000 or 10,000 lire at SIP offices, airports, railroad stations, newspaper stands, or tobacconists. (Buy them when you are in a major urban area; smaller towns are unlikely to have them.) The card is inserted in the phone box, and its remaining value is shown on a screen. An alternative is to use the telephone with a meter (*telefono a scatto*), which each town has in a bar (café) if you ask around; you pay the proprietor when you're through.

Regular calls within the same city cost 200 lire; tokens (*gettone*) are required less frequently these days, but it helps to keep a few with you.

In Rome, the main telephone center is located in piazza San Silvestro.

The Post

Mail service in Italy is rotten. Use the telephone or fax whenever feasible. Urgent letters should be sent by DHL, UPS, or another guaranteed service. When in Rome, try to do most of your mailing from the Vatican, which has its own—excellent—mail service. (Italian stamps are not valid at the Vatican.)

Local Time

Italy is six hours ahead of Eastern Standard Time, one hour ahead of Greenwich Mean Time, and nine hours behind Sydney. During the changeover to and from daylight saving time there are a few days when Italy is an extra hour ahead or behind, so double-check relevant hours near that period.

Electric Current

Italian current is 220 volts, 50 cycles; a converter/adapter is necessary for North American appliances. Most hardware stores, electronics outlets, and computer dealers in this country have them.

Currency

The monetary unit is the Italian *lira,* plural *lire,* written Ł. Notes are issued in denominations of 1,000; 2,000; 5,000; 10,000; 20,000; 50,000; and 100,000 lire. Coins are 10 (rare); 20 (rare); 50; 100; 200; and 500 lire. The exchange rate is subject to daily change; check with banks and daily newspapers for the current rates. As of this writing, lira is valued at about 1,250 to the U.S. dollar, 990 to the Canadian dollar, 2,200 to the British pound, and 880 to the Australian dollar. On arrival at Rome's Fiumicino airport, you can change money just after clearing passport control, before claiming your luggage.

Traveller's checks are changed in banks at (usually) better rates than elsewhere. American Express offices in Rome, Milan, Florence, and Venice cash personal checks for members carrying their cards. Few hotels will accept a personal check, and some do not accept credit cards.

Cambio (exchange) offices vary in rates. Check the posted sign and ask about the commission charged.

Many banks throughout Italy give Visa and MasterCard cardholders cash advances. MasterCard advances are made in banks with Eurocard ("EC") stickers on the door. (Eurocard is equivalent to MasterCard for other purposes as well.) Try to obtain such an advance in larger cities, as not all small towns are prepared for this service and you may have to travel to ten banks, waving your card, to find out whether any do. (An advance is an *anticipo*.)

Take your cash machine ID number with you, and ask your credit card company for a list of their automated teller machines in Italy.

Business Hours

Learning Italian business hours would require a university course. They vary from region to region, with the North adhering in general to more European hours and the South keeping the siesta tradition of closing for most of the afternoon and reopening in the evening; "normal" business hours in the South would be from 9:00 A.M. to 1:00 P.M. and 4:00 P.M. to 8:00 P.M. Many shops are closed Monday mornings. Banks are open usually from 8:30 A.M. to 1:30 P.M. and sometimes from 3:00 or 3:30 P.M. to 4:00 or 4:30 P.M., but individual differences require that you double-check. Exchanges (*cambio*) keep store hours. Local post offices are open from 8:00 A.M. to 2:00 P.M., and the central office is usually open late in the evening in large cities. Barbers open from 8:00 A.M. to 1:00 P.M. and 4:00 P.M. to 8:00 P.M. and are closed Sunday afternoons and Mondays. Women's hairdressers are open 8:00 A.M. to 8:00 P.M., but most close all day Sundays and Mondays.

Museum and Church Hours. State museums are open mornings all week but close on Mondays. Double-check the specific museum you want to visit before setting out. Churches that are open to the public at specific hours are usually open mornings only, although some open afternoons as well. The dress code for churches is: no bare shoulders or bare legs, for men or women. Many churches require a 100 or 200 lire coin in the light box to illuminate certain dark chapels or paintings. Keep a supply, preferably in a tube such as those used for camera film; Italian coins are large and heavy.

Holidays

Offices and shops in Italy are closed on the following dates: January 1 (New Year's Day); January 6 (Epiphany); Easter Monday; April 25 (Liberation Day); May 1 (Labor Day); August 15 (Assumption of the Virgin); November 1 (All Saints Day); December 8 (Day of the Immaculate Conception); December 25 (Christmas Day); December 26 (Saint Stephen).

Banks, offices, and shops may also be closed for local feast days, such as April 25 in Venice (Saint Mark), October 4 in Bologna (Saint Petronio), June 29 in Rome (Saints Peter and Paul), and June 24 in Florence, Genoa, and Turin (St. John the Baptist). While you might not be able to do any banking that day, these holidays are often colorful and festive, and the celebrations, especially in the smaller towns, are worth seeking out.

Note: Beware of *ponte* (bridge) weekends—the three-day weekends that include a holiday, when banking and other services will be closed. Remember that on Labor Day, May 1, absolutely *everything* in Rome and many other cities closes. This means the bus and subway lines as well, and taxis are far from plentiful. Few restaurants are open, but hotel restaurants and a few others will keep you from starving.

When banks are closed, you can change money in an emergency at the airport or railroad station or, with a higher service charge, at your hotel.

Safety

A great many problems are easily solved by purchasing or making a money belt or a small undercover silk or cotton pouch. Carry a credit card and enough cash for the day. Small towns are far safer (from thieves) than cities; and northern cities, with the exception of Milan and Turin, are safer than those in the south, including Rome, where thievery is a major problem at present. Be sure your homeowner's or renter's policy covers your valuables when travelling. Many do.

Keep a list of all important document, credit card, and

traveller's check numbers separate from those items. Or leave the numbers with someone at home whom you can call in case of theft.

If you *must* transport valuables, do so in a plain plastic shopping bag, or one from Upim or Standa, Italy's five-and-dimes. Cameras are easily cut off if you wear them around your neck. Pickpockets thrive in buses (in Rome the No. 64, which goes to and from the Vatican, is notorious) and other crowded areas. Gypsy children (with parental supervision) are among the most obvious; don't read any cardboard signs they put in front of you or your wallet will disappear. They normally work the railroad station areas, among others. Vespa-riding thieves, boys or girls, grab shoulder bags. The final word: Don't leave your valuables unguarded, even in St. Peter's.

The Emergency phone number throughout Italy is 115. For an ambulance, call 118. (Foreigners are not charged for emergency care.)

Restaurants

Eating out in Italy, even in the out-of-the-way places, can be an expensive proposition. To avoid unpleasant surprises—and to alert you to unusually inexpensive options—we have tried to indicate the general, relative cost of a meal (first course, second course, dessert, and house wine) at the restaurants we describe. Any meal that comes in under 35,000 lire is inexpensive; from 35,000 to 50,000 lire we consider moderate. Most restaurants are in this category, and whenever we don't mention the price range you can assume it's moderate. When the prices move from 50,000 to 100,000 lire, it's definitely expensive; and over 100,000 lire is devil-may-care territory. All restaurants charge a minimal cover charge, from 1,000 to 4,000 lire at inexpensive restaurants, and on up according to the menu prices.

All restaurants are required by Italian tax law to issue a *ricevuta fiscale,* a computerized cash-register receipt that you must carry with you upon leaving. You can be fined if you don't have it.

Day Hotels

Many services are offered by day hotels (*alberghi diurnali*), which are generally located near the main railroad stations. They are handy for day-trippers, providing baths, showers, barbers, hairdressers, shoeshines, dry cleaning, telephone, baggage checking, writing rooms, and private rooms for brief rest periods (overnight stays are not permitted). Information desks in railroad stations or airports can tell you where day hotels are located. Usually signs indicating "diur-nali" are clearly posted.

Hotels

Hotels are awarded stars by the government on the basis of amenities. If you don't need a television or a swimming pool, a deluxe hotel may not be required. (Deluxe hotels charge 19 percent IVA [value added] tax; others charge 9 percent.)

Ask your travel agent about independent packages, which often reduce hotel charges considerably.

The *pensione,* officially, is no more. They are categorized as hotels now. Some "hotels," therefore, will be located on a separate floor of a building. (The name "pensione" has been retained by some hotels.)

Motels

If you don't require traditional charm, Italian motels are excellent, and some have very good restaurants. AGIP and ACI are the organizations that operate motels, which are found near the main highways. (See the Tourist Office information booklet, below, for a listing.)

Youth Hostels

For a listing, see the Tourist Office information booklet, below, or contact the Associazione Italiana Alberghi per la Gioventù, via Cavour 44, 00184 Rome; Tel: (06) 46-23-42; Fax: (06) 47-41-26.

Country Living

A delightful way to see Italy is through the Agriturist organization, which arranges for stays in country houses that range from beautifully groomed villas and ancient castles to rough-and-ready farms. At present some Agriturist offices are not set up for English-speaking people, but if you can communicate in Italian, do write or call. The main office in Rome is located at corso Vittorio Emanuele 101, 00186 Rome; Tel: (06) 651-23-42. There are many individual provincial offices also. Their addresses can be obtained from the Italian Tourist Office (see the booklet listed below) or the main Agriturist office. The booklets *Guida dell'Ospitalità Rurale* and *Vacanze e Natura,* both published by Agriturist, list farms with descriptions and pictures.

Campgrounds and Mountain Cabins

More than 1,700 official campgrounds are in operation in Italy, varying from the simple to the well equipped, some with cottages. Write or call the Tourist Office (see below) for a current directory.

Longer Visits
If you are staying in one city for a week or longer, your best bet may be a *residence,* a hotel apartment that enables you to have your own living room and kitchen, usually for less than the price of a hotel room for that period. Many hotels have suites that are rented on a weekly or monthly basis as well. Contact the Italian State Tourist Office or local tourist authorities for a list of residences; in Rome, the Tourist Office booklet *Here Is Rome* lists residences there.

Apartments and houses can be rented in Italy through offices called Immobiliari, listed in the Yellow Pages. In Rome the newsletter *Wanted in Rome,* available at the Lion Bookstore (via Condotti 181), and at major newsstands, runs classified ads for those seeking and offering rentals in the city and throughout the country.

Many U.S. and British agencies handle villa and apartment rentals. The Italian Tourist Office lists a number of these (see below). This can be a great lira saver and a nice way to feel part of a community.

Cooking Classes
The ever-growing interest in Italian *cucina* has spawned a number of excellent cooking schools. These classes offer a long-lasting souvenir of your trip.

Giuliano Bugialli's Cooking in Florence. Bugialli's professional kitchen in Florence is the usual site of classes, although he also organizes trips to other regions. His books include *The Fine Art of Italian Cooking* and *Foods of Italy.* Contact him at P.O. Box 1650, Canal Street Station, New York, NY 10013; Tel: (212) 966-5325; Fax: (212) 226-0601.

Marcella Hazan, author of the best-selling *Classic Italian Cookbook* and *Marcella's Italian Kitchen,* conducts her classes in Venice. Information is available from Hazan Classics, P.O. Box 285, Circleville, NY 10919; Tel: (914) 692-7104; Fax: (914) 692-2659.

Lorenza de' Medici's Tuscan Cooking School, at her comfortable villa near Siena, brings to life the pages of her beautiful book *The Renaissance of Italian Cooking.* Contact Judy Terrell at (214) 542-1530.

Tourist Offices
Don't leave home without the booklet "General Information for Travelers in Italy," published annually by the Italian State Tourist Office. Major offices are located at:

630 Fifth Avenue, New York, NY 10111; Tel: (212) 245-4822; Fax: (212) 586-9249.

500 North Michigan Avenue, Chicago, IL 60611; Tel: (312) 644-0990; Fax: (312) 644-3019.

12400 Wilshire Boulevard, Suite 550, Los Angeles, CA 90025; Tel: (310) 820-0098.

1 Place Ville Marie, Suite 1914, Montreal, Quebec H3B 3M9, Canada; Tel: (514) 866-7667; Fax: (514) 392-1429.

1 Princes Street, London WIR 8AY, England; Tel: (0441) 408-12-54; Fax: (0441) 493-6695.

BIBLIOGRAPHY

JAMES S. ACKERMAN, *Palladio*. A scholarly introduction to the most imitated architect in the world.

HAROLD ACTON, *The Last Medici*. Melancholy, irony, and sympathy in equal parts, for a fascinating account of the gradual guttering out of a once brilliant family.

MICHAEL ADAMS, *Umbria*. One of the best books about the region.

BURTON ANDERSON, *Vino: The Wines and Winemakers of Italy*. Even though it was published in 1980, it is still the best book on its subject—and with interesting asides on food, too—covering all 20 regions of the country.

VERNON BARTLETT, *Introduction to Italy*. An amusing and unusually comprehensive overview of the country's history from ancient times to the present day.

LUIGI BARZINI, *The Italians*. Dr. Barzini explains his countrymen, with wit and knowledge based on deep affection.

JAMES BECK, *Italian Renaissance Painting*. A comprehensive and readable survey of one of the most important aspects of Western civilization.

BERNARD BERENSON, *Italian Pictures of the Renaissance*. One of the essential guides to Renaissance art.

————, *The Passionate Sightseer*. Illustrated diaries of this essential art historian.

EVE BOORSOOK, *Companion Guide to Florence*. An excellent, detailed guide to the city.

GENE A. BRUCKER, *Renaissance Florence*. An excellent one-volume survey of the social, political, and economic history.

JACOB BURCKHARDT, *Civilization of the Renaissance in Italy*. Remains a classic work on that period, though it represents a somewhat old-fashioned type of history.

————, *At the Court of the Borgia*. The days of Pope Alexander VI (father of Cesare and Lucrezia).

CHARLES BURNEY, *Music, Men, and Manners in France and Italy 1770*. Burney's account of his travels is one of the classics of the history of music.

BALDASSARE CASTIGLIONE, *The Book of the Courtier*. An eyewitness account of one of the smaller ducal courts of the Renaissance and a penetrating excursion into Renaissance thought.

BENVENUTO CELLINI, *The Life of Benvenuto Cellini*. One of the most fascinating autobiographies; Renaissance truth is as interesting as Renaissance fiction.

EDWARD CHANEY, *Florence: A Traveller's Companion*. Sites in the Tuscan capital as seen by writers throughout the centuries.

ELEANOR CLARK, *Rome and a Villa*. A novelist's portrait of the capital.

TOBY COLE, ED., *Florence: A Traveler's Anthology* and *Venice: A Portable Reader*. Both are compilations of literary depictions.

DANTE ALIGHIERI, *Divine Comedy*. Heaven, Purgatory, and Hell, peopled with the author's candidates for each.

CHARLES DICKENS, *Pictures from Italy*. Evocative portraits of scenes encountered.

UMBERTO ECO, *The Name of the Rose*. An intriguing novel set in the time of the Avignon papacy.

CAROL FIELD, *Celebrating Italy*. More than a cookbook, this sensitive and highly readable volume is an exciting adventure into the heart of Italy through its many legends, feasts, food, and mysteries.

E. M. FORSTER, *A Room with a View*. Florence as a setting for personal revelations.

SIDNEY J. FREEDBERG, *Painting of the High Renaissance in Rome and Florence*. The two volumes of this history by the former Harvard professor are as highly personal as they are scholarly, the prose rising at times to near-poetic vividness.

EDWARD GIBBON, *The Decline and Fall of the Roman Empire* (1776–1788). It is not commonly known that this classic work—hard to find in an unabridged edition—ends with the 15th century, not the 5th, and so has much discussion of the Visigoths, Byzantines, Arabs, Carolingians, Lombards, and other peoples who figured in the transition from Augustus to the early Renaissance. Gibbon—still—should be read by anyone interested in Italy.

JOHANN WOLFGANG VON GOETHE, *Italian Journey.* One of the most important Italian journals of its time.

RONA GOFFEN, *Piety and Patronage in Renaissance Venice.* An extraordinary close-up study of the specific dynastic and political purposes behind the masterpieces by Bellini, Titian, and others in the Venetian church of the Frari.

ROBERT GRAVES, *I, Claudius.* An imagined autobiography by the classical poet and translator.

JULIEN GREEN, *God's Fool: The Life and Times of St. Francis of Assisi.* A loving and sensitive account of the saint and his contemporaries.

FERDINAND GREGOROVIUS, *Lucrezia Borgia.* A biography of Lucrezia, her family, and the Renaissance. Indispensable.

PETER GUNN, *A Concise History of Italy.* True to its title.

AUGUSTUS HARE, *Augustus Hare in Italy.* A compilation of the author's travel writings in turn-of-the-century Italy.

BARBARA GRIZZUTI HARRISON, *Italian Days.* A noted essayist and fiction writer takes us on her personal journey through the country of her ancestors and rewards us with an affectionate but razor-sharp view of everything from history and politics to food and local lore.

HOWARD HIBBARD, *Bernini; Michelangelo;* and *Caravaggio.* Biographies of the artists by one of the most respected art historians.

PAUL HILLS, *The Light of Early Italian Painting.* This recent book is that rarity, art history capable of an immediate and powerful impact on the reader's visual perceptions.

PAUL HOFMANN, *O Vatican! A Slightly Wicked View of the Holy See.* An insider's appreciation.

————, *Rome: The Sweet Tempestuous Life.* Sketches of all aspects of life in the Eternal City.

————, *That Fine Italian Hand.* A revealing, shrewd, and amusing study of the Italian character: at work (or avoiding it), within the family (including the Mafia), always enjoying life.

HUGH HONOUR, *The Companion Guide to Venice.* The author, an English art historian, takes us through Venice in the company of the distinguished foreign visitors who have preceded us, from Montaigne and Walpole to Ruskin, Henry James, and Proust; their reactions provide a counterpoint to the pictures and buildings.

DEBORAH HOWARD, *The Architectural History of Venice.* A solid, readable one-volume account, with useful illustrations.

HENRY JAMES, *Italian Hours.* His love affair with Italy. "At last—for the first time—I live!" he wrote.

WERNER KERNER, *The Etruscans.* A scholarly look, with illustrations.

D. H. LAWRENCE, *Etruscan Places* and *Twilight in Italy.* Two travel journals written with the Lawrencian passion.

GIULIO LORENZETTI, *Venice and Its Lagoon.* The wonderfully detailed guide in translation; the bible of Venetian art historians.

NICCOLO MACHIAVELLI, *The Prince.* Biography of the Renaissance as seen by a major player.

GEORGINA MASSON, *The Companion Guide to Rome.* One of the best guides to Rome, divided by neighborhoods.

———, *Frederick II of Hohenstaufen.* A fine biography worth searching for.

———, *Italian Villas and Palaces.* A picture book full of good information.

MARY MCCARTHY, *The Stones of Florence* and *Venice Observed.* Books that have lost nothing through time. Essential.

AUBREY MENEN, *Speaking the Language Like a Native.* Lightness of touch and modesty of scale by no means preclude serious insight in this witty volume of social sketches by the Anglo-Indian-Irish writer, a long-time resident of Rome.

MICHEL DE MONTAIGNE, *Travel Journal.* The 16th-century essayist's Renaissance insights into church, state, tepid baths, and tough crayfish.

CHARLES DE SECONDAT, BARON DE MONTESQUIEU, *Considerations on the Grandeur and Decadence of the Romans* (1734). Published 42 years before Gibbon's *Decline and Fall,* Montesquieu's commentary focuses on the ancient Roman republican virtues and the institutions behind them—and of course on how and why they weakened, with the well-known result.

ALBERTO MORAVIA, *The Woman of Rome*. A novel of a prostitute under Fascism. Moravia's later works usually show Rome's bourgeoisie at calculated play.

JAN MORRIS, *The Venetian Empire*. An expanded look at Venice.

———, *The World of Venice*. Amusing and insightful impressions by one of the best writers on travel.

H. V. MORTON, *A Traveler in Italy* and *A Traveler in Rome*. Both are filled with the lore and musings of the beloved tale-teller.

PETER AND LINDA MURRAY, *The Architecture of the Italian Renaissance*. Not every fact here *is* a fact, but the writing is clear, the illustrations judiciously chosen, and the book probably the best short introduction to the subject for the general reader.

WILLIAM MURRAY, *The Last Italian: Portrait of a People*. An updated variation on Barzini's *The Italians,* written by a resident foreigner.

JOHN JULIUS NORWICH, *A History of Venice*. An exhaustive study of La Serenissima.

———, *The Italians: History, Art and the Genius of a People*. A comprehensive cultural history.

IRIS ORIGO, *The Merchant of Prato*. Essential reading about the birth of modern mercantilism—whether or not you go to Prato.

AENEAS SYLVIUS PICCOLOMINI (Pope Pius II), *Memoirs of a Renaissance Pope*. Classical humanism and backstage realpolitik blend in unexpected ways in this fascinating autobiography of the 15th-century Tuscan nobleman and pontiff.

GEORGE PILLEMENT, *Unknown Italy*. Up-to-date and off the beaten track, with a focus on architecture.

PLINY THE YOUNGER, *Letters*. Those that deal with his uncle's death at Vesuvius are riveting.

JOHN POPE-HENNESSY, *Italian Gothic Sculpture; Italian Renaissance Sculpture;* and *Italian High Renaissance and Baroque Sculpture*. These standard surveys distill the insights of one of the greatest connoisseurs in history. A straightforward main text is accompanied by informative appendices to each volume.

FREDERICK WILLIAM ROLFE ("Baron Corvo"), *The Desire and Pursuit of the Whole*. This mannered *roman à clef* is not just the paranoid fantasy of an aging pederast; it's also the most vivid evocation in existence of the genteelly "aesthetic" Anglo-American expatriate community in Venice just after the turn of the century.

WAVERLEY ROOT, *The Food of Italy*. Anecdotes and a pleasurable introduction to the country's food and wine.

JOHN RUSKIN, *The Stones of Venice*. The classic appraisal of the city's art history.

KATE SIMON, *Italy: The Places In Between* and *Rome: Places and Pleasures*. Both are full of insightful observations.

D. MACK SMITH, *Cavour and Garibaldi 1860*. The definitive English-language study of the Risorgimento.

WILLIAM JAY SMITH and DANA GIOIA, EDS., *Poems From Italy*. Almost 800 years of Italian poetry in parallel text form.

LAURENCE STERNE, *A Sentimental Journey Through France and Italy*. Musings on the Continent by the 18th century's top wit.

ALEXANDER STILLE, *Benevolence and Betrayal*. An illuminating and deeply moving account of the ordeal of five Italian Jewish families during the Fascist period.

ADRIAN STOKES, *The Stones of Rimini* and *The Quattro Cento*. Elaborately wrought, powerfully evocative travel writing-cum-criticism (of art and of life). The scholarship on which the English writer pinned his theories is dated beyond repair, but the unique sensibility and tone of voice remain fresh and stimulating.

IRVING STONE, *The Agony and the Ecstasy*. An evocative if fictionalized portrait of Michelangelo.

SUETONIUS, *The Twelve Caesars*. He told what he knew and didn't know with great candor.

ITALO SVEVO, *A Life (Trieste)*. An antihero in turn-of-the-century Trieste.

RACHEL ANNAND TAYLOR, *Invitation to Renaissance Italy*. A vivid and highly entertaining account of the Renaissance and its major players and themes, forcing us to reconsider some strongly held notions of those fluid times.

LIONETTO TINTORI AND MILLARD MEISS, *The Painting of the Life of Saint Francis in Assisi*. A unique study of the physical, day-by-day process by which a great fresco cycle came into being.

GIORGIO VASARI, *The Lives of the Artists*. The life and times of the Renaissance masters; gives a sense of how they were judged by their peers.

GIUSEPPE VERDI. *Letters of Giuseppe Verdi*. The composer, politician, and national hero is revealed in a generous collection of letters.

JOHN WHITE, *Art and Architecture in Italy: 1250–1400*. A thorough study of the period that immediately preceded the Renaissance.

FAITH HELLER WILLINGER, *Eating in Italy*. A superb guide to northern Italian food, invaluable to the travelling gourmet, from novice to advanced palate. Specific foods are clearly explained and restaurants are recommended.

RUDOLPH WITTKOWER, *Art and Architecture in Italy, 1600–1750*. The noted Baroque historian's scholarly examination of the period.

———, *Architectural Principles in the Age of Humanism*. Not easy going, but possibly the single most influential modern interpretation of the theoretical basis of Renaissance architecture.

If the book you want is out of print or hard to find, stop when in Rome at **Books on Italy**, via Giubbonari 30, 00186 Rome, near campo dei Fiori. Call first for an appointment (Tel: 06-654-5285), or write to Louise McDermott at that address for her mail-order catalogue.

In the United States, an excellent source is the Traveller's Bookstore, 75 Rockefeller Plaza, New York, NY 10019; Tel: (212) 664-0995. Ask for their catalogue of travel books and related literature. Another good source is the Complete Traveller, 199 Madison Avenue, New York, NY 10016; Tel: (212) 679-4339; their catalogue costs $1.

VIDEOGRAPHY

Some of Italy's artworks are films, many of which are now available on videotape, dubbed or with subtitles.

Of the early classics, *Bicycle Thief* (De Sica, 1949) and *Umberto D* (De Sica, 1952) are among the most shattering, painful, and powerful films ever made, great works of art and of human compassion. Another fine wartime film, *Open*

City (Rossellini, 1946), gives neo-realistic views of postwar Rome. A later (1971) De Sica film, *The Garden of the Finzi-Continis,* photographs in exquisite color the elegant prewar world of a Jewish family as an unthinkable future descends.

Other directors who have brilliantly dominated the scene are:

Luchino Visconti (*Rocco and His Brothers*),

Federico Fellini (*Nights of Cabiria, La Strada, 8½, La Dolce Vita, Amarcord, Juliet of the Spirits*),

Michelangelo Antonioni (*Red Desert, L'Avventura*),

Paolo and Vittorio Taviani (*Night of the Shooting Stars, Padre Padrone*),

Giuseppe Tornatore, the young Sicilian director whose *Cinema Paradiso* won an Oscar as Best Foreign Film, and

Lina Wertmuller (*Seven Beauties, Swept Away,* and, in an unusual collaboration with Franco Zeffirelli, *Brother Sun and Sister Moon,* a life of Saint Francis, well played against a lyrical Umbrian landscape).

I, Claudius is a fascinating, brilliantly acted series made for BBC-TV. Based on Robert Graves's novel, this look at imperial Rome and its intrigue won many awards. A PBS video release.

ROME

By Louis Inturrisi and Barbara Coeyman Hults

Louis Inturrisi, the contributor to the Accommodations, Dining, Nightlife, and Shopping sections, is a writer, journalist, and longtime resident of Rome. His articles on Italy appear regularly in the New York Times, *the* International Herald Tribune, *and* Architectural Digest. *Barbara Coeyman Hults, who contributes to the Rome narrative and Getting Around sections, is the editorial consultant for this guidebook.*

Fountains whirling their watery arcs; Romans shouting and gesturing wildly; cars, buses, and motor scooters hurtling like chariots on a life-and-death course—Rome rushes at you. It can be overwhelming, overblown, exaggerated. Colossal as the Colosseum, pompous as the Baroque popes, melodramatic as a street vendor. But just when you've had enough and given up on it, something unexpected happens. You see the Tiber sparkling sapphire in the night light, a waiter brings you a fresh taste from the oven as a gift, you're charmed by a cat admiring a column once reserved for the Caesars, the apricot glow of a building warms you, and you decide to reconcile.

Federico Fellini once praised the city's expansive aspect: "Rome allows you all sorts of speculation, vertically. Rome is a horizontal city, made of water and earth, spread out, and is therefore the ideal platform for flights of fancy. Intellectuals, artists, who always live in a state of friction between two different dimensions—reality and fantasy—here find an appropriate and liberating stimulus for their mental activity, with the comfort of an umbilical cord that keeps them solidly attached to the concrete. Because Rome is a mother—the ideal mother because she's indifferent. She's a mother who has too many children and who, not being able to take care of any one of them, doesn't ask anything of you, doesn't expect anything of you. She welcomes you when you come, lets you go when you leave."

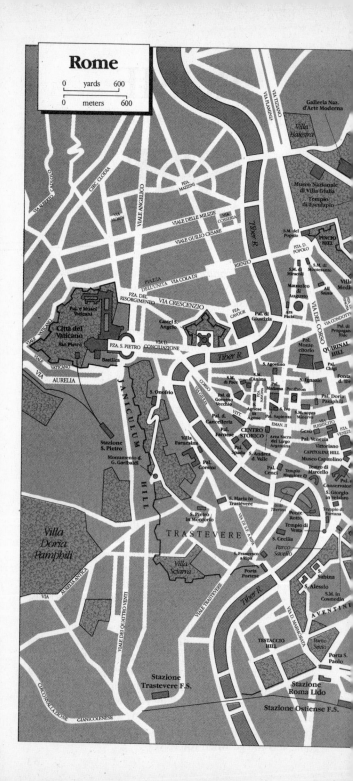

Though quoted when he made his film *Roma* in the early 1970s, Fellini's words have an ageless quality about them—as befits the Eternal City. They recall the flights of fancy that created the legend about the foundation of Rome by Romulus and Remus, nursed by the she-wolf, the original mother of Rome.

Throughout the city the ancient and the modern are juxtaposed: A classical column protrudes from a building erected centuries later. A sleek, modern train station abuts a Roman bath that was redesigned by Michelangelo as a church.

Between the deep red of the ancient brick and the stark white of modern marble and concrete are the mellower tones, now fixed by law, that dominate Rome and might have come out of a fruit basket in a Caravaggio painting. Peach, apricot, pomegranate, and honey hues decorate its palazzos and villas, the colors made even more striking in combination with the stately Renaissance style imported from Florence, or the exuberant Baroque born in Rome and favored by the popes. Rome's present look is a blend of all such styles, with a touch (but just a touch) of order added when the government of a newly united Italy lined the Tiber with travertine embankments when the city became its capital.

Rome's principal attractions are highlighted in the narrative below, but don't expect—or even attempt—to see everything the first time around. The jumble of the centuries is simply too confusing, even to longtime residents, who are used to the distractions of the unexpected church closures, the signs announcing *chiuso per restauro* (closed for restoration) and *chiuso per mancanza di personale* (closed for lack of personnel), the delightful tangent of discovering a hidden courtyard, witnessing a dramatic bit of street theater (though it's just the Romans going about their daily business), or lingering a little at table over a meal enlivened with good wine and better conversation.

Today's residents often pronounce the city *invivibile* (unlivable), with its endless traffic jams and pollution. But like New Yorkers and Londoners, they seem never to leave. However, apartment rents have soared, sending residents out into the peripheral parts of the city, and thus making transportation still more difficult. In the Centro Storico (the historic center, which in Rome refers to that part of the city across the Tiber from the Vatican), rents of $3,000 a month and more for an ordinary apartment are not unusual. These apartments are furnished and are offered to foreigners only, because foreigners will pay the rents and they can be evicted. (Italians, once in, can rarely be gotten out.)

Begin your visit on a leisurely note and let Rome's charms wash over you slowly. Include a Sunday or public holiday in your plans in order to see the city free of the traffic that normally engulfs its streets and monuments despite legislation attempting to restrict it. If it's a nice day (and it usually is, for the South begins in Rome, as evidenced by the palm trees and the slower pace), rent a bicycle (see details below), or sit in one of the cafés or restaurants in piazza Navona and watch the drama unfold in front of you against the piazza's Baroque backdrop. As a visitor, you'll be as much a part of the street scene as the "real" Romans, whose heroine Anna Magnani personified their fierce vitality on film. For despite laments among many residents that the real Romans have been over-run by other Italians drawn to the capital to take patronage jobs, they are still here—at least in campo dei Fiori and Trastevere, the only areas where you are likely to see Romans whose grandparents were born in Rome.

And the city, which together with the Vatican is capital of church and state, is just as intensely bureaucratic and chaotic as any Fellini fantasy. But don't let it overwhelm you. Above all, take your time. Toss a coin into the Trevi Fountain to ensure you'll be back, for that oft-quoted expression about Rome, *non basta una vita* (one life is not enough), is true.

MAJOR INTEREST

The Roman Forum

The Palatine Hill

Trajan's Column

The Colosseum

The Pantheon

Piazza Navona's Baroque splendor

Walking through the Centro Storico (Old Rome, the historic center) for its large and small architectural pleasures

Piazza del Popolo's churches and cafés

The Spanish Steps

Shopping in the via Condotti area

The especially Roman areas of campo dei Fiori and Trastevere

Rome's restaurants, cafés, and bars

The museums at Villa Borghese, Palazzo Barberini, the Capitoline Hill, the ancient Roman Terme di Diocleziano, the Vatican (including the Sistine Chapel), and elsewhere

St. Peter's basilica and piazza

The visitor is constantly confronted with visual reminders of more than two thousand years of history: from the outline left by the Circus Maximus, built in the second century B.C., to the Stadio Olimpico, refurbished for recent World Cup soccer finals. The Sabine and Etruscan kings ruled for more than two centuries (traces of the fortifications known as the Mura Serviane—traditionally attributed to the Etruscan king Servius Tullius, who ruled from 578 to 534 B.C.—may still be seen near the Mercato di Traiano [Trajan's Market]), until the Republic was founded around 500 B.C. The defeat of Carthage in 146 B.C. coincided with the conquest of Greek colonies in southern Italy, thus beginning the Greek influence on monumental Roman architecture, which expanded greatly during the Empire (27 B.C.–A.D. 395). It was during this era that most of what we see of ancient Rome was built, as well as when the engineering feats of the Aurelian Wall in the city (270–282) and the roads and aqueducts throughout the Empire were constructed.

Despite a series of sacks of Rome (by the Goths in 410, the Vandals in 455, the Saracens in 845, the Normans in 1084, and the German troops of Charles V in 1527), the papacy steadily established itself in the city, raising religious monuments and palazzi. The popes' effective political power began under Gregory I (590–604), but the development of the Holy Roman Empire—established when Leo III, in Rome, crowned Charlemagne emperor in 800—led to a series of conflicts between popes and emperors and eventually to the transfer of the papacy to Avignon (1309–1378). Rome's political and cultural importance was greatly diminished during this period.

With the end of the pope/antipope schism, and beginning with Martin V in 1417, Rome entered the Renaissance, and the popes began to commission great works from such artists as Michelangelo and Raphael. Sixtus V (1585–1590) began the first serious planning and development in the city in centuries, with straight roads, and under Urban VIII (1623–1644) and Innocent X (1644–1655) the Baroque we so associate with Rome today reached its zenith. During the relatively quiet political period that followed, such 18th-century works as the Spanish Steps and the Fontana di Trevi were built. Napoléon's troops occupied the city in 1798, and the French taste for Neoclassicism, typified by the works of Antonio Canova, Napoléon's favorite sculptor, also invaded the city's arts.

Following the defeat of Napoléon in 1814, the Italian revolution (Risorgimento) began, and Rome became the capital of the united Kingdom of Italy in 1870. The overblown monument to King Vittorio Emanuele, completed in 1911, set the stage for Mussolini's march on Rome in 1922, and the Fascist government he established imposed its order on the city by destroying entire neighborhoods to create triumphant boulevards like via dei Fori Imperiali and via della Conciliazione.

The liberation of Rome by the Allies in 1943–1944 brought about the Italian Republic we know today, and except for such scattered modern buildings as the New Audience Hall and a few hotels, the most important contribution to postwar building in Rome seems to be the Grande Raccordo Anulare (the 44-mile-long highway that rings the city)—an impressive feat of engineering, given Roman bureaucracy, almost in the tradition of the ancient Romans.

The discussion of the city that follows begins at the beginning, with *ancient Rome*. It continues chronologically with the monuments of the *Pantheon* and *piazza Navona* (formerly Diocletian's stadium), in the area where the mixture of ancient, Baroque, and Renaissance is most apparent: the *Centro Storico*. You'll then go south of the Centro Storico and see how the real Romans of today live, in the lively neighborhoods of *campo dei Fiori* and—across the Tiber—*Trastevere*. Then we return to ancient history in the *Capitoline* and *Aventine* hills back across the river west of the Roman Forum.

After a breather in Rome's largest park, *Villa Borghese,* you can trace the presence of foreigners in Rome (among them Napoléon's sister Pauline, who lived in the Villa Borghese); then, from the *piazza del Popolo,* stroll to that high point of the Grand Tour, the *Spanish Steps,* and from there go on to the haunt of the Hollywood stars in the 1950s and 1960s, the *via Veneto.* That area becomes a springboard to the city's Christian past, in the general neighborhood of the *Quirinal* and *Esquiline* hills, beginning with the Palazzo Barberini, built for Pope Urban VIII, and then heading generally south (into the area east of the Roman Forum) and back in time to Michelangelo's conversion of a portion of the Terme di Diocleziano into a church, to early Christian churches, and to two of Rome's major basilicas, Santa Maria Maggiore and San Giovanni in Laterano. Finally, you'll traverse the Tiber once again to the separate state surrounded by the city of Rome—*the Vatican.*

ANCIENT ROME

Traces of old Rome—an arch, a column, a fragment of sculpture, or even the colossal marble foot that gave via di Piè di Marmo its name—are strewn about the modern city. The ancient city itself, however, inhabits its very own zone. Behind the Vittorio Emanuele monument radiate the forums and the Palatine Hill, the Colosseum, the Circus Maximus, and the Terme di Caracalla. It is a world of venerable ruins intersected by avenues of rushing Roman traffic.

Before entering, pick up a copy of the red loose-leaf book titled *Rome: Past and Present,* with plastic overleafs that show the Forum now and then; it is essential to re-creating the whole from the assembly of stray columns and fragments you'll see before you. (Buy the book in a store as opposed to a stand near the monuments, where it will be double the price.)

The Palatine Hill evokes the Rome of Classical fantasy, umbrella pines shading fragments of ancient palaces. It's reached from the Roman Forum, whose main entrance is around to the left of the Vittoriano, as Romans call the modern-day monument, and is the best place to get an overview of the otherwise complicated Forum before you explore it on ground level. When you reach the Forum grounds from the main entrance on via dei Fori Imperiali, you will see the Palatine ahead of you, rising above the ruins, an irregular mass of pine, oleander, and cypress interspersed with yawning arches. These arches are the ruins of the grand palaces that lined the hill (which gave us the very word "palace"): residences of Augustus, Nero, Caracalla, Tiberius, and Domitian. To reach the belvedere of the Palatine, from which you'll have a grand overview of the Forum, walk left through the Forum to its far side and then follow the path up the hill. Turn right and take the steps up to the terrace.

The Roman Forum

Few monuments so clearly represent the history and life of an entire civilization as does the great complex usually called the Roman Forum (Foro Romano). There are many forums, and the Roman is only a small part of the entire archaeological site, but for clarity the Roman Forum is considered to be that section entered from via dei Fori Imperiali through the admission gate.

Built in the valley between the Capitoline and Palatine hills, the Roman Forum reached the peak of its importance under

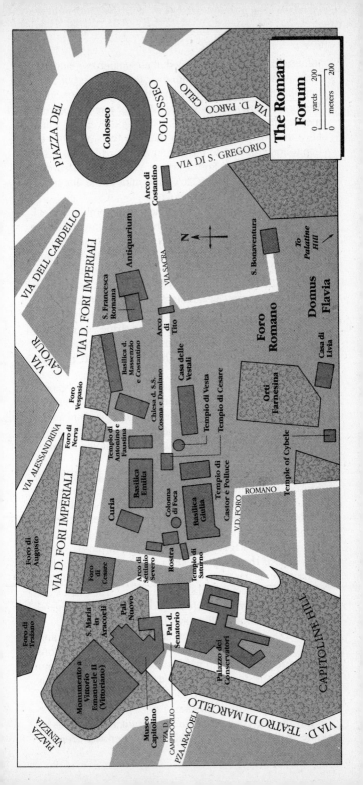

The Roman Forum

```
0        yards        200
0        meters       200
```

Colosseo

PIAZZA DEL COLOSSEO

VIA D. PARCO CELIO

VIA DI S. GREGORIO

VIA DELL CARDELLO

VIA D. FORI IMPERIALI

Arco di Costantino

Antiquarium

S. Francesca Romana

VIA SACRA

S. Bonaventura

N

To Palatine Hill

Basilica d. Massenzio e Costantino

Arco di Tito

Domus Flavia

VIA CAVOUR

Foro Vespasio

Chiesa d. S.S. Cosma e Damiano

Casa delle Vestali

Casa di Livia

Foro di Nerva

Tempio di Antonino e Faustina

Tempio di Vesta

Tempio di Cesare

Foro Romano

VIA ALESSANDRINA

Basilica Emilia

Orti Farnesina

Curia

Colonna di Foca

Basilica Giulia

Tempio di Castor e Polluce

Temple of Cybele

VIA D. FORI IMPERIALI

Foro di Augusto

Arco di Settimio Severo

Rostra

Tempio di Saturno

ROMANO

V.D. FORO

Foro di Cesare

Foro di Traiano

S. Maria in Aracoeli

Pal Nuovo

Pal. d. Senatorio

CAPITOLINE HILL

VIA D. TEATRO DI MARCELLO

Monumento a Vittorio Emanuele II (Vittoriano)

Palazzo dei Conservatori

PIAZZA VENEZIA

Museo Capitolino

PZA D. CAMPIDOGLIO

PZA ARACOELI

Julius and Augustus Caesar. Both these emperors—and later ones—enlarged the area with their own forums, but it was here at the original Roman Forum that the framework of Western civilization was forged. Much of our own government system derives from this forum, and even the names here are standard in Western thought: "capitol" from the Capitoline Hill next to the Forum; the word "forum" itself; "rostrum" from the Rostra, where Mark Antony delivered Caesar's eulogy; "money" from the mint at the Tempio di Giunone Moneta on the Capitoline.

The original Forum predates most of the buildings you'll see, which were built during the time of Augustus, the beginning of the Roman Empire. At the right, just past the entry ramp, stand the ruins of the **Basilica Emilia**. It was built in 179 B.C. and was later nearly destroyed by fire and the Vandals. The original basilicas had no religious purpose; they were commercial buildings with halls for conducting business. The building style was primarily functional, allowing light and air to circulate inside. The shape was rectangular and monumental, with two aisles and frequently a row of clerestory windows on top—the form adopted by many early Christian churches.

At the Emilia there were shops occupied by money changers—still an important profession for the tourist in Rome. When you walk up closer, in the nave you can see round green stains in the marble pavement, caused by copper coins dropped when the Goths set Rome ablaze in 410.

In front of the Basilica Emilia stands the original Forum as devised by Tarquin, the Etruscan king of Rome, in the eighth century B.C. He and other kings brought the tribes that inhabited these marshy hills together to complete a communal project—draining the malarial marsh of the Forum area. This done, the stage was set for the first forum—really an early piazza. The **Tempio di Vesta** on the east side was there at that time, as was the original Curia—next to the basilica—which was the meeting place of the senate. The black stone called *Lapis Niger,* in a sacred enclosure, covers the legendary site of the tomb of Romulus, founder of the city.

The look of the place at that time was of modest buildings made of tufa with a stucco coat and terra-cotta decorations. Since wars laid claim to much of Rome's vitality for centuries, little was done to beautify the Forum until Augustus, who then boasted that he'd found a city of brick and transformed it into a city of marble.

City life was concentrated in the Forum, and all roads led there. Political candidates addressed the crowds from the once grand **Rostra**, now just a stone platform behind the Column of Phocas. The Rostra was named for the prows (*rostra*) of ships captured as war booty and lined up here as war trophies. A later trophy would be Cicero's head and hands (43 B.C.), when he got on the bad side of Mark Antony. It was also at this spot that Caesar was cremated and Mark Antony delivered the funeral oration. Elections were held nearby, and victorious generals paraded along the **Via Sacra** (the oldest street in Rome, currently being excavated by an international team of archaeologists) to the Capitoline Hill, where the **Tempio di Giove** (Temple of Jupiter) stood.

Plautus, in his comedy *Curculio,* described the crowds: "In case you want to meet a perjurer, go to the Comitium; for a liar and a braggart, try the temple of Venus Cloacina; for wealthy married spendthrifts, the Basilica. There will be harlots, well-ripened ones . . . while at the fish market are the members of the eating clubs." But Roman society of that time—well before the wild days of Tiberius—was relatively reserved in dress and manners. Women were forbidden to wear jewelry or expensive clothes, partly because of the war efforts. Later, when Carthage was subdued in the Punic wars and Gaul was pacified—both events that filled the treasury—Rome changed, and its first capitalist class was born, for whom wealth was not in land but in money. After that, temples and basilicas sprang up in all the forums, including the adjacent Foro di Cesare and the Foro di Traiano—Trajan's Forum— across the present-day via dei Fori Imperiali (built by Mussolini and covering further riches known at this moment only to the gods).

Beyond the basilica stands the **Curia**, a brick building begun by Sulla in 80 B.C. that replaced the original Curia thought to have been built by King Tullius. Before the days of the Empire senators had considerable power. Judgments were sometimes helped along by augurs, who revealed the workings of fate by reading patterns in flights of birds or in the feeding movements of chickens. The Curia was a consecrated building, with an altar and statue to a pagan god of victory. Christians hundreds of years later objected to the statue, and Saint Ambrose, archbishop of Milan, finally had it removed by appealing to reason: "Where was Jupiter [when the Gauls attacked]?" he asked. "Was he speaking to the goose?"

In A.D. 203 the **Arco di Settimio Severo** (for Septimius Severus, born in Africa, who led Rome to victory in Syria and later in the British Isles) was erected and on top of the arch was placed a sculpture of Septimius and his two sons in a chariot. One of his sons, however, was Caracalla, who murdered his brother, Geta, to ensure that he himself would become emperor—and erased Geta's name from this and other monuments throughout Rome, though the original inscription can still be made out under the obliterated fourth line across the top of the arch. Romans often used columns decoratively rather than structurally, which can be seen in the freestanding examples of the arch's portico.

To the side and slightly behind the Arch of Septimius Severus is the **Tempio di Saturno**, whose eight columns can still be seen. Dedicated to the god Saturn, it was the site of the Saturnalia, celebrated in December of each year, a time of wild public festivities and gift giving, with the quality and amount of the gifts no less carefully observed than they are today.

In front of the Rostra is the **Colonna di Foca**, dedicated to the tyrannical Eastern emperor who gave the Pantheon to Pope Boniface IV in 608. Next to the Temple of Saturn is the **Basilica Giulia**, named for Julius Caesar, who was murdered (not in the Forum but in Pompey's Theater, then near Largo Argentina) before its completion. Some of the stones in the pavement were used as ancient gaming boards, traces of which can still be seen.

The most beautiful fragment in the Forum comes from the **Tempio di Castor e Polluce**: the three elegant columns east of the basilica, often photographed as a symbol of Classical grace. The temple was created during the fifth century B.C. after Roman troops saw the divine twins Castor and Pollux (the Dioscuri) fighting at their side in battle far from Rome. Then the heavenly twins appeared at this site, proclaiming the Roman victory.

The round **Tempio di Vesta** nearby, where the goddess's flame was kept burning by the Vestal virgins, is a favorite site, and was modeled on the circular hut used by the area's earliest known inhabitants. The Vestal virgins, women of noble birth pledged for 30 years to this cult, were charged with never letting the flame die. If it went out, they were severely thrashed; if they lost their virginity, they were buried alive after being driven in a covered hearse through the streets and forced to descend to their own tomb on a ladder. Because they enjoyed great privileges in Rome, it is sometimes assumed that Vestal virginity was a sought-after honor, but Suetonius tells of noble families doing everything to keep their daughters' names from getting on the list when a virgin died.

The house of the Vestal virgins was like a luxurious convent, a self-contained unit surrounding a central garden court with pools and statues of the virgins. The name Claudia has been erased below the figure of one who converted to Christianity, an eternal reminder of her ignominy.

The **Tempio di Antonino e Faustina** (at the right of the entrance to the Forum area) is named for the emperor and his wife who adopted Marcus Aurelius and ruled after Hadrian in A.D. 138. Impressively set atop a long staircase, Etruscan style, it has nicely carved columns and a fragment of a statue on the porch. Alongside it is the church of **Santi Cosma e Damiano**, once part of the Vespasian Forum. If the Forum-side entrance is open, you can see a delightful Neapolitan *presepio* (an exuberant, expansive Nativity scene). The church also merits a visit to see its sixth-century mosaics, among the earliest in Rome. Christ as the Lamb Enthroned is on the triumphal arch.

The name of the large **Basilica di Massenzio e Costantino** makes it sound as if the building were a collaborative effort, but it wasn't. It was begun under Maxentius, but after Constantine defeated him at the battle of the Milvian bridge in 312 it was given his name as well. Its original form is easy to imagine, and part of the coffered ceiling can still be seen. In the Museo Capitolino lie some disembodied fragments of the 40-foot statue of the emperor Constantine that once stood inside the basilica. Encountering the enormous head and hand is an unforgettable Roman experience.

Three massive cross vaults of the nave rose 114 feet above the floor, their lateral thrust strengthened by concrete piers 14 feet in diameter. A Barberini pope appropriated the bronze tiles for St. Peter's, giving rise to the saying, "What the barbarians didn't take, the Barberini did." One of its gigantic marble columns ended up in front of Santa Maria Maggiore on via Cavour. This sort of papal modularism makes it seem probable that everything is really still here in Rome, if only massive rearranging could be done. But of course the jumble of the centuries is part of Rome's charm.

The **Arco di Tito** (Arch of Titus) at the end of the expanse of the Forum was built in A.D. 81 to celebrate the sack of Jerusalem by the emperor; the friezes show the spoils, including the altar from Solomon's temple and the seven-branch candlestick (menorah), being transported back to Rome in A.D. 70.

Next to the church (Santa Francesca Romana) between the basilica of Maxentius and Constantine and the Arch of Titus is the **Antiquarium**, a museum that has some interesting objects excavated from the Palatine and models of the huts in sarcophagus form. (A complete model of ancient Rome is on display at the Museo della Civiltà Romana in the suburban district of E.U.R.—but it is often closed; Tel: 592-61-35. E.U.R. is accessible by Metro.)

The Palatine Hill

But now look at the Palatine Hill behind you.

> Come and see
> The cypress, hear the owl, and plod your way
> O'er the steps of broken thrones and temples.
> Ye whose agonies are evils of a day
> A world is at our feet as fragile as our clay.

This atmosphere of antiquity that enchanted Byron when he wrote *Childe Harold* is readily evoked on the Palatine. Here you can wander amid the umbrella pines of Rome that must have inspired Respighi, and for the moment the world is perfect in classical beauty. The Farnese spread gardens along the hill, fragrant with roses and orange blossoms in the spring.

Although the Palatine Hill inspires dreaming under a tall pine or an ilex, it is the site of some of Rome's most interesting traces of civilization and merits exploration. In back of the splendid Farnese Gardens, down the steps, lie the remains of the **temple of Cybele** (also called Magna Mater, the Great Mother). This temple to the Mediterranean earth goddess was dedicated in 204 B.C. when the Romans learned from the Sibyl that they must build it in order to win a critical battle in the Second Punic War. In it they were to place an idol to be brought from Asia Minor, a black stone said to have fallen from the sky. (Phallic stones represented the goddess's fertility attribute.) You can see parts of a podium and a stairway from the original temple; the temple itself was rebuilt several times.

The huts being excavated in this area date from the eighth century B.C., at the time Romulus and Remus founded the city, according to tradition. They were circular huts of the Iron Age, similar to that reproduced in the Palatine Museum.

The legend of Rome's founding precedes Romulus and Remus, however. When Troy was sacked, Aeneas, son of Aphrodite, carried his crippled father out to safety and on to Italy. A female descendant, a priestess sworn to virginity, met the war god Mars, and the twins Romulus and Remus were the result. She was put to death when the births were discovered, and the twins were set afloat on the Tiber. They came aground at the Palatine Hill, where a compassionate she-wolf found them and nursed them (as you've no doubt seen on thousands of souveniers of Rome). The wolf lived in a cave, the Lupercal, a facsimile of which was venerated during the time of Augustus at the Feast of the Lupercal.

Near the temple you'll find a partly subterranean corridor called the **Crytoporticus**, the main branch of which is about 400 feet (130 meters) long. These passages linked the palaces of the hill, and if they could talk, even today's gossip gluttons might be shocked. (Read or watch Robert Graves's *I, Claudius* for a taste of those times.) On a corridor wall near the house of the evil Livia, fine white stuccoes contain figures of Cupid and floral motifs. The upper floor of **Livia's House** is fascinating, decorated with Egyptian frescoes (things Egyptian were coveted then). In another part of the house, three painted rooms show an interesting mix of fantasy and reality. The nymph Galatea flees Polyphemus upon a seahorse, while Polyphemus looks at her with unveiled thoughts. Elsewhere the architectonic aspects of the frescoes, although often unreal, give a good idea of the decorative scheme used. In the right wing a low frieze glows with a variety of scenes, one of the largest and best examples of landscape painting in Roman art: men and women practicing religious rites; fishermen; a man with a camel; and other scenes.

Nearby, the **Domus Flavia**, the reception area for the emperor Domitian's palace (A.D. 1), stretches in front of the modern building at the edge of the hill (the former Monastery of the Visitation). The large open area, with a fountain surrounded by a columned portico, is well preserved.

To the east, at the hill's edge, the **Paedogogium** was a slave quarters. Ancient graffiti on the wall can still be seen, but the most famous, a donkey crucified, thought to mock the early Christians, is now in the Antiquarium (Palatine Museum) nearby. An inscription reads "Alexamenos worships his God."

The Circus Maximus

Although an oblong field, with wildflowers here and there, is all that's left of the Circo Massimo's great chariot track, it is enjoyable to walk where four chariots raced together for seven laps around the two and a half miles. Originally, as many as 385,000 spectators sat here amid marble columns—nothing Rome did was less than colossal. Caligula loved the chariots, and during his reign the number of races doubled to 24 per day. In the stands, touts and wine-sellers worked the crowds. The last race was held in A.D. 549.

The Arch of Constantine

On a nice day you'll notice lots of people on the Palatine buried in books (or in one another's arms) under the trees, and you may want to follow suit. Otherwise walk back down the hill past the Arch of Titus and out on the via Sacra to via di San Gregorio and the Arch of Constantine (Arco di Costantino), the largest and best preserved of the ancient arches. It was erected to the emperor after his successful encounter with Maxentius. That battle is famous partly because of the vision that Constantine had before it began: He saw a flaming cross formed in the sky and heard the words, "*In hoc signo vinces*" ("In this sign thou shalt conquer").

The arch's unusual collection of reliefs was partly assembled from various other Roman monuments. On the inside of the central archway are reliefs from the frieze of a monument that commemorated Trajan's Dacian victories, but Constantine's head has been substituted for Trajan's. The frontality of the figures, a Byzantine convention, here foreshadows Constantine's transfer of the imperial capital from Rome to Byzantium (rebuilt as Constantinople) in 330, and the end of the glory days.

Beyond the arch looms the great oval mass that is the Colosseum, which may be contemplated alfresco at the **Hostaria Il Gladiatore** on the piazza in front of the Colosseum entrance.

The Colosseum

It was its colossal size that gave the Colosseum its name, but it was its games of bizarre cruelty that made this the most famous building in Rome. Tourist buses rattle its old stones hundreds of times each day, leading Romans to predict that it will soon "crumble like breadsticks," echoing an eighth-century prediction quoted by the Venerable Bede: While the Colosseum stands, Rome will stand. When the Colosseum falls, Rome will fall. The Empire had many coliseums, and some exist today in better condition than Rome's, but this will always be *the* Colosseum. During the years when Christians were literally thrown to the lions, along with other "criminals," Claudius used to arrive at dawn to see the spectacle.

The building was begun in A.D. 72, during the reign of the emperor Vespasian, on the site where Nero had excavated a lake for the gardens of his Golden House (now in ruins across the street and rarely open). Outside stood a colossal

96-foot statue of Nero. Vespasian's spectacles of persecution were so sadistic that Romans turned from them in disgust.

The niches that now seem to be open arches on the sides of the Colosseum were actually created to house Greek sculpture—including athletic motifs from Greece's unbloody games. The Greek athletic contests were introduced to the Romans but were apparently too tame in an age when combat to the death was the daily diet. Roman architects used niches not only for statuary but also to glorify the massiveness of the walls by emphasizing their depth—something Greek architects with their airy colonnades would never have dreamt of.

The Colosseum was built of blocks of travertine excavated from quarries near Tivoli and brought to Rome along a road created just for that purpose. It was apparently modeled after the Teatro di Marcello (see below), built during Julius Caesar's time. It rises in three levels, each decorated with columns, from the plain Doric at the bottom to Ionic and Corinthian; the fourth level held the cables that supported the huge awnings that could be billowed out across the spectators to protect them from rain or excessive sun. Scents were also sprayed on the crowd to keep the smell of blood away from their delicate nostrils.

At the first row of seats we can still see the names of important boxholders. In the second circle sat the plebians, with women and then slaves at the back. Galleries constructed between the seats and the outer walls provided a place to mill during intermissions. The Roman use of the crossed vault made such galleries possible.

Almost 50,000 could be seated with enviable efficiency. There were 80 entrances (four for the select boxholders), and each had a number that corresponded with the game-goer's ticket. Leaving was also facilitated by the vomitoria that "disgorged" the crowds down numerous ramps. Every detail was ingeniously worked out by the architects, who were sensitive to public comfort even as they watched gladiators and animals die agonizing deaths.

The games, too, were organized carefully. Gladiators were recruited from the ranks of those condemned to death and war prisoners—both groups with little to lose but the possibility of a dazzling future. They were housed nearby in the recently excavated *ludus magnus*. The floor could be flooded to create *naumachiae* (sea battles), and sometimes the gladiators fought in the water. (Not every program was just filled with gladiatorial strife, of course. There were circus acts with panthers pulling chariots and elephants that wrote Latin inscriptions with their trunks.)

During gladiatorial combat, participants sauntered around the arena, nonchalant, with their valets bearing their arms. They wore purple embroidered with gold, and when they came to the emperor's box they saluted by raising their right arm and saying, "*Ave Imperator, morituri te salutant*" ("Hail, Emperor. We who are about to die salute you"). The crowd screamed and cheered at each blow: *Verbera!* (Strike!) and *Ingula!* (Kill!). To ensure that a fallen warrior was dead, he was struck on the head with a mallet. A gladiator unable to continue could lie on his back and raise his left arm in appeal. Then the crowd could wave their handkerchiefs and show their raised thumbs to the emperor, who might take their advice and raise his, granting life. Or they might consider him cowardly and turn thumbs down. The emperor's down-turned thumb could not be contested.

Winners were given gold and the adoration of young girls. Cicero thought it a good way to learn contempt for pain and death, and Pliny the Younger thought the trials fostered courage. (Cicero and Pliny, however, did not have to fight.) What was fostered among the spectators was something basic to the Empire: Rome was about conquering.

Of all the forms created by Greek and Roman architects, the amphitheater, a huge bowl structure such as the Colosseum, has, in today's sports stadiums, been the most imitated. Maybe that's because it dovetails so neatly with our own modern sensibilities—in its utilitarianism as well as in its striving for and achievement of grandiose and overwhelming effects. In general, Rome's greatest contributions to architecture were practical: aqueducts and waterworks, roads and city plans.

Trajan's Column and the Imperial Forums

Successive emperors laid out their own forums, and most are found across the via dei Fori Imperiali, Mussolini's idea of a triumphal highway, which split the forums into two parts.

The **Foro di Cesare** (Caesar's Forum) is mostly on the Roman Forum side of the avenue. On the far side, close to the Vittoriano, is the **Colonna Traiana** (Trajan's Column), a depiction of the emperor's battle (triumphant, of course), long classified as one of the wonders of the world. Its spiral frieze rises 100 feet, and it would, if marble could be unrolled, extend some 215 yards. This masterpiece of intricate composition contains 2,500 figures and was once more easily seen by a spiral staircase. Now binoculars would be handy.

Although you can see the column and much of the several forums by walking along the sidewalk, go inside the **Foro di Traiano** (Trajan's Forum; entrance at via Quattro Novembre 94), because then you can see the **Mercato Traiano** as well; besides, there is often an exhibition going on. Trajan's Market has the intimate fascination of ordinary places. It was a mall of 250 small shops on three levels where oil and wines, perfumes and shoes could be bought, and much of the original structure is well preserved. The forum itself is newly restored and will be the site of modern sculpture exhibitions.

Beyond the Foro Traiano is the **Foro di Augusto** and then the **Foro di Nerva**—where two fine Corinthian capitals have been restored above a relief of Minerva; the friezes tell the story of Minerva's jealousy of Arachne when she heard the peasant girl could spin more beautiful garments. She slit the web Arachne had created, and Arachne hanged herself in shame. Repentant Minerva changed her into a spider, restoring her skill in spinning.

Returning to the Mercato Traiano to leave, you'll see the **Torre delle Milizie** rising above it, part of what was the fortress of Gregory IX (pope from 1227 to 1241). The hilly streets that radiate from here and around nearby piazza del Grillo (off via di Sant'Eufemia) are so medieval in aspect they could be part of an Umbrian town, especially on Sunday when traffic is slow. The glimpses they afford of the forums through windows and arches and from parapets dramatize the ancient by contrasting the eras. From piazza del Grillo you can enter the **Casa dei Cavalieri di Rodi**, ancient seat of the crusading Order of St. John of Jerusalem. Go inside if it is open for the excellent view of ancient Rome from the loggia.

In December *presepi* (Nativity scenes) are displayed in churches throughout Italy, with lights, music, and even water effects. Now, a museum located near Trajan's Forum, open from October through May, displays more than 3,000 presepi from 29 countries, including Brazil, Palestine, and Madagascar. Lessons on constructing them are given during the month of November (in Italian). Open Wednesdays and Saturdays from 6:00 to 8:00 P.M., longer hours at Christmas. Call or write for an appointment: Museo Internazionale del Presepio, 31/AA via Tor de' Conti; Tel: 679-61-46.

The Baths of Caracalla

For more of ancient Rome, take a bus or taxi to the Terme di Caracalla south of the Colosseum. They were luxurious even for imperial Rome, their massive space shining with multi-colored marble, the pools filled by jets of water spouting from marble lions' mouths, the nymphaeum of gardens and pools and statues, gyms, theaters, and libraries. Everyone—rich and poor—went to the baths to socialize and gossip. Caracalla began this project in 212, and his successors added to the glamorous surroundings. The ruins today, the evocative site of Rome's summer opera season (see below), provide important insights into the social organization of ancient Rome.

THE CENTRO STORICO

The Centro Storico, Rome's historic center, is the name traditionally given to the part of the city that occupies the bend of the Tiber across from the Vatican, where the Pantheon, piazza Navona, and a world of Renaissance palaces and piazzas, Baroque drama, and spacious courtyards unfold—sometimes gradually but often abruptly, seducing the senses.

Begin at Palazzo Venezia, on the right corner of the via del Corso facing the Vittoriano, where the traffic is so frenetic that crossing brings on what Italians call *lo stress*. A traffic light eases some of the trauma, and once across you can weave a splendid path for yourself through streets that hold surprises even for those who tread their cobblestones daily. Most palaces along the way were created for noble families that numbered cardinals and one or even more popes among their members.

Peek into courtyards and look up at building decorations and tiny shrines. The traffic in this area is dreadful, so you might consider walking through it on a Sunday. Shops will be closed then, but almost everything else on this walk will be open, including the churches, though you will have to stop just before or just after mass to find them open to nonworshipers. If you can rent a bicycle to sail the virtually car-free streets, so much the better. Saturday morning strollers, on the other hand, can have a glimpse of noble Roman life at the **Palazzo Colonna**, via della Pilotta 17. It's closed all other days and in the month of August. The gallery maintains a fine collection, including 17th-century landscapes by Dughet and portraits by Titian and Veronese. But the Renaissance palace itself is the most fascinating part. The great hall's ceiling is decorated with stories of Marcantonio Colonna and family. A private chapel keeps a canopy and throne ready in case the pope should drop by. (One often has, particularly since Pope Martin V was a Colonna. His portrait hangs in the chapel.) The family church today is the church of the Santi Apostoli, on the adjoining piazza of the same name. An irreverent cool beer can be found at a beer hall of that name a few doors away.

Palazzo Venezia's crenellated, fortresslike mass was once the home of the Venetian Pope Paul II, but now it's better known for its balcony, at the center of the façade, from which Il Duce told Rome the Empire would rise again. Inside you sometimes can see his war room (Mappamondo). The museum in the palazzo has a good medieval collection and hosts frequent shows and exhibitions. In 1564 the pope gave the palazzo to Rome as the Venetian Embassy, but now it belongs to the Italian Republic.

Tucked almost out of sight behind the palace is one of Rome's Byzantine jewels, the basilica of **San Marco**. On its porch the popes once blessed the crowds as they do now from St. Peter's, but this small church usually escapes notice in a city where everything is grandiose.

The interior glows with mosaics and a coffered ceiling of blue and gold, with the heraldic crest and the crossed keys that always signify a pope. In the apse is a ninth-century mosaic of Pope Gregory IV offering Christ this church.

Across via del Plebiscito is the **Palazzo Doria Pamphilj** (Pamphili), still partly inhabited by the noble Doria family, whose anti-Fascist resistance during World War II is remembered by Italians. The Genoese admiral Andrea Doria is a prominent ancestor. Cross via del Plebiscito and follow the little street behind the palace around to its inner courtyard and the museum, which is well worth seeing not only for the paintings but also for the apartment tour, a rare opportunity to see the interior of a Roman palace. (You must wait for a small group to be assembled, but you can see the paintings in the meantime.) The paintings have numbers only, so you may want to buy a catalogue.

Among the highlights of the collection are *Salome* by Titian, and Caravaggio's *Penitent Magdalen* and *Rest on the Flight to Egypt* (the angel is superb but the gallery lighting isn't—it takes angling to see the painting without glare). Farther along is Parmigianino's *Adoration of the Shepherds;* then the bizarre *Olimpia Maidalchini,* whose less-than-sweet face, in a bust by Algardi, is found at the corner. The brother-in-law she bedeviled is around the corner: Innocent X, as

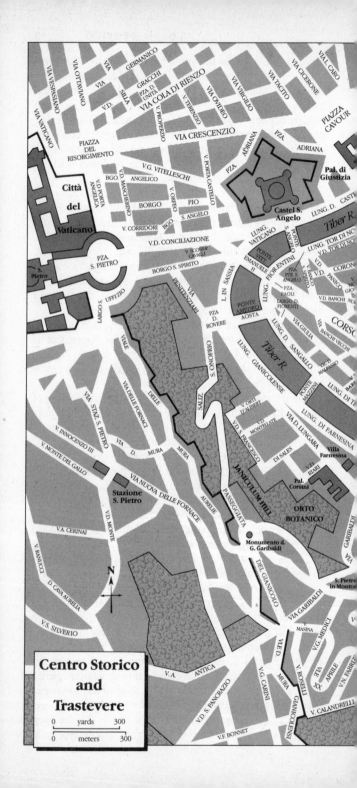

Centro Storico
and
Trastevere

| 0 | yards | 300 |
| 0 | meters | 300 |

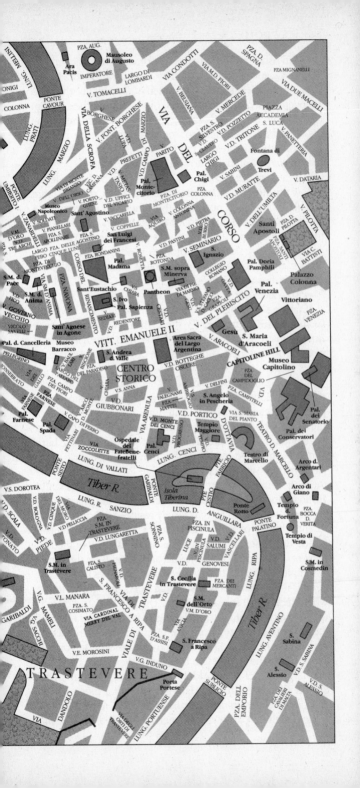

seen in one of the greatest portraits ever painted, by Velásquez, and also in a portrait by one who knew him better, Gianlorenzo Bernini. We owe much of the neighborhood to Innocent's forcefulness—that is, until Olimpia cheated him out of all worldly goods, taking his last coin when he was on his deathbed, according to some reports. Notice also, in Room IV, the lunettes by the Carracci family and the *Flight into Egypt* by Annibale Carracci.

For a leap into 20th-century luxury, when you leave, follow the street in front, via di Piè di Marmo, past the large marble foot planted nonchalantly at the side of the street. A clothing designer known to *tutta Roma* has a small shop in the piazza in back of the famous foot. **Teresa Trushnach** creates dresses, slacks, and blouses in sensuously beautiful fabrics and colors. Some ready-made clothes are also on display at her shop (via Santo Stefano del Cacco 27, Tel: 67-97-450). Take your Italian dictionary.

If fabric shopping is on your itinerary, turn left at via del Gesù to **Bises** at number 93, the 17th-century palace where Roman matrons have purchased fine yard goods for many years. The frescoed ceilings serve as a remembrance of times past.

At the Gesù intersection, you'll see **piazza della Minerva** rearing its lovely obelisk, placed atop Bernini's small elephant. The elephant seems quite undisturbed by the size of the obelisk on his back; his trunk curls out cheerfully, like a horizontal bazaar snake. The obelisk was found near here and presumably came from the Temple of Isis that stood close by this spot. In fact, the marble foot (above) may be the only remaining part of the figure of Isis. The beautiful **Holiday Inn Crowne Plaza Minerva**, on the piazza, has reopened—perhaps too dazzlingly restored to luxury status.

The church of **Santa Maria sopra Minerva** has a plain façade that hides its considerable riches. It's one of the few ancient Gothic churches in Rome, and it stands on the site of a temple to Minerva (as the name indicates), Isis, and Serapis—Egyptian religions having been brought to Rome when the Empire spread to Egypt. The first Christian church on the site was built during the eighth century, and much of the existing one dates from the 13th century—the work of Dominican brothers Fra Sisto and Fra Ristoro. As you advance along the impressive but dark aisle on the right, the first large chapel is the Aldobrandini crypt, where the parents of Clement VIII were laid to rest with a memorial by Giacomo Della Porta and Girolamo Rainaldi. At the transept is the delightful Carafa chapel, merrily frescoed with the life of Saint Thomas Aquinas by Filippino Lippi between 1488 and 1492.

To the right of the high altar is the Capranica chapel, with a *Virgin and Child* attributed to Fra Angelico. Beneath the altar is the crypt of Saint Catherine of Siena, the main patron saint of Italy and a Doctor of the Church. She lived near here and was instrumental in persuading the popes to return from their "Babylonian captivity" in Avignon. At the left is the tomb of the mystical Fra Angelico. Beyond is *Christ with the Cross* (1514–1521) by Michelangelo, apparently finished by another when the master found a flaw in the marble. Cardinal Bembo is buried at the altar (there's a plaque in the floor), as are popes Leo X and Clement VII, in tombs sculpted by Sangallo the Younger. Works of art are clearly not lacking in this church; an inexpensive booklet is for sale here, detailing each of them, or take a look at the diagram near the entrance. Behind the altar you can see a small museum and some rooms once occupied by Saint Catherine.

The Pantheon

As you walk toward the right, the mass of the Pantheon seems to sit in wait for you, as it has for millions of admirers over the centuries. Its massiveness is what seizes you first, followed by the grace of its columns and the piazza (piazza della Rotonda) that opens in front. The obelisk-topped fountain of wonderfully absurd faces spraying water, the young people sitting at the base, the open windows—always someone leaning out—make this one of the loveliest piazzas in Rome for people-watching. Have a drink or coffee at one of the cafés while you pay your respects to the Pantheon, the best preserved of all Rome's ancient buildings.

Across the top of the Pantheon's façade you'll see the name Agrippa in the inscription, signifying the son-in-law of Augustus, who built the original temple (27 B.C.), which later burned down. The existing structure is the work of the always-building Hadrian, and was begun in A.D. 118. In 609 it was consecrated as a Christian church, having originally been a temple to all the gods.

The outside gives little hint of what's to come—there is nothing like it in the world. The circular opening, way on top—with clouds passing some days, or even raindrops or an occasional snowflake—comes as a shock. The immensity of the round space so high above and the coffered ceiling around it are awe-inspiring. The tomb of Raphael, especially, and of the Italian kings Vittorio Emanuele II and Umberto I are impressive, of course, but it is the space that hushes chattering visitors when they come through the door. In fact, it was the first building ever conceived as an interior space, aided by the use of concrete and cross vaults that allowed Roman architecture to soar.

Walk around the Pantheon to the left as you leave, until you see the stag's head and antlers of the church of **Sant'Eustachio**, the saint being the nobleman who converted to Christianity when hunting. His bow and arrow were aimed at a stag when suddenly Christ's face appeared in the antlers, according to the legend. Have coffee or cappuccino at the **Caffè Sant'Eustachio**, long considered by many the best in Rome. Take a few steps into the piazza and you'll see one of Rome's most exquisite sights, the white swirling tower of Sant'Ivo (see below).

Continue to the right into via della Scrofa for two streets to the church of **San Luigi dei Francesi** (Saint Louis). You'll want to run inside to see the Caravaggio paintings, but stop outside for a moment to see a bit of drollery. At the bottom right of the façade is a salamander that bears the head of François I of France. The salamander was his insignia, but in his version did not bear his face.

Inside, the Caravaggio canvases are in the last chapel on the left. *The Vocation of Saint Matthew* glows with unreal light that hits each figure in a different way, some to follow Christ, some to remain in shadow. *Saint Matthew's Martyrdom* is one of the most dramatic of his works in terms of lighting effects. (The plumed figure at the top left is thought to be the artist himself.) *Saint Matthew and the Angel,* painted in 1602, shows Matthew writing what the angel dictates.

Turn left from the church of San Luigi for two blocks, then left again to the church of **Sant'Agostino** for Caravaggio's *Madonna di Loreto*. This painting was not at all what was expected, because he used the poor and humble as her supplicants instead of the usual rich patrons. The model for the Madonna was a local woman who had rejected a lawyer who sought her hand. The lawyer called Caravaggio a "cursed ex-communicant" for painting her; the artist, in turn, wounded him with a sword and had to escape to Genoa until things cooled down. Raphael painted the *Prophet Isaiah* in fresco here after he had seen the Sistine ceiling; the high altar is the work of Bernini.

From San Luigi it's a short walk south on via della Scrofa to Sant'Ivo. Turn right into corso del Rinascimento. Ahead, the well-guarded **Palazzo Madama** was named for Madama Margaret of Austria, illegitimate daughter of Charles V, who married a Medici and then a Farnese. The palace is now the Palazzo del Senato, named for the government body whose traditions go back to the Curia of the Forum.

Just beyond, at number 101, is the **Palazzo della Sapienza**, whose Renaissance façade is the work of Giacomo Della Porta. Inside are the Vatican archives, but the reason to enter is to see Borromini's newly restored tower and church of **Sant'Ivo** and the courtyard there that Borromini also designed. The Barberini bees that have been worked into the design indicate that a Barberini pope, Urban VIII, was the instigator. The courtyard is elegantly planned to lead the viewer to the campanile's upward movement. The church, constructed from 1642 to 1660, is an intricate play of convex and concave shapes inside, with a hint of the Rococo. Borromini's search for geometric perfection as a spiritual state comes close to fulfillment here.

Piazza Navona

Just across the street, behind a row of palaces, is piazza Navona. The façades that grace the piazza make the owners of these buildings among Rome's most envied residents. The piazza is beautiful in all lights and moods: in early morning when the street-sweepers swoosh through, and by the golden light of sunset when shadows make casual encounters seem dramatic. On Sundays it is still the village piazza, with the entire family here to watch the youngest balance his first two-wheeler while papa hovers above him. Artists set out their paintings, Africans sell belts, pigeons swoop, and rendezvous are agreed on with the eyes.

Festivity has always characterized piazza Navona. In ancient Rome it often took the form of *naumachiae,* when the piazza was flooded to create a sea for real ships to play war in—but it was not play, and deaths were part of the "excitement." During that era the piazza was the stadium of Domitian, which accounts for its elongated shape. Athletic contests (*agone*) were frequent, and gave the name to the church facing the center, **Sant'Agnese in Agone**.

Pope Innocent X, wanting a symbol of his family to be indelibly imprinted on Rome, as well as to beautify the city, called in Bernini to create a monument, stipulating that an obelisk be fetched from the Circus Maximus to be part of the design. Bernini's **Fontana dei Quattro Fiumi** shows four rivers and their continents, each represented by a person. The head of the figure representing the Nile was covered to indicate that the source was then unknown, but Romans said it was because Bernini's statue couldn't bear to look at his rival Borromini's dreadful façade on the church of Sant'Agnese. The Danube's outstretched arm, meant to connect the fountain visually with the façade, was said to be raised to ward off the church's imminent collapse. The Plate and the Ganges complete the quartet. Bernini himself, it's thought, finished the horse, rock, lion, and palm while working here in situ. His poetic use of realistic objects in an exuberant style has made the Fountain of the Four Rivers symbolic of Rome itself.

The other two fountains in the piazza were finished by Bernini and his studio: Fontana del Moro con Tritone (the Moor) and Fontana del Nettuno (Neptune); the latter was largely rebuilt during the 19th century.

Inside the church of Sant'Agnese is a bas-relief of Saint Agnes by Algardi, showing the miracle in which she was stripped naked in preparation for martyrdom, only to be covered immediately by her long, luxuriant hair, which suddenly grew to conceal her body from her persecutors.

Piazza Navona is the place to eat a delicious chocolate ice cream called *tartufo* at **Tre Scalini**—so what if it's crowded with tourists; the *tartufo* and Bernini together are not to be scorned. **Mastrostefano**, the terrace restaurant on the piazza, is another good place to sit and observe the piazza life, and the food can be surprisingly good for such a heavily visited location. Prints are found at **Nardecchia**, a 30-year-old institution at number 25.

The streets off the western side of the piazza are popular with the young and trend-conscious. Wine bars and shops have sprung up, enlivening the area at night. Walk down to the north end of piazza Navona (on your right when facing Sant'Agnese), turn left to the church of Santa Maria dell'Anima, designed by Giuliano da Sangallo, past the charming vine-covered Hotel Raphael—protected by *carabinieri* because of its government guests—to the lovely church of **Santa Maria della Pace**. Be there just after 10:30 mass on Sunday morning to see the Raphael frescoes of the sibyls. If it's closed, the façade and the polygonal piazza are delightful anyway. Its cloisters, Bramante's earliest Roman creation, are open every day.

So popular it's often overflowing, the **Bar della Pace** on nearby via Santa Maria dell'Anima is a trendy, pleasant place to have an expensive drink.

One block north of Santa Maria della Pace is the merry **via dei Coronari**, an antiques-sellers' street that holds regular antiques fairs, when it is carpeted as if for royalty and festooned with flowers, banners, and candles. Paralleling the street to the north is the medieval via dei Tre Archi, and all around for strolling are delightful streets near the banks of the Tiber.

Nearby, **Jeff Blynn's** New York–style bar at via Zanardelli 12 may inspire you to order a cool martini in its posh surroundings.

Along the river at piazza di Ponte Umberto I is the **Museo Napoleonico**, with Bonaparte family portraits and the chaise on which Pauline reclined for her famous statue by Cavona (now in the Museo Borghese; see below).

From here you can follow the via dell'Orso (the Street of the Bear) as it makes its romantic meanderings. The **Hosteria dell'Orso** is as atmospheric a place as Rome has to offer—a medieval hostelry where you can stop for a drink at the beautiful bar on the ground floor or dine upstairs (though the food does not match the decor in quality). At night the lights from the river make the window views softly romantic.

Continuing back to the via del Corso, you may want to get an ice cream at Rome's venerable *gelato* institution, **Giolitti**. If so, make a detour when you reach via degli Uffici del Vicario. The *semi-freddo* (partly frozen) varieties and fresh fruit flavors are sought after; for pastry-lovers, the *bigne allo zabaglione* (a cream puff bursting with Marsala-laced custard) is one of its rich specialties. Farther along the same street, the **Gelateria della Palma** is a relative upstart favored by younger *gelato* aficionados.

Via degli Uffici del Vicario leads to piazza di Montecitorio, where, in the **Palazzo Montecitorio**, the lower house of parliament meets—thus the heavy security and milling journalists when congress is in session. The palace itself was completed by Fontana in 1634, as requested by the ubiquitous Pope Innocent X Pamphili. The back of the palace has one of the few Art Nouveau touches in Rome—the stairway and portal designed by Ernesto Basile, the Sicilian master of Liberty style, as Art Nouveau is called in Italy.

The obelisk at the center of the piazza was brought to Rome by Augustus, according to Pliny in his *Natural History;* it is one of the 13 that remain out of the nearly 50 that once graced the cityscape.

At the far end of the piazza a short street leads to **piazza Colonna**, dominated by the **Palazzo Chigi**, where the cabinet offices of the government are located. The Chigi Palace was designed by Giacomo Della Porta in 1562 for the Aldobrandini family, but the famous Chigi family of banking interests bought it. During the 18th and 19th centuries this piazza was sufficiently off the beaten track for coffee to be roasted here in the open air; the scent was then considered disagreeable. The column (recently restored) for which the piazza is named commemorates the campaigns of Marcus Aurelius and his victory over the Germanic tribes. The emperor's statue at the top was replaced by one of Saint Paul in 1588.

At some point along the way you'll doubtless notice people carrying portable phones (*telefonini*). Italians, for whom discourse on anything is as essential as pasta, took to these phones in record numbers. An informal survey revealed that 80 percent, despite their professional-looking briefcases, were talking of love and its modalities and most of the rest were registering their opinions on food. When the new president tried to call the parliamentary delegates to order in 1992, he was drowned out by ringing phones; phones are now prohibited during sessions.

For a grand finale to your walk, cross the via del Corso to the right of the arcaded Galleria and continue straight ahead until the rush of water tumbling over boulders tells you that the **Fontana di Trevi** is near. This Baroque version of a nymphaeum, bursting with gods and steeds, was just another fountain until Hollywood, with *Three Coins in the Fountain,* and Fellini, who splashed Anita Ekberg in it in *La Dolce Vita,* made it part of the standard itinerary. Recently restored to an almost too pristine whiteness, it's most magical at night when fewer tourist cameras are clicking. Tradition dictates that you toss a coin into it from over your shoulder to ensure a return to Rome.

Near the fountain, the **Academy of San Luca**, in a small square of that name, exhibits works by Titian, Rubens, van Dyke, Guido Reni, and others. The *Madonna di San Luca* is attributed to Raphael.

THE REAL ROMANS:
CAMPO DEI FIORI TO
TRASTEVERE

The Counter-Reformation, when the Roman Catholic church was attempting to draw back the parishioners who had strayed northward, was a time when popes commissioned artists, notably Bernini and Borromini, to seduce the viewer into the church's mysterious excitement. Façades waved convex and concave, statues gestured, putti cavorted over ceilings and dangled chubby legs from balustrade perches. What realism didn't accomplish, trompe l'oeil did.

No art form better expressed Italy's own vitality, and

especially the famed exuberance of the people from Rome southward. To see the Baroque at its most opulent, start at the church of Sant'Ignazio (Saint Ignatius, founder of the Jesuit movement) and continue to the Gesù, where the saint is buried. The contrast between today's Jesuits—sometimes condemned by the Vatican for their leftist policies—and the priests who accumulated the Gesù's gold and precious stones is as dramatic as the art itself.

The church of **Sant'Ignazio** is near the Palazzo Doria, on a piazza best appreciated on a car-free Sunday. Sit on the church steps and you will discover yourself on a stage, the center of attention for the palaces that curve around the piazza, palaces whose waving convex and concave lines caused critics to call them "the bureaux"; the name spilled over into the tiny adjoining street, via del Burrò.

The church's visual impact starts with its façade, designed by the Jesuit Father Orazio Grassi, Algardi, and others, and financed by Cardinal Ludovisi, whose collection of antiquities is exhibited at the Museo Nazionale. Inside, a blaze of marble, stucco, and rich altar decorations sets the tone. Algardi created several large statues for this church, but the pièce de résistance is the nave's vault, entirely frescoed by the Jesuit Andrea Pozzo and showing Saint Ignatius's ascent into Paradise. Stand at the marble disc on the floor for the trompe l'oeil effect. (Baroque churches relied on viewer participation.)

The expensive trattoria **Cave di Sant'Ignazio**, with an outdoor terrace on the piazza, is still a favorite with Romans at night, when the setting is even more scenic.

Several blocks south of the church is the via del Plebiscito. Turn right into it and soon you will see the church of the **Gesù** (now behind scaffolding), whose opulence makes Sant'Ignazio seem stark. The façade was designed by della Porta in collaboration with the Jesuit Father Valeriani. The church is the prototype for Counter-Reformation churches, with room for the congregation to hear the priest's address comfortably and wide aisles for seating. The church was designed by Vignola for Cardinal Alessandro Farnese, and the idea was to lead the spectator into contact with the mystical by artistic means.

Father Pozzo again created a great ceiling in the chapel. The master of the quadrature painters, who treated entire ceilings as canvases, he organized the groups of heavenly participants by dark and light areas. Bernini's influence is seen here in the rays of light at the center, to which your eyes gravitate. There also appears the monogram IHS, signifying the Name of Jesus, a subject for contemplation in

Ignatian meditation. But not everyone saw it as mystical: The grand duke of Tuscany said it meant "*Iesuiti Habent Satis*"— "the Jesuits have enough."

Another story attached to the church is that of the devil and the wind. The two were out walking in Rome when they came upon this church. "Wait for me," said the devil, entering the Gesù. Since he never came out, the wind is still waiting, which explains why that corner is one of the windiest in Rome.

Continue along corso Vittorio Emanuele II to the **Area Sacra del Largo Argentina**, where some of Rome's oldest buildings, temples from the period of the Republic (fourth century B.C.), can be seen—in the traditional home of Rome's largest stray cat colony, whose benefactors are numerous. Near the via di Torre Argentina stood the Curia Pompeii, where Julius Caesar was murdered. To visit the grounds at Largo Argentina (most of it can be seen from the street), apply to Ripartizione X, via del Portico d'Ottavia 29; Tel: 671-038-19.

Continuing on the same street, on the left is where *Tosca* begins: the church of **Sant'Andrea della Valle**, designed by Carlo Maderno but publicized by Giacomo Puccini and, later, Franco Zeffirelli. Domenichino's contribution was considerable: the frescoes of the *Life of Saint Andrew*. The dome is the second highest and largest (after St. Peter's) in the city. A recently canonized saint of the family of Tommaso di Lampedusa (author of *The Leopard*) is buried here to the right of the high altar. Along corso Vittorio Emanuele II and off to the left on via Baullari (the trunkmakers' street) are the busy streets that surround piazza Campo dei Fiori.

The **Museo Barracco**, farther along on the Corso, occupies an elegant Renaissance palace and houses excellent collections of Egyptian artifacts and classical sculpture.

The Campo dei Fiori Area

On sunny mornings there is no merrier market scene than the one in this piazza—a medieval Covent Garden of cheeses and meats, fruits and flowers, greens and vegetables like none you've ever seen before, and all fresh from the fields, with the bakery **Il Forno** to provide fragrant bread and the **Enoteca campo dei Fiori** for wine. Prices at the luggage stands and flower stalls are usually lower than in stores. On gray or stormy days the campo is more fascinating and moody. Then the atmosphere of the Middle Ages at their most intense permeates the area around the statue of Giordano Bruno, who was burned here as a heretic in 1600. **Da**

Francesco on the piazza is a good trattoria for lunch; the crowded **Carbonara** rests on its shaky old laurels. The **Grotte del Teatro di Pompeo** on via Biscione is a favorite in the evening for its fiery *penne all'arrabbiata* (flat tubes of pasta with a red-peppery sauce), *liguine al radicchio* (narrow ribbon pasta with a spicy chicory sauce), and the pizza from its wood-fired oven.

To the north of the campo is the lovely **Palazzo della Cancelleria**, whose court with a double loggia is a Renaissance masterpiece and is thought to be partly the work of Bramante. (A glimpse through the gate may be all you'll get, though its hallowed halls ring with chamber music during the Christmas season.) To the southwest of the campo, the next square is the **piazza Farnese**, reached from the via del Gallo. There stands one of the most influential of Renaissance palaces—it was reproduced all over Europe. The **Palazzo Farnese** was begun by Sangallo the Younger for Cardinal Alessandro Farnese, who would become Pope Paul III. Exactly what part Michelangelo played is disputed, but it appears that the central balcony, the cornice, and the third floor were his contribution. The palace is today the French Embassy; for admission, which may or may not be granted, apply to the French cultural attaché. While on the piazza, have a look at the tiles in the **Galleria Farnese** boutique. If you are antiques hunting, stroll along the via Giulia, which runs parallel to the Tiber.

Continue along via di Monserrato southeast to the **Palazzo Spada**, in piazza Capo di Ferro. The piazza was designed by Francesco Borromini, who built a wall to screen the palace's resident, Cardinal Spada, from prying eyes. Windows later broke the wall, however, and the fountain was replaced by a more modest one.

The palazzo's busy façade blends whimsy and artistry, and depicts heroes of ancient Rome fêted with garlands of stucco. The palace was built about 1550, but Borromini wasn't called in until 1632. Because the Italian Council of State is the present occupant, access is not easily obtained, but the gallery and the garden are open. When you enter the courtyard—a fantasy of tritons, centaurs, and delicate garlands—stop at the custodian's corner office and ask him to show you the gardens (*giardini*) and the palace (*palazzo*). He often waits to assemble a small group—so you will know whether to stay there or head into the gallery, which has regular hours. (The custodian expects a tip.)

The garden has a charming secret—a colonnade that leads to a life-size figure . . . but no, it's an illusion created by diminishing columns; the figure is only about a foot tall in reality. We owe this fancy to the Augustinian priest Giovanni Maria da Bitonto (1653), not, as was thought until recently, to Borromini.

If you can enter the sumptuously decorated palace, you'll see the statue of Pompey under which Caesar was murdered (or a reasonable facsimile thereof). It's the "dread statue" to which Byron addressed this question: "Have ye been victors of countless kings, or puppets of a scene?" Borromini's stairway, the Corridor of Bas-Reliefs, and the state rooms are appropriately impressive.

The gallery is interesting partly because it is housed in its original setting, four rooms of the cardinal's palace. Of the artworks note especially Titian's *Musician,* the *Visitation* by Andrea del Sarto, a portrait of Cardinal Spada by Guido Reni, and works by Brueghel and Lorenzo Lotto. (A piece of paper enclosed in plastic, found in each room, lists the surrounding works.)

The Ghetto and Isola Tiberina

From piazza Mattei, south of the Area Sacra, via Sant' Ambrogio leads south to **via del Portico d'Ottavia,** named after the monument at the end of the block to the left (currently being restored). Augustus rebuilt the second-century B.C. portico of Cecilius Metellus, which surrounded the temples to Jupiter and Juno, and created two libraries—one Greek and one Latin—dedicating the portico to his sister, Octavia. It became a fish market (*pescheria*) during the Middle Ages, and now houses the fishmongers' church, Sant'Angelo in Pescheria, named in the fishmongers' honor.

Today, via del Portico d'Ottavia is the main street of what was Rome's Jewish **Ghetto,** one of the least touristed and most evocative sections of Rome. Formerly residents of Trastevere, the Jews of Rome moved to the Isola Tiberina following the pillage of Rome in 1084. Then, crossing over the ponte Fabricio (which was once known as the pons Iudeorum, or the Bridge of the Jews), they moved into the area next to the Portico d'Ottavia, ironically the very site where Vespasian and Titus had convened the senate the day Rome conquered Jerusalem. Paul IV officially confined the Jews to the Ghetto in 1555, and although much of it was razed in 1885 to destroy what had become a crowded and insalubrious district over the centuries, many of Rome's Jews chose to remain here. People still come to the area for its characteristic cuisine, which may be sampled at **Da Luciano** or **Da Giggetto** on the via del Portico d'Ottavia, or more expensively at **Piperno** on via del Monte dei Cenci. There is also an excellent pastry shop, **Il Forno del Ghetto**, at number 119. Try the ricotta cheesecake.

Another unfortunate site nearby is the **Palazzo Cenci**, in piazza Cenci. Never a part of the Ghetto, the palazzo was the home of the bloody Cenci family. In a 16th-century scandal, the brutal and perverted Francesco Cenci was murdered by a killer hired by his wife and three of his twelve children. Although public opinion held that this was legitimate self-defense, his wife and daughter Beatrice were beheaded near the ponte Sant'Angelo, his son Giacomo was drawn and quartered, the other son was sentenced to life imprisonment, and the pope confiscated all the family property. The Cenci exploits inspired many literati, including Shelley and Antonin Artaud, and every year on the anniversary of their deaths a mass is celebrated for the repose of Beatrice's soul in the church of San Tommaso, next to the palazzo.

One block away is lungotevere Cenci, where, to your left, is the **Tempio Maggiore**, Rome's synagogue. Built in 1904, it also houses a museum of Roman Jewish memorabilia (Tel: 656-46-48; closed Saturdays). Across from it is the boat-shaped island called the **Isola Tiberina**, reached by ponte Fabricio, Rome's oldest standing bridge, which dates from 62 B.C. (Farther downstream may be seen the remains of the older ponte Rotto, or Broken Bridge, which collapsed in 1598, the year Francesco Cenci was murdered.) The Isola Tiberina was sacred to Aesculapius, the god of medicine, and had hospitals on it long before the present-day Ospedale dei Fatebenefratelli (literally, the do-good brothers).

Trastevere

After walking through the ever-rushing crowds in the center of the city, crossing the Tiber to Trastevere (tras-TAY-var-ay) can be like entering a country town (first the speedway along the Tiber must be bested; push buttons for lights are found about every 50 feet). Go to Trastevere late in the afternoon, when the light on the buildings glows rose and gold, and at night (money belt–only zone). You can stroll through lanes where green tufts of grass sprout from little cracks in thick-walled buildings; tiny shrines are lit to the Madonna; the smell of fresh bread entices; artisans repair statues, sand tables, solder tin pots; children play in long smocks and dark stockings; fountain steps harbor meetings; and on enviable roof gardens the long arm of gentrification is seen. The people of Trastevere consider themselves the true Romans and have made little accommodation to the "foreigners" who have adopted their quarter, although they themselves are warm and friendly by nature.

Start in the southern part of Trastevere at the church of **Santa Cecilia in Trastevere**, whose large, tranquil courtyard is frequented by local mothers watching their *bambini* taking their first steps. Life was far from tranquil for Santa Cecilia, however, who lived in a patrician villa on the site (excavations have been made of her rooms below ground; entrance from inside the church). Her husband, Saint Valerian, was beheaded because, as a Christian, he refused to worship the Roman gods. Cecilia was locked in the steam room of her house, which was then heated by a roaring fire; instead of dying, she was found singing in a heaven-sent shower. Three days of heat did not kill her, and even the blows of an ax failed. By the time she died, hundreds had converted, inspired by her courage. Thus armed with the legend, enter the church to see her statue by Stefano Maderno at the high altar, a figure lying down with her head turned away, as she was when her sarcophagus in the catacombs was opened. On November 22 concerts are held in her honor, and the Academy of Santa Cecilia in Rome, among the most prestigious of music academies, was named for her. During the late afternoon, you may hear the nuns singing mass from behind the grate.

In the nearby **piazza in Piscinula** (named for an ancient Roman bath) stands the 12th-century Palazzo Mattei (now private), once the home of the family that reigned over this neighborhood in medieval days by force of intrigue and murder. Though both acts were common in the Middle Ages, apparently the Mattei went too far and were thrown out of Trastevere. They landed on their feet, however, amassing a great fortune and a cluster of palazzi at piazza Mattei across the river near the Fontana delle Tartarughe.

The spiritual side of the Middle Ages is also well represented at the piazza, with the church at the opposite side built above the house where Saint Benedict spent his childhood, and which he left to create one of the most widespread monastic organizations in the world. The tiny campanile (the smallest in Rome, with the oldest bell) can be seen to best advantage along via in Piscinula, leading from the piazza. Ceramics from all over Italy are beautifully displayed at the **Galleria Sambuca** on via della Pelliccia, several blocks to the west and just north of piazza Santa Maria in Trastevere, a good place for gift buying.

Stop at nearby via dei Genovesi 12 and ring for the *custode* to see the *chiostro,* one of the loveliest small cloisters in the city. Follow via Anicia south from via dei Genovesi, past the church of Santa Maria dell'Orto, with the

odd little obelisks on its façade, to piazza San Francesco
d'Assisi. Here the church of **San Francesco a Ripa** shelters
Bernini's statue of *Blessed Ludovica Albertoni,* strikingly
similar to his more famous Saint Teresa. Bernini was in his
seventies when he made this statue but was still in command
of his formidable powers. The chapel is a domed space,
strangely illuminated over the body of the saint lying in her
final agony. Howard Hibbard, in his book *Bernini,* describes
it in terms that recall a host of Baroque scenes in Rome:
"The waves of draperies in front echo her position, their
heaving billows reflect her agony, their colors accentuate
her pallor . . . the chiaroscuro of this drapery and the diago-
nal of Ludovica's arms, broken by [the position of] her
hands, create an almost symphonic treatment of physical
suffering and death . . . the frieze of bursting pomegranates
below the painting signifies the immortality to which her
soul is passing."

A living Baroque scene takes place daily (except Sundays)
at the produce market in **piazza San Cosimato**, across the
viale di Trastevere (a major bus artery) from the church of
San Francesco. If the market doesn't have something to
entice you, the streets that surround it are likely to. On **via di
San Francesco a Ripa**, which runs from piazza Santa Maria to
San Francesco, you'll find freshly made mozzarella and ricotta, banks of new cheeses to try, fresh bread, pizza squares,
and pastries—the *bignè* (cream puffs) *con zabaglione* are
rich with Marsala. On Sunday mornings the bakeries are
open and filled with people seeking the traditional *cornetti,
sfogliatelle* (a Neapolitan transplant), and their more sugary
associates.

Come early (8:00 or 9:00 A.M.) on Sunday morning for the
Porta Portese **flea market**, which extends for blocks and is
filled with sometimes interesting antiques, old books and
prints, stacks of jeans and shoes, fresh coconut and raw fava
beans (*fave*) to munch on, and a liberal assortment of
pickpockets. Roman authorities would close the market, but
the *populus Romanus* yells a resounding no. Stop first at the
bakeries on via di Francesco a Ripa (above) for fresh *cornetti*
and coffee to fortify you. After 11:00 A.M. only the crowd-
loving need apply—it's the thing to do on Sundays for many
Romans. The entrance where the "antiques" dealers ply their
trade, off via degli Orti di Trastevere, is the easiest. The
section around Porta Portese, on the Tiber, is often mobbed
by 11:00. (Remember that state museums are open Sunday
mornings, however.)

From here to the famous **piazza Santa Maria in Trastevere**
is only a short walk. Its dominant feature, the church of **Santa**

Maria, is enchanting, especially at night, when the façade mosaics glisten. By day it's a mini–piazza Navona, with crowds of local residents and visitors, soccer games, and entangled lovers on the fountain steps.

The church's portico, embedded with ancient relics, was built by Carlo Fontana in 1702. Its campanile (restored) has surveyed the piazza since the 12th century. Although the church we see dates from then, it was erected over what is traditionally thought to be the oldest church (first century) in Rome dedicated to the Virgin Mary. Inside is a gilded ceiling designed by Domenichino; the wonderful polychrome marbles and mosaics sparkle above the Cosmatesque pavement. In the mosaic of the *Madonna with Christ,* a very real woman sits with her son's arm about her in touching tenderness.

A few streets north, on via della Lungara, you'll arrive at the **Palazzo Corsini,** which houses an impressive collection of Renaissance and later masterworks from Fra Angelico to Poussin (open every morning). Across the street, the **Villa Farnesina** contains several rooms frescoed by Raphael with voluptuous and dramatic tales of the gods. The villa was built (1508–1511) for the Sienese banker Agostino Chigi, whose bedroom on the upper floor is frescoed with scenes from the marriage of Alexander the Great and Roxanna. No mere banker's fantasies for him. Given to drama, he once had the servants throw all the gold and silver utensils into the Tiber, outside the dining room, when dinner was finished. The startled guests didn't know that wily Chigi had laid nets in the river to catch his finery.

Stop also at the fine print collection on the second floor, called the **Gabinetto Nazionale delle Stampe.** The Farnesina is closed Sundays but open Mondays.

Near the Farnesina and perfect for a hot day's escape is the **Orto Botanico,** at largo Cristina di Svezia 24, an enchanting garden with greenhouses of orchids and cactus. On its higher level some of the ancient oaks and beeches that once covered the Janiculum have miraculously survived the onslaught of centuries. Open daily except holidays from 9:00 A.M. to sunset; Saturdays and Sundays until noon.

For a Trastevere evening, **Sabatini's** on the piazza is a popular place to dine, especially for the view, or stop at **Noiantri,** another landmark nearby. The English-speaking (or -learning) crowd in Rome turns out in force at the Pasquino, a second-run movie house on vicolo del Piede. **Vicolo delle Cinque** to the north is an attractive old street of stylish boutiques and trattorias. On via della Scala the **Birreria della Scala** is the spot for jazz and beer. Trastevere has several jazz clubs (Billie Holiday, Folkstudio, Big Mama) with American musicians in regular attendance. For a more elegant note, sit in the garden at the **Selarium** (just off via dei Fienaroli) and listen to live music. When it's late, **Yes Brazil** at via Francesco a Ripa 103 will follow up with Brazilian music; the crowd is young and Roman.

Janiculum Hill

High above Trastevere to the northwest, and overlooking the Centro Storico on the other side of the river, the Gianicolo (Janiculum Hill) is frequently climbed (or driven) not only for the superb views of Rome it affords but also for the church of **San Pietro in Montorio,** built over the spot west of Santa Maria in Trastevere where Saint Peter was once believed to have been crucified. In the courtyard is Bramante's lovely Tempietto, smug with Renaissance harmony. Beatrice Cenci is buried in the church, within sight of her place of execution on the ponte degli Angeli.

If you walk farther west up via Garibaldi and then to the passeggiata del Gianicolo, you'll see the monument to Garibaldi, hero of a united Italy. The passeggiata continues past the statue of his wife, Anita, who fought and died at his side.

CAPITOLINE HILL TO AVENTINE HILL

An exhilarating walk (mostly downhill) leads with very few street crossings from the piazza Venezia to the Tiber (stopping off at the Capitoline museums, Santa Maria d'Aracoeli, and piazza Bocca della Verità) and then turns up the Aventine Hill, where during the warmer months the simple charms of early Christian basilicas are entwined with the scent of rose gardens and the orangery, exquisite in spring.

The monument to Vittorio Emanuele II, or the **Vittoriano,** as it is frequently called, has few redeeming architectural features, and its never-darkening white marble in a city of apricot and honey tones is a shock. But to the Italian tourists who come to Rome to see their capital of only a little more than a century, it is a powerful image of unity and durability. The Tomba del Milite Ignoto (Tomb of the Unknown Soldier), midway up the steps and guarded 24 hours a day by the military, adds to its nationalistic appeal. An oddity just in front on the left is a fragment of ancient wall—left there because, when the area was being razed for the monument, it proved to be the tomb of one Caius Publicius Bibulus, who died about 2,000 years ago. Since graves had to be outside the city limits, this provided a historical clue to the configuration of the first century B.C. city walls.

Around to the right as you face the monument are the steep steps that lead to the Aracoeli church. These are suitable for penitents on their knees, but if you feel guilt-free you might opt for Michelangelo's Cordonata, the sloped staircase on the right that leads to the Capitoline Hill's summit and piazza del Campidoglio.

The church of **Santa Maria d'Aracoeli** (pronounced ara-CHAY-lee, or -SHAY-lee in Roman dialect) was built on the site of an ancient temple to Juno Moneta and to Jupiter—a holy place above the Forum where every Roman offered sacrifices. The earliest church on the site dates from the sixth century. In the ninth century a Byzantine monastery occupied the hill, and the present basilica was built around that time. Saint Bernard of Siena lived here, and his life is celebrated inside in a series of frescoes by Pinturicchio. The flight of 124 steps was built by the architect Simone Andreozzi, in gratitude for being spared from the plague in 1346; the parishioners contributed the funds. The church's name, which translates as Saint Mary of Heaven's Altar, is derived from the 12th-century *Mirabilia,* which tells of the time when the emperor Augustus consulted the sibyl about a problem: The senate wanted to deify him, but the idea didn't appeal to him as it had to his predecessor Julius Caesar. The sibyl prophesied that "from the sun will descend the king of future centuries." At that moment the Virgin Mary with the Christ Child in her arms descended from heaven and voices said to him: "This is the Virgin who will receive in her womb the Savior of the World—this is the altar of the Son of God." On that spot Augustus created the altar that was called the Ara Coeli. Later chroniclers mention the altar, which is now lost. A column in the church came from Augustus's bedroom in his palace on the Palatine Hill. It's marked *a cubiculo Augustoranum* and stands third on the left in the nave.

The sumptuous ceiling of gilt-coffered panels was built to honor the victory at Lepanto, which ended the Turkish fleet's rule of the Mediterranean (the papal fleet had taken part in the rout).

Pinturicchio's frescoes of Saint Bernard, painted in 1486, are among the best examples of the artist's work. In the right transept is a Roman sarcophagus festooned with fruit and flowers. Across from it at left is the octagonal tomb of Saint Helen, mother of Constantine. The altar beneath her burial urn is what was thought to be the Ara Coeli but is instead a fine 13th-century work that depicts the miracle. Also in this transept is the tomb of the 13th-century Cardinal Matteo d'Acquasparta, an exceptional work by Arnolfo di Cambio.

In the sacristy, or in the left aisle at Christmas, is the little gold- and gem-encrusted figure of the *Santissimo Bambino* (the Most Holy Child), whose intercession is still sought. Among the many legends surrounding the Bambino is one of a very wealthy woman who was so ill she wanted desperately to keep the Bambino with her through the night. In the morning she felt better but decided she couldn't part with him and had a replica made to return to the church. One medieval night, stormy to be sure, the monks at the church were aroused by a loud knocking at the outer door. It was the Bambino come to his rightful home. At Christmas every year, children come to the church and recite poetry to him; and Christmas Eve mass here is among the most festive celebrations in Rome.

Piazza del Campidoglio

The adjoining piazza del Campidoglio is one of the most pleasant places in Rome to sit, and especially so in the evening. The museums here are open certain weeknights and Saturday evenings. Though you may have to make do with a bit of curbing to sit on, the beauty of the piazza and the lack of cars make it exceptionally conducive to a respite. Since Michelangelo was the planner, this is not entirely surprising. Even the approach along the Cordonata alerts the senses to something out of the ordinary at the top.

The Campidoglio (Capitoline Hill) is the smallest of Rome's famous seven hills, but it is the most imposing because it was the spiritual and political center of the Roman world—the Forum was built on its slope—and it remains the seat of city government to this day. It is especially brilliant each April 21, when the city celebrates its birthday by illuminating the façades of the buildings with hundreds of dish candles.

The equestrian statue of Marcus Aurelius that once graced the center of the piazza (the only equestrian statue that has survived from Imperial Rome) has been relocated to a side courtyard after restoration, and the dramatic if less brilliant statues of Castor and Pollux stand at the top of the steps. At the right is the **Palazzo dei Conservatori**, in which the Conservators' Palace Museum is found. Its courtyard is unmistakably Roman; the enormous head and hand of Constantine, and odds and ends of limbs from the statue that was in his basilica in the Forum, line the warm apricot walls of the court.

On the stairs is the figure of Charles of Anjou, whose ambitions were ended by the Sicilian Vespers revolt; it is the only medieval portrait statue in Rome. In this extensive Classical collection—the statues are mainly copies of Greek originals—the *Thorn Extractor* is notable, but the portrait busts from Augustus to Nero and Tiberius are the prizes. Here Roman art did not follow the Greek patterns but showed the rulers in unidealized portraits. The Etruscan bronze statue of the she-wolf with the nursing twins, Romulus and Remus, that Pollaiuolo added, is also here; its imprint is on everything in Rome, from state seals to sewer covers. The Museo Nuovo wing is devoted to the Renaissance: paintings by Bellini, the Carracci, Caravaggio, Lotto, Reni, and others.

Directly across the piazza, in the Palazzo Nuovo, is the **Museo Capitolino**, where the ancient god Marforio lies in seductive indolence in the courtyard. His name is assumed—he's one of the "talking statues" to which verses were attached, usually satiric poems directed at the celebrities of the time.

Hadrian's villa at Tivoli was awash with splendid mosaics, and some of them are now here, in the Room of the Dove. The theme is Love: Eros and his Roman counterpart, Cupid, with Psyche and the Capitoline Venus. Among the fine statuary are the poignant *Dying Gaul;* the *Marble Faun* (a satyr figure attributed to Praxiteles, and the marble faun of Hawthorne's last novel); and the *Wounded Amazon* (a copy), which was sculpted for a competition at Ephesus, where the cult of Diana thrived.

The remaining building on the piazza is the Palazzo del Senatorio, where the local government meets. In back of it splendid views of the Forum unfold (by day and night).

Toward the Aventine Hill

To the west a couple of blocks on the via del Teatro di Marcello, in front of piazza del Campidoglio, is the **Teatro di Marcello**, Julius Caesar's first contribution to the dramatic world. Its impressive if fragmentary current state is enhanced by the oddity of its having apartments above. Known as the Palazzo Orsini, it is still inhabited by the Orsini family, who have perhaps the best view in Rome. (The stylish **Vecchia Roma** restaurant is close by, and is recommended for lunch.)

Down via del Teatro di Marcello toward the Tiber, before piazza Bocca della Verità, stands the sturdy, newly restored **Arco di Giano** (Arch of Janus) in a valley (now behind a parking lot) where cattle dealers gathered in the days of the Empire, sheltering themselves inside the arch. On the far side of the arch is the delightful church of **San Giorgio in Velabro**, named for the marsh in which Romulus and Remus were found. (The Palatine Hill is just beyond.) The church often bears the red carpet that awaits a wedding party, presided over by 13th-century frescoes.

The beautifully sculpted arch adjoining the church, erected in A.D. 204 in honor of Septimius Severus and his sons, is called the **Arco degli Argentari** (Arch of the Money Lenders). And again, after Caracalla murdered his brother, Geta, he removed Geta's name from the arch, as on the Arch of Septimius Severus in the Forum. On the pilasters contemporary views of the Forum provide the background.

As you turn back toward the Tiber, across the broad boulevard is the exquisite round marble **Tempio di Vesta**, really a temple to Hercules, some think, and the so-called **Tempio della Fortuna Virile** (both second century B.C.).

At the end of the street is the medieval church of **Santa Maria in Cosmedin**, famous for the open mouth of truth, the *Bocca della Verità,* on the porch. Hordes of tourists wait in line to see if it will snap off their hand if they tell a lie. The face was a medieval drain cover, but its appeal is not diminished by that knowledge. The sixth-century church was later enlarged and given to the colony of Greek refugees. The floor is a rare example of mosaics produced by the Cosmati themselves, most floors being only Cosmatesque; geometrical designs signal their work.

The Aventine Hill

Turn left at the corner by Santa Maria and walk to the next wide street, via del Circo Massimo. Across it, a winding road from the piazzale Romolo e Remo ascends the Aventine Hill; by following it you'll see the loveliest rose gardens in Rome (in May) and the orange trees of the church of **Santa Sabina**—and the view of Rome from the balustrade in the little Savello park by the church. The church is an elegant example of a fifth-century basilica, wonderfully lit by clerestory windows and impressive-looking with its Corinthian columns, but the drama is in its simplicity. In 1222 it was given to Saint Dominic, who was founding a new religious order, and the Dominicans still preside here. On the porch is a carved cypress door (under glass); the crucifix at the top left is apparently the oldest known representation of Christ on the Cross.

Continue southwest after Santa Sabina to **piazza dei Cava-**

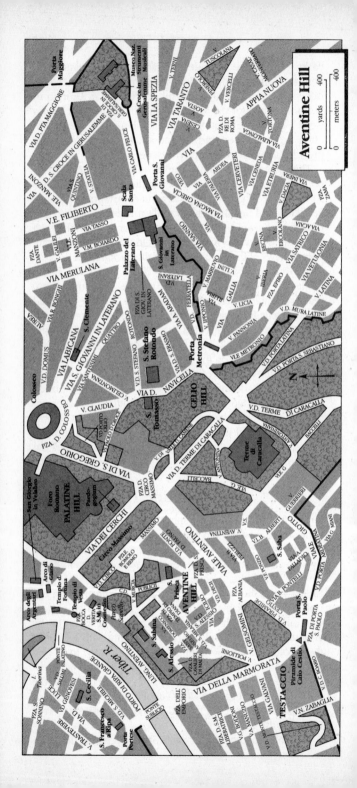

lieri di Malta, a Piranesi-designed space most famous for the keyhole at number 3 that frames St. Peter's dome so beautifully. The Aventine is an obviously wealthy residential neighborhood (money belts advised), and it is a joy to stroll up and down its slopes, away from the hubbub of the city. If you have time, stop also at the ancient churches of Santa Prisca, built over a Mithraic temple (being excavated), and San' Saba, on the other side of piazza Albania to the southeast of the hill.

For lunch, go across via della Marmorata from the Aventine to the outskirts of **Testaccio**, an old neighborhood where the slaughterhouses once stood, and that is still famous for restaurants that specialize in cooking innards. Wonderful vegetables are also a specialty of the inexpensive trattorias that dot the area. **Perilli** is a favorite on via della Marmorata, which leads from the ponte Sublicio to the Porta San Paolo, but stop first up the street at **Volpetti** (number 47) to see one of the most marvelous (and expensive) shops for cheese and other delicacies, including a mortadella like no other. Try the very strong Pugliese *ricotta forte* and varieties of fresh mozzarella; tasting is encouraged. Rome's housing shortage has brought the young and chic to this once-funky neighborhood. See it before the wine bars move in.

ROME'S LEGACY OF FOREIGNERS

Begin one of your days in Rome early, at the **Museo Borghese** in the small palace of the **Villa Borghese** (not a villa but a large park built for Cardinal Scipione Borghese, the pleasure-loving nephew of Pope Paul V, on the Pincio Hill). Today the Villa Borghese, just north of the Spanish Steps/via Veneto area, is one of the greenest and most relaxing public places in Rome, a favorite spot for a picnic, a trip with the children to the zoo, or a promenade to its piazzale Napoleone I on the west side of the **Pincio** for a traditional view of Rome over piazza del Popolo. Bicycles can be rented on via di Villa Giulia, but you must leave your passport.

For the purpose of this one early morning visit, however, go primarily for the museum, where the cardinal amassed, by patronage and plunder, an extensive collection of paintings (temporarily closed to the public) and sculpture. The display begins dramatically, if not scandalously, with the statue of Napoléon's sister Pauline, who, when she married Prince Camillo Borghese, commissioned it from Antonio Canova as a wedding present for her husband. She insisted on posing as

Venus, almost entirely in the nude. When asked how she could have done so, she replied, "Oh, there was a stove in the studio," anticipating Marilyn Monroe's remark about having a radio on in similar circumstances.

Scipione Borghese was an early patron of Bernini, a number of whose most outstanding sculptures are on display here, including *David, Apollo and Daphne,* and *Pluto and Persephone.*

From the museum it is a pleasant walk (or, perhaps better for scheduling your time, taxi ride) to Villa Giulia at the northwest corner of the park, which actually *is* a 16th-century suburban villa, built after a design by Michelangelo and Vignola for Pope Julius II. It houses the **Museo Nazionale di Villa Giulia**, an outstanding collection of the art of the mysterious Etruscans who once inhabited central Italy. Highlights include the *Apollo of Veii,* found in the excavations here, and the *Bride and Groom,* a sarcophagus depicting a smiling, dreamy-eyed couple reclining as if at a banquet with an equality that shocked other ancient societies. Upstairs are attenuated bronze statues and other objects covered with drawings that, to our eyes, look strikingly modern. The Castellani collection of antique jewelry also is superb.

If modern art is what interests you, head next to the **Galleria Nazionale d'Arte Moderna**, which you passed on your way from the Museo Borghese. It contains works of modern painters such as De Chirico, Boccioni, Modigliani, and Pistoletto, as well as some foreign works.

Piazza del Popolo Area

From Villa Giulia, ride or walk west to the ancient via Flaminia; turn south on it and you'll be entering Rome as travellers have traditionally for centuries, through the grand gate called the **Porta del Popolo**, at piazza del Popolo. One such arrival was that of Queen Christina of Sweden, who converted to Catholicism and came to Rome in 1655, an occasion for which Bernini decorated the inside of the great arch and Pope Alexander VII composed the arch's inscription: *Felici faustoque ingressui MDCLV.* Across the piazza are the twin churches of **Santa Maria di Montesanto** (on the left) and **Santa Maria dei Miracoli** (on the right), playful exercises in the art of illusionary design begun by Carlo Rainaldi. The church on the left is narrower than that on the right, so Rainaldi topped the left church with an oval dome and the right with a round one in order to make them look symmetrical—and they do. Good news is that the glamorous piazza is being cleaned and polished, and that the central Egyptian obelisk will be floodlit. Even better news is that it is closed to traffic.

Immediately to the left of the gate is the church of **Santa Maria del Popolo**, which was constructed with funds from the *popolo* (people) and gives the piazza its name. It was built originally in the Middle Ages over what was thought to be Nero's grave, in order to exorcise his malign spirit. Best known for its two paintings by Caravaggio, *The Conversion of Saint Paul* and *The Martyrdom of Saint Peter,* it also contains the Cappella Chigi by Raphael and works by Pinturicchio, Annibale Carracci, Sebastiano del Piombo, and Bernini (who was responsible for the restoration of the church).

Between the twin churches runs the renowned **via del Corso**, named after the horse races that were run during Carnival along its entire length between piazza del Popolo to the north and piazza Venezia and the Vittoriano to the south. One new addition to the otherwise static street is the **Fondazione Memmo**, a private foundation that hosts art exhibitions in the Palazzo Ruspoli (via del Corso 418, Tel: 683-21-77). Between shows, continue your tour by looking left (south) at via del Babuino (which leads to piazza di Spagna) and to the right at via di Ripetta. Either of the cafés at the beginning of these streets is a nice place to pause for some morning refreshment. Most evocative of the *dolce vita* era is **Canova**, on the left, since it is modern in style and popular with employees of the nearby Italian television office, RAI, across the river. **Rosati**, on the right, with its original Art Nouveau decor, comes alive at night, when it is frequented by slick young lotharios on the prowl in noisy sports cars and motorcycles.

Follow the narrow **via di Ripetta**. For a look at the building where Antonio Canova once created his masterpieces, turn onto via Antonio Canova, the third street on the left. You'll find his former studio on the right, a low building with bits of classical sculpture set into its apricot-colored façade, which also has a bronze copy of a self-portrait bust of the artist.

Two streets ahead on via di Ripetta is the **Ara Pacis Augustae**, an altar finished in 9 B.C. to celebrate the Augustan peace, which not only brought peace to the Empire but also ushered in the Augustan Age lauded by Virgil in the *Aeneid* and by other writers such as Livy, Ovid, and Horace. Much of the altar was rediscovered in Rome in the 1930s and transported to its present site, now covered with a

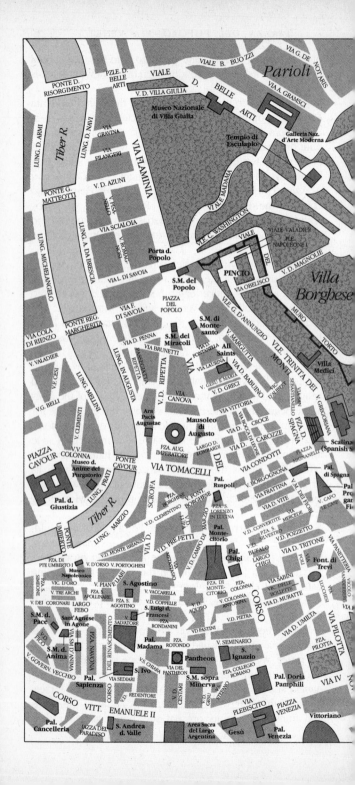

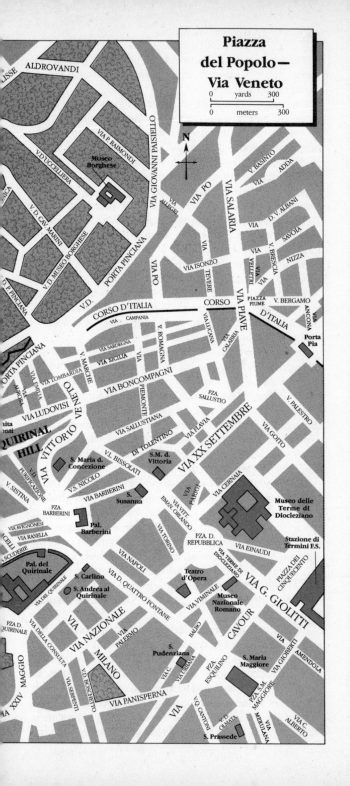

protective piece of Fascist-era architecture. Missing segments were reclaimed from museums throughout the world or replicated.

On one side of the altar, Augustus walks first but remains, modestly, almost unseen in the procession. Sir Mortimer Wheeler wrote of the marble, "If we would understand the Augustan period—its quiet good manners and its undemonstrable confidence—in a single document, that document is the Ara Pacis Augustae." As a work of art it is brilliant, and as a portrait gallery it gives us an image of the Augustan *dramatis personae*. His daughter Julia (banished to the Tremiti Islands for her sexual exploits) and her husband, Agrippa, who built the temple that Hadrian later transformed into the Pantheon, are at the center. The scenes of everyday life here are superb: A child pulls at his mother's robe and a woman silences a chattering couple with a finger to her lips. The child who wears the laurel crown would eventually be grandfather to Nero. The intertwined floral motifs on the far side are some of the finest examples of decorative art created in Roman times.

Across the street is the odd mound that is the **mausoleum of Augustus**. Now stripped of its original travertine covering and obelisks, it was once counted among the most sacred places in Rome. Like Hadrian's tomb (Castel Sant'Angelo), it took the cylindrical Etruscan form, and Augustus's ashes and those of his family were buried within. At his funeral pyre, which was nearby, an eagle was released when the emperor's body was committed to the fire, symbolizing his immortal soul soaring to divine heights.

Hold this thought and cross the Tiber at Ponte Cavour, where Rome's most curious museum awaits. Under glass are the face of a soul in purgatory that was printed on a wall; handprints of the dead priest Panzini that appeared on various objects, among which (without comment) was the chemise of Isabella Fornari, abbess of a convent; and other supernatural manifestations. Ask the sacristan if you may visit this **Museo delle Anime del Purgatorio** (Museum of the Souls in Purgatory) in the church of Sacro Cuore, lungotevere Prati 18.

Continuing along via di Ripetta, the first piazza you will encounter is **piazza Borghese**. Here, in the morning, stalls are filled with antique books and prints, often of high quality and reasonably priced. Nearby on via della Lupa is **La Grapperia**, a bar dedicated to the consumption of hundreds of varieties of the Italian aquavit, grappa. Back at the beginning of the street, via del Clementino and via Fontanella Borghese lead to the Corso, across which begins via Condotti. Lined with designer shops, **via Condotti** is Rome's most famous shopping street, though the two streets parallel to it on the south—via Borgognona and via Frattina—are lined with equally luxurious shops. If you're interested in serious shopping (see "Shops and Shopping," below), avoid the area on a Saturday, when the nearby metro stop of piazza di Spagna disgorges hordes of young people from the suburbs who look but don't buy, much to the consternation of the owners of Gucci, Ferragamo, Fendi, and other shops in the area.

Via Condotti goes straight to the Spanish Steps. Along the way, peek into number 68, the palazzo where the Sovereign Military Order of the Knights of Malta has its headquarters. Granted extraterritorial rights by the Italian state, it issues a limited number of passports and license plates with its S.M.O.M. insignia. If the Vatican is the world's smallest inhabited state, this is the only one entirely enclosed in a palazzo.

The Spanish Steps

Piazza di Spagna is laid out in the shape of a butterfly—without doubt a mellow subtropical species. The tall palms that greet you immediately and the languid crowds on the steps are beautiful reminders of how balmy Rome really can be. The piazza takes its name from the Palazzo di Spagna at number 57, the Spanish Embassy to the Holy See. Many other foreigners, however, have been active in the area. The Spanish Steps (Scalinata della Trinità dei Monti), which rise in the middle of the piazza, actually were paid for by the French to create an easier access to the church of Trinità dei Monti, built by their kings at the top of the hill, and the piazza once was known locally as piazza di Francia. The whole area, in fact, was called *er ghetto del'Inglesi* by the Romans, assuming that all foreigners were English, just as the Greeks before them had referred to all outsiders as barbarians. Keats lived and died in the house at number 26 piazza di Spagna, and is commemorated with a death mask and cases full of memorabilia (as are Shelley and Byron) in the Keats-Shelley Memorial there, where you can purchase tiny volumes of the poets' works.

Goethe and Dickens also knew the Spanish Steps. In his *Pictures from Italy,* Dickens described the characters of the day who went to the steps to hire themselves out as artists' models. "There is one old gentleman, with long hair and an immense beard," he writes, "who, to my knowledge, has gone through half the catalogue of the Royal Academy. This is the venerable, or patriarchical model." He then goes on to describe other colorful types who posed as "the *dolce far niente* model," "the assassin model," "the haughty or scornful model," and writes that "as to Domestic Happiness, and Holy Families, they should come very cheap, for there are lumps of them, all up the steps; and the cream of the thing, is, that they are all the falsest vagabonds in the world, especially made up for the purpose, and having no other counterparts in Rome or in any other part of the habitable globe." The theatricality of the Italian street scene is nothing new. These days, though, you're likely to encounter all sorts of vendors as you climb the steps, for amid the pots of azaleas in the spring, the Nativity scene at Christmas, and all over the steps throughout the year are the people selling crafts and offering modern-day Daisy Millers a coffee that turns out to be drugged, as the tale of their robbery will reveal in Rome's daily *Il Messaggero* the next morning. Like large metropolises everywhere, Rome is not immune to crime, and the Spanish Steps have been getting their share lately, particularly at night.

Yet the steps are still a welcome resting place for tourists. Romans know that spring has come when large pots of azaleas are brought from the Villa Celimontana, where they've wintered and budded, and are hoisted into place on the steps and in the surrounding streets.

You'll need some sustenance to scale the 137 steps, however. Fortunately, the historical presence of travellers and the piazza's contemporary guise as a center for luxury shops (increasingly affordable, it seems, only to Italians) have ensured a number of cafés and restaurants in the area. If you're feeling fancy, try **Ranieri's** on via Mario dei Fiori, a remnant from the Grand Tour days. Otherwise, the pleasant outdoor courtyard of **Otello alla Concordia** on via della Croce is a fine spot for lunch. For a postprandial pickup, the antique **Caffè Greco** on via Condotti has been offering coffee and other refreshment since the early 18th century. **Babington's**, to the left of the steps in the piazza, serves high-priced tea, and the bar at the Hotel D'Inghilterra, as well as **Baretto** at via Condotti 55, serve as watering holes for the elegant locals.

Or you may simply want a sip of water from the fountain called the Fontana della Barcaccia, at the base of the steps. Designed by Pietro Bernini, or possibly his son Gianlorenzo, it takes its shape from the boats that once came to the papal port of Ripetta, formerly nearby on the Tiber.

Before making your ascent up the steps, follow via del Babuino off the piazza to the left. Turn right on vicolo d'Alibert to the charming **via Margutta**, which is lined with an open-air art show every spring and fall (and art galleries year-round), and double back at via della Fontanella to via del Babuino, where amid the elegant antiques shops you'll notice the statue of Silenus, dubbed by residents "the baboon" and giving the street its name. The Anglican church of **All Saints** is at number 153, the English-language **Lion Bookstore** is at number 181, and, if you're in need of some refreshment, try the ultramodern **Café Notegen** at number 159. Cross piazza di Spagna to its southern triangle, where you'll see the column dedicated to the Immaculate Conception. Here each December 8 the pope crowns the statue of the Virgin with a garland of flowers; its height requires that the deed be performed by a member of Rome's trusty fire brigade from the ladder of a truck. The building behind the column is the **Palazzo di Propaganda Fide** (Palace of the Propagation of the Faith), the missionary center of the Catholic world. Bernini and Borromini both worked on its façades, but not at the same time. The side facing the piazza is the work of Bernini, and his rival's concave façade is to the right.

Perhaps braced with another sip of water from the Fontana della Barcaccia, you're now ready to climb the delightfully curving travertine steps to Trinità dei Monti, with its views of the shoppers below. In honor of the Trinity, the staircase is divided into three landings; each in turn is divided into three. The French occupy not only the church but the adjacent **Villa Medici**, just to the left as you face the church, on viale della Trinità dei Monti. It was here that Louis XIV established the Académie de France and the Prix de Rome in 1666. French artists still come to study at the academy within, which also hosts important art exhibitions. The street eventually leads to the view from the Pincio, but come back at sunset to enjoy that at its best, preferably from the **Casina Valadier** café-restaurant. Now is the time to turn around and head down via Sistina to piazza Barberini and the beginning of via Veneto. The centerpiece of the piazza is the Fontana del Tritone (Fountain of the Triton) by Bernini, and at the corner of via Veneto is the Fontana delle Api (Fountain of the Bees), named after its numerous symbols of the Barberini family, who commissioned the work from Bernini. (The Palazzo Barberini here is the starting point of our "Centuries of Christianity" section below.)

Via Vittorio Veneto

The shady curves of via Vittorio Veneto recall the days when it was a cow path only a century ago but mask the more frenetic activity that has taken place there in recent years, most infamously in the 1960s, when it was the stage for the extravagances of international film stars working at Rome's film studio, Cinecittà. The way of life was dubbed *la dolce vita* (the sweet life) and fictionalized by Fellini in a movie of the same name. Before musing on that time, however, stop into the church of **Santa Maria della Concezione** for a memento mori about where the sweet life eventually leads. Its five chapels were decorated in bizarre Rococo patterns formed by the bones of some 4,000 Capuchin monks.

These days the street scene is quieter, interrupted occasionally by the clicking heels of the (usually transvestite) prostitutes who walk the street at night and the cars that screech to a halt to meet them. But the overall atmosphere is peaceful, and the street activity can be taken in over leisurely refreshment at **Café de la Paix**, the best-known café from the days of the sweet life.

The Veneto ends in glory, however, with piazza Barberini's restored statue of **Il Tritone**—a masterwork by Bernini, who understood the exuberant sensuality of his city.

CENTURIES OF CHRISTIANITY

Ever mindful of museum hours, begin one day's tour on via delle Quattro Fontane at the entrance to the **Palazzo Barberini** (number 13). Begun in 1625 for Pope Urban VIII (Maffeo Barberini) by Carlo Maderno, construction of the palazzo was taken over by Borromini, who was responsible for the oval stairs on the right, and then by Bernini, who designed the central façade and the rectangular staircase on the left. The palazzo remained in the hands of the Barberini family for years. Among its tenants was the American sculptor William Story, who entertained the Brownings, Henry James, and Hans Christian Andersen in his apartments here. In 1949 it was sold to the Italian government and now houses the **Galleria Nazionale d'Arte Antica**, which is not a gallery of antique art at all. The gallery contains paintings by such artists as Fra Angelico, Filippo Lippi, Bronzino, Caravaggio, Tintoretto, and El Greco, as well as Raphael's portrait of *La Fornarina,* the baker's daughter who was his mistress. The sumptuous Baroque and Rococo decoration of the rooms, especially Pietro da Cortona's ceiling fresco *Allegory of Divine Providence* (note the ever-buzzing Barberini bees in the center) in the salon, gives some idea of the splendor in which the popes lived.

Southeast up via delle Quattro Fontane, where it intersects via del Quirinale, are the four facing Baroque fountains for which the street is named. This is also the crossroads of the wide streets laid out under Sixtus V (1585–1590), with sweeping views leading to Porta Pia to the northeast and to the obelisks of the Quirinal Hill to the southwest, the Esquiline Hill to the southeast, and Trinità dei Monti to the northwest.

On the far corner of via del Quirinale is Borromini's church of **San Carlo alle Quattro Fontane**, known affectionately as San Carlino, with a lovely adjacent cloister. The geometric complexity of the church's interior provides an obvious contrast (and convenient comparison) to the interior of Bernini's church of **Sant'Andrea al Quirinale** just down the street, which is relatively simple in spite of its rich marble and gilt decor.

Farther down the street is the **Palazzo del Quirinale**. Designed by Maderno, Bernini, and many others, it was formerly a summer residence of the popes and was later used by the kings of Italy. It is now occupied by the president of the republic. Its rich decoration by such artists as Melozzo da Forlì and Pietro da Cortona can be seen only by permission (write the Ufficio Intendenza della Presidenza della Repubblica, via della Dataria 96, 00187 Rome). No appointment is necessary, however, to see the *corazzieri,* the presidential guard, all over six feet tall and dashing in their crimson and blue uniforms, gleaming boots, and shining helmets with tossing plumes. The changing of the guard takes place every day at 4:00 P.M.

Take via della Consulta south off piazza del Quirinale and turn left on bustling via Nazionale, where you'll pass the recently reopened **Palazzo delle Esposizioni** at number 194, where interesting art exhibitions are held, and the Neo-Gothic American church of St. Paul on the corner of via Napoli. The street leads to piazza della Repubblica, with its tall spray of water shooting out of the Fontana delle Naiadi, an 1885 bronze fountain by Alessandro Guerrieri of naiads cavorting with sea monsters. The piazza is commonly called piazza Esedra because the arcades of the two curving palaces around it are built where the *exedrae,* or semicircular benches, of the Terme di Diocleziano (Baths of Diocletian) once existed. (Coincidentally, the ring around the fountain is still a popular trysting place.)

Baths of Diocletian Area

Begun by Maximilian and completed by Diocletian, the baths (*terme*) were the largest of all such Roman facilities, able to accommodate 3,000 people and covering an area of

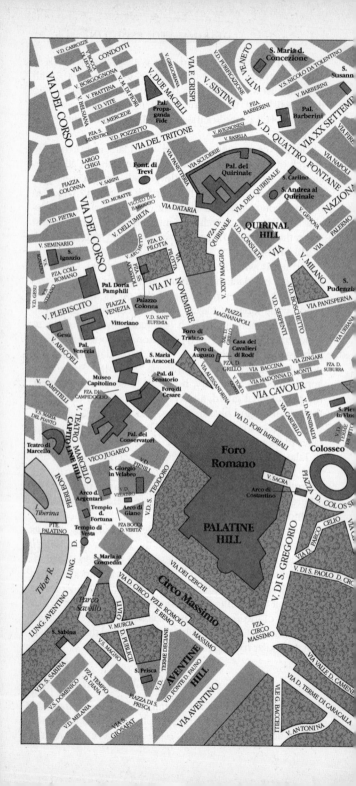

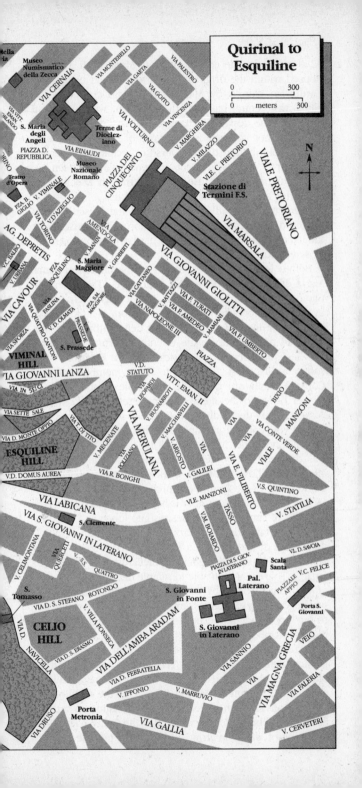

Quirinal to Esquiline

0   300

0   meters   300

N

...ella
..a

Museo Numismatico della Zecca

VIA CERNAIA

VIA MONTEBELLO

VIA GAETA

VIA PALESTRO

VIA GOITO

VIA VOLTURNO

VIA VINCENZA

VIA MARGHERA

V. MILAZZO

VLE. C. PRETORIO

VIALE PRETORIANO

VIA VITT. EMAN. ORLANDO

S. Maria degli Angeli

PIAZZA D. REPUBBLICA

Terme di Diocleziano

VIA EINAUDI

Museo Nazionale Romano

PIAZZA DEI CINQUECENTO

Stazione di Termini F.S.

VIA MARSALA

...RINO

Teatro d'Opera

PZA. B. GIGLIO

V. VIMINALE

V.D AZEGLIO

VIA D. VIMINALE

VIA TORINO

VIA AMENDOLA

VIA MANIN

VIA GIOBERTI

VIA GIOVANNI GIOLITTI

AG. DEPRETIS

V.C. BALBO

V. URBANA

PZA. ESQUILINO

S. Maria Maggiore

VIA CAVOUR

VIA PAOLINA

PZA S.M. MAGGIORE

VIA CATTANEO

VIA RATTAZZI

VIA F. TURATI

VIA P. AMEDEO

VIA NAPOLEONE III

V. MAMIANI

VIA P. UMBERTO

VIA QUATTRO CANTONI

VIA SFORZA

V.D. OLMATA

PRASSEDE

S. Prassede

VIMINAL HILL

VIA GIOVANNI LANZA

VIA IN SELCI

V.D. STATUTO

PIAZZA VITT. EMAN. II

VIA LEOPARDI

VIA BUONARROTI

BIXIO

MANZONI

VIA SETTE SALE

VIA T. DI TITO

V. MECENATE

VIA MACCHIAVELLI

VIA MERULANA

VIA POLIZIANO

VIA ARIOSTO

VIA

VIA CONTE VERDE

VIALE

ESQUILINE HILL

V.D. MONTE OPPIO

VIA R. BONGHI

V. GALILEI

VIA E. FILIBERTO

V.S. QUINTINO

V.D. DOMUS AUREA

VIA LABICANA

VLE. MANZONI

V.M. BOIARDO

TASSO

V. STATILIA

VIA S. GIOVANNI IN LATERANO

S. Clemente

V. CELIMONTANA

VIA QUERCETI

V. SS. QUATTRO

VL. D. SAVOIA

S. Tomasso

VIA D. S. STEFANO

ROTONDO

V. VILLA FONSECA

PIAZZA DI S. GIOV. IN LATERANO

S. Giovanni in Fonte

Pal. Laterano

Scala Santa

PIAZZALE APPIO

V.C. FELICE

Porta S. Giovanni

CELIO HILL

VIA D. NAVICELLA

VIA D. S. ERASMO

VIA DELL'AMBA ARADAM

S. Giovanni in Laterano

VIA SANNIO

VIA MAGNA GRECIA

VEIO

VIA D. FERRATELLA

V. IPPONIO

V. MARRUVIO

VIA

VIA FALERIA

VIA DRUSO

Porta Metronia

VIA GALLIA

V. CERVETERI

32 acres. Today the church of **Santa Maria degli Angeli** is housed within the original Tepidarium. It was begun as a Carthusian church by Michelangelo, who converted the baths' vast central hall into the nave, but when Vanvitelli took over the design he changed the nave into a transept. What has not changed is the sense of space, a uniquely Roman contribution to the course of architectural history. The church and its adjacent convent have just been restored to house the **Museo delle Terme di Diocleziano**, displaying art from the late Roman Republic.

Coin collectors will want to stop at the **Museo Numismatico della Zecca**, at via XX Settembre 97. Because it's in the Italian Treasury Building, your passport will be required; closed Sundays.

Before leaving the area, stop into the church of **Santa Maria della Vittoria** on via XX Settembre. (The American Catholic church of **Santa Susanna**, with a magnificent façade by Maderno, presently under restoration, is in the next block.) The interior of Santa Maria della Vittoria also was designed by Maderno in the Counter-Reformation style of the Gesù, and Bernini's theatrical Cappella Cornaro is Baroque at its most flamboyant. Here, members of the Cornaro family are portrayed in marble as spectators in theater boxes to the statue of Saint Teresa of Avila, whose ecstasy seems decidedly secular. If her sensuality gets the best of you, cool off in front of the horned statue of Moses in the Fontana del Mose around the corner. The fountain was designed by Domenico Fontana, who allegedly died after seeing how badly his work compared to Michelangelo's statue of Moses in the church of San Pietro in Vincoli (see below), though the story is held to be apocryphal.

Better to sublimate your desires into lunch and take the five-minute taxi ride from piazza della Repubblica in front of the Terme di Diocleziano a few long blocks south to the simple setting of the restaurant **Cicilardone** at via Merulana 77. There you'll be able to sample the endless varieties of homemade pasta by ordering *assaggini* (little tastes), which go a long way. (A less expensive alternative would be to buy provisions at the boisterous food market in nearby piazza Vittorio.)

If you haven't already done so on your travels, give a passing glance to **Stazione di Termini**, the railroad station often overlooked in the context of the city's more venerable architecture. Begun under the Fascists, as the neo-Roman side sections show, the construction of the station unearthed part of a wall built after the invasion of the Gauls in A.D. 390, the ruins of which in front of the station provide a stark contrast to the sweeping travertine curve of the entrance. Today the piazza in front serves as a gathering place for immigrants from Asia and Africa, a phenomenon reminiscent of the farthest-flung days of the Roman Empire. Gypsies will no doubt be interested in your *lire* here. Beware—especially of children carrying signs designed to distract you.

Santa Maria Maggiore

From Cicilardone take via Merulana to the double-domed basilica of Santa Maria Maggiore, one of the four so-called major basilicas of Rome, this one built on the Esquiline Hill. Many myths and legends surround the basilica, which was dedicated to the Virgin Mary after the Council of Ephesus in A.D. 431 affirmed that she was the mother of Christ. One of the most charming is that the Virgin appeared on this site on the night of August 4, 352, saying that her church should be built on an area she would cover—and did—with a snowfall the following morning. The event is commemorated each August 5 with a pontifical mass in the Cappella Borghese, accompanied by white flower-petal flurries from the dome of the chapel as a simulated snowfall in the piazza at right. (The chapel is also where the tiny coffin of Pauline Borghese lies.) The basilica preserves the relic (displayed each Christmas) of the Holy Crib in which the infant Jesus was laid, mentioned by Petrarch in a letter to Pope Clement VI in Avignon as one of Rome's sacred treasures to lure the papacy back.

The basilica has a magnificent vaulted ceiling covered with what is supposedly the first gold to have arrived in Europe from the New World, but even more precious are its mosaics, best seen with binoculars. The nave mosaics contain scenes from the Old Testament; the triumphal-arch mosaics depict the infancy of Christ; and the apse mosaics illustrate the Coronation of the Virgin. In the afternoon it is also likely you'll find a sacristan to admit you to the oratory of the manger beneath the Cappella Sistina, which houses the remains of Arnolfo di Cambio's original 13th-century decoration.

Outside, notice the campanile, which is the tallest in Rome. Its bells are said to speak in Roman dialect. When they ring, try to make out the words *Avemo fatto li facioli, avemo fatto li facioli* (We made the beans). The bells of San Giovanni in Laterano then ask, *Con che? Con che?* (With what?), and Santa Croce in Gerusalemme responds, *Co' le codichelle, co' le codichelle* (With *cotechino* sausage).

Nearby are **Santa Prassede** and **Santa Pudenziana**, two early Christian churches dedicated to sister saints, the daughters of a Roman senator named Pudens, who was a Christian and a friend of Saint Peter. Off the piazza di Santa Maria Maggiore is the side entrance to the brick church of Santa Prassede, on via Santa Prassede. The church was once a *titulus,* a private residence where Christians were sheltered and rituals took place during the time of persecution. In the apse mosaics the sisters are being presented by Saints Peter and Paul to the Redeemer, but the most spectacular Byzantine mosaics entirely cover the Cappella di San Zenone, which contains a column, brought from Jerusalem, on which the flagellation of Christ is believed to have taken place. Many relics are found in the church, among them a circular porphyry stone under which Santa Prassede is said to have placed the blood and bones of thousands of Christian martyrs.

On the other side of Santa Maria Maggiore, off piazza del Esquilino (with its obelisk that originally stood in front of the Mausoleo di Augusto), you'll find via Urbana, where the church of Santa Pudenziana stands. Its apse contains one of the oldest mosaics in Rome, dating from the fourth century.

San Pietro in Vincoli Area

Follow via Urbana down the hill to piazza degli Zingari, which means Gypsies in Italian, a reminder that bands of Gypsy pickpockets roam the area (and much of Rome)—so be alert. The street then leads to piazza della Suburra, named after the most notorious district of ancient Rome—which today seems quite peaceful, even trendy, with restaurants and rents both rapidly on the rise. Taking the steps up to via Cavour (where you could slip into **Enoteca** at number 313 for an afternoon refresher), cross the busy street, and on your right locate the steep staircase to the church of **San Pietro in Vincoli**. The church preserves a relic said to be the chains (*vincoli*) that shackled Saint Peter during his imprisonment in Jerusalem as well as in Rome, but most people come here to see Michelangelo's statue of Moses. (The horns are an artistic convention meant to indicate the subject's status as a prophet.) The figure is part of Julius II's ill-fated tomb, originally intended for St. Peter's and supposed to contain some 40 statues but never finished; some of its statuary was dispersed to the Louvre and to Florence's Galleria dell'Accademia. The *Moses* was completed, however, and Vasari writes about how the Jews of Rome went there "like flocks of starlings, to visit and adore the statue."

Many legends surround the statue: The mark on the knee supposedly comes from Michelangelo throwing his hammer at it, commanding it to speak.

Descend the Esquiline Hill on via degli Annibaldi and take the stairway that leads to piazza del Colosseo; around to your left, via San Giovanni in Laterano will bring you east to piazza di San Clemente. On the left is the fascinating **Basilica di San Clemente**, a three-level house of worship run by Irish Dominican brothers since the 17th century. Its upper level has a lovely 12th-century marble pavement by the Cosmati family, 12th-century mosaics, and 15th-century frescoes by Masolino da Panicale. Underneath, and reached by the right aisle, is the lower church, which has frescoes dating from the ninth century. Beneath it, and accessible at the end of the left aisle, are the remains of a first-century *domus* and third-century Mithraic temple, which has a bas-relief representing the sun god Mithras slaying a bull. And even farther below is another evocative phenomenon: If you listen carefully, you'll hear the Charonic sounds of an underground river, which leads to Rome's ancient Cloaca Maxima sewer.

San Giovanni in Laterano

Continuing along via San Giovanni in Laterano, lined with nondescript residential apartment buildings, you will soon come across another of the major basilicas of Rome, San Giovanni in Laterano (Saint John Lateran). It is the cathedral church of Rome and the titular see of the pope as bishop of Rome; he usually celebrates Maundy Thursday services here. The basilica takes its name from the patrician family of Plautius Lateranus, whose huge estate on the site was confiscated by Nero but later was returned to the family and became the dowry of Fausta, wife of Constantine, who built the original basilica here. (Constantine later had her drowned in her bath.) It subsequently underwent a series of disasters: a fifth-century sacking, a ninth-century earthquake, and a 14th-century fire; as a result, the present church has more historical than aesthetic appeal. The original Palazzo del Laterano next to the church was the residence of the popes until they moved to Avignon, and many important events in the history of the church took place here, including the 1123 Diet of Worms. (The current palazzo dates from the 16th century and is the seat of the Rome vicariate.)

Today you see an 18th-century façade on the church, crowned with gigantic statues of the saints surrounding Christ. Borromini designed the nave and aisles of the interior, which has a magnificent ceiling and statues of the apostles by followers of Bernini. Among the other sights of the church are a heavily restored fresco by Giotto in the Cappella Corsini; reliquaries containing (legend has it) the heads of Saints Peter and Paul and a piece of the table on which the Last Supper took place; and cloisters dating from the 13th century. Next door, **San Giovanni in Fonte** (the Baptistery of St. John) was the first of its kind, built by Constantine (the one who drowned his wife) in about 320. Its octagonal form became the prototype for baptisteries throughout Italy.

The Scala Santa, on the opposite side of the Palazzo del Laterano from the baptistery, contains the **Sancta Sanctorum**, the old private chapel of the popes, and, leading up to it, what are believed to be the steps Christ climbed in Pilate's house, brought to Rome by Saint Helena, Constantine's mother. Today the faithful still climb them on their knees.

Farther on, at the other end of via Carlo Felice, is the church of **Santa Croce in Gerusalemme**, one of Rome's seven pilgrimage churches. It contains two 15th-century works of art worth stopping for—an apse fresco, *The Invention of the True Cross* (the church was built to house the relics of the True Cross brought back from Jerusalem: three pieces of wood, a nail, and two thorns from Christ's crown), and a mosaic in the Cappella di Santa Elena—as well as another lovely marble floor by the Cosmati. The **Museo Nazionale degli Strumenti Musicali** next to the church, at piazza di Santa Croce in Gerusalemme 9A, houses an impressive collection of musical instruments from ancient times to the 17th century (closed Sundays).

Cannavota, Rome's oldest fish restaurant, is found in piazza San Giovanni in Laterano, near the obelisk. The restaurant itself is worth a dinner reservation (Tel: 06-77-50-07; closed Wednesdays). If you need to cast about beforehand, have a look at the colorful street market outside Porta San Giovanni in via Sannio, or check out the local branch of Italy's Coin department-store chain.

THE VATICAN

If all roads lead to Rome, they soon after lead across the Tiber to the Vatican. Since 1929, when Benito Mussolini and Cardinal Pietro Gasparri signed the Lateran Treaty between Italy and the Holy See, Vatican City—the seat of the Roman Catholic church and the cradle of all Christendom—has been an independent state ruled by the pope, the only

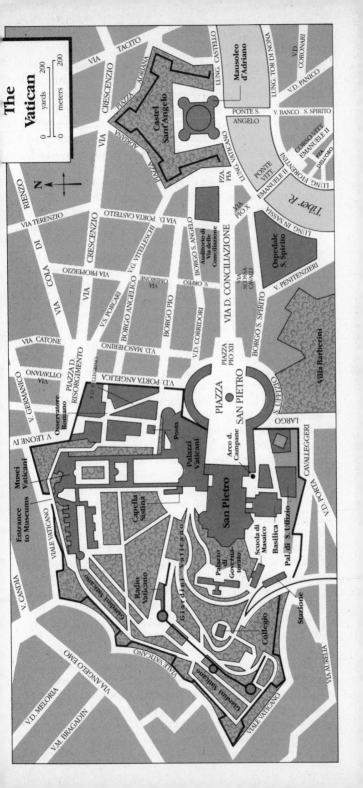

The Vatican

yards 200
meters 200
0

N

VIA TACITO
VIA CRESCENZIO
VIA RIENZIO
VIA TERENZIO
VIA COLA DI RIENZO
VIA CRESCENZIO
VIA PROPERZIO
VIA CATONE
VIA GERMANICO
V. OTTAVIANO
V. LEONE IV
V. CANDIA
V.D. MELORIA
V. ANGELO EMO
V.M. BRAGADIN

PIAZZA ADRIANA
VIA ADRIANA
LUNG. CASTELLO
LUNG. TOR DI NONA
V.D. CORONARI
V.D. PANICO
V. BANCO S. SPIRITO
Mausoleo d'Adriano
Castel Sant'Angelo
PONTE S. ANGELO
PONTE VITT. EMANUELE II
CORSO VITT. EMANUELE II
LUNG. FIORENTINI
LUNG. IN SASSIA
Tiber R.
PZA PIA
LUNG. VATICANO
VIA PIO X
VIA D. PORTA CASTELLO
VIA D. PORTA ANGELICA
BORGO S. ANGELO
V. ORFEO
V.G. VITELLESCHI
VIA OMBRONE
V.S. PORCARI
BORGO ANGELICO
BORGO PIO
V.D. CORRIDORI
V.D. MASCHERINO
Auditorio di Via delle Conciliazione
VIA D. CONCILIAZIONE
VIA SCOSSA CAVALLI
BORGO S. SPIRITO
V. PENITENZIERI
Ospedale S. Spirito
Villa Barberini
PIAZZA PIO XII
PIAZZA D. RISORGIMENTO
V.D. PELLEGRINO
Osservatore Romano
Musei Vaticani
Entrance to Museums
VIALE VATICANO
Posta
Palazzi Vaticani
Capella Sistina
PIAZZA SAN PIETRO
Arco d. Campane
S. UFFIZIO
LARGO
Radio Vaticano
Palazzo di Governatorato
San Pietro
Scuola di Mosaico
Basilica
Pal. di S. Uffizio
V.D. PORTA CAVALLEGGERI
Giardini Vaticano
Collegio
Stazione
VIA AURELIA

absolute sovereign in Europe. The Vatican, as it is most commonly known, has its own flag and national anthem, mints its own coinage, prints its own postage stamps (many Romans have more faith in its postal system than in Italy's, and go to the Vatican just to mail their letters and packages), has its own polyglot daily newspaper (*L'Osservatore Romano*), Latin-language quarterly (*Acta Apostolicae Sedis*), multilingual radio station, and plans for a television station. (The pope, it's said, gets his news from an all-Latin news show broadcast by Finnish shortwave.) All these activities take place in an area of just over 100 acres, a considerable part of which is taken up by St. Peter's, the world's greatest basilica in the world's smallest state. In addition to establishing the sovereign territory contained within the high walls of the Vatican, the Lateran Treaty granted special extraterritorial privileges to the churches of San Giovanni in Laterano, Santa Maria Maggiore, and San Paolo Fuori le Mura. Together with St. Peter's they constitute the four major basilicas of Rome.

Because of the limited visiting hours of many of the Vatican's attractions, you'll need careful planning to see the sights in the span of a day. *Begin early,* on Italian territory in piazza ponte Sant'Angelo across the Tiber from the Castel Sant'Angelo. You will be facing Rome's most beautiful bridge, the glorious ponte Sant'Angelo, which Gianlorenzo Bernini intended as the initial part of the approach to St. Peter's. Statues of Saints Peter and Paul greet you as you walk over the Tiber, virtually escorted by ten statues of angels, each carrying a symbol of Christ's crucifixion, to herald your visit.

The massive round object across the Tiber, topped with a statue of the Archangel Michael, is **Castel Sant'Angelo**. The ancient mausoleum of Hadrian, it was once landscaped, clad in travertine, covered with sculpture, and topped by a bronze statue of the emperor himself. In the Middle Ages it became part of the Aurelian Wall, and through a gate on the castle grounds called Porta San Pietro became the main point of entry to the Vatican for religious pilgrims. It also has served as a refuge for the popes, who entered it through a private passageway from the Vatican, and as a prison. One of its illustrious captives was the Renaissance goldsmith Benvenuto Cellini, whose escape is one of the most gripping moments of the dashing life he recounted with bravura, if not braggadocio, in his *Autobiography*. Bypass the castle's grim displays of weapons and prisons and opt for the sumptuous papal apartments on the top floor instead. The painting collection includes Lorenzo Lotto's *Saint Jerome* and works by Mantegna and Signorelli. From there take the staircase that, after a display of military paraphernalia, leads to the terrace familiar from the last act of *Tosca,* the one from which the heroine jumps to her death in the Tiber. (The river today is too far from the castle for her to have made it.)

The terrace has one of the best views of Rome and offers a close-up of Peter Anton Verschaffelt's 18th-century bronze statue of the Archangel Saint Michael, commemorating Pope Gregory the Great's vision during the plague year of 590, when Saint Michael appeared over Hadrian's tomb sheathing his sword, an act that signified the end of the plague and gave the castle its name. (Castel Sant'Angelo is open Monday afternoons as well, in case you want to see it later in the day.)

In Bernini's day, a walk down the narrow medieval streets from Castel Sant'Angelo directly west through the area known as the Borgo led to the delightful surprise of his expansive piazza at St. Peter's. Now, however, the grandiose **via della Conciliazione**, named after the Lateran accord, has ludicrously overextended the welcoming arms of Bernini's colonnade and ruined the dramatic element of turning suddenly into piazza San Pietro. In all fairness, a monumental boulevard had been planned since the middle of the 15th century; it was unfortunate that *domani* finally came in 1936 under Fascism. The wide swath, with double obelisks goosestepping along either side, was completed in 1950, just in time for a Holy Year (they officially occur every quarter century but can be declared as often as the pope wishes, as seen in recent years). Walk quickly and fix your gaze on St. Peter's, heading straight for the tourist information office in the colonnade on your left as you face the basilica.

The **Vatican Gardens** are now open to guided tour groups only, so make the most of your time if not your money (the price of admission to most things at the Vatican is lofty) and get to the office no later than 10:00 A.M. to sign up for the daily tour. The cost is Ł15,000 on Tuesdays, Fridays, and Saturdays. On Mondays and Thursdays the tour includes the Sistine Chapel and costs Ł27,000. (Between November and February, tours take place only on Saturdays.) The tour begins at the Arco delle Campane (Arch of the Bells), watched over by the Swiss Guards, whose red-yellow-and-blue striped uniforms—supposedly designed by Michelangelo—add a playful air to the increasingly serious job of protecting the pope. From there, guides escort visitors to a number of sights on the extensive grounds, given an occasional assist by a minibus. Included in the tour are sights most visitors to the Vatican have not seen—**Circo di Nerone,** where the first Christian martyrs (including Saint Peter) met their deaths; the 18th-century mosaic studio, which still sells stones as souvenirs; the train station (used primarily for the delivery of duty-free merchandise to fortunate employees and friends of the Vatican); the Palazzo del Governatorato, where the governor has his office; the radio station; and the prison. The most pleasant part of the tour is the gardens themselves, meticulously groomed and presided over by cypresses, umbrella pines, and—most magnificently—the only good views of the largest brick dome in creation, part of Michelangelo's original plan for St. Peter's.

The garden tour ends back at the tourist information office, and whether or not you've gone on it, this is where you should take the bus to a side entrance of the Vatican Museums. This bus also goes back through the gardens and is a pleasant alternative to the long walk from St. Peter's Square around the walls to the main museum entrance on the viale Vaticano to the north.

The Vatican Museums

The Vatican Museums have become so crowded that the authorities have had to resort to four color-coded tours to impose order. The only one that covers all the important sights is the yellow tour, which supposedly lasts five hours, but by following the yellow route and stopping only at the highlights listed below you can cut that time in half. (Ticket sales stop at 1:30 P.M. except at Easter and from July to September, when they stop at 3:30. The museums are closed on Sundays, except for the last Sunday of the month, when they're free. Wear comfortable shoes; take binoculars and a fan.)

The Egyptian Museum. Head straight for Room V, where the most impressive relics are the colossal granite statue of Queen Tuia, mother of Ramses II, and the sandstone head of Pharaoh Menuhotep across from it. Before leaving the room, peek through the door into the outdoor niche, which contains the giant bronze fir cone found near the Thermae of Agrippa, and to which Dante compared the giant's face ("just as wide as St. Peter's cone in Rome") in the *Inferno.*

Braccio Nuovo. Here stands the famous statue of Augustus, found in 1863 on the grounds of the dread Livia's estate at Prima Porta.

Chiaramonti Museum. Rather than dwelling on any single work of art here, take a look at the display, which was laid out in the early 19th century by Neoclassical sculptor Antonio Canova. The realistically human portrait busts of ancient Romans are the prized objects here.

Pio-Clementino Museum. Two of the most celebrated antique sculptures in the world are exhibited in Room VIII. The undisputed star is the *Laocoön*, described by Pliny the Elder as "a work to be preferred to all that the arts of painting and sculpture have produced." The first original Greek work of art to be discovered in Rome (it was unearthed in 1506 on the Esquiline Hill), it depicts a passage from the *Aeneid* in which Virgil describes the wrath the gods released on the priest Laocoön for warning the Trojans about the horse, sending two serpents to destroy him and his two sons. In the same room is another famous work, the *Apollo Belvedere* (a Roman copy of a fourth-century B.C. Greek statue once displayed in the Agora in Athens), which influenced Canova's nearby Perseus. Apollo's face came to symbolize beauty incarnate.

Father Nile is a favorite, resting on a cornucopia and a sphinx, dotted with babies. Other highlights of this museum are the *Apollo Sauroktonos* (Room V), the *Cnidian Venus* (Room VII), the *Belvedere Torso* (much preferred by the Romantics and Pre-Raphaelites to the Apollo Belvedere; Room III), the *Jupiter of Otricoli* (Room II), and the sarcophagi of Helen and Constantia, mother and daughter, respectively, of Constantine (Room I).

Gregorian-Etruscan Museum. Highlights in this newly reopened section are the Etruscan Regolini-Galassi Tomb (Room II) and *Mars of Todi* (Room III), the Greek *Head of Athena* and funerary stele (Room of Greek Originals), and the Greek amphora of *Achilles and Ajax Playing Morra* (Room XII).

Stop in the Sala della Biga (Chariot Room) for a sweeping view of St. Peter's from the window.

Raphael Rooms. These four rooms were the official apartments of Julius II, who commissioned frescoes from Raphael, the masterpiece of which is *The School of Athens*. According to tradition it contains portraits of Leonardo as Plato, Michelangelo as Heraclitus, and Raphael himself as the figure in the dark cap second from the extreme right. Truth, beauty, and justice were his themes throughout.

The Borgia Apartments. Here, Alexander VI had Pinturicchio paint frescoes, of which the richly decorated Room of the Saints is considered the major work.

Sistine Chapel. The chapel has been undergoing cleaning for a decade. Its most famous feature—the ceiling, which depicts scenes from the Book of Genesis—has been uncovered to reveal the brilliant colors of Michelangelo's original palette. The scaffolding at the end wall partly covers his *Last Judgment,* the success of whose restoration will not be up for our judgment until completion in 1994.

The Apostolic Library. Two paintings predominate here, the Greek Odyssey landscape series and the Roman *Aldobrandini Wedding.* In addition, temporary exhibits display the wonders of the library's rare book and manuscript collection.

Pinacoteca. Paintings by Giotto, Melozzo da Forlì, Raphael, Bellini, Reni, and Domenichino will delight the retina still capable of retaining anything after having seen the rest of the museums. Leonardo's unfinished *Saint Jerome,* although poorly restored, conveys the saint's pathos. Caravaggio's *Deposition* and Poussin's *Martyrdom of Saint Erasmus* present an interesting comparison—the former's immediacy contrasting with the latter's academic distance.

Before leaving, have a look at the museum gift shop, which, among its many reproductions and religious articles, sells men's ties patterned with papal coats of arms.

The sin of gluttony is not exactly catered to around the Vatican. However, take via del Pellegrino from the museum exit to **Borgo Pio**, the east–west street running parallel to via Corridori/via Borgo Pio to the south, where you'll find a number of prim little restaurants, such as **Marcello**, with tables in a vine-covered courtyard during the warmer months and, like its neighbors, serving a standard Italian menu. Fancier and more imaginative is **Papalino** at Borgo Pio 170 (Tel: 686-55-39; closed Mondays).

St. Peter's Square

After lunch, return to the immense oval of piazza San Pietro, which can now be enjoyed at a leisurely pace without having to worry about the pearly gates of the morning's attractions slamming shut. At noon on Sundays Pope John Paul II gives a blessing from his window in the Apostolic Palace, the second from the right on the top floor. At variable times on Wednesday mornings he holds an audience. In the summer, until the pope moves to his summer residence at Castel Gandolfo (see the Lazio chapter), it takes place in the piazza. In the winter the audience is held in the new audience hall designed by Pier Luigi Nervi in 1971, for which permission must be received by writing to the Prefect of the Pontifical Household, Città del Vaticano, 00120 Rome, or applied for in advance and in person at the bronze door to the right of the piazza.

On audience days the square is filled with religious pilgrims, often grouped together and carrying banners announcing their places of origin. Even at other times the square is bustling with large-scale activity, as befits a monumental space. Tight phalanxes of black-clad nuns and priests scuttle back and forth on official Vatican business. Schoolteachers lead groups of their uniformed charges and try to distract them from the surrounding grandeur with lectures. Fatigued tourists squint at the immensity of the piazza and the façade of St. Peter's. And the occasional self-contained honeymoon couple from the provinces wanders dazedly toward the basilica. Keeping watch upon it all are the 140 stone saints above Bernini's colonnade and the 13 giant statues over the façade of St. Peter's. For aerial variation, flocks of pigeons swoop freely to and fro, and if you're especially fortunate, it's all topped off by the colossal clusters of cumulus clouds that God seems to have designed especially for Baroque Rome.

The focal point of Bernini's oval piazza is the obelisk at the center, originally from Alexandria, where it had been erected by Augustus, and brought to Rome by Caligula. Not until much later was it erected on its present site; in 1586, chroniclers tell us, 900 men, 140 horses, and 44 winches accomplished the feat. Another account tells of a Ligurian sailor who, defying the papal order to remain silent during the dangerous enterprise, saw that the ropes were about to give out and cried, *"Aigua ae corde!"* an admonition to wet the ropes. He thus saved the day and Pope Sixtus V not only spared his life but rewarded him by starting the tradition of supplying the palms for Palm Sunday from his native port of Bordighera. Apocryphal as the tale may be, it is a charming example of the innumerable secular legends that surround the Vatican.

On either side of the obelisk spout the jets of two Baroque fountains, and between the two fountains and the colonnades is a circle of black marble in the pavement. If the squealing schoolchildren will allow you to stand on it, look toward the colonnade and you'll see the four rows of columns blend into one.

St. Peter's Basilica

Built under Constantine on the site of the tomb of Saint Peter, the original St. Peter's basilica, constructed in 326, was a sumptuous early Christian edifice almost as large as the present one. When the basilica began showing signs of age, the popes decided to build a new one and appointed a succession of architects to supervise the project. Bramante, Raphael, Sangallo, Michelangelo, and others were involved at one point or another, and their designs alternately called for Greek- and Latin-cross plans. Michelangelo's design for a Greek cross and dome was being carried out at the time of his death in 1564, but under Paul V it was decided to extend the front portion to conform to the outlines of Constantine's original basilica. This unfortunately makes Michelangelo's dome appear to sink as you approach the entrance, although it is the glory of the Roman skyline from elsewhere in the city. Carlo Maderno designed the façade and portico (where Giotto's *Navicella* ceiling mosaic from the old basilica was installed) in an early Baroque style.

As you step inside (you will not be admitted wearing shorts, skirts above the knees, or sleeveless dresses—St. Peter's dress code is stricter than Lutèce's or Claridge's, but the ambience is worth it), the effect is as dazzling as was intended. Perfect proportions mask the vastness of St. Peter's, but spotting the minuscule forms of other visitors beneath the gigantic statues, or a look at the comparative lengths of other European churches—traced in metal on the floor of the nave—confirms its enormous size. The immensity of history is also immediately present at the round porphyry slab set into the pavement in front of the central door: On this stone, on Christmas in the year 800, Leo III crowned the kneeling Charlemagne the first emperor of the Holy Roman Empire.

In the first chapel on the right, Michelangelo's **Pietà** stands behind the glass erected after the sculpture was assaulted in 1972. At the right end of the nave is Arnolfo di Cambio's bronze statue of *St. Peter Enthroned,* its foot worn by the touches and kisses of the faithful over the centuries. Over the high altar soars Bernini's gilded bronze **baldacchino**, its four fluted columns spiraling up to support a canopy crowned by an orb and cross a hundred feet above the floor. Be sure to note the more down-to-earth, human dimension of the carvings of a woman's features in the marble pedestals that support the columns; the facial expressions become progressively more contorted, culminating in the smiling visage of a newborn infant. Legend has it that Pope Urban VII asked Bernini to add the sequence in gratitude for his favorite niece surviving a difficult childbirth.

Bernini was entrusted with the decoration of the interior of St. Peter's, and his works abound throughout. In the apse behind the *baldacchino* is his reliquary of the throne of Saint Peter, topped by a stained-glass representation of the Holy Spirit. His tomb of Alexander VII in the passage leading to the left transept is but one highlight among many magnificent monuments in the church by other artists. The Treasury, reached from the left aisle near the transept, houses a valuable collection of sacred relics. Room III contains Pollaiuolo's tomb of Sixtus IV.

Back near Arnolfo's statue of Saint Peter is the entrance to the **Vatican Grottoes**, a dimly lit church containing a number of chapels and tombs. Beneath them are the famous excavations of what is held to be the original tomb of Saint Peter, where in the 1940s an ancient crypt containing bones and the remains of a garment fitting the description of Saint Peter's were discovered by archaeologists. Permission to enter must be obtained from the Ufficio Scavi, at the left of the Arch of the Bells, in piazza San Pietro (Tel: 698-53-18; open from 9:00 A.M. to 5:00 P.M.). They will call to confirm your visit, so make sure you have your phone number with you.

For a final survey of your visit to the Vatican, take the elevator at the front of the left aisle for a walk on the roof. Inspired souls may then continue up the 537 steps to the lantern for a last inspirational view of the Vatican, Rome, the Alban Hills, and the surrounding blessed countryside.

GETTING AROUND

International flights generally land at Leonardo da Vinci Airport in Fiumicino, about 30 km (18 miles) southwest of Rome. A train leaves the airport for the center of Rome every 20 minutes and takes about 25 minutes, with a stop in Trastevere, to reach its destination, Ostiense, near the Pyramid of Cestius. From there you can take the B line metro to the main train station (four short stops) or catch a taxi.

Tickets for the train from the airport cost 5,000 lire and must be purchased before boarding from a booth in the arrivals area or from machines at the turnstiles (requiring exact change). Tickets must be retained for on-board control. The train operates from 6:30 A.M. to 12:45 A.M., after which there are night buses into the center of Rome every hour on the hour until 5:00 A.M.

Rome's other airport, Ciampino, is about 16 km (10 miles) southeast of the city and is used mainly by charter flights. ACOTRAL buses provide service to the Cinecittà metro stop, which will take you into the center of Rome. But unless you are familiar with the metro, taxis are your best bet. Take only authorized "yellow" cabs, make sure the meter is turned on, and be forewarned that cabdrivers are entitled to charge a 10 percent surcharge when travelling to or from either airport. In addition, there are late-night rates, Sunday and holiday surcharges, and a small fee for each piece of luggage you put in the trunk.

International (and most national) trains arrive at Rome's central station, Stazione Termini, where you can catch a bus, a taxi, or the subway. Some trains arrive at Stazione Tibertina or Stazione Trastevere; these are less central but are served by taxis and buses.

Driving in Rome is best left to those who can trace their ancestry back to a charioteer or two. Crossing the street should satisfy anyone's taste for the heroic, but if you must have a car and want to rent it, make all the arrangements before coming to Europe to avoid paying the hefty value-added tax.

Rome's two subway lines, A and B, are inadequate and inconveniently located. Expansion is always in the air, but screeches to a halt every time the digging unearths another major artifact. Nevertheless, the *Metropolitana* (marked by a large M at the entrances) connects many of Rome's main tourist sights and runs from 5:30 A.M. to 11:30 P.M. (line B stops at 9:00 P.M.). Tickets can be purchased in major subway stations from machines, which require the exact change in coins, or from tobacconist shops, newsstands, and bars.

Rome's public bus system is extensive and relatively cheap. Various types of tickets—as well as a routes map—are available at the ATAC information booth in the parking area in front of Stazione Termini, the main train station. (Telephone information is available by dialing 469-51.) Tickets are good for unlimited use on any bus line for a 90-minute period. There are also daily, weekly, and monthly passes that permit unlimited travel on any bus line (but not the metro). In addition, passes allow the passenger to enter from the front of the bus, which is convenient during rush hours. Otherwise, buses are boarded from the rear and exited from the middle doors. (Passes for the metro are available at the ticket office next to the metro entrance on the lower level of Stazione Termini.)

Once you board the bus, place your ticket in the validating machine, which will stamp it with the time, date, and bus number. Failure to display a correctly stamped ticket or a pass to the controllers, who can board buses at any time and any place, could result in a hefty 50,000-lire fine—payable in any currency.

The same rules apply to the more limited tram service. A ride on tram 30 is an excellent way to get to know the city. The tram passes most of the major monuments and takes about an hour. If you have a 90-minute ticket, you can get on and off as many times as you want, so long as you stamp in your last ride before the time limit is up.

Each bus or tram stop, called a *fermata,* has a yellow sign that lists all the stops on the route and shows you where you are—provided you can read the small type. Most buses run from 5:00 A.M. until midnight, although some stop at 9:00; the hours are indicated at the bottom of each route listing. Popular routes have a night service listed under the *servizio notturno* column. Night routes often differ from day routes, so check carefully. Night buses have conductors who sell tickets.

A special tourist bus gives tours of the city every day at 2:30 P.M. The tour is a real bargain (about $5.00) because it lasts three hours and includes all of the major sights. Tickets are available at the ATAC information booth in front of the Stazione Termini (Tel: 469-51), which is also the departure point for the bus.

Rome is not a good taxi city; cabs are few and far between, expensive, and not air-conditioned, and they cannot be flagged down. The meter starts at 6,000 lire. The average fare in the city is 10,000 lire. On the plus side, tipping is optional. Taxis are found at stands throughout the city or may be called by dialing 35-70, or 49-94.

Whatever means of public transport you use, do not underestimate pickpockets. They are extremely enterprising with their hands, razor blades, and other means of getting into your pocket or purse. Make photocopies of your documents for easy replacement and leave the originals and any other valuables you don't really need in your hotel safe.

Violence is rare in Rome, but petty crime is not, so keep your money in a money belt or neck pouch and don't carry a bag or a conspicuous camera case. If your bag is snatched by a passing motorcyclist, do not hold on to it or you may incur more injury than the bag is worth. Report the loss to the police and the embassy, as very often the bag, minus the money, turns up in a post box or somebody's back yard.

Rome's hills, heavy traffic, and cobblestones make the city less than ideal for bicycles, but in some cases a bike can be the best way to explore the city. Bicycles can be rented for 3,000 lire an hour, 10,000 lire a half-day, or 15,000 lire a day at piazza San Lorenzo in Lucina off via del Corso, at piazza Sonnino in Trastevere, and at St. Peter Moto at 43 via Porta Castello near the Vatican (Tel: 687-57-14). Other locations are just outside the metro at piazza di Spagna and in the Borghese Gardens. A nine-mile bike path traces the Tiber, on the Trastevere–Vatican City side, beginning north of Ponte Cavour.

Rome city tourist offices are located in the customs area of both airports, in the track area of Stazione Termini (Tel: 487-12-70), and at via Parigi 5, behind the Grand Hotel between the train station and via Veneto (Tel: 488-37-48).

ACCOMMODATIONS

The rates given below are projections for 1993; always check for up-to-date information before making reservations. Wide ranges may reflect the differences between low- and high-season rates. Unless otherwise noted, the figures indicate the cost of a double room (per room, not per person) with bath. Air-conditioning is included in the price except when a surcharge is specified, as is breakfast. The service charge is included in the rate; inquire about the tax.

The telephone and fax area code for Rome is 06. When telephoning from outside the country, omit the zero in the city code.

"We were well accommodated with three handsome bed-rooms, a dining room, larder, stable and kitchen," wrote Montaigne's secretary of their lodgings in Rome. It's possible to get an idea of the value of the 20 crowns a month they paid in the 16th century when Monsieur le secretaire goes on to estimate that the beds in their rooms must have cost between four and five hundred crowns apiece. In that light, the room was a real bargain, especially when you consider that nowadays, the price—in dollars—of a room in one of Rome's top hotels is closer to what the beds cost—and without the larder, stable, or kitchen.

The Eternal City, in case you haven't heard, is no longer the *dolce vita* dreamland of cheap lodgings and gargantuan meals for a song. You have to hunt around and choose carefully now, but it is still possible to find reasonably priced accommodations, especially if you are willing to compromise on location or forego the stable and larder and some of the other conveniences of home.

The hotels in the following list are arranged according to neighborhoods. The Centro Storico (Old Rome) area offers proximity to the major monuments; the Villa Borghese area skirts the park; piazza di Spagna is close to Rome's elegant shopping district; via Veneto has the highest concentration of luxury hotels and an active nightlife; and the area near Stazione Termini, the central train station, is convenient for those who need to come and go in a hurry.

Centro Storico

A windy medieval street off the via della Scrofa opens into a tiny piazza where two enormous stone angels blow Judgment Day trumpets atop the Portuguese national church. Tucked into a corner of the church is the 150-year-old **Albergo Portoghesi**, a small, relatively inexpensive hotel that at first glance looks like a Paris bistro decked out in wrought-iron fencing and bunches of white globe lamps. Inside, the Portoghesi has kept its somewhat eclectic charm in spite of a recent effort to update. There are 24 rooms on three floors, all with antique furnishings, private bath, and air-conditioning. An elevator rises to the rooftop terrace, where breakfast is served in good weather and from which you can almost touch those trumpeting angels next door. Via del Portoghesi 1, 00186; Tel: 686-42-31; Fax: 687-69-76. £130,000; £10,000 extra for breakfast and £20,000 for air conditioning.

Discretion is the rule at the vine-covered **Raphael**, a favorite of journalists and Italian politicians. The somewhat gloomy lobby unsuccessfully blends antiques with modern furniture, and although most of the 85 rooms are small and far from luxurious, the views of piazza Navona from the upper floors are quite expansive—and expensive. The service is professional—down to the pink terry-cloth robes. Largo Febo 2, 00186; Tel: 65-08-81 or 683-88-81; Fax: 687-89-93; £385,000. £22,000 extra for breakfast.

Sole al Pantheon claims to be the oldest hotel in Rome (1493). Plaques attest to stays here of the poet Ariosto and the composer Pietro Mascagni, who wrote *Cavalleria Rusticana*. The Sole was also a favorite of Jean-Paul Sartre and Simone de Beauvoir, and one can see why just by opening the shutters onto the Pantheon—one of western architecture's most venerated monuments. The neighborhood teems with cafés, restaurants, and crowds of late-night revelers, so you'll appreciate the double glass in the windows and the central air-conditioning because you won't be able to open your windows—at least on the piazza side—and sleep in summer. Nor will you lament the Jacuzzi in the bath after a long day of sightseeing and shopping. Via del Pantheon 63, 00186; Tel: 678-04-41; Fax: 684-06-89. £250,000–£380,000.

Even closer to the Pantheon and more moderately priced is **Hotel del Senato**. Its jazzy postmodern lobby leads to less jazzy but serviceable rooms. The tiny elevator is an appropriate prelude to the size of the rooms, but when you open your window and look down over the Pantheon, you'll probably stop counting square feet. Piazza del Pantheon 73, 00186;

Tel: 679-32-31; Fax: 684-02-97. £110,000–£146,000; £18,000 extra for breakfast; £22,000 a day for air-conditioning.

Toward the back of the Pantheon, the **Holiday Inn Crowne Plaza Minerva** recently reopened after the property, once a hotel where George Sand and Marie-Henri Beyle (Stendhal) slept on separate occasions, was renovated and modernized. You'll pay handsomely for business-traveller-style amenities, such as nonsmoking rooms and satellite TV, but the convenient location, panoramic rooftop terrace, and barbecue lunches may make it worthwhile. Piazza della Minerva 69, 00186; Tel: 684-18-88; Fax: 679-41-65. £438,000–£492,000; £30,000 extra for breakfast.

For much less, the 97-room **Hotel Santa Chiara**, just across the street from the Minerva, has rooms furnished with antiques, recently completely renovated to include air-conditioning, color TVs, refrigerator, and lavish marble bathrooms. Via di Santa Chiara 21, 00186; Tel: 654-01-42; Fax 687-31-44. £76,000–£150,000; £25,000 extra for breakfast; £20,000 for air-conditioning.

Teatro di Pompeo is located in a tiny piazza near Campo dei Fiori and is built on top of the ruins of the Theater of Pompey, where Julius Caesar was assassinated on the Ides of March in 44 B.C. (and not in the Forum, as many think, because the Curia, like many public buildings in Italy today, was closed that day for renovation). Breakfast is served either in your room or in the cavernous cellars of the notorious theater. The 12 rooms are tastefully understated with their white walls, dark-beamed ceilings, and terra-cotta floors accented by hand-painted tiles and colorful geometric rugs. The rooms on the top floor look out onto the dome of the adjoining church, which seems to be coming right into the room. Central air-conditioning, refrigerator, and color TV are included. Largo del Pallaro 8, 00186; Tel: 687-28-12; Fax: 654-55-31. £175,000; £21,000 extra for breakfast.

The **Hotel Forum** has a stunning view over the imperial forums, particularly from its rooftop terrace and bar. The hotel is a converted convent, and part of its ancient bell tower forms part of the lobby, along with various capitals and other fragments from the surrounding archaeological zone. The air-conditioned rooms are done up in polished woodwork and brocade and are small but comfortable. Via Tor de' Conti 25, 00184; Tel: 679-24-46; Fax: 678-64-79. £300,000–£400,000; £25,000 extra for breakfast.

Near the antiques stores on via Giulia and the outdoor market in Campo dei Fiori is **Ponte Sisto**. The best rooms look out onto a large, palm-shaded courtyard where breakfast is served in good weather and where a bar crowd holds court at night in summer. Some of the 129 rooms (room 601 in particular) have views of St. Peter's and the Janiculum hill; most do not, but if you value large luminous rooms more than sweeping vistas, Ponte Sisto is where you'll get the most for your money. There is no air-conditioning, but parking is available. Room 107 has a large terrace. Via dei Pettinari 64, 00186; Tel: 686-88-43; Fax: 654-88-22. £146,000; £13,000 extra for breakfast.

Hotel delle Nazioni is just a coin's throw from the newly restored Trevi Fountain. It has small but comfortable rooms with air-conditioning and its own restaurant-pizzeria. If you come off-season, you get a 20 percent discount. Ask for one of the top rooms with a terrace—far from the 24-hour crowd at the fountain below. Via Poli 7, 00187; Tel: 679-24-41; Fax: 678-24-00. £225,000–£330,000.

Budget choice: Around the block from piazza Venezia and just off the Corso is the ideally located **Pensione Coronet**, a leftover from the era of cheap pensioni that still provides clean, functionally ugly rooms in a glorious setting overlooking the garden of the Palazzo Doria Pamphili. Piazza Grazioli 5, 00186; Tel: 679-23-41. £86,000; £10,000 extra for breakfast. No credit cards.

Villa Borghese

Perhaps due to its past as a house of ill-repute, the sumptuous **Valadier** has some of the largest bathrooms in Rome. Situated just below the Pincio hill, near the trendy piazza del Popolo, the hotel also has spacious air-conditioned rooms and lounges tastefully accented with gleaming marble, polished brass, mahogany, and fresh flowers. Ask for one of the three rooms that have terraces. There is a 20 percent weekend discount if you book in advance. Via della Fontanella 15, 00187; Tel: 361-19-98; Fax: 320-15-58. £270,000–£405,000.

Villa Borghese looks—outside and inside—like a country house set in the middle of the park, but there is no air-conditioning, and it gets noisy in summer when the windows are open. In the fall and winter, however, it's one of the coziest spots in Rome and far from the noisy crowds. Via Pinciana 31, 00198; Tel: 844-01-05 or 854-96-48; Fax: 844-26-36. £160,000; £28,000 extra for breakfast.

On a side street facing the venerable brick walls that the emperor Aurelius built in the third century A.D. to protect Rome is the **Hotel Victoria**, a small hotel with a solid reputation for comfort and good service. The air-conditioned rooms on the top floors have splendid views of the Villa Borghese park, which is convenient for joggers and strollers—but only during the daytime. Via Campania 41, 00187; Tel: 473-931; Fax: 487-18-90. ₤240,000–₤280,000.

Piazza di Spagna

The **Carriage** is named after the street in which the touring carriages of yesteryear used to stop for repairs. The Old World atmosphere is still evident in the gilded furnishings of this small bur comfortable hotel. All rooms are air-conditioned, but the best are clustered around a terrace on the top floor; number 32 has an enormous bathroom. Via delle Carrozze 36, 00187; Tel: 699-24-01 or 679-33-12; Fax: 678-82-79. ₤185,000; ₤25,000 extra for breakfast.

Rooms with views of the tile rooftops and domes of Rome are part of the offering at the newly renovated **Condotti**, just off Rome's super-chic shopping street of the same name. The 21 small rooms also are drop-dead chic, in cheerful peach and gray or light blue moiré silk. Some rooms on the top floor have terraces, while those on the second and third have small balconies. Via Mario de' Fiori 37, 00187; Tel: 679-46-61; Fax: 679-04-57. ₤133,500; ₤25,000 extra for breakfast; ₤20,000 a day for air-conditioning.

With its Oriental rugs, crystal chandeliers, and marble tables, the **De la Ville Intercontinental** at the top of the Spanish Steps is for many the quintessence of Old World charm. Its upper floors and roof-garden terrace (which offers a Sunday brunch) have spectacular views, while the rooms on the lower floors overlook a central courtyard. If you book in advance, there are special weekend and August rates. Via Sistina 69, 00187; Tel: 673-31; Fax 678-42-13. ₤415,000–₤484,00.

The **D'Inghilterra** used to be a refuge for writers in Rome (Henry James, Mark Twain, and Ernest Hemingway all stayed here), but its prices nowadays have placed it beyond most writers' means. It can be noisy and the rooms are small, but it has one of the best bars and by all accounts the best bartender in Rome. Via Bocca di Leone 14, 00187; Tel: 672-161; Fax: 684-08-28. ₤335,000–₤446,000; ₤22,000 extra for breakfast.

The **Hassler–Villa Medici** is the preferred hotel of many distinguished visitors, from American presidents to movie stars, but if you do not fall into a similar category, the service can be cold and unfriendly. Right at the top of the Spanish Steps, the Hassler is crowned with one of the city's most elegant restaurants. At these prices, ask for a room with a view of the Steps or the gardens behind. Piazza Trinità dei Monti 6, 00187; Tel: 678-26-51; Fax: 678-99-91. In U.S., Tel: (212) 838-

3110 or (800) 223-6800; Fax: (212) 758-7367. In U.K., Tel: (0800) 18-11-23; Fax: (071) 353-19-04. Ł400,000–Ł600,000; Ł25,000 extra for breakfast.

Opposite the Hassler and sharing the same views for a lot less money is the **Scalinata di Spagna**. Reservations are strictly required in this small family-run hotel. The two rooms on the top floor share the rooftop terrace and are usually filled by honeymooners. Breakfast is served in your air-conditioned room or on the flower-filled rooftop terrace, where you can bask in all the Roman standards: red-tiled rooftops, cascading geraniums, and a landscape of domes, large and small, in the distance. Piazza Trinità dei Monti 17, 00187; Tel: 679-30-06; Fax: 684-05-98. Ł130,000–Ł260,000. No credit cards.

Down Via Sistina, the **King** is a dependable, reasonably priced hotel in the Spanish Steps area. Its sparsely decorated rooms are nonetheless comfortable, and the rooftop terrace has more of those wonderful views. Via Sistina 131, 00187; Tel: 488-08-78; Fax: 487-18-13. Ł145,000; Ł25,000 extra for breakfast; Ł25,000 a day for air-conditioning.

Located at the top of the Spanish Steps in a former convent on the street that houses many of Italy's high-fashion ateliers, the small, stylish **Gregoriana** was decorated by Erté, and the doors of each room bear his anthropomorphic letters rather than numbers. Rooms F, M, and R have small balconies overlooking an inner courtyard, and room C preserves elements of what was a chapel in the days when the Gregoriana was a convent. (The leopard-skin wallpaper in the halls was added later.) There are only 19 rooms, which are often booked solid by models or rag-trade buyers, and the service is legendary. Via Gregoriana 18, 00187; Tel: 679-42-69; Fax: 678-42-58. Ł85,000–Ł142,000; Ł25,000 extra for breakfast; Ł20,000 a day for air-conditioning. No credit cards.

The newest of the small elegant hotels in the Spanish Steps area is the **Hotel dei Borgognoni**, on a narrow street where the inhabitants of Burgundy settled in Rome in the 17th century. The 50 rooms are small but richly decorated; some overlook a glass-enclosed, flower-filled inner courtyard. Number 109, 110, and 112 have small terraces. There are the usual amenities—air-conditioning, color TV, refrigerator, room safes, and a private garage—and the Borgognoni also offers a free baby-sitter service. Via del Bufalo 126, 00187; Tel: 678-00-41; Fax: 684-15-01. Ł330,000–Ł390,000.

Nestled in among the deluxe hotels at the top of the Spanish Steps is the unassuming **Albergo Internazionale**, which has long been considered one of the city's best-run hotels in the moderate price category. Parts of the building date from the 16th century, which accounts for the ornately carved wood furnishings and frescoed ceilings in some of its 40 rooms. Rooms on the fourth floor have terraces, and a few on the ground floor have whirlpool baths. All of the rooms have satellite TVs, and free parking is available. Via Sistina 79, 00187; Tel: 679-30-47; Fax: 678-47-64. Ł160,000–Ł220,000; Ł25,000 extra for breakfast; Ł20,000 a day for air-conditioning.

On a tiny, quiet side street off Via del Babuino and a few yards from the foot of the Spanish Steps is the **Margutta**, a small, inexpensive hotel, decorated in bold colors that reflect the artistic spirit of the nearby street from which it takes its name. Two of its 26 rooms are on the roof and come with fireplaces and private terraces that overlook palaces, bell towers, and the Pincio gardens. Via Laurina 34, 00187; Tel: 679-84-40 or 322-36-74. Ł94,000; Ł10,000 extra for breakfast.

Budget choice: Reflecting its name, the **Suisse** (Swiss) is an efficiently run, moderately priced hotel with large rooms furnished in both antique and modern styles. A charming terrace, a loyal clientele, and low rates make reservations well in advance a must. Via Gregoriana 56, 00187; Tel: 678-36-49. Ł80,000–Ł88,000; Ł12,000 extra for breakfast.

Via Veneto

Opposite the American Embassy, the **Ambasciatori Palace** offers 150 large, luxurious rooms in a modern setting and impeccable service. It has a lively bar, popular with embassy people. Via Vittorio Veneto 70, 00187; Tel: 474-93; Fax: 474-36-01. Ł400,000; Ł30,000 extra for breakfast.

The **Excelsior** was the preferred residence of Elizabeth Taylor and other Hollywood luminaries during the *dolce vita* era. Most of its roomy, luxurious suites and well-appointed rooms decorated in French Empire style still live up to its glamorous past. Via Vittorio Veneto 125, 00187; Tel: 47-08; Fax: 482-62-05. In U.S., Tel: (212) 935-9540 or (800) 221-2340; Fax (212) 421-5929. In U.K., Tel: (071) 930-41-47 or (0800) 289-234; Fax: (071) 839-15-66. Ł392,000–Ł619,000; Ł30,000 extra for breakfast. Pets accepted.

Offering the most discreet service of the Via Veneto luxury hotels, the **Flora** is a favorite of many for its Old World charm, spacious rooms, and traditional service. It is just inside the Aurelian walls and across the street from the Villa Borghese park, which is convenient for joggers. Via Vittorio Veneto 191, 00187; Tel: 48-99-29 or 482-03-51; Fax: 482-03-59. Ł330,000–Ł500,000; Ł35,000 extra for breakfast.

The **Hotel Alexandra** is a charming 19th-century mansion

at the bottom of Via Veneto that has been managed by the same family for four generations. All 45 rooms have recently been renovated and sound-proofed against the traffic on Via Veneto. Breakfast is served in an antiques-filled salon of faded gentility decorated with black-and-white photos of turn-of-the-century Rome. Air-conditioning, refrigerator, color TV, free parking restaurant, bar, and room service. Via Vittorio Veneto 18, 00187; Tel: 488-19-43; Fax: 487-18-04. Ł140,000–Ł200,000; Ł20,000 extra for breakfast; Ł20,000 a day for air-conditioning.

La Residenza, on a quiet street one block from Via Veneto, was a private villa and then a convent before it became a hotel. Seven of the 27 rooms have terraces; others have only small balconies but are larger. The public rooms have Louis XVI furniture, fireplaces, and Baroque mirrors. Many claim that the breakfast buffet here is the best in Rome. Via Emilia 22, 00187; Tel: 488-07-89; Fax: 485-721. Ł210,000; Ł25,000 extra for breakfast; Ł30,000 a day for air-conditioning. No credit cards.

Near the Station

The Neoclassical grandness of **Le Grand Hotel** is not diminished by its location near the train station, which used to be one of the most fashionable areas of the city. The Grand boasts majestic rooms and suites whose elegance is matched by the appointments in the public areas, where an elaborate tea is served each afternoon, and Roman matrons lunch to harp music and eat finger sandwiches and petits fours. Via Vittorio Emanuele Orlando 3, 00185; Tel: 47-09; Fax: 474-73-07. In U.S., Tel: (800) 223-6800 or (212) 838-3110; Fax: (212) 758-7367. In U.K., Tel: (0800) 18-11-23; Fax: (071) 353-19-04. Ł390,000–Ł624,000; Ł30,000 extra for breakfast.

The **Mediterraneo** is one of five hotels in the Bettoja hotel group that offer accommodations from luxury to reasonably priced. Situated on the Esquiline Hill, the highest of Rome's seven hills, the hotel has a roof-garden terrace, where breakfast is served in summer, that provides sweeping views of the city. The rooms are traditionally furnished but have modern conveniences like direct-dial telephones and satellite TVs. The concierges at the Mediterraneo have a long-standing reputation for service and knowledge. Via Cavour 15, 00184; Tel: 488-40-51; Fax: 474-41-05. In U.S., Tel: (800) 223-9832 or (212) 599-8280; Fax: (212) 599-1755. Ł180,000–Ł360,000; Ł20,000 extra for breakfast.

The recently refurbished **Hotel Nord** is another Bettoja hotel in a more economical price range. It faces the new Roman Archaeological Museum and is within walking distance of the train station and the opera house. Free parking is available. Weekend and off-season discounts are available when you book through a travel agency. Via G. Amendola 3, 00185; Tel: 488-54-41; Fax: 481-71-63. In U.S., Tel: (800) 223-9832 or (212) 599-8280; Fax: (212) 599-1755. £210,000; £30,000 extra for breakfast.

The Vatican

The most creature comforts–oriented hotel in the area is the modern **Atlante Star**, which also has a lush roof-garden restaurant with close-up views of St. Peter's and a unique policy (which it shares with its less expensive sister hotel, **Atlante Garden**) of picking up its guests at the airport free of charge. Via Vitelleschi 34, 00193; Tel: 687-32-33; Fax: 687-23-00. £240,000–£420,000; £27,000 extra for breakfast. Atlante Garden: Via Crescenzio 78, 00193; Tel: 687-23-61; Fax: 687-23-15. £180,000–£295,000; £27,000 extra for breakfast.

Formerly the Renaissance palazzo of Pope Julius II's family, the **Columbus**—even though due for renovation—abounds in red velvet drapes, antique tapestries, and frescoed ceilings in some of the rooms (number 221), although the management has opted for efficient simplicity in most of the others. That combination and the fact that the Columbus is on the main avenue leading into Vatican City make reservations in advance a must. Free parking. Via della Conciliazione 33, 00193; Tel: 686-54-35; Fax: 686-48-74. £140,000–£220,000; £30,000 extra for breakfast; £20,000 a day for air-conditioning.

Hotel Sant'Anna is a small hotel located 50 yards from St. Peter's Square on a busy street crowded with restaurants, food stores, and souvenirs shops. The 20 rooms are very small but attractive. Breakfast is served in a frescoed dining room or around the courtyard fountain. There's no elevator to take you there, but ask for one of the spacious blue-and-white attic rooms, each with its own tiny terrace. Borgo Pio 143, 00193; Tel: 654-16-02; Fax: 68-30-87-17. £150,000; £30,000 extra for breakfast; £20,000 for air-conditioning.

Budget choice: The **Alimandi** is a clean, well-run pensione with a charming breakfast terrace, and it's only a short walk back—for tired feet—from the Vatican Museums. Via Tunisi 8, 00192; Tel: 38-45-48; Fax: 31-44-57. £80,000–£110,000; £13,000 extra for breakfast. No air-conditioning.

Elsewhere in Rome

With a pool, tennis courts, and a famous restaurant, the **Cavalieri Hilton** is such a self-contained unit that many of its guests never leave it for very long. Moreover, its privileged position atop Monte Mario (north of the Vatican) gives it

ACCOMMODATIONS   115

some of the best views of Rome at night. A bus regularly shuttles guests (and their dogs and cats) to the Spanish Steps and back. Via Cadlolo 101, 00136; Tel: 315-11; Fax: 315-122-41. Ł395,000–Ł540,000; Ł30,000 extra for breakfast.

On a quiet side street between piazza del Popolo and the Tiber, the very low-key **Locarno** is many people's favorite small hotel in Rome. Although it has lost some of its finer fin-de-siècle features to modernization, the Locarno is still a good example of a Roman hotel that has managed to retain some of its original charm while yielding to the demand for color TVs, refrigerator, and air-conditioning. There are Belle Epoque touches in the lobby, such as Tiffany-style lamps and sinuous beveled glass doors, and in winter the open fire, dark woodwork, and brass ornaments give a warm glow to the parlor. In good weather breakfast is served in the garden under the ubiquitous Roman *umbrelloni*. A unique feature: The Locarno provides free bicycles. Via della Penna 22, 00186; Tel: 361-08-41; Fax: 321-52-49. Ł160,000; Ł25,000 extra for breakfast; Ł20,000 a day for air-conditioning.

In the exclusive residential neighborhood of Parioli behind the Villa Borghese, the luxurious **Lord Byron**, decorated in subtle tones and bursts of fresh flowers, attracts a well-heeled clientele. Moreover, it boasts a restaurant that many say is Rome's best. Via Giuseppe de Notaris 5, 00197; Tel: 322-04-04; Fax: 322-04-05. In U.S., Tel: (800) 223-6800 or (212) 838-3110; Fax: (212) 758-7367. In U.K., Tel: (0800) 18-11-23; Fax: (071) 353-19-04. Ł510,000; Ł25,000 extra for breakfast.

Somebody at the **Viminale** went to hotel school, because here you get all the extras—valet parking, remote-control color TVs, credit card keys, room safes, adjustable air-conditioning, and a newspaper slipped under your door in the morning. The 46-room hotel is in a converted Art Nouveau villa near the basilica of Santa Maria Maggiore. Most of the rooms have been fully restored, but there are still a vintage 1920s cage elevator on the inside and graceful Art Nouveau—or "Liberty," as Italians call the style—touches on the outside. Via Cesare Balbo 31, 00184; Tel: 488-19-10; Fax: 474-47-28. Ł155,000; Ł27,000 extra for breakfast; Ł20,000 a day for air-conditioning.

The **Plaza** is halfway between piazza del Popolo and piazza Venezia and has been catering to a sophisticated clientele since 1860. Its Old-World grandeur has not diminished since the queen of Mexico inaugurated it. The Belle Epoque reception room, with its potted palms and stained-glass ceiling, has recently been restored to its former Art Nouveau glory. The best rooms (number 257, for example) are set around a cool, quiet inner courtyard. Via del Corso 126, 00186; Tel: 67-21-01; Fax: 684-15-75. £255,000–£310,000; £18,000 extra for breakfast; £15,000 a day for air-conditioning.

Many people claim that the residential area on the Aventine hill above the Circus Maximus is the quietest in Rome, and for that reason the **Sant'Anselmo**, although a bit out of the way, has become popular. The garden breakfast terrace and afternoon bar reflect the lush, hushed surroundings of the area, where sleeping peacefully at night is never a problem. No air-conditioning. Piazza Sant'Anselmo 2, 00153; Tel: 574-35-47; Fax: 578-36-04. £90,000–£147,000; £18,000 extra for breakfast.

Also outside the center (but a quick bus or taxi ride away) are several hotels along via Nomentana, a wide tree-lined boulevard bordered by parks and private villas. Two hotels are the best in the area:

Villa delle Rose is a venerable old villa set back from the avenue with a tranquil, leafy garden and a gurgling goldfish pool. Once the residence of a series of wealthy Roman families who built their villas on what was then the outskirts of the city, Villa delle Rose has kept some of that atmosphere in its rooms and parlors. Via Vicenza 5, 00185; Tel: 445-17-88. £136,000; £17,000 extra for breakfast; £11,000 a day for air-conditioning.

Hotel Villa del Parco is a converted 19th-century villa set back from the street by a tree-lined drive, which gives it the air of a Mediterranean country house. The cozily furnished rooms have high ceilings and large double-door windows. In addition, it offers air-conditioning, refrigerator, color TVs, free parking, and a garden where breakfast is served. For joggers there is the ample Villa Torlonia park next door. Via Nomentana 110, 00161; Tel: 855-56-11; Fax: 854-04-10. £136,000–£202,000; £23,000 extra for breakfast; £20,000 a day for air-conditioning.

Budget choices: The 22-room **Pensione Parlamento**, off the central via del Corso, has the kind of relaxed, run-down atmosphere that some people find charming, and that (along with its rooftop terrace) has made it a favorite among expatriates. Via delle Convertite 5, 00187; Tel: 678-78-80. £62,000–£95,000; £12,000 extra for breakfast.

Located in the quiet Prati quarter north of the Vatican, the comfortably furnished **Forti's Guest House** is a block from the Tiber and convenient to all forms of public transportation. The Italian-American management is friendly and helpful and sometimes even prepares family-style meals for guests. Via Fornovo 7, 00192; Tel: 320-07-38; Fax: 321-22-22. £85,000–£95,000; £14,500 extra for breakfast.

Residences

If you are planning to spend at least a week in Rome, you should look into staying in a *residence* instead of a hotel or pensione. Residences are mini-apartments that include an outfitted kitchen, a bedroom and bath, and a parlor. The advantages are that you can have breakfast whenever you want, cook your own simple meals, and entertain guests in a living room instead of a bedroom. During the off-season, many residences let you stay for less than a week.

The best in this category is the **Palazzo al Velabro**, a vine-covered palazzo at the bottom of the Palatine Hill on a quiet street between the Tiber and the Circus Maximus (where you can go jogging). The 35 mini-apartments have a modern, functional decor, and some of them have terraces that over-look a lush inner courtyard that has the Palatine Hill as a backdrop. The £1,600,000-a-week price includes linens, kitchen utensils, color TV, air-conditioning, and maid ser-vice. Via del Velabro 16, 00186; Tel: 679-34-50; Fax: 679-37-90.

Ripa Residence in Trastevere is next door to Rome's renowned Sunday morning flea market. It offers monthly as well as weekly rates and boasts all the comforts of a hotel plus the privacy of your own home. The comforts do not include an iota of aesthetic charm and the (sometimes noisy) dog pound is nearby, but the convenience, location, and price may entice you to ignore the downside. Via degli Orti di Trastevere 1, 00153; Tel: 586-11; Fax: 581-45-50. £1,000,000 a week; £2,700,000 a month.

Monasteries and Convents

Another alternative to commercial hotels is a monastery or convent. These are not former houses of worship that have been converted into trendy hotels, but religious communi-ties that take in guests for a nominal fee (no credit cards) that sometimes includes meals. Accommodations are spartan but immaculate. Some monasteries have an 11:00 P.M. cur-few, but the ones listed here give guests their own keys, so they are free to come and go as they wish. The following accept families as well as single men and women of any or no faith.

The **Franciscan Sisters of Atonement** is an American or-der of nuns whose motherhouse is in Garrison, New York. All rooms have private baths; there is a dining room; and parking is available. There is also a spacious pine-shaded garden to stroll about in. (This convent is recommended by the Vatican City Tourist Information Office.) Via Monte del

Gallo 105, 00165; Tel: 53-07-82. Ł60,000 per person for room with full board; Ł45,000 for half board.

The **Convent of Santa Brigida** is in one of Rome's most beautiful Renaissance piazzas—piazza Farnese. The rooms are more expensive than at the other religious establishments that lodge guests but cheaper than in a hotel. Guests must eat at least one meal here. The rooms—all with private baths—are modest and spotlessly clean. The guest house is operated by an order of Swedish sisters who also have guest houses in Farfa and Assisi. Piazza Farnese 96, 00186; Tel: 698-52-63. Ł90,000 per person for room with full board; Ł70,000 for half board.

The **Casa di Santa Francesca Romana** is in the heart of Rome's bohemian quarter—Trastevere—a short distance from the Tiber Island. The pensione is housed in what was once a noble Roman family's vast palazzo, and it offers hospitality to groups, families, or individuals in single, double, or triple rooms with private baths. There is central heating (but no air-conditioning), an elevator, and a cool inner courtyard. Rooms 23 and 35 have picturesque views of Trastevere. Via dei Vascellari 61, 00153; Tel: 581-21-25. Ł87,000 for a double with bath.

The **Casa Kolbe** at the foot of the Palatine is a religious guest house that caters mainly to groups of pilgrims, but it sometimes has vacancies. The rooms are very basic, but the location is perfect and the public rooms and garden are quiet and relaxing. Via San Teodoro 44, 00186; Tel: 679-49-74; Fax: 684-15-50. Ł70,000–Ł82,000 for a double with bath; Ł7,000 extra for breakfast.

—*Louis Inturrisi*

DINING

Despite the abundance of roads leading to Rome, remarkably few culinary influences have flowed into or out of the Eternal City in its more than 2,000 years of existence. The sprinkling of non-Italian restaurants in the capital today (mostly Chinese) are looked upon with suspicion (and rightly so), while the others offer more or less the same Roman standards, none of which—with the possible exception of spaghetti *alla carbonara*—has ever achieved international recognition. The result is that although it is rare to eat badly in Rome, it is also true that the food is not very exciting—unless you count knuckles, shanks, and tails among the world's epicurean delights.

Roman cooking, like the people who created it, is simple, straightforward, and unpretentious: In a word, it is eminently practical—as befits a people better at road construction and plumbing than at painting or sculpture. It doesn't bother with subtle cream sauces or expensive ingredients like truffles because it didn't come out of the kitchens of the emperors or the popes, but out of the *cucina povera*—the good, solid home cooking of the common people. This characteristic still survives in the plain and hearty Roman dishes made from whatever was left over, whatever they could get their hands on, or whatever pieces of meat or fish nobody else wanted. It also accounts for the preponderance of tripe, brains, innards, and intestines in Roman cooking, as well as the ubiquitous presence of preservatives like hot peppers and garlic.

A complete meal in a Roman restaurant, osteria, or trattoria (there is not much difference nowadays) includes a first course (*primo*) of pasta, rice, or soup; a *secondo* of meat, poultry, or fish; and a dessert of fresh fruit, cheese, or, less often, sweets. The meal often begins with an antipasto of appetizers selected from a table near the entrance of the restaurant where a variety of grilled vegetables, cold cuts, and shellfish are displayed. Another favorite Roman appetizer is *bruschetta* (slices of toasted garlic bread topped with chopped tomatoes and sprinkled with olive oil).

The most common Roman *primi* are spaghetti *alla carbonara* (bacon, egg yolk, Parmesan, and black pepper), said to have been invented by coal (*carbone*) miners to satisfy their need for a simple sauce that could be prepared without cooking; *bucatini all'amatriciana* (long, narrow pasta tubes in a sauce of salt pork, onions, tomatoes, and grated sheep's-milk cheese); *penne all'arrabbiata* (short pasta with a peppy tomato and garlic sauce, topped with fresh parsley); spaghetti *alla puttanesca* (the sauce made from tomatoes, capers, and black olives), which tradition says was popular with whores (*puttane*) because of its lack of garlic; and *gnocchi* (potato dumplings), which are traditionally served every Thursday topped with one of the two standard Roman sauces: *sugo* (tomato and basil) or *ragù* (tomato and ground beef). If you can't decide which pasta to order, ask for *un assaggino* (a taste) of two or three. If it all sounds like too much, ask for *una mezza porzione* (a half portion).

The most common *secondi* are *saltimbocca alla romana* (literally, "jump-in-your-mouth" veal filets topped with prosciutto and a few sage leaves and then sautéed in butter); *coda alla vaccinara* (oxtail stewed in wine, onions, tomatoes, and celery); *peperonata* (chicken stewed in roasted peppers); *osso buco* (braised veal shank in tomato sauce); and *abbacchio al forno* (roast baby lamb served with roasted potatoes and rosemary). There are also *secondi* of grilled steaks and chops, the veal in Rome being especially good and reasonably priced. Try *lombata di vitello,* a veal chop that is best grilled over charcoal and doused with fresh lemon.

Fish is also available in most restaurants, but it is not a Roman specialty and the distance from the sea makes most claims to freshness suspect. Remember also that fish served on Mondays anywhere in Italy can't be fresh, as the fishermen do not take in a catch on Sunday.

To accompany the *secondi* there are a wide variety of *contorni* (raw or cooked vegetables) and salads. Some traditional Roman vegetables you should try if they are in season are: *puntarelle,* the crunchy stalks of the chicory plant, which are unknown outside the Rome area and are served in a dressing of anchovies, crushed garlic, olive oil, and vinegar; *rughetta,* a wilder variety of what is called rucola or arugula in other parts of Italy (and rocket in England) for the peppery nutlike flavor it adds to salads; and the tender, sweet, chopstick-thin wild *asparagi* (asparagus), which appear in early spring and are served with lemon or butter and Parmesan or *alla Bismarck*—with a fried egg on top.

To accompany the meal, try one of the wines from the Castelli Romani, the hills southeast of Rome, with names like Colli Albani, Frascati, and Marino. Most of the house wines served in trattorias come from the Castelli. The whites are very raw, but cheap; the reds are better—among the best are Torre Ercolana and Colle Picchioni.

Many Romans, like other Italians, like to end the meal with a *digestivo,* an alcoholic herbal brew that settles the stomach after the onslaught of three courses. The most common *digestivo* is an *amaro,* which means bitter, and you'd better believe it. *Amari* range from the mildly musty herbal flavor of a Montenegro or an Averna to the cough-medicine-gone-bad taste of the bracing elixir known as Fernet Branca. Nevertheless, they do seem to work at relieving the heaviness.

Other after-dinner drinks include the sweet anise-flavored Sambucca, which is served *alla mosca*—with three *mosce* ("flies") floating in it. These are really coffee beans to crunch on. There are also a wide variety of *grappas* (fruit brandies) that are kept near-frozen in summer and come in bottles full of pieces of fruit.

Romans eat lunch between 1:00 and 3:00 P.M.; dinners don't begin until 8:00. In summer, it is not at all bizarre to start a meal just before midnight.

In between, Romans snack on *pannini* (sandwiches in buns), *tramezzini* (half-sandwiches on slices of bread), or rice croquettes stuffed with mozzarella (*arancini*) or tomato sauce and ground meat (*supplí*) and deep-fried. Take-out pizza is available throughout the day; it's sold by weight in rectangular rather than triangular slices. In addition to the well-known red-sauce pizzas, there is also pizza *bianca* (white pizza), covered only with olive oil and salt or rosemary. Another favorite snack is sandwiches made with slices of *porchetta* (roast suckling pig), sliced before your eyes from the propped-up animal (with his or her head but minus the trotters).

As a rule of thumb, when choosing a restaurant always look for a handwritten daily menu, a fresh display of antipasti on the table inside, and an appreciative local crowd. Avoid places that display menus in five languages or with pages of dishes too numerous to prepare well. Another sure sign of low quality is a place that offers concoctions like pasta *allo champagne* (white wine) or risotto with kiwi.

The tap water in Rome is drinkable everywhere, but most people prefer to drink bottled mineral water (*aqua minerale*) with bubbles (*gassata*) or without (*non gassata*).

Since only the owner of a restaurant or trattoria is entrusted with writing the bill, it often takes more time than you would expect for it to arrive, depending on who and where the owner is. If you are in a hurry, ask for the bill when you order dessert or coffee and remind the waiter when he brings it. Even so, it could take up to 20 minutes or more to get the bill. Heading for the door, as a last-ditch effort, causes a commotion but produces results.

On the bill, in addition to what you ordered, you will find a small cover charge (*pane e coperto*) and a service charge of 10 to 15 percent. If the bill does not include the service charge, add it to what you pay; if it does, one usually leaves an additional Ł1,000 per person on the table for the waiter.

A note on Roman waiters: Roman waiters are a breed apart. They are not there to cajole the public. They are salaried and therefore do not perform for tips. Moreover, they are more or less assured of lifelong employment, so service with a smile is not one of their priorities. Threats to bring your business elsewhere go over their heads. On the plus side, they do not give lengthy biographies or wish you a nice day.

In the following list—arranged according to neighborhoods—a three-course dinner with a house wine in an inexpensive Roman restaurant or trattoria will cost about Ł25,000; in a moderately priced restaurant, Ł27,500–Ł47,500; and in an expensive restuarant, between Ł50,000 and Ł97,500. The very expensive category, such as hotel

dining rooms and three-star restaurants, starts at about
Ł100,000 and keeps on going.

The Pantheon

On a side street leading from piazza del Gesù toward the
Pantheon is **Chianti Corsi**, one of the few inexpensive
trattorias in the area that serves good Roman food. Corsi is
filled to capacity at lunchtime with politicians, shop assistants, and workmen, so go early. A typical Corsi lunch begins
with pasta in an artichoke cream sauce, goes on to roast veal
or meat loaf with gravy and roast potatoes flavored with
rosemary, and ends with dessert. But you don't have to order
all of it. One of the best items on the Corsi menu is the
insalata completa—an Italian version of Niçoise. Via del
Gesù 88. Closed Saturdays and Sundays; lunch only. Tel: 679-
08-21.

Da Fortunato is an expensive restaurant just off piazza del
Pantheon; it's popular with Italian politicians from the
nearby parliament and American journalists eavesdropping
on them. Veal from the milk-fed calves in the Campania
grazing lands south of Rome is a must to sample. The
scaloppine (flour-dusted veal filets sautéed in white wine or
lemon) at Da Fortunato is always tender. If you order an
orange for dessert, the waiter will peel it at your table and
turn it into a work of art. Reservations are required in
summer, especially if you want one of the outdoor tables
with a slice of the Pantheon to look at during your meal. Via
del Pantheon 55. Closed Sundays; no credit cards. Tel: 679-
27-88.

If you must eat fish in Rome, **La Rosetta**, with a Michelin
star to its credit, is a good place to have it. It claims a fresh
catch arrives every day from Sicily, but you will pay dearly
for that privilege. Forget about spaghetti with clam sauce—
that you can get anywhere. Concentrate instead on
tonnarelli alle uova di spigola (homemade spaghetti with
sea-bass roe) or *risotto all'aragosta* (lobster risotto). Via
della Rosetta 9. Reservations required; closed Sundays, Monday lunch, and August. Tel: 686-10-02.

Hostaria L'Angoletto is located on a little corner—which
is what its name means—in the maze of side streets that
leads out of the piazza where the Pantheon holds reign. In
addition to serving a variety of seafood and wild mushrooms
in season, it is one of the few moderately priced restaurants
in the center that serves food after midnight—or as long as
the customers keep coming. Piazza Rondanini 51. Closed
Mondays. Tel: 686-80-19.

La Cave di Sant'Ignazio is tucked into a corner of the

miniature piazza in front of Sant'Ignazio, which has so many entrances and exits that it looks like an opera set. Arrive early to get one of the outdoor candlelit tables to enjoy the show. The owners of this expensive restaurant claim that the fish arrives fresh from the port at Fiumicino every day. Try spaghetti with shrimp, garlic, tomato sauce, and fresh parsley, but leave room for the chocolate soufflé with vanilla sauce, which you should order at the beginning of the meal because it goes very quickly. Piazza Sant'Ignazio 169. Closed Sundays; reservations recommended. Tel: 679-78-21.

Piazza Navona

Many consider **El Toulà** the best all-around luxury-class restaurant in Rome. The decor of softly lit earth tones, comfortable armchairs, and glimmers of color in the antique paintings and Baroque flower arrangements is elegant but discreet. The cuisine is predominantly from the Veneto, so the rice dishes are especially well prepared. One of its Veneto specialties is *radicchio alla griglia,* grilled radicchio—the long, feathery variety that is grown in Treviso in the Veneto. Via della Lupa 29. Reservations required; closed Saturday lunch, Sundays, and August. Tel: 687-37-50 or 687-34-98; Fax: 687-11-15.

If you join the Sunday morning cappuccino-sipping, newspaper-reading, crowd-watching group in piazza Navona, you'll be glad to know about **Fiammetta**, one of the very few inexpensive trattorias open for lunch on Sundays. Just five minutes from the southern curve of the piazza, Fiammetta makes one of the best eggplant parmigianas in Rome. Get there early (it opens at 12:30) for one of the outdoor tables under an arbor. Piazza Fiammetta 8. Closed Tuesdays. Tel: 687-57-77.

Once a famous inn for the privileged, **Hosteria dell'Orso** has hosted, among others, Dante, Leonardo Da Vinci, and Rabelais. The 13th-century palace still retains much of its medieval splendor, and there is no lack of faded tapestries, gilded mirrors, and red velvet. This is the place to go if you want to dress up and have a special night in a very expensive restaurant. Many diners go from the dinner table to the Cabala discotheque upstairs. Via del Soldati 25. Reservations required; dinner only; closed Sundays. Tel: 686-42-50.

La Maiella specializes in dishes from the Abruzzi region east of Rome, such as *maccheroni all chitarra* (pasta cut into strings by pressing it through a guitar-like cutter)—but its risottos (*verdi,* with spinach, or *fiori di zucca,* with zucchini blossoms) make a visit to this expensive restaurant worthwhile, especially at night when the outdoor tables are crowded with Roman glitterati. Piazza Sant'Apollinare 45. Closed Sundays. Tel: 686-41-47.

Of the restaurants in the piazza, the best—and it is a qualified best at that—is **Mastrostefano** on the east side of the piazza. The view of Bernini's Fountain of the Four Rivers and Borromini's undulating church façade behind it is what puts this place in the expensive category, but the food, especially the *abbacchio* (roast suckling lamb), at least resembles the Roman food you find in less tourist-trodden areas. Piazza Navona. Closed Mondays and the last two weeks in August. Tel: 654-28-55.

Tucked away in a tiny piazza off via dei Coronari, which is lined with elegant antiques stores, **Osteria L'Antiquario** serves refined and unusual dishes that you won't find elsewhere, like *lasagne con melanzane al sugo di anatra* (lasagna with eggplant in duck sauce) or *coscio di anatra alle erbe in casseruola* (herbed thigh of duck in casserole). The price is high, but the candlelight and surrounding Renaissance palaces make it one of the most intimate outdoor dining experiences in Rome. Piazza San Simeone. Dinner only; reservations recommended; closed Sundays. Tel: 687-96-94.

Next door to the church of Sant'Agostino south of the piazza is the tiny eight-table, family-run **Da Pietro**, but this is not a cheap ma-and-pa operation. The food is expensive but prepared with exquisite care according to old family recipes. Among the best is *manzo al barolo* (very tender beef in a Barolo wine sauce). Via dei Pianellari 19. Closed Sundays. Tel: 686-85-65.

Campo dei Fiori

Besides being set in the ancient diamond-shaped brick ruins of the theater Pompey built to celebrate his triumph in 61 B.C., **Costanza** offers some of the most imaginative Roman cooking in town, two examples of which are *risotto con fiori di zucca* (risotto with zucchini blossoms) and *ravioli con carciofi* (artichoke-stuffed ravioli). The grilled meats are also good in this expensive restaurant—especially *abbacchio scottadito* (tiny grilled lamb ribs), which are best eaten with your fingers. But be careful not to "burn your fingertips," which is what *scottadito* means. Piazza del Paradiso 65. Closed Sundays and August. Tel: 686-17-17 or 654-10-02.

Filetti di Baccalà, in a tiny piazza off via de' Giubbonari, is always filled with young people, especially on Friday nights when they come to taste the Roman specialty for which the restaurant is named—baccalà—battered and deep-fried salt cod filets, which are served at paper-covered communal tables and accompanied by cheap raw Castelli wine. You may never want to eat one again, but the experience is pure Romano. Largo dei Librari 88. Closed Sundays and August. Tel: 686-40-18.

Il Pianeta Terra di Patrizia e Roberto is an elegant, very expensive restaurant run by a Tuscan rugby player and his Sicilian laywer wife. Its inventive, somewhat nouvelle menu has earned it a Michelin star and includes such rarities as *ravioli d'oca al barolo* (ravioli stuffed with goose in wine sauce) and *petto d'oca in salsa di prugne* (breast of goose in plum sauce). Via Arco del Monte 94. Dinners only; closed Mondays and August. Tel: 686-98-93.

Il Drappo means the drape and there are a lot of them, especially on the ceiling, in this expensive Sardinian restaurant. Sisters Angela and Valentina, together with their brother Paolo, have produced loving variations on the hearty cuisine of their native island. Try the *maialino arrosto* (roast piglet) accompanied by the flat, crunchy disk-shaped Sardinian bread called *carta da musica* (sheet music). For dessert try *sebada,* cheese-filled deep-fried dough balls. Vicolo del Malpasso 9. Reservations recommended; closed Sundays. Tel: 687-73-65.

If you're tired of pasta or want just a salad, try **L'Insalata Ricca,** which is next door to Sant'Andrea della Valle, the church in which the first act of Puccini's *Tosca* takes place. Salads come in both small and super sizes in this inexpensive restaurant. One super has olives, feta cheese, and artichoke hearts. There are also some pasta dishes in case you are still hungry afterward. Largo dei Chiavari 85. Closed Wednesdays; no credit cards; no smoking indoors. Tel: 654-36-56. There is also a **L'Insalata Ricca II** in piazza Pasquino, near piazza Navona; closed Mondays; Tel: 68-30-78-81.

If you get to **Hosteria Romanesca** early enough to get a table outdoors, you can get a moderately priced lunch and watch the vendors dismantle the outdoor food market in the campo, which closes shop every day (except Sundays) at about 1:30. As its name indicates, this trattoria serves heaping bowls of traditional Roman home cooking that has not been doctored to appear upscale or thinned down to accommodate tourists. Campo dei Fiori. Closed Sundays. Tel: 654-89-73.

Da Giovanni ar Galleto is on a street that connects campo dei Fiori with piazza Farnese and its magnificent Renaissance palace, which you can admire from an outdoor table. This moderately priced trattoria specializes in game and wild mushrooms (also truffles when they are in season), so be sure to try the *gallina faraona* (guinea hen) or the *galletto alla diavola,* a whole Cornish hen flattened and spiced and then baked to crispy perfection. Piazza Farnese 102. Closed Sundays; no credit cards. Tel: 686-17-14.

At **Pallaro** there is a fixed menu that includes three courses and wine for Ł26,000. The menu changes each day and the seating is family style, but the price is hard to beat in Rome these days. Largo del Pallaro 15. Closed Mondays. Tel: 654-14-88.

One of the liveliest places for outdoor dining is **Pierluigi**, on a side street near piazza Farnese. The *ravioli di pesce* (ravioli stuffed with seafood) and the *straccietti* (strips of sautéed beef) with raw *rughetta* on top are reason enough to reserve a table, but you may also be attracted by the fact that Pierluigi is one of the few expensive restaurants in Rome in which you can find homemade chocolate cake with whipped cream for dessert. Piazza dei Ricci 144. Closed Mondays; reservations recommended. Tel: 686-13-02 or 686-87-17.

In spite of what Shakespeare or Hollywood may have claimed, Julius Caesar was not killed in the Forum on the Ides of March in 44 B.C., but rather in the Teatro di Pompeo, because the Curia in the Forum where the Roman Senate usually met was closed for renovation (sound familiar?). The dining room of the **Da Pancrazio** restaurant is housed in the vaulted brickwork remains of the same Teatro di Pompeo, which once covered the whole area from the campo to largo Argentina. The ambience tends to be better than the food in this expensive restaurant, so it's best to stick to standards like *spaghetti alla carbonara.* Piazza del Biscione 92. Closed Wednesdays. Tel: 686-12-46.

Trevi Fountain

The pomposity of the owner of **Al Moro** was legendary even before he played to type in Fellini's *Satyricon,* but it has never stopped Fellini and a host of other luminaries from sampling what many people consider the best-prepared *funghi porcini* in Rome. The noise is unbearable, the waiters are schooled in the owner's protective disdain, and the smoke will kill you—but the wild mushrooms in this expensive trattoria are almost worth dying for. Vicolo delle Bollette 13. Closed Sundays and August; reservations recommended. Tel: 678-34-95.

Al Piccolo Arancio is on a *vicolo* (alleyway) off via del Lavatore, around the corner from the fountain. It has the most reliable menu of the eateries in this heavily trafficked area and offers fresh fish on Tuesdays and Fridays. Try *fusilli alla melanzana* (corkscrew pasta with an eggplant and tomato sauce) and the lemon mousse for dessert. Vicolo Scanderberg 112. Closed Mondays and August. Tel: 678-61-39. The same owners have two other moderately priced restaurants, **Da Settimo all'Arancio** (via dell'Arancio 50; Tel: 687-61-19) and **Arancio d'Oro** (via Monte d'Oro 17; Tel: 686-50-26), which also serves pizza. Both are closed on weekends.

The Colosseum

La Taverna dei Quaranta (The Tavern of the Forty) is a cooperative run by 40 would-be actors who take turns operating it. Located about a block away from the Colosseum, it has a rustic trattoria atmosphere and is popular with workmen and students. The offerings tend to be hearty Roman standards like *polenta* or *carbonara,* but there are always some interesting new ideas like risotto with radicchio. Via Claudia 24. Closed Sundays; no reservations; moderately priced. Tel: 73-62-96.

Osteria da Nerone is located on a hill just above the Colosseum and is one of the few moderately priced restaurants in the area that still serve good food. Try, for example, the homemade ravioli stuffed with ricotta cheese and spinach, garnished with melted butter and tiny sage leaves. The house specialty, *fettucine al Nerone* (ribbon pasta with peas, mushrooms, egg, and salami), seems well suited to an emperor (Nero) who is remembered for his excesses and whose house lies under the hill on which the restaurant sits. Via delle Terme di Tito 96. Closed Sundays. Tel: 474-52-07.

The Ghetto

Da Giggetto is the least fancy of the Ghetto restaurants and the most reasonably priced. It serves all the traditional Roman-Jewish specialties, mostly batter-dipped and deep-fried fish and vegetables, as well as *carciofi alla giudia* (a Jerusalem artichoke that is flattened so it looks like a chrysanthemum and then deep-fried until it is both crunchy and tender—a hard balance to achieve, and sometimes the artichokes are hard and greasy). The best of the offerings fried in this manner, however, is *mozzarella in carrozza,* tiny pieces of bread soaked in broth, dipped in egg, filled with mozzarella, and deep-fried to a golden crisp. Via del Portico d'Ottavia 22. Closed Mondays. Tel: 686-11-05.

The most celebrated restaurant in the Ghetto is **Piperno**, which is on a little hill in the corner of a tiny piazza next to the palazzo where Beatrice Cenci plotted her famous parricide. Piperno is pricey, but if you want exemplary (though non-kosher) versions of the Jewish classics such as *fritto* *misto* (a mixture of batter-fried delicacies) in a quiet, charming setting, this is the place. For dessert, ponder *le palle di nonno* (grandfather's balls), two hot cream puffs filled with sweetened ricotta cheese and chocolate bits. Monte de' Cenci 9. Closed Mondays, Sunday dinner, and August. Tel: 654-06-29.

Al Pompiere is the place to go if you want to sample one of the glories of Ghetto cuisine: *fiori di zucca ripieni* (batter-fried zucchini blossoms stuffed with tiny pieces of mozzarella cheese and anchovies). This moderately priced restaurant shares a part of the *piano nobile* of the Cenci Palace, which has several legends surrounding it and was a frequent goal of the English Romantic poets, who saw in Beatrice Cenci one of their ideal tragic heroines. If that doesn't interest you, consider that this is the only place in Rome that serves a pasta dish as delicate and tasty as *pennette* with lemon sauce. Via Santa Maria dei Calderari 38. Closed Sundays. Tel: 868-83-77.

The Roman artichoke is bigger and tenderer than those found in other countries. Nowhere is it better prepared than at **Da Evangelista**, where they do not deep-fry it, as they do elsewhere in the Ghetto, but rather flatten it between two bricks and then bake it in the oven—a method the owner's grandfather invented. The result is light and greaseless and melts in your mouth. Via delle Zoccolette 11. Closed Sundays and August; expensive. Tel: 687-58-10.

The excellent food and charming outdoor setting recommend the expensive **Vecchia Roma** in spite of the waiters' rudeness, which is so extreme that it has become a joke among customers. It is less amusing when they tamper with the bill. Nevertheless, the candlelight, the looming chiaroscuro background of the surrounding palaces and churches, and especially the sorbets made from whole fresh fruit are so memorable that they often make people more forgiving than usual. Piazza Campitelli 18. Reservations recommended; closed Wednesdays. Tel: 656-46-04.

Trastevere

If you prefer fish restaurants with a refined setting and excellent quality, at **Alberto Ciarlà** you will find everything from Maine lobster to Scottish salmon and Normandy oysters. The olive oil and wine (Bianco di Velletri Vigna Ciarlà) come from the owner's own property, and the sea bass with almonds and raw sea bream with ginger are just two of his excellent creations. Piazza San Cosimato 40. Reservations recommended; dinner only; closed Sundays; very expensive. Tel: 581-86-68; Fax: 688-43-77.

When **Augusto** fills up, which is almost every day and night in summer, the customers are expected to take things into their own hands, which often means getting your own bread and wine or replacing the paper tablecloths. The food in this family-run trattoria near piazza Santa Maria in Trastevere is hearty, healthy, and heaping and the price low, but don't go if you are in a hurry. Piazza de Rienzi 15. Closed Sundays. Tel: 688-57-21.

Ciak gets its name from the owners' passion for the movies (*ciak* is the "clack" sound the "take" board makes). It also explains the old movie posters and photos on the walls. This moderately priced restaurant near piazza Trilussa specializes in Tuscan cuisine. Start with an appetizer of mixed *crostini* (circles of bread spread with pâté, olive paste, or mushrooms). Then move on to *ribollita*—a hearty Tuscan vegetable soup with pieces of bread on top. A Florentine steak (with olive oil, lemon, and black pepper) could come next, or *spiedini* (skewers of grilled meat, sausage, bay leaf, and peppers). Vicolo del Cinque 21. Dinner only; closed Mondays. Tel: 589-47-74.

Da Lucia is a moderately priced trattoria located in a part of Trastevere that has not yet become so gentrified that it has nothing left but fake charm. The surrounding apartments and street-level shops, often festooned with the colors of rival soccer teams, testify to the fact that it is still a vibrant neighborhood of working-class Romans, and the menu reflects their interests. One of the best items, *penne all'arrabbiata* (short pasta in a spicy hot tomato and garlic sauce, garnished with fresh parsley), is a common Roman dish—rarely prepared as well these days as it is at Da Lucia. Via del Mattonato 2; Closed Mondays. Tel: 580-36-01.

At the moderately priced **Osteria-Pizzeria da Anna** just off viale Trastevere, you can eat outdoors or inside the air-conditioned dining room. The menu features all the Roman standards, which are prepared by the owner and served by her two daughters. Papa makes the pizzas at a wood-burning oven. Try *fettucine alla burina* (ribbon pasta with peas, tomatoes, mushrooms, and ham) or pizza with gorgonzola and rughetta. Via San Francesco a Ripa 57. Closed Thursdays. Tel: 589-39-92.

Eating in Trastevere's beautiful neighborhood living room, piazza Santa Maria in Trastevere, is a very expensive affair nowadays, but just around the corner is the moderately priced **Hosteria-Pizzeria Der Belli**. The view from the outdoor tables is not as picturesque as it is in the piazza, but the food is always good and sometimes inventive—like *formaggio arrosto con miele*—grilled cheese steaks with coarse honey. Piazza Sant'Apollonia. Closed Mondays. Tel: 580-37-82.

Il Ponentino ia named after the cool evening breeze that blows into Rome from the Alban hills in late afternoon in summer, so alfresco dining is one of the benefits of this inexpensive restaurant, which serves both pasta dishes and pizzas (in the evening). Try its *spaghetti alla Trasteverina,* made with cream, mushrooms, and peas. Piazza del Drago 10. Closed Mondays. Tel: 588-06-88.

One of the best restaurants in Rome in the moderately priced category is not Roman, but Sicilian. You will be hard bent to find better pasta in the capital than **La Gensola**'s rigatoni with broccoli, or its penne with eggplant and tomatoes, or the exquisite Arab-Sicilian *pasta con le sarde* with sardines, pine nuts, and raisins. The *secondi* in this small trattoria off piazza in Piscinula are typical Sicilian dishes like grilled swordfish or *involtini* (braised veal rolls stuffed with bread crumbs, parsley, and cheese). It also makes the lightest greaseless *calamari fritti* anywhere. Via della Gensola 15. Closed Sundays; reservations recommended. Tel: 581-63-12.

For many tourists, dining in Trastevere still means **Sabatini**, right in the piazza facing the church and sparkling fountain. The main dining room has beamed ceilings and frescoed walls, but even better are the crowded and noisy outdoor tables where you can indulge in some people-watching between courses. The food at Sabatini and its twin around the corner, **Sabatini II** (closed Tuesdays), is not any better than at less expensive Roman restaurants, and nothing on the menu has ever won critical acclaim, but what you really pay for is the view. Piazza Santa Maria in Trastevere. Closed Wednesdays. Tel: 581-20-26.

The full name of **Tentativo** reads like the title of a Lina Wertmuller film: *Tentativo di Descrizione di un Banchetto a Roma* (Attempt at a Description of a Banquet in Rome). The creative and very expensive menu includes such un-Roman entrees as *ravioli d'anatra* (duck-filled ravioli) and *fileto di manzo affumicato con funghi porcini* (smoked beef filet with porcini mushrooms). The setting is intimate and free of the usual operating-room lighting that abounds in most Roman eateries. Via delle Luce 5: Dinner only; closed Sundays and August; reservations necessary. Tel: 589-52-34.

Piazza del Popolo

The late Roman restaurateur Alfredo, self-proclaimed king of fettucine and creator of *fettucine all'Alfredo,* was popular with American tourists from the day he served his pasta dish to Douglas Fairbanks and Mary Pickford with a golden spoon and fork. **Alfredo alla Scrofa** continues the tradition (for much more than the fettucine, butter, cheese, and cream could ever cost) with what they say are the original utensils, and with a lot more show than class. (The drama is enhanced by live music.) Via della Scrofa 104. Closed Tuesdays. Tel: 654-01-63.

The location of **Casina Valadier**, on the Pincio Hill in the Villa Borghese gardens and overlooking piazza del Popolo, makes its outdoor terrace the perfect place for Sunday brunch. The prices are high but the view of the domes and rooftops of Rome is perfect, as is the carefully prepared *caprese* (Capri-style) salad of mozzarella balls, cured ham, and fresh tomatoes dressed with basil and olive oil. Save room for the vanilla ice cream topped with bits of caramelized orange peel. Piazza Valadier. Closed Mondays; reservations recommended for Sunday lunch. Tel: 679-20-83.

Dal Bolognese, right in piazza del Popolo, specializes in the cuisine of Bologna, which many say is Italy's finest. The pasta is all homemade and you should order it *al ragù*, with the meat sauce typical of Bologna. Though *cotolette alla bolognese* (breaded veal cutlet covered with a slice of prosciutto and melted cheese) is a standard, also try the *bollito misto,* a sampling of boiled meats and poultry accompanied by a green sauce of parsley, capers, and chopped onion. Piazza del Popolo 1. Closed Sunday dinner and Mondays; reservations recommended. Tel: 361-14-26.

La Buca di Ripetta, a moderately priced family-run trattoria two blocks from piazza del Popolo, is one of the few in that category that is air-conditioned and open for Sunday lunch. Go early because there are no reservations and it is small. Ask about the daily specials, which do not appear on the menu. On any Thursday, try the traditional Roman Thursday standard, *gnocchi* (potato dumplings). Via di Ripetta 36. Closed Sunday evening, Mondays, and August. Tel: 321-93-91.

Al Ristorante 59, on a street leading out of the piazza, is a fine clublike restaurant popular with journalists and businessmen who often meet there for interviews or power lunches. The most popular item on the excellent Bolognese menu is *tortelli di zucca,* little pockets of pasta filled with pumpkin squash and garnished with butter and sage leaves—it's the only place in Rome where you can get them. Via Angelo Brunetti 59. Closed Sundays; no credit cards. Tel: 321-90-19.

Piazza di Spagna

Tucked away on a side street behind the American Express office is **Alla Rampa**, where lunch is an enormous smorgasbord that includes everything from stuffed olives to eggplant parmigiana. This moderately priced restaurant also has pasta dishes and outdoor tables under the typical Roman canvas *ombrelloni* (umbrellas). If you want to sit outdoors, go early, because La Rampa does not take reservations. Piazza Mignanelli 18. Closed Sundays and Monday lunch. Tel: 678-26-21.

Nino, on a street leading out of the piazza, is what many consider the finest Tuscan restaurant in Rome. Its white bean soup (*zuppa di fagioli*) steamed in bottles (*al fiasco*) is a perennial favorite of regulars, especially in winter. Nino also makes excellent *bistecca alla fiorentina* (a huge charcoal-grilled steak with a bit of olive oil, lemon, and black pepper)—to be eaten with the excellent house Chianti *a consumo*, meaning you pay only for what you drink from the carafe on the table. Via Borgognona 11. Closed Sundays and August; expensive. Tel: 679-56-76.

Via Margutta, off via del Babuino, which leads out of the piazza in the direction of piazza del Popolo, is lined with artists' ateliers and is the site of an annual art fair in May. The small vegetarian restaurant **Margutta** has a warm, inviting atmosphere. The entrées, like tagliatelle with avocado and mushrooms, are generally expensive, but at lunch there is an economically priced buffet that includes an interesting assortment of vegetables and cold pastas. Via Margutta 119. Closed Sundays and August. Tel: 678-60-33.

Otello alla Concordia, on another side street leading out of the piazza, is a moderately priced trattoria that provides both indoor seating and outdoor tables beneath a vine-covered pergola. It serves classic Roman dishes, with a few concessions from other parts of Italy, and is very popular with office workers and shop assistants in the area. The cannelloni—always a chancey dish because you never know when it was prepared—is excellent here, but save room for *melone e lampone*—fresh melon with raspberries for dessert. Via della Croce 81. Closed Sundays; no reservations. Tel. 679-11-78 or 678-14-54.

The Hotel d'Inghilterra has opened its own expensive restaurant, **Roman Garden**, which has quickly become a popular spot for business lunches. Among the refined Italian dishes it serves are *insalatina di sogliola e salmone con spinaci* (a sole and salmon spinach salad) and *tortelli di anatra al tartufo* (duck-filled dumplings with truffles). Via Bocca di Leone 14. Open seven days. Tel: 67-21-61.

Via Veneto

A creative menu, flawless service, and an intelligent wine list have earned **Andrea**, an expensive diplomats' and business-men's restaurant, a faithful clientele. Among its best dishes are lobster bisque and *straccetti di manzo con porcini e tartufi* (strips of sautéed beef with porcini mushrooms and truffles). One eats very well here. Via Sardegna 26. Closed Sundays and Monday lunch. Tel: 482-18-91.

The hearty specialties of Emilia-Romagna are served in a quiet country trattoria-like setting at **Colline Emiliane** near piazza Barberini at the foot of via Veneto. Homemade pasta (rolled out before your eyes) is what to order here, or one of the boiled meat dinners that are a signature piece of the region. There is an excellent selection of Lambrusco and other Emilia wines. Via degli Avignonesi 22. Closed Fridays. Tel: 481-75-38.

The best thing to do at **Piccolo Abruzzo** is to let the owner, Eduardo, keep bringing the food until you can't eat anymore. That's what he'll do anyway. He usually passes around the tables with a bowl of whatever has just come out of the kitchen (shrimp risotto or spaghetti and eggplant) and insists that you try a little. You can stick to the standard menu, but the bill in this moderately priced trattoria featur-ing food from Abruzzo won't be that different. Via Sicilia 237. Closed Saturday lunch. Tel: 482-01-76.

For those looking for an "international" atmosphere, **Sans Souci** is the very expensive answer. A black-and-gold decor sets the scene for elaborate Italian-based dishes, often heavy-handed, such as the *ravioli di pesce* (fish-stuffed ravioli), which come swimming in a lake of heavy cream. But Miche-lin has given the filet of sole with strawberries a star. Via Sicilia 20. Dinner only; reservations recommended; closed Mondays and August. Tel: 482-18-14.

Others

The **Abruzzi**, located at the far end of piazza Santi Apostoli, a short walk from piazza Venezia, is an inexpensive restaurant that consistently serves well-prepared, dependable dishes from both Rome and the Abruzzo region east of Rome. You will always find here, for example, a delicious homemade *stracciatella* (chicken soup with ribbons of egg batter and Parmesan cheese floating in it). Via del Vaccaro 1, Closed Saturdays. Tel: 679-38-97.

In the warren of alleys that constitutes the area between corso Vittorio and the bridge to Castel Sant'Angelo is the tiny (seven-table) inexpensive trattoria called **Alfredo e Ada**, which remains one of the few trattorias in the old-fashioned "ugly, banal look" that has not been given a new glazed-over white-pine update. The quality of the good old-fashioned Roman food like *spezzatino* (veal stew) or *seppie con piselli* (baby squid with peas) hasn't changed either. There is no menu, and Ada does everything from cooking to serving to writing up the bill, so relax and enjoy it. Via Banchi Nuovi 14. Closed Sundays; no credit cards; no telephone.

Al Ceppo is located in Rome's elegant residential area, Parioli, near piazza Ungheria. The atmosphere is rustic: wood-beamed ceilings, dark wood tables, and an open-grill fireplace stocked with tree stumps, which is what *ceppo* means. The food is geared toward pleasing Italian families out for a good (and expensive) meal who expect entrées that are a little more special than what they prepare at home—such as cannelloni stuffed with pumpkin or giant ravioli filled with eggplant purée. Via Panama 2. Closed Mondays. Tel: 841-96-96 or 855-13-79.

Keep **Ambasciata d'Abruzzo** in mind when you are ready for a big meal. For a blanket price of £30,000 including wine, you can eat all you want and the waiters will still keep bringing the food. After a while you don't taste anything, but the outlay is impressive and induces lots of camaraderie with fellow diners, who exchange friendly grimaces and groans. When you sit down, there is a basket of sausages and bread already waiting. Skip it and make some selections instead from the antipasti table—keeping in mind that you will have to sample at least three pastas, two meat dishes, and as many desserts as your heart can take before you finish. Via Pietro Tacchini (in Parioli). The best way to get there is by cab; closed Sundays. Tel: 807-82-56.

One of the best all-time, old-time restaurants in Rome is **Cannavota**, near San Giovanni in Laterano. Its specialty is seafood, but the dish that has kept generations of neighborhood families coming regularly to this moderately priced restaurant is *bucatini alla cannavota,* pasta with a secret tomato-and-cream seafood sauce that is mildly spicy and delicious. Piazza San Giovanni in Laterano. Closed Wednesdays; reservations recommended. Tel: 77-50-07.

For a special evening in Rome, have dinner on a barge in the Tiber at **Canto del Riso**, just below the Ponte Cavour bridge. There are both outdoor and indoor tables, but get one of the outdoor candlelit ones and watch the sun go down while you sip an aperitivo. The food will pale by comparison, but try the seafood risotto or the salad with mozzarella, fresh tomatoes, and basil. Lungotevere Mellini 7. Closed Mondays; reservations recommended in summer; expensive if you order fish; Tel: 361-04-30.

The chicest place these days to sample the various Roman innards is **Checchino dal 1887**, auspiciously located across the street from the former slaughterhouses in the newly gentrified section of Testaccio, near the Ostiense train station. The owners claim their ancestors invented the Roman specialty *coda alla vaccinara* (oxtail stew), which has more bone than tail to it, but the pasta garnished with the same sauce is another matter. Checchino has two sommeliers in charge of one of the best wine cellars in Rome, downstairs carved out of the mountain of pottery shards that gives the area its name. And for dessert? Gorgonzola and coarse honey with a glass of very good Marsala. Via di Monte Testaccio 30. Closed Sunday dinner, Mondays, and August; reservations recommended in summer; expensive. Tel: 574-63-18.

Coriolano, just off via Nomentana, is an expensive classic Roman restaurant near Porta Pia that has kept its fan club of gourmets because of its absolute adherence to quality and freshness. The very small dining room is decorated with antiques the owner's father collected from Switzerland and Germany. The daughter speaks English and will explain the menu, which includes perfectly prepared items like *tagliolini all'aragosta* (very thin fettucine with lobster sauce). Coriolano is especially proud of its secret way of preparing porcini mushrooms. It's a shame the restaurant ruins it by passing out cigars and allowing smoking everywhere. Via Ancona 14. Closed Sundays and August; reservations recommended. Tel: 855-11-22.

Severino a Piazza Zama is beyond the Baths of Caracalla, but many Romans and travellers alike go there to sample the Roman dish it is justly famous for—*saltimbocca alla romana* (literally, "jump-in-your-mouth" filets of veal covered with prosciutto and cheese and then braised). If you order this dish, you get to take the decorated plate home with you. Piazza Zama 5. Closed Sunday dinner, Mondays, and August; reservations advised; expensive. Tel: 700-08-72.

La Campana, on a side street of the same name off via della Scrofa, began as an inn 500 years ago and has been consistently serving high-quality Roman dishes for more than 100 years. That makes it one of the oldest continual in-service restaurants in Rome. The food is still good. Take, for example, *vignarola,* a thick vegetable stew that is a meal in itself. But its pasta with artichoke cream sauce and homemade ricotta cheesecake are what have won this restaurant a loyal clientele. Vicolo della Campana 18. Closed Mondays and August. Tel: 687-52-73.

An Alternative to Restaurant Dining

If you find the traditional Roman three-course meal overwhelming for both your stomach and your pocketbook, one solution is to eat in wine shops that serve food (*enoteche*). These are not wine *bars,* but wine *stores* that have converted part of their establishment into a lunchroom. Most have only a few tables with paper tablecloths, a limited menu, and no service, but others have taken the idea upmarket by adding creative menus, waiter service, and a sophisticated ambience.

Most enoteche are open only for lunch, but some serve food until late at night. Another benefit is that you can try different wines and buy a bottle of what you like on the way out. Enoteche are quick, cheap, and ideal for those times when you want more than a sandwich or a pizza and less than a three-course meal.

Da Benito (via dei Falegnami 14; lunch only; closed Sundays) is a tiny one-room shop in the Ghetto with a few tables and a counter. The food is hearty (*gnocchi*—potato dumplings—every Thursday) and cheap and the atmosphere is crowded and harried. At **313 Cavour** (via Cavour 313; closed Sundays), however, you can take your time and choose from a wide selection of salads, pâtés, and *torte rustiche*—vegetable pies made from organically grown vegetables. The same is true at **Cul de Sac** (piazza Pasquino 73; closed Mondays; Tel: 654-10-94), near piazza Navona, where the wine bottles lie in racks over the tables and the red lentil or white bean soup is especially good with the warm homemade bread.

The most recent incarnation of the eat-in wine shop is a model in which the food is as important as the sale of wine. These smart in-places cater to young professionals and are more expensive. Among the best are **Spiriti** (via di Sant'Eustachio 5; closed Sundays), which features combination platters of daily specials like Greek salad, Sardinian lasagna, or grilled eggplant; and **Semidivino** (via Alessandra 130; closed Sundays), which is very upscale and offers such rarities as smoked breast of goose, sturgeon carpaccio, and rabbit pâté with truffles. But the best of the new enoteche is **La Bottega del Vino** (via Santa Maria del Pianto 9; lunch only; closed Saturdays and Sundays), where the wine cellar has been converted into a smart dining area and the menu features items like smoked salmon rolls filled with crabmeat and ricotta cheesecake from a bakery in the nearby Ghetto.

Pizzerias

The outdoor pizzerias at the beginning of viale Trastevere are still as loud and blindingly lit as they were in Fellini's

Roma, but they are the place to go if you want to sample the Roman version of Italy's most famous culinary invention. Roman pizza is flat, wafer-thin, and crunchy, because it is usually baked in a wood-burning oven so that the crust blisters and it acquires a slightly smoky flavor. In addition to the standards—*margarita* (tomato sauce, cheese, and basil), *napoletana* (cheese and anchovies), *funghi* (mushroom), and *salsicce* (sausage)—Romans have invented *la capricciosa,* a capricious blend of just about everything, including a hard-boiled egg. Most pizzerias do not open for lunch and do not take reservations.

Among the best—and therefore the most popular and most crowded—are **Baffetto** (via del Governo Vecchio 114; closed Sundays and August) near piazza Navona, where the lines are long but the turnover fast; **Da Ivo** in Trastevere (via San Francesco a Ripa 157; closed Tuesdays), which is well known for its meat-and-sausage–filled *calzone* (covered pizza); **Da Gildo** in Trastevere near Porta Settimiana (via della Scala 31; closed Sundays), which charges more but serves large pizzas with unusual toppings like shrimp or salmon; **La Capricciosa** at the end of via Condotti (largo dei Lombardi 8; closed Tuesdays), which claims to have invented the *pizza capricciosa* described above; **Le Volte,** located in a frescoed 16th-century palazzo (piazza Rondanini 47; closed Tuesdays) near the Pantheon; **Corallo** (via del Corallo 10; closed Mondays) off via Governo Vecchio, which also serves *foccacia;* **Osteria Picchioni** off via Nazionale (via del Boschetto 16; closed Wednesdays), which serves very expensive pizzas with truffles and sun-dried tomatoes; **Tulipano Nero,** a boisterous, busy outdoor pizzeria in Trastevere (piazza San Cosimato; closed Wednesdays) that serves large, inexpensive pizzas of all kinds; and **Taberna Piscinula** in piazza in Piscinula (number 50; closed Mondays), which is very upscale and expensive and offers far-out toppings like corn niblets or crabmeat at outside tables or in an air-conditioned inside room.

—Louis Inturrisi

NIGHTLIFE

Nightlife in the Eternal City is not as varied as it is in other, more cosmopolitan capitals. The symphony still lacks a permanent auditorium, there is no national ballet company, art galleries are few and unvaried, most cinemas are expensive and closed in summer, and the museum situation is legendary. However, recently the situation has shown positive signs of improvement. Wildcat strikes, inferior quality, and totally inconvenient ticketing, which often discouraged people in the past, occur less frequently; many theaters have adopted air-conditioning and computerized ticketing; the opera has a new inventive impresario; and there is even a museum (Palazzo delle Esposizione on Via Nazionale) that stays open until 11:00 P.M.

Rather than looking at after-hours as a time for partying, young Roman professionals put on their best clothes, take a walk or—less often these days—a ride into the center, have an aperitif at one stop, a meal at another, and a digestivo at a third, then go to a disco or to a piano bar to hear live music.

Activity in cafés and bars starts picking up after dinner at around 10:00 P.M. Piano bars and clubs begin to get lively at midnight, and nightclubs don't even open until after midnight in summer. Most of the clubs charge a cover, and some require a membership fee. In summer Roman nightlife can easily extend into the wee hours of the morning.

Information on what's happening in Rome can be found in Italian in the Rome daily *Il Messaggero* and in the Thursday supplement of *La Repubblica,* or in English in two biweekly English-language magazines, *Wanted in Rome* and *Metropolitana.* Both of the latter are available at kiosks and English-language bookstores.

Opera, Symphony, Theater

The **Rome Opera** season runs from December to May (box office: piazza Beniamino Gigli near via Viminale; Tel: 675-957-25 in English); in summer it mounts productions outdoors at the Terme di Caracalla, which always include a spectacular version of Verdi's *Aida.* The **Accademia di Santa Cecilia** symphony orchestra (via delle Conciliazione in front of the Vatican; Tel: 654-10-44) has regular concerts from October to June and moves outdoors to the Villa Giulia near the Modern Art Museum in summer. The **Teatro Argentina**, in largo Argentina (Tel: 654-46-01), mounts stage productions in Italian of classical and modern playwrights like Pirandello and Goldoni from October to June. Musicals in both Italian and English (by international touring companies) are performed at **Teatro Sistina** near the top of the Spanish Steps (via Sistina 129; Tel: 482-68-41) regularly throughout the year.

Cinema

All foreign films in Italy are dubbed. But the dubbers are carefully chosen (and sometimes become celebrities themselves), so that you would swear Woody Allen had grown up in Italy. Nevertheless, films are shown daily in English exclusively at the **Pasquino Cinema** (vicolo del Piede 19; Tel: 580-

36-22) just off piazza Santa Maria in Trastevere, and on Mondays at the **Alcazar Cinema** (via Cardinale Merry del Val 14; Tel: 588-00-99) near piazza Sonnino in Trastevere. Cinemas do not open until around 4:00 P.M. and close for lack of air-conditioning and customers in August.

Cafés and Bars

The mecca of serious people-watching has shifted recently from the bars on via Veneto like **Café de Paris** (number 90) or **Doney** (number 145) to **Rosati** and **Canova** on the curve of piazza del Popolo. The men here tend to be Roman, the women foreign. The opposite is generally true of the bars on via Veneto. In Trastevere, **Caffè-Bar di Marzio** in piazza Santa Maria is packed at night and on Sunday mornings, when you can't see the customers for the open newspapers. The best cappuccino in Rome is still at **Bar Sant'Eustachio** in the piazza of the same name near the Pantheon, but you have to tell the waiter *senza zucchero* if you don't like it sweet. Young professionals and students like **Vineria** in campo dei Fiori (number 15), whereas would-be actors and actresses prefer **Bar della Pace** in front of Cortona's fanciful Santa Maria della Pace or its new rival, **Bar Bramante**, across the street. Purists still go to **Caffè Greco** on via Condotti (number 86) near the Spanish Steps to revel in the atmosphere that once attracted the likes of Mark Twain, Dickens, and Buffalo Bill. At **Biancaneve** (Snow White) in piazza Paoli at the end of corso Vittorio, a young crowd sits at night on the side facing the illuminated Castel Sant'Angelo and munches on *mele stregate* (bewitched apples)—balls of *zabaione* ice cream coated in dark chocolate. Two cafés that have good panoramic views are **Cafe Ciampini**, across from the Villa Medici at the top of the Spanish Steps, and **Zodiaco**, on Monte Mario near the Hilton Hotel, which has a spectacular overview of Rome (viale di Parco Mellini 90).

Gelaterias

In Juvenal's time, Roman citizens used to collect snow from the foot of the outlying hills and mix it with honey and fruit to make libations they called *nix dulcis*—sweet snow. Modern Romans do not travel quite so far in their pursuit of *gelato,* but they are still very particular about how and where they enjoy their sweet snow. Rome, in fact, holds the title for ice cream consumption in Italy—more than five gallons per person. In summer it is part of the *passeggiata* (ritual evening stroll) to wind up at one of the following crowded gelaterias, currently considered among the best. (Remember, they are all closed on Monday.)

The mecca for serious gelato eaters is the via del Pantheon, a crooked street that leads out of piazza del Pantheon. Home of four of the best gelaterias in Rome, it has been nicknamed "ice cream alley." The first—and best—is **Fiocco di Neve** (number 51), which offers a limited number of fresh homemade flavors as well as a few in which rice has been added. Try *riso alle fragole,* which combines strawberry ice cream and rice. Farther down the opposite side of the street (which changes names) is **Gelateria della Palma** (via della Maddalena 20), a slick, high-tech gelateria that specializes in exotic fruit-flavored ices. Continuing to the end of via della Maddalena and turning right will bring you to **Giolitti** (via degli Uffici del Vicario 40), one of the oldest and most respected ice-cream parlors in Rome. Its *coppa olimpica* is an expensive combination of ice creams, sherbets, and whipped cream and a wafer chimney that weighs in at half a kilo.

Elsewhere in Rome, **Tre Scalini**, in piazza Navona, is justly famous for its *tartufo,* a ball of rich dark chocolate ice cream that includes chunks of even richer chocolate and a cherry in the middle, all smothered under dollops of whipped cream.

Other gelaterias in the center where you can find fresh homemade gelato are **Gelofestival** in Trastevere (viale Trastevere 27), which also has ice-cream sandwiches; **Pasticceria Cecere** (via San Francesco a Ripa 153) in Trastevere, which is famous for its *zabaione;* **Fassi** at via Nomentana 127; **Al Ristoro della Salute** (behind the Colosseum), which also makes fresh-fruit milkshakes; **Bar Europea** in piazza San Lorenzo, where you can get Sicilian specialties like *cassata* ice cream; and **Alberto Pica** (via della Seggiola), between largo Argentina and the Garibaldi bridge.

As an alternative to gelato, try a *granita* (crushed ice that has been made from fresh fruit juice) or a *grattachecca* (shaved ice over which a variety of syrups or fruit juices are poured). Most bars have *granite* in summer, and you will find *grattachecche* at the kiosks along the Tiber. A good way to lift flagging spirits is to order a *granita di caffè,* a coffee ice topped with whipped cream, or a *granita di limone,* with fresh lemon juice. **Tazza d'Oro**, at via degli Orfani 84, near the Pantheon, makes the best of both.

Piano Bars and Live-Music Clubs

For live music the choices are wide and scattered throughout the city. **Big Mama** (vicolo San Francesco a Ripa 18, in Trastevere), true to its name, is the leading jazz club in

Rome, but there are many others. The **Mississippi Jazz Club** (borgo Angelico 16, near the Vatican), **Music Inn** (largo dei Fiorentini 3, off via Giulia), and **Billie Holiday Jazz Club** (via degli Orti di Trastevere 43, in Trastevere) are all just as well established. **Saint Louis** (via del Cardello 13/a, near the Colosseum) is still enormously popular, but lately has been displaced by **Caffè Latino** (via di Monte Testaccio 96, in the trendy Testaccio neighborhood) as the current favorite.

For other kinds of music, there's **Four Green Fields** (via Morin 40, near the Vatican) for Irish music; **Yes Brazil** (via San Francesco a Ripa 103, Trastevere) for Brazilian; **Makumba** (via degli Olimpionici 19, near the ponte Flaminio) for African reggae and salsa (weekends only); and **Folkstudio** (via Sacchi 3, in Trastevere) for folk.

Birrerias

Romans are not about to forsake *vino,* but beer (*birra*) is becoming a popular drink, especially in summer. Imported beer is expensive; Italian brands like Nastro Azzurro and Peroni are less expensive but not as good. Nevertheless, an evening in a crowded Roman *birreria* can be a boisterous, rowdy, fun-loving affair. One of the most popular these days is **Birreria della Scala** in Trastevere (piazza della Scala 58; closed Wednesdays), which has live music and serves pasta as well. Other lively birrerie are **Birreria Bavarese** (via Vittoria 47; closed Mondays) and **Birreria Wiener** (via della Croce 21; closed Wednesdays) near piazza di Spagna; **Birreria Dreher** in piazza Santi Apostoli; and **Birreria Peroni** (via Brescia 24; closed Mondays), which dates from the turn of the century.

Nightclubs

Nothing is eternal about Rome's nightlife, which has become increasingly trendy. Jaded jet-set types still frequent **La Cabala** and the **Blue Bar** (via dei Soldati 25), both upstairs from the Hostaria dell'Orso restaurant near piazza Navona. More "in" at the moment, however, are **Gilda** (via Mario de' Fiori 97, near the Spanish Steps), and, especially, the recently opened **Alien** (via Velletri 13/19, near piazza Fiume), both frequented by beautiful people from the worlds of politics and entertainment. The poor rich kids of the Parioli residential district north of Villa Borghese—so much a cultural phenomenon that *pariolini* has become the Roman term for "gilded youth"—are dragging themselves to the new **Krypton** (via Luigi Luciana 52) with renewed lack of enthusiasm. And the latest gay hangouts for both sexes are **L'Angelo**

Azzurro (via Cardinal Merry del Val 13, in Trastevere) and **Hangar** (via in Selci 69/A, near Santa Maria Maggiore). But who knows when the new emperors of entertainment will turn their thumbs down on what Cicero called the *aura popularis* (popular breeze) of these "in" establishments. Before you go, you'd better have your hotel check to make sure they're still in business.

—*Louis Inturrisi*

SHOPS AND SHOPPING

Though T. S. Eliot's women may "come and go, talking of Michelangelo," when shoppers come and go in Rome today the talk is more likely to be of Valentino, Fendi, and other designers who keep their ateliers here. For despite Milan's prominence in the ready-to-wear fashion world, Rome still reigns supreme for *alta moda*.

Rome's sartorial splendor extends to men as well. The fabrics of made-to-measure shirts rival anything you'll see on Savile Row, and the tailoring is often superior. Quality, and the traditions of pomp and circumstance running from the ancients through the popes and now to the headquarters of Italy's major television networks and film industry, are what distinguish shopping in the capital.

Shops in Rome generally are open from 9:00 or 10:00 A.M. to 1:00 or 1:30 P.M., unless they're on *orario no-stop* (chic Italian for nonstop schedule); they reopen between 4:00 and 5:00 P.M. and stay open until between 7:00 and 8:30 P.M. All shops are closed Sundays and Monday mornings, except around Christmas. Food shops close Thursday afternoons in fall and winter and Saturday afternoons in spring and summer. In addition to national holidays, many shops close on Rome's birthday, April 21.

Most of the shops listed below accept credit cards, but if you find that you need cash outside of normal banking hours, try one of the new automatic machines in the center or Banca Nazionale del Lavoro (via Veneto 11; Tel: 482-44-21) or 482-76-60), which stays open *no-stop* until 6:00 P.M., including Saturdays.

The most elegant (and expensive) shopping in Rome centers around the streets leading out from piazza di Spagna. Less expensive—but by no means less crowded— are the shops on via del Tritone and via Nazionale. Other, less-trafficked shopping streets are via Cola di Rienzo (near the Vatican), via dei Giubbonoari (near campo dei Fiori), via Salaria, and the daily open-air market specializing in used clothes along via Sonnio next to San Govanni in Laterano.

Spanish Steps

Before leaving the piazza to shop in the side streets, you may want to stop at **American Express** (number 38). Having put your credit cards and money safely in a waist pouch, not in a shoulder bag or wallet, you are ready to do some serious shopping.

Begin by wandering up **via Babuino**, off the piazza to the north, where two designers have their less expensive boutiques: the **Armani Emporium** at number 140 (his more-expensive men's and women's lines are at via Condotti 76) and Valentino's **Oliver Boutique** at number 61 (his women's store is at via Bocca di Leone 15; his men's, on the corner of via Condotti and via Mario Fiori). On the same street, along with women's wear by **Missoni** (number 96/a; his men's shop is in the piazza at number 78), you will find some of Italy's leading antiques dealers. **Antonacci** (number 146) and **W. Appolloni** (number 133) are the most famous. If you're looking for a painting, double back down the parallel **via Margutta** and have a look into the art galleries that line that street.

Return to the piazza and go down fashion's most famous shopping street, **via Condotti**, where you will find internationally known stores like **Richard Ginori, Gucci, Cartier, Bulgari, Beltrami**, and **Hermes. Ferragamo** has a men's shop at number 66 and a women's shop at number 74. **Trussardi** is at number 49; **Barilla** (number 29), which makes classic hand-sewn shoes for men and women, and **Battistoni** (number 61), which makes made-to-measure menswear, are less well known but worth visiting. The hairstylist **Sergio Valente** has his salon at number 11.

Via Borgognona and **via Frattina** are two more streets leading out of the piazza where you will find more famous name showrooms. The **Fendis** have their shop at number 36; **Gianni Versace** has his men's shop at number 29 (his women's shop is at via Bocca di Leone 26); and **Gianfranco Ferrè** has a men's shop at number 6 and a women's shop at number 42/b. At number 4/d is the black-and-white shop of the publicist **Franco Maria Ricci**, where you can purchase elegant cards, art books, and copies of his very expensive art magazine *FMR*. Finally, if you love stationery stores that are full of bric-a-brac and cleverly designed office supplies, have a look in the two **Vertecchi** stores on via della Croce (numbers 38 and 70) before leaving the area.

Specialty Shops in the Center

Antiques and engravings. Besides the daily outdoor print market in piazza Fontanella di Borghese, some reputable shops that sell antique prints are **Roberto Boccalini** (via del Banco di Santo Spirito 61), **Casali** (piazza del Pantheon 82), **Cascianelli** (largo Febo 14), **Nardecchia** (piazza Navona 25), and **Giuliana Di Cave** (piazza di Pietra 24), near the Pantheon.

The largest concentration of antiques dealers is on via dei Coronari, and if you are there in May or October, you will see the street decked out in carpets and torches for the two annual antiques fairs. Some exceptions to the mostly 19th-century English furniture in the shops are **Mario Morisco** (number 136), which sells French Empire furniture; **La Mansarde** (number 202), which deals in Piedmontese period furniture; and **Metastasio** (number 33), which sells unusual nautical paintings. Other streets where antiques are sold are via Giulia near piazza Farnese and via del Babuino off piazza di Spagna.

Crafts and ceramics. Via dell'Orso, just off Ponte Umberto, is lined with crafts shops and holds an annual fair every October. Elsewhere, the antique craft of tile making is still practiced at **Galleria Farnese** (piazza Farnese 50); mosaic tiles may be made to order at **Opificio Romano** (via dei Gigli d'Oro 9), and **Canguro** (via di Campo Marzio 45) sells high-quality yarns.

Expensive handmade beeswax candles are available at **Pisoni** (corso Vittorio Emanuele 127); master bookbinding is the specialty of **Mario Rossini** (via dei Lucchesi 25); and **Papiro,** near the Spanish Steps (via Capo le Case 55), makes a wide line of products from handmade marbleized paper. If pottery from Deruta, Vietri, or Apulia, or country furniture from Umbria and Tuscany interests you, **Galleria Sambuca** near Santa Maria in Trastevere (via della Pelliccia 30) has the most representative line of both in Rome.

Housewares. **Croff Centro Case** has well-designed Italian housewares and furniture (via Cola di Rienzo 197); **Spazio Sette** (via Barbieri 7), near largo Argentina, has inventive hi-tech everything from soup spoons to floor lamps; and **De Sanctis,** at number 84 in piazza Navona, has all the latest Alessi home products as well as De Simone folk pottery. The housewares department in the basement of the piazza Fiume branch of **La Rinascente** department store has a good selection of espresso pots and pasta makers.

Men's made-to-order. **Caleffi** (via Colonna Antonina 53) has been making men's shirts, suits, and ties for three generations. **Caraceni** (via Marche 1 and via Campania 61/b) is another respectable family dynasty in custom tailoring; and **Camiceria Piero Albertelli** (via dei Prefetti 11) specializes in men's nightwear.

Bargain outlets. **Discount dell'Alta Moda** (via Gesù e Maria), between piazza di Spagna and piazza del Popolo, and **Discount System** (via del Viminale) near the Basilica of Santa Maria Maggiore sell designer clothes and accessories from the top names in Italian fashion at a 50 percent reduction.

Linen and embroidery. **Frette** (piazza di Spagna 10 and via del Corso 381) is an old, very respected vendor of quality linens; **Cir**, at largo Susanna 88, has fine handmade embroidery.

Leather goods. **Bottega Veneta** (via San Sebastianello 18) just off piazza di Spagna has very distinctive—and expensive—bags and wallets; jackets and other clothing can be found at moderate prices at **Gerard** (via San Silvestro 55); excellent hand-crafted belts, bags, and luggage can be custom ordered at **Polidori** (via Piè di Marmo 7) near the Pantheon, and gloves are available in all sizes at a tiny store without a name at via di San Claudio 70, near La Rinascente department store and piazza Colonna.

Children's toys and clothes. There is a children's toy store at either end of piazza Navona: **Al Sogno** (number 53) sells gigantic stuffed animals, and **Berte** (number 108) has hand-carved Pinocchios (with exchangeable noses) and a variety of children's games. **La Cicogna** (via Frattina 38) and **Cir** (piazza Barberini 11) are expensive children's clothes boutiques. For less expensive clothes, try **Chicco** (via della Penna 16) near piazza del Popolo. **Mondo Antico** (via dei Pianellari 17) sells miniature stage sets and puppets.

Books. **Rizzoli** is in the Galleria Colonna at largo Chigi; the **Economy Book & Video Center** (via Torino 136) near the opera house sells English books and rents English-language videos; the largest English-language bookstore is **Lion Bookstore** (via del Babuino 181). Also recommended for English and American books are the **Anglo-American Bookstore** (via della Vite 57) near the Spanish Steps and the **Corner Bookshop** at via del Moro 48 in Trastevere.

Department stores. Romans have never gotten the hang of department stores. They prefer their neighborhood boutiques, where they can count on personal service and a discount. As a result, the department stores in Rome are very low-key. **La Rinascente** has a branch in piazza Fiume and another in piazza Colonna; **Coin**, in piazzale Appio near San Giovanni in Laterano, is more upscale; and **Upim** (via del Tritone 172) sells cheap clothes, household goods, and cosmetics.

Unusual shops. Via dei Cestari runs between largo Argentina and the Pantheon, and the shops on it specialize in religious articles, statues, and gilded angels. For more mundane purchases, **Art'è** (piazza Rondanini 32) sells witty replicas of urban architecture; Rome's only magic shop is **Curiosità e Magia** (via Aquiro 70); **La Gazza Ladra** (via del Bianchi Vecchi 29) has an extensive stock of 19th-century walking sticks; **Ai Monasteri** (piazza delle Cinque Lune 76), near piazza Navona, sells liqueurs, honeys, and herbal elixirs made by monks and nuns; **Olfottoteca** (piazza della Cancelleria 88) mixes perfumes to order; **Giovanni Borghi** (via della Scrofa 52) sells trilobites and other fossils; **Borsolino** (via del Corso 39) sells hats, straw or otherwise; **Postcards** (piazza del Pantheon 69) has postcards from every region and of every famous artwork in Italy; **Moriondo & Gariglio** (via della Pilotta 2) is Rome's oldest and best fancy chocolate store; **Trimani** (via Giotio 20) has the best selection of wines, olive oil, and balsamic vinegar at affordable prices; **Numismatica** (via Sistina 10) sells ancient Roman coins; **Pineider**, the elegant Florentine stationers at via Due Macelli 68, will help you design your own stationery; **Arte del Pane** (via Merulana 54) sells every kind of bread imaginable; F.A.M.A.R. (piazza dell'Unità 51) has blazer buttons with designer logos on them, and there's a taxidermist, **L'Imbalsamatore**, with a stuffed cobra, at via Sant'Agostino 5, near piazza Navona.

Finally, for a Sunday morning shopping event, there is the open-air flea market at Trastevere's Porta Portese, where you can browse among everything from vintage postcards to fake Etruscan pottery. The pickpockets make the most money, they say, and it has become a common dictum that if your wallet is stolen on the way in, you can buy it back on the way out.

—*Louis Inturrisi*

LAZIO
DAY TRIPS FROM ROME

By Barbara Coeyman Hults

Lazio (LA-dzio), a land of forests, castles, and ancient abbeys, is rarely experienced by tourists, except when they hurry along the crowded and rarely attractive major arteries to Rome. Besides Rome, the Villa d'Este is apt to be the only part of the region visited. (The Roman name for Lazio, Latium, is sometimes used in English.)

This isolation has been a great boon to Lazio, for it has been able to go its own way, for the most part without the click of cameras or the exclamations of the adoring to make the region self-conscious. Actually, Lazio is one of the most beautiful parts of Italy, with a rare mystical quality all its own, born of monasticism and pine forests, mountain grottoes worn deep in the porous tufa rock, lakes and spas, and quiet towns. As to its superlatives, Lazio has more lakes than any other region of Italy—still, shadowy volcanic lakes in the midst of thick forests.

Lazio's boundaries extend north to Viterbo and the borders of Umbria and Tuscany, south beyond Anzio and Gaeta to the border of Campania, and east to the mountainous Abruzzo.

Its castles and abbeys are often rugged and isolated on mountaintops covered with pine and *macchia,* the pervasive Mediterranean shrub. Its gastronomy has the same simple, fresh, and hearty character: rice or pasta with beans, pasta *all'amatriciana* (with *pancetta* and the local pecorino cheese) or *all'arrabbiatta* (in a tomato sauce made "angry" with hot peppers), lamb or pork roasted outdoors, chicken done in hundreds of ways, roasted artichokes, oxtail stew, tripe, and Rome's famous *saltimbocca* (slices of veal, cured ham, and sage leaves in a tangy sauce).

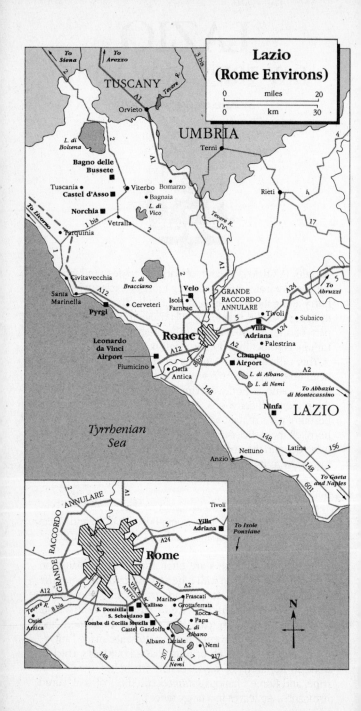

Autumn is Lazio's season, when a cool breeze picks up the scent of wood fires and the red wine is uncorked.

MAJOR INTEREST

The Catacombs
Archaeological excavations at Ostia Antica and
   Palestrina
Tivoli for Villa d'Este and Villa Adriana: frescoes,
   gardens, fountains
The Castelli Romani, castles and villas in the Alban
   Hills: Frascati, Castel Gondolfo, and others
Viterbo
Major Etruscan sites: Tarquinia, Cerveteri, and Tus-
   cania
The ancient Benedictine Abbey of Montecassino
The gardens of Ninfa
The island of Ponza

THE CATACOMBS

Shaded with cypress trees, the graceful symbol of death, numerous elaborate tombs of wealthy ancient Romans border the Appian Way (*Via Appia*), the consular road built by the censor Appius Claudius and opened in 312 B.C. to link Rome with the south. In the early years of Christianity, the bodies of several saints were buried in the tombs, and soon others wanted to be interred alongside them. They became places of worship for Christians, but there is no evidence that they were also hiding places.

Catacombs are systems of underground galleries on several levels, extending often for miles. The openings to the tombs were closed with slabs of marble, and a name—originally in Greek, later in Latin—was carved into them. Over the centuries the tombs have been looted by invaders and local thieves, but much of interest remains. Saints' bones have been removed to churches in Rome.

Caveat: Many of the catacombs are dark, most of the steps are uneven, skulls and bones are quite visible, and retreat is often impossible once inside—and some people do want to retreat.

The **Catacomb of San Callisto** is one of the most important. Named after Saint Calixtus (the slave who became pope), who was appointed guardian of the site by Pope Zephyrinus (199–217), it constituted the first specifically designated cemetery of the early bishops of Rome and was the burial place of the early popes (but not of Calixtus, who was perhaps crowded out) as well as Saint Cecilia, who is commemorated by a copy of the Carlo Madreno statue in the crypt. It is also the most extensive of the catacombs, stretching some 15 miles underground, and has not yet been fully explored. Just behind the catacomb of San Callisto is the **Catacomb of Santa Domitilla**, which contains the fourth-century basilica of San Nereus and Sant'Achilleus, as well as some beautiful paintings, including the first known representation of Christ as the Good Shepherd, painted in the second century.

The **Catacomb of San Sebastiano**, a few minutes away, developed around the spot where Saint Sebastian was martyred and buried, and is also where the bodies of Saint Peter and Saint Paul were first buried. It is an enormous structure on four levels, much visited over the centuries, partly because during the Middle Ages Saint Sebastian was thought to have influence against the Black Plague. The tunnels are covered with graffiti. In the room honoring Peter and Paul words invoking the apostles can be seen. A beautifully decorated pagan tomb adds to the mix.

Along the Appian Way at number 119A is the entrance to the **Jewish Catacombs**, where names and symbols can still be seen on the tombs. For permission to visit, ask at the Synagogue in Rome, Lungotevere Cenci 9.

The best-known of the Roman burial monuments is the **Tomb of Cecilia Metella**, a vast circular shape created for the daughter-in-law of the triumvir Crassus, who shared office with Caesar and Brutus. The crenellated top was part of a fortified castle built around it during the 14th century. Unlike most monuments of the period it has been preserved with much of its marble facing intact, and is decorated with charming relief scenes. Nearby is the restaurant **Cecilia Metella** (via Appia Antica 125; Tel: 06-513-67-43; closed Mondays), which makes for a pleasant (moderately expensive) outdoor lunch or dinner during the warm weather.

The number 118 bus from the Colosseum stops at the Catacomb of San Callisto; the other sites are all within walking distance from San Callisto. Each catacomb closes on a different day, and they all close from 12:00 to 2:30 P.M. daily.

OSTIA ANTICA

If the Palatine Hill is one of your favorite places in Rome, Ostia Antica will be your favorite excursion. To the charm of umbrella pines and ancient ruins is added the complexity of a city, with apartments and storehouses, fish markets and shrines.

The extensive excavations of the ancient commercial and military seaport precinct of Ostia are most important to archaeologists for their examples of Roman residential architecture, ranging from the patrician villa, called the *domus* (much more common at the wealthy resort town of Pompeii), to the apartment block called the *insula*. Set in a park unbothered by the intrusions of the centuries and gracefully landscaped with cypresses and umbrella pines, the site gives a more vivid picture of everyday life in the Empire than anything in Rome does. From the entrance, follow the Decumanus Maximus, the town's main street, to the **Terme di Nettuno** (Baths of Neptune), where mosaic marine monsters cavort with cupids and naked deities. Continue on to the theater and the tree-shaded piazzale delle Corporazioni, the former business district, where the mosaic pavement in front of the various offices depicts the nature of the businesses inside. Several blocks later you'll reach the **Capitolium**, a large temple dedicated to Jupiter, Juno, and Minerva. Behind it is the **Museo Archeologico Ostiense,** housing well-displayed sculptures from the excavations, noteworthy among them *Cupid and Psyche, Family of Marcus Aurelius,* and *Lion Attacking a Bull.* Farther on are some remarkable mosaics in the ancient residences called the **Casa delle Muse** (House of the Muses) and the **Domus dei Dioscuri** (House of the Dioscuri). Nearby, at the Marine Gate, go up into the former tavern if sexually explicit material doesn't bother you. At the farthest end of the excavations are the remains of one of the oldest synagogues yet discovered, dating from the first century. Buy an illustrated guidebook at the gift shop to identify the buildings.

The most picturesque way of getting to Ostia is on the boat sponsored by the Amici del Tevere, which leaves from the ponte Marconi in Rome. Otherwise, take metro line B to the Magliana stop, where a connecting train goes to Ostia Antica. The crowded-in-season resort Lido di Ostia, which leaves much to be desired as a beach, can be reached by metro or on foot. Lido di Ostia has a number of seafood restaurants, of which **Da Negri** is among the nicest (via Claudia 50; Tel: 06-562-22-95; closed Thursdays; fairly expensive).

TIVOLI AND VILLA ADRIANA

Medieval in appearance, the town of Tivoli (30 km/19 miles east of Rome) is the bastion of the Renaissance **Villa d'Este,** built for Cardinal Ippolito II d'Este (son of Lucrezia Borgia) by Pirro Ligorio. The villa itself contains frescoes by 16th-century artists, but more noteworthy are its gardens, where hundreds of fountains freshen the air and add water music. Though the *giochi d'acqua,* the sprays of water that surprised unsuspecting visitors, are no longer in use, the fountains themselves are just as wondrous. The Organ Fountain, Terrace of the Hundred Fountains, Ovato Fountain, Little Rome (a tiny replica of Rome's Tiber Island), and Dragon Fountain are but a few. Dry for centuries, the fountains have been restored by the Italian government, which also illuminates them at night during the summer.

Tibur (Tivoli's ancient name) was founded, some say, by the Siculi, and later became an important resort for wealthy Romans. It was here that the Sybil Albunea, whose shrine was sacred to her cult, was consulted.

The most pleasant warm-weather dining option in the area is **Sibilla** (via della Sibilla 50; Tel: 0774-202-81), a regional restaurant whose outdoor garden overlooks the temples of Vesta and Sibilla. Seeing the fountains at Villa d'Este is perhaps best combined, however, with a surreptitious picnic dinner at **Villa Adriana** (Hadrian's Villa), 4.5 km (3 miles) south of Tivoli. Now in ruins, it was once the largest villa in ancient Rome (180 acres). The Emperor Hadrian built it for his retirement, reconstructing some of his favorite sights from around the world to keep him company. Among them were the entrance colonnade, called the Poikile, from Athens, and the Canal of Canopus from Egypt. The Maritime Theater is a round building inside which a moat surrounds a small island. On the island, a miniature villa contains a reception room and of course a bath. Hadrian could receive or shut out guests by merely raising or lowering the drawbridges. Finding the emperor at the Villa Adriana took connections of a high order.

The **Antica Trattoria del Falcone** (via del Trevio 34; Tel: 0774-223-58; closed Mondays), where Lazio's dishes—such as chick-pea soup, baccalà, and fresh fruit pies—as well as pizza are featured, is a refuge for the weary visitor.

ACOTRAL provides regular bus service from Rome (via Gaeta, near the piazza dei Cinquecento) to Tivoli, depositing passengers near the entrance to the Villa d'Este; buses stop about a mile from the entrance to the Villa Adriana. The local CAT bus in Tivoli goes near the Villa Adriana stop as well. Taxis from the town of Tivoli go to the door.

PALESTRINA

Known to the ancient Romans as Praeneste, Palestrina was founded, according to legend, by the son of Ulysses and Circe. Then the site of the oracle at the **Temple of Fortuna Primigenia** (the first daughter of Jupiter)—one of the richest and most elaborate sanctuaries of antiquity and the largest Greek-style building in Italy, dating from 80 B.C.—today the town is visited for the archaeological excavations surrounding the temple, magnificently located on the slopes of Monte Ginestro, 37 km (23 miles) east of Rome. Its adjacent museum, the **Museo Archeologico Prenestino** (in the Palazzo Barberini), houses material from the excavation, the highlight of which is a second-century B.C. mosaic depicting the floodwaters of the Nile.

Music lovers might want to have a look at the monument to the town's most famous native son, 16th-century composer Giovanni Pierluigi da Palestrina, in the main piazza. Just outside town (via del Piscarello, Tel: 06-955-77-51) is the restaurant **Trattoria del Piscarello**, where you can enjoy a classic Roman menu—in an outdoor setting in fair weather.

ACOTRAL buses leave Rome regularly for Palestrina from piazza dei Cinquecento; there is also train service from Stazione Termini to the Palestrina station, from which a local bus takes you to the town center.

East of Palestrina, the abbeys of Santa Scolastica and San Benedetto at **Subiaco** merit a visit.

CASTELLI ROMANI

The Castelli Romani (Roman castles) are, collectively, the 13 towns about 21 km (13 miles) southeast of Rome where wealthy Romans built castles and villas in the Colli Albani, or Alban Hills, best known today for their crisp white wine.

Frascati is the most popular of the Castelli Romani, and though its lovely 16th-century **Villa Aldobrandini** has spectacular views of Rome, it is best known as a gathering place for *fagottari,* people who buy or bring bundles of *porchetta* (pork roasted with herbs) and other delicacies to enjoy on open-air terraces next to the wine shops while drinking healthy amounts of the Frascati wine. **Cacciani** (via Armando Diaz 13; Tel: 942-03-78; closed Tuesdays) is an excellent restaurant here, with an expansive outdoor terrace from which to enjoy the scenery (expensive; reservations are recommended).

The woods and vineyards of **Grottaferrata** shelter the Abbazia, a Basilian abbey founded in 1004, where the Greek Orthodox rite was reinstituted with the pope's permission during the last century. The monks will show you around the grounds and the museum of religious artifacts, and also sell olive oil and a good local wine.

The elegant **Grand Hotel Villa Fiorio**, in its park of pine trees, is the place to stay and to dine, an ideal retreat unless it's to be a wedding party weekend—ask in advance (viale Dusinet 28; Tel: 06-945-92-76). In the town, the **Taverna dello Spuntino** is a charming spot to relax in over home-made pasta, veal with arugula, roast pig, and homemade desserts (via Cicerone 20; Tel: 06-945-93-66; closed Wednesdays). Both restaurants are fairly expensive.

The wine of **Marino** is considered the best of all the Colli Albani whites, and is especially celebrated during the Sagra dell'Uva (Festival of the Grape) on the first Sunday in October, when, after a procession and an offering to the Madonna, the Fontana dei Mori flows with wine, and so do the crowds.

Castel Gandolfo is believed to be the location of Alba Longa, the most powerful city in ancient Latium, founded by the son of Aeneas and destroyed by the Romans. The current town contains the church of **San Tommaso da Villanova** and a fountain, both by Bernini, in its main square. Its **Palazzo Pontificio** is part of the Vatican State and serves as the summer residence of the pope, who gives addresses here on Sundays and holds audiences on Wednesday mornings (apply for admission at the Vatican).

Albano Laziale is on a lake on the site of the Castra Albana, which was built by Septimius Severus for a Roman legion in the second century. Ruins of the ancient town and subsequent medieval additions may be seen.

The Nemus Dianae, or Grove of Diana, sacred to the primitive cult with which James Frazer opens *The Golden Bough,* gave its name to the town and lake of **Nemi**, today famous for its strawberries. Though very few of them are wild, they are all celebrated in the Sagra delle Fragole, or strawberry festival, in June. **Rocca di Papa**, named after the castle, or *rocca,* built by the popes, is the highest of all the Castelli Romani. The upper portion of the town is medieval, and if you ascend Monte Cavo above that (as did the Roman legions when the Temple of Jupiter Latialis was located here), you'll be treated to magnificent views of the Castelli, the lakes of Albano and Nemi, and the surrounding countryside as far as the coast.

The most convenient way to see the Castelli Romani in a

day is undoubtedly by car, beginning on the Roman via
Tuscolana (route S 215) and following signs for the individual towns; otherwise, select the one or two towns that appeal
most to you and check train and bus schedules. Trains from
Stazione di Termini serve Albano, Marino, and Frascati.
ACOTRAL buses from Cinecittà (a stop on metro line A)
serve all the towns.

The **gardens at Ninfa,** south of the Castelli, exude a melancholy magic from the 12th century, when the overgrown
ruins were a prosperous town. The gardens, with plants
brought from all over the world, are open the first Saturday
and the first Sunday of every month from April to October.
For admission, contact the Amministrazione Caetani, via
delle Botteghe Oscure 32, Rome (Tel: 06-686-61-01), or the
Oasi di Ninfa (Tel: 0773-432-31).

VITERBO

Few medieval cities convey their era as dramatically as
Viterbo. The priorities of the Middle Ages—defense, defense, and prayer—are met in Viterbo's massive walls and
brooding introspection. This mood doesn't extend, however, to the young soldiers in today's town, putting in their
year of compulsory military service at the Viterbo base.
Their preoccupations are predictable, and not very militant.

On rainy days the city seems too dour for some travellers,
like many cities of its time, but when the weather is fair it is
superb, flourishing at the foot of the Cimini hills. The tufa, a
soft, porous volcanic stone typical of central Italy, changes
color with the weather, absorbing foggy grays and warm sun
tones with equanimity.

The capital of its province, Viterbo is 104 km (50 miles)
northwest of Rome. It has been a city to be reckoned with
since the 13th century, when it was the papal seat during
strife between the papacy and the empire, and the place
where the first conclave in Catholic church history was held.

The heart of Viterbo is the **piazza del Plebiscito,** where
yesterday and today vie for supremacy, overlooked by tufa
lions. Here the **Palazzo dei Priori,** or Communale (town
hall), begun in 1460, still maintains the city's records. Its fine
Renaissance courtyard and loggia are usually open to visitors, and you can glimpse the current powers of Viterbo as
they pontificate within. The building with the clock tower is
the 13th-century Palazzo del Podestà (Mayor), the secular
authority of its time.

Across the square, near the door of the church of

Sant'Angelo, a Roman sarcophagus has been set into the wall. It is called the tomb of the beautiful Galiana, who was killed with an arrow by a Roman officer whom she'd refused, thus sparing the city from siege, we're told.

Along the via San Lorenzo, a twisting street through the ancient city, stands the imposing Renaissance form of the Palazzo Chigi, enhanced with a lovely court and loggia. Beyond it is what is now the Jesuit church of the Gesù, a simple 11th-century structure, but restored. Inside, it seems, two brothers of the Monforte family beat up Prince Henry of Cornwall during Mass, avenging the death of their father, which had been ordered by King Richard.

At the triangular piazza della Morte, probably the site of executions yet today green and cheerful, the vicolo Pellegrini leads to the Ponte del Duomo, set on an Etruscan base that can be seen if you descend the stairs at the bridge's side. The bridge united the city with an ancient castle.

Nearby, the beautiful 14th-century Palazzo Farnese, birthplace of the Farnese pope Paul III, has a stylish courtyard.

The cathedral of San Lorenzo is a 12th-century Romanesque building with a splendid campanile in Gothic form. The interior was severely damaged during World War II. In the left apse the *Madonna della Carbonara,* and in the sacristy the painting of *Christ Blessing the Saint,* both by Girolamo da Cremona, are among the treasures. On the altar, *Saint Laurence in Glory* is the work of the Baroque artist Giovanni Romanelli, who also painted the *Holy Family* in the right aisle.

In the piazza, the Palazzo dei Papi, with its open loggia, is the true cornerstone of the city. It was built between 1257 and 1266, and soon after was used to house the first Conclave. Even the Second Vatican Council is unlikely to have had a stormier session, and it was not a longer one (1268–1271). To end the impasse over the election of Gregorio X as pope, the Viterbese removed the roof of the congress hall. The Princes of the Church, sequestered beneath, erected tents and continued, until their subjects resorted to stones; holes can still be seen where they hit the floor. Gregory was thus pelted in, and despite this electoral process four more popes were elected here.

Returning to the piazza della Morte: The little street in front of the fountain will take you through the beautifully preserved 12th-century Medieval Quarter, with its pinnacle, the piazza San Pelligrino, considered the most comprehensive medieval piazza in Italy. The Palazzo degli Alessandri here is a typical example of an austere private palace. This section is the place to wander, on the lookout especially for the superb fountains that are typical of Viterbo and for other signs of the Middle Ages—towers, covered passageways, gently arched bifurcated windows, and dark streets. The **Fontana Grande**, off the via Cavour (near where you began), is one of the city's finest.

The **Museo Civico** at piazza Crispi is housed in the convent of the church of Santa Maria della Verità. The Etruscan objects on the ground floor reflect Viterbo's other dominant influence. To the west of Viterbo lie some of Italy's most important Etruscan sites, notably at Tarquinia, Cerveteri, and Tuscania; they are described below. In the gallery, the star is Sebastiano del Piombo's *Pietà,* based on a lost drawing by Michelangelo. There is also a lovely cycle of frescoes on the life of the Virgin by Lorenzo da Viterbo (1469). Currently closed for restoration, the museum is scheduled to reopen sometime in 1993.

The **church of San Francesco**, near the northern city walls and close to the Public Gardens, houses the tombs of Pope Clement IV and Hadrian V, the latter attributed to Arnolfo da Cambio.

Viterbo has one notable restaurant, **Il Richiastro**, which is open only Thursday through Sunday. The Scappucci family restored a 12th-century building for the atmosphere they wanted, and in 1981 opened this delightful trattoria. Here traditional recipes have been carefully researched, and the best of Lazio emerges. Hearty soups of beans and grains, steaks, and the less popular (in North America) cuts of meat are done to perfection. Many of the products, including the olive oil, are home-grown or homemade. Call to reserve (via della Marrocca 16–18; Tel: 0761-22-36-09; no credit cards; closed in August).

As to hotels, the best-appointed are the **Mini Palace** and the **Balletti Palace**. The **Tuscia** is fine for an overnight and within most budgets.

The **Villa Lante** at Bagnaia, a suburb of Viterbo, is a Renaissance treat, and its gardens are among Italy's finest. Also near Viterbo, the amazing **Parco dei Mostri** at Bomarzo suited the bizarre fancy of Prince Vicino Orsini. Massive stone ogres, harpies, mermaids, and a leaning tower make up an early Disneyland-on-the-edge (about 16 km/10 miles east of Viterbo, connected with ACOTRAL bus several times a day). In Bomarzo you might want to stay in a 17th-century castle, part of the Agriturist project, called the **Azienda Pomigliozzo**; its dining room uses its own products.

Rome's transit authority, again in its infinite wisdom, has

changed things around so that getting to Viterbo is a project. We can only hope that the situation will be changed by the time you want to go.

At present the way to get there is to go to Saxa Rubra, near Prima Porta, a stop on the Roma Nord line that starts near the Flaminia metro stop, just outside the gate of Rome's piazza del Popolo. (To save time and frustration, take a taxi to Saxa Rubra.) At Saxa Rubra a bus will take you on to Viterbo. The train will too, but the trip is long, although a nice way to see the countryside (unless you get one of the old wooden-seaters). In any case, leave as early as possible if you're making a day trip. In Viterbo, cars can be left outside the walls at piazza Martiri d'Ungheria.

On the way back you might want to dine in Saxa Rubra at the **Grotte di Livia**, a pleasant family-run restaurant on the grounds of a villa that Livia and Augustus shared during Rome's imperial golden age. Its homemade pasta is superb, and the steaks are excellent. On a hot evening in Rome, its outdoor dining is the right choice (piazza Saxa Rubra 9; Tel: 06-691-12-53; closed Mondays).

ETRUSCAN SITES

Most of the beautiful removable objects—sculpture, vases, and gold artifacts—unearthed from Etruscan necropolises over the last century are on display at museums such as the Museo Nazionale di Villa Giulia and the Musei Vaticani in Rome. The tombs themselves, however, which so fascinated D. H. Lawrence (he wrote about them in *Etruscan Places*) and others, are easy to visit from Rome, and a look at their faded frescoes and homelike arrangement makes the ancient civilization seem both closer and more distant.

The area west of Viterbo is one of the richest parts of Italy in Etruscan excavations. The principal sites, from northern Lazio to near Rome, can be seen in a day trip from Rome.

Begin at the site farthest from Rome, the medieval-looking town of **Tarquinia**, about 90 km (56 miles) up the coast, where the **Museo Nazionale Tarquiniese** has an extensive collection of Etruscan art from the nearby necropolises (about 3 km/ 2 miles west of town)—only a few of which are also open to the public (apply at the museum) on any given day because of their delicate condition and to protect them from grave robbers (*tombaroli*). The unrivaled collection of wall paintings gives a vivid impression of the partying afterlife that the Etruscans anticipated—perhaps the reason they are always smiling. (Open 9:00 A.M. to 2:00 P.M.; Tel: 0766-85-60-36.) Tarquinia today is home for hundreds of refugees from Eastern Europe, an unsettling experience for all concerned.

Toward Viterbo, more necropolises are to be seen surrounding the hill town of **Tuscania** as well as farther along the road at **Bagno delle Bussete. Castel d'Asso**, on a small road southwest of Viterbo, has a large cliffside necropolis, as does **Norchia**, to the west of Vetralla. From Tarquinia, the coastal road south is dotted with both Etruscan and Roman sites at Civitavecchia, Santa Marinella, and Pyrgi. **Cerveteri**, perched on a spur of tufa, enjoyed a comfortable Etruscan life during the seventh and sixth centuries B.C., if the paintings on the tombs don't lie. The **Museo Cerite**, located in the Orsini castle, exhibits objects from the surrounding tombs, including some fascinating sculpture and red-figured vases. But the **Necropolis**, on the hill called Banditaccia, about 2 km (1 mile) from the town's center, is the prize. Tombs are laid out in avenues here amid an attractive park of cypress trees and flowers. If you can arrange for a guide at the ticket office, do so, for many of the tombs with frescoes remain closed. The Tomba dei Rilievi (fourth century B.C.), for example, is decorated with scenes of everyday life, but can only be seen with a guide. (Closed Mondays.)

About 2 km (1 mile) south of Cerveteri is the oldest tomb, the huge tubular **Regolini-Galassi tomb**, dating from the seventh century B.C. Its conical top with tall grass growing on it was the typical tomb design, and influenced Hadrian's and Augustus's tombs in Rome.

You may want to picnic somewhere along the way, but good food can be had at the restaurant **Nazareno** (località San Paolo; Tel: 06-995-23-82).

Because many of the Etruscan sights are tombs in the open countryside, the best way to visit them is by car. Depending on how long you want to stay at the individual sites, this can take one lengthy day or two leisurely days, with the best accommodations for a stopover at Tarquinia's **Tarconte e Ristorante Solengo**, via Tuscia 19; Tel: (0766) 85-61-41; closed Wednesdays. Otherwise, buses leave from via Lepanto in Rome for Tarquinia and Cerveteri.

ANZIO AND NETTUNO

Anzio was the birthplace of both Caligula and Nero, a bloody legacy continued more recently by the landing in World War II of American and British troops. Today it and Nettuno are modern seaside resort towns with decent beaches and family-style accommodations, about 60 km (37 miles) south of Rome. In addition, Anzio boasts the excavations of the **Villa di Nerone** (Nero's Villa). Both towns are of particular interest for their cemeteries: The British Military Cemetery is located at Anzio, the American at Nettuno. Anzio also has a panoramic seafood restaurant, **All'Antica Darsena** (piazza Sant'Antonio 1; Tel: 06-984-51-46; closed Mondays); Nettuno's is **Il Gambero II** (via delle Liberazione 50; Tel: 06-985-40-71; closed Mondays and from September 15 to June 15).

ACOTRAL buses leave for Anzio from Rome at Cinecittà, at Osteria del Curato; trains from Stazione Termini.

ABBAZIA DI MONTECASSINO

The abbey at Montecassino as one of the most important outposts of Christian culture during the Middle Ages, when much of the world was dark. Begun in the sixth century by Saint Benedict, founder of the Benedictines, it has existed for more than 14 centuries, despite destruction by an earthquake in 1349 and the Allied bombardment of 1944, in which hundreds of tons of bombs were dropped to destroy a German stronghold. After the war an inspired work of reconstruction was begun, and today the monastery is almost restored to the original.

The abbey commands as dramatic a position as nature allows, atop a high peak that overlooks a breathtaking panorama of rolling hills and valleys. To reach it, hairpin curves must be executed along a 9-km (5-mile) road.

Saint Benedict, who had been living as a hermit in nearby Subiaco, was asked by a group of monks to be their abbot— but apparently things didn't work out, as they tried to poison him. When he returned to Subiaco he attracted a great number of disciples. An orderly man, he divided the monks among 12 monasteries, appointed a prior for each one, and made manual work a part of the program. Subiaco quickly developed as a center of spirituality and learning. Benedict left suddenly, apparently because of bad rapport with a prior, and settled at Montecassino, destroying the temple to Apollo on the mountaintop and constructing an altar on the site. In about 530 he began to build the monastery, attracting many disciples, whom he organized into a monastic community. He then wrote the Rule of Saint Benedict, prescribing a life of moderation in asceticism and a program of prayer, chastity, study, and work, in community life with one superior. Obedience, stability, and zeal were the watchwords, and his Rule has affected monastic life throughout the centuries since.

At the abbey's entrance three cloisters lead to the Loggia del Paradiso, from which the view of the valley is superb. The original loggia, which has been reconstructed exactly, was designed by Sangallo (who designed Orvieto's famous well). The basilica's altar, originally the work of Fanzago, has also been duplicated, as has Sangallo's tomb of Pietro de'Medici, the son of Lorenzo. The original crypt remains, where Saint Benedict was buried. A museum is open but the library, with thousands of the original books and manuscripts, is available only to those with requests for serious study.

Among nearby restaurants are **Boschetto**, via Ausonia 54 (Tel: 0776-30-12-27), with good local cooking, and **Canguro**, via Appia Nuova 8500 (Tel: 0776-442-59; closed Mondays). Both are inexpensive.

PONZA

Lazio's dramatically beautiful island of Ponza, off the coast of Anzio south of Rome, had been kept in the family until recently; foreigners didn't flock there, except perhaps in August when every puddle in Italy speaks a different language. In recent years easier transit, including hydrofoils, has changed all that, facilitating weekend trips. Yet despite it all, Ponza maintains a striking individuality.

The Pontine Islands (Isole Ponziane), of which Ponza is the largest and most important, are volcanic islands whose past extends to the Paleolithic era. Their early history followed the course of their supply of obsidian, the hard stone best suited for knives. Used first as a trading post, Ponza became a convenient isle for receiving those who had fallen out of favor with emperor Tiberius. Monks lived on the island through the Middle Ages, and colonists arrived during a tax-incentive program of the Bourbons in Naples. During World War II the island was again used for exiles—and also for Mussolini during a short period after the war.

The island's charm is its 6 miles of amazing configurations: Jagged, pale tufa cliffs rise high above the sea, and beaches and grottoes soften the rocky shoreline. The principal town, also called **Ponza**, is pastel-colored and simple. The island's interior is usually reached through tunnels, like the one the Romans dug to the **Chiaia** (kee-AY-ya) **di Luna** (Moonlight Bay), where a 300-foot-high crescent of cliff shelters a beach below (at low tide). A boat trip around the island circles grottoes and beaches, but the real joy is the drama of the island itself against the sea. If you climb **Monte**

Guardia to Punta della Guardia (1 hour) you will discover extraordinary, bizarre rock formations. At sea, scuba divers may find coral and sunken ships amid the sea creatures.

The **Grand Hotel Chiaia di Luna**, on a cliff that overlooks the bay, is an unusual complex of small buildings united by terraces and stairways. The beach is reached through a Roman tunnel, but the pool and bar, solarium, and restaurant are close at hand. The **Torre dei Borboni** takes a bit of walking to get to (they'll send a porter), but this hotel and its site in an old Bourbon fort are worth the effort, especially if your room is in the 18th-century castle that overlooks the port. Ponza's lobster (*aragosta*) is served in the sea-view dining room, and the hotel's private beach is down a stairway. The good budget-hotel choice on Ponza is **Gennarino a Mare**, with balconies overlooking the sea.

Ponza's festivals occur on the last Sunday in February and on June 20, both commemorating San Silverio, the pope who drew the wrath of the Byzantine empress Theodora, who backed another candidate. Legend has it that he was murdered on Ponza on June 20.

To arrive at Ponza from the port of Fiumicino (near Rome's airport), take the Medmar hydrofoil or ferry (about 40,000 lire); the trip takes about 6 hours. Reserve well in advance during the summer (piazza Barberini 5, 00187 Rome; Tel: 06-482-85-79; Fax: 06-481-45-01). Helios runs ferries from Anzio and Formia on the Lazio coast (Anzio: 06-984-50-85; Formia: 0771-70-07-10).

If you're held up at Fiumicino (the airport or the nearby harbor town), or if you need a respite between flights, stop at the **Ship Museum** near the airport on via Portuense at km 5, and at the **Isola Sacra** excavations of ancient Roman tombs, on the road to Ostia at km 3.5. For lunch at Fiumicino's port, stop at **Il Pescatore**, via Torre Clementina 154 (Tel: 06-650-51-89; closed Thursdays), or at the famous **Bastianelli al Centro**, on the same street at number 88 (closed Wednesdays; Tel: 06-650-50-95).

ACCOMMODATIONS REFERENCE

The rates given below are projections for 1993; always check for up-to-date information before making reservations. Wide ranges may reflect the differences between low- and high-season rates. Unless otherwise indicated, the figures indicate the cost of a double room (per room, not per person). However, half-board (mezza pensione) rates, which include breakfast and one other meal per day, are per person. The service charge is included in the rate; inquire about tax and breakfast.

▶ **Agriturismo Pomigliozzo**. 01020 **Bomarzo** (Viterbo). Tel: (0761) 92-44-66.

▶ **Balletti Palace**. Viale Trento 100, 01100 **Viterbo**. Tel: (0761) 34-47-77; Fax: same. £120,000–£143,000.

▶ **Gennarino a Mare**. Via Dante 64, 04027 **Ponza**. Tel: (0771) 800-71; Fax: (0771) 800-98. £70,000.

▶ **Grand Hotel Chiaia di Luna**. Via Chiaia di Luna, 04027 **Ponza**. Tel: (0771) 801-13; Fax: (0771) 80-98-21. Open at Easter and May 22–October 4. £150,000–£300,000; half board £100,000–£195,000.

▶ **Grand Hotel Villa Fiorio**. Viale Dusmet 28, 00046 **Grottaferrata**. Tel: (06) 945-92-76; Fax: (06) 941-34-82. £110,000–£160,000; half board £150,000.

▶ **Mini Palace**. Via Santa Maria della Grotticella 2, 01100 **Viterbo**. Tel: (0761) 30-97-42; Fax: (0761) 34-47-15. £120,000–£180,000.

▶ **Torre dei Borboni**. Via Madonna 1, 04027 **Ponza**. Tel: (0771) 801-35. £60,000.

▶ **Tuscia**. Via Cairoli 41, 01100 **Viterbo**. Tel: (0761) 22-33-77; Fax: (0761) 34-59-76. £64,000–£100,000.

UMBRIA AND THE MARCHES

By Joanne Hahn

Joanne Hahn has lived and studied in Italy and travels there frequently. Formerly on the staff of Travel & Leisure *magazine, she writes for several consumer magazines.*

Umbria is a landlocked fortress of medieval treasures built on the remains of an Italic, Etruscan, and Roman past. Somewhat overshadowed by Tuscany, its celebrated neighbor to the north and west, this land of saints and sinners, with its serene hills, tranquil lakes, silent valleys, and steep mountains, is more quietly seductive. Stepping into these medieval hilltop villages, you can experience life much as it existed hundreds of years ago, when the rising communes began cutting their feudal ties and experimenting with self-rule.

Perhaps the most striking feature of the area is its peacefulness. The landscape seems transcendent and perpetually shrouded in a blue-green haze, which may account for the impressive number of saints born here—said to number over 20,000—whose names read like a *Who's Who* of holiness. They include Saint Francis of Assisi, founder of the Franciscans, and his friend Saint Clare, who created a sister order, the Poor Clares; Saint Valentine, third bishop of Terni; and Saint Benedict of Norcia, whose monastic Rule helped spread Christianity and kept Western civilization from totally succumbing to the barbarians.

Noble cathedrals, graceful monasteries, and resplendent manors dot hills and cluster around tiny villages. Tradition is kept alive not only through crafts and festivals but in the converted monasteries offering comfortable lodgings and retreats from the congested cities—accommodations that range from a few rooms in a convent to a sprawling Benedictine monastery like Bevagna's.

Distances between towns are short, making it possible to visit major sights on day trips from such nearby major cities as Rome and Florence, though Umbria is quite appealing as a destination in itself. The more popular towns of Assisi, Perugia, and Spoleto can become crowded, especially during the summer festivals, but most of the other towns are off the beaten track—though easily accessible by car and bus—and therefore rarely thronged.

The Marches (Marche in Italian, pronounced MAR-kay) lie between Umbria to the west and the Adriatic coast on the east. The best-known city is Urbino, one of the great centers of early Renaissance humanism. Except for the Byzantine influence (from Ravenna to the north)—and some Venetian influence, too—the Marches were subjected to much the same historical movement as Umbria.

With Perugia as a starting point, we follow a clockwise elliptical track through the center of Umbria—Assisi, Spoleto, Todi, Orvieto—and then take another track north from Perugia to Gubbio and on to the Marches, Urbino, and the Adriatic.

MAJOR INTEREST IN UMBRIA

Perugia
Piazza IV Novembre and its Fontana Maggiore
Palazzo dei Priori (Galleria Nazionale dell'Umbria)
Collegio del Cambio (frescoes of Perugino)
Cathedral of San Lorenzo
Corso Vannucci (shops, cafés, people)
Musical events

Deruta (pottery)

Assisi
Basilica of San Francesco (frescoes of Giotto)
Basilica of Santa Chiara
Tempio di Minerva
Eremo delle Carceri
Religious festivals

Spello (Pinturicchio frescoes)
Montefalco (Gozzoli frescoes)

Fonti del Clitunno, Tempietto del Clitunno

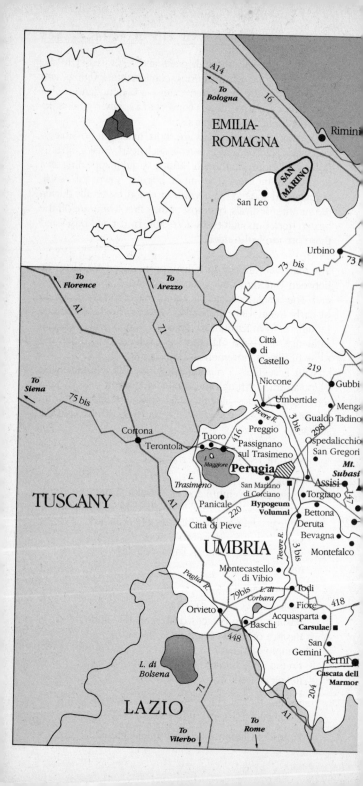

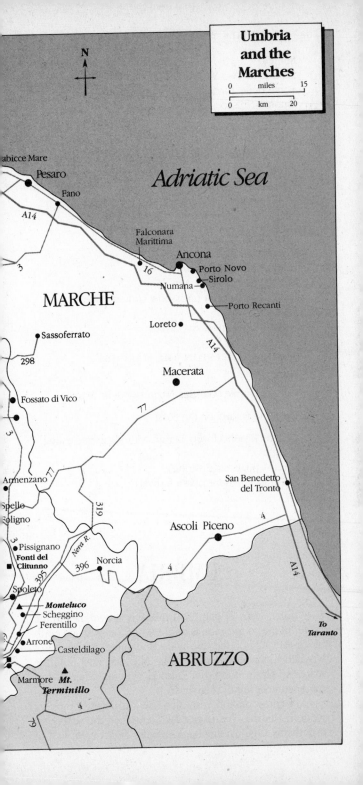

Spoleto
Festival of Two Worlds (music and art extravaganza)
Ponte delle Torri (Bridge of the Towers)
Duomo (frescoes of Filippo Lippi)

Todi (piazza del Popolo)

Lago Trasimeno (boating and fishing facilities)

Orvieto
Cathedral (frescoes of Fra Angelico, Gozzoli, and
   Signorelli)

Gubbio
Palazzo dei Consoli (Eugubine tablets)
Roman theater
Basilica of San Ubaldo
The Race of the Ceri, May 15
Palio della Balestra (crossbow contest), late May
Crafts
Frasassi caves, near Sassoferrato

MAJOR INTEREST IN THE MARCHES

Urbino
Palazzo Ducale (Galleria Nazionale delle Marche)

Fano and Pesaro, on the coast

Conero Riviera (lovely littoral with some interesting
   sights)
Loreto (pilgrimage shrine)
Macerata (outdoor opera festival)

UMBRIA

The "green heart of Italy," as Umbria is known, lies in the
center of the country and is bordered on the west and north
by Tuscany and on the east by the Apennines, that sweep of
wooded mountains and limestone hills that runs from the
maritime Alps to the tip of Calabria. (On the other side of
the Apennines are the Marches.)

Over three million years ago the sea covered most of
western Umbria. The largest lake left when the waters receded was **Lago Trasimeno**, a popular resort area west of

Perugia. This is where Hannibal outmaneuvered the consul Flaminius and slaughtered more than 16,000 Roman soldiers in 217 B.C. Trasimeno is rich in trout, pike, eels, perch, and the delectable *lasca,* a favorite fish of the popes since the Middle Ages.

Now you too can eat those same fish, along with the classic fish soup, *tegamaccio,* at the rustic **Ristorante da Luciano** on the north shore at Passignano sul Trasimeno (lungolago Aganoor Pompily 14; Tel: 075-82-72-10; closed Wednesdays). The main restaurant, overlooking the lake, is expensive prix fixe with several complete menus offered. Do ask to see the menus, for although the waiters are charming, they are smooth operators, and before you know it you will be avalanched with enough food to sustain the Italian army. Right next door is an adjunct where you can order à la carte and spend less (the same kitchen serves both rooms). Directly across from the restaurant, you can catch the ferry to **Isola Maggiore**, a beautiful moody island with the church of San Michele Arcangelo, which has 14th- to 16th-century frescoes. You can have a meal there at the modest restaurant **Sauro**, the island's only hotel/restaurant (Tel: 075-82-61-68; Fax: 075-82-51-30; closed January 11–February 19). You'll also find lovely examples of lace making, which the Irish servants of the Marchioness Guglielmi passed on centuries earlier.

North of the lake, about 10 minutes away by car, is the cozy **Residenza San Andrea al Farinaio**, in Terontola. Reached by a sliver of a road paralleling Route 71, the inn reflects the genial personality of its owner, Patrizia Nappi, with flowers and antiques played off against 13th-century walls. The spacious dining room, with exposed wood beams that frame walls decorated with colorful majolica and copper pots, invites you to linger over a meal in front of the fireplace. There are five bedrooms, three with private bath, and breakfast and dinner are served, though you must make reservations for the meals. The large room at the top of the stairs is especially attractive. In all, the accommodations are well priced, given the comfort level. The inn is open all year and is a perfect base for exploring the countryside.

For instance, you're only one-half hour away from **Cortona**, a Tuscan jewel of a hill town worth visiting. You might combine a visit here with lunch at the charming **Trattoria Dell'Amico**, on via Dardano 12. Bedecked in gay blue plaid and memorabilia, the restaurant serves simple but hearty meals at very modest prices. Try the grilled lamb with rosemary, if it's in season. Closed Mondays. (Tel: 0575-60-41-92).

From Lake Trasimeno, there's a glorious route (416) that

originates in the hamlet of Tuoro, just west of Passignano, and ends at Niccone, near Umbertide. The road slices through the picturesque countryside, where wild horses gallivant over the green fields. Niccone is home to the charming family-run **La Chiusa**. The kitchen here serves only organic food cultivated on its farm, but it's not the "beans and sprouts" cuisine you would expect from such an enterprise. Rather, this husband-and-wife team, Dada and Claudio Rener, cook up some sophisticated dishes, such as beef in a rich wine sauce. Their place is reached by a winding road, just off route 416, that you're sure goes nowhere. But continue on until you can't go any farther and you'll have reached your destination. Meals are served Friday and Saturday evenings (do a trial run finding the place in daylight, for the black velvet nights make for difficult going) and Sunday lunch, a popular family time, on a trellised terrace perfect for savoring nature's bounty. Reservations advised. (Address: S.S. del Niccone km 2, Tel: 075-930-31-48.)

For an authentic slice of Umbrian country life, a stay at **La Meridiana**, also in Niccone, is in order. Here, at this well-bred hillside farm that sits on acres of fields rich in olive and fruit trees, surrounded by glorious woods, you'll partake of age-old customs and take comfort in nature. The farm, which has a rustic charm, comprises three beautifully restored farmhouses with antique country pieces blended stylishly with workaday objects. The three houses, Casagrande (sleeps 7), Casa degli Archi (sleeps 5), and Il Casale (sleeps six) come furnished with bed linens, towels, cooking gear, and daily maid service; and the use of horses and bicycles is included in the price. Gas is charged at cost. Extra charges cover meals, babysitters, and cross-country day excursions, by Jeep or horseback. Marisa Berna, the owner, is a cultural maven and a great source of information on the area's events. (Ask her about the little-known music festival in nearby Preggio.) She also runs one-week cooking courses at the farm from May through September. The fee is $910 and includes accommodations in a double room, guided tours, five four-hour cooking classes, all meals—most at Maridiana—and cultural excursions.

The Tiber (*Tevere*), which transported Cleopatra on her visit to Julius Caesar in 46 B.C., meanders south through Umbria on its way to Rome and is joined by the Nera, which runs the width of Umbria. Critical to agricultural development during early settlement days, the Tiber was replaced as the main thoroughfare by the Flaminian Way, which the Romans built as they were consolidating their power throughout the region. They sited many of their military colonies throughout the Tiber valley as well as along this road, which runs north from Rome through Umbria before terminating at the Adriatic city of Fano. This well-travelled route has served popes, emperors, dukes, and armies. Today, route 3 (and 3 *bis*) more or less traces this ancient road and connects many of the region's cities and towns.

The Etruscans

The region is named for the Umbri, a rather peaceful tribe dispersed around 500 B.C. by the Etruscans, who travelled from the western coast to Tuscany, Latium, and Umbria, where they formed a religious and cultural federation. According to Herodotus, the Etruscans came from Lydia in Asia Minor, although some scholars believe they were indigenous. The Tiber was the ancient frontier; the Etruscans occupied the lands on the western side, while the Umbrians were pushed to the eastern side. Towns were built on hills, the so-called Etruscan position, to free the lowlands for cultivation and provide defense against invaders; Perugia and Orvieto are among the best examples.

Wars and truces with the Romans, who arrived in the fourth century B.C., greatly diminished Etruscan power, and many cities became Roman. Tombs record the losses of this period and are markedly more sober than the richly ornamented ones of earlier, prosperous times. The Etruscans' language, with Greek elements, continues to captivate scholars, and their sculpture, elaborate funerary objects, rich metalwork, and intriguing tombs reveal their vivid religious beliefs and preoccupation with the afterlife. To prevent the spirits from intruding into the world of the living, their burial cities (*necropoli*) usually were built some distance from their towns—which accounts for the discovery of *necropoli* in isolated locations.

Skilled engineers, the Etruscans cleared thickly wooded areas and used the timber to build ships and homes. Their advanced agricultural and engineering techniques proved invaluable to the Romans, who by 396 B.C. had captured the Etruscan city of Veii, near Rome. Orvieto and Perugia resisted the Romans for a while, but fell toward the end of the century. The glorious days of Augustus (40 B.C.–A.D. 14) brought great peace and prosperity to Umbria, the results of which can be seen in the numerous Roman bridges, amphitheaters, and temples that are incorporated comfortably into the medieval fabric of the Umbrian cities.

The Middle Ages

Umbria's arts and customs reflect its strong religious and papal ties. With the arrival of the barbarians and the fall of Rome in the fifth century, Umbria sank to a low point and turned in on itself. During this time, bishops exercised both ecclesiastical and civic responsibilities and fought against many of the barbarian kings, who later came to rely on their literary skills. The numerous wars decimated the countryside and made Umbria easy prey for the Lombards, who conquered the area, eventually became Christian, and established roughly a dozen duchies. Spoleto was one of the most important; it ruled most of Umbria from the sixth to the ninth century. From the fourth century on, with the Empire ruled from Constantinople, the popes began accruing power, as they marched in the imperial footsteps of the Romans.

While the Lombards fought the Byzantines, the papacy rose through the skillful rule of Pope Gregory the Great (A.D. 590–604); his pontificate established a high mark in the development of the papal states, which came to rule much of Umbria centuries later. Another ally of the papacy during this time was monasticism, which had arisen in the East during the early Christian era and had greatly diversified by the time it reached the West. Just a few years after the last Roman emperor was deposed, the tiny town of Norcia in southeastern Umbria gave birth to Saint Benedict, who in 529 founded the great monastery in Montecassino (between Rome and Naples) according to a strict Rule he had devised, which combined work with prayer and regulated almost every detail of a monk's life. This Rule of Saint Benedict became a model for other monasteries, and Benedictine monasticism spread throughout Western Europe. Cultural and civic lifeboats during those dark years, the Benedictine monasteries flourished, banishing the great medieval sin of *accidia* (sloth) and providing safe havens for the preservation of ancient and early Church thought.

Charlemagne's creation of the Holy Roman Empire set the stage for the papal and imperial rivalry that shaped the political arena for hundreds of years. A reading of the battlements that mark the skyline of the Umbrian cities reveals initial loyalties: square crenellations for Guelph (pope), swallowtail for Ghibelline (emperor). In Perugia, the papacy prevailed from 1540 to 1860. Reduced to its essence, the conflict was really the clash of the burgeoning capitalists and a feudal nobility.

In the late 12th and early 13th century, after the growth of commerce fostered ecclesiastical abuses, the Church took stock of itself morally, and a tidal wave of reform followed. Saint Francis of Assisi took the emotional lead, and his mendicant friars reached out to the confused masses. His spirit covered Umbria like a blanket of peace, turning ferocious medieval demons into sweet birds and bees, taming wolves, softening stoic Madonnas into tender ladies of love, and bringing the heavens down to earth by narrowing the gap between rich and poor.

The collapse of the Carolingian dynasty ultimately left a power vacuum that was quickly filled by merchants and landowners, and free communes arose. From the 11th through the 13th century, trade with the East (which the Crusades helped unleash) and with Flanders and France stimulated the growth of towns in Umbria. With this growth came a measure of freedom and local self-government. The towns fought each other with appalling regularity, however, and manipulated the ruling powers—either the pope or the emperor.

Cities trafficked in both goods and ideas. The introduction of Aristotle's works by Arab and Greek scholars—in contrast to the prevailing Christian Neoplatonism—and the revival of Roman law created an era of intellectual excitement and yielded new modes of abstract thinking, which were expressed in business, commerce, and religion. This ferment eventually led to the founding of universities.

Umbrian Food

Like their quiet countryside, Umbrians are reserved but friendly. They work in tandem with nature, producing a simple but royal cuisine according to the season's bounty. The labors of the months are celebrated in wonderful meat, game, and vegetable dishes, including *palombacci,* roasted wood pigeon, often in an intricate wine sauce; *gobbi,* fried cardoons; and *porchetta alla perugina,* roasted whole suckling pig with wild fennel, rosemary, and garlic. Spicy sausages are another treat and are usually served grilled or over pasta. Norcia, a mountainous region and butchering capital east of Spoleto, provides a sumptuous array of salamis—the most exotic being the *mazzafegato,* made with pork livers, pine nuts, raisins, sugar, and orange peel—and a rare variety of lentil, the size of a freckle, from the village of Castellucio.

In **Norcia**, southeast of Assisi and reached by the sinuous but scenic routes 77, 319, and 396, you can purchase the lentils directly from the farmers' cooperative that cultivates them: Consorzio Agragio, via della Stazione 2 (Tel: 0574-57-

17-65). The town, essentially Umbrian with its pink-beige coloring and Romanesque architecture, was home to Saints Benedict, founder of Christian monasticism, and Scholastica, his twin sister. Nursia, as the Romans called Norcia in A.D. 480, is replete with food shops, particularly *norcinerie* (pork shops), which sell a sterling array of products and all seem to have a stupefied boar's head gracing their portals. One of the best is **Frantelli Ansuini**, near piazza San Benedetto; the shop is festooned with sausages, prosciutti, and cheese, and ever so aromatic. The reason these pork products are so ambrosial is the pigs' diet—nothing other than truffles, Norcia's other main attraction.

If you hanker for a pork extravaganza, try dinner at the **Hotel Posta**, via Cesare Battisti 12, Tel: (0743) 81-74-34. Or if truffles tantalize you, **Dal Francese**, via Riguardati 16 (Tel: 0743-81-62-90), offers a five-course meal (*degustazione*) in which every dish features the black truffle (closed Fridays from October to June; expensive).

Wild boar, whose meat the Romans stewed in a mixture of honey and vinegar, remains popular here, and variations of the dish can be found at the **Ottavi Restaurant** in San Mariano di Corciano, just 6 km (4 miles) southwest of Perugia. The plaid rugs and wood paneling of this country-formal restaurant (located at via Anita Garibaldi 10, right off the main road that skirts the small hill town) enhance the memorable dishes created by Signor Ottavi's family. Don't miss the shrimp in a creamy dill sauce, the dazzling antipasti, or the homemade desserts (Tel: 075-77-47-18; Fax: 075-77-48-49. closed Sundays and August).

Black truffles from the area around Spoleto lace many dishes and frequently appear as fine shavings on top of hand-cut *stringozzi, ceriole,* or *manfrigoli* pasta or on *crostini.* Festivals celebrate these musty gems, which pigs used to ferret out and which scientists recently discovered contain a steroid similar to that secreted by pigs during mating. No wonder they squealed with delight during the hunt. This may also explain the huge consumption of truffles by Emperor Claudius and King Henry IV of France, who believed their sexual prowess would thereby be enhanced. Today dogs hunt them, though in a much less frenzied fashion.

The gnarled olive trees that hug the slopes yield the green-gold oil that culinary cognoscenti consider the finest in Italy. It is best sampled on *bruschette,* grilled slabs of oil-slathered bread that years ago were eaten to gauge the quality of oil. Farmers would immerse homemade bread in the oil, grill it on an open fire, and then suck the bread to test the flavor of the oil. In autumn, the peppery greens that grow wild in the fields—such as *crispigno, strigoli,* and *raponzoli*—accompany hearty *salmi,* or stews. In southern Umbria, the nutty wheat grain *farro,* which fed the Roman troops—and which Roman aristocrats sacrificed in cake form to the god Jupiter Farreus during wedding ceremonies—is used in soups and as flour in pasta and sweets.

The abundant walnuts here find their way into the Indian-type cornmeal pudding called *brustengolo* and the typical Christmas dish of *maccheroni con noci e cacao,* pasta with a walnut and cocoa sauce. And sinister-sounding desserts, such as *fave di morti* cookies and *serpentone* cake, which resonate with the region's turbulent and mythic past, add a sense of intrigue to dining. The most fertile Umbrian land, in the Tiber valley and lowlands between Perugia and Spoleto, is lined with olive trees and grapevines that look out over plains sprinkled with corn, wheat, tobacco, and alfalfa—the very plains that produce the flour for *schiacciata,* a delicious flatbread baked with olive oil and often enhanced with onions.

The rich vineyards produce a wide variety of wines, from the prized Orvieto—which the popes loved in its *abboccato* (sweet) form but which today is mostly dry—to the superb DOCs of the Colli Altotiberini and Montefalco and grand crus and rich Rubescos of Torgiano.

You can immerse yourself in the traditions of Umbrian cooking at the excellent **Cooking School of Umbria** in Todi. Run by Donaldo and Dino Soviero, a father-and-son team, the school is situated in a charming old farmhouse with warm terra-cotta tiles and rough-hewn beams stretching over an impressive kitchen that includes five professional ranges, with 22 burners and four ovens, plus two wood-burning ovens. Classes are small and are conducted in English. Accommodations on site. For information, contact The Cooking School of Umbria, 127 Casella Postale, 06059 Todi. Tel: (075) 88-73-70.

PERUGIA

Perugia, the capital of Umbria, is a logical place from which to explore the region. Easily reached from Rome, Siena, or Florence, Perugia offers excellent transportation to neighboring cities such as Todi, Gubbio, Assisi, Spoleto, and Orvieto. Rich in artistic treasures, Perugia is a gritty city with steeply canted streets, perfect for exploring the rich knotting of its Etruscan, medieval, and Renaissance past.

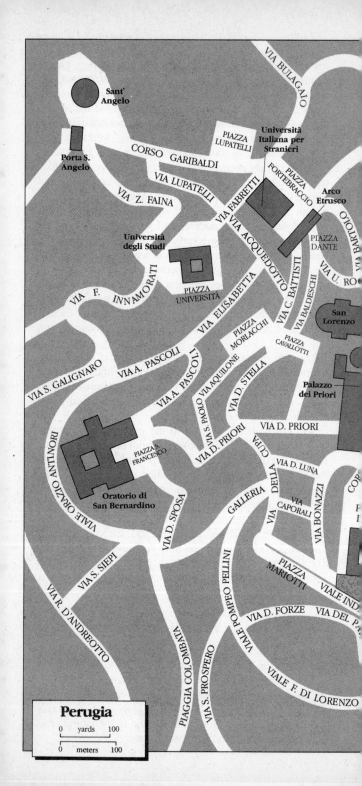

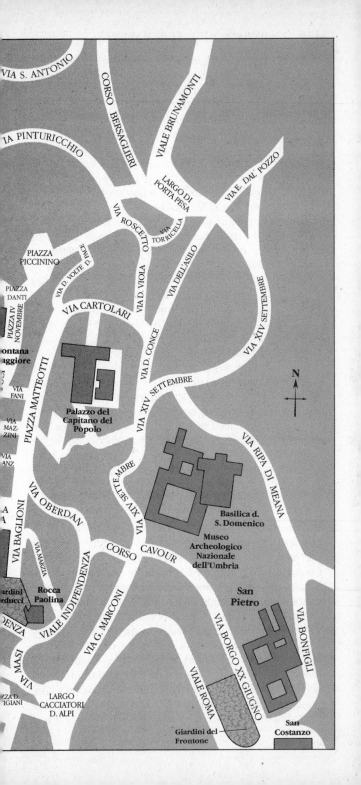

An important agricultural and commercial center, Perugia takes the lead now much as it did during its medieval period and its Etruscan period, in the sixth century B.C., when it was one of the most important strongholds of the 12 confederated cities. Fragments of those early times abound in the city, especially around the Old Town. Fine examples of Roman and Etruscan antiquities can be seen in the **Museo Archeologico Nazionale dell'Umbria**, in the monastery of the church of San Domenico at piazza Girodano Bruno in the southeast part of the city. Many of the objects in the collection were taken from Etruscan tombs. The chief attraction is the *Cippus Perusinus* slab, containing more than 150 Etruscan words.

Nearby is the basilica of **San Pietro**, which was built in the tenth century by the monks of Montecassino. Within its ancient basilican form you will see dramatic paintings by Vassilacchi; the melancholy *Pieta* by Perugino; a haunting Caravaggio, *Saint Francesca Romana;* the richly detailed *Pieta* by Bonfigli; a gossamer *Annunciation* by Sassoferrato; and an exquisitely carved altar by Mino da Fiesole. For a refreshing break, stroll through the lovely 18th-century gardens, **Giardini del Frontone**, across from the church.

Angered by Perugia's support of Antony following the murder of Caesar, in 40 B.C. Octavian (later called Augustus) ravaged the city, which he "starved into surrender," according to Suetonius. After he became emperor, Augustus rebuilt the city and inscribed his signature, "Augusta Perusia," on the Etruscan arch at the end of via Ulisse Rocchi. During the barbarian invasions, Perugia resisted the advances of Totila for seven years before succumbing in 546.

The Old Town

The medieval and Renaissance area of Perugia—site of its principal attractions—sits atop an uneven cluster of hills that rise high above the central Tiber valley. From the **Giardini Carducci**, which is graced by dark fir and ilex trees and located just off the corso Vannucci, you can take in the surrounding countryside, confirming Henry James's description of Perugia as the "little city of infinite view."

The scarcity of parking for cars at the top is relieved by several lots below, the most convenient being the one at piazza dei Partigiani, from which you enter the **Rocca Paolina**, the famous fort erected by Pope Paul III in 1540 to help control the city's despotic family, the Baglioni, whose scandalous behavior the pope couldn't tolerate. All but destroyed in 1860 when the Perugians shed the last reins of papal rule, the fort—designed by Sangallo, who blended the ancient Porta Marzia into the design—was later subsumed by a modern administrative building on piazza Italia. By taking a series of escalators that connect the lower and upper parts of the city, it is possible to view this subterranean Perugian Pompeii, which incorporates the remains of the rebel family's holdings and reveals traces of ancient roads, piazzas, and buildings. It stands as a symbol of papal authority over the Perugians, papal partisans who nevertheless rebelled against the pope's salt tax. (To this day, Perugia's bread remains saltless, as does most of the region's.)

During the papal exile in Avignon and the Great Schism that followed (which divided the Church and created rival factions, each claiming its own pope), princely despots began to menace the Umbrian cities. Perugia produced two families, the Oddi and the aforementioned Baglioni, whose shameless behavior sent tremors of fear throughout the region. The Baglioni, who eventually drove out the Oddi, wore their cruelty like a badge of honor. Even their names—Astorre, Grifone, Atalanta, Zenobia—have a mythic ring to them, suggestive of warriors of some dark saga; and their actions did at times seem superhuman. The historian Jacob Burkhardt described the climate of fear they created: "the city became a beleaguered fortress under the absolute despotism of the Baglioni, who even used the cathedral as barracks." The young artist Raphael, who was studying with Perugino at the time, witnessed these horrors and painted his world-famous *Deposition* (now in the Galleria Borghese in Rome) for the mother of one of the men killed in battle.

Both play and piety were tinctured by violence in Perugia, as the rather unpleasant game called *la battaglia dei sassi* (battle of the stones) suggests. Revived by the condottiere Braccio Fortebraccio, who controlled the city from 1416 to 1424, the game resembled a dress rehearsal for war—one lightly protected team, the *lanciatori,* would pelt the more heavily padded *armati* in a fight for control of the piazza.

The *battuti* (flagellants), popular during the reform movement in the Church, originated here, and in acts of great public penance they would whip themselves into a frenzy. Unlike the gentle followers of Saint Francis, they spread a tortured fervor throughout a good part of Europe before the pope halted them. The 15th-century Franciscan preacher Saint Bernardino of Siena also attempted to reform the city and delivered his impassioned pleas from the golden balcony that juts out from the cathedral. The **Oratorio di San**

Bernardino at piazza San Francesco, with wonderful bas-reliefs by Agostino di Duccio distinguishing its façade, is dedicated to this outraged Franciscan.

The City Center

Today the city's aggressions are sublimated in the production of the exquisite Perugina chocolates, and Buitoni pasta, and in the activities of the sizable university, whose students flood the city.

The hub of activity is the **corso Vannucci**—named after the city's master painter, known as Perugino (Pietro Vannucci)—a wide majestic street, its buildings scarred by time and human struggle, that is used as an open-air salon: people shop, students congregate, men and women debate the latest political intrigues, children play, and dogs scramble for handouts. The corso runs from the Giardini Carducci at the piazza Italia to the piazza IV Novembre and is closed to automobile traffic. To absorb the rich flavors of the city, begin with a coffee at the lofty 19th-century café **Sandri**, at number 32 on the corso. Available are traditional Perugian delicacies—*torciglione,* a pastry shaped like an eel, *crescia al formaggio,* a cheese brioche, and *rocciata,* a powdered-sugar–covered cake—which you may eat under a lavishly frescoed ceiling. In the back is a *tavola calda* offering hot prepared foods. Nearby, the **Bottega d'Arte** offers samples of Umbrian weaving and pottery, and the lovely shop of **Signor B. Paoletti** is famous for its hand-embroidered linens and baby clothes. The best hotel in town, the stately **Brufani** in the piazza Italia, is a throwback to the gilded days of the 19th century (but with every modern convenience) and is home to the **Collins** restaurant, serving haute Umbrian and Continental food. Adjacent to the Brufani, and enjoying the same prime location (and the same palazzo), but charging a fraction of the price, is the comfortable **Palace Hotel Bellavista**. Another moderately priced hotel in the area is **La Rosetta**, with a well-regarded restaurant. Try the ravioli with walnut sauce or have a drink on the sheltered patio, which affords a partial view of the avenue's goings-on. Alas, its interior is impersonal, with robotic waiters doing "their duty." You will eat just as well, for less money, at the bustling **La Taverna**, on via della Streghe 8, just off corso Vannucci. Housed on two floors of a historic building brimming with Perugian soul, the place specializes in Umbrian fare, serving ample portions of savory grilled pork and truffled dishes to loyal crowds. Closed Mondays; Tel: (075) 610-28.

Dominating the corso Vannucci is the Gothic **Palazzo dei**

Priori, with an eccentric staircase that fans out onto the square in front of the Duomo. Perugia's fearsome pride inheres in the symbols that surmount the doorway: a bronze griffin and Guelph lion support the chains of the gates of Siena, which fell to the city in 1358. This former home of the ruling magistrates is a somber, arrogant building that houses the **Galleria Nazionale dell'Umbria.** (The museum is on the third floor; the entrance is from the corso Vannucci.) The best works are by no means all Umbrian, but notable are the large 13th-century painted crucifix by Maestro di San Francesco and the Bonfigli works: the lovely *Adoration of the Magi,* the *Annunciation with Saint Luke,* and the animated fresco *The Siege of Totila,* recalling the city's barbarian phase.

Other impressive works here are Piero della Francesca's *Madonna with Angels and Saints* polyptych and his *Annunciation.* In the two rooms devoted to paintings of two Umbrian luminaries, Perugino and Pinturicchio, the mystical Umbrian countryside and fervent religious piety—hallmarks of Umbrian art—are distilled. Also worth noting are a collaborative work by Pinturicchio and Perugino, the *Miracle of the Saints,* which is rich in architectural detail, a superlative *Adoration of the Magi* by Perugino, recently restored, and the luminous *Madonna and Child* by Gentile da Fabriano; plus wonderful small gems of Giovanni Boccati of Camerino, a Marches native son who specialized in angelic choirs, putti, and flagellants.

Adjacent to the Palazzo dei Priori are the **Collegio della Mercanzia** and the **Collegio del Cambio.** Two of the most powerful guilds in the city were the merchants and the money changers, whose members were elected as priors. The richly carved audience room of the Collegio della Mercanzia precedes the real attraction in the Collegio del Cambio—the masterful frescoes of Perugino and his students, including Raphael, who is said to have painted the figures of Fortitude. Classical and Christian worlds are united in the portraits of ancient and biblical personages that mingle on the walls, all under the penetrating eye of the pudgy-faced Perugino, whose portrait presides over the scene from its vantage point atop the dividing pilaster. Vasari described Perugino as a man "of little or no religion, who could never bring himself to believe in the immortality of the soul."

North on the corso Vannucci is the piazza IV Novembre and the 13th-century **Fontana Maggiore,** built to celebrate the completion of an aqueduct that brought water to Perugia from Montepulciano in Tuscany. Its striking bas-reliefs by Nicola and Giovanni Pisano, whose works are amply represented in Pisa and Siena, illustrate the city's civic and religious pride on the upper basin and the rhythms of nature on the lower. Culinary pride is in evidence nearby as well, at the simple vaulted restaurant **Il Falchetto**, at via Bartolo 20, right behind the Duomo (Tel: 075-618-75; closed Mondays). They make a fine *pappardelle alla lepre* (pasta in a hare sauce), hearty *palombaccia al rubesco* (wood pigeon in a wine sauce) though sometimes the birds seem a bit bare-boned, and tasty *falchetti* (spinach dumplings). The Gothic cathedral of **San Lorenzo**, whose unfinished façade gives it an equivocal presence, is undistinguished except for the inlaid wooden choir, a particularly lovely *Deposition* painted by Federico Barocci, the beautiful altarpiece of Luca Signorelli (in the cathedral museum), the so-called onyx wedding ring of the Virgin (kept in a reliquary with 15 locks), and the elegant loggia of Braccio Fortebraccio, added by the *condottiere* in 1423.

To savor some truly ancient Umbrian cuisine in a setting of flowering archways, silver candelabras, and rich red banquettes framed in gleaming wood, try **Osteria del Bartolo**, via del Bartolo 30 (Tel: 075-61-461; closed Tuesdays and mid-January). Owner Walter Passeri offers a choice of two menus: one with dishes dating from the 15th century and earlier, including *piccione ripiena alla paesana* (stuffed pigeon), and the other a creative blend of the antique and the modern. Reservations suggested. (The prix fixe is moderately priced.)

Right around the corner from piazza IV Novembre, at via della Gabbia 13, is the homey, inexpensive trattoria **Cesarino**, where homemade pasta and spit-roasted lamb, poultry, and sausage are specialties. For starters here, order the *torta al testo,* a flat unleavened bread baked on a stone slab and stuffed with bitter greens and cheese. Outside terrace dining is available in spring and summer. (Closed Wednesdays, and Thursday lunch in summer; Tel: 075-662-77.)

Around the other side of the cathedral on piazza Danti is the via Ulisse Rocchi; at number 16 is the **Enoteca Provinciale**, where you can sample over 150 local wines. At the end of the street is the **Arco Etrusco**, where the Etruscans' engineering skill is immediately apparent. The massive stone blocks, blackened by the Octavian fire and surmounted by a 16th-century loggia, formed one of the seven gateways to the old city. Just beyond, at piazza Fortebraccio, is the renowned **Università Italiana per Stranieri** (Italian University for Foreigners), housed in the 18th-century **Palazzo Gallenga Stuart**. Opened in 1926, it is responsible for the international flavor of the city and has a superlative library of Italian, English, French, and German books. You might follow a few of the students to one of the best buys in town, the restaurant **Dal Mi' Cocco**. Head north on corso Garibaldi to number 12. The delightfully rustic trattoria offers seasonal menus featuring delectable *crostini,* hearty soups, rich pastas, and expertly grilled meats at an incredibly low prix fixe. (Closed Mondays and the second half of July; Tel: 075-625-11.) A walk is definitely in order after one of these meals; continue down the street to **Sant'Angelo**, a sweet, round, fifth-century church that was built on the site of an ancient temple, using 16 columns from the original structure.

The medieval streets in the old section brim with secrets. Among the best of them are the via delle Volte della Pace, a dark and mysterious covered walk, and the via della Gabbia, where criminals once dangled in cages from the Palazzo dei Priori. Close by is piazza Morlacchi, where the eponymous 18th-century Rococo theater hosts many of the city's musical events. A highlight of the music season is the chamber concert series, Amici della Musica, held in July at the Palazzo dei Priori. Throughout the summer the cloisters and piazza abound with dance and theater performances. The jazz festival in July electrifies the city—which is then soothed during a festival of sacred music in September. Check for listings with your hotel concierge or at the tourist office (via IV Novembre 3; Tel: 075-233-27).

Just outside Perugia, at Olmo in Corciano, reached by route 75 *bis* east, is the delightful **Osteria dell'Olmo**, serving distinctly Umbrian food in a rustic setting, including gracious outdoor dining (closed Mondays; Tel: 075-517-91-40). Also outside of Perugia is the handsome **Villa di Montesolare**, roughly 20 minutes away via route 220, southwest, in the direction of Città di Pieve. Located in the hamlet of **Panicale**, this restored 16th-century villa has eight guestrooms and two suites furnished with period antiques. But its prime hilltop position overlooking the wondrous countryside is the real hook. Lush grounds laced with lemon trees are perfect for strolling, tennis, or a horseback outing. The elegant dining room serves superb Tuscan food, and the hillside swimming pool is *the* spot for catching a Technicolor sunset. The place is open from April to November.

Outside Perugia

The Etruscan necropolis **Hypogeum Volumni**, about 6 km (4 miles) to the southeast on route 75 *bis* in the direction of ponte San Giovanni, evokes the mysterious charms of the

Volumni, an important Etruscan family of the second century B.C. A small green door marks the entrance to this tomb, which is shaped like an Etruscan house and has chambers dug directly into the volcanic rock containing Greek-stylized cinerary urns, many of which display images suggesting the intensely emotional Etruscan personality. Note the urn of Arunte Volumni, who reclines on the top in the manner of a bored Caesar. Although this tomb has none of the colors of the others, it is still worth a visit.

Wine enthusiasts will find the **Lungarotti Wine Museum** at Torgiano, which traces the history of wine through a wide collection of wine containers and geographic sites, appealing. It is roughly 16 km (10 miles) southeast of Perugia, off route 3 *bis*.

Torgiano, a peaceful hamlet, is dominated by the superb Relais & Châteaux hotel **Le Tre Vaselle**. This outstanding palazzo, set off from the verdant fields of the family's vineyards, was restored by the vintner Dr. Giorgio Lungarotti, who spared no expense in re-creating antique comfort without any hint of ostentation, although the dining room is a bit vast and impersonal. (Its new annex, **La Bondanzina**, with trompe l'oeil landscape murals that warm up this 19th-century country house, is just around the corner.) The renowned restaurant serves refined Umbrian fare, using ingredients from the hotel's farms. The boar steak grilled with fresh rosemary goes remarkably well with the fabulous wines of the family. And for dessert, the *cialde,* a whisper-thin crepe with custard gelato, rounds out the meal nicely. An ambrosial finale would be a glass of Vin Santo, a rich dessert wine served with crunchy biscotti (*cantuccini* or *brutti ma buoni*) for dunking. The hotel will arrange to pick up guests at the ponte San Giovanni train station in Perugia, or you can take a taxi. The **Lungarotti Osteria**, at corso Vittorio Emanuele 33, sells wonderful products that make fine gifts for cooking enthusiasts, including homemade balsamic vinegar and extra virgin olive oil.

Those interested in pottery will find **Deruta**—roughly 16 km (10 miles) south of Torgiano on 3 *bis*—a good place for the traditional *arabascato blu* and other designs, which are sold in the many outlet stores on the via Tiberina, the main street of the lower town. One venerable factory is **Ubaldo Grazia**'s, whose family has been making majolica since the Renaissance, and who will custom-design anything for you; via Tiberina 181. They accept traveller's checks but no credit cards. (Tel: 075-971-02-01; closed Sundays.) You should also visit the **Ceramic Museum**, which is lavishly stocked with majolica. And chamber music lovers will delight in the

International Chamber Music Festival, held during August and September in the little town of Città di Castello, north of Perugia. Charming for its sheer simplicity, the city has a few superior paintings in its museum, the Pinacoteca Comunale, including the dramatic and mysterious *Martyrdom of Saint Sebastian* by Luca Signorelli, some early works of Raphael, and a stunning *Coronation of the Virgin* by the workshop of Domenico Ghirlandaio. Città also hosts an annual white truffle fair in November. For information, contact the tourist office at via R. Cesare 2b (Tel: 075-855-48-17).

ASSISI

Only 25 km (15 miles) east of Perugia is Assisi, indelibly connected with Saint Francis, whose life is one of the greatest riches-to-rags stories ever told. Sitting on an imposing spur of Mount Subasio, the grand two-tiered basilica with the adjoining convent of San Francesco dominates the green plains below. From the basilica you can see the glistening dome of Santa Maria degli Angeli in the valley below, the imposing Baroque church that shelters the tiny stone hut known as the Porziuncola. The hut, gussied up a bit, was given to Saint Francis as his pastoral headquarters by the Benedictines in return for a yearly ration of fish—a bargain still honored today. Francis returned here to die, and it is also where he received Saint Clare into the Franciscan order after she fled her rich father and life of luxury: her hair shorn, her garb gray, her life one of sacrifice and poverty.

The rosy hue of Assisi is nature's doing—part sun, part pink limestone quarried from Mount Subasio, from which the entire city gets its unified character. Flowers and rosemary spill over ancient walls, providing extra color and fragrance, and along the steep and narrow streets cheerful brothers in flowing brown robes go about their business, oblivious to the crush of visitors.

The storm preceded the calm here; from the fall of the Roman Empire to the end of the 15th century, Assisi was the scene of occupation and warfare: Totila, Lombards, Perugian menace, the plague. During Saint Francis's time the town was divided politically into the nobles, who idled away at their estates; the merchants selling their wares; the artisans grouped in guilds; and the serfs, who labored in the fields. When Duke Conrad of Lutzen was finally driven out (four-year-old Frederick II, Barbarossa's grandson, was visiting at the time and barely escaped), the merchants attempted to overthrow the nobility, who quickly fled to

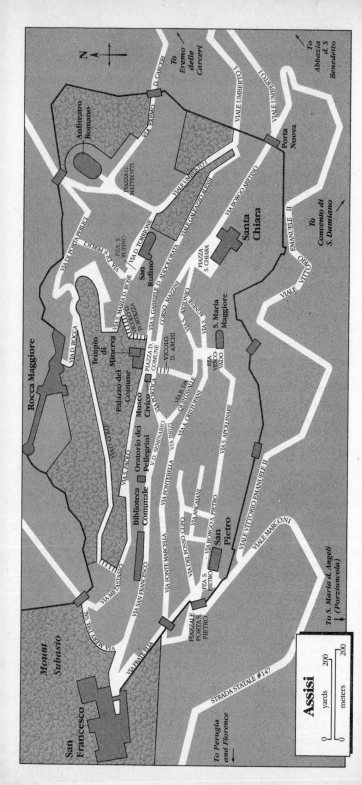

Assisi

To Eremo delle Carceri

To Abbazia d. S. Benedetto

Anfiteatro Romano

VIA D. CARCERI

VIA EREMO

VIALE UMBERTO I

VIALE UMBERTO I

VIA UMBERTO I

Porta Nuova

PIAZZA G. MATTEOTTI

VIALE UMBERTO I

VIA DI PORTA PERLICI

VIA GALEAZZO ALESSI

VIA BORGO ARETINO

PZA. S. RUFINO

VIA D. TORRIONE

Santa Chiara

San Rufino

VIA S. GABRIELE D. ADDOLORATA

PIAZZA S. CHIARA

CORSO MAZZINI

VIA S. ANTONIO

VIALE VITTORIO EMANUELE II

VIA S. MARIA D ROSE

VICOLO D. FONTEBELLA

VICOLO D. ARCHI

VIA S. AGNESE

VIA S. RUFINO

S. Maria Maggiore

VIA D. ROCCA

Rocca Maggiore

Tempio di Minerva

Palazzo del Comune

PIAZZA D. COMUNE

VICOLO D. COMUNE

PZA. VESCO VADO

VIA PORTICA

Museo Civico

VIA S. MARIA QUINTAVALLE

VIALE VITTORIO

Convento di S. Damiano

Oratorio dei Pellegrini

Biblioteca Comunale

VIA D. SEMINARIO

VIA S. PAOLO

VIA BRIZI

VIA A. CRISTOFANI

VIA S. APOLLINARE

VICOLO SBARRE

VIA FONTEBELLA

VIA D. FOSSO CIECO

VIA ANCAJANI

San Pietro

VIA FONTE MARCELLA

VIA SAN FRANCESCO

VIA BORGO S. PIETRO

Mount Subasio

VIA METASTASIO

VIALE F. MA

PZA. S. PIETRO

PIAZZALE PORTA S. PIETRO

VIALE MARCONI

VIALE VITTORIO EMANUELE II

To S. Maria d. Angeli (Porziuncola)

VIA FRATE ELIA

San Francesco

STRADA STATALE #147

To Perugia and Florence

yards 200

meters 200

Perugia for help—and Perugia was only too happy to feed its aggressive instincts. Fields were devastated and the peasants were terrorized.

The merchant class, to which Francis was born in 1182, was perhaps the best off. Son of the wealthy textile merchant Pietro de Bernardone, Francis was the town playboy, helped his father in the shop, and probably accompanied him to the south of France, where they would buy sumptuous fabrics. Passionate in play and love, he fought against Perugia and was captured and held prisoner for a year—during which he underwent his conversion to Christ. Knights, courtly love, and the Crusades shaped these times, and Francis, who referred to himself as the *jongleur de Dieu,* was very much a man of his time. His youthful vigor is best evoked during the riotous feast of Calendimaggio in the first week of May, when citizens dressed as jesters and troubadours reenact the pagan rites of spring. And his tender heart is recalled during the annual *Festa del Perdono* (Feast of Forgiveness) on August 1 and 2, which Saint Francis established to provide Catholics with a more peaceful alternative for gaining indulgences than hieing off to the Crusades for a little killing. Today, many come from near and far to partake of this feast and renew their faith.

Exchanging a cloak of silk for one of poverty did not endear Francis to his father, a businessman who gave credit to his customers and calculated the collateral of land he would have should they default. Besides, who would carry on the business? Nevertheless, the burgher's son transformed himself into the *poverello* (poor one), courting poverty the way Dante wooed Beatrice.

His divine madness attracted many, including some prominent noblemen who willingly renounced their wealth to follow him. In 1209 he petitioned Pope Innocent III to establish an order of preaching friars. The pope hesitated initially, partly because he understood the threat Francis's radical poverty would pose to the wealthy prelates. But he also realized its salutary effects. A dream in which Innocent saw the church of St. John Lateran falling and the barefoot Francis supporting it (chronicled in one of the Giotto frescoes in the basilica) coincided with Francis's desire, and the pope granted him oral approval.

In 1219 Francis accompanied the Fifth Crusade to Egypt, where he sought unsuccessfully to convert the sultan. His life has offered great aesthetic possibilities to artists, who for centuries have chronicled the saint's love of nature and mankind in ever-widening fashion. Two years after Francis's death Pope Gregory IX began building the great **Basilica**; it is one of life's ironies that a saint dedicated to simplicity and poverty should have such an imposing church erected in his name. Or, as Henry James comments in his *Italian Hours,* "the Saint whose only tenement in life was the ragged robe which barely covered him, is the hero of this massive structure. Church upon church, nothing less will adequately shroud his consecrated clay."

The basilica, actually two churches, one above the other, was constructed over a period of 25 years on the design of Brother Elia, Francis's right-hand man, who was not content with the more modest indexes of Francis's humanity. It seems to reflect the twists and turns of an increasingly humanized religion. The Romanesque lower church has short squat pillars and a vaulted ornamental ceiling, lightened only by an occasional sunbeam. The walls are covered with frescoes by Cimabue, Simone Martini, Giotto, and Pietro Lorenzetti. The body of Saint Francis, which the Assisans hid from Perugian body snatchers, lies in the crypt; it was only rediscovered in 1818. In sharp contrast, the Gothic upper church is a leap into light, both architecturally and literally. The faded but unforgettable Cimabue frescoes, particularly the *Crucifixion,* were done before the masterful 28-fresco cycle of Giotto, which captures the emotional intensity of the life of the saint and dominates the upper church.

From the basilica, you can almost touch the gracious **Hotel Subasio**, a converted monastery and the city's finest hotel, on via Frate Elia; it is adorned with antiques and flowers though the rooms are slightly conventual in flavor. From one of its balconies, the poet Gabriele D'Annunzio delivered his mock sermon to his lover, Eleanora Duse, to the applause of the forgiving Franciscans. Although the hotel fronts on a noisy, crowded street, the attractive restaurant and magical terrace offer a marvelous setting in which to enjoy a view of the countryside; the quietest rooms look out over the valley.

The via San Francesco, unfortunately festooned with tawdry memorabilia of Saint Francis, extends from the basilica and traverses the town's slope on its way to the piazza del Comune. At number 8 is the **Albergo Il Palazzo**, part of the larger Palazzo Bindangoli Bartocci, built in the 1500s. Recently renovated but retaining its original rustic beams and vaulted ceiling, the hotel has 12 simple but stylish rooms, many with views of the beautiful Spoletana valley. There are several interesting sights along the way, including the **Oratorio dei Pellegrini**, number 11, once a hospice for pilgrims and covered with exquisite frescoes; and the **Biblioteca**

Comunale, number 12, which contains the oldest copy of Saint Francis's nature poem, *Canticle of the Creatures*. Right before the entrance to the main piazza, you'll find the **Museo Civico**, where you can view the remains of the ancient Roman forum that lies directly under the piazza.

At the piazza del Comune, site of the old Roman forum, the soaring buildings of the 13th-century *comune*—the Torre, Palazzo del Comune, and Palazzo del Capitano del Popolo—look down haughtily on the tiny **Tempio di Minerva**, built during the reign of Augustus. Nevertheless, the temple inspired Goethe, who rhapsodized over its proportions: "just right for such a small town yet so perfect in design that it would be an ornament anywhere." He preferred this temple, which was converted to the church of Santa Maria in 1529, over the "monstrous basilica," as he described it. The piazza, where troubadours sang of idealized love and today grandmothers trudge on their daily marketing rounds, is within a stone's throw of many hotels and restaurants. Just beyond the temple, a steep flight of stairs leads to the family-run and inexpensive restaurant **La Fortezza** at vicolo della Fortezza 2b, a cozy refuge for simple but delicious fare. Try their creamy fava bean soup with mint and prosciutto and their grilled pork and *maccheroni alla Fortezza* (pasta in a rich green vegetable sauce). Tel: (075) 81-24-18; closed Thursdays. If picnic fare is what you're after, try the **Bottega del Buongustalo** at via S. Gabriele 17, just off the piazza. They stock fine local delicacies such as herbed and stuffed fresh breads and bear pâté.

The quiet, family-run **Hotel Umbra**, embraced by vine-covered walls and situated at the end of a cul-de-sac on vicolo degli Archi, right off the piazza, has that special Franciscan magic, with pleasant rooms, terraces, views, and reasonable prices. Its restaurant, though, misses the mark when it strays into the French arena. If you stick with strictly Umbrian fare, you'll be pleased. And you can't beat the serenity of the trellised garden, where meals are served during the summer by overattentive but good-natured waiters. Tel: (075) 81-22-40. (Closed Tuesdays and November 15 to December 15.)

Not too far away is another hotel/restaurant combination, the small, genteel **Hotel Fontebella**, on via Fontebella, housed in a 17th-century palazzo graced with antiques and comfortable rooms. Its restaurant, **Il Frantoio**, on vicolo Illuminati, occupies an old olive-oil pressing room and serves refined (and expensive) regional cuisine such as superb tortelloni with sage butter or plates of *crostini*. During the summer it's particularly pleasant to eat under the thatched roof of the terrace. Closed Mondays; reservations needed; Tel: (075) 81-29-77.

For chic medieval dining try **Medio Evo**, at via Arco dei Priori 4b, within a short walk from the piazza. In a setting befitting knights in shining armor, tuxedoed waiters roll out plates of steaming pasta with truffles and fragrant grilled meats to the sounds of soft live music. Reservations suggested; Tel: (075) 81-30-68. Closed Wednesdays, January, and July 3 to 21.

Restaurants close early in Assisi, but one that serves late and is a favorite of the locals is the little pizzeria **I Monaci**, just off the passageway between via del Seminario and via Brizi (Tel: 075-81-25-12).

From the piazza runs the corso Mazzini, a shop-lined street and the location of the **Hotel Dei Priori**, with 19th-century furnishings and 20th-century conveniences. Its prime location and moderate rates make it a good value. The street leads to the basilica of **Santa Chiara**, where the body of Saint Clare lies in a subterranean tomb. Impressive for its massive pink buttresses and lovely rose windows, it also contains a 12th-century crucifix said to have spoken to Saint Francis, urging him to "rebuild My church."

A short distance away, heading north, is the handsome Romanesque **Cathedral of San Rufino**, with rose windows that seem to twirl around a medley of carved saints and animals. Of special interest is the porphyry font where Frederick II and Saints Francis and Clare were all baptized with what were obviously very potent waters. A nearby path leads to the **Rocca Maggiore**, the castle built in 1174 where Duke Conrad of Lutzen made his headquarters.

The immense basilica of San Francesco may reflect the sweeping influence of Francis, but the convent of **San Damiano**, about 2 km (1½ miles) south of Porta Nuova, best expresses his simple, eloquent love of God through humanity. A lonely and silent place, it was here that Francis heard the voice of the crucifix and composed his *Canticle of the Creatures,* and where Saint Clare and her order lived. Another serene haven is **Saint Anthony's Guest House**, located a short walk from the main piazza. Perched on a hill, this simply furnished but comfortable home is run lovingly by the Franciscan Sisters of the Atonement from Graymoor, New York. The price is benign and the spirit all Saint Francis, with lovely untamed gardens, inviting library, chapel, and stunning views. Breakfast is served and there is also one midday meal, which is extra. There is an 11:00 P.M. curfew, but Assisi is hardly jumping at night, so this shouldn't pose a problem.

Assisi is a pilgrimage town that miraculously manages its crowds well. During Holy Week the Deposition is reenacted with a torch-lit procession through the streets. The Festa del Voto, celebrating the miracle of Saint Clare repelling the Saracens from the city, is on June 21. On October 3 and 4, the Transito di San Francesco commemorates the death of the saint with a simple service at sunset; the light from hundreds of candles gives the city a surrealistic glow. If you happen to be in Assisi during the last two weeks of July or the first week of August, you might enjoy getting tickets for one of the musical events of **Festa Musica Pro Mundo Uno**, a two-part festival, sponsored by the Accademia Musicale Ottorino Respighi in Rome (via Villa Maggiorani 20, 00168 Rome), which handles many musical events in Umbrian cities for the Festival. The second part (August 6 to 18) takes place in Orvieto. And what would a medieval town be without its crossbow contest? You can witness this hearty sport duriing the **palio of San Rufino**, which takes place in August, along with ballad singing, puppet shows, and other theatrical events, in the many squares throughout Assisi.

If you find yourself hard-pressed for a hotel in the city, try the wonderfully restored medieval fortress **Lo Spedalicchio**, 16 km (10 miles) away in the town of Bastia Ospedalicchio, equidistant from Perugia and Assisi. Although the hotel sits right off busy highway 147, once you pass through the grand doorway, present-day annoyances disappear. Capacious and comfortable, it might have as its its best feature its moderate, if not cheap, rates. But if you can tolerate more of a pinch to your pocketbook (though not much more), try **Castel San Gregorio**, a gem of a hotel in the town of the same name. Just 15 minutes northwest of Assisi, it is reached by a winding road that snakes through the gentlest terrain before reaching the path to the hotel, which itself is lined with pencil-thin cypress trees. Intimate, with wood-beamed ceilings that stretch over cozy sitting rooms, it has only 12 rooms and acres of lovely untamed gardens for strolling. Full pension available.

One especially pleasant place is the **Antichità "Three Esse" Country House** at S. Pietro Compagna 178, a short distance from the lower gates into Assisi. Silvana Ciammarvghi has furnished this cozy inn (just ten rooms) with antiques from her shop, which is adjacent to the inn, so "country antique" charm abounds. Inexpensive.

A rustic haven just 13 km (8 miles) east of Assisi, in Armenzano, is **Le Silve**, a converted old farmhouse sporting tiled floors, stone and whitewashed walls, beamed ceilings, and antique furnishings. This working farm produces its own cheese, oil, and meat, and has several independent suites on its grounds, about one mile or so from the main house. Facilities are plentiful, including pool, tennis, sauna, riding, and more.

The **Eremo delle Carceri** (Hermitage of the Prisons), just a ten-minute drive up forested hills, is also worth a visit. Saint Francis and his companions frequently sought solace at this monastery, which was nothing more than a few caves until Saint Bernardino built it up. The interior resembles an errant Henry Moore sculpture, and its stone terraces offer compelling views of the countryside. A steep flight of stairs inside the **Chapel of Saint Marie** leads to Saint Francis's stone grotto, the original core of the monastery, where you can see the saint's stone bed and oratory.

SPELLO AND MONTEFALCO

About 12 km (7 miles) from Assisi, southeast on route 75, is the charming town of Spello, known as Hispellum during its Roman days, a rosy oasis of narrow pristine streets and covered passageways nestled on a foothill of Monte Subasio. The main gateway at the bottom of the hill, the Roman Porta Consolare, with three "mature" statues dating from the Roman republic, introduces the town's history—which also inheres in the town's two other gates, the Porta Urbica and the best one, the Porta Venere, wonderfully preserved, flanked by two cylindrical towers and dating back to the age of Augustus. During the Augustan reign the city enjoyed wide territorial power (the poet Propertius lost much of his land during this time and was quite bitter over it). Through this gate, up via Consolare, you come to the main attraction of Spello, the 12th-century church of **Santa Maria Maggiore** on via Cavour, which contains the wonderful Pinturicchio frescoes painted for the Baglioni family of Perugia, a favorite of Pope Martin V, who gave Spello to them; the frescoes, as stunning as the ones he painted in Siena's Piccolomini library, are set off by brilliant Deruta majolica floors. Spello's rhythms are firmly rooted in the past; this is most evident during the feast of Corpus Christi in the first week of June, when the town's main piazza becomes a carpet of flowers that depict religious scenes for the festival known as the *Infiorata*. Many visitors to Assisi spend the night in Spello and find the comfortable lodgings and restaurants a good value. On via dei Molini, at the highest point in the city, is the "rustic modern" **Hotel Bastiglia**, with some hillside rooms and a fine restaurant in a lovely space enhanced by giant wooden beams and a fireplace. This small city boasts other good restaurants: for instance, **Il Molino**, in a converted 18th-century mill at the bottom of town at piazza Matteotti 6 (Tel: 0742-65-13-05; closed Tuesdays), where you can dine on perfectly grilled meats and superb homemade pasta without suffering financial ruin. One caveat: The outdoor terrace is right on the main road, so be prepared for noise. Although the area is ringed by shrubs, they are hardly an effective sound barrier. **Il Cacciatore**, via Giulia 42, offers terrace dining with sweeping views, plus several rooms. There's nothing fancy here, but all the food coming out of Signora Bruna's kitchen is the essence of Umbrian simplicity and freshness. Tel: (0742) 65-11-41; closed Mondays.

One pleasant and inexpensive restaurant, at via Cavour 2, is **La Cantina**, with a few good Umbrian dishes and some creative variations on regional themes as well (closed Wednesdays; Tel: 0742-65-17-75).

There are many diminutive towns in the hills close by. **Bettona**, still girded by Etruscan walls, is the site of the severe Palazzetto Podestarile, where you can see the works of Andrea della Robbia and Dono Doni. Soaring above the valleys of the Clitunno and Topino rivers is the Umbrian **Montefalco**, which sits like a medieval aerie on what seems to be the highest point in the region, earning it the title "balcony of Umbria." This old Roman colony, sacked by Frederick II and later taken by the papacy, is a sunny town where old men with sun-baked faces sit around playing the popular Italian card game *scopa* while their apron-clad wives stand vigil in doorways. Its pride is the former church of **San Francesco**, now a museum, which contains the superlative fresco cycle of Saint Francis's life by Benozzo Gozzoli, which is also featured in the church of San Fortunato. Be sure to have the museum guide show you the mysterious fresco that contains a Christ figure whose eyes follow you as you walk from one side of the fresco to the other.

For a spectacular view of the Umbrian landscape go to the Palazzo Comunale, where you can buy a ticket and climb the stairs to the bell tower. Follow up with a tasty home-cooked meal of pasta and grilled meats, washed down with a robust Rosso di Montefalco wine, at the warm and rustic **Trattoria Ringhiera Umbra**, corso G. Mameli (Tel: 0742-791-66). For something a bit more elegant, but not expensive, go to the **Coccorone**, largo Tempestivi, just off the central square at vicolo Fabbri, which specializes in pasta with truffles and such other earthy Umbrian dishes as *pappardelle al sagrantino*, wide noodles in a rich red wine and porcini mushroom sauce (Tel: 0742-795-35; closed Wednesdays). Or picnic in the inviting hills and take along a bottle of Sagrantino, a hearty local wine made from twice-pressed grapes. Montefalco is easily accessible by bus from Foligno, which is about 6.5 km (4 miles) northeast. Close by, a few miles northwest of Montefalco, is **Bevagna**, a quiet, faded town worth a visit for its two wonderful Romanesque churches, San Silvestro and San Michele, which face each other across the central piazza Silvestri. Once a flourishing Roman city, the town has a few impressive remains, including some Roman mosaics, which can be seen on via Porta Guelfa. Nearby, at piazza Garibaldi, is a simple but good inexpensive restaurant, **Da Nina** (Tel: 0742-621-61; closed Tuesdays and July). And for a taste of cloistered comfort, the Benedictine monastery at corso Matteotti 15 rents rooms that are simple, comfortable, and very inexpensive (from Ł45,000 half board and Ł55,000 for full board; Tel: 0742-36-01-33). Just 3 km (2 miles) east of Foligno is the solemn 13th-century **Abbadia di Sassovivo**, also worth a visit. You might combine a trip here with lunch at **Villa Roncalli**, located in the genteel town of **Foligno**, which holds the Quintana joust every second and third Sunday in September. The town has a number of interesting churches, including Santa Maria Infraportas, a Romanesque gem. The lovely 15th-century villa, on the outskirts of town, at via Roma 25, is very much a family affair. Wood-fired ovens turn out fragrant breads, and the handmade pasta and home-cured prosciutto should ensure a repeat visit. There are also ten sparely furnished but comfortable rooms and a pleasant sheltered garden. Closed Mondays and the first two weeks in August. Tel: (0742) 67-02-91; expensive.

Fonti del Clitunno

South of Spello on route 3 (the Flaminia Way), near the village of **Pissignano**, are the **Fonti del Clitunno**, the pure springs that were an ancient Roman religious outpost and the source of the river Clitumnus. The notorious emperor Caligula prayed here at his villa, which stood on the banks of this limpid pool rimmed by weeping willows and poplars. Its powerful effects have charmed many writers—Virgil exclaimed about its beauty, Byron included it in his *Childe Harold,* and Corot painted its sublime poetry. Nearby is the miniature **Tempietto del Clitunno**, built in the fifth century over a pagan oratory and containing the oldest frescoes in Umbria (seventh century). Its delicate proportions inspired Palladio.

When fall ushers in the game and mushroom season, stop where the Umbrians do, at the warm Umbrian inn **Le**

Casaline, just a few miles south at Campello sul Clitunno, for a sampling of its specialties (Tel: 0743-52-08-11; closed Mondays). There are also seven rooms, done up in rustic simplicity, that apparently are a diversion for the owner, Signor Zeppadoro.

SPOLETO

About 14 km (9 miles) south of Pissignano, still on route 3, and north of Rome via Terni, is Spoleto. The densely wooded hills of Monteluco, which rise over 2,000 feet, shelter this tiny gray town, so full of charm and cultural excitement each summer during the famous **Festival of Two Worlds**, launched by Gian-Carlo Menotti more than 30 years ago. Each summer, the festival turns this sleepy town into a Mediterranean Chautauqua, with famous artists in attendance. The extravaganza of music, dance, and theater eclipses the real Spoleto of still and quiet nights.

The giant Calder sculpture in the faceless modern part of town, where the train arrives, is the first clue to Spoleto's other nature. From here there are frequent buses to the central piazza della Libertà in the old part of town. If you expect to attend the festival, plan well in advance; tickets are snatched up early and hotels fill fast. (The festival runs from mid-June to mid-July; for information, contact: Festival dei Due Mondi, via Margutta 17, Rome; Tel: 06-678-3262. In Spoleto, the festival office is at via Giustolo 10; Tel: 0743-281-20.)

An episcopal see in the fourth century, Spoleto suffered under the barbarian Totila and subsequently became the headquarters of the Lombard duchy that ruled over most of Umbria for 300 years. For a while it was a fief of Countess Mathilda of Tuscany, but after the Guelph versus Ghibelline battles in the 14th century, Spoleto became part of the papal states.

As for evidence of ancient times, Roman ruins predominate, but the giant stones that form part of the wall surrounding the Rocca (see below) recall the Umbrians who lived here in the seventh and sixth centuries B.C. Fiercely loyal to the Romans, who had colonized the city in 241 B.C., Spoleto repulsed an attack by Hannibal. The **Porta Fuga**, near the Palazzo Pompili, commemorates this impressive victory, and the splendid theaters, basilicas, Roman baths, houses, and arches throughout Spoleto act as palpable guides to this rich Roman period.

The area from the Roman arch, Porta Monterone, around

to the Duomo and sweeping up to the Rocca includes the most interesting sights. Viale Matteotti, the main road, skirts the public gardens and passes the **Hotel Dei Duchi**, an agreeably modern place with an adequate restaurant and pleasant terrace. (It is a ten-minute walk from the center of town.) The street leads to the piazza della Libertà, once the private courtyard of a 17th-century palazzo and now the site of the tourist office. (The office offers good walking tours of the city, which include nature walks with altitudes indicated.) Off the piazza stands a first-century Roman theater that has been beautifully restored. Close by is a new hotel, the **Albornoz Palace**, in the public park on viale Matteotti, with 96 comfortable, tasteful rooms and well within easy reach of activities. From here the corso Mazzini, the main artery sprinkled with attractive shops, slices through the heart of town, passing the delightfully lively **Sabatini**, number 52/54, where you can dine on sumptuous *stringozzi* pasta with truffle sauce or tortellini with cream of nettle in either of two lovely garden terraces or in the main building, a 16th-century palazzo, frescoed with trompe l'oeils. (Tel: 0743-22-18-31; closed Mondays and the second half of January.) Try the *pan pepato,* a delicious spice cake, if it's available. Another restaurant loaded with charm is **Il Panciolle**, which recently relocated to new quarters in the heart of the medieval section at largo Muzio Clemente 4, just off via Fontesecche, which runs perpendicular to corso Mazzini. Fragrant lime trees embrace a small piazza where tables are set up during the summer. The house specialties include superb grilled lamb chops. Reservations are suggested, since this seems to be a favorite haunt for performers (Tel: 0743-455-98). There are also seven attractive rooms with bath. Another fine restaurant, in a more secluded spot, is the formal **Taverna il Tartufo**, located at the foot of corso Garibaldi at the city's exit point. (Tartufo is a healthy walk from Sabatini; Tel: 0743-402-36; closed Wednesdays and July 15 to August 5.) Specialties to try here are the game and truffle dishes. During the summer ask for a room in the basement, where it's cool.

A short drive or a 20-minute walk from the piazza Garibaldi is the basilica of **San Salvatore**, a remarkable fourth-century church built by Oriental monks from a Roman temple and modified in the ninth century. Its naked quality reflects the simple character of early Christian devotion and stands in contrast to its younger Spoleto counterparts, the 13th-century San Domenico (near piazza Collicola) and the 12th-century San Gregorio Maggiore at piazza Garibaldi, both of which are worth a visit.

Back in the center of town, off via Brignone, is the petite 12th-century church of **Sant'Ansano,** built into the remains of a Roman temple. Be sure to see the Romanesque frescoes in the crypt beneath the church. Alongside is the **Arco di Druso,** built in A.D. 23 by the Roman Senate in honor of Tiberius's son Drusus, who had repelled the barbarians.

The lively piazza del Mercato, once a Roman forum, is now the town's marketplace. Cafés and food shops line the square, where you can sit and watch the daily dramas unfold and perhaps buy a sandwich from the *porchetta* seller, whose spit-roasted pig adorns his countertop in a slightly indecent manner. From the piazza, a series of galloping steps, the via del Mercato, runs down to the piazza Collicola, where you will find parking and a few modest hotels, including the **Charleston,** at number 10.

At the end of piazza del Mercato, the via del Municipio leads to the piazza del Municipio, beneath which lie the remains of the home of Vespasian's mother. Enter the town hall, where the small **Pinacoteca** occupies the first floor. The unlabeled collection has a few well-regarded works: frescoes by Lo Spagna, a native son, and an eerie Mary Magdalene by Guercino. You must ask the museum attendant to admit you to the Vespasian home beneath. A short stroll from here is the brooding **Rocca,** a six-towered fort constructed in the 14th century by Gattapone on orders from the papal legate, Albornoz. The Rocca, which protected Totila (king of the Ostrogoths), also served as residence to papal governors and even to Lucrezia Borgia, whose father, Pope Alexander VI, appointed her governor of Spoleto in 1498. Plans are in progress for turning this into a historical museum covering the history of medieval and Lombard Spoleto. The garden path encircling the fort offers great views.

To the south of the Rocca is the overwhelming **ponte delle Torri** (Bridge of the Towers), spanning the ravine through which the river Tessino flows. The dramatic 14th-century bridge, built on the foundation of a Roman aqueduct that still carries water from the hills of Monteluco, has ten soaring arches and was one of Gattapone's greatest engineering feats. The bridge dwarfs the tiny white **Hotel Gattapone** —two stone structures, one for the restaurant, the other for lodging (13 rooms), that spill down the precipice. This gem has gleaming wood-paneled walls and elegantly furnished rooms; it overlooks rich green mountains studded with evergreens, oaks, and ilex, and dappled by wild sweet peas.

From piazza Campello (at the foot of the Rocca) head toward via Saffi and then turn right on via dell'Arringo, a lyric flow of steps named after the *Arringo,* the general assembly of men who decided the politics of the day. One of the prettiest walks in town, it brims with orchestras and chamber groups during festival time. The walk passes the little 11th-century church of **Sant'Eufemia** on the left, a fine example of Lombard architecture, which contains a seating gallery for women (*matronei*) and lovely Cosmatesque sculpture decorations. And on the right is the **Museo Civico**, located in a Renaissance palace, with a handsome collection of Romanesque and medieval sculpture. Note the third-century B.C. public notice forbidding the cutting of timber in a sacred grove in Monteluco.

The via dell'Arringo's wide fan of steps opens onto the piazza del Duomo, where the **Duomo** stands, adorned only by its great rose windows, which circle round the lovely fresco on the tympanum and the intricate carvings surrounding the main door. The Duomo was sacked by Frederick Barbarossa in 1155. Rebuilt and consecrated by Pope Innocent III some 40 years later, the church contains splendid frescoes by Pinturicchio and Annibale Carracci. But the major attraction is the peerless fresco cycle *Life of the Virgin* by Fra Filippo Lippi, the monk who wore his habit rather loosely and whose sweet Madonnas were inspired by his lover, a nun with whom he had two children. His son, Filippino Lippi, designed his tomb, which you can see here, and the Medici family paid for it. Actually, it was Lorenzo de' Medici who helped the monk out of some hot water during one of his amorous escapades and who landed him the commission to paint the frescoes. Also worth noting are the fine Cosmati pavement and the Santissima Icone (Madonna) brought to Spoleto from Constantinople.

Next to the baptistery is the 17th-century **Teatro Caio Melisso**, where the major performances of the festival occur and where Rossini once performed. During intermission you may wish to slip out for a quick bite, and the **Tric-Trac** restaurant right on via Duomo serves excellent pastas and will accommodate your schedule.

The **Teatro Nuovo**, near piazza San Domenico, is also the site of many performances during the festival and in September, when the Festival of Experimental Opera takes place here.

Spoleto, as you may have surmised, is a real crowd-pleaser during the festival, and it's the crowds that send people scouring in search of lodging outside the city. One splendid place that opened recently is the intimate **Barbarossa Hotel**, a classy farmhouse beautifully restored, with nine rooms and welcome spacious, shady grounds. It's a short drive from town.

Monteluco

Long held in reverence by the Umbrians and later the Romans, the sacred hills of Monteluco were also home to Saint Francis and Saint Bernardino of Siena. An excursion to Monteluco, just 8 km (5 miles) southeast of Spoleto on route 2, is a beautiful drive and takes you to the ancient church of **San Pietro**, built on the site of an old necropolis encircled by cypress trees. The carvings of beasts and imaginary creatures on the Romanesque façade are a stony guidebook to the medieval mind of faith and superstitions. Farther up the hill is the convent of **San Francesco**, a honeycomb of cells nestled beneath the sanctuary that Saint Benedict built. Today, Capuchin brothers use the hermitage, just as the saints and generations of brothers have before them.

South of Spoleto and Monteluco, off route 3 and a little to the southeast of Terni, is the **Cascata delle Marmore** (Marble Cascade). Built by the Romans, who diverted the waters of the Velino river to drain the Rieti marshes, the cascade drops about 500 feet in three successive waves over marble-lined clefts. A breathtaking view can be had of them, but only on weekends. During the week the falls are used to drive powerful hydroelectric turbines. The best view is from the belvedere in the village of Marmore. A short side trip from Terni northwest on route 3 *bis* will bring you to the fascinating **Carsulae**, the pure Roman town where you can walk unimpeded by any medieval structure among ruins of temples, baths, theaters, and arches.

Another pretty drive from Terni, this one northeast along route 209, takes you to **Ferentillo**, where you can see the mummies in the crypt of San Stefano, located in Precetto, the oldest section of town. A combination of soil and air naturally embalmed these poor souls. Just beyond Ferentillo and also worth a visit is the abbey of **San Pietro in Valle**, founded in the eighth century by Duke Faroald II of Spoleto. Along the way there is an excellent trattoria, the inexpensive **Rossi**, located in Casteldilago, near Arrone, in the magnificent Valnerina valley. Here is true home cooking, starring homemade pastas and the freshest local ingredients in a comfortable setting (Tel: 0744-781-05; closed Fridays).

Since you're in truffle paradise, you may want to visit the **Urbino factory** in Scheggino, a little way beyond Ferentillo on route 209. The largest producer of truffle paste in the world, the factory gathers truffles, both black and white, from every country and cleans and grades them before either selling them fresh or turning them into paste or some other form. The early winter months are the factory's busiest, but they'll be happy to show you around at other times; however, you must write or call first for an appointment (Tel: 0743-611-33).

TODI

Route 79 *bis* runs deep through the green rolling countryside and connects two of Umbria's most attractive cities, Orvieto and Todi. The steep streets of Todi, whose history is revealed in its three sets of walls—Etruscan, Roman, and medieval—make the city a study in the vertical. The gods had a hand in creating Todi: According to legend, an eagle swept over the plains and snatched the blueprints for the city and dropped them at the top of the hill. The superstitious Umbrians read this as an omen and re-sited their city at the summit, unwittingly making it an attraction for the Etruscans (400 B.C.)—who never could resist a hilltop village. When the Romans conquered Tutere (the Etruscan name), they changed the name to Tuder and shaped the town into a ferocious military power, endowing it with amphitheaters, forums, and many temples, some of whose fragments survive to this day. Todi contains one of the loveliest squares in Italy, the **piazza del Popolo**. Once a Roman forum, the piazza is surrounded by buildings whose stern walls summon up the vigorous civic and commercial life of the city: the **Palazzo del Capitano** (which houses a small museum that has been closed for restoration for some time but is scheduled to reopen soon), linked with the 13th-century Lombard **Palazzo del Popolo** (one of the oldest public buildings in Italy), and the **Palazzo dei Priori**, former seat of the *podestà* (mayor), which bears a sprawling bronze eagle on its façade. It's imperative to sit at one of the outdoor cafés as you take in the severe beauty of this architectural ensemble. The piazza Garibaldi, which adjoins the piazza del Popolo, offers some of the best views of the valley, as well as parking.

The 12th-century **Duomo**, standing at the end of the square where the temple to Apollo once stood, almost in defiance of the civic buildings, contains some fine Renaissance art and 16th-century inlaid stalls. Because of its strategically superior site and the clever ministrations of its bishop, Todi eluded the barbarian Totila—as it did Frederick II years later. The church of **San Fortunato**, at piazza della Repubblica, commemorates this period. Within is a crypt containing the tomb of Jacopone da Todi; a lawyer with a taste for luxury and excess, he became a Franciscan monk after the death of his wife—whom he discovered had been wearing a hair shirt for years under her fine clothing. He was a staunch critic of Pope Boniface VIII (his Frati Minori were instrumental in the final persecution of the pope) and an accomplished poet, composing biting *laude* (prayer ballads, and Italy's first protest songs) that exposed papal corruption. His devotional lauds, especially the *Stabat Mater Dolorosa* and the *Stabat Mater Speciosa,* are particularly beautiful and are performed here during Holy Week. Also within is the impressive fresco of the *Madonna and Two Angels* by Masolino da Panicale and a fine wood choir in the apse by Antonio Maffei of Gubbio. Just below the church, at via Ciuffeli 33, you'll find the attractive bar **Antartico**, where you can have a cheap light meal. The street also has several fine antiques/restorer shops.

As a center of woodworking and antiques, Todi hosts the national antiques fair each spring (April–May) and a national crafts fair in August and September. And during the first ten days of September, Todi also dons its cultural cap to host opera, ballet, and theater during its **Festival di Todi**. There are two good restaurants in town: the inexpensive **Jacopone da Todi** at piazza Jacopone 3 (Tel: 075-88-23-66; closed Mondays and July 15–30), which serves an excellent *pasticcio* (tubular pasta filled with cheese and spinach), and the very special (but moderately priced) **Umbria** at via San Bonaventura 13 (Tel: 075-88-27-37; closed Tuesdays). Try the Umbria's *spaghetti alla boscaiola,* with wild asparagus, and two local wines, Grechetto and Ciliegiolo. In good weather, eat outdoors on the terrace, which overlooks miles of spectacular landscape.

There are a few modest hotels in Todi; the more luxurious choices are a few miles outside of town. A rocky road leads to the **San Valentino Hotel**, south of town. Much money went into restoring this 13th-century monastery, nestled on a wooded hillside in the town of Fiore (and open year-round). Persian carpets and gleaming wood, plus gardens, swimming pool, and tennis courts, make for a pampered stay. Nearby, in Terminillo, there are respectable ski slopes. Another good choice, less than a mile west of town on the road to Orvieto, is the converted convent **Hotel Bramante**, with cozy rooms, modern facilities, medieval charm, and moderate prices. The hotel sits opposite the **Tempio della Consolazione**, a graceful Renaissance church with such pure lines that it is thought to have been designed by Bramante. Nearby is the quaint **Trattoria Cibocchi**, at ponte Martino 67, a favorite "no frills" spot for locals. Reached by a winding, bumpy dirt road running perpendicular to the main road that skirts the church, the restaurant abounds in local color. Large windows frame rolling hills and vineyards, and baskets of thick, homemade bread grace the tables. The menu changes daily and the food is very satisfying. Try the rabbit stewed in wine and olives, or the roasted fowl. Closed Fridays; Tel: (075) 88-29-49.

There's a good bed-and-breakfast not too far, a little north of Todi in Montecastello di Vibio. **Fattoria di Vibio** is made up of side-by-side stone houses that its owners, two Roman brothers, have imaginatively restored. There are ten double rooms altogether, done up with wrought-iron beds, terra-cotta floors, and local handicrafts. You can swim, hike, play tennis, or ride horseback here—or just laze poolside and sip Vin Santo on the panoramic terrace. There's a two-day minimum, and weekly rentals are available from mid-June to mid-September.

The drive from Todi to Orvieto via either route 79 *bis* (very scenic) or route 448 (scenic), passes through some transcendent terrain, the mood of which no doubt inspired the chef/owner of **Vissani**, hailed as one of the five best restaurants in Italy. Located in the town of Baschi, near Lago di Corbara, it is housed (actually it's a small room) within the larger, bustling **Il Padrino** (Vissani's father)—where you can enjoy excellent Umbrian food at moderate prices. The younger Vissani's creations, among them shrimp ravioli in orange oil, are cosmic, as are his prices; it's best to order the prix fixe dinner (six courses). The service is impeccable if surreal—but then, this is Italy. Depending on your mood, you will eat very well at either place. Reservations imperative. Tel: (0744) 95-02-06 for Il Padrino; (0744) 95-03-96 for Vissani; both closed Wednesdays.

ORVIETO

Talk about being placed on a pedestal! A giant upthrust of reddish tufa rock, a jagged remnant of volcanic days, lifts Orvieto some 900 feet above the wide valley of the river Paglia. Approached by route 71 from Lago di Bolsena to the southwest, the city appears to be a mirage, especially during the sizzling Umbrian summer when the air seems to wave like moiré fabric.

Although its cathedral and its wine take top billing, Orvieto's history stretches back to the Etruscans, whose sharp eye for defensive positions made this an important stronghold of their confederation in the sixth century B.C. Then known as Volsinii, this thriving pottery town developed a prosperous economy, trading widely with Greece, and established a powerful agricultural monopoly. The Romans sacked it in the third century B.C. and forced the inhabitants to build a new city, Volsinii Novi (modern Bolsena). Later the *urbs vetus,* or old city—from which Orvieto's name derives—was rebuilt. Numerous artifacts taken from Etruscan tombs are on view at the **Museo Archeologico Faina** in the Palazzo Faina across from the cathedral.

The Roman period was followed by the familiar bands of medieval marauders—Goths, Byzantines, and Lombards—the last of whom set up a duchy here in the sixth century A.D. During the Guelph–Ghibelline battles, the Monaldeschi and Fillipeschi families, whom Dante compared to the Montagues and Capulets, scandalized the city and their neighbors. The plague further stressed the city and made it easy prey for the takeover in 1354, when the papal legate, Cardinal Albornoz, annexed it to the Papal States.

Orvieto is quite flat up top, where it is laced with narrow streets sporting stately 13th-century palaces and shops that sell traditional majolica ware. Overwhelming the piazzale Cahen at the eastern edge of the city is the **Rocca Fortress**, built in 1364 by Cardinal Albornoz as a way of keeping the papal embers burning while the pope lived in Avignon. Nearby are the remains of an Etruscan temple and the **Well of San Patrizio**, designed by Antonio da Sangallo in 1530 and commissioned by Pope Clement VII, who, having recently fled Rome after Charles V sacked the city, wished to prepare the town should it be placed under siege. Two spiral staircases, which never intersect, descend into the well.

The **Duomo**, which stands in the spacious piazza Duomo directly across from the tourist office, is the town's centerpiece. With its striped sides and bejeweled façade, the cathedral is a masterpiece of exuberant details and dominates the entire city. Gothic architecture, introduced into Italy by the Cistercians, never really captivated the Italians (their version is always with a small "g"). Uncomfortable with Gothic proportions, which they considered inimical to the widely spaced Roman plan they loved, the Italians did what they were best at: They *decorated* the cathedral in Gothic style but never wholly embraced the Gothic form.

The Miracle of Bolsena gave birth to Orvieto's cathedral. A skeptical priest, Peter of Prague, doubted the theory of transubstantiation (a hotly debated issue in the Church at the time, when heresies were cropping up regularly), which holds that during the consecration of the host, the bread is transformed into the body and blood of Christ. Once while he was celebrating mass, his misgivings were relieved when the host spouted droplets of blood on the altar cloth. When Pope Urban IV, who was in Orvieto to escape the heat of Rome, heard about it, he declared an official feast day, Corpus Christi, and enlisted Thomas Aquinas—who was lecturing in theology at the convent of San Domenico—to write the sacred Office of the day. The plan for the cathedral took some 30 years to flesh out; in 1290 Pope Nicholas IV laid the cornerstone. Since 1264 the feast has been celebrated here every summer (on the ninth Sunday after Easter) with a lavish festival, during which buildings are draped, citizens don medieval costumes, and the sacred altar cloth, housed in an elaborate reliquary shaped like a little Duomo, is paraded through the streets.

The cathedral's construction, spanning three centuries, was begun in the Romanesque style by Arnolfo di Cambio; it took on a Gothic appearance when the Sienese architect Lorenzo Maitani began work in 1309. The façade, which was finally completed in the 17th century, is a symphony of color, harmony, and grace, lifted to the heavens by soaring pinnacles that divide the surface into a three-part scheme. The mosaics are spectacular at sunset, when the celebrated bas-reliefs by Maitano on the lower pilasters—telling the story of the Last Judgment—are highlighted. Orcagna designed the great rose window—gilding the "Golden Lily of Cathedrals," as the church is called. The modern hand of the Sicilian sculptor Emilio Greco (1964) created the richly ornamented bronze doors, whose themes of charity and mercy blend harmoniously into the overall design of the façade. The austere striped interior contains many marvels: the marble *Pietà* of Ippolito Scalza, in the north transept, against the nave pillar; a monumental organ with 5,585 pipes; and the gilt-and-enamel reliquary by the Sienese Ugolino di Vieri in the chapel of the Corporale, just left of the altar (the reliquary holds the famous stained linen cloth of the Bolsena miracle). Also within the chapel are the restored frescoes by Ugolino di Prete Ilario, depicting the miracle of Bolsena, and the stunning 14th-century *Madonna dei Raccomandati* by Lippo Memmi, a study in grace and mystery.

But the real drawing card over the centuries has been the incomparable frescoes of Fra Angelico, Benozzo Gozzoli, and especially Luca Signorelli in the cathedral's **Chapel of the Madonna of San Brizio**, to the right of the altar. Begun by Fra Angelico and Gozzoli around 1447, they were completed some 40 years later by Signorelli, who was responsible for the walls and who laced the works with a bit of personal history, inserting himself in the *Antichrist* fresco (he's the blond) and portraying his unfaithful mistress as the prostitute being carted off by the devil in the *Inferno* fresco. The human modeling in these frescoes is so superlative that Michelangelo came here to study them, as did Augustus John several hundred years later. One special attraction of the cathedral is the newfound and recently restored fresco of the Madonna and Child by Gentile da Fabriano. Stunningly transparent, this fresco, done in 1425, was recently discovered under another fresco of minor importance during some restoration work.

South of the cathedral is the severe-looking Palazzo Soliano dei Papi, which sheltered 32 popes in its time. Today it houses the **Museo dell'Opera del Duomo** and contains a fine collection of regional art.

Near the cathedral, off the Palazzo Faina on via Maitani, is the small first-class **Hotel Maitani**. Graciously appointed and skillfully managed, it offers a good view of the cathedral and the rooftops of Orvieto from its terrace. A few doors down from the Maitani, at number 10, a simple but reliably good meal can be had at **Trattoria Etrusca**. In a setting of white-washed walls and tile floors, you can dine on house specialties such as *coniglio all'etrusca* (rabbit in green sauce) and *umbrichelli al tartufo bianco* (pasta in a white truffle sauce). The tourist menu is a good value, and the restaurant occasionally has spontaneous wine tastings. (Tel: 0763-440-16; closed Mondays and January.) And at number 1, the **Cantina Barberani** wine bar is a good place to sample the local vintage. To the north of the cathedral, in the piazza, is the modern but tiny **Hotel Virgilio**, set in an ancient building (a good bargain). There is excellent shopping on via Duomo, the main street. At number 78 **Ristorante Maurizio** serves delicious *agnolotti* (pasta dumplings) stuffed with mushrooms (closed Tuesdays and January; Tel: 0763-432-12). You can pick up delicate handmade Orvietan lace at **Maria Luigia Moretti**, at number 55. Follow via Duomo to the corso Cavour. Take a leisurely stroll down Cavour past the attractive shops and medieval homes to the **Montanucci Bar** at number 21, which has a little garden in the back and serves *frullato,* a rich concoction of mixed fresh fruits blended to a creamy froth, sometimes spiked with vodka.

One of the charms of Umbria is its thriving artisan workshops. Perpendicular to the corso Cavour is the quaint artisan street of Bottega Michelangeli, named after the local wood sculptor whose works are abundantly featured in the shops. For a whimsical collection of handmade wooden puppets and dolls, stop at number 3. But a real live Geppetto is **Giuseppe Maccherini**, on via Ripa Serancia, whose charmingly cluttered workshop is filled with the most endearing Pinocchios.

At the western end of corso Cavour is piazza della Repubblica, where the Roman forum once stood; it is still the city's nerve center. On one side of the square is the 13th-century Palazzo Comunale, built over the remains of a sixth-century church. To the east is the lovely 11th-century church of **Sant'Andrea**, built over the remains of a Roman temple. It was here that Innocent III announced the Fourth Crusade and that Pope Martin IV was crowned in 1281 in the presence of Charles of Anjou. The sacristan will admit you to the Etruscan and Roman remains below.

Radiating out from the piazza is via Garibaldi, where the **Hotel Aquila Bianca** is located. This restored Renaissance palazzo, with coffered and painted ceilings, possesses an understated beauty. It is first-class but reasonably priced and well located. The quietest rooms face the courtyard. A short distance away, on via Cipriano Manente 16, perpendicular to via Garibaldi, is **Trattoria La Palomba**. This hilltop café has been catering to Orvietans for years, who congregate every afternoon and evening for *ombrichelle tartufate,* thick spaghetti with black truffle sauce and juicy grilled sausage. Moderately priced, La Palomba is closed Wednesdays. (Tel: 0763-433-95).

The medieval quarter stands at the western edge of the piazza della Repubblica and is dotted with old ocher churches and tiny homes clinging tenaciously to the hills. Bright geraniums and lilting sounds of families gathered for lunch add a gentle touch to a stroll. Via Ripa Serancia snakes through here and ends at the **Grotte del Funaro**, number 41, a cavernous but cozy restaurant located in a restored grotto—several rooms of old caves buried deep within volcanic rock. It is popular for its spicy sausage, beautifully grilled meats, and rich antipasti (Tel: 0763-432-76; closed Mondays). The piano bar (which opens at 10:00 P.M.) nicely prolongs an evening and offers an alternative to the only other form of nightlife, the *passeggiata* (promenade), which takes place in front of the cathedral. Things liven up a bit the first two weeks in August during the Festa Musica Pro Mundo Uno, featuring many musical events. (For information, see the section on Assisi's festivals.) At the end of via Malabranca is the 12th-century church of **San Giovenale**. Dedicated to Saints Giovenale and Savino, who first brought Christianity to Orvieto, it contains some faded but interesting frescoes by local artists and is currently being restored.

To capture the heart of the Orvietans, go to the **piazza del**

Popolo, which is wonderfully alive, especially during market days on Thursdays and Saturdays. The Palazzo del Popolo, an ecclesiastical palace right on the piazza, dating from Hadrian IV's pontificate (1157), faces the Bracci family palazzo, which is now the **Grand Hotel Reale**. The hotel *is* grand, and romantic, and a little worn—though there's ongoing renovation. For those who are willing to sacrifice a little convenience for the sake of charm and history, this moderately priced hotel offers good value.

Orvieto was a holy place for the Etruscans, and the **Croce del Tufo necropolis** (dating from the eighth to the third century B.C.), located at the foot of the city, offers an excursion into the world of the dead.

Just 5 km (3 miles) south of Orvieto is a former Christian abbey, today the incomparable **Hotel La Badia**. The eighth-century Benedictine abbey of Saints Severo and Martirio was for centuries a sanctuary for popes, cardinals, and nobles. Everything from the graceful courtyards to the splendid Romanesque architecture with flowing arches and elegant rooms (just 24, including a few suites) is designed to induce peace and comfort. The hotel's restaurant is also superb, and for the more active there are a small pool and tennis courts.

Another country haven is the small but engaging **Villa Ciconia**, at via dei Trigli 69, set in its own park about 3 km (2 miles) from strada Statale 71. A 16th-century farmhouse owned by the Petrangeli family, with coffered ceilings, murals, and a host of comfort zones, the hotel has nine tastefully furnished rooms with canopy beds and a fine restaurant specializing in Umbrian fare, using ingredients from the family's farm.

GUBBIO

Just over a stretch of the Apennines, about 40 km (25 miles) northeast of Perugia on the way to the Marches and Urbino via scenic route 298, stands Gubbio—hard and gray. You can't imagine a more quintessentially medieval town, so well preserved is it, probably because it's remote and can be reached only by car or bus (the nearest train station is at Fossato di Vico, 16 km/10 miles away—there is bus service from Fossato to Gubbio). Gubbio is pure escapism, a medieval Disneyland where you can indulge your taste for the mysterious, mystical, and earthy at the same time. The city began as an Umbrian town during the sixth and fifth centuries B.C., then became an ally of Rome. In the early years of the Roman Empire its position made it an important communications link between Rome and Ravenna, and it prospered greatly. The sprawling, well-preserved 2,000-year-old **Teatro Romano** that lies just outside the town walls recalls this period and is about a five-minute walk from the piazza Quaranta Martiri, named after 40 citizens shot by the Nazis in 1944, an entry point for cars and buses and a good place to park. The theater, with its solitary arches and columns, and set apart from the city like an exiled king, makes a comeback each year from mid-July to August, when classical plays are performed here (mostly in Italian). The frescoes of the city's celebrated painter, Ottaviano Nelli, the most important Umbrian representative of the 15th-century Gothic style, can be seen in the church of **San Francesco**, on the piazza. On the other side of the piazza, the weavers' loggia, the *tiratoio,* where 14th-century weavers stretched their textiles to dry, shelters the teeming fruit and vegetable stands of today's farmers.

Gothic invasions pushed the city up the treeless slopes of Monte Ingino, an event duly impressed upon you as you climb uphill to reach the major attractions. In 413 Gubbio was the seat of a bishopric, and in the 10th and 11th centuries it developed into a powerful free commune before being drawn into the Montefeltro Duchy of Urbino in 1384. The patron saint, Ubaldo, is credited with saving the city by convincing Frederick Barbarossa to release it from allegiance to the Holy Roman Empire. On May 15, the **Race of the Ceri** turns this "city of silence" into a riotous medieval pageant in honor of Saint Ubaldo's victory. During this eruption, it is easy to imagine the Gubbian knights marching off to join the First Crusade. Three neighborhood teams bearing towering *ceri*—half-ton wooden poles, each topped with the figurine of a saint—race up the hill to the saint's shrine in the **basilica**, which displays his withered remains in a glass-domed case. You can turn modern for a moment amidst this fanfare and take the pleasant funicular, which glides over colorful rooftops to reveal a spectacular tapestry of hills and valleys, up to the Basilica. No sooner does this frenzy subside than another turns up on the last Sunday in May: the spirited **Palio della Balestra** (Crossbow Competition). Pitted against their arch-rival, Sansepolcro, Gubbio's archers evoke centuries of passionate challenges, though good-naturedly.

From the central piazza you can see the **Palazzo dei Consoli,** grand dame of civic pride, which dominates the city from its lofty position on the piazza della Signoria, and which is strewn at times with stark modern sculptures that seem the only tie to the modern world. Built by Gattapone between 1332 and 1346, this elegantly proportioned palazzo contains the grand Salone dell'Arenga (top floor, and also site of the Communal Art Gallery), where the town's consuls met to plan the city's affairs. Their tenure was from two to six months, during which they were forbidden to have contact with the outside world, thus preventing influence-peddling. On the first floor is the **Civic Museum**, which contains the fascinating 2,000-year-old Eugubine bronze tablets, the Rosetta Stones of Umbrian culture. Written in Etruscan and Latin characters, they are sketchy clues to the language and sacred rites of this holy city, which was once governed by a council of priests. Also worth inspecting are the collection of Roman coins and sarcophagi; the sweet, faded frescoes of Nelli and Palmerucci; and the beautiful *Madonna of the Pomegranate,* attributed to Pier Francesco Fiorentino.

Several of the best hotels and restaurants in Gubbio are grouped near the Palazzo: the homey, ribbed-vaulted **Taverna del Lupo**, via Ansidei 21 (closed Mondays and January; Tel: 075-927-43-68; Fax: 075-927-12-69), which serves such typical Egubino fare as *imbrecciata* (a rich vegetable soup that is a winter specialty) and an excellent *cappelletti al tartufo;* and the gracious **Alla Fornace di Mastro Giorgio**, via Mastro Giorgio 2, which is noted for its exceptional truffle-laced dishes, soothing Baroque music, and elegant 14th-century quarters (Tel: 075-927-57-40; closed Sunday evenings, Mondays, and February; expensive). In fact, truffles get their just respect during Gubbio's lively Fiera del Tartufo (Truffle Fair) each year, which takes place on different dates during October and November. A good sampling of truffle products can be found at **Ghiottonerie**, right next door to Alla Fornace, and also at **Prodotti Tipici Gastronomici**, via dei Consoli 99, which stocks a trove of truffled products, including a delectable white truffle liqueur.

Close by, near the upper part of the town, is the old Palazzo Raffaelli, now the **Bosone Hotel**, perhaps the town's best hotel. Dante was a frequent visitor of the Raffaelli family, and his spirit seems to linger still. A new addition is the charming restaurant in the rear, which has the most delightfully perched terrace bursting with pots of fragrant yellow ginestra and serves some tempting updated Umbrian dishes. In addition to à la carte, there are two complete menus, one for L25,000 and the other for L40,000, that are real bargains.

There's also the simple but comfortable **Gattapone Hotel**, via Ansidei 6, with 13 rooms and a small garden.

Some visitors may find Gubbio slightly claustrophobic for spending the night, and luckily there's a new hotel no more than a mile or two outside of town. The **Park Hotel Ai Cappuccini** occupies a 17th-century Franciscan monastery set in a spacious park on via Tifernate. The sober, almost stark exterior belies the lavish interior, which sports every modern convenience, including a grand swimming pool, full fitness center, video room, many conference rooms, and more. Although tastefully decorated with expensive furnishings, there's a feeling of sterility—nothing evocative of conventual comfort. Rather, the hotel seems more oriented to the business class. And given its vastness, it definitely needs the softening touch of a full clientele. Moderate to expensive, depending on who's footing the bill—you or your company.

Medieval buffs hankering for a crossbow should go to the **Bottega del Artigiano di Antonio Bei** at via Borghetto Nuovo 9. (Crossbows penetrated with such force that in 1139 the Lateran Council voted to prohibit their use; the attempt was unsuccessful.) Bibliophiles will find a wide selection of books and old maps at **Gabriel,** via dei Consoli 24.

At the top of town the Palazzo Ducale and the Duomo face each other. The **Palazzo Ducale** is built on the remains of an older building where Charlemagne and Frederick II had stayed. Notable for its lovely Renaissance courtyard, a subtle blend of flowing arches and Corinthian columns, it was redone for Federico da Montefeltro, Duke of Urbino, who seized Gubbio during its waning days of independence. Across the small piazza is the **Duomo,** a 13th-century church with a graceful façade constructed of soothing lavender-gray brick. The interior is serenely beautiful, with an elegant geometry created by rows of Gothic arches, and lovely frescoes by Nucci, Doni, Gherardi, and Viti, as well as stunning 12th-century stained-glass windows.

The snug alleys and streets yield a host of surprises, like small gardens and homes with the strange *porte dei morti* (death doors). Tall and narrow, placed roughly four feet above street level, often with stairs leading to them, these doors, it was thought, were used as passageways for coffins. But another, less colorful explanation establishes them as safety entrances used during barbarian raids.

The most picturesque streets within the medieval center are the via dei Galeotti, via Piccardi, and via Baldassini, where, at number 28, the **Ceramiche Casagrande Giorgio** features the impressive ceramics for which the city is famous—particularly the black *bucchero* and lusterware. Unfortunately, the secrets of the ruby-red lusterware perished with the master ceramist Maestro Giorgio when he died. There are many ceramic and antiques shops along here, as well as a great little inexpensive trattoria, the **Rosticceria Gianna**, at number 26, perfect for grilled meats and true *cucina casalinga*. Another good shopping street is the via dei Consoli, behind the Palazzo dei Consoli.

Umbria is a beehive of artisans, who craft everything from hand-loomed tablecloths to gaily colored pottery and fine lace. **Gualdo Tadino**, southeast of Gubbio on route 3, is known for its rich polychrome and metallic pottery. The International Pottery Exhibition and Competition is held here every July and August.

A good excursion, northeast about 50 km (30 miles) via the Sassoferrato road, is to the fascinating **Frasassi Caves**, an extensive network of underground caves bristling with stalagmites, stalactites, and other incredible forms.

The emerald countryside surrounding Gubbio is composed of vast hills and valleys punctuated by the odd monastery or two and pleasant small villages. For a superlatively scenic road through this area, look for route 298, connecting Gubbio with Perugia. Also along here, at Mengara, you will find a good Agriturismo hotel/restaurant, the **Oasi Verde**, aptly named since it sits on lovely green grounds within a working farm. This is "no-frills" lodging, with clean, simple rooms (all with bath) and an occasional flourish in the public spaces. But the price is right, and it makes a good choice for families. And the location can't be beat.

THE MARCHES

Near Gubbio, route 3 heads north toward Urbino, which lies on the eastern edge of the Apennines in the area known as the Marches. The region, which abuts Umbria on the west, extends along the Adriatic side of the Apennines from Pesaro down to San Benedetto del Tronto; it is marked by a series of very high slopes paralleling the coast that gradually soften as they approach the sea. The coast is strewn with overcrowded, undistinguished seaside resorts, although there are some lovely hillside towns above that are worth exploring. The Gauls and Piceni, who had settled here, were incorporated early into the Roman hegemony, around the third century B.C. Some impressive Roman works remain, such as the **Arco d'Augusto** in Fano and the **Arco di Traiano** in Ancona, capital of the region. During the Middle Ages the

Lombards ruled the southern part; the northern area fell under the Byzantine exarchate of Ravenna. Later the entire region was handed to the pope as a gift from the Franks. The 12th and 13th centuries were followed by political and cultural activities of the powerful signorial families, including the Malatestas of Rimini and the Montefeltros of Urbino. The area's economy is largely agricultural. Ancona, the principal port, is a jumping-off point to Greece and Yugoslavia, and shows Venetian influence.

Food in the Marches

Regional cooking in the Marches reflects the humble tastes of its fishermen and shepherds. Along the coast from Pesaro to San Benedetto, the simplest trattorias serve *brodetto,* a hearty Italian bouillabaisse. Oysters and *bombi* (large sea snails) are treats of the area, and are served with a squirt of lemon at many seaside stands. *Cannelli* (razor clams) often appear as appetizers or on top of pasta along with the delectable *saraghine allo scottadino,* small fish that are grilled and eaten with the hands.

Olives feature richly in the cuisine of Ascoli Piceno, not only in the form of top-quality olive oil but also in the eccentric dish called *olive ascolane,* fried stuffed giant olives. *Maccheroncini di campofilone,* delicate egg noodles that absorb sauce well, and *vincisgrassi,* a sinfully rich lasagne, should more than satisfy your craving for something farinaceous. Prized lamb and pork dishes are simply prepared, usually grilled, and the delicate veal is especially good as *olivette,* rolled paupiettes in a seasoned wine sauce. For snacking, the soft, spreadable salami of Visso, called *ciauscolo,* is divine; and the pecorino, both fresh and aged, and caciotta cheeses are superb.

For gastronomic elegance, you can't beat the white winter truffle of the Metauro valley. The sprawling vineyards produce super red and white wines. The best-known white DOC is Verdicchio. Less well known but equally prized are the fruit-scented white wines Bianco dei Colli Maceratesi and Bianchello del Metauro, and the rich, full-bodied reds Rosso Conero and Rosso Piceno.

URBINO

The star of the region is Urbino, where, nestled between two hills, a court of humanistic splendor took shape toward the

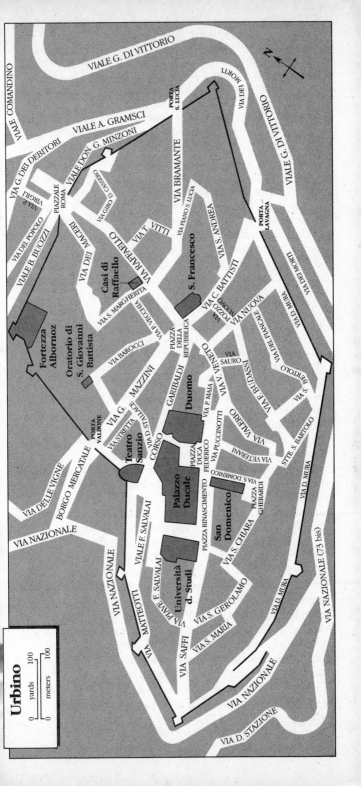

Urbino

0 yards 100
0 meters 100

VIALE G. DI VITTORIO

VIALE COMANDINO

VIALE A. GRAMSCI

VIALE DON G. MINZONI

VIA G. DEI DEBITORI

VIA P. VIRGILI

VIALE B. BUOZZI

VIA DEL POPOLO

PIAZZALE ROMA

VIA GIRO D. CASSERO

VIA DEI MACERI

VIA T. VITTI

VIA RAFFAELLO

Casa di Raffaello

VIA S. MARGHERITA

VIA P. VECCHIA

Fortezza Albornoz

Oratorio di S. Giovanni Battista

VIA BAROCCI

VIA G. MAZZINI

PORTA VALBONE

VIA STRETTA

VIA D. STALLACCE

Teatro Sanzio

CORSO GARIBALDI

BORGO MERCATALE

VIA DELLE VIGNE

VIA NAZIONALE

VIALE F. SALVALAI

VIA PAVE F. SALVALAI

Università d. Studi

VIA MATTEOTTI

VIA SAFFI

VIA S. GEROLAMO

VIA S. MARIA

PIAZZA RINASCIMENTO

Palazzo Ducale

PIAZZA DUCA FEDERICO

Duomo

PIAZZA DELLA REPUBBLICA

S. Francesco

PORTA S. LUCIA

VIA BRAMANTE

VIA PIANO S. LUCIA

VIA S. ANDREA

VIA C. BATTISTI

VIA POZZO NUOVO

VIA NUOVA

VIA DEI MORTI

PORTA LAVAGNA

VIALE G. DI VITTORIO

ORATORIO

VIA D. MURA

VIA DEL BERTOLO

VIA DEL PANORAMICA

VIA SAURO

VIA VENETO

VIA P. MAIA

VIA PUCCINOTTI

VIA VETERANI

VIA VALERIO

VIA E. BUOSSI

STTE S. BARTOLO

VIA S. BARTOLO

VIA S. DOMENICO

San Domenico

PIAZZA GHERARDI

VIA S. CHIARA

VIA D. MURA

VIA NAZIONALE (73 bis)

VIA D. MURA

VIA NAZIONALE

VIA D. STAZIONE

N

latter half of the 15th century—a singular occurrence whose effects would resonate throughout Western history.

The honey-colored city traces its origins to the Umbrians, centuries before Christ; it became a Roman municipality in the third century B.C., but its zenith came during the 15th century under the great condottiere Federico da Montefeltro, whom Castiglione described as the "light of Italy." The Montefeltros were appointed as overlords by the Holy Roman Empire after the Byzantine and Lombard invasions. During the growth of the free communes, Urbino became caught in the strife between the pope and emperor. The full flowering of the city came in 1444 when Federico, the philosopher-warrior, assumed control after the citizens murdered his tyrannical half-brother, Oddantonio. Federico's court exemplified the best in Renaissance style, and in the words of Castiglione, his palace "seemed more like a city than a mere place."

Federico, a remarkable man by any standard, divided his time between soldiering and scholarship. Along with his wife, Battista Sforza, he created one of the most illustrious cultural centers of his time. As a mercenary he was in great demand, serving both kings and popes, and earning a reputation for loyalty in a line of work synonymous with treachery. At one point Venice, which was at war with Ferrara (under whom Federico was engaged), offered him money to withdraw from fighting. He refused. Milan and Florence as well as the papacy were among his employers; Edward IV of England awarded him the Order of the Garter.

In addition to the great warrior-humanist, three other luminaries are associated with the city: the architect Bramante, who expressed his love of antiquity in many a palace and church in Italy, the painter Raphael (although only a few of his works are here), and the writer Castiglione.

Urbino is small and compact and is still girded by its great Roman walls. The scenic path of the via delle Mura, which traces these walls, offers splendid views of sloping manicured fields set off by rows of cypress. Because the city is a bit off the main travel routes, there are no grand hotels or restaurants. One of the city's best hotels is the Bonconte, which sits like a small jewel box on the via delle Mura and offers comfortable (though smallish) accommodations at reasonable prices. The front rooms afford a magnificent view of the undulating fields. The Bonconte is within walking distance of the town's center and is a stone's throw from Gabriele Monti's endearing restaurant, Vecchia Urbino, at via dei Vasari 3/5 (Tel: 0722-44-47; closed Tuesdays). Strictly a family affair, it serves some of the region's best dishes—try the *olivette alla pesarese,* a thin rolled veal cutlet with a paste of capers, or the *spaghetti alla chitarra "Vecchia Urbino,"* made with bacon, red pepper, and cheese—all prepared by the loving hands of Signor Monti's mother. Verdicchio, the leading wine of the Marches, goes well with these dishes. The dessert wine, Moscato, is superb.

The train station for Urbino is just over a mile south of the Old Town; there are buses to the piazza della Repubblica in the heart of town. The piazza, which draws the hip crowd as well as the town's elders, is the best place for watching the daily drill. Nothing fancy here, but you can take refreshments at one of the many cafés under the arches as you watch the crowds pass by. Just off the piazza at via C. Battisti 5, is the basement restaurant **Trattoria del Leone**, where you can dine on a tasty four-cheese risotto and rich *cicerchiata,* a sweet honey cake topped with almonds and cinnamon, without damaging your budget. The restaurant is closed on Sundays and the last two weeks in June; Tel: (0722) 32-98-94.

The Ducal Palace of Federico is the city's main attraction; it is only a five-minute walk from the piazza della Repubblica. As the corso Garibaldi snakes up from the piazza, you immediately become aware of the 16th-century university, which has a surprisingly complete bookshop where you can obtain translations of many of the classics.

The Ducal Palace

The Renaissance Palazzo Ducale, with its graceful courtyard, *Il Cortile d'Onore,* is located in the piazza Duca Federico. Commissioned in 1444 by the duke, who called in the Dalmatian architect Luciano da Laurana to incorporate the two existing and dismal Gothic palaces, it was completed by the Sienese Francesco di Giorgio Martini in 1482. Much of the palace is devoted to the **Galleria Nazionale delle Marche**. The masterpieces include *La Muta,* Raphael's strong and tender portrait of a lady possessing a Leonardesque mystery; Piero della Francesca's compelling *Flagellation,* a triumph of perspective and scale; and his *Madonna of Senigalia,* a ferociously silent portrait with a deep emotional gravity. Other interesting works include Paolo Uccello's *Profanation of the Host,* the *Ideal Town,* an architectural rendering, and a fine *Madonna and Child* by Orazio Gentileschi. The wonderful collection of Federico Barroci's paintings reveals the artist's superb manipulation of light and space and his emotionalism, which greatly influenced the development of 17th-century Baroque art. One of his masterpieces, the enormous *Last*

Supper, captures a bracing psychological truth, although many feel the Christ figure is a little saccharin.

During the duke's reign the palace brimmed with the best art and furnishings, and scholars, poets, and artists flocked here. Today imagination is needed to recall those lively times, since most of the furnishings were carted off when the popes took control and are now on view in the Vatican Museum. However, the space itself is masterful; it captivated both Lorenzo de' Medici and Montaigne.

The throne room contains magnificent 17th-century Gobelin tapestries, but it is the duke's study that is riveting. Lustrous wood inlay work designed by Botticelli and Pontelli manifests the ideals of the Renaissance. The room is a triumph of trompe l'oeil, with books and armor that seem to spill magically out of closets. Pedro Berruguete's portrait of the duke perhaps best sums up his character: Bedecked in shimmering armor and silk robes, the duke sits reading serenely, his small son, Guidobaldo, at his knee.

During the reign of Guidobaldo, Federico's son, the poet and diplomat Baldassare Castiglione was in service at Urbino, and conceived his famous book *The Courtier* here. Written in the form of conversations and consciously modeled after Plato's *Republic,* it examines the ideal of the perfect courtier and was considered required reading for a gentleman.

The **Duomo**, near the palace, is a Neoclassical reworking of an older church and contains some interesting works by Federico Barocci. The diocesan museum, the Albani, has a good collection of ceramics, vestments, and chalices. A little beyond the Duomo, along via Saffi, you'll see signs for the bar/pizzeria **Le 3 Piante**, located on one of the side streets at via Voltaccia della Vecchia 1. The interior is Spartan, but the pleasant vine-covered terrace overlooking sloping hills is the perfect retreat after a morning of museums. The pizza is tasty, as are the other simple Marchegiana dishes. For something a bit fancier, try the new and inexpensive **Pasta a Gogò**, via Valerio 16. Small and attractive, it features traditional Marchegiana fare, including the hand-rolled pasta called *strangolapreti* with a zesty tomato-sage sauce, and in the fall, wild boar. (Tel: 0722-29-42; closed Mondays.) Off the piazza della Repubblica, via Raffaello snakes up a steep hill, passing the house at number 57, open to view, where Raphael spent his youth. Right next door, at via Santa Margherita 38–40, is the hotel **Raffaello**, which occupies a 500-year-old building. The renovated interior is modern and the rooms attractive. There's no restaurant but breakfast is offered, although at about triple the cost of breakfast at the local café.

The street crests at piazzale Roma; just to the west, the public gardens and the great fortress of Cardinal Albornoz offer a superb view of the city. Also from the piazza della Repubblica, via Barocci leads to the **Oratorio di San Giovanni Battista**, where the colorful frescoes depicting the life of Saint John the Baptist by the Salimbeni brothers can be seen.

The surrounding hills of Urbino are as beautiful as those of Tuscany, and greener. Ensconced on the summit of one of these hills is the attractive **Beauty Farm**, the creation of Isabella Giuriatti, a transplanted aesthetician from Cortina D'Ampezzo. Her stone farmhouse is outfitted with antiques and a touch of the new; the beauty ritual for guests includes facials and massages in which her own natural herbal creams are used. The area makes a good base for day trips into the countryside and nearby historic towns and sights. You can drive to the picturesque town of **San Leo**, medieval to the core, with requisite fortress. Set on the highest rock (2,096 feet), the fortress enjoys an impregnable position overlooking very sheer cliffs. An obvious selling point for the Inquisitors, who decided to imprison Count Alessandro di Cagliostro, master con man and magician of the 18th century, here. Even his chicanery was insufficient to defeat this place, in whose tiny cell, called *il pozzetto* (the shaft), he languished for four years before apoplexy claimed him. San Leo also has two fine churches worth visiting.

THE COAST

From Urbino, route 73 *bis* connects with route 3 and leads to the unpretentious seaside town of **Fano**, home to the Malatestas for more than two hundred years. Exhibiting some interesting Roman features, such as the first-century A.D. **Arco d'Augusto**, Fano is older than the Romans, and its name derives from the ancient goddess Fanum Fortunae, a statue of whom adorns the lovely fountain that stands in the central piazza XX Settembre. On weekdays the piazza bustles with food and clothing stalls that contrast greatly with the stately Renaissance **Palazzo della Ragione** facing it. Inside is the **Teatro della Fortuna**, where plays and musical events take place during the summer. From the palazzo, a Renaissance arcade leads to the courtyard of the Palazzo Malatesta (which contains the Museo Civico and Pinacoteca). Fano has several good seafood restaurants: Feast on succulent grilled scampi at the **Ristorante da Pep**, at via Garibaldi 21, or on pasta with clams at **Da Giulio**, viale Adriatico 100

(Tel: 0721-80-56-80; closed Tuesdays and October). But if you want to eat where the fishermen do, go to **Trattoria Da Quinta**, viale Adriatico 42. Favored by locals who come for the owner's delicious pasta with mixed seafood or marinated anchovies, the restaurant is lively with true piscatory panache. Closed Sundays and August. (Tel: 0721-80-80-43.) And it is right next door to **Pesce Azzurro**, a bustling cafeteria run by the fishermen's cooperative, where you can get a five-course fish dinner for 10,000 lire—surprisingly good—and eat outside in semicommunal style.

A half hour north along the coastal highway is the charming resort town of **Pesaro**, birthplace of Rossini and former home of the Sforzas and Della Roveres. The city is handsome; its main artery, corso Rossini, which becomes viale della Repubblica closer to the marina, is lined with attractive shops and runs past the composer's home (to which a small museum is attached). The great **Palazzo Ducale**, a relic from the signorial days, is particularly noteworthy. During the 16th century, Pesaro was known for its fine ceramics, examples of which can be seen at the **Museo Civico** (which includes the **Museo della Ceramiche** and the **Pinacoteca**) on via Toschi Mosca (but don't miss the stunning *Coronation of the Virgin* by Giovanni Bellini inside). An excellent shop for first-class ceramics is **G. Molaroni**, via Luca della Robbia 17/19 (Tel: 0721-331-81; closed Monday mornings). And for leather goods for the home, such as trays and ice buckets, you should visit the **Arte Cuoio** shop at via Saffi 12 (Tel: 0721-255-27; closed weekends). Hotels are plentiful in Pesaro, and most are moderately priced, if undistinguished. One near the seaside promenade, the century-old villa **Vittoria** on piazzale della Libertà, recalls a more charmed life. Lovers of bel canto will delight in the Rossini Opera Festival, which takes place from August 16 to September 8 at the Teatro Rossini. If you are fluent in Italian and a film fancier, you'll enjoy Pesaro's New Film Festival (mid-September to the end of October). **Lo Scudiero**, via Baldassini 2, in the heart of old Pesaro, is a charming but pricey place to savor the treasures of the sea (Tel: 0721-641-07; closed Thursdays and July). If your heart is set on a room with a view for dining, then you'll like the **Hotel Principe–Da Teresa**, viale Trieste 180. The food (also expensive) and the views make for a memorable experience (Tel: 0721-300-96; closed Mondays).

One of the most spectacular drives, though, is north from Pesaro in the direction of Gabicce Mare. The majestic hills here, crowned with wild flowers and pines, offer an oasis of silence and beauty. Exploration of the hills and valleys will reveal many wonderfully preserved medieval towns and graceful monasteries, as well as the delightfully secluded **Capo Est** hotel, set high on a hill at Gabicce Monte, with glorious vistas and its own private elevator directly to the beach. (Open May through September.) Another scenic drive in the Marches follows the Conero Riviera, extending from Ancona south through the towns of Porto Novo, Sirolo, and Numana. The stretch of the Apeninnes that plunges toward the sea creates beautiful isolated villages that hover over white sandy coves. Some of the most pristine places are nestled between Porto Novo and Numana, such as the little beach of **Due Sorelle**, reached only by a small boat. A night at the intimate hotel **Emilia**, ensconced on a hill at Porto Novo, will work the magic of this unspoiled area on you, with breathtaking views of Monte Conero and the rugged coast. Reasonably priced, it has a good restaurant specializing in fresh seafood dishes. Although the decor is somewhat spartan, softened only by flowers and wicker, the dramatic views compensate. Many like dining at **Fortino Napoleonico**, a stony white structure incorporating part of a fortress built by Napoléon that fronts the beach. Meals, taken in two beautiful rooms that capitalize on the stunning sea views, tend to be a little fancy and pricey, including items like shrimps with fennel and gnocchi with caviar. There are also 15 rooms done in wicker and three suites furnished with period antiques. And the rooftop terrace is the best tanning salon. One caveat: The bar plays music that not only can be heard but also felt from the surrounding rooms. However, if you ask the management to turn it down, it willingly obliges. Tel: (071) 80-11-24.

North of Ancona, about 13 km (8 miles) directly on coastal route 16, is the town of Falconara Marittima. Here you'll find the attractive **Villa Amalia**, via degli Spagnoli 4, which makes a perfect stop for dining. The villa has three intimate dining rooms, and a few bedrooms should you wish to spend the night, but the real appeal is Signore Ceccarelli's cooking, which relies on truly local seafood that she transforms into small works of art. Lamberto, her son, is the sommelier, and you'll appreciate his recommendations. Do eat out on the verandah, weather permitting (Tel: 071-91-20-45; closed Tuesdays).

The drive south from Numana takes you to Porto Recanati. From here, if you drive inland just 20 minutes, you reach **Loreto**, one of the most popular pilgrimage shrines in Italy. A tiny city ringed by high walls, Loreto lives on the mystery of the House of Mary, or *Santa Casa*, as it is known, located in the grand **Church of Mary**, which is part of the sprawling sanctuary. Legend has it that the little house, originally situated in Nazareth, was carried in 1291 by angels who, in retreat from the Moslems, took it first to Istria and then across the Adriatic to the "laurel woods," or Loreto. The church that shelters the house is superb and took more than 100 years to complete. It sits in the piazza della Madonna, which is enclosed by an elegant loggia by Bramante and includes a fountain by Carlo Maderna, one of the architects of St. Peter's. The interior of this Baroque church has a sterling group of international chapels lining the aisles. Directly under the dome of the church stands the *Santa Casa,* a simple brick structure dressed in marble by Bramante, with exquisite marble reliefs by Sangallo. An eerie black statue of the Madonna and Child stands on the altar of the tiny chapel. The numerous pilgrims who throng to the sanctuary in hope of a cure lend Loreto a poignant appeal.

When it comes to eating in Loreto, **Orlando Barabani**, via Villa Costantina 93, is a hunter's paradise (Tel: 071-97-76-96; closed Wednesdays and July). The inside decor is bland, but there's a pleasant garden out back, and the *papardelle* with venison sauce, the roast pigeon, and the thrush are great.

In nearby Macerata, from July 14 to August 14, the city opera rings out with sounds of its **opera festival**, with performances at the grand open-air Sferisterio theater. There's also a host of other music and art events. Check with the tourist office for information on tickets: piazza Libertà 12; Tel: (0733) 23-48-07. Or call the Sferisterio theater: (0733) 407-35.

There are few hotels of distinction in Macerata, but north of the city in Montecassiano (take the scenic route 361) is the serene **Villa Quiete** in Località Vallecascia. Set in lushly shaded grounds that include a pool, the 18th-century villa has a decidedly Tuscan tone, with antiques, drab sitting rooms, some comfortably furnished rooms, and as its name suggests, quiet. South of here a bit, at Montanello, is a fine restaurant, the **Floriani**. In a beautiful setting of vineyards and olive trees, this rustically elegant place serves traditional dishes, with a slight creative flair, that are based on recipes over 400 years old (Tel: 0733-42-92-67; closed Mondays).

Right in Macerata, the **Da Secondo** restaurant, via Pescheria Vecchia 26, is a lively, popular spot known for tasty lamb dishes as well as superb *vincigrassi,* that sinfully rich lasagne (Tel: 0733-449-12; closed Mondays and the end of August).

GETTING AROUND
There is no airport in the region, the nearest one being Rome's. There are several ways to explore the area, however. Most of the interesting sights and cities can be visited

following a circular route. For instance, as we've laid out our narrative, a tour by car might begin at Perugia, continue to Assisi, down to Spoleto, across to Todi and Orvieto, back up to Perugia, and on to Gubbio before heading to Urbino.

Or you can start at Orvieto and proceed to Todi and Spoleto, then up to Assisi and Perugia before continuing on to Gubbio and Urbino.

If you are travelling by rail, there are two daily trains making the three-hour trip from Rome to Perugia on the Rome–Ancona line. Change at Foligno for the train to Perugia and Assisi. There are frequent trains directly from Rome to Orvieto on the Rome–Florence line; the train arrives beneath Orvieto's Old Town; buses and taxis take you up to the piazzale Cahen or piazza Duomo. There are also trains from Florence to Perugia.

The F.C.U. (Ferrovia-Centrale Umbra), one of Italy's few remaining privately operated railroads, has a route that begins in Terni (an uninteresting industrial town) in southern Umbria and follows the valley of the upper Tiber through the heart of Umbria. Terni is about an hour and a half from Rome by train. It is fun—if not always entirely comfortable—to travel on these trains, packed as they are with housewives and students on their way to Perugia. Schedules tend to be "flexible," so allow plenty of time. The train passes through some ancient towns, like the spa towns of San Gemini and Acquasparta, and proceeds to Todi, Deruta, and Perugia. F.C.U. schedules are available in the Italian Railways' *Orario Generale,* a large train schedule book found in most train stations. Local bus service between towns is good, with stations in all the major centers.

ACCOMMODATIONS REFERENCE

The rates given below are projections for 1993; always check for up-to-date information before making reservations. Wide ranges may reflect the difference between low- and high-season rates. Unless otherwise indicated, the figures indicate the cost of a double room (per room, not per person). However, half-board (mezza pensione) rates, which include breakfast and one other meal per day, are per person. The service charge is included in the rate; inquire about tax and breakfast.

▶ **Albergo Il Palazzo**. Via San Francesco 8, 06081 **Assisi**. Tel: (075) 81-68-41. Ł115,000.

▶ **Albornoz Palace Hotel**. Viale Matteoti, 06049 **Spoleto**. Tel: (0743) 22-12-21; Fax: (0743) 22-16-00. Rooms Ł210,000, half board Ł200,000.

▶ **Antichita "Three Esse" Country House.** S. Pietro Compagna 178, 06081 **Assisi.** Tel: (075) 81-63-63; Fax: same. £115,000.

▶ **Barbarossa Hotel.** 06049 **Spoleto.** Tel: (0743) 22-20-60 or 436-44; Fax: (0743) 22-20-60. £240,000 off-season; £300,000 during festival.

▶ **The Beauty Farm.** Località Pozzuolo 60, Montesoffio, 61029 **Urbino.** Tel: (0722) 571-83. Half board £75,000.

▶ **Bonconte.** Via delle Mura 28, 61029 **Urbino.** Tel: (0722) 24-63; Fax: (0722) 47-82. £155,000.

▶ **Bosone Hotel.** Via XX Settembre 22, 06024 **Gubbio.** Tel: (075) 922-06-98; Fax: (075) 922-05-52. Closed February. £135,000; half board £125,000.

▶ **Brufani.** Piazza Italia 12, 06100 **Perugia.** Tel: (075) 625-41; Fax: (075) 202-10. £420,000.

▶ **Capo Est.** Località Vallugola. 61011 **Gabicce Monte.** Tel: (0541) 95-33-33; Fax: (0541) 95-27-35. Open May–September. £290,000; half board £200,000.

▶ **Le Casaline.** Campello sul Clitunno, 06049 **Spoleto.** Tel: (0743) 52-08-11. £85,000.

▶ **Castel San Gregorio.** Via San Gregorio 16, 06081 **San Gregorio Assisi.** Tel: (075) 803-80-09; Fax: (075) 803-89-04. Closed January 15–30. £108,000; half board £103,000.

▶ **Charleston.** Piazza Collicola 10, 06049 **Spoleto.** Tel: (0743) 22-00-52. £110,000.

▶ **Emilia.** 60020 **Porto Novo.** Tel: (071) 80-11-45; Fax: (071) 80-13-30. Open March–November. £110,000; half board £150,000.

▶ **Fattoria Di Vibio.** Località Buchella-Doglio, 06057 **Montecastello di Vibio.** Tel: (075) 878-03-70 or 874-96-07. Full board £95,000–£115,000.

▶ **Fortino Napoleonico.** 60020 **Porto Novo.** Tel: (071) 80-11-24; Fax: (071) 80-13-14. £150,000; half board £140,000.

▶ **Gattapone.** Via Ansidei 6, 06024 **Gubbio.** Tel: (075) 927-24-89; Fax: (075) 927-12-69. £80,000.

▶ **Grand Hotel Reale.** Piazza del Popolo 25, 05018 **Orvieto.** Tel: (0763) 412-47; Fax: same. £135,000.

▶ **Hotel Aquila Bianca.** Via Garibaldi 13, 05018 **Orvieto.** Tel: (0763) 412-46; Fax: (0763) 422-73. £125,000.

▶ **Hotel La Badia.** Località La Badia, 05019 **Orvieto.** Tel: (0763) 903-59; Fax: (0763) 927-96. Closed January and February. £275,000; half board £205,000.

▶ **Hotel Bastiglia.** Via dei Molini 7, 06038 **Spello.** Tel: (0742) 65-24-07; Fax (0742) 65-12-77. £110,000; half board £100,000.

▶ **Hotel Bramante.** Via Orvietana 48, 06059 **Todi.** Tel:

(075) 894-83-81; Fax: (075) 894-80-74. Ł215,000; half board Ł165,000.

▶ **Hotel Dei Duchi**. Viale Matteotti 4, 06049 **Spoleto**. Tel: (0743) 445-41; Fax: (0743) 445-43. Ł215,000; half board Ł130,000.

▶ **Hotel Fontebella**. Via Fontebella 25, 06082 **Assisi**. Tel: (075) 81-28-83; Fax: (075) 81-29-41. Ł200,000; half board Ł165,000.

▶ **Hotel Dei Priori**. Corso Mazzini 15, 06081 **Assisi**. Tel: (075) 81-22-37; Fax: (075) 81-68-04. Open March–November. Ł113,000; half board Ł120,000.

▶ **Hotel Gattapone**, Via del Ponte 6, 06049 **Spoleto**. Tel: (0743) 22-34-47; Fax: (0743) 22-34-48. Ł165,000.

▶ **Hotel Maitani**. Via Maitani 5, 05018 **Oriveto**. Tel: (0763) 420-11; Fax: same. Closed January 7–22. Ł170,000.

▶ **Hotel Subasio**. Via Frate Elia 2, 06081 **Assisi**. Tel: (075) 81-22-06; Fax: (075) 81-66-91. Ł200,000; half board Ł170,000.

▶ **Hotel Umbra**. Vicolo degli Archi 6, 06081 **Assisi**. Tel: (075) 81-22-40. Closed January 10–March 15. Ł100,000.

▶ **Hotel Virgilio**. Piazza del Duomo 5/6, 05018 **Oriveto**. Tel: (0763) 418-82. Ł150,000.

▶ **La Meridiana**. Niccone 173, 06019 **Umbertide**. Tel: (075) 930-32-34. One-week stays: Ł550,000–Ł850,000.

▶ **Oasi Verde**. Albergo Ristorante Agrituristico, 06024 **Mengara**. Tel: (075) 92-01-56. Ł75,000.

▶ **Palace Hotel Bellavista**. Piazza Italia 12, 06100 **Perugia**. Tel: (075) 207-41. Ł108,000.

▶ **Il Panciolle**. Largo Muzio Clemente 4, 06049 **Spoleto**. Tel: (0743) 455-98. Rates unavailable.

▶ **Park Hotel Ai Cappuccini**. Via Tifernate, 06024 **Gubbio**. Tel: (075) 92-34; Fax: (075) 922-03-23. Ł300,000; half board Ł210,000.

▶ **Raffaello**. Via Santa Margherita 38–40, 61029 **Urbino**. Tel: (0722) 48-96; Fax: (0722) 32-85-40. Ł135,000–Ł140,000.

▶ **Residenza San Andrea al Farinaio**. San Andrea al Farinaio 118, 52040 **Terontola di Cortona**. Tel: (0575) 67-77-36. Ł150,000.

▶ **La Rosetta**. Piazza Italia 19, 06100 **Perugia**. Tel: (075) 208-41; Fax: same. Ł170,000; half board Ł150,000.

▶ **Saint Anthony's Guest House**. Via Galeazzo 10, 06081 **Assisi**. Tel: (075) 81-25-42. Ł73,000 with breakfast.

▶ **San Valentino Hotel & Sporting Club**. 06059 **Fiore** (Todi). Tel: (075) 894-41-03; Fax: (075) 894-86-96. Open March–November 15. Ł400,000; half board Ł280,000.

▶ **Sauro**. 06060 **Isola Maggiore**. Tel: (075) 82-61-68; Fax: (075) 82-51-30. Closed January 11–February 19. Ł75,000; half board Ł60,000.

▶ **Le Silve**. Località Armenzano, 06081 **Assisi**. Tel: (075) 801-90-00; Fax: (075) 801-90-05. Ł250,000; half board Ł180,000; reductions for children.

▶ **Lo Spedalicchio**. Piazza Brunno Buozzi 3, Ospedalicchio, 06083 **Bastia**. Tel: (075) 801-03-23; Fax: same. Ł110,000; half board Ł105,000.

▶ **Le Tre Vaselle**. 06089 **Torgiano**. Tel: (075) 98-24-47; Fax: (075) 98-52-14. Ł300,000; half board Ł280,000.

▶ **Villa Ciconia**. Via dei Trigli 69, 05019 **Orvieto Scalo**. Tel: (0763) 906-77; Fax: same. Ł170,000; half board Ł157,000.

▶ **Villa di Montesolare**. 06064 **Panicale**. Tel: (075) 83-23-76; Fax: (075) 835-54-62. Half board Ł110,000–Ł125,000.

▶ **Villa Quiete**. Località Vallecascia S, 62010 **Montecassiano**, Tel: (0733) 59-95-59. Ł120,000.

▶ **Villa Roncalli**. Via Roma 25, 06034 **Foligno**. Tel: (0742) 39-10-91. Ł125,000; half board Ł125,000.

▶ **Vittoria**. Piazzale della Libertà 2, 61100 **Pesaro**. Tel: (0721) 343-43; Fax: (0721) 688-74. Ł265,000.

FLORENCE

By Anne Marshall Zwack

Anne Marshall Zwack, who lives in Tuscany and Hungary, has written extensively for magazines and for the travel section of the New York Times, *and is now writing her first book.*

Florence does not evoke love at first sight, unlike other Italian cities such as Venice and Rome. And yet it is the most Anglo-Saxon of Italian cities, where expatriates from Robert and Elizabeth Barrett Browning onward have felt most at home. It is, as Mary McCarthy writes in *The Stones of Florence,* "a manly city, and the cities of art that appeal to the current sensibility are feminine." The three dominant figures of the Renaissance—Donatello, Brunelleschi, and Michelangelo—were, after all, bachelors. There are no sweeping vistas in Florence, with the exception of the Technicolor sunset from the piazzale Michelangelo; the *palazzi* are forbidding. "Magnificently stern and somber" are the narrow streets, according to Charles Dickens, streets crammed today with honking vehicles between token sidewalks and frowning eaves. Ezra Pound claimed that Florence—Firenze—was the most damned of Italian cities, with no place to stand or sit or walk.

Likewise, the Florentines themselves, compared with the extroverted, warm southern Italians, are a dour folk who tolerate tourists as a necessary evil. The Florentine is iconoclastic and frugal, not to say stingy. Dante, himself a Florentine, called them *"Gente avara, invidiosa e superba"* (a stingy, envious, and proud people). They are also well groomed, well educated, and very civilized. Florence is a Northern European city where—though since Mussolini the trains may not always run on time—people are punctual, reliable, and hardworking. Indeed, the Florentines' under-

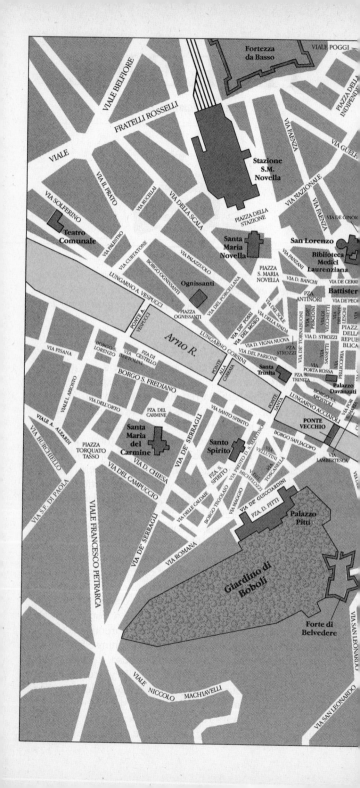

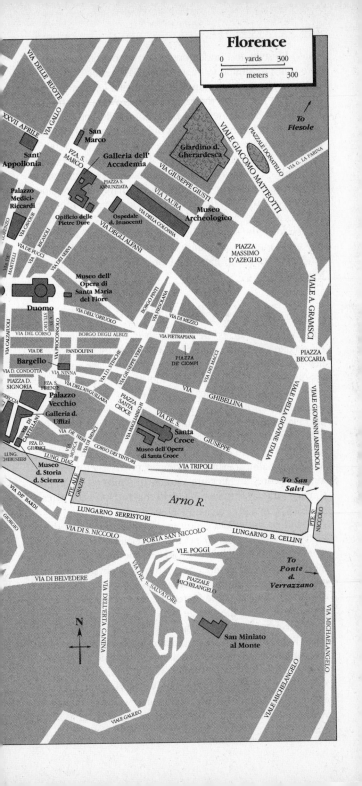

stated lifestyle and undemonstrative, almost puritanical nature is not dissimilar to the so-called WASP ethic.

Florence is not an industrial city—within less than half an hour from the center the Chianti wine-growing country is at hand—and hence there has been no mobile population to melt in the Florentine pot. Not only the aristocracy, known as the *dugento* (meaning "descending from the 1200s"), who still live in their patrician palazzi, but also the clerks and tradespeople have been Florentines for centuries, since before the *Mayflower* landed, and they have the arrogance of people who know that their ancestors invented the modern world. Now as then a Saint Bernardino of Siena could preach from the steps of the church of Santa Croce, "Italy is the most intelligent country in Europe, Tuscany the most intelligent region in Italy, and Florence the most intelligent town in Tuscany."

The Renaissance

Florence, after all, *is* the Renaissance, the first city to be raised like Lazarus from the dead when the rest of us were, if not exactly painted blue, still plunged in the Dark Ages. "It is inside these walls," exclaimed the young Stendhal as he rode over the Apennines into Florence, "that civilization began again." It is interesting to reflect on the fact that Michelangelo, the culminating figure of the Florentine Renaissance, died the year Shakespeare was born. "This century, like a Golden Age, has restored to light the liberal arts, which were almost extinct—grammar, poetry, rhetoric, painting, sculpture, architecture, music, the ancient singing of songs to the Orphic lyre—and all this in Florence," wrote Marsilio Ficino, protégé of the Medicis, in 1492.

For three and a half centuries, Florence and larger-than-life figures like Leonardo da Vinci and Galileo Galilei set the world a new standard, not only in the arts but also in medicine, science, engineering, astronomy, physics, political thought, even economics (there were 72 banks in the center of the city alone, and the Florentine florin was the dollar or deutsche mark of the Middle Ages). Dante and the Florentines invented the Italian language as it is spoken today, while Florence also pioneered mapmaking. By following the Florentine Toscanelli's map, Columbus was able to discover the New World, although both thought it was a new route to Asia. Another Florentine, Amerigo Vespucci, disproved this and gave his name to two continents, while Giovanni da Verrazzano sailed up the North American coast as far as Nova Scotia, calling new landmarks by Tuscan names such as

Vallombrosa and San Miniato. It could thus be argued that many of us—Old World or New—have roots in Florence, and that, as ex-mayor Massimo Bogianckino said when criticized for not stemming the increasingly overwhelming flood of tourists, "Florence belongs to the world."

"When one great genius is born, it is in the very nature of things that he shall not stand alone." So observed Vasari, Renaissance architect and chronicler, when writing about Masaccio. His theory is that Renaissance men were "impelled by nature and refined to a certain degree by the *air they breathed* to set to work, each according to his own talent." It is nevertheless difficult to explain how so many great talents lived in this "Etrurian Athens," as Byron called it, at the same time. It may simply be that the 15th century was an age of individualists, many of whom happened to be artists. Florence was as modern and as aggressively progressive in the quattrocento as New York is today—one might even say the Medicis were the Rockefellers of the Renaissance.

The River Arno

Florence is divided, like Paris, into a right and left bank, here by the yellow river Arno—and indeed yellow is the dominant color in Florence. "She sits," says Henry James, "in the sunshine beside her yellow river like the little treasure city that she has always seemed"; the "sallow houses" vary in shade from ocher to withered lemon, while the roofs and domes are a rusty orange.

In the 13th and 14th centuries the foundations of Florentine wealth were built on wool, a full quarter of the population being involved in the many facets of the cloth trade. Artisans washed and rinsed their fleeces in what a perennially disgruntled Dante called that "cursed ditch," the river Arno. Even Mark Twain thought it would be "a very plausible river if they could pump some water into it." The Arno sinks so low in summer that the fish die, while in winter it can rise so high that it floods its banks, as in 1966, when much damage was done to the city and its works of art. (You will see plaques all over the city showing the height of the floodwaters.) In the old days carts came rumbling over the ponte alla Carraia (from *carro,* meaning cart), bringing wool from the English Cotswolds and from France and Flanders to be dyed and spun in Florence; the cloth guilds, the Arte della Lana and the Calimala, were so wealthy they could finance the building of the Duomo, the Baptistery, and the basilica of San Miniato.

The Medici family, who ruled Florence officially and unofficially from 1434 until 1737, with only a few interruptions—

such as Savonarola's ascendancy and several attempts at a true republic—were merchants, lords of commerce rather than an aristocracy, and it is due to their affluent patronage that so much of the city was built and adorned. Their coat of arms, a varying number of balls, surmounts many a portal and cornice to this day. (It has been suggested that these balls are meant to be pills, a pun on the name Medici, which means doctors.)

The two banks of the Arno are linked by a number of bridges, of which only one, the **ponte Vecchio** (Old Bridge), spanning the river at its narrowest point, survived the war. Hitler fell so in love with the kitsch conglomeration of jewelry stores lining its sides that the Luftwaffe was ordered to spare it for posterity. It is called the Old Bridge to distinguish it from the ponte alla Carraia, which was "new" (in 1220), although the present structure of the ponte Vecchio dates from 1345. Goldsmiths and jewelers have plied their trades on the bridge since the 16th century, in stores that were once a bazaar for butchers, hosiers, green-grocers, and blacksmiths.

Other, more beautiful bridges, like the **ponte Santa Trinita**, whose arches were drawn by Michelangelo, had to be fished piece by piece out of the river after the war and rebuilt with funds raised by the sale of tickets for individual bricks and stones; $160,000 was collected by a committee led by Bernard Berenson. (This legendary figure in the world of art and art history bequeathed his beautiful villa to Harvard University, and it is now the Florentine branch of the university.)

The right (north) bank of the Arno is the more pompous, monumental side of the river, where you will find all the banks, boutiques, and car-rental and travel agencies, the train station, and most of the museums and churches.

MAJOR INTEREST ON THE RIGHT BANK

Galleria degli Uffizi (comprehensive collection of Renaissance art)

Palazzo Vecchio (Florence's town hall)

Galleria dell'Accademia (Michelangelo's *David*)

Museo Nazionale del Bargello (sculpture by Donatello and others)

Duomo, Baptistery of San Giovanni, the Campanile, and the Museo dell'Opera di Santa Maria del Fiore (Donatello's organ lofts, Michelangelo's *Pietà*)

Church of Santa Croce (Giotto frescoes) with the Museo dell'Opera di Santa Croce

Church of Santa Maria Novella (Uccello frescoes in
   the Green Cloister)
Monastery of San Marco (Fra Angelico frescoes)
Church of San Lorenzo and the Cappelle Medicee
   (sculpture and architecture by Michelangelo)

SPECIAL INTEREST

Palazzo Davanzati (medieval nobleman's home)
Museo di Storia della Scienza (Galileo's telescopes
   and memorabilia)
Cenacoli (frescoes depicting the Last Supper)
Opificio delle Pietre Dure (Renaissance workmanship
   in semiprecious stones)
Palazzo Medici-Riccardi (Gozzoli frescoes)
Museo Archeologico
Biblioteca Medici Laurenziana

The left (south) bank, or *Oltrarno* (literally, "over the
Arno"), is traditionally the poorer side of the river, the
artisan quarter, and the greener side of Florence.

MAJOR INTEREST IN THE OLTRARNO

Palazzo Pitti with the Galleria Palatina, Museo degli
   Argenti, and Giardino di Boboli
Church of Santo Spirito
Church of Santa Maria del Carmine (Masaccio
   frescoes)
Piazzale Michelangelo (panoramic view of Florence)
Church of San Miniato al Monte (Romanesque
   architecture)

In Florence the major museums—the Uffizi, Pitti, Bargello,
and Accademia—are literally crammed with works of art,
leaving just enough space for the light switch. It is therefore
inadvisable to attempt more than one museum in a day. Most
are open from 9:00 A.M. until 2:00 P.M. except Mondays,
unless otherwise noted here; on Sundays and public holidays, until 1:00 P.M. Churches are open from 7:00 A.M. until
noon and 2:30 or 3:00 to 6:30 or 7:00 P.M. (Visits during
church services are sometimes actively discouraged, especially on feast days.)

THE RIGHT BANK

Although central Italy was first civilized by the Etruscans, and the little hilltop village of Fiesole was an Etruscan settlement, Florence itself is a Roman town. The main thoroughfares used to converge on the corner where Upim, the city's main department store, stands today; the piazza della Repubblica is on the site of the Roman Forum; and it was long believed that the Baptistery was originally a temple to Mars, built to celebrate the Roman victory over the Etruscans in Fiesole. No traces of its Roman past remain in contemporary Florence, however, although excavations have recently been carried out in the piazza della Signoria, when further evidence of the buried Roman city came to light. Florence today remains overwhelmingly Renaissance, her treasures still lived in and part of everyday life. "The ancient city of the 15th century still exists and constitutes the body of the city," remarked the 19th-century philosopher Hippolyte Taine, without being "enveloped in medieval cobwebs," while someone else has said that Florence is "like a town that has survived itself."

It is to the architect Arnolfo di Cambio that the Duomo (Cathedral), the Palazzo Vecchio (Town Hall), and the church of Santa Croce have all been attributed. He was the son of a German "Maestro Jacopo" who was invited to Florence after building a Franciscan church in Arezzo and was immediately rechristened "Lapo," a local name still very popular in Florence today. In Florence Jacopo built the Palazzo del Bargello, which housed the law courts (now a museum containing the Medici sculpture collections), while his son Arnolfo, born in 1232, was responsible for as much progress in architecture, according to Vasari, as Cimabue was in painting. At the age of 30 Arnolfo was considered the best architect in Tuscany.

Il Duomo

The word "Duomo" comes from the Latin *Domus Dei* (House of God). Even today the cathedral of Santa Maria del Fiore looks inordinately large, but in 1294, when the cornerstone was laid, the project must have seemed as vast and wondrous as the launching of the *Titanic* 600 years later. Even now, no building in Florence may be built higher than the cathedral, which dwarfs the rest of the city, as Mark Twain says, "like a captive balloon." Vasari claimed, "The ancients never dared so to compete with the heavens as this building seems to do, for it towers above the hills which are around Florence." The city fathers had decided that their cathedral should be *"più bello che si può"* (as beautiful as can be), a requirement stipulated in this and subsequent Florentine building contracts throughout the Renaissance. Italians today are still city patriots rather than nationalists; in those days there was a definite one-upmanship among the rival cities of Tuscany as to which would have the biggest and the best. When Arnolfo di Cambio died, the Florentine elders were left with the problem of raising the biggest dome since the Roman Pantheon above his vast edifice. A competition was held for the design, but before Filippo Brunelleschi's project was finally accepted, many decades were spent in theorizing and arguing. One scheme was to build a mound of earth full of coins, construct the dome above it, and then invite the townspeople to scavenge for the coins. Meanwhile, to finance the building a tax was levied on anyone caught blaspheming—a bad habit still notoriously rife among Florentines today.

Genius and Beauty do not always go hand in hand. Both Brunelleschi and Giotto were ill-favored youths—and apparently even Michelangelo had protruding ears—but Vasari comforts us with the notion that "under the clods of earth, the veins of gold lie hidden." Brunelleschi's father wanted his son to become a notary like himself and was impatient with the doodlings of someone who was to give the world "the most noble, vast, and beautiful building of modern times" (Vasari). Like many Renaissance artists—Ghiberti, Botticelli, Donatello, Uccello, Verrocchio, and Luca della Robbia—he was first apprenticed to a goldsmith. Donatello was Brunelleschi's best friend, and together they went to Rome to dig up and measure the art and architecture of antiquity. Contemporary Romans, who had not yet awakened to the importance of their Classical past, thought the two of them eccentric treasure-seekers. Filippo came back with his project for the biggest dome in Christendom: to build *two* cupolas, one within the other, bearing each other's stresses and strains—an idea that initially made him the laughing-stock of Florence. Fourteen years later, when several marble quarries had been depleted in the process of building it, the laugh was on the other side. Overcoming all opposition, Brunelleschi supervised the building, which began in 1420, down to the minutest details, personally designing the pulleys and hoists and constructing kitchens and wine shops between the two walls so that the masons need not descend for lunch. He illustrated his answers to architectonic queries submitted by the craftsmen by whittling away at a handy turnip. Today visitors can walk around the dome between the double walls, 300 feet above the ground, every day except Sundays.

The maintenance of the Duomo is a full-time job. Around the corner in the via dello Studio, a little band of crafts-people called the *scalpellini* work on damaged buttresses or cornices and on the strips of green and white marble from the cathedral's façade all year round. The dome is currently supported by scaffolding—serviced by pulleys that would have been the envy of Brunelleschi—because some telltale cracks have appeared on the ceiling. The central part of the façade is also undergoing restoration.

The Renaissance architect Alberti wrote of the dome that, rising above the skies, it was "large enough to shelter all the people of Tuscany in its shadow." As you walk in the echoing interior of the cathedral today this is believable, especially since all the statuary and furniture have been moved to the nearby Museo dell'Opera di Santa Maria del Fiore. As an 18th-century traveller observed, "The architect seems to have turned his building inside out; nothing in art being more ornamented than the exterior, and few churches so simple within." The **Museo dell'Opera di Santa Maria del Fiore** (the cathedral museum) must have the worst labeling in Florence, but in it are the splendid organ lofts, or *cantorie,* by Luca della Robbia and Donatello, whose *putti* are surely the most roguish urchins of the Renaissance. Here too is a Michelangelo *Pietà,* one of his four great sculptures of the mourning Madonna receiving the body of Christ from the Cross (the others are in St. Peter's in Rome, the *Pietà da Palestrina* in the Galleria dell'Accademia in Florence, and the *Pietà Rondanini* in the Castello Sforzesco in Milan). The one here was never finished, and Michelangelo actually tried to destroy it, although he had originally intended it as his own funerary monument. The figure of Nicodemus support-ing the body of Christ is a self-portrait. The museum is open every day until 6:00 P.M. in winter and 7:30 P.M. in summer.

Unlike many cathedral squares, the piazza del Duomo has never been the heart of Florence—an honor reserved for the piazza della Signoria. A sea of tourists swirls between the Duomo and the Baptistery in the wake of tour guides bran-dishing deflated Knirps umbrellas. In summer, equally de-flated tourists subside onto the cathedral steps in sweaty disar-ray. Only partially closed to traffic, the square is also invaded by lumbering orange municipal buses and vicious mopeds.

Baptistery of San Giovanni

The Baptistery, or Battistero, opposite the cathedral, was called the "bel San Giovanni" by Dante, who was baptized here—as were all the children born in Florence during the year—in a communal ceremony, a practice still in use today. Every time a boy was born a black bean was dropped into an urn in the Baptistery, while a girl was recorded by a white bean, thus establishing the annual birthrate. The structure, a pure octagon, is above all remarkable for its **Ghiberti bronze doors**, notably the famous "Gates of Paradise," as Michelangelo called them.

Brunelleschi and Lorenzo Ghiberti were rivals. When, in 1400, the Calimala (cloth guild) announced a competition to see who would forge the doors of the Baptistery, Brunelleschi was 23 years old and Ghiberti 20. Ghiberti won. It took the Ghiberti bronze foundry 24 years to finish the Gates of Paradise, during which time many leading Renaissance artists, such as Donatello, Uccello, Michelozzo, Gozzoli, and Antonio Pollaiuolo, passed through his workshop, the artists of the Renaissance being first and foremost superb craftsmen. Both the casting in bronze of the Ghiberti doors and the raising of Brunelleschi's cupola were unprecedented technical as well as artistic achievements. The Gates of Paradise visible today are copies of the originals, which are now housed in the Museo dell'Opera di Santa Maria del Fiore to protect them from pollution.

The Campanile

In 1334 a public decree announced the building of a *campanile* (bell tower) in these terms: "The Florentine republic desires that an edifice shall be constructed so magnificent in its height and quality that it shall surpass anything of its kind produced in the time of their greatest power by the Greeks and Romans." The project was assigned to Giotto, who, when asked by Pope Benedict IX to submit samples of his work, drew a perfect circle in red pencil. If the seeds of the Renaissance can be said to have been sown somewhere, it is with Giotto, a pupil of the great Cimabue, whom he surpassed and, again according to Vasari, "threw open the gates and showed the path to that perfection which art displays in our age." Although Giotto did not live to finish it (he died in 1336), the Campanile remains, to quote Longfellow, "the lily of Florence blossoming in stone." Visitors can climb to the top of it for a bird's-eye view of the city.

Unlike the Duomo and the Baptistery, the bell tower, right next to the cathedral, is open all day every day (not closing for lunch), until 5:30 P.M. in winter and 7:30 P.M. in summer.

Ospedale degli Innocenti

The exploration of space, be it of a canvas, a continent, the celestial realms, or the concentric circles of the Inferno, was a Florentine fixation from Dante to Galileo. Brunelleschi himself represents a transition from two- to three-dimensional architecture. Although his most famous achievement is the *Cupolone,* as the dome is called, Brunelleschi was also responsible for the Ospedale degli Innocenti (foundlings' hospital), the Old Sacristy of San Lorenzo, the church of San Lorenzo, the Pazzi chapel in Santa Croce, and the church of Santo Spirito, west of the Palazzo Pitti in Oltrarno.

The Ospedale degli Innocenti, on the piazza Santissima Annunziata northeast of the Duomo along via dei Servi, was the first Renaissance building in Florence. Begun in 1419, the hospital shows Brunelleschi's debt to the Classical and Romanesque past in its colonnaded loggia.

The hospital also has a picture gallery that is worth a visit for an inhabitant's view of a pure Renaissance building, as well as for the *Adoration of the Magi* by Ghirlandaio, who was Michelangelo's mentor. In color and detail it is magnificent, with sheep grazing on the Tuscan hills in the background and the Arno seemingly flowing on forever behind the stable in Bethlehem. The bearded, richly accoutred figures were all members of the silk guild, the *Arte della Seta,* who were the orphans' affluent benefactors. (Closed Wednesdays.)

Many Brunelleschian designs are enhanced by roundels in glazed terra-cotta, such as the swaddled infants that line the façade of the Ospedale degli Innocenti, by Andrea Della Robbia, who died in 1525. The Della Robbias were the only "dynasty" of the Renaissance—Luca's nephew Andrea had three sons, Luca, Girolamo, and Giovanni, all of whom were sculptors. It was Luca who invented the terra-cotta glaze that gave this fragile medium an almost endless durability. The Della Robbias have works in nearly every museum and church in Florence.

Church of San Lorenzo

In the Old Sacristy in the church of San Lorenzo, between the Duomo and the train station, Brunelleschi used a basic design—a circle within a square—that formed the basis of quattrocento architecture. Renaissance people believed strongly in the mysticism of mathematics: The geometrical figures of the circle and square corresponded exactly to the symmetry of a human figure with all four limbs out-stretched; the Deity could best be represented by a tri-angle. Mankind belonged to a lucid, geometrically ordered universe.

Brunelleschi also designed the main body of the church of San Lorenzo, a virtuoso exercise in perspective. The church is a geometrical progression of columns, arcades, cornices, and window frames in *pietra serena* (the local stone that is the hallmark of Florentine Renaissance interiors), each element echoing the central theme and receding into a well-ordered distance, as though rippling toward the same vanishing point.

The **Cappelle Medicee** (Medici Chapels) in the church of San Lorenzo were designed by Michelangelo, who was given what amounted to a state funeral in this church when he died in 1564.

Most of the Renaissance artists came from simple back-grounds, village boys brought up among the stonecutters. Even Michelangelo, the only one from the minor nobility, maintained that he had imbibed his genius with the milk of his wet nurse, a stonecutter's wife from Settignano.

Michelangelo believed that architecture was fundamen-tally based on anatomy, with man as the measure of all things. He himself said, "Those who do not know the human body cannot be good architects." Indeed the architecture of these chapels, which were built as a Medici final resting place, can be described, like their creator, as superhuman—in concept and design. Until Michelangelo, sculpture was considered an ornament to architecture; in the Medici cha-pels the roles could be said to be reversed—Michelangelo's architecture *is* sculpture.

On the tombs the figures are not reclining, their feet in floppy chain mail, as on earlier funerary monuments, but are sitting up ready for the Resurrection, with Michelangelo's statues of *Day* and *Night, Dawn* and *Dusk,* signifying the passing of time, at their feet. Much has been written about the statue of *Night,* perhaps most poignantly by Walter Pater, who said, "No one ever expressed more truly than Michelan-gelo the notion of inspired sleep, of faces charged with dreams."

While you are visiting the church of San Lorenzo and the Medici chapels, it is worth pausing in the **Biblioteca Medici Laurenziana** (Laurentian Library), in the piazza San Lorenzo. Most remarkable for its staircase, also designed by Michelangelo, the library houses priceless manuscripts and codices, including the *Medici Virgil*. (Closed Sundays.)

Galleria dell'Accademia

Michelangelo's most famous work in Florence is the **David** in the Galleria dell'Accademia, on the via Ricasoli leading off the piazza del Duomo. Carved out of an 18-foot block of marble, the *David* was called by contemporary Florentines *Il Gigante* (the Giant), which makes you wonder how large Goliath would have been. Indeed, Michelangelo believed that the artist should have his measuring tools in the eye rather than in the hand, as it is the eye that judges, and he saw his *David* as a civic symbol. The arrogant youth is Florence, the little city on the Arno, triumphing over a whole cast of Goliaths—the papal court, the Medici power, and the rest of the world put together. *David* remains to this day the most popular Florentine, as D. H. Lawrence said, the "presiding genius of Florence." Last year, *Il Gigante*'s big toe was attacked by an unbalanced tourist, renewing fears for the statue's safety in these days of mass tourism. A glass screen is to be erected as a protection.

The Galleria dell'Accademia also contains two other works by Michelangelo, *The Slaves* from the tomb of Pope Julius II and *Saint Matthew* from the Duomo, as well as a rich collection of works by well-known Florentine artists from the 13th to the 18th century. The museum is open in the morning year-round, and until 7:00 P.M. during the summer.

Monastery of San Marco

An entirely different figure from Michelangelo was Fra Angelico, an unworldly and retiring monk—he once refused a bishopric, pleading unworthiness—from the Dominican monastery of San Marco. He was commissioned by Cosimo de' Medici to paint frescoes in the cloisters and chapter house of San Marco (across piazza San Marco from the Galleria dell'Accademia), and to him we owe what is perhaps the most reproduced **Annunciation** of all time. However, despite the delicacy and pastel colors of Fra Angelico's paintings, he shares with the architects of his day (the first half of the 15th century) a keen architectonic sense; there is depth and perspective in the colonnades that frame the Angel Gabriel appearing to Mary.

A fellow Dominican, whose cell here can be visited, was Fra Girolamo Savonarola, whose rabid puritanism, which urged artists to throw their works onto his Bonfire of Vanities, almost nipped the blossoming Renaissance in the bud in the last years of the 15th century. Even such great artists as Botticelli fell under the spell of his thundering sermons. It was his spirit that inspired the Florentines to suggest putting a golden fig leaf on Michelangelo's *David,* much to the artist's distress.

Museo Archeologico

If you are not planning to include important Etruscan centers like Volterra or Chiusi in your itinerary, you may want to visit the Museo Archeologico in Florence; officially it is in the piazza Santissima Annunziata, although the main entrance is now in a side street, via della Colonna. Here are the alabaster ash chests from Volterra and little bronzes of startling artistic merit, as well as the most famous Etruscan bronze in Tuscany, the Chimera. A mythical creature—part lion, part goat, its tail like a snake biting one of its own horns—this statue was found in Arezzo and restored by Cellini. If you are lucky you may catch one of the exhibitions that the museum, a world center for restoration, holds periodically of works restored after being rescued, usually from the bottom of the sea; in recent years these have included the Riace bronzes, the gilded bronzes of Cartoceto, and the gold and gems of the Medicis and the Hapsburg Lorraines. The museum is open from 9:00 A.M. to 2:00 P.M. (1:00 P.M. on Sundays); closed Mondays.

Opificio delle Pietre Dure

The art of semiprecious stone inlay flourished under the Medicis and is still very popular in Florence today, although instead of the lapis lazuli, jasper, sardonyx, porphyry, agate, and chalcedony of the Renaissance, the materials used now are more likely to be marble, alabaster, or even stones from the bed of the Arno. Although the workmanship is still excellent, it can't compare with the days when there was a Medici patron to foot the bill. At that time there was an artisan whose sole function was to select the semiprecious stones to fit the designs of wreaths of flowers, baskets of fruit, and miniature Tuscan landscapes. At the Opificio delle Pietre Dure (via degli Alfani 78, near piazza Santissima Annunziata) you can see the workmanship of the Renaissance on tables and panels where the garlands of roses have an almost velvety sheen, with pearly drops of dew among the petals, the pips of the pomegranates juicy and red. (Closed only on local feast days.)

Palazzo Medici-Riccardi

This was the Medicis' private home, completed in 1460, where Cosimo, Piero, and Lorenzo all lived, although Cosimo complained that it was "too large a house for so small a family." Later they moved into the Palazzo Vecchio and then, as grand dukes of Tuscany, to the Palazzo Pitti.

Benozzo Gozzoli was a quattrocento Florentine painter who studied under Fra Angelico and whose fresco of the *Procession of the Magi* in the tiny chapel of the palazzo is perhaps his best work, among the most unforgettable of the many frescoes in Florence. His approach to his work was lighthearted: When Piero ("the Gouty") de' Medici complained about two little seraphim on the horizon, he was told not to worry, "two little cloudlets will take them away." The *Procession of the Magi* contains more Florentines than Wise Men, with the depiction of the Medicis and their courtiers. There is Piero the Gouty himself, his motto, *Semper,* engraved on the horse's trappings. The three Medici girls are dressed as pages with feathers in their caps, and Gozzoli has painted himself into the procession together with his mentor, Fra Angelico. The frescoes have been restored in time for the 500th anniversary of Lorenzo Il Magnifico's death. His is the splendid gilded figure in the center, although it is not a good likeness: The magnificent nose has been much toned down for the portrait.

Palazzo Vecchio

Goethe concluded that for Florence to have accumulated such a rich heritage of art and architecture she must have enjoyed "a long succession of wise rulers." And yet throughout the 13th century Florence was split by bitter strife between the two warring factions, the Guelphs and the Ghibellines. Like the Montagues and Capulets of *Romeo and Juliet,* some families belonged to the Guelphs, the merchant party with allegiance to the pope, others to the Ghibellines, the aristocratic and feudal party whose sympathies were with the Hohenstaufen Holy Roman emperors. These feuds were carried on between cities as well—Guelph Florence against Ghibelline Siena, Pisa, and Arezzo. However, even among the Guelphs themselves there were bitterly opposed White Guelphs and Black Guelphs. Depending on which party momentarily held sway, Florentines of the opposite allegiance were forced, as Dante (himself a White Guelph) was, to eat what he called "the bitter bread of exile."

The Palazzo Vecchio was built to celebrate a definitive Guelph victory at Benevento in 1266. The tower, which has variously been compared to a rocket or a hypodermic needle, soars upward from the **piazza della Signoria**, the center of Florentine civic life, the square that was paved over the ruins of Ghibelline property so that they could never set foot in their palazzi again. Later the Palazzo Vecchio became the official residence of the Medicis, acquiring the epithet "*Vecchio*" (old) when Cosimo de' Medici moved into his new apartments in the Palazzo Pitti. Today it is still Florence's town hall, where births and deaths are registered and where Florentines are married—the bride always being presented with a bouquet of *gigli,* or irises, the city's emblem. (Today 20 percent of the marriages at the Palazzo Vecchio are of Americans—marriage being surprisingly free of red tape for foreigners in Florence.) Seemingly endless flights of stairs lead up to the great rooms, seat of the city's administration in the 15th century, and to the Medici apartments, all of which can be visited, from 9:00 A.M. to 7:00 P.M. (8:00 A.M. to 1:00 P.M. on feast days), except on Saturdays.

Galleria degli Uffizi

The Galleria degli Uffizi, next to the Palazzo Vecchio, was once the offices, or *uffizi,* of the Medici government. The building was designed by Vasari, who also built a corridor to enable the reigning grand duke to leave his apartments in the Palazzo Pitti and cross the ponte Vecchio without ever having to descend to street level. It was completed in only five months and claimed five lives in the building. Today the gallery houses the most important collection of Renaissance art in the world. The museum is open afternoons as well as mornings, from 9:00 A.M. to 7:00 P.M. Monday through Saturday, and a half day on Sunday.

The main gallery, on the top floor, starts with the early Sienese painters (almost Byzantine in style), including Duccio, Lorenzetti, and Simone Martini, and continues through the International Gothic style of Gentile da Fabriano and Lorenzo Monaco to the early Renaissance. Here Masaccio is joined by Masolino, who also collaborated on the frescoes in the Brancacci chapel in Santa Maria del Carmine (see below), and Uccello, with what is often considered his masterpiece, the *Battle of San Romano*. This battle scene, which used to hang in Lorenzo de' Medici's bedroom, is one of three panels—the other two are now in Paris and London.

The two best-known paintings of the Uffizi are surely the **Birth of Venus** and **Primavera** by Sandro Botticelli—huge canvases that once hung in a Medici villa outside Florence. Botticelli's popularity is a relatively recent phenomenon; he was rediscovered during the Victorian Grand Tour period at the end of the last century. In his own lifetime he would have died a pauper on crutches if Lorenzo de' Medici had not supported him during his last years (he died in 1510).

Both the *Birth of Venus* and the *Primavera* would seem to be pagan subjects, but they are in fact offshoots of the Neoplatonic thought subscribed to almost slavishly at Lorenzo the Magnificent's court—interpretations of the Venus myth in Christian terms. The *Primavera* is an allegory of civilized living, while *Venus* is a pagan Madonna. Marsilio Ficino, tutor to the Medici children, wrote to one of his charges that Venus symbolizes humanity, "herself a nymph of excellent comeliness."

Two newly restored works were unveiled to the public in 1990: Duccio's *Maestà* and *The Crowning of the Virgin* by Botticelli, accompanied by an exhibition of restoration techniques.

Another recently restored work is the *Tondo Doni,* a round picture of the Holy Family that Michelangelo painted for Agnolo Doni, who, like a good Florentine, haggled over the price (it was a new idea that artists should be paid differently from artisans, who got so much per hour); the patron was shamed into paying double. (During a similar argument, Donatello smashed a statue to pieces, declaring that his patron was obviously more used to purchasing beans than art.) In the *Tondo Doni,* the only canvas he ever completed, Michelangelo shows his mastery of contour, his sculptural style emphasizing movement and expressive line.

The Uffizi also houses an *Annunciation* by Leonardo da Vinci, one that, like most Annunciations, seems to have taken place in Tuscany, with cypress trees and umbrella pines punctuating the skyline. Leonardo's treatment of the angel's wings is highly innovative, studied in detail from real birds' wings; the folds of the Madonna's draperies were copied from an actual piece of cloth.

Leonardo was the archetypal Renaissance man, who excelled at everything he turned his hand to. The illegitimate son of a village squire, he was the first to apply reason to everything in the universe. He discovered the meaning of fossils, understood the solar system far ahead of his time, realized a hundred years before it was pronounced a certainty that the blood circulated in the body, understood optics and the role of the retina, and nearly invented the airplane. At the Antico Setificio in San Frediano the silk weavers still use a giant bobbin invented by Leonardo to wind the silk—no one has yet thought of a better system.

Leonardo was so busy inventing he had little time for painting, where perhaps his greatest genius lay. He himself wrote, as an afterthought when offering his services as an architect and an engineer, "In painting I can do as much as anyone, whoever he may be." To Leonardo we owe the tender, mysterious smiles not just of the Mona Lisa but of all his female figures, sacred or otherwise. He conceived objects as bathed in space, inventing *lo sfumato,* in which he defined his forms without abrupt outlines. When just a youth he was apprenticed to Verrocchio and painted the left-hand angel in a canvas of his master's *The Baptism* (now here in the Uffizi), after which it is said that a chagrined Verrocchio vowed never to paint again, concentrating on sculpture from then on. Also in the Uffizi is Leonardo's *Adoration of the Magi,* which, with its pyramidal composition—a solution to the problem of cramming a picture with spectators around the central group of the Madonna and Child—is considered a watershed in Renaissance art: a break with all that had gone before, and one of the most important works in Florence in the last quarter of the 15th century.

The Uffizi collection includes works by Filippino Lippi, Mantegna, Perugino, Raphael, Bellini, Giorgione, Correggio, Titian, Rubens, Veronese, Caravaggio, Tintoretto, and every other major Renaissance painter in Italy and abroad. With the waning of the High Renaissance, we find the Mannerism of Pontormo and Bronzino, including the latter's portraits of Medici courtiers, in a magnificent circular room with a mother-of-pearl inlaid domed ceiling. Agonizingly long lines tend to form outside the museum, especially in the high season.

Palazzo Davanzati

The **Museo della Casa Fiorentina Antica**, a few streets to the west of the piazza della Signoria, is a unique example of a domestic building of the 14th century, when the medieval tower was evolving into the Renaissance palace, the fortress into the home. Once the house of a noble family, the Palazzo Davanzati has been restored as it was in the days when Florentine matrons sat at the loom or the spinning wheel, filling their bedroom chests with hand-spun linen, their kitchen shelves stacked with the utensils and crockery typical of the time, all of which is here on view. The Palazzo

Davanzati is also remarkable for its *agiamenti,* a genteel Renaissance word for toilet—a rare luxury in those days.

Bargello

The Bargello, just across the piazza San Firenze from the Palazzo Vecchio, built 50 years before the Duomo and the Palazzo Vecchio, was originally the seat of the *podestà,* or chief city magistrate. Criminal offenders were often hung out of the windows of the tower, and their pictures were painted on the walls of the tower and inner courtyard by well-known artists like Andrea del Castagno, who acquired the nickname Andreuccio degli Impiccati, or "Andy of the Hanged." Medical students and investigators such as Leonardo could claim the bodies of the condemned men for dissection, as long as the condemned had been born more than two miles beyond the city walls and were therefore "foreigners."

The Museo Nazionale del Bargello today is to sculpture what the Uffizi is to painting. Here are Michelangelo's *Drunken Bacchus* and *Brutus;* Cellini's *Perseus* in a number of poses: with his mother, Danae, slaying the Medusa, and rescuing Andromeda; Giambologna's *Mercury;* and two more *David*s: bronze statues by Verrocchio and Donatello, the latter reputedly the first nude statue of the Renaissance.

Donatello's *David* is very different from Michelangelo's. It is a boyish, almost effeminate statue, with curly locks and a dandyish hat—in many ways a flashback to the Classical past in which Donatello found his inspiration. At the same time, it is not a mere copy of Roman art but the work of an equal who is doing very much "his own thing." Verrocchio's *David,* on the other hand, is typical of the late quattrocento in its elegance and finesse of workmanship and is said to have been inspired by his pupil, the young Leonardo.

Donatello was, after the death of Masaccio, the major Florentine artist of the 15th century. Sculpture at that time was a question of either accepting Donatello's ideas or reacting against them; the latter solution usually meant following in the more conventional wake of Ghiberti. Donatello challenged the subordinate role of sculpture as mere decoration of architecture. His work has a dramatic quality and a passionate sense of tragedy, especially in works like his *Maddalena* in the Museo dell'Opera di Santa Maria del Fiore (see above).

On the first floor, Donatello's *David* is flanked by his magnificently austere *Saint George* and his irresistible *Amore*—a cupid in wading trousers reaching up to be hugged, his *Marzocco* lion of Florence, a *Saint John the Baptist* by Desiderio da Settignano, and some of the better-known Della Robbias.

To the right of the Bargello, a narrow street leads to the via Isola delle Stinche and some of the best ice cream in Florence, at **Vivoli's**. After which you round a corner into piazza Santa Croce, dominated by the striped marble façade of the church for which it is named.

Although devoid of green, piazza Santa Croce—once the sight of tournaments under the Medicis—is a neighborhood square where mothers walk their children, pigeons waddle between the benches, and vendors absent-mindedly sell postcards or balloons, while the occasional North African known as the *"Vuu' compra'"* sits dolefully cross-legged, surrounded by his wares. (*"Vuu' compra'"* is a distortion of *"Vuoi comprare"* or "Do you want to buy?" This is often the only Italian they know, as they stoically wander up and down the streets and beaches of Italy. They have now been joined by Albanian refugees, while the over-enthusiastic windshield cleaners at the traffic lights are mostly from Poland.)

Church of Santa Croce

Dante left Florence, never to return, and is buried in Ravenna—a fact to which the Florentines are still not reconciled. But there is a commemorative plaque to Italy's greatest poet in the Franciscan church of Santa Croce, together with flamboyant marble tombs of great Italian figures such as Galileo, Rossini, and Michelangelo. Santa Croce, at the eastern edge of the city center near the river, is Florence's Pantheon, a center for the cult of famous men. The most beautiful tombs are of two chancellors of the Republic and prominent humanists, Leonardo Bruni and Carlo Marsuppini, which face each other on either side of the nave. Humanism in the Renaissance was *humanitas,* a word that Leonardo Bruni, who was chancellor in 1427, borrowed from Cicero, meaning studies that are "humane," worthy of the dignity of mankind. It is therefore appropriate that the portrait of the man himself dominates each tomb, the Bruni monument being the more austere of the two, the solemnity of the Marsuppini tomb relieved by some entrancing little *putti* blithely standing guard.

The church of Santa Croce is where Lucy Honeychurch of E. M. Forster's *A Room with a View* finds herself at a loss without a Baedeker while looking for the frescoes of Giotto, "in the presence of whose tactile values she was capable of feeling what was proper." With these frescoes in the **Peruzzi** and **Bardi chapels**, Giotto, who flourished in the early 14th century, imposed a new and more human vision of the arts of Western Europe. Not since antiquity had the human body been represented in such a realistic way. He also had a genius for selecting the most dramatic psychological moment in a story and making every component of the fresco echo this. His people are experiencing real emotion; the grief-stricken brothers mourning the death of Saint Francis are human in their suffering at a time when faces in painting were only conventional masks. The epitaph on a monument to Giotto erected by Lorenzo the Magnificent reads in Latin, "I am he by whom the extinct art of painting was revived."

The flood of 1966 did much damage to the church of Santa Croce, especially to the frescoes and to the giant 13th-century crucifix by Cimabue—widely pictured in the press dragging in the mud when the waters had receded. What is left of it is in the **Museo dell'Opera di Santa Croce**, in the old convent refectory next door (open from 10:00 A.M. to 12:30 P.M. and 2:30 to 6:30 P.M. in summer, 10:00 A.M. to 12:30 P.M. and 3:00 to 5:00 P.M. in winter; closed Wednesdays). At the far end of the cloisters the Cappella dei Pazzi can be admired, a classic example of Brunelleschi's circle-within-a-square style. The leather school that adjoins the church was founded by the monks and is now, besides a school, a series of workshops where you can purchase leather goods and have them initialed on the spot.

Museo di Storia della Scienza

Galileo was the last of the great Florentines (1564–1642) at the end of a Golden Age. He originally wanted to be a painter, but his father discouraged this as an unprofitable profession. Instead, Galileo's work on the science of dynamics and statics, and his discovery and formulation of the laws of motion, are the basis of modern engineering, even of spacecraft. Such avant-garde ideas brought him into conflict with the Church, and he spent much of his life trying to justify his theories before the Inquisition. He lived out his last years, blind and embittered, in exile at his villa in Arcetri on a hill above Florence, where the Florentine observatory stands to this day. The Museo di Storia della Scienza (Museum of the History of Science) contains Galileo's telescopes, compasses, and astrolabes and the lens with which he first identified Jupiter and the "Medici" planets, as he christened them. There is his armchair, his telescope stand—and even the pickled third finger of his right hand. Open daily from 9:30 A.M. to 1:00 P.M., and from 2:00 to 5:00 P.M. on Mondays, Wednesdays, and Fridays; closed Sundays.

Church of Santa Maria Novella

Paolo Uccello was obsessed by perspective. His wife said that he would crawl into bed late at night saying, *"O, che dolce cosa è questa prospettiva"* (how fair a thing is this perspective). He was called *Uccello* (bird) because of the many birds and beasts that appeared in his paintings. Although he relied largely on illustrations of birds and beasts, the animals featured in Renaissance paintings often were drawn from life. Lions were caged behind the Uffizi from the 13th century onward, and a camel, a giraffe, and other exotic animals arrived in the retinue of the Emperor John Palaeologus when the Western and Eastern churches met in Florence. This momentous event, sponsored by the Medicis, was immortalized by Benozzo Gozzoli in his *Procession of the Magi* in the chapel of the Palazzo Medici-Riccardi.

Uccello spent a disproportionate number of hours (scolded for it not just by his wife but by his friend Donatello) studying the perspective of the *mazzocchi,* the intricate straw scaffolding used for the extravagant headgear of the time, as shown in the equestrian portrait of Niccolò da Tolentino by Andrea del Castagno and in Uccello's twin fresco of Giovanni Acuto, the English mercenary whose real name was John Hawkwood. (The two frescoes are side by side in the Duomo.) Typically parsimonious, the Florentines owed this condottiere a memorial, but to save money they commissioned Uccello to do a fresco giving the illusion of sculpture.

Paolo Uccello's 15th-century studies of perspective are most evident in his frescoes in the **Green Cloister**, adjacent to the church of Santa Maria Novella, in the piazza Santa Maria Novella. These depict scenes of the Creation and the Universal Deluge, the panic and anarchy in the latter enhanced by a vanishing focal point that seems to act like a magnet, drawing in the entire biblical cast.

The Green Cloister is so called because of the *terra verde,* or greenish grisaille, that was Uccello's favorite medium for frescoes. The cloister follows most Florentine museum opening and closing times but is closed Fridays.

Leading off the Green Cloister is the **Cappellone degli Spagnoli** (Spanish Chapel), "Spanish" because the Spanish retinue of Eleonora of Toledo, wife of Cosimo de' Medici, used to hear mass here. The chapel's murals, painted by Andrea Bonaiuti and others around 1366–1368, were the most ambitious work of pictorial theology of their time. Salvation, they suggest, is possible if sinners listen to the Dominican monks to whom Santa Maria Novella and the cloister and neighboring pharmacy all belonged. "Dominicans" was said to mean *"Domini Canes,"* hounds of the Lord; the Dominicans fought heresy mercilessly. No doubt when the Black Death of 1348 struck Florence and more than half the population of the city died, many townsfolk must have felt a cold wind blowing "I told you so" down their necks.

The side chapels in the church of Santa Maria Novella, which is across the piazza della Stazione from the train station, were all financed by leading citizens thankful for survival or in memory of their dear departed: for example, the **Strozzi Chapel** with frescoes by Filippino Lippi and the **Tornabuoni Chapel** with frescoes by Ghirlandaio, who also made the magnificent stained-glass window that dominates the nave. (The exquisite blonde noblewoman paying her respects to Saint Elizabeth after the birth of Saint John the Baptist is in fact Lucrezia Tornabuoni, mother of the magnificent Lorenzo.)

The church is very badly lit, or as Edward Hutton politely puts it, "full of a sort of twilight," which can be illuminated by inserting some coins into a machine. You must seek out *The Trinity* by Masaccio in the main nave. Here Brunelleschian architectural forms are used—the arch is an exact copy of part of the façade of the Ospedale degli Innocenti— as a setting for figures that are represented for the first time in a human dimension rather than larger than life, as divine figures traditionally were. Above the door in the sacristy, where postcards are on sale, is an ample, very beautiful wooden cross by Giotto and his school (both the painting and the cross are currently under restoration).

Look, too, for Brunelleschi's crucifix, which hangs with an almost chilling solemnity in a chapel all by itself. Hereby hangs the tale of the competition between Donatello and Brunelleschi as to who would carve the most beautiful crucifix. When Brunelleschi pronounced Donatello's Christ "a boor," Donatello is supposed to have answered, "Take wood, then, and make one yourself," a saying that became a byword in Renaissance Florence. Some time later, the two friends came back to Brunelleschi's studio, having shopped for lunch. Donatello was so bowled over by the just-completed ascetic Christ hanging on the wall that he dropped the provisions—eggs, cheese, and all—out of his artisan's apron onto the floor.

The **Pharmacy** of Santa Maria Novella at via della Scala 16, originally run by the Dominican monks, has been functioning since 1612. It still makes and sells herbal remedies 400 years old. In times of plague the pharmacy made a lotion called *Aceto dei Sette Ladri* (Seven Thieves Vinegar), an unguent that was rubbed on the body to prevent contagion, named after the seven thieves who used to go around the city at night to rob the corpses of unfortunate victims of the plague. The pharmacy still does a surprisingly brisk trade in this lotion, which it sells as smelling salts. It also sells soaps, colognes, and potpourris in old-fashioned packaging that make unusual gifts to take home. (There is similar merchandise, cheaper but not so distinctively packaged, in another old Florentine pharmacy, **Il Cinghiale**, opposite the Straw Market.)

Piazza Santa Maria Novella has become the established meeting place for the Filipino community, which makes up most of the domestic staff of Florence, every affluent Florentine household employing at least one. They give life to an otherwise transient square, congregating around the Serravezza marble obelisks supported by turtles by Giambologna.

The Cenacoli

Florence has a number of *cenacoli,* or frescoes of the Last Supper, painted on the walls of monastery refectories. The first Renaissance refectory in Florence belonged to the Benedictine nuns of **Sant'Appollonia**. The *Last Supper* by Andrea del Castagno here, at via Aprile XXVII, just off the piazza San Marco, is a tense, dramatic work with a very sinister Judas sitting alone on one side of the pristine tablecloth. Andrea del Castagno was a glowering peasant painter, what the French call *ténébreux,* and his bloodthirsty reputation may be due in part to his appearance, in part to the harsh realism of his work. He is one of the most important painters to follow in Masaccio's footsteps, although he owes the linear rhythms and dramatic quality of his work to Donatello.

A very different *cenacolo* is the *Last Supper* by Domenico Ghirlandaio in the refectory of **Ognissanti** at borgo Ognissanti 42 (the street runs almost parallel to the lungarno on the right bank), where Jesus and his apostles are enjoying a peaceful domestic reunion, with pewter flagons on the floor and a beautifully embroidered cloth on the table. In the background, songbirds wheel above the lemon trees. (Open till noon on Mondays, Tuesdays, and Saturdays.) Domenico Ghirlandaio was the son of a goldsmith whose craft also gave the family their name: *Ghirlande* means garlands, or wedding crowns. Ghirlandaio was the master of the young Michelangelo, who as a mere boy was drawing at his feet while he was painting the Tornabuoni chapel in Santa Maria Novella, causing the elder painter to exclaim, "but he knows more than I do!"

Andrea del Sarto painted his *Last Supper* at **San Salvi** much later, in the mid-16th century. The ballooning draperies and flamboyant gestures of the apostles are typical of the High Renaissance. Although he was among the best draftsmen of his time, and Michelangelo is said to have told Raphael, "There is a little fellow in Florence who would make you sweat if he ever got a great commission to do," Andrea del Sarto had a weak character. He married a shrew, but unlike Petruchio he never tamed her, and with Madonna Lucrezia he had, says Vasari, "his work cut out for him for the rest of his days." However, every woman that Andrea painted—"his handsome vague-browed Madonnas," as Henry James called them in his *Florentine Notes*—had something of his wife in her, because not only were she and her numerous and demanding family always before him, but "he carried her image in his heart."

The painter died of the plague at the age of 44, untended by his wife, who was scrambling to leave the city. The church of San Salvi is at via Andrea del Sarto 16, a short taxi or bus ride from the center of Florence (take bus number 6, which can be caught in piazza San Marco).

THE OLTRARNO
Palazzo Pitti

The Pitti Palace is the largest, most overwhelming palazzo in Florence. It was built by Luca Pitti, who was the equivalent of a modern-day industrialist and self-made man who wanted to have a bigger and better home than any of the noble families of Florence, especially the Medicis. The Pitti was criticized at the time, as there was already a housing shortage in Florence, and never before had a private residence been conceived on such a large scale, with blocks of stone that to Taine seemed more like "sections of mountains." Never before, too, had a palazzo been built, as Machiavelli complained, in such royal isolation, although this proved an advantage later on when the Pitti became the palace of the ruling families of Tuscany, from the Medicis onward. The Medicis were followed by the Hapsburg Lorraine archdukes, in the days when Florence was part of the Austro-Hungarian Empire, and by the House of Savoy when Florence was briefly capital of Italy. Today it houses no fewer than six museums, of which four—the Monumental

Apartments, as they are called, and the carriage museum, as well as the porcelain and costume museums—are temporarily closed.

The **Museo delle Porcellane** and the **Galleria del Costume** are both well worth a visit if you are a buff in either genre—especially the former, which is housed in the Casino del Cavaliere, built for a son of one of the Medicis, with its formal garden and a view over the hills of Florence. (Visits by appointment. Tel: 21-25-57.) If you are on a tight schedule, however, you may have time only for the Galleria Palatina and the Museo degli Argenti—the same ticket gives access to both.

The **Galleria Palatina** houses pictures from the High Renaissance by Raphael, Titian, Tintoretto, and Andrea del Sarto, as well as some beautiful landscapes by Rubens. Apart from Andrea del Sarto, none of these masters was born in Florence, even though Vasari describes Raphael as a "Florentine painter born in Urbino," perhaps because his stay in Florence and his study of the works of Masaccio, Leonardo, and Michelangelo had a lasting effect on his work. "I must not fail to mention that Raphael so much improved his manner after his visit to Florence that he seemed to be an entirely different and much greater artist," says Vasari.

The **Museo degli Argenti** (Silver Museum) is chiefly remarkable for the collection of vases and *orfèvrerie* that belonged to Lorenzo de' Medici. Unlike his father, Cosimo, he was not a patron of large works of art, preferring to collect ornaments and accessories. For him love was the *appetito di bellezza,* the appetite for beauty. Don't miss the jewels of Maria Luisa de' Medici in a little alcove of their own.

Behind the Pitti Palace is the **Giardino di Boboli** (Boboli Gardens), which is open to the public from 9:00 A.M. until sunset every day. This is a Classical Italian garden with ilex walks, box parterres, and a whole cavalcade of statuary, such as the grotesque pot-bellied figure of a dwarf, Cosimo's court jester Morgante, astride a turtle. The gardens are the favorite venue of children and their nannies in the mornings and are an ideal place to picnic, with an 18th-century coffeehouse halfway up the hill. The Medicis planted a plethora of imported seeds and bulbs in the gardens; even today when a child says, "*Voglio* . . ." (I want), he will be told, "The grass called 'I want' doesn't even grow in the Boboli gardens." There is a controversy raging over whether visitors should be required to pay an entrance fee to the gardens—intended to stem the increasing vandalism to which Florence is vulnerable.

The Medicis also sponsored every aspect of the arts, and

goldsmiths, silversmiths, engravers in crystal and cameos, seamstresses, wood-carvers, leather craftsmen, and artisans working in baser metals like bronze and copper all flocked to the Medici court and competed to produce the jewels, the trinkets, the knickknacks and ornaments that adorned the ruling family's apartments.

Today this thriving artisan life still exists in the streets that fan out at the feet of the Palazzo Pitti. One of the joys of the Oltrarno is to lose yourself on purpose in the narrow little streets and peer into dingy workshops where wood shavings fly and strong smells of glue and varnish assail the nose. As Mary McCarthy says, "The Florentine crafts, out of which the arts had grown, the severe tradition of elegance that goes back to Brunelleschi, Michelozzo, Donatello, Pollaiuolo has been transmitted to the shoemaker and the seamstress."

With the death of Galileo in 1642, the Golden Age of Florentine arts and architecture came to an end, but Florence is still a world center for craftspeople and for art restoration. There are artisans like **Bartolozzi**, at via Vellutini 5R, whose workshop pieced together and recarved the abbey of Monte Cassino after it was bombed by the Americans during World War II. Inch by inch it took 30 artisans ten years. Or **Brandimarte**, whose workshop at via Bartolini 18 rings with the sound of chisels like the chorus from *Il Trovatore,* making timeless silverware, goblets, and large silver plates ringed with fruit and flowers that could have graced the tables of Lorenzo the Magnificent himself. Next door, the **Antico Setificio Fiorentino** is still working with looms more than a century old, into which up to 40,000 hairlike strands of silk are threaded by hand, one by one, while the patterns are punched on wooden blocks, the quattrocento version of a computer. Emilio Pucci is president of the Setificio; to this day only women, and only women from the Oltrarno San Frediano district of Florence at that, can work here.

The Churches of Santa Maria del Carmine and Santo Spirito

These two churches are west of the Pitti in neighboring squares bearing their names. In the Carmine is the **Cappella Brancacci,** famous for its frescoes by Masaccio.

Masaccio's real name was Tommaso, but he was called Masaccio, which means "Slovenly Tom," because of his disregard for appearances. Masaccio was a people's painter, with the straightforward honesty of a Florentine artisan. About a century after Giotto, Masaccio revived the earlier artist's approach to fresco painting. He painted in a sculptural way, departing from the International Gothic style by emphasizing mass and light over line and color.

Masaccio was the first painter of his time to apply the new principles of perspective worked out by sculptors and architects such as Donatello, Ghiberti, and Brunelleschi. Although he died at the age of 27 (in 1428), in only five or six years he managed to revolutionize Florentine painting. He used the new knowledge of anatomy to paint, as Vasari says, "many attitudes and movements that had never before been painted." The tax collector collecting the tribute money from Saint Peter is appropriately avid; Adam and Eve express their shame with gaping mouths as they are expelled from the Garden of Eden. Adam and Eve are now as Masaccio painted them—without the fig leaves of puritanical afterthought—recently unveiled after restoration. There is a separate entrance to the frescoes, to the right of the church; and there is usually a line, as only a certain number of people are admitted at one time.

No lesser painters than Filippino Lippi, Andrea del Castagno, Verrocchio, Ghirlandaio, Botticelli, Leonardo da Vinci, Perugino, Michelangelo, and Raphael recognized Masaccio as a master and came to study these frescoes in the Brancacci chapel. (Open 10:00 A.M. to 5:00 P.M.; 1:00 to 5:00 P.M. on feast days. Closed Tuesdays.)

The church of **Santo Spirito** was Brunelleschi's last church, which he did not live to finish. It belonged to an Augustinian order whose members gave up lunch for half a century in order to finance its building. Even though Brunelleschi's designs were not entirely carried out, it is still, according to Vasari, "almost the most perfect church in Christendom." There is a fine altarpiece by Filippino Lippi, as well as a small, eye-catching painting quaintly called *Saint Mary of the Relief,* with a Madonna in a magnificent orange gown brandishing a wooden club at a sour-looking little orange devil, who stamps his foot on an orange-checkered marble floor.

Piazza Santo Spirito is a neighborhood square, with old men dozing on benches while their wives knit and gossip and children, dogs, and pigeons tumble about the fountain. In the mornings there is a market for vegetables and, among other things, shoes and secondhand clothes. In the evenings it is the more sinister venue of the flotsam and jetsam of the Florentine drug culture, although the municipal police are doing what they can, with a police car stationed there permanently. This should not deter the younger, more venturesome visitor from enjoying a cheap bohemian pizza at **Borgo Antico** (closed Sundays) or an ice cream at **Caffè Ricchi**. **Cabiria** is one of the trendiest bars in town (closed Tuesdays).

Church of San Miniato al Monte

The church of San Miniato is reached by a steep but very rewarding climb, up steps behind the Porta San Niccolò (one of the old gates to the city), less than a mile east of the Pitti. It is the most beautiful Romanesque church in Florence and dominates the city, sharing with the nearby **piazzale Michelangelo** the view to end all views, especially at sunset, "when the sun from the west, beyond Pisa, beyond the mountains of Carrara / Departs, and the world is taken by surprise" (D. H. Lawrence).

San Miniato himself was the first Christian martyr in Florence. After having been decapitated in the arena, he carried his head up the hill and across the river to the present site of the church, which is built on an early Christian cemetery. The mosaic floor with its zodiac symbols dates from 1207. At 4:45 P.M. sharp every day the monks sing Gregorian chants in the crypt; the doors are shut the moment they begin, so be punctual.

Music and Literature
in Florence

Not all of the greatness of Florence lies in its paintings, statues, and buildings. The city was also cradle to the humanities, to music, and to literature. Under Lorenzo de' Medici, Florentines sought a "rationale" for God and man in the study of the ancients. Poliziano, the poor student from Montepulciano who became tutor to the Medici children, wrote that the young nobility of Florence were so fluent in Greek that it was as though Athens, instead of being destroyed by barbarians, had been detached from the Greek peninsula and incorporated into the city on the Arno. Marsilio Ficino, the son of Cosimo's doctor, was only 18 years old when the old Medici duke requested him to translate Plato. In 1459 Cosimo founded the Accademia Platonica. Ficino's "Christian" interpretation of Plato dominated Florentine thought until the arrival in 1484 of Giovanni Pico della Mirandola, whose ideal was to unite all philosophies and all religions into one intellectual concept.

His so-called Oration on the Dignity of Man is considered the manifesto of the Renaissance.

The seeds of opera as we know it today were sown in Florence in 1580 at the house of Count Giovanni Bardi—the same family as Dante's Beatrice—when a group of musicians, together with Vincenzo Galilei (father of Galileo and a composer), decided to revive the ancient music dramas of the Greeks. In former times there had been no song catchier than the "Kyrie Eleison" until the troubadours brought love ballads to the courts of Italy and France. Slowly, *musica profana* in the form of madrigals, and choral singing in general, took over from psalms and religious chants; the angels in Renaissance painting are equipped more often than not with lutes and mandolins, while Boccaccio's *Decamerone* resounds with joyous voices singing worldly songs in unison.

La Camerata Fiorentina, as it came to be called, went one step further, and in works like *Dafne* by Jacopo Peri (1594) and *Euridice* (1600) by Peri (with Caccini), the dramatic values of the story were enhanced by the expressive quality of the music, inventing musical speech, or "recitative," gradually to be enriched by arias, duos, and set choral pieces. In this way the groundwork was laid for Claudio Monteverdi at Mantua, who in turn opened the way for the later great operatic composers such as Gluck, Mozart, Rossini, Verdi, and Wagner.

Florence's **Teatro Comunale** has an opera season in the fall and features ballet and concerts in the spring. The musical director is Zubin Mehta, but other famous conductors as well as singers and performers come to Florence all year round, especially in May and June during the Maggio Musicale (Musical May Festival).

Dante Alighieri, born in 1265, was a Florentine and the first great figure of the Renaissance. He was not only a poet but a philosophical thinker, a politician, and a religious visionary. He gave expression to the mind and spirit of an age in which the conflicting realms of religious thought and an Aristotelian vision of the cosmos formed the basis of contemporary writing—writing which, because it was expressed exclusively in Latin, was available only to a scholarly elite. In *De vulgari eloquentia* Dante advocated the use of Italian, and his *Divina Commedia* was written in the language of his native city's streets.

Exiled from Florence in his early 30s because of his political activities, Dante was a wanderer until the end of his life, in 1321. Don't bother to visit his house in Florence; it is a 19th-century reconstruction, not to say a fake.

Giovanni Boccaccio, one of the world's greatest storytellers, half French, half Tuscan, was born in 1313. He grew up in his family home of Certaldo, between Florence and Siena. He was a great admirer of Dante, and one of his earlier works was a biography of Italy's leading poet. In his last years he received an allowance from the city of Florence as public expositor of the *Divina Commedia*. The Florentine gardens of the Villa Schifanoia were the setting for his famous *Decamerone*.

GETTING AROUND

Shod in a pair of comfortable shoes, you can see the whole city on foot. A car is a liability because of a trigger-happy civic system for towing away vehicles that have strayed from the straight and narrow paths and parking lots. Recently, to combat traffic anarchy and pollution, most of the "historic center" has been closed to all vehicles, and female police, like Scylla and Charybdis, bar your way at every turn. This is known as the *zona blu*, or blue zone. (A German traffic whiz-kid has been called in by the authorities to extend this zone still farther—leading, needless to say, to even more chaos.) If you do have a car, your only hope is to try to park on the lungarno in the piazza di Cestello in the Oltrarno or in the parking lot in the Porta Romana. If you can find the devious route into the midst of things, there is also parking outside the church of Santa Maria del Carmine. At all of these lots, the hourly rate escalates as every hour goes by.

The only destinations that might call for a bus are the *cenacolo* of San Salvi (line number 6) and the church of San Miniato and piazzale Michelangelo—although there are magical, albeit strenuous, steps leading up here from the Porta S. Niccolò (line number 13). Tickets can be purchased at tobacconists. The main bus stops are outside the main train station or near the Duomo in the stretch of via de'Martelli that runs into via Cavour, or in the piazza San Marco.

Taxis are yellow and fairly ubiquitous; they can also be summoned by telephone from a bar: 47-98.

When to Go

Florence lies in a hollow ringed by hills, which makes it one of the hottest cities in Europe in summer. It is to be avoided if possible during July and August—which is also when a huge number of tourists swarm into the city like locusts. Most Florentines decamp in August, leaving behind a ghost city with shuttered stores and hot pavements. Spring and autumn are the best times to come; the discerning traveller should avoid summer altogether. Winter is relatively mild and short-lived, from December to mid-March, when it rains rather than snows and the queues in front of museums almost disappear. A Florentine proverb is: *Natale con i tuoi, Pasqua con chi vuoi* (Christmas with your own folks, Easter with whomever you want). So beware—many Italians, especially schoolchildren, seem to descend on Florence at Eastertime.

Arrival at Major Gateways

For years the only airport near Florence was at Pisa, which has a rail service direct from the airport to Florence. Florence now has its very own airport, called Peretola—which has become Italy's third busiest airport, after Rome and Milan. Neither Pisa nor Peretola is an intercontinental airport, but they handle most European flights and link Florence to Milan and Rome for overseas travel. If you are arriving directly from North America, you will have to land in Rome or Milan and take another plane or a fast train to Florence. The slowest train in Italy used to be called an *accelerato,* followed by a *diretto,* then a *direttissimo,* an *espresso,* a *rapido,* and finally the super-superlative *super-rapido* and *inter-city,* which will get you to Florence in under three hours from Rome or Milan (sometimes first class only, but worth the extra money). A supersonically fast train, taking only 90 minutes, is being studied for the near future.

ACCOMMODATIONS

The rates given below are projections for 1993; always check for up-to-date information before making reservations. Wide ranges may reflect the differences between low- and high-season rates. Unless otherwise indicated, the figures indicate the cost of a double room (per room, not per person). However, half-board (*mezza pensione*) rates, which include breakfast and one other meal per day, are per person. The service charge is included in the rate; inquire about the tax.

The telephone and fax area code for Florence is 055. When telephoning from outside the country, omit the zero in the city code.

Finding room at the inn in Florence is never easy; when the tourist season is over, the buyers come pouring in for the various Pitti fashion shows, while the *Maggio Musicale,* the annual music festival in May and June, fills the hotels in spring.

Florence has a number of large hotels, including two belonging to the CIGA group, the Excelsior and the Grand, both on piazza Ognissanti on the right bank, west of the center. (It has recently been announced that the Aga Khan, owner of the group, has put them up for sale.) After a hibernation of over a decade, the **Grand Hotel** reopened a few years back, the bedrooms redecorated in pristine pink-and-white Napoleonic stripes. The reception rooms, including the magnificent Winter Garden, still echo the architectural themes of the end of the 19th century, when the Grand was built. While the freshly redecorated rooms of the Grand are superior to those of its sister hotel, the **Hotel Excelsior** has a livelier lobby with the old-fashioned charm of great old European hotels. The piano bar is still the place to find Florence's aging playboys after 6:00, and the restaurant, **Il Cestello**, has one of the best rooftop views in the city (the winter version of Il Cestello is on the ground floor). The Grand inaugurated its restaurant in the Winter Garden last year. Grand: Piazza Ognissanti 1, 50123. Tel: 28-87-81; Fax: 21-74-00 (changing to 28-87-84 this year). Ł630,000. Excelsior: Piazza Ognissanti 3, 50123. Tel: 26-42-01; Fax: 21-02-78. Ł536,000. In U.S. for both, Tel: (800) 221-2340 or (212) 935-9540; Fax: (212) 421-5929. In U.K. for both, Tel: (0800) 28-92-34 or (071) 930-4147; Fax: (071) 839-1566.

The most exclusive, the most elegant of the five-star luxury hotels is the **Hotel Regency**, in the quiet piazza Massimo d'Azeglio at number 3 (50121), east of the Duomo near viale Gramsci. More like a stately town house than a hotel, the expensive Regency has an almost sinister chic, with William Morris–style wallpapers and dusky mirrors. A twin hotel to the Byron in Rome, the Regency has a very good restaurant. Tel: 24-52-47; Fax: 234-29-37. Ł385,000–Ł525,000, suites Ł570,000–Ł600,000. In U.S., Tel: (800) 223-6800 or (212) 838-3110; Fax: (212) 758-7367. In U.K., Tel: (0800) 18-11-23; Fax: (071) 353-1904.

Expense should be no object either at the **Hotel Villa San Michele**, a former monastery halfway up the Fiesole hill, northeast of the center. The villa was designed by Michelangelo, who today has a suite with a marble Jacuzzi tub named after him. Flowers are everywhere, with wisteria tumbling down the walls; there is also a heated pool. Not all the exquisitely furnished rooms share the spectacular view of Florence with the restaurant under the loggia. Via di Doccia 4, 50014 Fiesole. Tel: 594-51; Fax: 59-87-34. Ł640,000–Ł850,000. In U.S., Tel: (800) 223-6800 or (212) 838-3110; Fax: (212) 758-7367. In U.K., Tel: (0800) 18-11-23; Fax: (071) 353-1904. Closed November through March.

If you like the idea of that setting but can't afford the

prices, the **Pensione Bencistà**, a little lower down the hill at via Benedetto da Maiano 4, 50014 Fiesole, offers the same view and the same wisteria for less money in a Tuscan country-house atmosphere. However, one meal of home cooking per day is an obligatory part of the service. Tel: 591-63; Fax: same. Ł85,000 per person without bath, Ł110,000 per person with bath. The Villa San Michele has a private bus, while the Bencistà has to rely on the services of the municipal number 7. No credit cards.

Prices at the four-star hotels are still high, but reasonable for the service and location offered. The **Hotel Berchielli** at lungarno Acciaiuoli 14, 50123, west of the ponte Vecchio, was an old-fashioned hotel with that brand of well-worn gentility beloved of middle-aged English tourists in flat heels. It has been entirely revamped and modernized and brought almost too forcibly into the 20th century, but it should now appeal to a much wider clientele. Tel: 26-40-61; Fax: 21-86-36. Ł385,000. No restaurant.

Almost facing the Berchielli, on the Oltrarno side of the river, is the **Hotel Lungarno**, with one leg knee-deep in the river and the other in the quaint little street of borgo San Jacopo, at number 14, 50125. The Lungarno has become something of a cult hotel with a large international following, many of them buyers, who will stay only here, even if it means a room without a view. The little downstairs sitting room looking onto the river is a cheerful, comfortable place to meet, and there is a garage next door. Tel: 26-42-11; Fax: 26-84-37. Ł280,000. No restaurant.

Another hotel that has enjoyed a radical face-lift is the very central **Hotel Bernini**, behind the Uffizi gallery in the piazza San Firenze 29 (50122). When Florence was the capital of Italy, from 1865 to 1870, members of parliament met in the magnificent room that is now the breakfast room, and portraits of heroes of the Risorgimento stare down from the frescoed and stuccoed ceiling, which has been restored to its former splendor. The rooms are elegantly furnished, and some of them offer a view out over the rooftops at the Palazzo Vecchio or toward San Miniato. There is a small garage. Tel: 28-86-21; Fax: 26-82-72. Ł270,000–Ł300,000, with breakfast. No restaurant.

The **Hotel Helvetia & Bristol** was a well-known landmark during the era of the Victorian Grand Tour, when it was decorated in the slightly stuffy, understated chic of the period. It reopened last year after extensive restoration, during which everything was changed except the atmosphere. No two rooms or suites are furnished in the same style, be it Baroque or Biedermeyer. The bar—palm trees and wicker furniture—is an ideal place for a light lunch. There is also a very good restaurant. Less expensive than the larger hotels, it could not be more centrally located. Via dei Pescioni 2, 50123. Tel: 28-78-14; Fax: 28-83-53. Ł475,000–Ł510,000 with breakfast.

A relative newcomer on the scene is the **Loggiato dei Serviti**, in a privately owned Renaissance palace opposite the Ospedale degli Innocenti in piazza SS. Annunziata (number 3, 50122). Elegantly furnished by the aristocratic owners, the Loggiato is reasonably priced. Tel: 28-95-92; Fax: 28-95-95. Ł200,000 with breakfast. No restaurant.

Alternatively, the **Grand Hotel Villa Cora** is a five-star hotel in the viale Niccolo Machiavelli (number 18, 50125), one of the sweeping, tree-lined avenues that wind up toward the piazzale Michelangelo in Oltrarno. A grandiose 19th-century edifice, Villa Cora looks like a Beethoven concerto cast in stone and gilded stucco. The rooms, furnished in fake Victoriana to match, look out on the park and a poolside restaurant, the **Taverna Machiavelli**. Tel: 22-98-451; Fax: 22-90-86. Ł630,000, suites Ł695,000–Ł1,150,000, with "full American breakfast."

Cheaper and less luxurious accommodations are to be had in Florence's various pensioni, of which there are many, and these are becoming more and more popular now that Europe in general, and Florence in particular, has become so much more expensive for visitors from the United States. The **Pensione Beacci Tornabuoni**, one of the better ones, has hotel prices but a pensione atmosphere; cozy little sitting rooms and old-fashioned Tuscan country-house-style furniture right on the via de' Tornabuoni (number 3, 50123), Florence's main shopping street. The rooms vary greatly in size, but you can pay extra for a large one. There is a pleasant little restaurant, and although the Beacci is usually fully booked months ahead, the management will give preferential treatment to those who want half or full board. Tel: 21-26-45; Fax: 28-35-94. Half board Ł125,000–Ł150,000.

Also perched among the roofs of the via Tornabuoni is **La Residenza**, at number 8. Less glamorous but comfortable, with a dowdy charm. Tel: 21-86-84; Fax: 28-41-97. Ł170,000 with breakfast. A small restaurant provides wholesome breakfasts and evening meals.

The *Room with a View* was filmed in the **Pensione Quisisana & Pontevecchio**, Lungarno Archibusieri 4, 50122. Tel: 21-66-92 or 21-50-46; Fax: 26-83-03. Ł150,000 with breakfast.

The **Hermitage** is tucked away among the rooftops above

the ponte Vecchio, a delightful dollhouse of a pensione that would be almost claustrophobic were it not for the flowered terraces overlooking the Arno. It could not be more centrally located, but it is not for light sleepers, as the double windows are no real match for the nightly noise from the Lungarno. At Vicolo Marzio 1 (50122), at the corner of piazza del Pesce opposite the warren of little goldsmiths' workshops called the Casa dell'Orafo, the Hermitage accepts only Visa credit cards. Tel: 28-72-16; Fax: 21-22-08. £165,000; £200,000 with breakfast.

The **Monna Lisa** is a quieter alternative—not quite so central, it is a five-minute walk east of the Duomo. Although often styled as a pensione, the Monna Lisa is really an elegant and expensive small hotel with a distinctly patrician Florentine ambience. (Monna is in fact the correct spelling of what is universally known as Mona Lisa. The word derives from "Madonna," which was a medieval way of saying Missus.) Some of the rooms look out on the garden, and chairs are set out in the shade of the magnolia tree. Borgo Pinti 27; Tel: 24-79-751; Fax: 24-79-755. £330,000 with breakfast; special rates available during the winter months.

One of the few pensioni in Florence to retain its sensibly shod character—a clientele in pursuit of culture, rather than comfort, at affordable prices—is the **Splendor**, in the via San Gallo, at number 30 (50129), a ten-minute walk north of the Duomo. Tel: 48-34-27; Fax: 46-12-76. £150,000 with breakfast.

Hidden away behind the Piazza SS Annunziata and the Archaeological Museum in the quiet via Laura at number 50, 50121 (Tel: 23-44-747; Fax: 24-80-954), is the **Hotel Morandi alla Crocetta**. Once a monastery, the hotel is currently being expanded and renovated, albeit preserving its old-fashioned charm, and a cinquecento fresco has been uncovered in one of the bedrooms. £140,000 for a double without breakfast.

Surely the most delightful place to stay in Florence is at the **Torre di Bellosguardo** on the hill of the same name above the city, where the Baron and Baroness Franchetti have transformed their ancestral home into a small, personal hotel. Furnished in exquisite taste, the old villa is surrounded by well-tended gardens. Via Roti Michelozzi 2, 50124. Tel: 22-98-145; Fax: 22-90-08. £330,000. No restaurant.

However, the most economical way to visit Florence is to stay in a convent, which differs from a pensione only in that it is staffed by nuns. Piety is an option, but credit cards reek of the ungodly. Not all of the convent/pensioni relish being mentioned in guidebooks, as they have their own faithful clientele, but one particularly pleasant one is the **Pensione**

Villa Linda at via Poggio Gherardi 5, 50135, between Maiano and Settignano (a car is advisable). Tel: 60-39-13. Ł40,000 per person with breakfast.

DINING

The Florentines, of course, also invented cuisine. When Catherine de' Medici went to France as the bride of King Henri II d'Orléans, she is said to have taken a flagon of olive oil and a bag of beans with her, and she reputedly introduced the French court to the use of forks and the subtleties of canard à l'orange and sauce béchamel. When it comes to cooking, the Florentines are reactionary in the extreme. Any variation on the food that *la mamma* or *la nonna* made is viewed with suspicion, and menus in the typical restaurants and trattorias in Florence tend to be much the same.

Florentine food is, however, always full of flavor, whether it is the tart taste of new olive oil on toasted bread (*fetta unta*) or on white beans (*fagioli*), the fragrance of fresh basil garnishing *la pappa al pomodoro* (a local soup made with tomatoes), the full-bodied taste of red meat in the *bistecca alla fiorentina* (T-bone steak), or the piquancy of *pecorino,* the local sheep's-milk cheese.

Italy, said D. H. Lawrence, "is like cooked macaroni—yards and yards of soft tenderness raveled round everything." Yet although pasta is on every menu, the real Tuscan start to a meal is a bowl of soup such as *ribollita,* made out of cabbage and yesterday's bread.

Although only two hours from the sea, Florence is a meat-eating city, and fresh fish is served in very few restaurants. The many varieties of hand-picked salad, of which arugula is only one, are very tasty; vegetables are always ordered separately, under the menu section *Contorni.* Desserts are not Florence's strong point, except in the better restaurants. All the frothy confections of *profiterolles* and meringue in town look as though they are made by the same person, who delivers them to the restaurants every morning.

Florence is surrounded by the Chianti wine-growing area. The best local wine is the Chianti Classico, the bottle with a little black rooster on the neck label. Chianti Putto (with its little *putto,* or cupid, on the neck of the bottle) is grown in a less restricted area and can also be a very palatable table wine. Many restaurants have an unlabeled house wine that you pay for *al consumo*—according to how much you drink.

The prices quoted include a pasta course, a meat or fish dish with extra vegetables, and dessert or fruit. Often the house wine and mineral water are covered as well. In Italian restaurants, unless it is a pizzaria, you are expected to eat the main dish, although you are forgiven for skipping the pasta or soup. Ordering pasta as a main dish is frowned upon, even at lunch—although restaurateurs can be mollified if you order a vintage cru with it!

The only restaurant in Florence with two Michelin stars is the *very* expensive **Enoteca Pinchiorri**, which is rather like attending a reception at a society wedding. Waiters, like ushers, whisper in your ear, and there are hot-house blossoms everywhere: in the vaulted dining room and in the palazzo courtyard—five bouquets in the ladies' room alone. Annie Féolde is French and is the power behind the scenes in the vast kitchens, which have recently introduced a Tuscan *nouvelle* menu. Her husband, Giorgio Pinchiorri, is in charge of the 70,000 bottles in their cellars, which you can visit upon request. It is best to take the *dégustation* menu, which gives you a little taste of everything. Closed Sundays, Monday lunch, February, and August. Via Ghibellina 87; Tel: 24-27-77; Fax: 24-49-83.

Il Cibreo is just around the corner from one of the two main food markets and halls (the Mercato S. Ambrogio, northeast of Santa Croce). It is a small, pleasantly bohemian restaurant like a sophisticated downtown bistro, Fabio and Benedetta being the kind of people who reject plushness on principle rather than from necessity. Both decor and food bear the stamp of their very individual style. There is no pasta, but instead an array of unusual, mouth-watering antipasti, a choice of delicious soups, and some very good homemade desserts. Quite expensive (£130,000 for two with a not outstanding wine) but good value for the money. Reservations are a must. (Closed Sundays and Mondays.) Via dei Macci 118; Tel: 234-11-00. There are a few cheaper tables at the back of the Cibreo for students, locals, and the New Poor. Fabio also has a fascinating gourmet store around the corner from the restaurant, and this year has opened a café across the road for breakfast and light lunches. After 10:00 P.M. it is an animated bar for drinks and do-it-yourself piano entertainment.

Another culinary couple are Giuliano and Sharon, at **Garga**, in a little street between the train station and the river. He is the chef with the basset-hound jowls and the almost tangible Tuscan accent. Sharon is Canadian and can explain their personal brand of Tuscan cooking in transatlantic terms, dishes such as their *crostini,* a traditional Florentine antipasto, chopped chicken livers on crisply toasted peasant bread; their excellent risottos; and pasta dishes like

Il Magnifico. They have enlarged their tiny restaurant in 14th-century premises next door, and Garga is now less of a squash, but make reservations anyway. Closed Mondays; open evenings only; moderately priced. Via del Moro 48R; Tel: 239-88-98.

A contradiction in terms—a quiet, restful trattoria—is **Le Quattro Stagioni** (no relation to New York's Four Seasons), where the food is well prepared, the service smooth and polite, the decor blandly unobtrusive. It is the only restaurant in the via Maggio, once the main thoroughfare of Renaissance Florence (Maggio is a shortening of Maggiore) and now the antiques-store row, around the corner from the piazza dei Pitti. Piero, the diminutive chef/owner, whose ruddy face beams from under his chef's hat, makes different kinds of *gnocchi* for every season, as well as a Renaissance version of a Caesar salad, called, of course, the Catherine de' Medici salad. Dinner for two will run about Ł80,000 with wine. Closed Sundays and August. Via Maggio 61R; Tel: 21-89-06.

Cammillo, on the other hand, is very noisy and bustling, the way Italian trattorias usually are. In the Oltrarno part of town, it has been family-owned for generations. Father sits behind the old-fashioned cash desk while son weaves in among the crowded tables, and the waiters in long white flapping aprons boom orders into the kitchen with voices like foghorns. *Always* bursting at the seams, not just with Florentines but with an increasing number of Americans and Japanese, for whom Cammillo has become a landmark. They may not yet have managed to turn it into a tourist restaurant, but they have succeeded in inflating the prices, although it is still within the same range as the establishments already mentioned (Ł100,000 for two with the house wine). Just about the only restaurant of note open on a Sunday, Cammillo is closed Wednesdays, Thursdays, and August. Borgo San Jacopo 57R; Tel: 21-24-27.

A light, vinous lunch is to be had at the **Cantinetta Antinori** in the palazzo of the same name, belonging to the Antinori wine-making family, in the piazza Antinori, southeast of the piazza Santa Maria Novella. Although a fancy menu is now available, the Cantinetta is at its best in its original role of patrician snack bar, providing food as accompaniment to the wine. Medium priced, if you stick to the snacks; otherwise a full meal will cost Ł100,000 for two without wine. Closed Saturdays, Sundays, and August. Piazza Antinori 3; Tel: 29-22-34.

Typical of Florence are what could be described as "kitchen" restaurants, with white-tiled walls, communal tables, a quick turnover of patrons, clanging of saucepans, and a noisy, steamy, convivial atmosphere. The most famous of these is **Sostanza**, around the corner from the Excelsior Hotel. This is a Florentine institution where it is important to remember that it is they who are doing you a favor and not vice versa. Closed Saturdays and Sundays. Via del Porcellana 25R; Tel: 21-26-91; closed Saturdays and Sundays. Dinner for two with wine will cost about Ł80,000. A lesser-known "kitchen" restaurant is **Alla Vecchia Bettola**, on the other side of the Arno on the piazza Torquato Tasso—closed Sundays and Mondays. Viale Ludovico Ariosto 32R. Tel: 22-41-58. At "kitchen" restaurants it is impossible to make reservations, and you may end up standing in line. They often don't serve coffee—and can't cope with credit cards. They are cheaper than some of the restaurants given above, but not as cheap as you might think they would be (Ł80,000 for two).

The newest in this genre is **La Baraonda**, just down the road from the Enoteca Pinchiorri, at via Ghibellina 67R (Tel: 234-11-71), where you will find simple dishes masterfully prepared for a discerning international clientele in very much a "designer kitchen" decor. Closed Sundays and Monday lunch. You can expect to pay Ł110,000 for two with wine.

A restaurant beloved of professional Florentine businesspeople—always the most discerning and demanding eaters—is the **Taverna del Bronzino**, behind the piazza della Indipendenza. It is difficult to find without a taxi but decidedly worth the detour for excellent food and an impressive wine selection. The decor is sober, solid, and unostentatious—the way Florentines like it—with serious food such as their black tortellini (the pasta dough is tinted black with the lining of walnut shells) and steak baked whole in the oven, sliced, and served with a green pepper sauce. This is also the place to try one of Italy's northern Piedmont wines. Closed Sundays and August. Via delle Ruote 27R; Tel: 49-52-20. The prices are serious too: Ł120,000 for two with wine.

L'Antico Fattore, just around the corner from the Uffizi gallery, features typical Tuscan food and is very good value for the money (Ł80,000 for two with a house wine). With a bare-bones trattoria atmosphere, well-worn white tablecloths, dark wood furnishings, and bottles standing to attention against whitewashed walls, L'Antico Fattore has a groaning board of antipasti and fresh-tasting, well-cooked food. Closed Sundays and Mondays. Via Lambertesca 1; Tel: 238-12-15.

Very few restaurants in Florence have a garden for outdoor dining in summer; you may want to escape the city heat north toward Fiesole and **Le Cave di Maiano**, although this involves an expensive taxi ride. Here the stone tables are like petrified toadstools, and fireflies wink among the cypresses. Cave di Maiano has been serving the same menu for more than 20 years (running to Ł110,000 for two with wine), and for old-time habitués a certain staleness has crept into the atmosphere. Tel: 591-33; closed Thursdays and Sunday evenings. Farther up the road at via delle Cave di Maiano 20 is the cheaper (Ł60,000 for two), more basic **Trattoria da Graziella**, in a simpler setting but with good wholesome food and a cool breeze in summer. Closed Mondays.

Another very pleasant little trattoria with outdoor dining, abundant antipasto, and a loud and friendly atmosphere is **Osvaldo**, at Ponte a Mensola on the way to Settignano and near Berenson's (now Harvard's) Villa T Tatti. It's in the moderate price range.

A new favorite with Florentines in search of respite from the summer heat is **Giogoli Rossi** in via di Giogoli (number 10), a country road on the way to Cerbaia. Above Galluzzo near the Certosa monastery, it is a 15-minute drive from the center of Florence. Tel: 25-77-877. Closed Mondays, Tuesday lunch, and August. Dinner for two: Ł80,000 with wine.

If you must have fish in red-meat country, **La Capannina di Sante**, "Sante's little cabin" on the banks of the river Arno east of the center at the ponte da Verrazzano, serves just that—and only that—excellent fresh fish from the Tyrrhenian Sea for every course except dessert. Fresh fish, as opposed to frozen, or *congelato,* is always expensive, but not outrageously so, and Sante also has a very good white wine list. Like Moses' basket of rushes, Sante's cabin looks as though it might float down the river at any moment, although care has been taken with details, such as soft lighting and a red rose on every table. When the restaurant is full the service can be flustered. And, despite Guernica tactics, the mosquitoes are not always kept at bay. Ponte da Verrazzano; Tel: 68-83-45. Closed Sundays, Monday lunch, and August 15–early September. Expect to spend about Ł180,000 for two people with wine.

Giuseppe Alessi used to run one of the Florentine restaurants most sought after by gourmets from far and wide. Reservations had to be made months in advance, and every one of a wealth of dishes was set before the reverent diners accompanied by a dissertation on its exact historical and gastronomic context. Today this very talented chef has made a full somersault and now runs an inexpensive neighborhood club with an annual membership of Ł10,000 (payable at the entrance). Only wines made by the members are served—no commercial labels. Simplicity is the order of the day, and Alessi's club is among the best buys in town at ₤20,000 per person, everything included. The few dishes are wholesome and tasty, especially the riotous salads. No reservations and no credit cards; closed Sundays. Via di Mezzo 24R; Tel: 24-18-21.

The **Ristorante Corsini**, on the lungarno of the same name, has an arresting decor with murals and artifacts enhancing the elegant, palatial interior. The place to go for a quiet, pampered, air-conditioned lunch on a hot and dusty day. Tel: 21-77-06; closed Mondays; moderately expensive.

The most scenic pizza place in town is **Le Rampe**, a restaurant on a bend in the road that winds up from the river to the piazzale Michelangelo, with terraces overlooking the city's best profile. There is a regular menu as well as a choice of pizzas (pizza is cheap wherever you go; here, you'll pay only ₤20,000 per person for pizza, wine, and dessert). Closed Mondays. Viale Poggi 1; Tel: 681-18-91.

Two really cheap but clean family-run trattorias are **La Casalinga**, just around the corner from piazza Santo Spirito (via del Michelozzi 9R; Tel: 21-86-24; closed Sunday and first half of August; no credit cards), and **Da Benvenuto**, via Mosca 16R, a five-minute walk from the Uffizi gallery (closed Wednesdays, Sundays, and August; no credit cards). Be prepared to share a table with other diners. Again, ₤20,000 pays for a simple meal at both.

A trendy new lunch place (it is also open for dinner) is **Mirò**, at 57/59R via S. Gallo (closed Sundays; Tel: 48-10-30). Via S. Gallo is a street that specializes in, among other things, weighing machines, and young Florentine mothers come here to rent scales for weighing their infants. It is also near the Palazzo Medici Riccardi and the Monastero di San Marco. Lunch for two runs around ₤40,000.

For a sandwich in town off the main shopping street, the via de' Tornabuoni, go to via del Parione 19R, where three steps down is a simple little *alimentari* (grocery store) that makes copious sandwiches to order with crusty baguette-type bread. Try the prosciutto with *mascarpone* cream cheese and nuts, downed with a glass of very ordinary wine. Cheap. Open 8:00 A.M. to 3:00 P.M. and 4:30 to 7:30 P.M.; closed Wednesday afternoons and Sundays.

BARS DURING THE DAY

The three most famous bars in Florence are **Gilli**, in the only unattractive square in the city, piazza della Repubblica; **Giacosa**, at via de' Tornabuoni 83R; and **Rivoire**, in the piazza della Signoria. All are reasonably priced if you take your refreshment standing up, and all become ruinously expensive the moment you sit down at one of the little tables with pink tablecloths.

Gilli has Belle Epoque ceilings, a dab hand at cocktails, very light lunches, and in the evenings music that wafts over the hedge from a little palm-court orchestra at a neighboring bar. Closed Tuesdays. Piazza della Repubblica 39R; Tel: 21-38-96. Giacosa is ideal for shoppers, with dainty pastries to combat that buying fatigue, as well as expensive light lunches. Closed Sundays. Tel: 29-62-26. Rivoire has the best location in town, being the wateringhole nearest to the Uffizi gallery, with sidewalk tables in the square facing the Palazzo Vecchio. Its specialty is hot chocolate topped with an over-sized wedge of double cream. Closed Mondays. Piazza della Signoria 5R; Tel: 21-44-12.

Also in the via de' Tornabuoni, at number 64R, is **Leopoldo Procacci**, a deluxe grocer who sells English marmalades and superior cookies behind glass-fronted cabinets. There is also a small, old-fashioned bar dispensing truffle-paste-filled sand-wiches with your aperitif, hence the musty smell of truffles that fills the store. Closed Sundays and Wednesday after-noons, Procacci follows a timetable of its own: 8:30 A.M. to 1:00 P.M. and 4:30 to 7:45 P.M. Tel: 21-16-56.

Doney—the restaurant and bar and meeting place for Florence's boulevardiers—has recently reopened in the pi-azza Strozzi at number 18R. The original Doney's, once the haunt of prominent Anglo-Florentines like the Brownings and Mrs. Keppel, was turned into yet another shoe shop a few years ago, but its successor, which Giorgio Armani has launched next door to his Emporio, has the original furni-ture and some of the original charm. Ideal—and not as expensive as might be expected—for a light lunch or cock-tail although it has yet to become the institution that its namesake was.

ICE-CREAM BARS

The most famous is **Gelateria Vivoli** in via Isola delle Stinche at number 7R, on the site of an old debtors' prison. The Vivoli family is an institution in Florence, and the bar is a major landmark for visiting Americans, too. The large assort-ment of ice creams and *semi-freddi*—Piero Vivoli maintains you can make ice cream out of *anything*—is labeled in English as well. Closed Mondays in summer, Mondays and Tuesdays during the winter.

Not as well known, but just as good, is the **Gelateria Villani** at the piazza San Domenico number 8, halfway up the Fiesole hill (by the number 7 bus). There are a few tables outside where the ice cream is served in parfait glasses and smothered in fruit. You can also take it out in little cardboard cups. The specialty is Crema Villani, a creamy caramel flavor. Closed Mondays.

Not far away, also on a hillside above Florence, is the newly opened **Fattoria di Maiano**, near the Cave di Maiano restaurant. This very popular ice cream bar is open until late at night. Specialties include ice cream made with pignoli nuts, and ice cream "pizzas"!

FLORENCE BY NIGHT

Florence is becoming increasingly trendy *la notte*. Once an early-to-bed-and-early-to-rise city, compared with the *dolce vita* and high life of Rome and Milan, Florence is now almost too swinging, with vehicles choking the *lungarni* until the early hours and the streets filled with exotic denizens of the night, many of whom come in from Prato and Pistoia and whom one never sees during the day. In summer many of them converge on the Cascine, the large city park where children bicycle along the shaded paths by day and where the tennis club hosts an international tennis tournament in May and June. By night the *lucciole,* or glowworms, appear—a poetic term for streetwalkers and the breathtaking *viados,* transsexual glowworms from Brazil. There is also **Central Park**, a huge disco, recently revamped, with room for hundreds of dancers under the stars, as well as the brand-new **Meccanò**. For the less energetic, there is the **Rex Bar** in via Fiesolana, a trendy meeting place with a disc jockey and *the* rendezvous for Florence's younger set, while for all ages, **Montecarla** in via dei Bardi is an ideal venue for drinks after the theater or movies in an outrageously kitschy decor. For jazz aficionados there is a jazz club, **Mood**, in corso dei Tintori, around the corner from piazza Santo Croce.

SHOPS AND SHOPPING

After Milan, Florence is the number-one shopping city in Italy, more elegant and with more variety and verve than either Venice or Rome. Above all, much of what you see in the stores has been produced in or around Florence itself. It is enough to say that over 90 percent of the "Made in Italy" output exported to North America comes from Tuscany, and the city is full of buying offices for all the major stores.

Florentine stores are open from 9:00 A.M. to 1:00 P.M. and from 3:30 or 4:00 P.M. to 7:30 or 8:00 P.M., and close on Monday mornings throughout the winter, Saturday afternoons in summer. All the larger stores take credit cards. (Some of the smaller boutiques tend to open later in the morning.)

The Bond Street/Fifth Avenue of Florence is the north–south **via de' Tornabuoni**, which leads down to ponte S. Trinita, along with streets such as the via della Vigna Nuova branching off to right and left. Here you will find local fashion landmarks like Gucci and Ferragamo, both of which are based in Florence, side by side with big fashion names from all over Italy and a few French intruders as well: Valentino couture from Rome, Armani and Versace from Milan, Ermenegildo Zegna from Piedmont, the sadly missed Neapolitan Mario Valentino for shoes, as well as the Fendi sisters, Yves Saint-Laurent, Vuitton, Cartier—the list goes on. For the very fashion-conscious, two local stores called **Alex** and **Emmanuel Zoo**, both in the via della Vigna Nuova, 5R and 18R, have a very up-to-date collection, while the real style-seekers go to **Luisa** in via Roma at 19–21R. All the avant-garde clothes labels are to be found there. For the fashion-conscious "fauché," three branches of **Grandi Firme** have opened in via Verdi, via dei Castellani, and Borgo degli Albizi; here you can buy designer labels from previous years at a fraction of the original cost. The ultimate in casual fashion is at **Enrico Coveri**, via della Vigna Nuova 27–29R, or—for designer work shirts—at **Ermanno Daelli**.

The **borgo San Jacopo** is a fascinating shopping street in the Oltrarno for people for whom the designer label is not everything. There is Giachi for bags, La Bottega Artigiana for shirts, Lo Spillo for Victorian jewelry and knickknacks, the gourmet store Vera, stores selling everything from fun clothes, shoes, and prints to hams, together with a cluster of bars and restaurants. Also here are **Pagliai** for period silver and **Manetti**, one of the last artisan goldsmiths in Florence.

Leather

Florence has always been famous for its leather. To judge from the streets of Florence, it would seem that the only things locals shop for are shoes and pizza by the slice. One of the sad things about Florence today is that whenever an old-fashioned store closes, the space is instantly snapped up by a shoe store or a snack bar. Leather magnates like Beltrami and Raspini have stores all over the city selling not only shoes but bags and leather clothes; you must remember that the prices include their not inconsiderable frontage costs. **Mantellassi**, in the piazza della Repubblica 25R, still produces handmade shoes—at a price—but you will find cheaper stores, too, around the market in the borgo San Lorenzo or in the Oltrarno.

The best leather store in Florence is **Cellerini**, at via del

Sole 37R. Cellerini is an artisan of a kind that has survived from the days of the Medicis; his upstairs workshop is littered with soft, supple strips of different colored leathers and patterns of bags for the famous people he has been serving for the last 30 years. **Taddei**, in the piazza dei Pitti 6R, is a tiny workshop making solid leather objects such as boxes, frames, and jewelry cases, a painstaking process involving the pressing of different layers of leather, like the soles of good shoes, over molds and then highly polishing them until they look like wood. **Il Bisonte** is a leather store at via del Parione 11 that now has branches in other cities in Europe and whose goods are also sold in a few select stores in the United States. A Falstaffian figure, the creator of Il Bisonte makes bags, suitcases, and belts out of natural leather, and multicolored canvas bags for summer.

Jewelry

Florence has been a city of goldsmiths since Renaissance times, although nowadays much of the gold and gems sparkling behind the storefronts is factory made. The most famous jeweler in Florence is **Settepassi**, who has merged with a Milanese jeweler, Faraone, and moved off the ponte Vecchio—the goldsmiths' traditional home since the 16th century—to via de' Tornabuoni 25R. The bridge is still the place to go for gold, new and antique jewelry, some silver, and necklaces of coral, ivory, and semiprecious stones. Each tiny store has its own personality, its own history, its own prices. The ponte Vecchio is like a bazaar, and it continues on into via Por San Maria on the right bank. **Bijoux Cascio** at via Por San Maria 1R and via de' Tornabuoni 32R makes costume jewelry so perfectly it looks like the real thing, and **Angela Caputi** at borgo San Jacopo 78 and 82 makes stunning parures out of plastic.

Linens

In the last century, young girls came from all over Europe, assiduously chaperoned, to buy linens in Florence for their trousseaux. Today few can afford to pay for genuinely hand-embroidered linens trimmed with handmade lace, and much of the merchandise displayed in the windows of via Por San Maria is machine made or imported from the Orient. Some is still handmade by the seamstresses of Greve, an hour away from Florence, however; you just have to pick and choose. **Cirri's**, at via Por San Maria 38–40R, makes smocked dresses and sailor suits for the kind of children who are seen but not heard, while **Bruna Spadini**, on the lungarno Archibusieri 4–6R, makes very fine linens for the table, boudoir, and bed. The undisputed grande dame of the boudoir, however, is **Loretta Caponi**, at borgo Ognissanti 12R, who makes nightgowns from the stuff that dreams are made of. She has opened a store opposite with a second entrance at lungarno Amerigo Vespucci 11, with enchanting outfits and gifts for babies and little girls.

Antiques and Crafts

"In Florence, even the stonemasons have a sense of aesthetics," Sir Harold Acton said. Here you can have anything and everything repaired, restored, matched, mended, custom-created, carved, chiseled, woven, or welded by expert artisans. **Pagliai**, in borgo San Jacopo, will match a missing teaspoon from a set; **Signora Locchi**, in via Burchiello (number 10), will find exactly the right crystal stopper for a headless decanter; **Baldini**, at 99/105R via Palazzuolo, will make bronze handles for the drawers of antique commodes … and the list goes on. There is infinite choice in passementerie stores, like **Valmar**, 53R via Porta Roassa. And **Quercioli & Lucherini** is a haberdashery in via Calimala that has changed little in style since the days of *Sense and Sensibility*.

Florence is also a center for antiques, old and new, with antiques stores on either side of the via Maggio in the Oltrarno as well as in the borgo Ognissanti and via dei Fossi.

The *settore degli inganni* (trompe l'oeil) has long been one of the minor Florentine arts—a plaster column can be made to look like Carrara marble, a fireplace like chalcedony. At **Ponziani Mario**, via Santo Spirito 27, what at first glance seems an expensive antiques store is in fact a rambling workshop where artisans hand-paint in a variety of styles, from chinoiserie to Old Florentine, on furniture that is then treated to look like the most precious of antiques. There are workshops specializing in marbleizing, such as **Cappellini Marino** at via Presto di San Martino 10R, while at stores such as **Giannini** in piazza Pitti 37R, or at **Il Papiro** all over the city (via Cavour 55R, piazza Duomo 24R, lungarno Acciainoli 42R), you can buy Florentine paper in an infinity of marble look-alike shades pasted onto frames, boxes, pencils, bookends, diaries, and so on.

Markets

An important part of Florentine shopping is provided by the markets. The main market is in **piazza San Lorenzo**, where stalls are set up every day selling souvenirs, gloves, bags, belts, sweaters, tee-shirts, shoes, and jeans, around the corner from the main food hall and fruit-and-vegetable market—

which is itself well worth a visit to see the profusion of local produce.

The Straw Market, **Mercato del Porcellino**, is in the little square at the end of via Por San Maria under covered arches. "Bring me a straw hat from Florence..." used to be a popular song, but today the straw goods probably come from the Orient—the market sells cheap linens, bags, umbrellas, small leather goods, and fake Gucci bags instead.

Otherwise, every space in Florence large enough to qualify as a piazza has a morning market for fruit and vegetables and a few other odds and ends thrown in. On Tuesday mornings there is a huge market at the **Cascine**, the big public gardens on the right bank of the Arno west of the center, where you can buy unhemmed Gucci scarves (seconds), antique nightshirts, all manner of clothing, and kitchenware for unbelievably cheap prices. Finally, in **piazza de' Ciompi**, four blocks north of Santa Croce, there is a permanent flea market; bargains are rare but rummaging is fun.

TUSCANY

By Anne Marshall Zwack

Italy is better known for her cities than for her countryside, and indeed few Italian landscapes live up to the beauty of the Eternal City—no one ever wanted to "see Latium and die"—while all the Veneto has in common with Venice is the first syllable. The transcendent exception is Tuscany (Toscana), which some people actually prefer to the Renaissance grandeur of Florence.

MAJOR INTEREST

Etruscan sites at Volterra, Cortona, Arezzo, and elsewhere

Wines and country restaurants around Siena in Chianti, Montalcino, and Montepulciano

Trecento art and architecture in Tuscan hill towns

Siena's art and architecture

L'Argentario and other southwest coastal resorts

The islands: Giglio, Giannutri, Elba

Fra Filippo Lippi's works at Prato

Thermal spas at Montecatini

Walled medieval city of Lucca

Marble artisans at Carrara and Pietrasanta

Pisa's campo dei Miracoli (Leaning Tower, cathedral, Baptistery, cemetery)

Tuscany is a word with a unique resonance that conjures up alluring vistas, so much so that a perfume has been named after this region of central Italy. Beautiful as they are, no perfume could ever be named after England's Lake District or France's valley of the Loire.

Despite the inroads of the 20th century—concrete posts now support the vines that once clung to the trunks of olive trees or trailed along wooden stakes; tractors have replaced the white wide-horned oxen that used to pull the plows; and

the autostrada has made a gash through the Tuscan hills—
Tuscany is substantially the same as when Lorenzo de' Medici, a fervent Tuscan, wrote: *"Tiene il cipresso qualche uccel*
segreto . . . l'uliva in qualche dolce piaggia aprica/Secondo il
vento par or verde, or bianca" ("Shelters the cypress a secret
bird . . . the olive on its gentle sun-warmed slope blows first
green, then white with the wind").

The carefully husbanded hills, combed with vines and
crested with cypress trees, still look like the landscape in the
Allegory of Good and Bad Government, painted over three
walls of the Palazzo Pubblico in Siena by Ambrogio Lorenzetti
in the 14th century. Indeed, while painters from other Italian
cities are essentially urban, the great Tuscan painters of the
Renaissance fill their paintings with the familiar landscapes
and rural scenes in which they grew up. Many of those whom
we call Florentine painters are in fact Tuscan village boys—
Leonardo from Vinci and Masaccio from San Giovanni
Valdarno. Madonnas and saints pose before backdrops of
vineyards, the banks of the Arno, and umbrella pines. Tuscany
has always attracted artists, now as then. "You learn for the first
time in this climate what colors are," said Leigh Hunt.

As Curzio Malaparte says in his *Maledetti Toscani:* "Anyone coming to Tuscany will immediately realize that he is in
a country of peasants. And being a peasant for us is not just
knowing how to dig, to hoe, to plough, to sow, to pound, to
reap, to harvest: above all it means to mingle the clods of
earth with the clouds, and to make one of heaven and earth."
Tuscans are as rooted in their soil as the century-old olive
trees that dot the slopes; their philosophy of life is based on
the country proverbs of their forefathers. Theirs is a crusted
charm. The Tuscans are, as a 17th-century traveller wrote,
"ravished with the Beauty of their owne Countrey," and
although they may have seen the rest of the world only on
television, Tuscans are convinced that the Arno valley is this
side of Paradise. Country people forced to leave their land
following the decline of agriculture come back a generation
later to restore the broken-down farmhouses, called *case*
coloniche, as do Milanese and expatriate English, Germans,
and Americans.

Tuscan food has an immediacy, a straight-from-the-*orto*
(vegetable garden) flavor about it. Soups such as the *pappa*
al pomodoro or *ribollita,* both good ways to use up old
bread, are topped off with a flourish of olive oil. The herbs
are always fragrantly fresh, the salads often hand-picked wild
greens. The beef for the famous *bistecca alla fiorentina*
comes—when it is not imported—from the Chianine cattle
raised in the Maremma region; the homemade pasta is filled

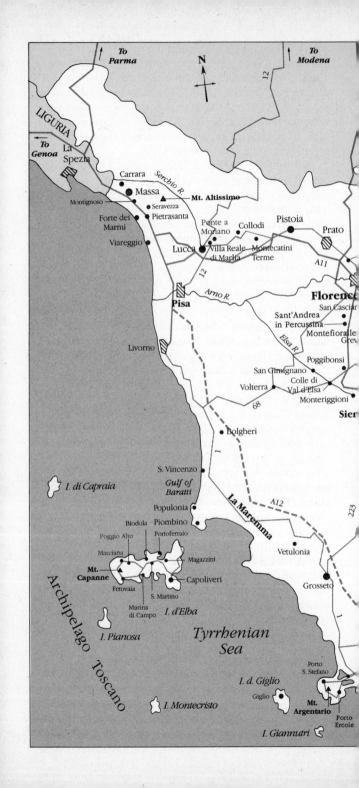

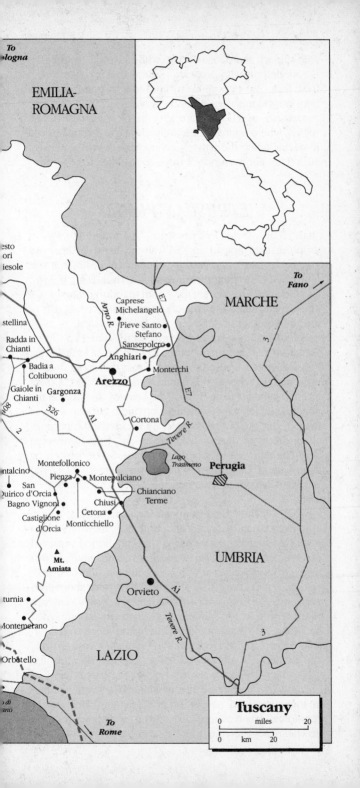

with spinach and ricotta cheese, while a typical Tuscan meal is rounded off with *pecorino* (a local sheep's cheese) and fresh fruit. You eat well in any little country trattoria, and so here we will mention chiefly the more elusive and exclusive restaurants, which often are also the most expensive, in a region where eating is relatively cheap. A medium-priced meal, including the house or a nonvintage wine, will cost 50,000 lire per person for a three-course menu.

ETRUSCAN PLACES

"Italy today," wrote D. H. Lawrence, "is far more Etruscan in its pulse than Roman and will always be so." The word *Tuscany* comes from *Etruscan,* the ancient civilization that flourished between the river Arno, the river Tiber, the sea, and the Apennines during the eighth to fourth centuries B.C. The Greeks called the Etruscans *Tirreni;* hence this part of the Mediterranean is known as the Tyrrhenian Sea.

We still do not know where the Etruscans came from. Some say that they are from the lost city of Atlantis, or that they emigrated from the north, or that they originated in Lydia and fled after a great famine struck Asia Minor. Others claim that the Etruscans came from Lemnos, an island in the Aegean, and left when the smiths of Vulcan became short of iron, or that they were Phoenicians who settled in colonies along the coast during their navigation of the Tyrrhenian Sea. The most likely is perhaps the thesis put forward by Dionysius of Halicarnassus in the first century B.C.: "The Etruscans emigrated from nowhere. They have always been there."

Wherever they came from, the Etruscans were as culturally advanced and commercially affluent as the Greeks who colonized southern Italy (Magna Graecia). Etruria consisted of a league of 12 cities, called the *dodecapolis,* among which were the Tuscan cities of Volterra, Populonia, Chiusi, Arezzo, Vetulonia, and Cortona. Fiesole, the hilltop town above Florence, was Etruscan until subdued by the Romans, as was Saturnia with its hot sulfur springs. Each city was governed by a king, called a *lucumone.* The Etruscans grew grain in abundance on what Livy called the *"opulenta arva Etruria"* and bequeathed polenta to Italian cuisine. They planted vines; their Trebbiano is still one of the grapes used in Chianti wines and in the Tuscan whites. They were the first to mine iron and copper on the island of Elba and at Populonia, where there are still iron pebbles on the beaches. They were sufficiently advanced architecturally to invent the cupola, and the paintings they have left on vases and amphorae are of astonishing artistic merit.

The Etruscans believed that mankind was governed by an implacable destiny, as was the life of an individual or an entire civilization. They thought Etruria would, like the Third Reich, last a thousand years. They shared with the National Socialists and the ancient Romans the belief that the state and the city were more important than the individual, who could be sacrificed to the general good. The Roman symbol of power, subsequently the symbol of the Italian Fascist party, was the fasces, borrowed from Etruscan lore.

Nonetheless, the Etruscans were a joyous, insouciant folk, with a passion for music and dancing and with what D. H. Lawrence called "an inner carelessness" that, although crushed by the heel of the advancing Roman legions, has survived to the present day. Sumptuous banquets were followed by theatrical performances; *ister,* the Etruscan word for actor, has given us our word *histrionics.*

Most of what we know of the Etruscans comes from objects excavated from their tombs. Although their dead were always cremated, the Etruscans believed in taking everything with them when they went. There are tombs at, for instance, Populonia, Vetulonia, and Chiusi—but on the whole, when you've seen one Etruscan tomb, you've seen the lot. (Henry James also complained about the "trudging quest for Etruscan tombs in shadeless wastes.") The more fascinating Etruscan heritage is to be found in the contents of these tombs—the painted amphorae and carved funerary urns, which D. H. Lawrence in his *Etruscan Places* called "little ash chests"—in the splendid Museo Archeologico in Florence, as well as in museums in Volterra, Chiusi, and Cortona. Incidentally, the Etruscans were never buried without a bottle of good wine.

Volterra

Volterra, said Lawrence, is "on a towering great bluff of rock that gets all the winds and sees all the world," a walled, almost menacing hilltop town with black, still specks of birds hovering above its ramparts. Perhaps these are the "gray-hooded carrion crows" mentioned by Lawrence, who clearly did not like Volterra, perhaps because he visited the town (southwest of Florence and west of Siena) on an inauspiciously cold and rainy day. Gabriele d'Annunzio, who lived in Volterra for a while, called it a "city of wind and boulders," a buffer between the wind from the sea on the one side and from the mountains on the other. It is interesting to note that the Etruscans thought the winds came from hell.

Lawrence cheered up considerably in the **Museo Etrusco Guarnacci** and confessed to getting more pleasure from the ash chests of Volterra than from the Parthenon frieze, preferring the immediacy of the portrait effigies that decorated these little alabaster sarcophagi to what he calls the "boiled down" effect of Greek aesthetic quality, "too much cooked in artistic consciousness." Because the top half of the ash chest, with its effigy of the departed, often seems ill-matched with the lower, sarcophagus half, Lawrence speculated whether people in Etruscan times went to the funeral parlor and chose a casket, much as we do today, while the effigy was executed after death and depended on what end your implacable destiny had in mind for you. The museum is open every day from 9:30 A.M. to 1:00 P.M. and 3:00 to 6:30 P.M.; from 8:00 A.M. to 2:00 P.M. between November and March.

Lawrence was scathing, on the other hand, about Volterra's main activity, the quarrying and transformation of alabaster into "all those things one does not want: tinted alabaster lampshades, bowls with doves on the rim," and so on.

Alabaster lends itself to an infinite variety and fluidity of designs, as it is one of the softest stones. Its greatest popularity was in the 18th and 19th centuries, when merchants braved the oceans of the world to bring their wares to marketplaces as far away as Bombay. In Volterra you can walk down the narrow cobbled streets and peer into workshops where artisans sit at their workbenches, chipping away at a vase or the head of a horse, almost up to their ankles in snow-white shavings that crunch underfoot. Although much of the output answers to Lawrence's description, Volterra has many gifted artisans who can execute orders to your specifications relatively cheaply.

Fun gifts to take home are the alabaster ice creams, coffee cups, fried eggs, etc., that *Vogue* calls "half pop, half metaphysical," made by the young **Marco Ricciardi** in his workshops at via Guarnacci 26 and via Porta Diana 9.

The rather grim aura of Volterra perhaps comes partly from the high-security prison within its ancient walls. In Lawrence's day, two imprisoned artisans managed to escape by carving old bread into realistic effigies of their faces—curls, warts, and all—that fooled the guards while they made their getaway. Today the prison houses some of Italy's most notorious terrorists, including members of the Red Brigades.

Eating in Volterra is wholesome rather than awesome at

any of the several restaurants spilling out into the narrow medieval streets. The medium-priced **Etruria,** opposite the Palazzo dei Priori, is the best known; Prince Charles was taken here on one of his sketching tours of Tuscany, and you can sit outside in Volterra's main square. Tel: (0588) 860-64; closed Thursdays, January, and two weeks in June.

The **Villa Nencini,** at borgo Santo Stefano 55, is a little country hotel just outside the city walls.

Populonia

There is not much left of the grandeur of Etruscan Populonia except its splendid isolation and the view. From the top of a hill covered in Mediterranean scrub, where wild boar snuffle for acorns, Populonia overlooks the coastline and the island of Elba. And yet in Etruscan times it was important enough to be able to send 600 men to the aid of Aeneas, as Virgil tells us in the *Aeneid.*

Populonia was named for the Etruscan god of wine, Fufluns, which became Fofluna and eventually Popluna. Vestiges of the Etruscan walls are still visible in this one-street, one-coffee-shop village, which belongs in its entirety to a doctor living in Rome. Two years ago an elegant and correspondingly expensive little restaurant called **Il Lucumone**, in honor of an Etruscan monarch, opened in the main street (Tel: 0565-294-71; closed Mondays during the winter). The Populonian necropolis is at the foot of the hill, near the gulf of Baratti, which was the port for Etruscan Volterra and where now in summer flocks of yachts and fishing craft come to roost. The gulf of Baratti has a beautiful beach ringed with umbrella pines; it does get very crowded, however, in the summer.

The working of iron ore moved from Elba to Populonia in the fourth century B.C., when wood for fuel became scarce on the island. It is estimated that the area occupied by the furnaces was about 40 acres, while the mountain of *scoriae* (tailings) accumulated to around two million tons. Populonia became famous throughout the Mediterranean, and as Phoenicians and Ionians came with ships full of artworks to exchange for tools and arms, the city grew in stature and prestige. Just how elegant the villas and temples of Populonia became can be seen from the statue of Apollo, now in the Louvre, that was found in the bay, tangled in seaweed, by a group of 19th-century fishermen.

Populonia is in the **Maremma** region, where cattle are raised and wild boar still hunted. The hillsides below Populonia are a wild boar reserve, and the young can be seen feeding every evening just outside the city walls. Bristly heads with awe-inspiring tusks adorn many a restaurant wall, and menus here lean heavily to red meats and wild-boar roasts or stews. Surprisingly few restaurants serve fresh fish from the Tyrrhenian Sea, although one exciting—and very expensive—exception is the **Gambero Rosso** in San Vincenzo, a ten-minute drive north from Populonia (piazza della Vittoria 13; Tel: 0565-70-10-21). The young Fulvio Pierangelini has emerged as one of Italy's most talented chefs, and food guides award him the highest accolades of chef's hats and rosettes. For those who shun the sophistication and expense of Il Gambero Rosso he has opened a more casual beach restaurant just next door, **Il Bucaniere** (via Marconi 8; Tel: 0565-70-33-87). Both restaurants have superlative fish menus, and both are closed on Tuesdays. (Only the Gambero Rosso takes credit cards.)

Chiusi

Chiusi was one of the most important centers in Italy, especially during the seventh century B.C. Porsenna, legendary king of Etruscan Chiusi, summoned goldsmiths from all over the known world to make him a golden sarcophagus adorned with 5,000 golden chicks and a mother hen, and drawn by 12 golden horses—the Etruscans have been compared to the oil sheikhs—a much-sought-after treasure that has never been found. There are, however, over 1,000 exhibits in the **Museo Nazionale Etrusco**, and even these are only a fraction of the objects—scattered today among museums all over the world—found in Chiusi's Etruscan tombs.

Leading art historians have maintained that the art of the Renaissance owes much to its Etruscan forebears: There is a funerary urn in Chiusi that bears a striking resemblance to the Palazzo Strozzi in Florence, while the aloof, quizzically smiling female figures—Etruscan women lived alongside their men, the first feminists of history—contain the same enigma as the Mona Lisa. (Milan Kundera, in his latest novel, *Immortality,* maintains that these smiles are not "a response to some particular, momentous situation, but a permanent state of face, expressing eternal bliss.") Chiusi is most famous for its *canopi,* jars with lids in the shape of human heads. In the summer, the museum is open from 9:00 A.M. to 1:40 P.M. on weekdays, until 12:40 P.M. on Sundays.

Here, if anywhere, would be the place to visit Etruscan tombs. In the "Monkey Tomb" the frescoes are amazingly well preserved: The dear departed, a female figure, sits under her umbrella—or perhaps parasol?—while funerary games are played in her honor, and a monkey on a leash is tied to a nearby tree. Sadly, for their own protection, the painted tombs are no longer on public view.

Today, apart from the museum, Chiusi seems a dusty little country town, with women from the surrounding villages waiting patiently for the *corriere,* the rattling blue local bus, to take them home after a morning's shopping.

Chiusi shares a railway station, however, with the very different **Chianciano Terme**. This busy, modern spa is about 120 km (75 miles) from Florence and 65 km (40 miles) from Arezzo. *"Benvenuti a Chianciano,"* reads the sign as you arrive, *"Fegato Sano"*—a healthy liver—and *"Arrivederci a Chianciano Fegato Sano"* as you leave. Porsenna was among the first to seek a *fegato sano* in Chianciano, and Horace also mentions it in his writings.

Today Chianciano has over 200 hotels, including the **Spadeus Grand Hotel "Il Club,"** a health farm where you can lose weight and gain a radiant new attitude to life under the eagle eye of strapping gymnasts from California.

At **La Foce**, 10 minutes from Chianciano, **L'Oasi** (via della Vittoria 90) is a typically Tuscan restaurant featuring hearty grilled steaks and robust wines at moderate prices. Tel: (0578) 75-50-77; closed Wednesdays; no credit cards.

Cetona

Only about 15 km (10 miles) from Chiusi and Chianciano, Cetona has become famous in recent years thanks to Padre Eligio, a Franciscan brother who used to be the chaplain of the Milan soccer team. He has since started a restaurant, **La Frateria di Padre Eligio**, in the **Convento San Francesco**, a restored monastery outside the Etruscan village of Cetona. Here the graduates of his Mondo X drug-rehabilitation program not only cook and serve in the restaurant but tend the vegetable gardens and orchards as well as the surrounding farms. They produce everything served in the extremely well run restaurant except the wines, which are carefully chosen from Italy's finest vintages. Each dish is garnished with exotic blossoms from the manicured monastery gardens where immaculate lawns surround a helicopter pad. There is nothing in the faces of the waiters smiling above brisk bow ties to suggest that these are all people who have been to hell and back, except an almost excessive desire to please. What could have been just a laudable exercise in philanthropy has become one of Italy's better (and very expensive) restaurants, for which gourmets make a detour. A few rooms in the monastery offer very unmonastic comfort to diners who do not wish to attempt one of the lovelier, more curvaceous drives back to their hotel. They will be rewarded in the morning by breakfasts of homemade bread and an impressive array of La Frateria's jams. Tel: (0578) 23-80-15; closed Tuesdays.

Cortona

Cortona, a town near Lago Trasimeno, south of Arezzo and east of Siena and the autostrada, has long been something of a cult corner of Tuscany for expatriate intelligentsia. Even older than Troy, Cortona was a flourishing little township well before the Etruscans colonized it. During the Renaissance it basked in the reflected glory of its most famous native son, Luca da Cortona, or Luca Signorelli, whom Bernard Berenson called "the Great Illustrator." Fra Angelico also lived here for some ten years and painted an *Annunciation* that makes an interesting comparison with the one in the monastery of San Marco in Florence. This painting and some of Luca Signorelli's work are in Cortona's **Museo Diocesano** (open 9:00 A.M. to 1:00 P.M. and 3:00 to 6:30 P.M. in summer; to 5:00 P.M. in winter; closed Mondays). The most striking painting in the museum, and one of the most beautiful of the 1400s, is Bartolomeo della Gatta's *Assumption*.

Luca Signorelli was considered one of the most important artists in the mid-15th century—he was commissioned to paint a whole cycle of frescoes for the Sistine chapel in Rome, as well as for the cathedral at Orvieto. He was much influenced by his time in Florence, and his obsession with the dramatic possibilities of the male nude harks back to Masaccio and forward to Michelangelo. A pupil of Piero della Francesca, he shows a wild imagination and rude vigor in his best work; his later paintings, churned out together with his school during his retirement in Cortona, are somewhat wooden.

Luca Signorelli was something of a "swinger" in contemporary terms, socially outgoing and spendthrift. He once borrowed money from Michelangelo and neglected to give it back until the Florentine master appealed to the courts of Cortona. The great tragedy of his life was the death of his 30-year-old son, also a painter, who is depicted in Signorelli's *Compianto sul Cristo Morto* ("Grieving for the Dead Christ") in the Museo Diocesano. Two other works of note in this museum are the *Parato Passerini,* a liturgical vestment designed by Andrea del Sarto, and a Roman sarcophagus that so impressed Donatello while on a visito to Cortona that he rushed back to Florence to inform Brunelleschi of his discovery. The latter "wasted no time, not even pausing to change his clothes or tell anyone of his intentions," Vasari relates, and instantly undertook the hundred or so kilometers on the back of a donkey to go to Cortona to view this marvel for himself and to sketch it *con la penna in disegno*—as a pen and ink drawing.

Today Cortona is a magical town, "perched on the very pinnacle of a mountain, and I wound and doubled interminably over the face of the great hill, while the jumbled roofs and towers of the arrogant little city still seemed nearer to the sky than to the railway station," as Henry James put it in his *Italian Hours.* The via Nazionale is the only horizontal street—the locals call it the *Rugapiana,* or flat wrinkle—in the whole of Cortona. Although only as wide as a New York sidewalk, it is the main street, with the most important stores, and the Cortonesi walk up and down here on Sundays after mass in any one of the diminutive churches conceived before the days of spires and vaults. From the air, Cortona looks like a nicely browned pie crust, cracked by a maze of little streets, which, splashed with the color of potted plants dangling around the doorways, climb inexorably upward toward the sun. It is worth the long haul to the top for churches like the **Chiesa di San Niccolò**, where Luca Signorelli painted an altarpiece on both sides of the canvas. As in many small Tuscan churches, a guardian can be summoned by a bell and rewarded with a 1,000 lire note. When you have finished admiring the *Deposition of Christ,* he will push a secret button and the whole picture will swing out from the wall, as in a Gothic novel, to reveal the *Madonna with Saints Peter and Paul* on the back.

Another church, which is perhaps the most important architectural feature of Cortona and one of the most perfect Renaissance churches in Tuscany, is **Santa Maria al Calcinaio**, its octagonal cupola dominating the Val di Chiana from a bend in the road leading up to Cortona. It was Luca Signorelli who suggested entrusting the building to Francesco di Giorgio Martini and who personally went to Urbino to invite this architect to Cortona. Among other treasures, there is a stained glass window by William de Marcillat, who was responsible for some of the splendid *vetrate* of Arezzo.

Cortona also has its share of Etruscan tombs and an archaeological museum—the **Museo dell'Accademia Etrusca**—whose most important exhibit is a bulbous Etruscan lamp from the fifth century B.C. The museum is closed on Mondays.

Restaurants and hotels in Cortona are disappointing. **Il Falconiere** makes up for a somewhat erratically inventive

cuisine with its setting in a patrician villa and garden overlooking Cortona (località San Martino; Tel: 0575-61-26-79.
Closed Wednesdays; medium-priced.) The one recommend-
able hotel—the Gugliemesca, 10 km (6 miles) away on a
wooded hillside—is closed for an indefinite period.

Saturnia

Saturnia, between Orvieto and Grosseto about 220 km (135
miles) south of Florence and frequented more by Romans
than by Tuscans, is the Etruscan equivalent of a Jacuzzi tub.
At the **Cascatelle del Mulino** hot sulfurous water cascades
down the hillside, while the banks are lined with the kind of
mud that would cost $20 a thimbleful in London or New
York. In winter, whole families strip off fur coats and down
jackets and wallow in natural pools at temperatures of 100° F,
leaving the skin like satin, well-being oozing from every
pore. And although the cascades are public, there is room
for everyone and no need to fight over the mud, especially
on weekdays. Some 7 km (4 miles) south at Montemerano is
Laudomia, a rustic, moderately priced trattoria with rooms,
which offers very good food. Try the *acqua cotta,* a delicious
Tuscan vegetable broth served with an egg. The trattoria is in
the capable hands of Laudomia's granddaughter, an archetypal Italian *mamma* who also makes jams and cakes to take
home. Tel: (0564) 62-00-62. Rooms are also available in the
little village at very reasonable rates.

For the more luxury- and (health-) conscious, the **Hotel
Terme di Saturnia** offers not only comfort but a number of
thermal treatments, beauty programs, and "anti-stress" so-
journs at a price—but worth it.

Arezzo

Although Arezzo was one of the chief cities of the Etruscan
league, today we go to this little Tuscan town 80 km
(50 miles) southeast of Florence to see the work of Piero
della Francesca. The fifth centenary of the great maestro's
death was celebrated in 1992. Piero, called "della Francesca"
because he was the son of a woman who was widowed
before he was born, painted a cycle of frescoes in Arezzo's
church of **San Francesco** that are among the most beautiful
in Italy. They have a moonlit quality, an unearthly austerity
and immense expressive power. Giorgio Vasari, himself a
native of Arezzo, says that in this work "Piero shows the
importance of copying things as they really are"—a novel
concept at the time. The frescoes tell the legend of the

"Triumph of the Cross," a tale comprising many countries and characters, including the superlative scene of Constantine dreaming in his tent. These frescoes are being restored and will not be visible for at least two more years.

Piero was first and foremost a mathematician, "a most zealous student," we are told, "using a knowledge of Euclid to demonstrate the properties of rectilinear bodies better than any geometrician." His other painting in Arezzo is a *Saint Mary Magdalen* in the cathedral, but it is worth driving the 40 km (25 miles) northeast to his birthplace at **Sansepolcro** to see his most famous work, *The Resurrection*. The sleeping soldier at the feet of the risen Christ in this painting is said to be a self-portrait by Piero, a sad reminder of the painter's destiny: By the age of 60 he was completely blind. In his diary a local lamplighter remembers, as a young boy, guiding the aging artist around the streets of Sansepolcro. Piero della Francesca remained faithful to this little town in his painting and in his heart until the day he died— October 12, 1492, the day Columbus discovered America. Some 17 km (10 miles) south of Sansepolcro at **Monterchi** is another Piero della Francesca masterpiece, the *Madonna del Parto,* or *Madonna of Childbirth*.

Giorgio Vasari, the first art critic in history, whose house at via XX Settembre 55 he himself lovingly furnished and frescoed, is another famous Aretine. Petrarch was born here (his house has now become an academy), as were Maecenas (in 68 B.C.) and the humanist Leonardo Bruni, whose tomb is one of the loveliest in the church of Santa Croce in Florence. Many Renaissance figures were born and grew up in the surrounding countryside, among them Michelangelo, Masaccio, and Paolo Uccello. Said Lady Morgan, travelling in the early 19th century: "Its subtile air has been asserted to be peculiarly favorable to genius."

Besides San Francesco, another church to be visited is **San Domenico**, for the Cimabue crucifix over the main altar, similar to the much damaged cross of the church of Santa Croce in Florence (now in the adjoining museum), and a beautiful *Annunciation* by another native of Arezzo, Spinello, also known as Aretino.

No Tuscan city worth its salt is without a sloe-eyed Madonna by Pietro Lorenzetti. His earliest work, the haunting polyptych in the **Pieve di Santa Maria**, shows the Madonna in an ermine-lined mantle looking at her guileless bambino with a passionate, almost foreboding, intensity.

Lastly, William de Marcillat, the famous stained-glass artist, lived out his last years in Arezzo, and some of his best work is to be found in the cathedral.

The best time to come to Arezzo is the first Sunday (and preceding Saturday) of every month, when an antiques fair is held in the town's medieval center. Stalls are set up in the piazza San Francesco and continue past the church into the piazza Grande or piazza Vasari and around the corner up the street leading to the Duomo.

On the first Sunday of September every year a tournament called the "Saracen Joust" is held, a tradition going back to the 13th century. The breast-plated Saracen is armed with a whip that he uses to lash at charging horsemen wearing the colors of the four medieval neighborhoods of Arezzo.

There are quite simply no good restaurants in Arezzo. The modern travelling salesman–style **Minerva** hotel just outside the walls of the old city is comfortable and clean and offers perhaps the most honest food in the city, catering to local businesspeople rather than tourists (via Fiorentina 4, Tel: 0575-37-03-90; medium-priced). Otherwise, the best policy would be to grab a sandwich at the bar under the Vasari loggia in the main square and plan to stay 28 km (17 miles) southwest of the city at **Gargonza**, a tiny 13th-century village belonging to Count and Countess Roberto Guicciardini, of one of the oldest families in Florence. You can either rent one of the renovated doll-like medieval houses for the week or stay in the guesthouse for a night or two. In summer the Guicciardinis organize music festivals. In addition the **Castello di Gargonza**, 11 km (7 miles) from the Monte San Savino autostrada exit, boasts a medium-priced, welcoming trattoria, also called **Castello di Gargonza**. Closed Tuesdays; reserve only in high season. Tel. (0575) 84-42-38. The **Locanda Sari** is a small, inexpensive hotel and restaurant 16 km (10 miles) from Sansepolcro. The restaurant is closed on Tuesdays.

If you are following a Piero della Francesca itinerary east of Arezzo toward Sansepolcro and Monterchi, it is worth making a detour to pay homage to the birthplace of Michelangelo, at Caprese Michelangelo, a hilltop village 26 km (16 miles) from Sansepolcro. The hotel and restaurant **Fonte della Galletta** is rather like a mountain refuge, a welcome escape in summer from the hot valley, where creature comforts are scarce but where the food, leaning heavily toward *porcini* mushrooms from the surrounding woodland, is good and inexpensive. Tel: (0575) 79-39-25.

Another simple trattoria in the area is the **Castello di Sorci**, 3 km (2 miles) from Anghiari (clearly signposted), for a hugely satisfying, very inexpensive meal. Closed Mondays; Tel: (0575) 78-90-66.

Near Arezzo, at Monterarchi (Tel: 055-970-70-45), Jenny

Bawtree of **Rendola Riding** takes horseback riders on treks all over Chianti country. This is one of the better known of several similar riding centers in the area.

THE WINE-GROWING AREAS OF TUSCANY

The word *Chianti* comes from the Etruscan name *Clante*. Chianti wines as such have been grown throughout the heart of Tuscany since the 12th century; Chianti Classico, most prized of the Chianti wines, grows in a more restricted area between Florence and Siena. Chianti Classico has a black rooster on a gold background as its neck label, an emblem inspired by a Vasari painting on the ceiling of the Sala del Cinquecento in the Palazzo Vecchio in Florence. Only those wines that are grown within strict geographical confines and meet the exacting regulations of the Gallo Nero (Black Rooster) Consortium may call themselves "*classico*." "Riserva" on the bottle means that the wine has aged for at least three years.

The quickest route from Florence to Siena is the Superstrada. But the via Chiantigiana (route 222) will give you more of the feel of Tuscany, especially as you near Radda and Gaiole east of 222. Every bend in the road (and these are frequent) brings more undulating hills combed with vines and more rows of cypresses that seem to march up the slopes and then stop abruptly halfway, as though pausing to get their bearings. Silver-green olive trees still peep over the old stone walls lining the route. Alternating with the trees is a tangle of bushes and stunted oaks, highlighted in spring with a blaze of yellow broom and in winter by red rose hips and old man's beard.

In Tuscany, as in Italy as a whole, it is almost inconceivable to consume food and wine separately. That may explain why, despite the large quantities of grapes grown and consumed each year, public drunkenness is virtually nonexistent. It also means that where there are vines, there are restaurants, too many to mention, where it is difficult to encounter a bad meal.

Greve

This town, about a third of the way to Siena on route 222, is considered the capital of Chianti Classico, and every year in the second half of September a wine fair is held here.

Individual growers preside over stands where you can sample and compare the different Chianti wines. In the main square, with its sloping arches on three sides, there is an *enoteca* (wine-tasting boutique) open year-round, as well as a butcher, Falorni, where they still make their own sausage and prosciutto the old way, curing the meat on the ashes of a wood fire.

The Chianti region has always been very industrious, as opposed to industrial, although small industries have mushroomed in recent years. The road to Greve takes you through the area where the huge terra-cotta vases for the lemon trees are produced, as well as the bricks and tiles—some still made by hand—that are used for so many Tuscan floors. In Greve itself the women are famous for their needlework. They can spend up to three years on a tablecloth, which they then bring to stores like **Azina Valoriani** on via C. Battisti, just off the main square, to be sold at prices that may sound high but are in fact a fraction of their real worth.

Just above Greve is the tiny village of **Montefioralle**, paved with rugged flagstones and dating from the 11th century. Montefioralle is the birthplace of Amerigo Vespucci, who gave his name to both Americas. This is such an unusual rock pool of history, left behind by the tides of time, that it is worth stopping here at the otherwise undistinguished little **Trattoria del Guerrino** for a simple but fragrant Tuscan lunch. Open Thursday to Sunday. No credit cards; reserve in season. Tel: (055) 85-31-06.

South of Greve

Two delightful hotels are at Castellina on 222 and Radda to its east. The **Tenuta di Ricavo** at Castellina, once a medieval village, has old stone houses tucked away among gardens, trees, and bushes around two swimming pools—the ultimate in getting away from it all. The Swiss management ensures that everything works and that guests are on time for meals. Closed from October to Easter.

The newly opened **Relais Fattoria Vignale** at Radda was once the manor house of a wine-growing estate, now faithfully restored so that a stay in the almost monastic elegance of its rooms and lounges grouped around the pool is like Tuscan country life when people could afford to live it up in style. It was here that the Gallo Nero Consortium was formed in 1924, and the Relais is still the legal headquarters of Chianti Classico. Neither of these hotels is expensive for what it offers, and both are near enough to Florence and Siena to permit easy day trips.

The sleepy little country town of Radda also has a restaurant called **Vignale**. Although not part of the hotel—a two-minute walk away—the restaurant is equally well run, offering ambitious and hence relatively expensive meals in a clean and welcoming country-restaurant atmosphere. Closed Thursdays and November 16 to February. Tel: (0577) 73-80-94.

From Radda to Gaiole the road winds past the entrance to vineyard after vineyard, most of which can be visited; some wine makers sell their wine directly from their cellars (signposted *vendita diretta*) as well as sending it all over the world. The **Castle of Brolio**, since 1141 the seat of the Ricasoli family, who make Brolio Chianti, is open to the public every day and is well worth a visit for a walk along the castle walls. A left turn as you leave the castle will take you to Badia a Coltibuono, a tiny village grouped around the ancient tower of the Benedictine monastery, now privately owned by the Badia a Coltibuono wine-making family (Lorenza de' Medici, the owner's wife, runs a well-known cooking school in spring and fall). The restaurant outside the monastery's thick walls is also called **Badia a Coltibuono** and is now managed by the family, offering fresh ingredients from the surrounding countryside, including *porcini* mushrooms that grow in the woods behind the restaurant. Closed Mondays. Tel: (0577) 74-94-24.

A right turn from the castle, on the other hand, will take you to Villa a Sesta, to the **Bottega del Trenta**. This restaurant has a courtyard at the back where you can sit in summer and where the villagers come once a year, on Saint Catherine's Day, to cook a festive dinner in the 150-year-old wood oven. All the ingredients, especially the olive oil on toasted bread, called *fett'unta*, and the tiny homemade sausages, are of the best quality, and the peasant soups and hearty pastas are the kind of fare Tuscans serve at home. The bearded Franco waits at tables, while his Parisian wife, Hélène, brings exotic touches such as the excellent chocolate cake that tastes like a baked *mousse au chocolat*. No credit cards accepted, but the Bottega is not expensive. Tel: (0577) 35-92-26; closed Tuesdays and Wednesdays.

Within three minutes of each other are two very different kinds of accommodation near Gaiole in Chianti. The **Castello di Spaltenna** has been transformed by a talented young Irishman into a very comfortable country hotel with four-poster beds with hand-painted drapes and a couple of Jacuzzi tubs. The rooms are grouped around the medieval castle courtyard, above a restaurant where the atmosphere and food are more typical of an English Relais & Châteaux hotel than of the Tuscan heartland. The hotel now also boasts a pool. Not as expensive as the disapproving locals say it is, or as you might expect it to be. Closed Monday evenings and Tuesday lunch.

For the more bohemian traveller, the **Park Hotel Cavarchione** is delightfully situated on a hillside in a renovated old Tuscan farmstead. Mozart ripples from the open windows, which look out onto woodland and vines. Adrian, in a magnificent Valentino waistcoat, entertains his guests, Champagne glass aloft, under Camp Tahiti sunshades grouped around the pool. No restaurant, but ample breakfasts and snacks are available.

San Casciano

If, instead of route 222, you take the Superstrada south from Florence, your first exit will be at San Casciano, a busy market town. Machiavelli wrote his treatise *The Prince* only 3 km (2 miles) away at **Sant'Andrea in Percussina**. He spent the days of his country exile snaring thrushes, selling wood from his estate, and reading Dante and Petrarch while lunching on "such food as this poor farm and my slender patrimony provides." The afternoons were spent with the locals at the inn, where Machiavelli would "act the rustic for the rest of the day," playing cards until the ensuing arguments could be heard as far away as San Casciano. In the evening he would strip off his muddy workaday clothes and change into his court robes to work on his masterpiece, "plumping and grooming" it for four hours every day.

Also in Sant'Andrea in Percussina (on the floor below the Macchiavelli museum) are the offices of the Consorzio Chianti Classico, where travellers can obtain information about the different wine estates in Tuscany, some of which rent apartments and holiday homes by the week or month all over Chianti country, for people who are contemplating a longer stay (and have a car). One of the most charming of these is **Fattoria La Loggia**, with restaurant, swimming pool, and horses for guests, at Montefiridolfi, 4 km (2.5 miles) south of San Casciano. This form of travel is called *agriturismo,* and there are agencies operating all over the territory that specialize in rentals, such as the **Cuendet** in Cerreto, near Monteriggioni. (See also "Useful Facts" in the Overview.)

Colle di Val d'Elsa

Another worthwhile stop close to the Superstrada is Colle di Val d'Elsa (about two-thirds of the way to Siena), a glassmaking town since the Middle Ages. Since the 18th century, when an Alsatian firm chose Colle as its headquarters because of the abundant supply of wood for the furnaces, the town has specialized in crystal. Today there are about a hundred artisans working in glassblowing, engraving, and cutting crystal in and around this walled medieval town, which was the birthplace of Arnolfo di Cambio, architect of Florence's cathedral.

Every year in September there is a crystal fair here. Because this is the countryside, the fair is more like a village festival than a trade fair, but you will get a good idea of the range and artistry of these glass artisans, whose work is as fine as any produced in Europe today (a fact the Tuscans themselves do not even know, Tuscany being a land that rarely honors its own). There is a glass store in the center of town called **Mezzetti**, where you can buy work by all the factories and engravers in Colle di Val d'Elsa.

There are three good restaurants in town, but perhaps the best is **L'Antica Trattoria**, on three floors with an Art Nouveau decor. L'Antica Trattoria serves unusual dishes such as *risotto verde all'ortica* (green risotto with nettles), which, despite its name, is delicious (piazza Arnolfo 23; closed Monday evening and Tuesdays; Tel: 0577-92-37-47).

The **Villa Belvedere**, 2 km east of Colle di Val d'Elsa, is an 18th-century villa, once the favorite venue of Ferdinand III, the archduke of Tuscany. Now open all year round, it has 15 rooms, all with sweeping views of the Tuscan hills and vineyards. At 25 km (15 miles) from Siena, it is ideally situated for people wandering through Tuscany by car.

San Gimignano

The Poggibonsi exit off the Superstrada leads you west to San Gimignano, home of one of Tuscany's few white wines, the Vernaccia. The wine is golden yellow, dry, fresh, and smooth in taste, with a hint of bitter almond; it should be drunk young and cold.

San Gimignano is one of the few Tuscan towns that still has its towers, which appear on the horizon like a mirage or a fairy castle as you round a bend. It has changed not a whit since the end of the 1300s, as we can see from the painting in the Museo Civico of San Gimignano in his bishop's miter, cradling the city in his lap as though on a tea tray. Of the legendary 72 towers, only 14 remain; the highest, like the "Rognosa," which was once the courts of justice and prison, are more than 160 feet high. The others belonged to leading San Gimignano families—the higher your tower, the more important you were—like the rival Ardinghelli and Salvucci families, one Guelph, the other Ghibelline. From the holes in the walls that are still visible, ramps and passageways were constructed so that friendly families could visit one another without venturing out into the streets. San Gimignano was involved in all the important battles between Guelph and Ghibelline cities, such as the Battle of Montaperti, when—according to Dante—the waters of the river Arbia ran red.

San Gimignano was an important stopping place for pilgrims on their way to Rome and was such a bustling trade center that the to-ing and fro-ing of mules bearing merchandise must have looked not unlike the prosperous township in Ambrogio Lorenzetti's *Allegory of Good and Bad Government* in the Palazzo Pubblico in Siena. (One of the principal thoroughfares of Europe, the *Francigena,* passed through the city.) Besides wine, one of the main products handled here was saffron, used in cooking, dyeing, and medicines. The merchants of San Gimignano traded far and wide; one of the Ardinghelli family is recorded as taking his wares to Egypt, Libya, and Syria.

Where there is prosperity there is art, and the cathedral of **San Gimignano** is a treasure trove of artworks. The cathedral contains two wooden statues by Jacopo della Quercia: a very Aryan-looking Angel Gabriel announcing the birth of Jesus to a masterfully self-effacing Madonna. Taddeo di Bartolo's dire vision of Hell here verges on the grotesque, not to say the obscene. Barna di Siena was one of the few artists of the late trecento who can bear comparison with the earlier innovators, like his maestro, Simone Martini. The cycle of frescoes in the cathedral, depicting episodes from the life of Christ, was Barna's last work; he fell off the ladder while stepping back to admire his portrayal of the Crucifixion, with fatal consequences.

Benozzo Gozzoli did some of his best work during his last years in San Gimignano, in the church of **Sant'Agostino**. In this cycle of frescoes it is the *bambini* who charm us most, whether the infant Saint Augustine and his fellow students being handed over to a Nicholas Nickleby–type schoolmaster, or the baby Christ himself, petulantly playing with a wooden spoon while the mature Saint Augustine holds forth on the mysteries of the Trinity.

An important figure in San Gimignano's lore and legend was Santa Fina, a little saint who was as delicate as the violets that bloom on the towers on the anniversary of her death in 1253. There are pictures of this saint in the Museo Comunale and in the cathedral; Ghirlandaio painted the 15-year-old Santa Fina on her deathbed being comforted by a vision of Saint Gregory borne aloft by crimson-winged cupids. To Ghirlandaio we also owe another *Annunciation,* showing a very bookish Madonna surprised at her studies, under the arches of the piazza Pecori next to the cathedral.

The **Museo Comunale** is the forbidding palazzo to which the Torre Grossa, or Big Tower, belongs. Among the many artworks housed here is a *Maestà* by Lippo Memmi—more than a pupil, an alter ego of Simone Martini—in what is sometimes called "Dante's Hall" because Dante spoke here in 1300 to drum up support for the Guelph party. The theme of the *maestà,* the majestic Madonna holding sway over both heavenly throng and earthbound Tuscans, is dominant in 14th-century lore, when all the leading cities of Tuscany were fiercely independent and republican, answering to no despot, monarch, or temporal authority but only to the dictates of the Divine. (The ticket for the museum also allows access to Saint Fina's chapel in the cathedral.) Open 9:30 A.M. to 12:30 P.M. and 3:00 to 6:00 P.M. (2:30 to 5:30 P.M. from October 1 to March 31, when it is also closed Mondays).

San Gimignano also has a high-security jail girded by the ancient walls (as does Volterra to the west). In medieval cities like these a jail doesn't seem out of place, and the thousands of tourists who crowd into San Gimignano every year scarcely cast a glance in its direction as they shop in the many stores selling very tempting and tasteful basketware and ceramics, or eat in the main square overlooking the 13th-century *cisterna* (cistern), which gives the square its name. This well was still in use until 50 years ago; you can see the marks of seven centuries of ropes chafing against its sides.

The hotel-restaurant **Cisterna** is located in one of the most picturesque squares in Italy. The restaurant offers an unambitious but pleasant meal with a view, at affordable prices. Closed Tuesdays and Wednesday lunch. Tel: (0577) 94-03-28. Visitors wishing to stay overnight would be better advised, however, to go 3 km (2 miles) southwest from San Gimignano to the **Hotel Pescille**, a large manor house surrounded by vines, with windows looking out toward the famous towers. The hotel is open from March to November and has a delightful restaurant.

Wine cellars beckon on both sides of the narrow main street, where you can sample the different Vernaccias and buy a bottle or two to take home. One of the best is called Guicciardini Strozzi, from a vineyard belonging to the princely Tuscan family of the same name.

Monteriggioni

The last stop going south on the Superstrada before you reach Siena is tiny Monteriggioni, another miragelike fortress with squat square towers punctuating the six-foot-thick walls that surround the flagstoned square and the well, or *pozzo,* that gives the one restaurant its name. Built in the early 13th century, Monteriggioni merits a passing mention in Canto 31 of *L'Inferno: "Come in su la cerchia tonda/di Montereggion di torri si corona"* ("As with the circle of turrets Monteriggioni is crowned").

Il **Pozzo** is a family-run restaurant with a welcoming atmosphere and good food prepared by the owner's wife. The dishes include *panzerotti,* a bubbling-hot mixture of crêpes and cream, and also meat grilled over an open fire. A meal, accompanied by the house Vernaccia, is not cheap, but it is good value. Closed Sunday evenings, Mondays, January, and part of August. Tel: (0577) 30-41-27.

Vino Nobile di Montepulciano

First mentioned in documents dating from the eighth century, the Vino Nobile di Montepulciano is less well known than Chianti, but experts from the Farnese Pope Paul III onward have been effusive in its praise. The papal verdict was: *"Questo vino ha odore, colore, e sapore"* ("This wine has bouquet, color, and taste"). It is a more purplish red than Chianti Classico and has a delicate bouquet of violets. It becomes Riserva after three years' aging.

In the old streets of **Montepulciano**, southeast of Siena and not far from the A 1, are several cellars where you can taste and buy the Vino Nobile. Among the most prestigious are the Avignonesi wines in the cellars of the 16th-century palace of the same name in Montepulciano's main street, the Corso. The cellars are opposite a modest and inexpensive family-run hotel, Il **Marzocco**, which gets its name from the Marzocco lion atop a column before its windows. (Montepulciano was involved in a tug of war between Florence and Siena for centuries, and the Marzocco lion, a symbol of Florentine dominion, replaced the she-wolf of Siena in 1511.)

Montepulciano has always been an aristocratic town, one of the best-preserved historic centers in Italy. Tradition says that it was founded by dissident nobles from Etruscan Chiusi. Cosimo I de' Medici elevated Montepulciano to the status of *città nobile,* and every façade lining the narrow streets of this "pearl of the 500," as it is called today, harks back to its Renaissance past. The imposing façades of the Bucelli, Gagnoni-Grugni, and Cervini palaces belonging to the once powerful local families seem too large for the narrow Corso, which winds up the hill with medieval dignity, past the Michelozzo façade of the church of Sant' Agostino to the spacious, grandiose **piazza Grande** that commands a view of the valley.

The **Palazzo Comunale** (town hall), also by Michelozzo, is a squatter version of the Palazzo Vecchio in Florence, a symbol of the town's allegiance to Cosimo de' Medici's Florence. Medici influence can also be seen in the square, where the well by Antonio Sangallo the Elder is surmounted by the famous Medici coat of arms, supported by Florentine lions, while the griffins of Montepulciano stand respectfully to one side.

The dusky interior of the **Montepulciano Cathedral** contains a number of interesting artworks, including a funerary monument to a certain Bartolomeo Aragazzi, bits and pieces of which are distributed all over the church. A frieze of putti and garlands, once the base of the monument, is now in the main altar, which is surmounted by a magnificent triptych of the Assumption, painted in 1401 by one of the most gifted of Sienese painters, Taddeo di Bartolo. In one of the panels Saint Antilia is shown carrying the 14th-century town of Montepulciano on a large tray, as if it were a ceremonial cake.

The piazza Grande, with its splendid square palazzi Nobili-Tarugi and Contucci, is also the location of a **school for mosaics** whose works are on sale to the public.

Montepulciano's most famous son was Angelo Ambrogini, known as Poliziano, one of the leading poets and humanists of his time (1454–1494). When he was 16, his translations of Homer earned him the tribute *juvenis Homerus,* or young Homer. Lorenzo de' Medici became his patron, and he was tutor to the Medici household and taught at the university in Florence. Among other things, he wrote the first play in Italian of any literary merit, *Orfeo,* one of the finer works of the Italian Renaissance.

The **Museo Civico/Pinacoteca Crociani** in the Palazzo Neri-Orselli is well worth a visit, especially for its earliest paintings, a *Saint Francis* by Margaritone d'Arezzo and the *Crowning of the Virgin* by Jacopo di Mino del Pellicciaio, with its almost Oriental hues. Closed Mondays and Tuesdays.

Halfway down the hillside is the abbey of **San Biagio**, masterpiece of Antonio da Sangallo the Elder and once a place of pilgrimage for its miraculous frescoed Madonna, whose eyes were said to move. Today the hallowed precincts should still be visited for a 16th-century architectural feast. Meanwhile, Montepulciano remains best known for a bit of Old World kitsch, a life-size figure of the Neapolitan clown Pulcinella, who chimes the hours on top of a 16th-century tower in the main street.

A 15-minute drive northwest from Montepulciano is **Montefollonico**, where Dania Lucherini has made a name for herself as one of the best chefs in Tuscany. Her food owes its flavor and flair to the freshness of the herbs and greens that come from her vegetable garden beneath the **Ristorante La Chiusa**'s walls; cheese and meats are supplied by country people from round about. La Chiusa has a few rooms, country-cottage style except for the bathtubs, which are pure California, large enough for a whole family to congregate in. Closed Tuesdays; very expensive.

Pienza

Enea Silvio Piccolomini, whose life story is told so vividly in the frescoes by Pinturicchio in the Libreria Piccolomini in Siena's cathedral, was born in the town of Corsignano, later renamed Pienza in his honor (west of Montepulciano on route 146). After he became Pope Pius II in 1458, he asked Bernardino Rossellino, architect of the Marsuppini tomb in Santa Croce, to transform his native town. Pienza was to be the first example of Renaissance urban planning, its piazza and adjacent buildings rebuilt according to Renaissance principles of architecture and lifestyle.

And so it remains today, a lived-in museum where you can visit the pope's palace and apartments, with their hanging gardens overlooking the rolling, misty green hills of the Val d'Orcia, with Monte Amiata in the background. No wonder Pope Pius insisted that the windows of the cathedral, which he called *domus vitrea,* look out toward what is perhaps the most uplifting and unspoiled vista in Tuscany, what Malaparte calls "the most feminine of Tuscan landscapes." He even threatened to excommunicate anyone who dared to modify the interior's decor; the pictures by Il Vecchietta, Sano di Pietro, and Giovanni di Paolo—which he commissioned—are still in their original places. These are the last works of the glorious Sienese era, which by the 15th century had faded into insignificance beside the bright star of Florence.

Pius himself was so pleased with Pienza that he forgave Il Rossellino for exceeding his budget, praising him thus: "You did well, Bernardo, in lying to us about the expense involved in the work. If you had told the truth, you could never have induced us to spend so much money, and neither this splendid palace nor this church, the finest in all

Italy, would now be standing." He then gave the architect an additional 100 ducats and a scarlet robe, an honor awarded to few.

The **Club delle Fattorie**, or Farmsteads' Club, is a very successful concern specializing in all-natural products from all over Tuscany. It has opened a store just inside the main gateway to Pienza, where you can buy the wines, honeys, jams, olive oils, pickled preserves, and other produce of the region. Pienza is famous for its cheese, perhaps because the sheep have rich pastureland in the Val d'Orcia and feast on herbs like absinthe, mint, and leopard's bane; the cheese is wrapped in walnut leaves while it seasons. Every year on the first Sunday of September there is a *cacio* fair, when local producers bring their cheese to town to be sold.

Monticchiello

Another little hilltop village, between Pienza and Monte-pulciano, is Monticchiello, famous for its *Teatro Povero* (Poor People's Theater), which puts on a play in the main square in the second half of July, entirely written, acted, and directed by the villagers. Although Monticchiello is the essence of "off the beaten track," its theatrical background has brought the villagers total literacy since the 1700s, unusual in a country community in the days when distances seemed greater and communication was slow. The 13th-century church once housed a very lovely *Madonna and Child* by Pietro Lorenzetti that—despite the severity of the trecento style—shows great tenderness and bonding between mother and child. Removed to Siena to be restored, the painting has never been returned to Monticchiello (a fact much resented by the villagers) and now hangs in the Pinacoteca in Siena. You can see a dog-eared postcard of the Madonna in most Monticchiello front rooms, including that of the store selling very attractive handwoven linens opposite the church.

If you prefer to stay for lunch in this hilltop hamlet, try the **Taverna di Moranda** at via di Mezzo 17, a rather dark but comfortable little restaurant that will serve you an honest, inexpensive Tuscan meal. Closed Mondays. Tel: (0578) 75-50-50; no credit cards.

The country roads of the Val d'Orcia, one of the most uncluttered, unspoiled corners of Tuscany, wind gently through fields of windswept wheat dotted with poppies where, even in high season, there are few cars on the road. It is worth taking your time, driving up to the ancient hilltop villages like **San Quirico d'Orcia** 10 km (6 miles) from Pienza for the crumbling majesty of its Collegiata, with splendid portals attributed to Giovanni Pisano and the Barili wooden intarsia choir stalls (currently under restoration). **Castiglione d'Orcia**, 9 km (5.5 miles) away, has another Pietro Lorenzetti Madonna in the church of Saints Stefano and Degna. The only tourists in the area converge on **Bagno Vignoni**, 6 km (4 miles) from San Quirico, especially on weekends—its main square is a rectangular reservoir of hot water bubbling up from a volcanic spring. Here Lorenzo de' Medici "*Il Magnifico*" came to cure his arthritis and Saint Catherine of Siena's mother brought her in the vain hope of distracting her from all this talk of saintliness. Undeterred, the young Saint Catherine would escape maternal vigilance and plunge into the hottest waters to scald herself as penance for her sins. To this day, an ethereal light appears sometimes on the surface of the waters, which locals call "Saint Catherine's Way."

More hedonistic bathers can wallow in the pool of the Hotel Posta Marcucci, while the place to stay is the **Albergo Le Terme**, a simple little hotel in a palazzo built for Pope Pius II by Rossellino. Incredibly cheap, it is especially recommended out of season when the waters in the square steam below the hotel windows and visitors are few.

Brunello di Montalcino

This wine, considered Tuscany's most "serious," grows around the town of **Montalcino**, 46 km (28 miles) south of Siena. Again a very old wine, Brunello is mentioned continually in documents narrating the vicissitudes of Tuscan history, such as the time the Maresciallo di Monluc rubbed it on his cheeks to give them color during the siege of Montalcino in 1553, so that the populace would not realize how serious the food shortage had become. It was the wine, we are told, that the Medicis preferred to send their popes, although Cosimo de' Medici complained more than once about the highly intoxicated state in which his guests left his dinner table after the Brunello had been flowing too freely.

Brunello is aged in casks for four years before bottling and continues to age in the bottle, becoming more full-bodied and velvety as time goes by. It can be called Riserva only after five years; it's one of those wines that really needs to breathe and should be uncorked up to a day before consumption. The most famous—and expensive—Brunello is Biondi Santi, but other, less-renowned Brunellos can be equally good. The **Fattoria dei Barbi Colombini** has opened a rustic restaurant a few minutes' drive from Montalcino. You can drink your fill of Brunello here during an inexpensive meal outside on benches in summer or around a log fire in winter. Reserve in summer and on Sundays. Closed Tuesday evenings in winter and Wednesdays year-round. Tel: (0577) 84-93-57. Alternatively, at the **Caffè Fiaschetteria Italiana**, a wine bar and coffeehouse left over from the Belle Epoque in the center of Montalcino, you can taste and compare different Brunellos by the glass. (No credit cards.)

Legend has it that Charlemagne laid the foundations of the abbey of **Sant'Antimo**, 9 km (5 miles) from Montalcino, one of the most beautiful Romanesque buildings in Italy. With its pale yellow stone and bucolic silence, Sant'Antimo is unforgettable, whatever your credo.

SIENA

Siena, south of Florence in the heart of the wine country of Tuscany, is a distillation of all things Tuscan, like a Cognac or, more to the point, a grappa. The Sienese speak the purest Italian (it is said that in their use of words, the Sienese prefer butter to Tuscan olive oil); their city has been a highly civilized place since the Middle Ages. The Madonnas in their 14th-century paintings are draped in ornate robes made of mouth-watering silks and damasks, and even today the velvets and brocades for the costumes used in the *Palio,* the historic horse race run twice a year in the main square, are handwoven and cost hundreds of dollars a yard. Unpolluted by industry and unspoiled by the locust sort of tourism that afflicts some of Italy's larger cities, affluent Siena has maintained the same high standards of excellence and elegance for centuries and needs no tourism to boost the city's economy.

For four centuries the city's archives were kept in wooden bindings called *Biccherna,* each painted by a leading artist of the time. (These are well worth a visit, in the **State Archives of Palazzo Piccolomini**.) Dante studied at the university in Siena, one of the oldest in Italy. The hospital, founded in the ninth century, is still one of the most important in the country, especially for ophthalmology (Mrs. Sakharov came from Russia for an eye operation here). Siena's own bank, the Monte dei Paschi di Siena, was founded in the 17th century, although its origins go back even further.

"The Siena of today is a mere shrunken semblance of the rabid little republic which in the 13th century waged triumphant war with Florence, cultivated the arts with splendor, planned a cathedral... of proportions almost unequaled and contained a population of 200,000 souls." So said Henry

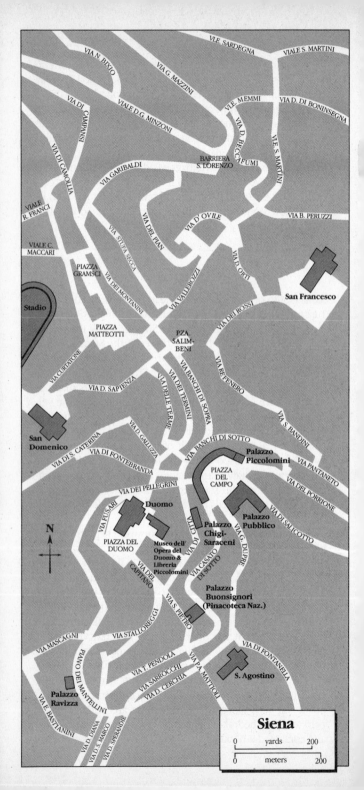

James, but the Sienese have none of the Madame Bovary complexes of provincial towns. In the 18th century Horace Walpole found Siena "very smug," and Ghibelline Siena still feels superior in every way to the rest of Tuscany—especially Florence, its traditional Guelph enemy. After all, was Siena not founded by Senus, son of Remus, one of the twin founders of Rome who was suckled by the she-wolf, Siena's symbol to this day?

The Sienese Trecento

In the 1300s it was Siena that led the way in painting and determined the course of Florentine art at the dawn of the quattrocento. "Like a leaven working through the whole lump, so the outstanding quality of Tuscan art during the fourteenth century slowly permeated the whole of Western European painting," wrote Peter and Linda Murray in *The Art of the Renaissance*.

However, the only Sienese artist who can withstand close comparison with Giotto is Duccio di Buoninsegna. He was an unruly genius; there are records of at least nine fines levied against this great painter, for a number of offenses. All the other leading figures in Italian art were pupils of someone or another, but Duccio seems to have blazed a trail out of nowhere, although he was certainly affected by the work of Nicola and Giovanni Pisano from Pisa, who at that time were working on the pulpit in Siena.

His most famous work in Siena is the *Maestà*, or *Majestic Madonna*, a supremely important figure for the Sienese, who revered her not just as the Mother of God but, more intimately, as patron saint of the Sienese Republic. This grandiose painting took three years to complete and cost 3,000 gold florins. It was, as Duccio himself wrote in his contract for the work, "the best I can and know how to do, the best the Good Lord will allow me." When it was completed in 1311, the people of Siena bore the painting in triumph to the cathedral, accompanied by the music of trumpets and bagpipes.

Originally the *Maestà*—now in the **Museo dell'Opera del Duomo**—was painted on both sides. The scene of the Madonna on her throne was backed by 60 panels, two of which are now in the United States, in the National Gallery in Washington and the Frick Collection in New York.

Another transcendent figure of the Sienese trecento is Simone Martini, a pupil of Duccio. He, too, painted a *Maestà* (recently unveiled after restoration), for a 40-foot wall of the Palazzo Pubblico, where she could observe the judicial procedure of the councillors of the Sienese Republic. Even more famous is his painting, on the opposite wall, of Guidoriccio da Fogliano, a knight and charger caparisoned in a rather loud black-and-yellow checked cloak (checks and plaids are very popular in Sienese painting), all the more remarkable because the horse is standing on two left feet. A few years ago a shudder went through the international art world at the suggestion (never proved) that this masterpiece of Simone's might be a fake.

Perhaps Simone's most brilliant work is his *Annunciation,* which, although painted for the cathedral in Siena, is now in the Uffizi in Florence. Also in Florence is his *Madonna* in the Guilds' church of Orsanmichele, while his polyptych—six panels surrounding a Madonna and Child—is in the Museo Nazionale in Pisa.

After Simone Martini's departure to Avignon (then the seat of the papacy), where he spent his last years, the brothers Ambrogio and Pietro Lorenzetti stepped into his shoes.

In 1340 Pietro was summoned by the Florentines to paint a Madonna for a church in Pistoia (that painting is now in the Uffizi). This would seem to confirm that in the century following Giotto's death and before the emergence of Masaccio—a period marked by a devastating plague—there were no Florentine artists to match the painters of Siena. Pietro's work is best represented in Siena by his *Birth of the Virgin,* now in the Museo dell'Opera del Duomo and remarkable, among other reasons, because it is a faithful reproduction of a bourgeois Sienese household of the mid-1300s.

Pietro's brother, the gentler, more introspective Ambrogio, has left Siena an incomparable masterpiece, the *Allegory of Good and Bad Government,* which covers three sides of the **sala della Pace**, also known as the sala del Nove (Room of the Nine), in the **Palazzo Pubblico**. Never before in the whole history of art had anyone attempted such an ambitious project, a detailed panorama of daily life in both city and countryside, and it is one of the most exciting things to see in Siena. (Another key painting by Ambrogio, also in the Uffizi, is the *Presentation in the Temple,* showing a depth and sense of architectural perspective that was revolutionary in those two-dimensional days, as was the expressive quality of the main characters.)

The gradual evolution in Sienese painting from the trecento onward can be seen in the **Pinacoteca Nazionale**, where Byzantine Madonnas slowly give way to rosier cheeked, ampler forms in the new perspective of the Renaissance, painted by artists like Giovanni di Paolo, Matteo di Giovanni, and Il Vecchietta. There are also the first pure landscapes, executed on wooden panels, to be painted in Europe: *City by the Sea* and *Castle on the Shore of a Lake* by Ambrogio Lorenzetti.

Frequently represented in Sienese painting is Saint Catherine of Siena (1347–1380), usually depicted with a lily, a flower generally absent from Sienese painting as it was the symbol of hated Florence. Although she never learned to read and write and had no formal education, Saint Catherine dictated learned treatises and missives to leading ecclesiastical figures (not least Pope Gregory XI, whom she persuaded to transfer the papal seat from Avignon back to Rome) and became a Doctor of the Church and later patron saint of Italy. Her house can be visited, although not much is left of the original decor except her cell, which contains a few personal belongings, including the walking stick that was necessary because of the arthritis she willed on herself in atonement for her father's sins. In the **Church of San Domenico** are further relics of this saint, frescoes by Sodoma of her swooning in ecstasy, and her only recognized likeness, in a chapel at the end of the nave.

The Piazza del Campo

Cars must be parked in the piazzas outside the center, as no motorized vehicles are allowed in the old flagstoned streets of Siena. The urban layout is like a Gothic game of Snakes and Ladders, with a magnificent finishing post, the piazza del Campo, acclaimed by Montaigne as the most beautiful square in the world. Don't attempt to visit Siena in high-heeled shoes; you'll either be slithering down the narrow streets that trickle toward the piazza, which fans out like a peacock's tail at the foot of the Torre del Mangia, or resolutely climbing up again.

Henry James, who regretted how few of the world's wonders can "startle and waylay," was quite bowled over by the piazza del Campo: "The vast pavement converges downward in slanting radiations of stone, the spokes of a great wheel." These spokes divide the piazza into nine segments in honor of the government of the Nine, leading merchants and bankers who ruled Siena from 1283 to 1353. The Nine was the only really stable government Siena ever enjoyed in that era; the city's history is otherwise punctuated by the internecine fighting between Guelphs and Ghibellines and its century-long feud with Florence. (In his dedication to the *Maestà,* Duccio wrote, "*Sis causa Senis requiet*" ("Bring peace to Siena"), and added: "and life to Duccio, who has painted you like this.") The Nine built the cathedral and the

Palazzo Pubblico, from which the Torre del Mangia, as Henry James saw it, "rises slender and straight as a pennoned lance planted on the steel shod toe of a mounted knight, and keeps all to itself in the blue air." Few things inspired James as much as the Torre del Mangia, "the finest thing in Siena," whose 332 steps you can climb today.

In the center of the square, where people sit and watch the pigeons scatter in clouds every time children or dogs gambol past, is a copy of a fountain surmounted by she-wolves by Jacopo della Quercia. This great Sienese sculptor (without whose heritage, the Sienese claim, Michelangelo could never have reached the exalted peaks of Mount Olympus) was one of the first, according to Vasari, "who showed that sculpture might make a near approach to nature." His *Fonte Gaia* (Gay Fountain), which took years to complete, earned him the nickname of "Jacopo della Fonte," although his best-known work is the tomb of Ilaria del Carretto in the cathedral in Lucca.

Siena Cathedral

Ruskin wrote that he found the cathedral "in every way absurd—over-cut, over-striped, over-crocketed, over-gabled, a piece of costly confectionery." For the non-purist, Siena cathedral is an architectural *Maestà,* an overwhelming edifice that inspired Wagner, during his Sienese sojourn, to write *Parsifal.* One of the most remarkable facets of this profusion of decorative arts is the cathedral floor, covered in elaborate graffito technique, while the **Libreria Piccolomini**, off the left nave, was a favorite haunt of Henry James, with its illuminated manuscripts, "almost each of whose successive leaves gives the impression of rubies, sapphires and emeralds set in gold and practically embedded in the page."

The Libreria Piccolomini is frescoed by the Perugian Pinturicchio, whose paintings narrate the life of that "most profanely literary of Pontiffs and last of would-be crusaders," Enea Silvio Piccolomini, who became Pius II. Much of the revenues of his papacy went into this library, and at times, judging from the fresco of his caravels lashed by a violent storm in the port of Genoa, the future pope lived dangerously. Later he was to rebuild the center of his native town, Pienza, one of the loveliest in Tuscany (discussed above). In this cycle of frescoes, reputedly Pinturicchio's best work, some of the rather stereotyped faces are of unusual quality and may have been painted by the young Raphael.

The Palio

Siena's famous horse race, an event that is in no way intended as a mere tourist attraction, is a dusty, noisy, tense, and sometimes frightening occasion that the townspeople relive every year with passionate fervor. Neighborhood feeling here is intense: Every child in Siena is baptized draped in the flag of its *contrada* (a little group of streets), which bears the name and colors of the local insignia—the Dragon, the Porcupine, the She-Wolf, the Noble Goose, and so forth. The first Palio was run in 1656; since then it has taken place twice a year, on July 2 and August 16—with full Renaissance panoply—and sometimes three times if there is a special event to commemorate, as when the first man walked on the moon. Every year, voices of protest condemn the riotous, unruly race around the main square on a thin layer of sawdust. Recently both Franco Zeffirelli and Brigitte Bardot joined the chorus. A riderless horse can win the race, no matter how or by whom the rider was unseated, and casualties, both human and animal, are not uncommon. If the horse dies in one of the fiercely disputed heats before the race, his hooves are ceremoniously paraded around the square on a silver tray. The winning horse is adequately rewarded, however, at the victory banquet of his *contrada,* when tables are set out in the narrow streets and he stands at the head of the table, his hooves painted gold, with an overstuffed nosebag of fodder and sugar. Every *contrada* has a museum that can be visited on application to the Azienda Autonoma di Turismo at via di Città 43.

Another major seasonal event is the **Accademia Musicale Chigiana**, the music festival held in the Palazzo Chigi-Saraceni every July, which draws music lovers and well-known musicians from all over the world.

Staying in Siena

A hotel in a magical position on a hill 3 km (2 miles) north of Siena is the **Park**, recently acquired by the Charming Hotels mini-chain (owners of the Helvetia & Bristol in Florence and the Inghilterra in Rome). They have transformed the Park into a showpiece hotel worthy of its setting, with an excellent restaurant supplied by its own vegetable garden.

Another choice, the beautiful **Certosa di Maggiano**, is a Relais & Châteaux hotel 3 km (2 miles) south of the city, in a converted monastery with the quiet elegance of a Tuscan country house—peach trees surround the pool, and old leather-bound books line the library walls.

If your budget doesn't rise to Certosa prices, try the **Pensione Palazzo Ravizza** in a charmingly old-fashioned 17th-century palazzo five minutes from the Duomo. Long *the* place to stay for the discerning tourist, the Ravizza offers quite acceptable accommodation—although it's not what it once was.

Food in Siena

Siena is better known for its culture than its cuisine, which, although palatable enough, has settled into a comfortable gastronomic rut—thanks no doubt to the undemanding tourists who hardly notice what they are eating as they sit out at tables in the piazza del Campo, one of the most splendid open-air dining rooms in the world.

A medium-priced restaurant a little out of the ordinary— and certainly trying harder—is the **Osteria Le Logge**, just around the corner from the Palazzo Pubblico. A bohemian place, the venue for Siena's university fauna and what could be described as swinging Sienese, it looks less like a restaurant than an Old Curiosity Shop, with old-fashioned glass-fronted cabinets around the walls; prewar radios and similar props punctuate the decor. Le Logge's food is imaginative, such as the *Terra di Siena,* veal baked with peperoncino and tomato, and a risotto with bacon and sweet corn. A good selection of *pecorino,* the local sheep's cheese, rounds off the meal, a perfect partner for the house wine, a Brunello del Paradiso. The owners of Le Logge have restored a 14th-century cellar beneath the restaurant, visible from above through glass. Closed Sundays. Tel: (0577) 480-13.

The real eager-beaver gourmet drives a little way out of the center of Siena (a taxi will also oblige not too ruinously) to the **Antica Trattoria Botteganova**. Here great care goes into the choice of dishes resuscitated from the menus of Siena's past, into decanting the impressive choice of wines, and into procuring the freshest ingredients, such as the *erbette* (herbs) that are an integral part of many dishes here. Allow the helpful staff to advise you on the constantly varying menus. The food is moderately priced—not as expensive as it could be. Closed Sundays and Monday lunch. Tel: (0577) 28-42-30.

Siena has Tuscany's sweet tooth. It's famous not only for its *panforte,* which tastes like a very solid mince pie, but also for cookies called *ricciarelli.* At **Nannini** in via Banchi di

Sopra you can sample all these local delicacies and also buy boxes in varying sizes to take home.

Siena is not known as a shopping town, but the elegant little boutiques on via Banchi di Sotto and via di Città, the streets encircling the piazza del Campo, are well worth a browse. You can pick up local pottery here, with designs inspired by the colorful flags of the *Palio,* at such stores as **Zina Provvedi**.

THE TYRRHENIAN COAST

There are 203 miles of coastline in Tuscany, not counting the islands—not quite enough to accommodate comfortably the many thousands of Italian holiday-makers and sun-worshippers from northern climes who descend on its beaches and coastal resorts, especially in July and August. The Versilia district, to the north, was once the haunt of artists and poets as well as the local aristocracy, who still have summer homes here. But a broad band of concrete has wedged itself between the mountains and the sea, leaving windswept pines to tower forlornly over the countless *villette* (bungalows) and hotel billboards.

A busy four-lane road roars past the beach, which is divided into different *bagni* where you have to pay, some-times through the nose, for your corner of a foreign land complete with deck chair and umbrella. At best, like the Bagno Piero at Forte dei Marmi, these *bagni* look a little like Deauville in Impressionist paintings; at worst, like Viareggio, which has become more famous for its spectacular carnival than for its seashore, they can verge on Coney Island.

Farther south is the **Maremma**, Tuscany's Camargue (see also the section on Etruscan Places, above), where people still raise white oxen and hunt wild boar and where, if you are lucky, you may still find local cowboys, called *butteri,* riding on old American-style saddles. However, the area's wild beaches, lined with dunes and dense Mediterranean *maquis,* are often part of wildlife protection areas, such as Capalbio, the Lago di Burano, and the oasis of Bolgheri—a medieval village about 50 km (30 miles) south of Livorno in the middle of an animal-conservation and wine-growing area. Those beaches readily accessible to visitors are always crowded in summer; few have the kind of hotels and facili-ties the discerning traveller is accustomed to.

L'Argentario

Travellers should therefore concentrate on the southern-most tip of the Tuscan coast, the Costa d'Argento (Silver Coast), more often called simply **L'Argentario** after the rocky promontory that dominates the coastline and the islands of Giglio and Giannutri. Sixteen miles of panoramic coast road on the Argentario dip and swerve around dazzling corners, linking Porto Santo Stefano and Porto Ercole, the two fash-ionable resorts on what is virtually an island joined to the mainland by narrow causeways. The Argentario is about the same distance south of Siena as it is northwest of Rome: 120 km (75 miles).

There are two sandy beaches here, the **Giannella** and, bet-ter still, the **Feniglia** (where Caravaggio is said to have died), but the real joy of the Argentario is to rent a boat and bathe in the blue depths of the rocky inlets or among the grottoes that corrugate the islands' coastlines—a paradise for deep-sea diving. The **Hotel Pellicano** in Cala dei Santi sits in a dream-like setting on a hillside; you can watch the yachts billowing by on their way to Cala Galera, a marina where up to 700 boats can moor in summer. The Pellicano is the kind of hotel where very rich people talk in hushed tones and even the children splash noiselessly in the pool dug out of the rock above the bay. Hidden away in the Mediterranean scrub, it is more like a private house where privileged guests can play tennis on manicured courts, or backgammon around the bar, or dine on the vine-shaded terrace where one plate of pasta costs $45.

Porto Santo Stefano and **Porto Ercole** are for people who love the sea and to be seen. The boutiques lining the port at Porto Ercole sell designer seamen's sweaters while the seafar-ing jet set step into their rope-soled shoes and off their yachts to go eat at one of the restaurants on the port—like the medium-priced **Il Gambero Rosso**, which, despite ups and downs over the years, is still the place to people-watch in Porto Ercole (closed Wednesdays; Tel: 0564-83-26-50). Or "Let's go to the Monastery," they say, and pile into cars to drive up to the Convento dei Frati Passionisti, where the food at **Il Sorgente** may be cheap and undistinguished, but the view of the lagoon of Orbetello glittering at your feet is priceless. After dinner there is dancing in the open air on top of a hill at **Le Streghe**, a small and intimate nightclub that has been the venue of chic young Romans for the past 20 years.

Another favorite haunt in Porto Ercole is **Bacco in Toscana**, originally an *enoteca* and now more like an intimate club with a charming hostess and an accomplished chef specializ-ing in fish and excellent homemade desserts. (Tel: 0564-83-

39-78; closed Mondays in season and open only on weekends out of season.)

While Porto Ercole retains its fishing village atmosphere, **Porto Santo Stefano** has been considerably built up, with hundreds of little red *villette* boxed around the port, in turn crammed with boatyards and honking vehicles. It is to Porto Santo Stefano that the owners of secluded villas tucked away among the wild vegetation on either side of the *panoramica* come to do their weekly shopping and buy bits and pieces for their boats moored in the turquoise bays below. It is also from Porto Santo Stefano that the public boats go to the islands of Giglio and Giannutri (the latter only in the summer season). Although the *panoramica* road is the best way to see the Costa d'Argento, be careful of the last five miles, which can be somewhat hair-raising unless you have a Jeep.

THE ISLANDS

The archipelago of the Argentario was a strategic stretch of coastline, a prey to Saracens and marauding pirates, including Barbarossa, who carried off 700 inhabitants of the island of Giglio in 1544 to sell as slaves at the market in Constantinople. The last time raiders came, so the story goes, they got drunk on Ansonaco, the famous wine of the island— Stendhal talks of it—and were ignominiously captured by the islanders.

Giglio

Giglio, 14 km (9 miles) from Porto Santo Stefano, is famous not only for its wine but also for its granite, out of which many Italian churches have been built, as has the medieval fortress of Giglio Castello that dominates the island. Here, at **Le Tamerigi** (Tel: 0564-80-62-66; closed Monday lunch and winter), you can enjoy a delicious and moderately priced meal of fish and the local wild rabbit and game. The most magical hotel on the island is the Hermitage; clinging to the rock face with the sea crashing below, it can be reached only by sea. (If you have no boat of your own, the hotel will pick you up at Giglio Porto.) Allowing for the inevitable drawbacks of its secluded position, **Hotel Pardini's Hermitage**, as it is called in full, is the perfect retreat and a base from which to sally out and discover the grottoes and hidden bays, where shoals of Mediterranean fish bask on the sandy seabed.

Rooms are also available in private houses on the island. Look—as everywhere in Italy—for *"Zimmerfrei."*

Giannutri

The Greeks called this island Artemis because it is shaped like a quarter moon. Fourteen miles from Porto Ercole by boat, it has no hotels or restaurants, but it does have fascinating sea depths where sunken Roman galleons, half submerged by sand, can be explored.

Elba

"Lucky Napoleon!" wrote Dylan Thomas to friends in 1947. Whether the Little Emperor shared his opinion is unclear; the most lyrical passage he writes about Elba in his *Memoirs* concerns his departure: "I left the island of Elba on the 26th February, 1815, at 9 o'clock in the evening. I boarded the brig *Inconstant,* which flew the white flag studded with bees throughout the journey."

Unfortunately a great many people seem to share the Welsh poet's enthusiasm. This largest island in Tuscany, reached by boat from the mainland town of Piombino (about 75 km/50 miles south along the coast from Pisa), is overrun by tourists—especially Germans—in the summer months. But it *is* possible to get far from the madding crowd by renting rowboats at the beautiful beaches of Cavoli or Fetovaia on the southwest coast and rowing around the headland to bathe in deserted coves.

There are two Napoleonic landmarks on Elba: his villa in San Martino, 5 km (3 miles) from Portoferraio, and the **Palazzina dei Mulini** in the historic center of Portoferraio. The villa has a pleasant setting and a good view, but there is little of Napoléon except for his bed, which probably looks the same as Napoléon's beds everywhere else, while at the Palazzina there are manuscripts, his library, the flag with three bees that he had made especially for his Elban interlude, and a picture of his dog.

Some of the most fascinating parts of the island, where the Etruscans mined iron ore—the Greeks called it Aethalia (Soot Island)—and where the Romans built their summer villas, are off the tourist track. At **Magazzini**, a small port on the north coast near Bagnaia, there are gardens like the Villa alle Palme, where almost every kind of palm tree grows, as well as exotic plants brought over the centuries from all around the world. At her estate in Magazzini, **La Chiusa**, Giuliana Foresi, one of the leading citizens of Elba, sells her wines from a centuries-old manor house, including the velvety dessert wine for which Elba is famous, Aleatico. In the hills above Marina di Campo is **Sant'Ilario**, a little village most tourists haven't even heard of, which has one of the most stable populations in Italy; for centuries no one has left his or her native village, nor have there been infiltrations from elsewhere. Here a man known as Pietro delle Pietre (Peter of the Stones; ask at Sant'Ilario's only bar) has accumulated one of the most interesting collections of semiprecious stones in the world.

Marciana, on the slopes of Monte Capanne, Elba's highest mountain (the 3,340-foot peak can be reached by funicular railway), boasts an interesting archaeological museum, the Antiquarium Comunale. In the neighboring medieval hamlet of Poggio Alto you can eat a hearty meal of wild boar and game at **Publius** (Tel: 0565-992-08; closed November 15 to March 15; moderately priced). The best restaurant on the island, however, is **Il Chiasso** at Capoliveri, which serves exquisitely prepared (and expensive) fish from the surrounding seas (Tel: 0565-96-87-09; closed in winter). The hotel with the most charm is the **Hotel Hermitage** on the gulf of La Biodola, with its own private beach set in dense native vegetation.

PRATO

Prato, 19 km (12 miles) from Florence to the northwest, is that city's industrial alter ego. It is the ladies of Prato whose sleek cars are parked outside the boutiques and jewelers of Florence's via de' Tornabuoni, something the Florentines with their old money and ancient heritage find—not without a tinge of envy—rather vulgar.

The Pratesi owe their wealth to wool, as Prato is the largest wool-producing city in the world. Known as *cenciaioli* (ragmen), the Pratesi invented the recycling of wool on an industrial scale. Huge trucks trundle through the center of the city carrying bales of rags destined for recycling into short-fibered wool, the kind most overcoats are made of. "Everything ends up in Prato," it is said: "the history of Italy and of Europe, all ends up in Prato—in rags!"

Less well known are the ancient origins of Prato and the considerable artworks within its 14th-century walls. "Prato," says Edward Hutton, "is like a flower that has fallen by the wayside, that has faded in the dust of the way." Squares like the piazza del Comune and the surrounding streets have the same medieval charm as Lucca or Arezzo, and the cathedral is a cornucopia of artworks. The statue in the middle of the piazza is of Francesco di Marco Datini, the first great merchant of Prato, who has gone down in the annals of commerce as the 14th-century inventor of the letter of credit.

Saint Stephen's Cathedral

Filippo Lippi was a Carmelite monk who spent his boyhood, brush in hand, studying the Masaccio frescoes in the Brancacci chapel. Despite his vocation, Fra Filippo was a hot-blooded youth, "so great a sensualist," we are told by Vasari, "that he would stop at nothing to gratify his immediate longings." His lusty nature no doubt interfered with his work, because his patron Cosimo de' Medici once locked him in his room until he had finished a painting. After two days, the frustrated artist tucked up his robes and shinned down a rope made of bed sheets. "And here you catch me at an alley's end," wrote Robert Browning in his poem "Fra Lippo Lippi," "Where sportive ladies leave their doors ajar."

While in Prato, Fra Filippo became enamored of a novice, Lucrezia, and (incredibly) persuaded her Mother Superior to let the young girl sit as a model for the Virgin in a painting on which he was engaged. One thing led to another, and Lucrezia bore him a son, Filippino, the next year. Brought to Florence by his father when he was ten years old and placed under Sandro Botticelli's wing, Filippino was destined to become one of the great masters of the Renaissance.

Meanwhile, his father the monk was being paid 2,000 florins, the highest fee ever earned by a Renaissance artist, to paint the main chapel of the cathedral at Prato with scenes from the lives of Saint Stephen and Saint John the Baptist, with an enchanting Salome dancing the dance of the seven veils. One of the stricken observers staring at Saint John's severed head is none other than Fra Filippo himself.

The cathedral, dedicated to Saint Stephen, is guardian of a precious relic, the *Cintola,* or girdle of the Virgin Mary. Legend has it that the Mother of Christ gave her girdle to Thomas, the doubting apostle, when she was assumed into heaven. Saint Thomas entrusted the girdle to a priest, whose daughter Maria fell in love with a boy from Prato who had come to the Holy Land as a crusader. The two eloped to Prato, with the girdle hidden in a basket of rushes. Today the girdle is shown to the populace five times a year from the circular pulpit on the right side of the cathedral's façade, which is decorated with a frieze of putti by Donatello, not unlike his frieze of gamboling urchins in the Museo dell'Opera del Duomo in Florence. The rest of the year the girdle is kept in the chapel of the Cintola, the altar surmounted by a small but very expressive statue of the *Madonna della Cintola* by Giovanni Pisano—the mother looks in mock severity at the Christ Child, who evidently is intent on pulling off her crown. An altogether better behaved *bambino* sits on the lap of the *Madonna dell'Ulivo* (*Olive-tree Madonna*), by Benedetto da Maiano, also in the cathedral.

Other churches well worth a visit are **Santa Maria delle Carceri**, by Giuliano da Sangallo, built according to the classical quattrocento plan (devised by Brunelleschi) of the circle within a square, and the convent of **San Niccolò**, with its Della Robbia–style lavabo in the sacristy and its nuns' private chapel. Knock on the door to the left of the main altar and the nuns will show you around; they appreciate a little offering in exchange.

If you have time, visit the **Museo Civico**. It contains, along with some beautiful works from the trecento, paintings by Prato's most famous son, Filippino Lippi, including his *Madonna del Ceppo,* with Francesco di Marco Datini kneeling at her feet, and the *Tabernacolo della Madonna del Canto di Mercatale,* surrounded by Saints Margherita, Antonio, Caterina, and Stefano, which the artist originally painted on the corner of the house he bought for his mother. When the house was bombed in 1944, the tabernacle was also smashed, but it has been reconstructed piece by piece (the scars are clearly visible) and has acquired over the centuries an almost talismanic significance for the Pratesi. The museum is open from 9:30 A.M. to 12:30 P.M. and from 3:00 to 6:30 P.M. except Sundays and holidays, when it is open mornings only. Closed Tuesdays.

For a change from art of the past there is the new **Prato Museum of Contemporary Art**, an immense exhibition space that resembles a sawtooth-roofed factory—and which has indeed been endowed by a textile industrialist, Luigi Pecci. The museum, the Centro per l'Arte Contemporaneo (Luigi Pecci), is known locally as "Il Pecci." Open from 10:00 A.M. to 7:00 P.M. Closed Tuesdays.

The **Metastasio Theater** draws avant-garde and exotic theater groups from all over the world; whether it is New York's Living Theatre, Chinese acrobats, or Russian puppets, it is very popular among Florentines and Pratesi alike. It's around the corner from the church of Santa Maria delle Carceri.

There is a delightful hotel, the **Villa Santa Cristina**, on a hill above Prato in a vine-covered villa. Left over from the days before Prato became the beehive of business it is today, the Villa Santa Cristina is furnished like an old-fashioned country house, with the modern rooftops of Prato far below. Tel: (0574) 59-59-51. The restaurant is closed Sunday evenings and Mondays.

People come especially to Prato to eat at Il Piraña, a fish restaurant with an unfortunate "executive suite" decor but with very good seafood dishes, such as spaghetti with lobster, a meal in itself. (Fresh fish is expensive everywhere in Tuscany.) The Piraña is in a rather unattractive part of Prato, at via Valentini 110; Tel: (0574) 257-46. Il Piraña is closed for Saturday lunch, Sundays, Monday lunch, and all of August.

MONTECATINI TERME

People have been "taking the waters" at the spa of Montecatini Terme since Roman times. One of the springs, the Tettuccio, has just celebrated its sixth centenary. The unforgettable scenes of turn-of-the-century spa life in the award-winning film *Oci Ciornie* (*Dark Eyes*) were shot here: Marcello Mastroianni in impeccable white trousers and spats walking with enviable sangfroid into the mud bath to retrieve his lady love's hat from among the water lilies.

Montecatini, off the A 11 west of Prato, is an unexpectedly lush and languorous corner of Tuscany, with a balmy atmosphere conducive to the healing of psyche and physique for which this spa is famous throughout Italy. Many Italian families take their holidays in Montecatini to unwind after the stresses and strains of the working year and to cure their gallstones and gastric ulcers in the most natural and congenial way.

It is difficult to talk about the beneficial effects of the waters of Montecatini without descending into the nether regions of the human anatomy. However, "the purgative effect only represents a part, and not the most important, of the activity of the Montecatini waters," the learned booklet issued by the spa assures us. Basically, Montecatini's springs are recommended for the treatment of diseases of the liver, digestive tract, and metabolism, including the extensive pathology of arthrosis. The waters can be classified into two groups: the salt-sulfate-bicarbonate-sodium for drinking purposes and the salt-iodine-sulfate-alkaline for thermal baths, irrigations, and showers. The beverage waters are mainly found in the Tettuccio, Regina, Excelsior, Torretta, and La Salute establishments, while mud cures, baths, inhalations, and so on are to be found in the Leopoldina, Excelsior, and Redi baths. These are not luxurious health farms but clinically utilitarian establishments focusing on your insides rather than your exterior. High season is from August 1 to October 15. The Excelsior establishment is the only one open all year round.

After a bracing shot of salt-sulfate water before breakfast, visitors to Montecatini evidently spend the rest of their time pampering themselves. For a small provincial town, Montecatini has an impressive array of boutiques lining the corso Roma and its continuation, the corso Matteotti, and there are also extensive facilities for sports, including golf.

A light but highly sophisticated lunch at the **Enoteca da Giovanni**, accompanied by a crescendo of local vintages, is hardly a dietician's dream and is expensive (Tel: 0572-716-95). Giovanni's more modest establishment next door, **Cucina da Giovanni**, is marginally less Lucullan and half the price (Tel: 0572-716-95). Both are closed Mondays. A funicular railway leaves Montecatini every half-hour for **Montecatini Alto**, an ancient hilltop hamlet 1,000 feet above the spa, where **Montaccolle** (via Marlianese 27; Tel: 0572-724-80) offers good local food with an even better view. Medium-priced, it is open only in the evenings and is closed Mondays, Tuesday lunch, and November.

In a restored Art Nouveau villa, Pier Angelo and his English wife, Roxana, recently opened a restaurant, **Pier Angelo**, which is magnificent in every detail and is fast becoming a mecca for Italian gourmets (via IV Novembre 99; Tel: 0572-77-15-52; closed Sundays, Monday lunch, and August). Not unexpectedly, it is expensive, and you must have reservations.

Cakes and coffee are an important part of the afternoon ritual here; Montecatini's specialty is *cialde,* plate-sized wafers filled with a nutty-tasting cream, to be sampled at, among others, the **Nuovo Caffè Biondi** on the corner of the main shopping street. The most famous *pasticceria* in Montecatini is **Giovannini** at corso Matteoti 4. In the evenings, visitors to Montecatini take a constitutional walk along spacious tree-lined avenues like the viale Verdi, where at the large outdoor **Caffè Gambrinus** a palm-court orchestra plays. Younger types go uphill to the new **Aria** disco, restaurant, and swimming pool on via delle Pietro Cavate, just below Montecatini Alto.

Montecatini has 500 hotels and pensioni, of which the most famous is the **Grand Hotel e la Pace** with its adjoining "natural health center" in five acres of luxuriant park. Built in 1870, this Belle Epoque palace was once the most exclusive "fat farm" in Italy, where the likes of King Farouk recovered from their excesses; it is correspondingly expensive, although special terms can be worked out at all times. (Open March to November.)

The **San Marco**, at via Rosselli 3, is a small but welcoming little hotel.

About 25 km (15 miles) west from Montecatini is the walled medieval city of Lucca.

LUCCA

From the air Lucca looks like a pinball game about the size of New York's Central Park, the tourist like the little lead ball dribbling along the tortuous jumble of streets and bouncing off churches at every corner. Lucca seems less a town than a film set for a medieval epic, the kind where halberds clash beneath mullioned windows. You will find yourself wondering why the men are not in doublet and hose, the ladies in high-necked ruffs—in every other way the city seems to be caught in a Gothic time warp. The corners of the narrow streets are so eroded by centuries of elbows brushing past that the walls are noticeably indented about three feet above the ground.

The Lucchesi have a reputation for being even stingier than the Florentines, but perhaps they are just careful of their wealth, as for centuries Lucca has been a prosperous town. Lucca was to silk what Florence was to wool in the Middle Ages, and under Paolo Guinigi (about whom more later) the silk industry reached its apogee. Silk is still woven in Lucca and sold at the **Tessiture Artistiche Lucchesi** at via Anfiteatro 15 and at via del Duomo 12. Luccan mastery of the art of wrought iron can still be seen in the 16th-century lanterns, doorknobs, and knockers that stud the façades of the city's palazzi.

The old center of Lucca is surrounded by two and a half miles of massive 17th-century ramparts and walls, so wide that the top has been turned into a tree-lined avenue. One of the most rewarding things to do in Lucca is to rent a bicycle and pedal along the top of this "circular lounging place of a splendid dignity," as Henry James called it, looking down at the city below. There is a certain snobbism among the Lucchesi as to who lives within and who without the city walls, the two "classes" being *Lucca fuori* and *Lucca dentro* (literally, Lucca out and Lucca in). As a visitor you will definitely be Lucca in, since everything you want to see is *dentro*.

Lucca used to be a very important city, despite its diminutive size, bristling with over 200 towers, each belonging to one of the leading families, with trees sprouting on top of them. Over the centuries these towers either have been demolished, the bricks recycled into other buildings, or have collapsed of their own accord. The only tower left standing, as opposed to a house-plus-tower like the Palazzo and Torre Guinigi, is the **Torre delle Ore** (Tower of the Hours), saved for posterity because it sported one of the two public clocks.

Castruccio Castracani, whom Machiavelli is said to have taken as his model for *The Prince,* was literally found in a cabbage patch here at the end of the 13th century by a widow who raised him as her son. He led Lucca into feats of valor that this placid little Tuscan city had never dreamed of, and became a local Napoléon, master of all of western Tuscany, from Pistoia to Volterra.

Another important Lucchese is the 15th-century artist Matteo Civitali, whose work is almost ignored by encyclopedias and art historians. His works adorn many of Lucca's churches, together with works by other members of his family: Vincenzo, Masseo, and Nicolao.

Lucca was originally a Ligurian settlement, which became Roman around 180 B.C. The city still retains its Roman layout, its *cardo* and *decumanus* (intersecting major streets) and, above all, the oval **Amphitheater** tucked away right in the center of the city, where you come upon it completely by surprise. The arches from which gladiators and hungry lions once issued into the arena are now little boutiques.

Lucca may not have given the world as much art as some other Tuscan towns, but it gave us more than its share of musicians. From the 16th century onward musicians such as Guami, Malvezzi, Gregori, Gasperini, Geminiani, and Boccherini left Lucca for the courts of Europe, while Giacomo Puccini's family had been Lucchesi for generations. You can visit the house on the via di Poggio where he was born and where, among other things, his *Turandot* piano and his greatcoat are preserved. (Open from 10:00 A.M. to 6:00 P.M. in summer and from 10:00 A.M. to 4:00 P.M. in winter. Closed Mondays.)

The **Villa La Principessa** is the only luxury hotel in or near Lucca, about ten minutes from the center in Massa Pisana, in what was once the country place of Castruccio Castracani. Surrounded by gardens, century-old trees, and a pleasant pool, the baronial halls with fires in the grates and roses in bowls are everything a princely country house should be. Unfortunately the hotel is not particularly well run, the service is well-meaning but slow-witted, and the decor in the rooms is in questionable taste. The **Hotel Hambros,** five minutes from Lucca, also in an old country villa, has fewer pretensions (and no restaurant) but is more reasonably priced. If you are without a car, the **Hotel Universo** right in the center of Lucca has the Old World, slightly dilapidated charm and rampantly stuccoed ceilings of Europe's Grand Tour hotels.

Food in Lucca does not differ substantially from that in the rest of Tuscany, but the Lucchesi do have their own wines— the Montecarlo whites—and their own olive oil, which many prefer to the classical Tuscan olive oil produced around Florence and Siena. Trattorias abound in the center of Lucca, all similar, so choose one that doesn't look too touristy and that has good smells wafting from the kitchen— such as the inexpensive **Da Giulio in Pelleria** (via delle Conce 37; closed Sundays, Mondays, and the first half of August; reservations are a must; no credit cards; Tel: 0583-559-48). However, some of the best food in Tuscany is to be had 10 km (6 miles) due north of Lucca at **Ponte a Moriano**, a hamlet on the banks of the river Serchio.

A predecessor of the **Ristorante la Mora** in Ponte a Moriano was probably offering refreshment to travellers on their way to Florence in Roman times, as the word *mora* is Latin for a stopping place. What is sure is that the great-great-uncle and -aunt of today's owners, Sauro and Angela Brunicardi, were already cooking for their guests in 1867. The restaurant serves traditional dishes from the Lucca region, including a thick soup called *gran farro* made from spelt, a type of wheat that grows on the local hills and was used in cooking by the Roman legionnaires as they tramped up the peninsula. Other dishes include chicken breasts in balsamic vinegar, beef with fresh *porcini* mushrooms (which are also good with *straccetti,* a local pasta), and what can only be described as a Tuscan cheesecake. Closed Wednesday evenings, Thursdays, and mid-October; expensive but worth every penny for a fine culinary experience. Tel: (0583) 571-09.

Another worthwhile gastronomic detour, 6 km (4 miles) from Lucca, is **Solferino** in località San Macario in Piano (via delle Gravine 50; Tel: 0583-591-18). Named after the famous battle, the restaurant offers all the makings of a historic evening (if not a cheap one). Closed Wednesdays, Thursday lunch, and most of August.

In Lucca the streets around the via Fillungo are the main shopping venue. The largest stores must be all of three yards across, and their names are still in traditional black and gold. There are jewelry stores in particular, such as **Carli** at via Fillungo 95, that look as though they haven't changed since they were founded—in Carli's case, in 1655. The coffeehouse **DiSimo** at via Fillungo 58 has been a haunt of litterateurs and artists since the days when Giovanni Pascoli, one of Italy's most famous poets, took his morning coffee here; the atmosphere is such that he could still be propping up the bar. In keeping with the pervading sense of antiquity in Lucca, the most sensible thing to buy is old prints at **Silvano Spinelli** at via Sant'Andrea 10. Another art connection in Lucca: Every other year, in November, a festival of cartoons brings cartoonists from all over the world.

Nightlife in Lucca is the streets, thronged with people as if they were in an outdoor salon until the early hours.

The Churches of Lucca

Lucca was reputedly the first city in Italy to receive the light of the Gospel and has 99 churches to its name, "ecclesiastical architecture being indeed the only one of the arts to which it seems to have given attention," said Henry James. But in this art it excelled. Even Ruskin wrote of one of the smaller churches, the Santa Maria Forisportam, better known today as Santa Maria Bianca: "Absolutely for the first time I now saw what Medieval builders were and what they meant. I took the simplest of façades for analysis, that of Santa Maria Foris-Portam, and thereon literally began the study of architecture."

You cannot visit all 99, but three churches are of prime importance: San Martino, San Michele in Foro, and San Frediano.

"All that is best in Lucca, all that is sweetest and most naive may be found in the beautiful Duomo," said Edward Hutton about **San Martino**. However, the cathedral's interior is so dark that it almost seems foggy, as though centuries of incense had stopped trying to filter out of the windows high up under the vaults. Take a handful of 100-lire coins to put into a machine that will illumine for an if-you-blink-you-miss-it moment the beautiful tomb of Ilaria del Carretto, the wife of Paolo Guinigi, who died in 1405. The figure of this child-wife, by the Sienese sculptor Jacopo della Quercia, looks as though she were asleep, with a little dog at her feet waiting expectantly for his mistress to wake up, "neither alive with the life of the body, nor dead with the death of the body." Gabriele d'Annunzio went so far as to call Lucca "the city within the wooded circle where the wife of Guinigi sleeps." This truly moving funereal statue is not just a work of art but conveys—as it did to Charles Morgan's Sparken-broke—a feeling of "private communication," as though "her silence had whispered in his ear." (Its recent restoration has evoked strong criticism, as has a project to move the monument from the church to a museum.) The *Last Supper* by Tintoretto, on the other hand, seems to shine with a light of its own, the table where the apostles are dining depicted vertically for once, instead of the usual transversal scene.

Among other things, Matteo Civitali worked on the octagonal chapel in the middle of the church that houses the wooden crucifix, or *Volto Santo,* which has been venerated in Lucca since 782. Legend has it that the crucifix with Christ's face was carved by Nicodemus (who helped to bury Christ) out of a cedar of Lebanon, the angels guiding his hand. To save the holy work from religious persecution, Nicodemus put it out to sea in a rudderless boat, which eventually beached on the coast near Lucca. The relic was brought to Lucca in a cart drawn by untamed oxen. Every year on September 13 and 14 the people of Lucca relive this tradition with the *Luminara,* a candlelit procession through the streets. The *Volto Santo* became famous throughout Europe in the Middle Ages, and even King William II of England used to swear, *"Per Sanctum vultum de Luca."*

The façade of the church of **San Michele**, typical of the Pisan style, is like a crescendo of notepad doodles, layer upon layer of blind arcades. It is crowned by one of the city's landmarks, a ten-foot-high statue of the Archangel Michael in bronze and stone, with a magnificent pair of wings and with the defeated dragon at his feet.

Matteo Civitali's contribution to this church, the *Madonna Salutis Portus,* erected to mark the end of the plague of 1476–1480, is outside, above a cornerstone.

Santa Zita is buried in the church of **San Frediano**, one of the best examples of Lucca's Romanesque style. Saint Zita, who died in 1278, is the patron saint of housemaids, mentioned by Dante in Canto 21 of *L'Inferno*. She was a maid in the household of the noble Fatinelli family, and her master discovered her distributing bread from his larder to the poor. When challenged, Zita held open her apron to find that, by divine intervention, the bread had been turned into flowers. On her feast day in April there is a ceremonial blessing of the newly blossomed daffodils, and the streets of Lucca turn into a flower market. In death, this homely saint joined the Irish Saint Richard, who died in Lucca on a pilgrimage in 722 and is also buried in this church. (These churches are open from 9:00 A.M. to noon and 3:30 to 5:00 P.M.)

Paolo Guinigi

Like the Medicis in Florence, Paolo Guinigi was a merchant and patron of the arts. He was only 24 when he became "Captain and Defender of the People," and he was Lord of Lucca for 30 years, from 1400 onward. It was he who brought Jacopo della Quercia from Siena to make a sarcophagus for his young wife, Ilaria. Commerce flourished during his rule. He had a monopoly of the local marble quarries, and his ox carts brought marble to Florence and Venice to build the cathedrals of Santa Maria del Fiore and San Marco. He brought a foretaste of Renaissance grandeur and an unfamiliar joie de vivre into the sober lives of the Lucchesi, traditionally an austere and parsimonious folk. His library boasted works by Dante, Boccaccio, and Petrarch, and he had a passion for precious stones, sending scouts to Paris and Venice to bring back gems for his collection.

The Guinigi tower, with its seven ilex trees growing on top, is a worthwhile climb to enjoy a view of what Hilaire Belloc called "the most fly-in-amber little town in the world," with its rust-colored roofs like crumbling gingerbread and the Apuan Alps in the background.

Paolo Guinigi also built the Villa Guinigi, today the **Museo Nazionale**. Again Matteo Civitali is represented, with a *Madonna and Child,* but the most interesting exhibits are a 13th-century crucifix reminiscent of Cimabue by Deodato Orlandi and a *Sacra Conversazione* by Fra Bartolomeo, as well as the carved wood and intarsia, some of which come from Paolo Guinigi's library and some from the cathedral of San Martino (especially the work by Cristoforo Canozzi de Lendinara, a friend of Paolo della Francesca, with his views of Lucca in different shades and grains of wood). The museum is open 9:00 A.M. to 2:00 P.M.; closed Mondays.

Outside Lucca

During Napoléon's occupation of Italy, he gave the city of Lucca to his sister Elisa, who was married to Felice Baciocchi. In 1811 she took over the **Villa Reale di Marlia**, about 15 km (9 miles) northeast of Lucca, redecorating all the rooms in Neoclassical style. (Open from 10:00 to 11:00 A.M. and 3:00 to 8:00 P.M.; closed Mondays.) Here she listened to concerts conducted by Niccolò Paganini, her private conductor, and supervised the embellishment of the villa's beautiful gardens, which can be visited all year; from July to September, they are open only on Tuesdays, Thursdays, and Sundays. Guided tours are offered five times a day.

A bit farther out to the northeast are some of the most famous gardens in Italy, at the **Villa Garzoni** at Collodi, birthplace of the author of *Pinocchio*. (Open from 9:00 A.M. until sunset year-round.)

CARRARA AND PIETRASANTA

A side trip from Lucca (or from Pisa) would be a visit to the Tuscan marble-quarrying areas northwest up the coast toward La Spezia in Liguria. The quarries of the Apuan mountains above Carrara and Pietrasanta have been providing giant blocks of marble for the façades of temples and churches, equestrian statues, and monumental flights of stairs from Roman times to the present day. In the old days the huge slabs were sent sliding down the mountainsides, hoisted onto carts, and dragged by the traditional Tuscan white oxen to the big cities or to the nearby seashore, where they were loaded onto ships and sent all over the world.

Today the quarrying still goes on day and night, and the mountains yield 700,000 tons of marble a year, much of which you can see stacked like packs of cards in the yards of the innumerable workshops huddled around the towns of Carrara and Pietrasanta in northwest Tuscany. It is worth driving up to the quarries of Monte Altissimo, 5,200 feet high, between the two towns. From the top of the sheer white marble face—said to be the source of the marble for many of Michelangelo's famous sculptures—you can see as far as the Côte d'Azur on a good day. (Take the Seravezza exit from the Via Aurelia, route 1.)

If you like marble in the kitchen—cutting slabs, rolling pins, pestles and mortars, and so on—there is a store in Carrara on via Piave called **Nuova Marmotecnica** that is well worth a visit.

On the other hand, if you have your heart set on a marble statue like the ones in the windows of Romanelli, the famous marble store on the lungarno Acciaiuoli in Florence, the artisans of Carrara or Pietrasanta will carry out orders to your specifications, however outrageous these may be. It is interesting to know that these marble artisans actually execute the giant masterpieces that adorn the main squares of cities all over the world and find their way into famous collections and art galleries. The sculptor submits a model in plaster or marble and the artisan here then reproduces it to scale in the outsize dimensions required, chiseling and honing the work to its finished perfection.

In the workshop of **Carlo Nicoli** at piazza XXVII Aprile 9, the oldest and best-known workshop in Carrara, are artisans who are responsible for some of the most famous works of art today. (You can join them at lunch in a very basic trattoria just down the road.) If your requirements are more modest, CAMP (the syndicate for artistic marble products and typical handcrafts from the town of Pietrasanta, at viale Marconi 5 in Pietrasanta) will send you to whichever artisan is most qualified to carry out the type of work you have in mind.

About ten minutes southeast of Carrara in Montignoso, in an unlikely setting tucked away among small industrial centers, is **Il Bottaccio**, which would be impossible to find if the signs along the road were not so good. At this supremely elegant Relais & Châteaux hotel, white Persian cats prowl around the indoor fish pond in the dining room in an atmosphere redolent of the early James Bond (perhaps the vaguely ghoulish waiters who hover at your elbow, assiduously pouring vintage wines, feed recalcitrant diners to the exotic fish lurking beneath the water lilies). The five suites also have a Hollywood setting: The rooms are on several levels, and high-tech four-poster beds share the space with an antique stone oil press (where Dr. No gets ground up in the final scene?) and a mosaic-lined, sunken Jacuzzi tub. Very expensive—for an unforgettable experience.

PISA

The people of Pisa believe in keeping their jewels in the bank and use their front parlor only on Sundays. Pisa's "jewels," or main sights, lie not on a velvet cushion but on the lushest of green lawns within the campo dei Miracoli (Field of Miracles), while the rest of the city leads a humdrum life outside its limits. Two-thirds of your time in Pisa will be spent at the campo, visiting the Leaning Tower, the Duomo, the Baptistery, and the cemetery.

It should not be forgotten that Pisa—due west of Florence near the coast, and now its poor relation visited chiefly for the Leaning Tower—is one of the oldest cities in Europe and was a great maritime republic long before the Florentine Renaissance. Florentine sculpture and architecture owe much to architects like Buscheto, who started work on the cathedral here in 1063, 200 years before the Duomo in Florence, while sculptors like Nicola Pisano and his son Giovanni gave Tuscany its most beautiful pulpits—not to be overshadowed even by those of Donatello—in the 13th century.

Despite a succession of overlords, Pisans have always

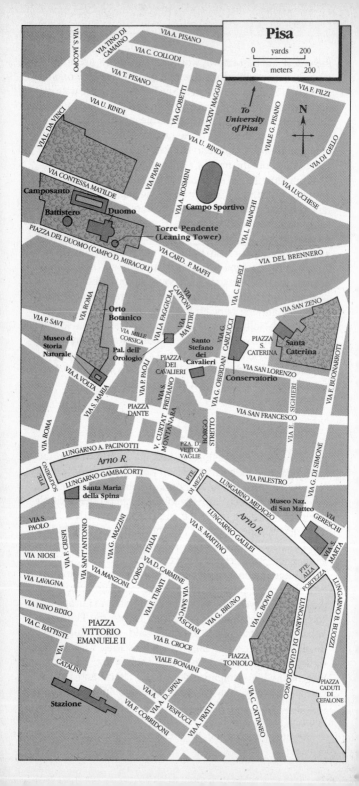

remained Pisans rather than Etruscans, Romans, or even Tuscans. From earliest times they have turned their backs on the rest of Italy and looked toward the sea that gave them the medieval equivalent of an empire. Their supremacy on the sea and their victories over the Saracens provided Pisa with the funds to build the campo dei Miracoli and influenced the so-called Pisan style that was imitated by so many later Tuscan architects: the black-and-white striped marble and the lacy tiers of blind arcades that are Gothic and Romanesque with a strain of Muslim.

All the great Pisan sculptors are called quite simply Pisano, although they are not all related—Bonanno, who was the original architect of the Leaning Tower; Nicola and his son Giovanni; Andrea da Pontedera and his sons Nino and Tommaso. Nicola, helped by the young Giovanni and his pupil Arnolfo di Cambio (later the architect of Florence's Duomo), was responsible for the pulpit in the Baptistery, while Giovanni executed the breathtaking pulpit, or *pergamo,* in the cathedral itself. Later they were all called to Siena to work on the pulpit for the cathedral there.

Pisano works adorn nearly all the churches in Pisa, such as the lovely church of **Santa Maria della Spina** (Saint Mary of the Thorn; so called because it once housed a thorn from Christ's crown) on the banks of the river Arno. Together with other treasures of Pisan sculpture and painting, the works of the Pisano sculptors—including the nursing *Madonna of the Milk* by Nino Pisano—are to be found in the impressive **Museo Nazionale di San Matteo**, on the lungarno Mediceo (open 9:00 A.M. to 7:00 P.M., to 1:00 P.M. on Sundays; closed Mondays), and in the **Museo dell'Opera del Duomo** in the campo dei Miracoli, supposedly the best place to view the tower (open 9:00 A.M. to 1:00 P.M. and 3:00 to 7:00 P.M.).

Pisa, said Shakespeare, is "renowned for grave citizens." The **University of Pisa** on via XXIX Maggio, still one of the most important parts of city life, is among the oldest in Italy—founded in the 12th century—and was frequented by, among others, Galileo Galilei. Hanging from the magnificent ceiling of the Duomo is the "Lamp of Galileo," which, according to popular legend (as in Newton and the apple), inspired the great astronomer's theory of the movement of the pendulum.

Campo dei Miracoli

"Pisa and its monuments," according to Henry James, "have been industriously vulgarized, but it is astonishing how well they have survived the process." Despite the fact that the tower has become one of the seven wonders of the world and an outsized cliché, you will not be disappointed by a visit to the campo dei Miracoli. After the hollow emptiness of Florence's Duomo, the Pisan **Duomo**'s rich and busy interior will come as an uplifting experience, not just for the pulpit but, among other things, for the Byzantine-style mosaic in the apse, the last work of Cimabue, who died in Pisa in 1302; for the oval dome; and for the bronze doors by Bonanno Pisano. The cathedral is open from 7:45 A.M. to 1:00 P.M. and from 3:00 to 7:00 P.M.

Another jewel, more like a giant marble tiara, is the **Battistero**, with its beautiful octagonal font for baptism by total immersion and its ascetic statue of John the Baptist (open from 8:30 A.M. to 8:00 P.M. in summer, 9:00 A.M. to 5:00 P.M. in winter). The Baptistery has remarkable acoustics: If you bribe a choirboy to sing for you, suggests Edward Hutton, you will hear "a thousand angels singing round the feet of San Raniero." (San Raniero, or more correctly, San Ranieri, is the patron saint of Pisa, and on the eve of his feast day—June 16—the entire city, including the tower, is lit up with flaming torches. The next day the whole town takes part in the medieval *Gioco del Ponte,* a mock battle held on the ponte di Mezzo, Pisa's main bridge over the Arno.)

The enclosed **Camposanto** (cemetery), built on earth brought back from Mount Golgotha by the crusaders, was enriched by the seafaring Pisans with souvenirs of their travels to foreign lands, making the cemetery's cloister the oldest museum in the world. During World War II it was badly bombed, and the splendid frescoes by Benozzo Gozzoli and the unknown Maestro del Trionfo della Morte were severely damaged. Restored, they now hang in a special room here (open from 8:00 A.M. to 7:00 P.M., 5:30 P.M. in winter).

The most remarkable thing about the **Leaning Tower** is, of course, that it leans. As Herman Melville said, we wait for it to crash, like a pine cone poised to hit the ground. It continues to tilt, a millimeter more every year. Should it topple, 14,500 tons of marble will come crashing down onto the green lawns of the campo dei Miracoli. It was closed to the public several years ago to prevent just such a catastrophe, and for the time being cannot be climbed while extensive tests are carried out on the surrounding soil. The latest project is to encase the tower in a sort of steel corset.

A small museum, also in the Campo, well worth a visit is the **Museo delle Sinopie** (open from 9:00 A.M. to 1:00 P.M. and from 3:00 to 7:00 P.M.), where the original red chalk cartoons of the frescoes in the Camposanto museum are housed.

These were revealed by the bombing during World War II and show a free hand and refreshing vigor sometimes lacking in the frescoes themselves.

Piazza dei Cavalieri

The campo dei Miracoli continues into the piazza dei Cavalieri, site of the **Church of Santo Stefano dei Cavalieri**, with its spectacular wooden ceiling by Vasari. The Knights of Saint Stephen were a military order founded by Cosimo I de' Medici, whose statue stands in the square. Opposite is the **Palazzo dell'Orologio** (Clock Palace), once two towers with sinister associations for the Pisans. Pisa, like many Tuscan cities, once bristled with towers—10,000, according to the chief European rabbi at that time, Beniamino da Tudela, although surely this was an exaggeration. In one of these towers, the Pisan Ugolino della Gherardesca, considered responsible for a resounding naval defeat, was starved to death along with his sons and grandsons, while the *Pasquareccia*—one of seven bells atop the Leaning Tower—rang to announce his end, an episode that inspired both Dante and Shelley.

Shelley was also inspired by the river Arno, one of the few jewels that the Pisans do wear every day. The river winds its way in an elegant curve through the center of the city, and nearly everything you will want to see here (besides the campo dei Miracoli) is on the river. One place not to miss is **Sergio**, the best restaurant in Pisa, a welcoming, unpretentious trattoria famous all over Tuscany. Sergio offers menus at varying prices—none of which you could actually call moderate—based on fish from the nearby shore, seasoned with local herbs like wild fennel and *santoreggia,* a kind of thyme. Closed Sundays and Monday lunch. Tel: (050) 58-05-80. The **Caffè dell'Ussaro** in the Agostini Palace is also a landmark where patriots and poets gathered in the last century.

Although the leading hotel in Pisa is **Dei Cavalieri**, opposite the train station, it is worth sacrificing its undoubted comfort for the turn-of-the-century charm of the somewhat dilapidated second-category **Hotel Victoria**, overlooking the river. This hotel has been in the same family since 1839 and was, in its heyday, the best hotel in Pisa; members of the English royal family, the Iron Duke of Wellington, and Shelley all stayed here. Some rooms (211 and 212) still have the original frescoes and old tiled bathrooms, which hopefully still work.

The port of Pisa has long been silted up, but the city today has a melting-pot, casbah atmosphere. There is none of

Florence's understated chic in the **corso Italia**, Pisa's main street. Behind the Hotel Victoria is the market square, the **piazza delle Vettovaglie**, more North African than Italian, where the fishmongers sell *cee,* Pisa's main specialty in winter—baby eels. You can eat here with the vendors themselves in the cheap and unceremonious **Trattoria della Mescita,** tucked between two market stalls.

Another restaurant renowned for its good food, especially the homemade pasta and fish soups, is **Al Ristoro dei Vecchi Macelli.** *Macello* means abattoir, and the restaurant is at 49 via Volturno, a street leading off lungarno Simonelli just around the corner from the old slaughterhouses. But fish, not meat, is the order of the day and therefore relatively expensive, as fish tends to be in Tuscany. Tel: (050) 204-24. Closed Wednesdays and Sunday lunch.

The **Villa di Corliano** hotel is located in Rigoli, 8 km (5 miles) from Pisa and 10 km (6 miles) from Lucca. At the end of a tree-lined avenue, the late-Renaissance villa is set in the middle of lawns studded with palms, against a backdrop of hills. The best rooms and the reception rooms are frescoed and furnished with antiques (not all rooms have a bath).

GETTING AROUND

Barcelona, Brussels, Munich, Paris, and Vienna maintain regular air service to Florence. Intercity trains connect Florence with Rome in two hours.

The Etruscan sites and the winegrowing areas around Siena are best seen by car, rented in Florence or Siena (or better, in advance in the U.S.).

Volterra is difficult to get to without a car. From Florence, take the Superstrada down to Colle di Val d'Elsa, where you can have lunch, and then drive half an hour west on route 68 through an unspoiled Tuscan landscape up the hill to Volterra.

Cortona, also an Etruscan town, is two hours by train from Rome and about one and a half hours from Florence. It is roughly the same distance by car; there's an autostrada exit at Arezzo, which is only 30 km (18 miles) from Cortona.

Siena is an hour's drive from Florence south along the Superstrada, and SITA buses leave regularly from the Florence bus station, opposite the main train station. Tour buses usually make a stopover at San Gimignano on the way.

L'Argentario on the coast is about two hours by car from Rome and three and a half hours from Florence. The train stop for l'Argentario is at Orbetello.

Ferries to the islands of Giglio and Giannutri leave from Porto Santo Stefano. For Giglio the ferry company is Società

Toremar; Tel: (0564) 81-46-15. For Giannutri, call Naval Giglio; Tel: (0564) 81-29-20 or 80-93-09.

Elba is an hour by car ferry (Toremar and Navarma lines) from Piombino, and 30 minutes by Hovercraft. In summer there are flights to Elba from Pisa.

Montecatini Terme is about 40 km (25 miles) from both Pisa and Florence, 27 km (17 miles) from Lucca. It is an easy drive, or bus or train trip, from each.

Lucca is about 70 km (45 miles) west of Florence and less than 25 km (15 miles) northeast of Pisa; it's easily accessible by train or by car on the Autostrada. The city is so small that the only way to visit it is on foot. (The author of this chapter literally got stuck in a Mercedes between the narrow sides of a street in Lucca, like Winnie-the-Pooh in the rabbit hole.)

Pisa has its own airport, with flights to all major European cities, and is an important railway junction. It is an hour's drive from Florence, but parking is a problem in Pisa— which is small enough to be seen on foot anyway.

ACCOMMODATIONS REFERENCE

The rates given below are projections for 1993; always check for up-to-date information before making reservations. Wide ranges may reflect the differences between low- and high-season rates. Unless otherwise indicated, the figures indicate the cost of a double room (per room, not per person). However, half-board (mezza pensione) rates, which include breakfast and one other meal per day, are per person. The service charge is included in the rate; inquire about tax and breakfast.

Tuscany boasts a wealth of good and inexpensive accommodations in castles and farmhouses. Contact the Agriturist office in Rome or Florence (see below).

▶ **Agriturismo.** Agriturist Associazione Regionale Toscana, piazza S. Firenze 3, 50122 **Florence**. Tel: (055) 28-78-38. (This is the official government agency. See also Cuendet, below.)

▶ **Albergo Le Terme.** 53027 **Bagno Vignoni S. Quirico d'Orcia.** Tel: (0577) 88-71-50; Fax: (0577) 88-74-97. Half board Ł61,000 off-season; Ł66,000 in season.

▶ **Il Bottaccio.** 54038 **Montignoso.** Tel: (0585) 34-00-31; Fax: (0585) 34-01-03. Suites Ł450,000–Ł680,000.

▶ **Castello di Gargonza.** Count and Countess Roberto Guicciardini, Castello di Gargonza, località Gargonza, 52048 **Monte San Savino** (Arezzo). Closed in January. Tel: (0575) 84-70-65 or 84-42-38; Fax: (0575) 84-70-54. Ł160,000; houses in the *foresteria* Ł623,000–Ł1,449,000 per week.

▶ **Castello di Spaltenna**. 53013 **Gaiole in Chianti**. Tel: (0577) 74-94-83; Fax: (0577) 74-92-69. Closed January 15–February 28. ₤220,000 with breakfast.

▶ **Hotel Cavalieri**. Piazza della Stazione 2, 56125 **Pisa**. Tel: (050) 432-90; Fax: (050) 50-22-42. In U.S., Tel: (800) 221-2626 or 247-1277; Fax: (212) 213-2369. In U.K., Tel: (0800) 28-27-29; Fax: (0923) 89-60-71. ₤322,000–₤347,000 with breakfast.

▶ **Park Hotel Cavarchione**. 53013 **Gaiole in Chianti**. Tel: (0577) 74-95-50; Fax: same. ₤170,000 with breakfast. Open Easter to November. ₤160,000 with breakfast; no credit cards.

▶ **Certosa di Maggiano**. Strada di Certosa 82, 53100 **Siena**. Tel: (0577) 28-81-80; Fax: (0577) 28-81-80. ₤460,000 with breakfast; suites ₤600,000–₤1,000,000.

▶ **La Chiusa**. Via della Madonnina 88, 53040 **Monte-follonico**. Tel: (0577) 66-96-68; Fax: (0577) 66-95-93. Closed January 6–March 25 and November 5–December 5. ₤240,000 with breakfast; suites ₤340,000–₤390,000.

▶ **Convento San Francesco** (La Frateria di Padre Eligio). 53040 **Cetona** (Siena). Tel: (0578) 23-80-15; Fax: same. ₤250,000; no credit cards.

▶ **Cuendet & Cie**. Località Il Cerreto/Strove, 53035 **Monteriggioni** (Siena). Tel: (0577) 30-10-53. In U.S., Destination Cuendet USA, 165 Chestnut St., Allendale, N.J. 07401; Tel: (201) 327-2333; Fax: (201) 825-2664.

▶ **Fattoria La Loggia**. Via Collina 40, 50020 **Montefiridolfi** (Florence). Tel: (055) 82-44-288; Fax: (055) 82-44-283. ₤1,600,000–₤3,000,000 per week for apartments with two to six beds. No credit cards.

▶ **Fonte della Galletta**. Località Alpe Faggeto, 52033 **Caprese Michelangelo** (Arezzo). Tel: (0575) 79-39-25. ₤52,000. For a stay of more than three days, this rate includes full board.

▶ **Grand Hotel e La Pace**. Via della Torretta 1, 51016 **Montecatini Terme**. Tel: (0572) 758-10; Fax: (0572) 784-51. In U.S., Tel: (800) 223-6800 or (212) 838-3110; Fax: (212) 758-7367. In U.K., Tel: (0800) 18-11-23; Fax: (071) 353-1904. Open April–October. ₤250,000–₤420,000. Half board ₤300,000; full board ₤320,000.

▶ **Hotel Hambros**. Via Pesciatina 197, 55010 **Lunata**. Tel: (0583) 93-53-55; Fax: same. ₤110,000.

▶ **Hotel Hermitage**. La Biodola, 57037 **Portoferraio** (Elba). Tel: (0565) 93-69-11; Fax: (0565) 96-99-84. Open April–October. Half board ₤105,000–₤285,000.

▶ **Hotel Pardini's Hermitage**. 58013 **Isola del Giglio**. Tel: (0564) 80-90-34; Fax: (0564) 80-91-77. Half board ₤85,000–₤140,000. Full board in high season ₤90,000–₤130,000. Open Easter–September.

▶ **Hotel Pescille.** Località Pescille, 53037 **San Gimignano** (Siena). Tel: (0577) 94-01-86; Fax: same. Open March–November. ₤105,000; half board ₤215,000 for two.

▶ **Hotel Terme di Saturnia.** Via della Follonata, 58050 **Saturnia** (Grosseo). Tel: (0564) 60-10-61; Fax: (0564) 60-12-66. Full board with use of thermal baths ₤240,000 per person.

▶ **Hotel Universo.** Piazza del Giglio 1, 55100 **Lucca**. Tel: (0583) 49-36-78; Fax: (0583) 95-48-54. ₤118,000; half board ₤100,000.

▶ **Hotel Victoria.** Lungarno Pacinotti 12, 56100 **Pisa**. Tel: (050) 94-01-11; Fax: (050) 94-01-80. ₤110,000 with breakfast.

▶ **Laudomia.** Località Poderi. 58050 **Saturnia**. Tel: (0564) 62-00-13. ₤60,000–₤70,000.

▶ **Locanda Sari.** Via Tiberina km 177, 52036 **Pieve Santo Stefano** (Arezzo). Tel: (0575) 79-91-29. Half board ₤70,000.

▶ **Il Marzocco.** Piazza Savonarola 18, 53045 **Montepulciano**. Tel: (0578) 75-72-62; Fax: (0578) 75-84-02. ₤75,000.

▶ **Pensione Palazzo Ravizza.** Piano dei Mantellini 34, 53100 **Siena**. Tel: (0577) 28-04-62; Fax: (0577) 27-13-70. Half board ₤230,000 for two.

▶ **Park Hotel.** Via di Marciano 18, 53100 **Siena**. Tel: (0577) 448-03; Fax: (0577) 490-20. ₤245,000–₤330,000.

▶ **Il Pellicano.** Località Sbarcatello, via Panoramica, 58018 **Porto Ercole** (Grosseto). Tel: (0564) 83-38-01; Fax: (0564) 83-34-18. Open Easter–November 3. ₤210,000–₤580,000.

▶ **Relais Fattoria Vignale.** Via Pianigiani 9, 53017 **Radda in Chianti**. Tel: (0577) 73-83-00; Fax: (0577) 73-85-92. Open May–October. ₤230,000–₤270,000 with buffet breakfast.

▶ **San Marco.** Via Rosselli 3, 51016 **Montecatini Terme**. Tel: (0572) 712-21; Fax: (0572) 77-05-77. Half board ₤110,000.

▶ **Spadeus Grand Hotel "Il Club."** Via le Pianè 35, 53042 **Chianciano Terme** (Siena). Tel: (0578) 632-32; Fax: (0578) 643-29. ₤440,000 (₤380,000 single), everything (food, treatments, etc.) included.

▶ **Tenuta di Ricavo.** 53011 **Castellina in Chianti**. Tel: (0577) 74-02-21; Fax: (0577) 74-10-14. Open April–October. ₤265,000 with breakfast; suite with terrace ₤340,000 with breakfast.

▶ **Villa Belvedere.** Località Belvedere, 53034 Colle di Val d'Elsa. Tel: (0577) 92-09-66; Fax: (0577) 57-02-52. ₤154,000 with breakfast; half board ₤230,000.

▶ **Villa di Corliano.** Via Statale 50, Rigoli, 56010 **San Giuliano Terme** (Pisa). Tel: (050) 81-81-93. ₤90,000; suites ₤160,000.

▶ **Villa Nencini.** Borgo Santo Stefano 55, 56048 **Volterra**. Tel: (0588) 863-86. ₤90,000.

▶ **Villa La Principessa**. 55050 **Massa Pisana**. Tel: (0583) 37-00-37; Fax: (0583) 37-90-19. Closed in January. ₤320,000; suites ₤480,000 and up.

▶ **Villa Santa Cristina**. Via Poggio Secco 58, 50047 **Prato**. Tel: (0574) 59-59-51; Fax: (0574) 57-26-23. Closed in August. ₤150,000 with breakfast.

EMILIA-ROMAGNA

By Michele Scicolone

Michele Scicolone contributes articles on travel and food to Gourmet *magazine and to the* New York Times. *She teaches Italian cooking in New York City, and is the author of* The Antipasto Table *and* La Dolce Vita, *on Italian desserts.*

Emilia and Romagna are two ancient provinces that were wed in 1860, when lush, coastal Romagna joined the seriously artistic and gourmand plain of Emilia, which skirts the Apennines, the mountain chain that separates this region from Liguria and Tuscany. Although World War II caused considerable damage in this part of industrialized Italy, a more thriving region is hard to imagine. Busy Bologna rivals Milan in achievement; productivity and a high standard of living are the rule.

For centuries, Romagna was Roman in every possible sense: It was part of Rome when Emilia was still a series of colonies; later, under the Visigoths and then the Byzantines, its leading town of Ravenna served as what was to be the final capital of the Western Empire. Roman again during the Renaissance, along with Ferrara and Bologna, the area ended up as the property of the Papal States.

The historic cities of Emilia—Piacenza, Parma, and Modena—line the ancient Roman road that not only gives the territory its name but passes through the center of Bologna as well. The project of Marcus Aemilius Lepidus in 187 B.C., the **Via Emilia** connected the present Piacenza to Arminium (Rimini) on the Adriatic. The cities of the Via Emilia are not distant from one another, and the road is straight (now paralleled by a modern autostrada), so time is no problem

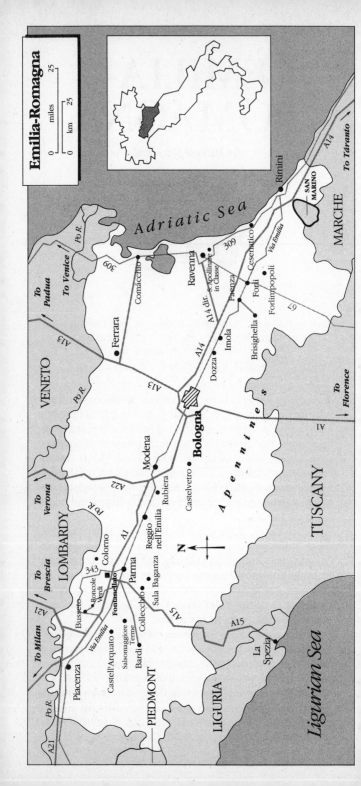

until the traveller reaches them and finds that for architecture, for history, and for art they are a delight to visit.

The Food of Emilia-Romagna

No gastronomic tour of Italy would be complete without a visit to Emilia-Romagna, considered by many food lovers to be the home of some of Italy's finest cooking. Although others may challenge that assertion, few, if any, would disagree that it is Italy's richest regional cuisine. Cows grazing in the Enza Valley between Parma and Reggio Emilia account for much of the country's milk, cream, butter, and cheese, especially Parmigiano-Reggiano, the "king" of Italian cheeses. Pigs— whose presence is due to the Romans, for whom pork was far and away the favorite meat—contribute luscious pink prosciutto and a vast variety of sausages. In warm weather a cornucopia of fruit is produced in the fertile plains, including peaches, cherries, and apricots.

An assortment of *salumi* (cold sliced meats) is the typical starter for lunch or dinner. The selection may include thin, silken slices of moist prosciutto ham; *spalla cotta,* cured pork shoulder; *culatello,* the choicest part of the prosciutto; *mortadella,* inspiration for our baloney; and various types of salami, often served with crispy puffs of fried dough called either *crescentina* or *gnocco fritto.*

Emilia-Romagna's pride is its excellent fresh pasta, hand-made with only eggs and flour as opposed to the dried macaroni, made with flour and water, that is eaten in other parts of Italy. According to Marcella Hazan, author of *The Classic Italian Cook Book* and a native of Emilia-Romagna, dried spaghetti and macaroni were nearly unknown until recently. She writes, "The only pasta consumed was home-made pasta, and it was made fresh daily in virtually every home." Though modern lifestyles have made this less of a reality, fresh pasta is still considered something of an art form, one that can be sampled in many of the region's wonderful restaurants, served in rich capon broth, tossed with butter and Parmesan cheese, or dressed with lusty Bolognese-style meat and tomato *ragù.*

Meats are the typical second course, particularly *bollito* and *arrosto misto,* a selection of mixed boiled or roasted meats and poultry, served with a zesty green sauce or *mostarda,* fruits candied in a sweet-hot mustard syrup. *Zampone* and *cotechino,* two large, savory sausages served sliced with cheesy mashed potatoes or lentils, are cold-weather favorites. Near the coast seafood takes precedence, especially eels from the salt flats at Comacchio.

For dessert there are many choices, but one not to be missed is *torta di taglierini,* an almond cake topped with skinny pasta strands baked until crunchy.

The region's wines are not often counted among Italy's best, but they can complement the local foods nicely. Many are *frizzante* (slightly sparkling) and are meant to be drunk young. On the Emilian side of the region, from Piacenza to Bologna, the principal wine is Lambrusco, dark red and fruity, and much drier than the kind that is usually exported. The Romagna side of the region contributes red Sangiovese and two whites, Trebbiano and Albana di Romagna. Trebbiano is light and fresh and it can be made either still or sparkling, according to the taste of the winemaker; Albana is quite dry with a slight almond flavor. Sangiovese is a light red wine, though those from the *superiore* zones can age and develop complexity as *riserva.*

As in most of Italy, dining out in Emilia-Romagna can put a serious dent in your wallet—but most food lovers agree that the region's outstanding cuisine is worth the investment. Where a menu approaches the heart-stopping price category, we've indicated as much.

Romagna is Italy's greengrocer. Travel through the countryside in spring and summer, and you'll find fruits and vegetables feted at their peak seasons. The Sagra di Pesca (peach festival), the Sagre di Piselli (pea festival), and such feature their star attraction cooked in an amazing number of ways. The regional tourist office will let you know where the *sagre* are (see below for address).

We cover the two most important cities of Romagna first: Ravenna, on the coast, and then Ferrara, inland. Next we go west to Parma and move southeast from there along the old Via Emilia through Modena to Bologna.

MAJOR INTEREST

Food and restaurants (Emilia)
Mosaics and frescoes; festivals (Romagna)

Ravenna
Byzantine and Visigothic mosaics and architecture
Basilica of Sant'Apollinare in Classe

Ferrara
Renaissance palazzi
The Castello: Ducal suite
The Duomo (façade and Cosmè Tura panels)
Palazzo dei Diamanti painting gallery

Parma
Galleria Nazionale in Palazzo della Pilotta (Correggio,
    Leonardo)
Convent of San Paolo (Correggio)
Romanesque cathedral (Correggio, frescoes)
Church of San Giovanni Evangelista (Correggio,
    Parmigianino)
Farnese palace at Colorno
Verdi pilgrimage
The Parma castles

Modena
Galleria Estense (paintings)
Biblioteca Estense (illuminated manuscripts)
Duomo
Fini restaurant

Bologna
Pinacoteca Nazionale (Raphael, Giotto, others)
Streets of palaces
Medieval piazza Maggiore
Byzantine-Romanesque church of Santo Stefano
Basilica of San Petronio (exterior, paintings)
Church of San Giacomo Maggiore (Costa frescoes,
    chapel)
Church of San Domenico (dell'Arca, Pisano
    sculptures)
Pescherie Vecchie market
Visit to Brisighella

RAVENNA

Of all the towns of Emilia-Romagna, Ravenna remains the
most evocative and the most unusual. Set apart from the Via
Emilia on the Adriatic coast, it retains a distance both in place
and in time. Nowhere else can you find so many vestiges of
Byzantium as in this town of marble, ivory, and gold that was
to be the final bastion of the Western Empire. Its mosaics
and their images outshine everything of a similar period in
Istanbul—where every representation of the human counte-
nance was destroyed in the Iconoclastic Rebellion—or in
Greece, where centuries of earthquakes and Turkish occupation have left little. So you must come to Ravenna to view a
record of those fifth and sixth centuries A.D. that signaled the
fall of the empire in the West. And every stage of that empire
was witnessed here: from its beginning, when Ravenna was
the headquarters of Caesar for his march on Rome, to its

Golden Age, when Augustus created the thriving port of Classe (marked now by the lone basilica of Sant'Apollinare), and then—in a wave of invasions—to the end.

In the fifth century the Visigoths moved their capital from Milan to Ravenna, then a city protected by marshes and lagoons and crisscrossed by canals—an early version of Venice. This was an intelligent move that was to prolong the life of the empire by hundreds of years. The monuments of that capital can be seen almost chronologically, one near the other.

Those sights that remain most deeply in the mind are connected with two amazing women. One monument is the **Tomb of Galla Placidia**, off via San Vitale in the northwest corner of the city; the other is next door, the **mosaic** in San Vitale depicting the Empress Theodora and her court. Galla Placidia's history was by far the earlier. Born to a patrician Roman family, she was captured in the sack of Rome by Alaric in 410 A.D. and was present at his burial in the river Busento, in Calabria. To the horror of Roman aristocratic society, she married his successor, Ataulf. From then on, she never looked back. The Visigoths by no means considered themselves barbarians; they felt that the mantle of Rome had fallen on their shoulders, and this highly ambitious woman was to take the fullest advantage of that legacy. She ended up as regent to her son, Valentinian III, who became emperor at the age of six; for 20 years she ran the Western Empire. This included most of Spain, where her name appears on more streets and squares than in Italy; her palace in Barcelona lies below that of Ferdinand and Isabella. In Ravenna she is buried with her son and her husband (whose reign was brief) in a tomb that glows with blue and gold lapis, with stars on the ceilings and mosaic panels in the naturalistic manner of Rome's early Christian churches. Of Galla Placidia's many palaces and basilicas, this small mausoleum is all that remains, but its impact exceeds its size.

The Visigothic empire in Spain lasted until the Arab invasion; in Ravenna its life was shortened by a crusade from the East, sparked by the view of the Orthodox Catholic Church of Byzantium (and in particular the Emperor Justinian) that its Arian form of Christianity was a heresy. Justinian launched a war both with generals and with architects. The generals, of whom Belisarius was the most capable, took Ravenna in 540 A.D. The architects, years before, had started pouring money from the imperial treasuries into structures in Ravenna that would illustrate the true faith, and of these the most spectacular remains the church of **San Vitale**. Distinctly Oriental in design, like the churches of Syria, its interior walls are lined with marble and porphyry; mosaics cover the ceilings and arches, incorporating two panels of imperial portraits that are the finest left to us by Byzantium: On one are Justinian and his court; on the other his empress, Theodora, with her ladies-in-waiting. San Vitale was finished in the year of the death of this *Basilissa,* who sports a halo hardly earned by her past. By no means of noble birth like Galla Placidia, Theodora was born into the circus—then a sort of burlesque. Even that sounds fine compared with Gibbon's immortal description of her in his *Decline and Fall.* She rose to dominate both emperor and empire with just the sort of hard, strong character that is apparent in her image here in San Vitale.

Among the other attractions at the town center is **Sant'Apollinare Nuovo,** built by Theodoric during the sixth century for the Arians and expanded three centuries later with a graceful cylindrical campanile. The mosaics are among Ravenna's most famous—the processions of the virgins, preceded by Magi, toward the Madonna and angels, and of the martyrs going from Ravenna toward Christ. The nearby **Battistero degli Ariani** (Baptistery of the Arians), also sixth century, contains a fine mosaic *Baptism of Christ and Procession of the Apostles.* Behind the Duomo, the **Museo Arcivescovile** boasts the great ivory throne of Maximilian, chef d'oeuvre of sixth-century Alexandrine artists.

Northeast of the city, just past the railroad tracks, is a monument imposing in solemnity. Theodoric, the sixth-century Ostrogoth king, was buried, presumably, in this mausoleum bearing his name, **Mausoleo di Teodorico.** Set alone in a cypress grove, it was built in monolithic style—using huge stones and no mortar and covered with a dome.

San Vitale might be the most unusual of Ravenna's churches, but the basilica of **Sant'Apollinare in Classe,** near the pine woods that have grown over the silted-up Roman port and reached by frequent bus service from the train station, is in its way the most beautiful. Serene and spacious, built on the plan of an early Christian basilica, it has sides that are lined with marble columns and sarcophagi leading up to a golden blaze of mosaics dominated by a cross against a sea of stars. The pine forest itself was once a haunt for the horse-riding Byron, when he was living in Ravenna in the palazzo (still there) of his mistress, Teresa Guiccioli, with her, her complaisant husband, and his own menagerie of animals. (This affair is lucidly described in Iris Origo's impeccable book *The Last Attachment.*) Ravenna's other guest-poet, Dante, exiled from Florence, died of marsh fever right in town. The citizens of Ravenna used every subterfuge to retain his body, and he still lies here in his domed marble tomb.

With all its museums, baptisteries, and basilicas, Ravenna is difficult to see on a day trip, except perhaps from Ferrara. The churches are best seen in the morning light, so it is a good idea to spend the night. The two most attractive hotels are the **Centrale-Byron** and the **Bisanzio**, both quiet and central—but small, so reserve. Ravenna itself has had an economic revival, thanks to the discovery of methane gas on its outskirts, in what is now an industrial landscape (immortalized by the director Michelangelo Antonioni in *The Red Desert,* one of his many attempts to drive his leading actress, Monica Vitti, mad).

The Old Town itself is intact; it has a delightful miniature piazza from the Middle Ages, the **piazza del Popolo**, with columns like those near San Marco in Venice supporting the town's two favorite saints, who look down on the café tables. There are two good restaurants in Ravenna, both expensive. One, the **Tre Spade**, alongside the cathedral at via Rasponi 37 (Tel: 0544-323-82; closed Mondays and August), was started a few years ago by young people who admired Imola's San Domenico. In their neo-Venetian Rococo decor they have done well indeed; carpaccio, tagliolini with smoked salmon, and crepes with artichoke hearts are a few of the specialties. The food of Romagna is akin to that of Venice (the same sea is at hand): *fritto misto* of fish, scampi grilled or boiled, and risotto with *gamberetti.* Some of these last dishes are available at the **Bella Venezia** (via 4 Novembre 16; Tel: 0544-217-46; closed Sundays), which is more of a trattoria in style than the Tre Spade. Because the best Trebbiano is produced in the Ravenna area, and because it goes well with all of this food, it is the wine to order.

For an inexpensive lunch or supper in this area look for one of the many blue-and-white-striped roadside stands selling *piadina,* Romagna's answer to the pizza. *Piadina* is a savory flat bread baked on a stone griddle and served hot, either plain or folded around cooked vegetables (called *crescione*), sliced meats, or cheese. In Ravenna the **Cà de Ven**, housed in what was once a 14th-century palace at via Corrado Ricci 24, serves made-to-order *piadinas* as well as local wines by the carafe or bottle.

THE EMILIA-ROMAGNA COAST

The Adriatic coast of Emilia-Romagna, a long stretch of beach resorts and pine woods, is very popular with summer tourists, especially from Germany and Great Britain. There are many hotels to choose from here, though a day trip to the beach can be arranged easily from Ravenna. The beaches are fine, but the region suffers from a chronic problem with algae, which takes the form of a thick green slime the Italians call *mucillagine,* which clings to the shoreline. It is not considered dangerous, but it is unsightly and efforts are being made to control the problem. Climatic conditions affect its recurrence, so the situation changes from year to year. Check the local newspapers, if possible, before going.

About midway between Ravenna and Rimini is the town of Forlimpopoli, birthplace of Pellegrino Artusi, sometimes called the Italian Fanny Farmer. Artusi was the author of a classic Italian cookbook, *Scienza in Cucina e L'Arte di Mangiar Bene,* which has sold more than a million copies both in the original 1891 version and as revised. Just outside of town in Selbagnone is a highly regarded restaurant, **Al Maneggio**, in a restored 17th-century villa (Tel: 0543-74-20-42, closed Sunday evening and Mondays). Owners Bruna and Giorgio Sebastiani are earnest advocates of local ingredients and present a meticulously choreographed (and expensive) menu, by reservation only.

Rimini, at the southern end of Emilia-Romagna's coast and the largest of the beach towns, was an important Roman outpost. In the 13th century it became the province of the ruthless Malatesta family, immortalized by Dante in the *Inferno.* Nowadays during the summer months it is packed with tourists who come for the fine white-sand beaches.

FERRARA

Ferrara is a city of Emilia but is set apart from the Via Emilia. Though founded by the inhabitants of the ancient, now ruined, port of Spina in the Po delta, it had a sizable population only after the fall of Ravenna to barbarians in the sixth century A.D., when an influx of refugees made its riverfront a working commercial port. By 1208 Ferrara had been taken over by the Este family, and they ran it in a manner that was to make it a center for arts and learning known to all of Europe. Within their castle, which dominates the city center, they did most of their bloody deeds—the most famous being the execution by Marchese Niccolo III of his young wife, Parisina Malatesta, and his son Ugo, when he caught them in flagrante delicto thanks to a window mirror.

More innovative were the broad, sunny streets of gardens and palaces laid out by Ercole I in the 15th century, making Ferrara one of the first planned cities anywhere. The most advanced contributions to the civilization of the Renaissance came first from the small courts such as those of Ferrara and Mantua, developments that were copied later in Florence and Rome. The Estes had their castle—just as the Bourbons later had the Bastille in Paris—but for pleasure and entertainment they used their outlying palaces, and it was in them that they received the Humanist writers and philosophers, such as Tasso, Ariosto, and Petrarch, who were to turn their town into a cultural phenomenon. One of their random inventions was the theater as we know it, with a curtain going up and a play performed in front of an audience.

Thanks to Borso d'Este, an able administrator and avid protector of the arts, we have the **Palazzo Schifanoia**, near the town walls on via Scandiana, with frescoes that he commissioned from the three painters who first formed the School of Ferrara: Cosmè Tura, Ercole de' Roberti, and Francesco del Cossa. Cossa's frescoes give us an idea of the pastimes and pleasures of Borso's court, and in them one notes the large part that women played in Este society. Two of the most remarkable were the daughters of Ercole I: Isabella, who was to marry a Gonzaga and become marchioness of Mantua, and Beatrice, who was to marry Ludovico Sforza and become duchess of Milan. They exported their background with them, with results that have filled art galleries and libraries. (In painting alone, Isabella was patron to Mantegna, and Beatrice to Leonardo.)

Apart from the Schifanoia there are three palaces in Ferrara that are not to be missed. (Ferrara's attractions are easy to enjoy, for the flattish city is comfortable to walk and a joy for bicyclists, who count among their numbers many local residents of all ages.) One was built for the retirement of Ludovico il Moro, Beatrice's husband, but fate was to decree an early death for her and prison for him after the French, largely at his instigation, descended into Italy. At via XX Settembre 124, the **Palazzo di Ludovico il Moro**, with its rose gardens and painted ceilings, now houses the Greco-Etruscan finds from Spina. Not far from it is the **Palazzina di Marfisa d'Este**, decked out with furniture and paintings of its period, and with a garden theater where the plays of Marfisa's friend, Torquato Tasso, were performed. The airiest and most pleasant of the three palaces is the **Casa Romei** (north of the Palazzo di Schifanoia and reached by the borga Vada), built by the merchant husband of Polissena d'Este and later enlarged by the same Cardinal Ippolito who built the Villa d'Este at Tivoli, outside Rome. It is now a museum for the sizable number of frescoes, sculpture, and paintings rescued from convents and churches in Ferrara after the arrival of Napoléon.

Casa Romei also served as a second home to Ferrara's most famous duchess, Lucrezia Borgia, who married Duke Alfonso I. By this alliance the duke appalled the Italian aristocracy, since by his time the Estes had become pillars of genteel society, whereas the Borgias were looked upon as something akin to a Spanish Mafia. As we now know, it was Lucrezia's bloodthirsty brothers who did the poisoning and the killing; but her record—one husband horribly murdered and the other warned in the nick of time to run for his life—was hardly reassuring. It was her stupendous dowry and fear of her loving, dangerous father—Pope Alexander VI—that ensured the marriage to Alfonso, and her entrance into Ferrara for her nuptials became one of the most recounted spectacles of Renaissance Italy. (The best biography of this fascinating woman is by Maria Bellonci; it reads like a novel of suspense.)

Lucrezia was then 20. She was not stupid, and she had a very appealing side to her character. She stayed on in Ferrara, much loved even after her family fell from power, until she died at the age of 39 giving birth to her seventh child. She had renovated part of the **Castello**, the main ducal residence, for her own apartments; today her *orangerie,* which served as her salon for artists and poets, has been restored, as have the frescoes of its loggia. Gone, though, is her brocaded bathroom; her mania for bathing, most likely a Hispano-Moresque legacy, had scandalized the Italians right from the start, when her mammoth wedding cavalcade stopped for 24 hours on its way from Rome so that she could wash her hair. Her conquests in Ferrara were ardent but most likely platonic, her three suitors having been Pietro Bembo, the dashing poet who was to become a cardinal; Ercole Strozzi, the Florentine who helped her set up the *orangerie;* and finally Alfonso Gonzaga, the husband of her worst enemy, Isabella d'Este. Isabella could never forgive Lucrezia for having so much money; on the other hand, Lucrezia's attempt at a learned court could never rival Isabella's at Mantua because she simply did not have Isabella's education. But she did have a personal warmth perhaps sorely needed by the nonintellectual Gonzaga, who had been treated with nothing but contempt by his bluestocking wife.

Near the Castello is the **Duomo**, with its handsome pink marble façade—an amalgam of Romanesque and Gothic styles—and the **Museo del Duomo**. In this neighborhood of squares and courts is a welter of welcoming cafés and restaurants. The best of the latter are the least pretentious. The **Grotta Azzurra** (piazza Sacrati 43; Tel: 0532-20-91-52; closed Wednesdays) serves *passatelli alla Romagnolo,* spaetzle-like noodles made from bread crumbs, eggs, and Parmigiano in a rich broth, as well as *stinco di suino,* tender braised pork shank.

North of the center along corso Ercole is one of the most handsome of Ferrara's palaces, **dei Diamanti**, so called for the diamond-shaped marble facets on its façade. It now houses Ferrara's painting museum, or **Pinacoteca**, which contains a creditable collection of the School of Ferrara. Even so, the finest Cosmè Turas are his panels in the Museo del Duomo; the best Cossas are his frescoes in the Schifanoia; and a lot of the best of everything was hauled off to Modena when the Estes had to leave Ferrara at the end of the 16th century thanks to a papal refusal to accept their last possible heir as duke. Many an illegitimate Este had been recognized over the centuries, but Rome had long coveted Ferrara and so in 1598 refused to accept the grandson of Alfonso I as heir. When the family left, they were in quite a bad mood and took just about everything movable with them, including their vast libraries and lots of paintings. Something else that left with them was the luck of Ferrara; ineptly administered by cardinal legates, the city fell victim to flood and plague, then to the depredations of Napoléon's troops—and finally to the bombings of World War II.

Ferrara was one of the worst-bombed cities in Italy, sharing the fate of the other towns of Emilia-Romagna that happened to be incorporated in the German "Gothic Line." The miracles lie in what was saved and in the restoration of the rest.

From the corso Ercole you can walk to **Il Ristorantino** at vicolo Agucchie 15, one of Ferrara's most attractive restaurants specializing in traditional fare. Try the classic *cappelletti alla zucca*—you'll never believe the base is pumpkin. Ferrara has a way of giving pumpkins and apples an unexpected glamour. Tel: (0532) 76-15-17.

Ferrara is worth a night's stay, being perfect for evening walks, whether around the animated squares of the medieval section or in the nostalgic shadows of the later palaces and the greenery of its more open areas. These nighttime scenes will remind you, in their perspectives, of Giorgio de Chirico—who spent years of his early life here. These pink and ocher palaces have become familiar through his artistic vision. Their gardens turn up in a book and film of our own time—*The Garden of the Finzi-Continis*—set in Ferrara.

The most convenient central hotels are the **Ripagrande**, installed in a palace in the medieval section, the gracious and quiet **Astra**, and the recently renovated **Annunziata**. The last two are located near the Castello.

THE CITIES OF THE VIA EMILIA

The road built by Marcus Aemilius Lepidus began at the Roman town of Placentia, where it was crossed by the Via Postumia running from the Roman equivalent of Genoa to Concordia in the Veneto. Placentia became a very busy town; **Piacenza**, the city that later replaced it, remains a commercial center, and—with its sturdy Palazzo Communale fronted by two Farnese equestrian statues on their pillars—a monumental one at that. It has one very good restaurant, the **Antica Osteria del Teatro** (via Verdi 16; Tel: 0523-237-77; closed Sunday evenings, Mondays, and August), which is housed in a beautifully restored 15th-century palace complete with wooden ceilings and honey-colored walls. The contrast of modern decor with antique/rustic lines works well here, creating a formal but relaxed atmosphere. There are three intimate dining rooms and the food is innovative, sometimes fussy, expensive, but well done. The regional menu is quite fine.

Midway between Piacenza and Parma is the handsome medieval hill town **Castell'Arquato**. Situated in the foothills of the Piacentine Apennines, the town was originally a Roman camp before passing into the hands of the bishops of Piacenza, becoming an independent city-state and then the feudal domain of the Viscontis and Sforzas. It has its obligatory battle scars, including the remains of a fortress. The main piazza Matteotti, at the top of the hill, has an impressive ensemble of medieval buildings, including the **Palazzo Pretorio** and a 12th-century Romanesque church, the **Collegiata**, both worth a visit. Fossil foragers will delight in the findings of the **Museo Geologico**, but a more modern attraction is the genial restaurant **Taverna del Falconiere**, right in the piazza, with a delightful covered terrace that takes full advantage of the views of the rich countryside, studded with farms. Its *tortelli,* stuffed with spinach, ricotta, and mascarpone cheese, are wonderful and go well with the local red wine, Carmianino (closed Mondays; Tel: 0523-80-31-55). Another spot for enjoying Piacentine fare is **La Rocca—da Franco** (via Asilo 4; Tel: 0523-80-31-54; closed Wednesdays, January, and July), where you might try tasty *burtlêina,* a thin egg-and-lard fritter eaten with salami as an appetizer; or *anvein,* anolini stuffed with bread crumbs, cheese, eggs, and nutmeg served either in broth or with butter and cheese.

Southwest of Parma is **Salsomaggiore Terme**, a resort town popular the year round with Italians who come to bathe in its thermal waters. The quiet streets are lined with flowers and there are a number of pleasant cafés to relax in. In the central piazza, the **Terme Bezieri** is housed in an ornate Art Nouveau building. Among the many hotels, the **Grand Hotel et de Milan** is the finest, with beautifully land-scaped gardens and a swimming pool. The lively **Osteria del Castellazzo**, in the medieval center (borgo Castellazzo 40; Tel: 0524-782-18), offers a varied menu of unusual dishes such as colorful *tortelli di carote,* spinach pasta with a carrot-and-ricotta filling in butter sauce, and asparagus with fried eggs and Parmesan.

Because Salsomaggiore is only 33 km (20 miles) from Parma, its hotels often serve to supplement those of Parma when the latter city is inundated with visitors to one of its many trade fairs, such as Cibus, an annual spring food-and-wine extravaganza that attracts 1,500 exhibitors and 100,000 visitors. For information on Cibus and other trade fairs, contact E. A. Fiere di Parma, via F. Rizzi 3, 43031 Baganzola.

Parma

The city of Parma, laid out with such spacious elegance by the Farnese family, has a history that is not just the usual one of survival: It is a success story. The Farneses, during their centuries of rule, united with a bridge the two towns that now make up Parma, opened up the medieval sections with avenues and parks, and made their duchy a powerful force in the international politics of Europe. When Isabella Far-nese assumed the throne of Spain in the early 18th century, though, the Farneses left—taking even their furniture with them. Their town could easily have gone the way of Ferrara, which, with the departure of the Estes, simply fell to pieces, like a clock with the center of its mechanism removed.

A flood of lucky events kept Parma on the map. The begin-ning of the 19th century brought Marie Louise, the Hapsburg wife of Emperor Napoléon, to rule the duchy when her husband was sent into exile. Both she and her consort, Marshal Neipperg, were efficient administrators. Devoted to music, painting, and literature, they soon set their noble city back on its feet—commercially, too, and in the most various ways. Parma's violets had always been celebrated; Marie Lou-ise created a perfume industry around them. Parma's hams had been produced since Roman times; now they became *jambons de Parme* and were exported as the region's main product. The local cheese, Parmigiano, had been made by the Romans, too; now it became a sine qua non for Italian pasta everywhere. (To watch Parmigiano and prosciutto being

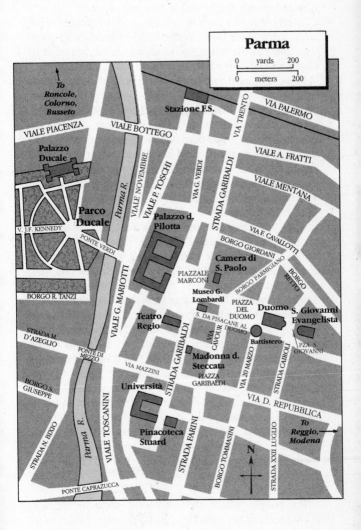

Parma

| 0 | yards | 200 |
| 0 | meters | 200 |

To
Roncole,
Colorno,
Busseto

VIALE PIACENZA

VIALE BOTTEGO

Stazione F.S.

VIA TRENTO

VIA PALERMO

VIALE A. FRATTI

Palazzo
Ducale

VIALE NOVEMBRE

VIALE P. TOSCHI

VIA G. VERDI

STRADA GARIBALDI

VIALE MENTANA

Parma R.

Parco
Ducale

V. J.F. KENNEDY

PONTE VERDI

Palazzo d.
Pilotta

VIA F. CAVALLOTTI

BORGO GIORDANI

Camera di
S. Paolo

BORGO PARMIGIANO

BORGO RETTO

PIAZZALE
MARCONI

BORGO R. TANZI

VIALE G. MARIOTTI

Museo G.
Lombardi

PIAZZA
DEL
DUOMO

Duomo

S. Giovanni
Evangelista

S. DA PISACANE AL DUOMO

STRADA M
D'AZEGLIO

Teatro
Regio

STRADA GARIBALDI

VIA CAVOUR

Battistero

PZA. S.
GIOVANNI

STRADA CAIROLI

PONTE DI
MEZZO

VIA MAZZINI

Madonna d.
Steccata

VIA 20 MARZO

BORGO S.
GIUSEPPE

PIAZZA
GARIBALDI

Università

VIA D. REPUBBLICA

Parma R.

VIALE TOSCANINI

STRADA GARIBALDI

Pinacoteca
Stuard

STRADA FARINI

BORGO TOMMASINI

To
Reggio,
Modena

STRADA N. BIXIO

N

STRADA XXII LUGLIO

PONTE CAPRAZUCCA

prepared—and to sample the goods—ask the tourist office in piazza Duomo to arrange a tour of one of the plants near Parma. Parma cheeses and other goods, everything from paintings to clothes, are for sale at the **Ghiaia**, an open-air market beneath the bridge at the end of strada Mazzini.) Cultural publicity was soon to come as well. A minor French functionary, Marie-Henri Beyle, came to see Parma's paintings; later, as the writer Stendhal, he set the action of *La Chartreuse de Parme* here.

Music, a passion with Marie Louise as it had been with her aunt, Marie Antoinette, was housed in a handsome new opera house, the **Teatro Regio**, which still exists today. Soon, in the hamlet of Roncole just to the north, a composer worthy of filling it was born. Giuseppe Verdi made Parma a place of pilgrimage for opera-lovers even to our day, and his last librettist, the composer Arrigo Boito, was to give his name to the local conservatory of music. The Parmigiani are possibly the world's most critical opera audience. They consider themselves to be the keepers of a proud musical heritage and have been known to strike fear in the hearts of performers. The *loggionisti,* as members of the Teatro Regio's gallery are called, lead the way, jeering singers who do not meet their standards. Stories are told of the diva who, mortified by the audience's reaction to her singing in *La Gioconda,* walked off the stage midway and continued on to the train station without changing her costume or makeup. In 1979 the audience was so infuriated by the conductor's performance and a singer's rendition of Violetta in *La Traviata* that they forced the theater to close at the beginning of the third act. But the passionate loggionisti can praise as enthusiastically as they criticize. When the great Birgit Nilsson sang at the Regio she was reluctant to take a curtain call because of the clamor from the audience until she realized that their cries of *Bis!* were actually a request for an encore, and not boos. Arturo Toscanini, the impassioned conductor, was born in Parma, and performed frequently at the Regio. His former home is now a small museum (borgo Tanzi 13; closed Mondays).

The painter whose work Stendhal came to see was Correggio, and his paintings can still be seen in the same places. One is in the **Galleria Nazionale** of the Farnese Palace, the **Palazzo della Pilotta** (open 9:00 A.M. to 2:00 P.M.; Sundays to 1:00 P.M.), on piazzale Marconi, where his paintings are joined by the works of Van Dyck, Leonardo, and many others, including works taken from various convents and villas and brought here for safety by Napoléon. Alongside the galleries is the **Teatro Farnese**—older than Vicenza's Palladian theater but, though damaged in the war, now thoroughly restored and used for concerts.

The most delightful work of Correggio, however, is found in the **Camera di San Paolo** near the Pilotta: frescoes the abbess commissioned for her dining room. The subjects are mythological, done as trompe l'oeil in colors as fresh as the day they were painted.

Correggio's most ambitious work in Parma remains his frescoed cupola in the **Duomo**, a masterpiece of light and perspective. The Duomo was of course started long before Correggio came along, as its 12th-century façade testifies. It is adorned with some of Italy's most interesting Roman-esque sculpture, mostly by one artist, Benedetto Antelami, whose neo-Byzantine reliefs grace the **Baptistery** as well. The latter, octagonal in form and built in pink Veronese marble, is remarkable for its bright 13th-century ceiling murals.

Nearby is the church of **San Giovanni Evangelista**, which is more Renaissance in style than the Duomo, with frescoes both by Correggio and by Parma's other major painter, Parmigianino, who did much to create the Mannerist style later developed by the school of Fontainebleau. San Giovanni also has a cloister sheltering a 13th-century pharmacy, its shelves laden with faïence medicine jars and mortars.

One of the joys of wandering about Parma is the number of cafés—for a cappuccino or a *frizzante*—set in squares all over the town (smaller ones are near the cathedral or the opera house, with the greatest expanse of tables on the **piazza Garibaldi**). After an *aperitivo* in piazza Garibaldi, you'll find **Parizzi** nearby at via della Repubblica 71. (Tel: 0521-285-952; closed Sunday evenings, Mondays, and July 21 to August 20). Entered through an alleyway, the restaurant is in a patio beneath a skylight. In the center of the space is a choice of antipasti: the best ham and charcuterie available—since the owners' family ran a *salumeria*—and a tempting choice of *ripiene* (stuffed zucchini, eggplant, and tomato). In season the local favorite, fresh asparagus *alla parmigiana,* is very much in evidence: with melted butter, grated Parmesan, and here with eggs boiled just to the point at which they can be chopped over the asparagus tips. In a city of great pastas, its potato-filled *tortelli* with a light sauce of *funghi porcini,* the incomparably meaty wild mushrooms, are a standout, and Parizzi's *tortelli d'erbetta alla Parmigiana,* filled with ricotta and Swiss chard, are a paragon of that classic dish. Roasted duck with thin shreds of carmelized lemon peel is a specialty and a delicious study in contrasts, while the lamb chops with balsamic glaze are a fine demonstration of one of the uses of the precious balsamic vinegar. The restaurant has an extensive national and regional wine list, though for local wines the surest bets remain Sangiovese for red and Trebbiano for white. After dinner, sample a *digestivo* such as Nocino, made from green walnuts, or the aromatic herb liqueur known as Erbe Luigia. Parizzi is moderately expensive.

If you leave the galleries of the Pilotta at lunchtime, you can walk right across the palace square to **La Greppia** at strada Garibaldi 39 (Tel: 0521-23-36-86; closed Thursdays, Fridays, and July), a bright white and pricey eatery where a plate-glass window at the end of the room fully reveals the kitchen, giving a concrete idea of the fresh pasta and vegetables at hand. These can be combined, as in a delicious pasticcio of asparagus. You can spend days in Parma without seeing a drop of tomato sauce; instead, the *agnolotti* and *tortelli* are served with *panna* (based on cream), or shaved white truffles, or just butter and freshly grated Parmesan. The main courses at La Greppia range from a smooth *vitello tonnato* to liver sautéed in sage. The desserts can feature the taste of bitter chocolate that the Hapsburgs took with them from Vienna to wherever they ruled, or perhaps something lighter, such as the white peach sorbet made from the fruit of the owner's home garden.

A simpler setting is that of the **Trattoria Vecchio Molinetto**, where meals are good and hearty—in the garden in summertime (viale Milazzo 39, Tel: 0521-526-72; closed Fridays, Saturday lunch, and August). On warm nights you can dine alfresco while gazing at the Romanesque façade of the duomo at **Angiol D'Or** (vicolo Scutellari 1; Tel: 0521-28-26-32; closed Sundays). The restaurant is beautifully decorated and rather formal, but the food can be uneven.

Near La Greppia and on the same strada Garibaldi is the **Museo Civico Glauco Lombardi**, dedicated to Marie Louise and filled with souvenirs, paintings, and furniture rescued from her town palace, which nestled alongside the Pilotta and was bombed off the face of the earth during World War II. As you can see here, she herself was an excellent watercolorist, taught, like her aunt, by Redouté. She and Marie Antoinette shared a problem: They were Austrian, one trapped in France by the Revolution and the other ruling in Italy when the Risorgimento was beginning to stir. In France Marie Louise had been confronted by the problem of replacing the enormously popular Joséphine de Beauharnais as Napoléon's wife, but in Parma her goodwill and good works won over the population. The Neoclassical tomb she built for Neipperg can be seen in the church of La Steccata, across from her opera house, surrounded by more frescoes by Parmigianino. Her second city palace has survived: the **Ducale**, or *dei Giardini,* with its shaded gardens in the style of Le Nôtre, across the river from the Pilotta.

Shoppers in Parma will want to bring home some of the beautifully packaged violet-scented soaps, sachets, and cologne made by **Borsari 1870**, at via Trento 30/A. Violets coated in crystallized sugar are another Parma specialty. The edible flowers are prized by pastry makers around the world and can be purchased at the elegant **Pasticceria Torino** at via Garibaldi 61. The mahogany-paneled pastry shop also sells excellent cakes and tarts that can be sampled over coffee at two tiny tables. If you're lucky you will arrive in time to taste a *torta di riso,* a rice pudding tart, still warm from the oven.

Tea-drinkers will enjoy the charming **Miss Pym Sala da Tè**, a British-style tearoom at borgo Parmigianino 5/B, not far from the fashionable shopping district behind piazza Garibaldi. There are dozens of exotic teas to choose from as well as snacks and cakes to go with them.

Parma seems to have conventions for just about everything, and its hotels are often full. The least pretentious of the grander hotels is the **Park Hotel Toscanini** (quiet in back, but front rooms have river views). The **Palace Hotel Maria Luigia** is the *grande dame,* located near the heart of the city. **Maxim's**, in the hotel lobby, offers an eclectic menu of regional Italian specialties in addition to traditional cuisine from Parma. A table by the entrance displays the fresh homemade pasta and vegetables of the day. (Closed Mondays and August; expensive.)

Outside Parma

Excursions from the town can combine lunching with sightseeing. At **Colorno**, about 15 km (9 miles) north of Parma, is the country palace used by Marie Louise. Built as a summer residence by the Farneses, it has been restored to something like its former state thanks to antiques fairs periodically held in it. And this **Palazzo Ducale** is worth preserving; it is a Baroque building set on the foundations of a former castle of the Sanseverinos, surrounded by trees and reflected in its river—an open invitation to romance.

This is just how it served in the case of Stendhal. Always searching through old papers and documents for ideas, he fell upon a history of the Farnese family and in it found the story of the seductive Giulia, a woman of few scruples who was infatuated with her young nephew Alexander. She was mistress to many, including a certain Cardinal Roderigo, who was to become Pope Alexander VI. Once installed in Rome she sent for her nephew, whose interests she energetically advanced, and from a libertine he was transformed into the serious man who was one day to become pope himself. Stendhal took these figures from history and put them into *La Chartreuse de Parme*. It should be reread by any traveller approaching these lands.

Stendhal—da Bruno, a restaurant on the site of the inn at which the author stayed, is a busy series of rooms aromatic with the scent of herbs on roasting lamb and pork. The restaurant moves outdoors in good weather and overlooks the stream below, which is a haven for fishermen. Both salmon and *fritto misto* of freshwater fish remain favorites on the menu. Tel: (0521) 81-54-93; closed Tuesdays.

Fans of Giuseppe Verdi have several choices for lunching in the country near places associated with the life of the composer. West of Colorno is **Roncole Verdi**, his birthplace, where his father's general store and tavern is now a national shrine. Next door to it is a very good restaurant called **Guareschi**, named after the author of the Don Camillo books but with musical tribute aplenty to the composer inside (Tel: 0524-924-95; closed Fridays). From Roncole the young Verdi moved to the town of **Busseto**, a few miles northwest. There he worked as organist in the church and was taken under the wing of Antonio Barezzi, a music-loving grocer of means who ran the local orchestra society and was able to help further the career of the already promising composer. Verdi's first wife, Margherita, was Barezzi's daughter; their marriage ended in the tragedy of her death and that of their two children when the couple was desperately trying to make good in Milan. Busseto remains a bustling, prosperous town. The atmospheric restaurant **I Due Foscari** is appropriately run by the singer Carlo Bergonzi (Tel: 0524-923-37; closed Mondays, January, and August 1 to 15). There are also rooms upstairs, inn-fashion, that must be reserved well in advance. For food, however, **Ugo** (Tel: 0524-923-07; closed Mondays, Tuesdays, and January), at via Mozart 3, is the better and less expensive place to go. While in Busseto try the local pastry specialty *spongata,* a hard, flat spice cake filled with nuts and candied fruits.

After his first success with *Nabucco,* Verdi's luck changed, and he returned to the environs of Busseto to build in 1849 the **Villa Verdi di Sant'Agata**, which was largely paid for by *Trovatore* and *Rigoletto*. His companion here was the well-known soprano Giuseppina Strepponi, who had befriended him in his early days and who was later to become his wife. Their marriage, however, took place only in 1859, and Verdi never forgave the people of Busseto for their bad treatment of Giuseppina. Sant'Agata, open to the public, is filled with mementos of Verdi and Giuseppina, including her favorite parrot, stuffed, and a portrait of his Maltese terrier. The house and gardens may seem gloomy to some, but the Verdi *appassionato* will be moved to tears. The hotel room in Milan where he died has been reconstructed here exactly as it was, and the romantic can imagine the stillness of the thousands who stood outside all night awaiting the dreaded news. Because of his participation in the movement for Italian independence Verdi was a national hero as few Italians have been, possessing more the stature of a George Washington than a composer. His last years at Sant'Agata were sad and lonely; Giuseppina and most of his friends had already died, and he had to count on the visits of his younger collaborators, among them Arrigo Boito and an enthusiastic young conductor from Parma, Arturo Toscanini.

Inside the **Rocca** (castle) at the center of the old town, the charming **Teatro Verdi**, where Toscanini and others conducted, is preserved and used regularly. The town of Busseto, where Verdi is still referred to, at least by the elders, as the Maestro, has a thriving tourist business in Verdiana, including hard-to-find tapes, fine woodcut prints, and plastic key chains with Giuseppe on one side and Giuseppina on the other (she is now loved, of course). A variety of musical presentations take place here; write or call the tourist office (piazza Verdi 24; Tel: 0524-924-87) for information. At Carnival and during the summer season there are regular celebrations, for which you can reserve by calling the Cooperativa Parmigianino; Tel: (0521) 82-11-39. The traditional Verdi tour begins at Roncole, where tickets can be bought for all three of his homes: Roncole, his birthplace; Busseto, where he lived in the **Palazzo Orlando**; and the Villa Verdi at Sant'Agata. Call the tourist office to see if a bus tour has been organized.

The Castles of Parma

Near Parma are several dramatic castles; among the most notable is **Fontanellato**, a few miles northwest of Parma. With moat, turrets, vast dining halls, and delicate frescoes by Parmigianino, it is a splendid place to spend an hour. (In fact, since it is not far from the Parmigiano cheese plant, you might indulge in both.) In the 15th century, the Sanvitale family transformed it from a fortress to the charming place it is today. (The castle now belongs to the municipality.) The frescoed room that is the prize was painted by Parmigianino in 1524 with scenes from the myth of Diana and Acteon, a story Ovid liked, in which the bathing Diana is inadvertently observed by Acteon. She changed him into a stag, and he was then torn to pieces by hounds. All involved, including the hounds, are poetically beautiful, and this is deservedly considered one of the artist's masterpieces.

If this whets your appetite for castles, go down to **Bardi**, 67 km (42 miles) southwest of Parma, where one of the most evocatively situated castles is perched high on a hill. Its 16th-century frescoes and wood-beamed ceilings have been well preserved. Check with the Parma tourist board or call the castle (Tel: 0525-713-21) to make sure it's open.

There are two good restaurants in this area. One is the elegant and fairly expensive **Ceci**, located in Collecchio (via D. Galaverna 28; Tel: 0521-80-54-89; closed Thursdays) in the Villa Maria Luigia, with its enormous trees and beautiful gardens. You can dine in a shady glass-enclosed terrace or out-of-doors in fine weather. Service is formal though friendly and the wine list is excellent, with some good buys. Don't miss the unusual *gelato di crema mantecato con balsamico,* ice cream whipped with balsamic vinegar, an unlikely combination that is tangy yet subtle. Far less formal, though not inexpensive, is the **Trattoria da Eletta** in Sala Baganza (via Campi 3; Tel: 0521-83-33-04; closed Mondays, Tuesdays, and the last two weeks in August), a cozy country restaurant. Eletta once cooked for the legendary Cantarelli in Samboseto, a now-closed restaurant that still operates as a specialty foods store and was a mecca for gastronomes during its heyday. But Eletta carries on the tradition, serving some of the tenderest and sweetest prosciutto, *culatello,* and salami imaginable. The pasta is excellent, but the specialty is the *savarin di riso,* a creamy molded risotto wrapped in prosciutto and topped with *porcini* mushrooms. Desserts are also outstanding.

From Parma the Via Emilia descends toward the southeast, passing through the rich commercial town of Reggio, which shares the honors with Parma in the production of Parmesan cheese. About halfway between Reggio and Modena is the town of Rubiera, home of the moderately expensive **Ristorante Albergo Arnaldo** (piazza XXIV Maggio 3; Tel: 0522-621-24), a warm, informal restaurant with comfortable modern rooms upstairs. The restaurant specializes in both *arrosto misto* and *bollito misto,* mixed roasted or boiled meats. The meats arrive on their own special warming cart so that diners can choose from the selection of five or more varieties of succulent poultry, veal, beef, or pork with assorted sauces. The pasta dishes are also excellent. About 12 km (7 miles) farther east of Rubiera is the ancient city of Modena.

Modena

The Via Emilia serves as the main street of Modena, which, of all the towns in the road's path, is perhaps the most exquisite, with a Romanesque cathedral that is a masterpiece; a superb museum of paintings; and streets of palaces, churches, arcades, and squares that have not changed since the days of Stendhal—so that the town itself is a work of art. Modena was scarcely hit in the last war; whatever damage has been done to the medieval quarter was perpetrated not by bombs but by the Este family when they arrived from Ferrara at the end of the 16th century. Modena was to be their new capital, Baroque was their style, and money was no object. New avenues were cut through the old city, and the **Palazzo Ducale**, second in size only to that of the Gonzagas in Mantua, was built to dominate the center, which it still does. Later a small, elegant opera house was built (both Luciano Pavarotti and Mirella Freni are Modenese). When the city walls came down after the unification of Italy they were replaced by tree-lined promenades. Many an avenue was once a canal—as is revealed by the names—and old Modena must have had a Venetian air; some of the piazzas near the cathedral still do. Like Venice, Modena is a city best appreciated when explored on foot.

The **Galleria Estense** is the painting museum, housed in the Palazzo dei Musei (at the far end of via Emilia Centro) along with the Este library. It took years to reorganize the picture galleries, but the result has been worth waiting for: one of Italy's best arranged collections. The Estes arrived— as would be expected—with cartloads of works of Cosmè Tura and the School of Ferrara, but they went right on collecting. Duke Francesco I went to Madrid and had his portrait painted by Velázquez (who in turn came to Modena on a buying trip for the king of Spain and was proudly shown the portrait in the palace). He also commissioned a flamboyant bust from Bernini, and that we see, along with a selection of Veroneses, Tintorettos, Guardis, and even an El Greco. On the floor below the gallery is the **Biblioteca Estense**, and though all of its 600,000 books and 15,000 manuscripts are hardly on permanent view, one room is open to the public to show the library's prizes. Featured is the Bible of Borso d'Este, with 1,020 pages illuminated by a team of artists, including Taddeo Crivelli. It is certainly the most valuable illustrated manuscript we have from the Italian Renaissance. It is in good company, with priceless Byzantine codices, French miniatures, and a fascinating collection of maps. One of the latter represents countries by their fauna; the coast of Brazil is the curved back of a green cockatoo.

Towering over Modena is the cathedral's Romanesque campanile, called the **Ghirlandina** thanks to the bronze garland on its weather vane; it reminded the Spanish Sephardim of their Giralda in Seville. The **Duomo** itself has been returned to its original Romanesque self, yet its interior has a Byzantine air, with its painted crucifix glowing over the raised main altar backed by arches and separated from the nave by a magnificent rood screen. The cathedral is closer to San Marco in Venice than to its Norman contemporaries in Apulia. It is a veritable museum of sculpture, with the work of the Lombard Wiligelmo later added to by the Campionese artists who came down from Lugano. There is even more in the **cathedral museum**, with its remarkable metopes brought down from the buttresses to rooms where they can be properly seen. More treasures surround the tomb of San Geminiano in the crypt, and lovers of wood intarsia shouldn't miss the Coro.

The lateral side of the Duomo facing the **piazza Grande** at the center of Modena is worth contemplation—best done over an aperitif in one of the cafés opposite (providing that it is not a weekend, when a hurly-burly antiques fair descends with its carts and stands). Modena's main shopping street is the **via Farini**, which leads to the dominating façade of the Palazzo Ducale.

The more fanatic gourmets who come to Modena look at nothing at all and head speedily for the famed **Fini** at rua Frati Minori 54. Practically an institution, Fini was founded in 1912 alongside a *salumeria;* since redecorated, it has retained its relaxed atmosphere and superior service. You would hardly suspect that the family has organized its own export service for many of the delicacies that find their way to your table here: their own salamis, hams, and pâtés; their *zampone,* or stuffed pig's foot (which is sliced like a sausage when served). The **Salumeria Telesforo Fini** is now located at corso Canalchiaro 139, in case you want some delicacies to take home.

Aceto balsamico, the heady vinegar for which the region is famous, also may be purchased at Fini. Authentic balsamico, made from Trebbiano grape juice, has a slightly caramelized flavor due to a long cooking process. The cooked juice is aged in a series of at least five casks made from different varieties of wood. The very best balsamicos are aged for decades. The concentrated nectar that results is very potent and would typically be offered as an after-dinner liqueur or a restorative. Lucrezia Borgia recommended it to alleviate the pain of childbirth. Nowadays balsamico is served drizzled over ice cream, berries, or other fruits, or even over Parmigiano-Reggiano cheese—but rarely in salad dressing.

The Finis have their own vineyards, where they produce the best of Lambruscos: the Sorbara. But in case this doesn't appeal to you, the restaurant has a wine list of 150 labels, both Italian and French, noted by province. Their pâté of prosciutto and chicken is an ideal opener; their pastas change with the season. If you are lucky, the menu will have a pasticcio of tortellini, served with a rich béchamel and encased in a crisp pastry shell. The cuisine of Modena—and the town considers it completely apart from that of Bologna and Parma—involves a great deal of labor. To accompany the boiled meats, *zampone,* and fowl of the *bollito misto* a bevy of sauces are wheeled up, among them *salsa verde,* then a *peperonata* of diced peppers, and the piquant mixture of preserved fruits known as *mostarda di Cremona.* Truffles lace the dishes here as they do all over the North, turning up in risottos, shaved over veal cutlets, or topping chicken already swimming in whiskey and cream. The dishes at Fini need not be heavy, though: Witness the lightly fried brains and sweetbreads, the kidneys *trifolati,* and the liver cooked with sage. A chocolate *semi-freddo* is one of the best desserts of the house; of course, all the cakes and tarts are made on the premises. Tel: (059) 22-33-14; Fax: (059) 22-02-47. Closed Mondays, Tuesdays, and August; expensive.

There are many other good restaurants in Modena. On the grand side there is the **Borso d'Este** (Tel: 059-21-41-14; closed Sundays and August) at piazza Roma 5, facing the palace; and in a more modest bracket, **Oreste** (piazza Roma 31; Tel: 059-24-33-24; closed Sunday evenings and Wednesdays) or **Enzo,** upstairs at via Coltellini 17 (Tel: 059-22-51-77; closed Tuesdays). Also good is **da Danilo**, located on a quiet side street at via Coltellini 31, where you can dine alfresco on *garganelli* (ridged pasta quills) in a light tomato and chicken sauce, or thick slices of rich *zampone* with tender beans perfumed with garlic. For morning coffee, stop at **Giusti**, near the piazza Maggiore (via Farini 75), for a cappuccino and warm chocolate-filled croissants. Next door, Giusti is also a gourmet shop, where excellent balsamic vinegar from a variety of producers, olive oil, dried *funghi porcini,* and other delicacies are sold. In back there is a tiny *osteria,* only five tables, where you can taste some of the best food in Modena. Reservations are a must (Tel: 059-22-25-33; closed Sundays, August, and December).

For the pleasure of walking in Modena, the more central your hotel, the better. (It should be noted that the Hotel Fini, on Modena's outskirts, is a completely separate establishment from the restaurant, which is in the middle of town.) A list of Italy's most beautiful hotels would have to include Modena's **Canalgrande**, set as it is in a former bishop's palace, its lobbies hung with Baroque portraits and sparkling with chandeliers, and its rooms overlooking the parterres of a small garden. There is a choice of simpler lodgings, in particular the **Roma**, right on the via Farini, and the **Libertà**.

In Castelvetro, 19 km (12 miles) south of Modena, you can dine at a hilltop castle at the aptly named **Al Castello** (piazza Roma 7; Tel: 059-79-02-76; closed Mondays, January, and one week in August), either outdoors on the pretty flower-decked terrace or inside in the lofty dining room. It is popular with families and young Modenese. *Fritto misto all'italiana* is a favorite—an assortment of fried foods that may include meats, zucchini, squash flowers, olives, potatoes, apple rings, and a creamy pudding, according to the season. In the front room, you can purchase the owner's homemade balsamic vinegar, which may be sampled drizzled on moist Parmigiano for an appetizer or over ripe strawberries (in season) for dessert.

Modena is the next city northwest of Bologna on the Via Emilia, a scarce 39 km (24 miles) away, a particularly pleasant town to stay in and far less expensive than Bologna. So if Bologna is packed because of one of its innumerable trade fairs, it can be visited from Modena quite easily.

Bologna

The capital of Emilia-Romagna and one of Italy's richest cities, Bologna was already celebrated in the Middle Ages—for its university. That same university still gives it a taste of youth that many a historic Italian town lacks. Its arcaded streets have remained wonderfully intact, all 21 miles of them. For urban conservation, Bologna is thought by many to be second only to Venice.

Luckily for visitors, not all of these leagues of arcaded thoroughfares have to be traversed. Walkers can easily manage the sights at the center of town by starting in the **piazza di Porta Ravegnana**, where the tallest landmarks of Bologna stand: the two medieval towers, **Due Torri**. From here, like

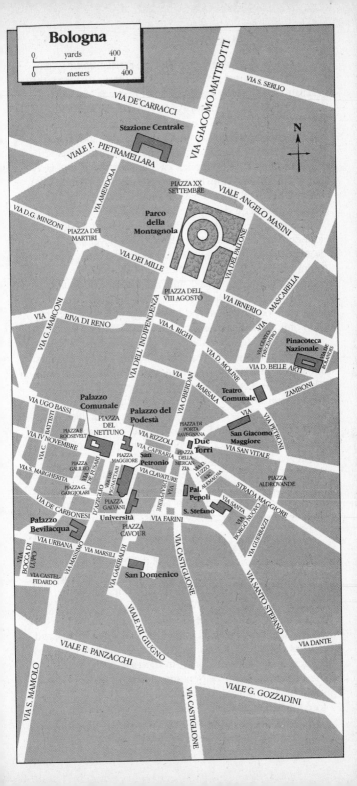

rays of a star in an older version of the Parisian *étoile* system, issue the streets that harbor most of the town's treasures: the **via San Vitale**, the **via Zamboni**, and the **strada Maggiore**.

You can follow the history of Bologna in the churches and palaces of these streets, beginning with the most ancient of all: the conglomeration of buildings that form the church of **Santo Stefano**. Bologna's San Petronio constructed this 12th-century church as a replica of the church of the Holy Sepulcher in Jerusalem; his version remains much more like the original than does the 19th-century hodgepodge of the actual sepulcher today.

By the time of Petronio, Bologna's university had been founded. It specialized in civil law (having developed from a Roman law school founded in A.D. 425), was modern to the point of having women teachers, and by the 13th century was attracting up to 10,000 students at a time from all over Europe. For this deluge of outsiders lodgings had to be created, food provided, and hostels opened, so the expansion of Bologna began as pure necessity. The town's arcaded streets served to leave the sidewalks open for commerce and discussion in any weather, while the center remained for traffic. Many of the students were by no means poor: Thomas à Becket was one, and later came many an English lord as well as the sons of Italian aristocrats. One of the latter was Ercole, the son of Isabella d'Este, who, like many, arrived to fill a rented house with his own furniture and paintings (with a mother who was the patron of Andrea Mantegna, one can imagine).

The 13th century also brought the wars between the papacy and the German emperor Frederick II. In Bologna, the papal, or Guelph, side won, and the emperor's son Enzo, already resident in Bologna, was taken prisoner and lodged—in luxury—in the palace on the **piazza Maggiore** that still bears his name. Then as now Bologna's central square, the piazza is the location of the Palazzo del Podestà, the Palazzo Comunale, and the basilica of **San Petronio**. The cathedral, planned to be larger than St. Peter's in Rome, was designed by Antonio di Vicenzo, who also provided the other major buildings of Gothic Bologna, including the Loggia dei Mercanti. Much of the piazza Maggiore is his, and here as elsewhere in town a certain medieval heaviness was lightened by later additions—in the case of the piazza, by the bronze fountain of Neptune, the work of the Flemish sculptor Jean Boulogne (Giambologna). It wasn't long before the Renaissance city began to take shape, with its colors of ocher, rose, and rust (from the terra-cotta trimmings); the copper domes of the churches lend a glow of sulphur green.

Bologna never remained for a long period under the dominion of any one family, unlike the Ferrara of the Estes or the Mantua of the Gonzagas. Here there were three important families: the Pepoli, the Visconti, and the Bentivoglio. These last, who intermarried with the Sforzas and modeled themselves on the Medici, were the most influential. Even they were so disliked that their palace was destroyed by a mob. It was situated across from their charming chapel in the church of **San Giacomo Maggiore** on the via Zamboni; the chapel's frescoes by Lorenzo Costa depict a day in the life of a Renaissance court.

During this period Bologna's artists were usually called in from elsewhere, the painters largely from Ferrara and the sculptors (Nicola Pisano, Jacopo della Quercia, and others) mainly from Tuscany. These artists turned the churches into veritable museums. Apart from San Giacomo, with its Bentivoglio chapel and oratory, there is **San Domenico** for Pisano and **San Petronio** for the sculptures over the doors and the paintings inside. One of the great pleasures of Bologna is the work of Nicolo dell'Arca. Inside the church of San Domenico one of his delicate angels flanks a robust early work of Michelangelo. His, too, is the bust of San Domenico in the sacristy. In the Pinacoteca (see below), his *Pietà* of life-size figures, raw with emotion, is on loan from its former home in Santa Maria della Vita. The finest palace of the Renaissance in Bologna is the **Palazzo Bevilacqua**, near San Domenico, where the Bentivoglios moved when their own palace burned down.

The quarrels of these reigning families and the communal government itself were to come to an abrupt end in 1506, when the papacy took over Bologna and ruled the town until the arrival of Napoléon. Here the reign of Rome was not to be as negligent as it was in Ferrara; a large portion of the city was given over to convents and monasteries. The popes had decided to make Bologna the Rome of the north, a decision concurrent with the beginning of the Counter-Reformation. Emperor Charles V already had been crowned here by the pope in 1530, and soon the Inquisition was to arrive. So did an era of prosperity, brought on by the production of silk and hemp in the city. A wave of Baroque architecture engulfed the city in churches and in palaces—which you must search out, because the arcades draw our attention instead to their courts, which regale us with splendor. Most palaces, such as the **Hercolani** and the **Pepoli Campogrande**, are on these same streets near the Due Torri; lovers of Baroque should get a list of the many others at the tourist office. The largest building of all was the Archiginnasio, built as the center of the **University of Bologna** behind San Petronio by the papacy. Its Anatomical Theater is splendidly preserved, with wooden benches for the students and a marble slab for the "subject" of the discourse. Baroque theater came later, introduced by Bologna's Bibbiena family, all ten of them, who were to construct theaters and settings for the courts of Europe and who left a gem in Bologna with their **Teatro Comunale**, on via Zamboni.

Most important of all here was Baroque painting: the school of Bologna started by the Carracci brothers and carried on by Guido Reni, Domenichino, and Il Guercino, among others. They—along with Correggio—were the Italian painters whose work the later visitors on the Grand Tour came to see, visitors such as Liszt, Goethe, Stendhal, Byron, and the Romantics. After a century of being shelved thanks to "modern" taste, these works are now featured in massive shows in London, New York, and of course in the very large **Pinacoteca Nazionale** on Bologna's via Zamboni. This gallery was founded by the city fathers in 1797 after the arrival of Napoléon and before the occupying forces could indulge in their favorite game of packing masterpieces and sending them back to the Louvre. The resulting museum gives a complete survey of Bolognese artists from the Gothic masters to the Baroque, as well as of the schools of Ferrara and of Giotto. The *Santa Cecilia* of Raphael, which sent many a 19th-century viewer into a swoon, remains the most famous picture here.

The French naturally moved the headquarters of the university from its Catholic cradle in the Archiginnasio into a building that had been used for physics and science. One of the later Bolognese graduates who studied there was the inventor Guglielmo Marconi. With the unification of Italy, the old city walls came down, Bologna's commerce expanded, and a period of bourgeois prosperity was ushered in. One of the chief things that these newly rich were interested in was food.

Bologna's smart shopping mall, the Galleria Cavour on via Massei, just off via Farini, shows off the household names of the fashion industry and also fine local craftsmen. One of the best of the latter is **La Selleria**, a store for quality handcrafted shoes and bags that don't need a label to affirm their worth (via Massei 2E). The horsey set, and those who enjoy that motif on clothes and accessories, will want to shop at **Ritz Saddler** and its branches **Ritzino** and **Ritzy** along via Farini. The **Swatch Store** on via D'Azeglio has hundreds of the latest designs of the eponymous wristwatch, suitable for collectors as well as those just looking for a new timepiece. A quaint hat store, the **Cappelleria Dante Barbetti** in via IV Novembre, has everything from classic Borsalino fedoras to children's wool caps and ladies' fashionable chapeaus.

Bologna has many fine bookstores. The **Feltrinelli** chain has several outlets around town; the one on the via Due Torri specializes in English and other foreign-language books. Don't leave Bologna without tasting the delicious chocolates from **Majani**, located at via de'Carbonesi 5B. The company, founded in 1796, makes creamy hazlenut and chocolate layers called *Fiat,* as well as dark chocolate sticks. After shopping you might want to stop at **Zanarini** in nearby piazza Galvani for refreshments at the lively bar or in its pretty tearoom in back.

For a foretaste of Bologna's table and to whet your appetite, there is nothing better than a stroll from the Due Torri to the streets surrounding the main market, the **Pescherie Vecchie**, and its satellites. There you can see *salumerie* without rival, their windows chockablock with the local mortadellas, salamis, and huge wheels of cheese from all over Emilia (note especially **Tamburini**, via Capraria 1). The pyramids of wild mushrooms, vegetables, and fresh fruit are worthy of any still life in the Pinacoteca. Nearby, **Paolo Atti** at via Drapperie 6 is famous for pasta, bread, and pastry. The **Aguzzeria del Cavallo**, a few shops down the same street, has a fascinating assortment of gadgets for riding, hunting, and fishing as well as for cooking. As for the restaurants, they are of such renown that they produce the same sort of "news" that flashes through Paris. On the high-priced end, the **Tre Frecce**, at strada Maggiore 19, is now considered one of Bologna's best restaurants. Housed in a medieval building, with thick-beamed walls and huge oil paintings in the dining room, the restaurant owes its laurels to owners Enzio and Annalisa Salsini (Tel: 051-23-12-00; closed Sunday evening, Mondays, and August).

Al Pappagallo (Tel: 051-23-28-07; piazza della Mercanzia 3/c), thanks to the Tre Frecce's owners, who are now the guiding lights, is again one of the most popular restaurants in town (closed Sundays and Monday lunch). The super-expensive **Notai** (via de' Pignattari 1; Tel: 051-22-86-94; closed Sundays) sits serenely elegant in its turn-of-the-century setting, while the somewhat less costly **Grassilli**, via del Luzzo 3, offers not only superb food but an additional treat for opera-lovers. Its walls are emblazoned with signed photos of its past clientele—Callas, Tebaldi, del Monaco, the names of some of them etched into brass plaques on the backs of the chairs they used to occupy—and a bust of Verdi presides over the main room (Tel: 051-22-29-61; closed Wednesdays and July 15 to August 15). In all of these restaurants the big three of Bolognese pasta are featured: tortellini, tagliatelli, and lasagna. When green (from being mixed with spinach), the last two are unbeatable. Pasta is treated in myriad ways; by no means do you have to stick to the local staple, *salsa Bolognese.* These pastas can be flavored with *funghi porcini* or topped, in season, with diced vegetables or sauces of green pepper *(pepe verde)* or cream *(panna).* Nor are you limited to the big three; gnocchi with a dressing of gorgonzola can be delicious, as are the Pappagallo's crêpes stuffed with *mortadella.* Of the main courses, the best known are the turkey breast *(tacchino)* or veal *costollete alla Bolognese,* richly cooked with grated Parmesan, butter, and sliced ham. Veal also turns up in *involtini* (veal birds) with mushrooms *(farcite)* or with truffles, sweetbreads, and chicken giblets (*in cassoto*).

Diana (via dell'Indipendenza 24; Tel: 051-23-13-02; closed Mondays and August) is a big, bustling, expensive trattoria that spills out onto the sidewalk during the warmer months. Under the green-and-white striped awnings you can enjoy classic Bolognese specialties. Ask for *bollito misto "magro"* (lean) if you prefer poultry and veal to the richer cuts of pork. Its homemade *crema* (custard) *gelato,* under a veil of warm dark chocolate sauce, is sensational; or in springtime you can end the meal on a lighter note with tiny, aromatic *fragoline di bosco* (wild strawberries).

At cozy **Da Silvio** (via San Petronio Vecchio 34 D; Tel: 051-22-65-57; closed Sundays), meals begin with a dazzling assortment of antipasti that vary with the seasons. Genial host Silvio Cavalieri personally waits on tables, bringing out bowls of homemade pickled artichokes and onions, several kinds of salads, and an irresistible mortadella pâté. The warm melted cheese with a topping of shaved mushrooms is a winter favorite. Pastas are excellent and there are several light main courses on the menu, including an arugula salad with sautéed *speck* (ham) and balsamic dressing. Save room for the procession of homemade desserts that follows, including a dense, moist chocolate cake and the *semi-freddo.*

Trattoria Re Enzo (via Riva di Reno 79; Tel: 051-23-48-03; closed Sundays and August; no credit cards accepted) is a moderate-to-expensive trattoria created by Enzo Coviello, a Neapolitan with an eye for winning combinations. The kitchen bows to the seasons, with traditional dishes with a modern twist, including *garganelli,* ribbed pasta quills in a zesty caponata sauce, and spinach pasta wrapped around tomino cheese. Classical music and animated crowds make for gracious dining.

In the suburbs of Bologna, north of the train station, the moderately expensive **Da Sandro al Navile** (via Sostegno 15; Tel: 051-634-31-00; closed Sundays, most of August, and a week at Christmas) is located on the banks of the Navile canal. The three dining rooms in this old farmhouse are set off with wood beams, and bottles and bric-a-brac adorn stuccoed walls, giving the place a rustic charm. The antipasto table will dazzle you, but it is the homemade pastas that draw the crowds. *Tortellacci verdi,* large green noodles stuffed with ricotta and porcini mushrooms, are divine. A good wine selection, too. And for dessert, try the *crema cotta* or *crema caramela,* both savory and rich. Next door is the restaurant's wine shop, worth a visit.

Cesari (via de' Carbonesi 9) is a relaxed and welcoming trattoria, where *cucina tipica* and *moderna* meet gracefully; don't miss the sweet dessert ravioli (Tel: 051-22-67-69).

There is no reason to precede a Rabelaisian meat dish with pasta; with a copious pasta dish you need only salad and dessert. Another escape route can be economical, too: lunch in a starred restaurant, but in the evening dine more simply with locals in a reliable trattoria such as **Leonida**, at vicolo Alemagna 2 (Tel: 051-23-97-42). To taste a variety of pasta dishes, take a short cab ride to **Da Angelo** at via Enrico Mattei 22 (Tel: 051-53-01-28; closed Sundays). Because of its young population, Bologna is great fun at night. Not all of the local *jeunesse* can afford the Pappagallo, and the trattorias are where the animation can be found.

Finish meals with a warming glass of smooth Vecchia Romagna, the classic Italian brandy made from trebbiano grapes. Vechia Romagna is produced in Bologna by Giovanni Buton & Co., and visits to the distillery, located just outside of Bologna, can be arranged for small groups; Tel: (051) 50-62-36.

Travellers interested in learning more about Italian cooking should consider the four- or seven-day courses offered by the **International Cooking School of Italian Food and Wine** located in Bologna. For information contact the owner, Mary Beth Clark, 300 East 33rd Street, Suite 10J, New York, New York 10016.

Of the hotels in the higher categories, the **Baglioni** is one of Italy's most exquisite. The comfortable home of Cardinal Lambertini during the 19th century, it was transformed into a hotel during the early 1900s. Closed for many years, it reopened in 1988, with its dazzling Carracci frescoes gracing the dining rooms. The next most appealing hotel is the **Internazionale**: It is old-fashioned in its decor and in its courteous service. On a small scale, but still with four stars, is the **Al Cappello Rosso**, on a pedestrian street a stone's throw from the piazza Maggiore, and thus convenient for sightseeing.

Of the smaller hotels, the **Corona d'Oro 1890** (but in a building dating from the 14th century) gets the gold crown, as its name implies. Freshly renovated—with Art Nouveau frescoes, feathery ferns, and a light atrium—this is one of Italy's prettiest. Two other hotels owned by the same management, the **Dei Commercianti** and the **Orologio**, have also been renovated but are more modern in appearance than the Corona d'Oro. All are centrally located.

The **Roma** is less expensive yet comfortable and the **Palace**, though somewhat tired-looking, is popular with businessmen and a good value. These last two have parking available, an important consideration if you are driving into this traffic-congested city.

Not far from Bologna is **Imola**, just 34 km (21 miles) southeast on route 9 (the Via Emilia), home of one of Italy's finest restaurants, **San Domenico**. Owner Gianni Morini is back after trying his hand at another San Domenico—in New York. That establishment is under separate ownership now, so Morini can once more devote his full attention to the original. Elegant yet inviting, this very expensive restaurant offers an elaborate tasting menu as well as à la carte choices of both traditional and creative recipes. A signature dish is the single giant raviolo stuffed with ricotta cheese and a soft-cooked egg yolk. When the raviolo is cut, the yolk breaks, blending with the truffled butter sauce. Tender gnocchi with a light vegetable sauce containing fava beans is also a good choice, as is the risotto topped with a concentrated veal broth. Duck breast is done in a peppery wine sauce with raisins. Desserts, like the pastry cornucopia filled with fresh fruit on a creamy sauce and the coconut and chocolate bombe, are beautifully presented. Wine-lovers will not want to leave without a visit to the cellar, although a meal at San Domenico is an excellent opportunity to sample some of the better local vintages, including those of Montericco–Pasolini Dall'Onda. The Pasolini winery, located just minutes away from the restaurant on via Montericco, produces a fine white Albana and a full-bodied Sangiovese di Romagna. (Via Sacchi 1; Tel: 0542-290-00; closed Mondays and August.)

On the way back to Bologna stop at the unusual medieval town of **Dozza**, where an art competition is held the second weekend in September in odd-numbered years. Artists come from all over Italy to paint the walls in brilliantly colored designs. At the town's summit is a castle that houses the **Enoteca Regionale** (wine library) of Emilia-Romagna, where wines may be tasted and purchased. On the first Sunday of June each year a wine festival is held and prizes are given for the most beautiful floral-decorated balconies.

Another dining temptation near Bologna is found at the castle-topped medieval town of **Brisighella**, about 13 km (8 miles) southeast of Imola. There you'll feast in a grotto restaurant that makes up part of the ground floor of the hotel **Gigiolè**. Pasta with rabbit sauce and game dishes as well as a handsome selection of vegetable dishes are specialties that lure Bolognese. Reserve ahead at the hotel and you'll see the morning mists unveil the enchanted town. Tiny alleys climb to the fortress on the hilltop, once the routes of mules bearing chalk to ceramics factories that supplied nearby Faenza, then the capital of porcelain production. All ceramics fanciers must go on to **Faenza**, about 13 km (8 miles) to the northeast, to see its exceptional museum of ceramics from early shards through Renaissance and contemporary splendor.

To the east the Adriatic beckons (or will, when its pollution problem is cleaned up). Go to **Cesenatico**, whose outdoor sailing ship museum is awash with multicolored sails as brilliant as any regal standards. Stay at the bright and modern hotel **Pino** in a garden near the port, or in any of the many pensioni that cater to summer beachgoers. Along the quai at the ship museum, dine at **Buca d'Amalfi**, where owner Stefano Bartolini prepares a clam and bean stew, seasoned with the sea air that enlivens this popular spot (corso Garibaldi 41; Tel: 0547-824-74).

Fans of both the architect Alberti and the painter Piero della Francesca will drive farther southeast to **Rimini**, at the very end of the Via Emilia, to see the **Tempio Malatestiano**, one of the great monuments of the Renaissance, a church glorifying Sigismondo Malatesta, who is buried within; and then perhaps dip down to Umbria. Others will take advantage of Bologna's rapid autostrada A 1 to head south over the Apennines to Florence and Tuscany.

Emilia-Romagna is favored with an excellent tourist office—a rarity in Italy. Write, call, or stop by in Bologna: APT, via Marconi 45; Tel: (051) 23-74-13.

GETTING AROUND

This region may be the best connected of all Italian regions. Most of the major cities are on train lines, with frequent service to one another. From Bologna there are many trains a day to Parma, Piacenza, Modena, Ferrara, Ravenna, and Rimini. The railroad is so thorough in its routing that buses are rarely necessary, except to visit the smallest towns.

Bologna is also well connected to Florence and Venice by train, and by air to all other Italian airports directly or with good continuing flight service. Alitalia's Volobus Bologna connects Bologna with Milan's Malpensa International Airport twice a morning. (Alitalia and the national airlines from London, Paris, Frankfurt, and Stuttgart offer regular service to Bologna.)

By highway Emilia-Romagna is on a direct line from Parma to Bologna and Rimini across the old Via Emilia, which is now approximated in part by route A 1, with clearly marked turnoffs for the western part of Emilia-Romagna.

ACCOMMODATIONS REFERENCE

The rates given below are projections for 1993; always check for up-to-date information before making reservations. Wide ranges may reflect the differences between low- and high-season rates. Unless otherwise indicated, the figures indicate the cost of a double room (per room, not per person). However, half-board (mezza pensione) rates, which include breakfast and one other meal per day, are per person. The service charge is included in the rate; inquire about tax and breakfast.

▸ **Annunziata.** Piazza Repubblica 5, 44100 **Ferrara.** Tel: (0532) 20-11-11; Fax: (0532) 20-32-33. ₤260,000.

▸ **Astra.** Viale Cavour 55, 44100 **Ferrara.** Tel: (0532) 20-60-88; Fax: (0532) 470-02. ₤260,000.

▸ **Baglioni.** Via dell'Indipendenza 8, 40121 **Bologna.** Tel: (051) 22-54-45; Fax: (051) 23-48-40. ₤490,000; half board ₤340,000.

▸ **Bisanzio.** Via Salara 30, 48100 **Ravenna.** Tel: (0544) 271-11; Fax: (0544) 325-39. ₤180,000.

▸ **Canalgrande.** Corso Canal Grande 6, 41100 **Modena.** Tel: (059) 21-71-60; Fax: (059) 22-16-74. ₤220,000; half board ₤190,000.

▸ **Al Cappello Rosso.** Via de' Fusari 9, 40123 **Bologna.** Tel: (051) 26-18-91; Fax: (051) 22-71-79. ₤330,000.

▸ **Centrale-Byron.** Via 4 Novembre 14, 48100 **Ravenna.** Tel: (0544) 222-25; Fax: (0544) 325-39. ₤95,000.

▶ **Dei Commercianti**. Via de' Pignattari 11, 40124 **Bologna**. Tel: (051) 23-30-52; Fax: (051) 22-47-33. Ł155,000.

▶ **Corona d'Oro 1890**. Via Oberdan 12, 40126 **Bologna**. Tel: (051) 23-64-56; Fax: (051) 26-26-79. Closed in August. Ł310,000.

▶ **I Due Foscari**. Piazza Carlo Rossi 15, 43011 **Busseto**. Tel: (0524) 923-37; Fax: (0524) 916-25. Ł110,000.

▶ **Gigiolè**. Piazza Carducci 5, 48013 **Brisighella**. Tel: (0546) 812-09. Closed in February. Ł52,000; half board Ł43,000.

▶ **Grand Hotel et de Milan**. Via Dante 1, 43039 **Salsomaggiore Terme**. Tel: (0524) 57-22-41; Fax: (0524) 57-38-84. Open April–November. Ł280,000.

▶ **Internazionale**. Via dell'Indipendenza 60, 40121 **Bologna**. Tel: (051) 24-55-44; Fax: (051) 24-95-44. Ł275,000.

▶ **Libertà**. Via Blasia 10, 41100 **Modena**. Tel: (059) 22-23-65; Fax: (059) 22-25-02. Ł100,000.

▶ **Orologio**. Via IV Novembre 10, 40123 **Bologna**. Tel: (051) 23-12-53; Fax: (051) 26-05-52. Ł155,000.

▶ **Palace Hotel**. Via Montegrappa 92, 40121 **Bologna**. Tel: (051) 23-74-42. Fax: (051) 22-06-89. Ł142,000.

▶ **Palace Hotel Maria Luigia**. Viale Mentana 140, 43100 **Parma**. Tel: (0521) 28-10-32; Fax: (0521) 23-11-26. Ł250,000.

▶ **Park Hotel Toscanini**. Viale Toscanini 4, 43100 **Parma**. Tel: (0521) 28-91-41. Ł200,000.

▶ **Pino**. Viale A. Garibaldi 7, 47042 **Cesenatico**. Tel: (0547) 806-45; Fax: (0547) 847-88. Ł120,000; half board Ł76,000.

▶ **Ripagrande**. Via Ripagrande 21, 44100 **Ferrara**. Tel: (0532) 76-52-50; Fax: (0532) 76-43-77. Ł255,000.

▶ **Ristorante Albergo Arnaldo**. Piazza XXIV Maggio 3, 42048 **Rubiera**. Tel: (0522) 62-124. Ł120,000.

▶ **Roma**. Via D'Azeglio 9, 40123 **Bologna**. Tel: (051) 22-63-22; Fax: (051) 23-99-09. Ł182,000.

▶ **Roma**. Via Farini 44, 41100 **Modena**. Tel: (059) 22-36-18; Fax: (059) 22-37-47. Ł100,000.

VENICE

By Paolo Lanapoppi

Paolo Lanapoppi, born and educated in Venice, was a professor of Italian literature and civilization at Cornell University, the City University of New York, and Vassar College for many years. He is now back in Venice as a travel writer for Travel & Leisure *and other magazines. His biography of Mozart's librettist Lorenzo da Ponte was published in France in 1991.*

The unique nature of Venice as a city has been acknowledged and celebrated since the very beginning of its existence. People were amazed: They had seen harbors and riverfronts and even small islands included in settlements, but a city rising in the middle of a lagoon, with water flowing between streets and squares, intruding in front of homes, churches, and shops—this seemed as weird 1,500 years ago as it seems today.

It would be wrong to believe that Venetians added to or took from the lagoon islands. The layout of the city was there from the very beginning: There was a large lagoon, well protected from the open sea, and in the middle of it there was a cluster of flat, barely emerging islands separated by canals; the canals were the result of tidal movements and of the action of freshwater streams flowing into the lagoon from the mainland. It was on top of those islands that the Venetians built their city (see below for building techniques). Even in the worst of storms the waves never rose higher than a couple of feet, while most of the time the water flowed quiet and clean (still in the beginning of our century, Marcel Proust marveled over the "splendid blue of the water").

One of those canals, the largest and deepest of all, ran through the clusters of islands as though it had been designed

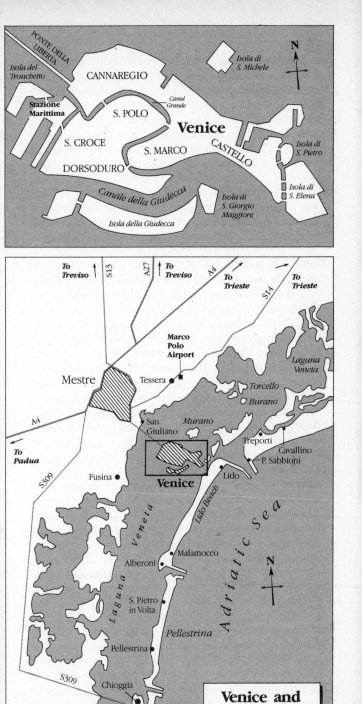

to touch on as many of them as possible. With its large, lazy curves it took two and a half miles to cover a straight distance of three-quarters of a mile. It was deep enough for the largest ships to navigate without danger. The richest merchants soon began to build their headquarters on its banks, so that vessels could load and unload the precious cargoes right under their own windows. The canal's banks became lined with elegant buildings that made its name famous all over Europe—Canal Grande.

This double communication network (streets for pedestrians, canals for passengers and merchandise) is as much in use today as it was in the early years of the city's life. Crates of Coca-Cola as well as construction materials and other goods are patiently loaded into large motorboats and skillfully navigated through the canals. As a result, the streets (usually called *calle*) are exclusively for us, the common pedestrians. Most European cities are now trying to recover this human dimension by excluding traffic from at least the oldest and most beautiful neighborhoods; by its very nature, Venice has always done so, and it may well represent our cities as they could be—or could have been.

The enormous wealth accumulated by the Venetians over the centuries put them in a position to decorate their houses and palaces, churches and squares, with the contributions of the best artists of various periods, although very little of importance has been added since the fall of the Republic in 1797. Yet the charm of the city does not depend exclusively on the major works of art and architecture. Many visitors, and most natives, prefer the so-called minor Venice, which consists of two-story homes along narrow canals with just a Gothic window here or a Byzantine bas-relief there to gently capture the attention of passersby. In these labyrinthine neighborhoods daily life goes on in relaxed, colorful ways, under the shade of imposing patrician palazzi and next to churches that contain priceless works of art. For a short stay, one of the following walks will give a very good feeling of Venice's atmosphere: The most highly recommended is Rialto–San Cassiano–San Polo–Frari, for the colorful life in the vegetable and fish markets as well as its charming bridges, streets, and squares very little known to tourists. The other is La Salute–San Gregorio–Accademia–Zattere, a "residential" neighborhood, quiet and charming.

So Venice is a place where a visitor can be duly impressed by magnificence, power, and wealth, yet it is also a city in which it is uniquely possible to stroll in total silence and isolation in front of a friendly body of water dotted by faraway cypresses and bell towers, or to sit on the steps of a lonely bridge and, yes, let a streak of romanticism surface for a while.

MAJOR INTEREST

Piazza San Marco: Basilica, Palazzo Ducale
The Canal Grande
The Gallerie dell'Accademia
Scuola di San Rocco (Tintoretto)
Scuola di San Giorgio degli Schiavoni (Carpaccio)
Ca' Rezzonico (Museum of the Venetian 18th Century)
Ca' d'Oro–Galleria Franchetti (Gothic palace and art collection)
Peggy Guggenheim Collection (contemporary art)
Island of Torcello (Veneto-Byzantine art)
Island of Murano (glass factories and the glass museum)
Island of Burano (lace)
Island of Lido (beaches)

From the fifth century on, Venice was built with an enormous display of military courage and business skill. The wars, first to conquer a vast empire, then to defend it (mostly against the Turks), were relentless and bloody; Venetians have been at war against every power in Europe—and on at least one occasion against a coalition of all of them. Meanwhile business was thriving; the Venetians are credited with inventing banks, income tax, and modern bookkeeping.

Have any of those qualities of persistence and competitiveness survived in the descendants of the city's fathers? To paraphrase a Venetian saying, too much water has flowed under the bridges since those glorious times. The character of contemporary Venetians has probably been shaped much more by the sad events that followed the loss of independence: French domination (1797–1815), Austrian domination (1815–1866), and finally reunion with the new kingdom of Italy as just one province among many. The change in times and in attitudes can easily be detected in the plays written by Carlo Goldoni in the second half of the 18th century: No more heroic figures, great admirals, and glorious battles—instead a world of merchants and bureaucrats with a clear premonition of impending doom. Goldoni's characters shine at best for their smiling wisdom tinged with cynicism, their constant self-irony, and their resigned acceptance of the world's ways.

This could also be called superior detachment, and it is in a way a civilized attitude. Venetians are fiercely but cynically attached to their past. They crowd the weekly lectures on Venetian art and history at Università Popolare, Ateneo Veneto, Venezia Viva, and other cultural clubs; many of them know, or think they know, their city stone by stone. But they remain ill at ease with the glorious past, as it clashes against a reality made of down-to-earth, unresolved problems; like the ruined offspring of ancient nobility, they have only a few old albums to show. The pendulum of history has swung hard for Venetians; they smile as they display the ancient glory, while present-day fatalism is the only protection they can afford—together with a subtle innuendo: Don't worry, they seem to be saying, it will swing for you too.

In the past 30 years the tourist boom has created a new breed of Venetians. They are the merchants and shopkeepers, often lured into Venice from the mainland, often not cultivated at all, and ready to exploit the thriving tourist trade. Cafés and restaurants, hotels and clothing shops are often run by this not-so-pleasant crowd. They make you think with regret of the courteous, even quixotic attitude of an antiques dealer quoted by Mary McCarthy in her 1961 book on Venice: "Eighteenth century?" she had asked him hopefully about a set of china on display. "No, nineteenth," he answered with firmness, showing off his expertise and losing the sale.

The Rise of the Republic

The unmistakable, fascinating Oriental look of the city is due to its geographically unlikely ties with Byzantium, capital of the eastern half of the Roman Empire. For many centuries after its founding, Venice seemed to ignore its immediate neighbors in Italy and Europe; its commercial, political, and military life was oriented toward the East, with resulting enormous influence on the arts.

From the time of its founding, Venice was a republic. Its citizens were as proud of their constitution as today's citizens of the United States are of their own. Even the founding of the city is credited not to one hero, as in most other cases, but to a group of equals. Their descendants, with proper and careful additions of new blood from time to time, continued to run it collegially for 1,300 years.

Official historians used to set the origin of Venice at the time of Attila, the cruel king of the Huns, who invaded Italy in A.D. 412, causing the population of the mainland to seek refuge in the lagoon islands. It has now been ascertained that at the time of the barbaric invasions a lagoon community was already established and functional; this is abundantly confirmed by archaeological material. The passage of invading populations just increased the importance of the existing community, both as a refuge and as a strategic stronghold for what was left of the Roman Empire.

With the collapse of Rome (A.D. 476), a few territories on the eastern coast of Italy, unconquered by the barbarians, remained attached to the Eastern Empire, which had its capital in Byzantium (Constantinople). Like Ravenna, the Venetian lagoon was one of these areas, and by the sixth century its inhabitants had formed a strong and well-organized community. They were formally under the protection and rule of Byzantium, and when Emperor Justinian decided to wage war against the Goths, who had conquered almost all the rest of Italy, they were in a position to offer very substantial help.

Cassiodorus, a scholar and prime minister at the service of the Goths, had words of high praise for the lagoon people: In a letter to their chieftains (537), he described in flattering terms their homes surrounded by water and their agile, maneuverable boats. In 551 those boats and the organization behind them were able to transport a Byzantine army of 25,000, successfully avoiding the Gothic armies that were ready to ambush them on the mainland.

Northern Italy was then conquered by the Lombards (seventh century), and yet again by Charlemagne, king of the Franks (end of the eighth century). In those war-ridden times the lagoon community was able to survive brilliantly by leaning mostly (but by no means exclusively) toward the Byzantine side. In 812 Pepin, the son of Charlemagne, officially acknowledged Byzantium's rule over the lagoon (and over southern Italy), in exchange for acceptance of his title of Holy Roman Emperor.

Until that time the chief islands of today's Venice were of little importance. Instead, the political and military center of the area was the island of **Torcello** (evidently a fortified town, as the name, derived from *torre* or *tour,* seems to indicate). And in Torcello the lagoon civilization of that period has left a few splendid monuments (discussed below).

The move to today's Venice took place in the eighth and ninth centuries, parallel with the increasing military power and wealth of the republic.

By the 12th century the importance of the lagoon community was widely acknowledged by Europeans. One episode, later exalted by state artists to the level of myth, underlined this in 1177: the meeting in Venice of the two great rivals in

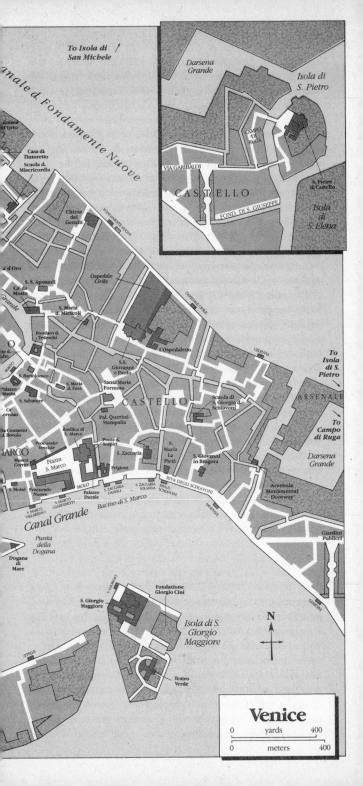

To Isola di
San Michele

Darsena
Grande

Isola di
S. Pietro

anale d Fondamente Nuove

donna
d'Orto

CAMPO
DI
RUGA

Casa di
Tintoretto
Scuola d.
Misericordia

Chiesa
dei
Gesuiti

VIA GARIBALDI

FONDAMENTE NUOVE

CASTELLO

S. Pietro
di Castello

FOND. DI S. GIUSEPPE

Isola
di
S. Elena

a'd'Oro

Ca'da
Mosto

S. S. Apostoli

Ospedale
Civile

rande

S. Maria
d. Miracoli

OSPEDALE CIVILE

To
Isola
di
S. Pietro

Fondaco d.
Tedeschi

L'Ospedaletto

CELESTIA

te d.
alvo

RIALTO

S. Bartolomeo

S. Maria
d. Fava

S.S. Giovanni
e Paolo

ARSENALE

Palazzo
Manin

S. Salvatore

Santa Maria
Formosa

Scuola di
S. Giorgio d.
Schiavoni

To
Campo
di Ruga

Ca
oredan

CASTELLO

a Contarini
d. Bovolo

Basilica di
S. Marco

Pal. Querini-
Stampalia

S.
Maria
La Pietà

S. Giovanni
in Bragora

Darsena
Grande

Procuratie
Vecchie

Ponte d.
Sospiri

S. Zaccaria

IARCO

Museo
Correr

Piazza
S. Marco

Prigioni

Arsenale
Monumental
Doorway

S. Molsè

Procuratie
Nuove

Palazzo
Ducale

MOLO

S. ZACCARIA
DANIELI

S. ZACCARIA
JOLANDA

RIVA DEGLI SCHIAVONI

S. MARCO
GIARDINETTI

RIVA D.
SCHIAVONI

ARSENALE

S. MARCO
VALLARESSO

Canal Grande

Bacino di S. Marco

Giardini
Pubblici

Punta
della
Dogana

GIARDINI

Dogana
di
Mare

S. Giorgio
Maggiore

Fondazione
Giorgio Cini

N

Isola di S.
Giorgio
Maggiore

S. GIORGIO

ZITELLE

Teatro
Verde

Venice

0	yards	400
0	meters	400

the fight for European supremacy, Pope Alexander III and Holy Roman Emperor Frederick I, called Barbarossa (the red-bearded). The reconciliation took place with a ceremony in the piazza San Marco, which had been enlarged by filling a canal that ran in front of the basilica.

A few years later the military and economic power of the community emerged in full strength with the Fourth Crusade (1202–1204): Venice obtained the contract for the transportation of all troops and materials to the Holy Land (4,500 horsemen, 9,000 squires, 20,000 infantrymen), and when the crusaders proved unable to pay the amount agreed upon, Doge Enrico Dandolo proposed that they work for Venice instead. There just happened to be a few coastal towns that didn't like the Venetian domination very much and needed to be taught a lesson. As those towns were just on the way to Jerusalem, the whole operation would require only a slight detour for the Christian armies. The crusaders agreed, but when the deed was accomplished the Venetians found other pretexts to keep these debtors busy in their favor and the whole enterprise turned into a war of conquest, climaxing with the siege and occupation of Byzantium itself.

Thus the old vassals conquered their former lords. The doge refused the title of emperor for himself or for other Venetians; the democratic tradition was already extremely strong in Venice, and primacy of one single family would not have been tolerated. He knew he had to answer to a group of solid, realistic merchants who were running the city's political life with an eye, or both eyes, to profit and security. In the final settlement with the crusaders, Venice obtained more than it had originally hoped for: large quarters in Byzantium, plus a maritime empire of cities and harbors on the eastern Adriatic and Greek coasts, enabling the city to secure its commercial ventures for centuries to come.

SAN MARCO

Entrance into Venice was carefully planned by the founding fathers of the city. It was, of course, by boat (the bridge over the lagoon was built in the 19th century, a controversial idea and a heavy price to pay for modern comfort), and not from the mainland side, but from the open sea. On those waters, beyond the frail, damlike islands of Lido and Pellestrina, the glory and wealth of the Republic had their base: the eastern coasts of the Adriatic, the Peloponnesus, Cyprus and Crete, plus countless harbors in the eastern Mediterranean—all under Venetian domination. From those exotic centers, ships would sail up the Adriatic to the narrow entrance of the Venetian lagoon; they would then raise their best flags, dress their sailors and officers in their most splendid uniforms, and be allowed through the narrow, heavily protected channel into the waters of the mother city.

Century after century, careful touches were added to the naturally grandiose stage setting. It was a matter of image, the importance of which had been discovered by this republic of merchants long before the advent of our public-relations wizards. As you sail in from the Lido (it can be done today by water bus), Venice's skyline is exactly what the ancient rulers wanted it to be. The lagoon waters are always quiet; often a slight mist veils the distant domes and bell towers, and the city seems to materialize out of the water. In the morning the sun rises beyond the visitor's shoulders and is caught and reflected by patches of gold finish: the angel on top of the **Campanile di San Marco**, the huge globe over the ancient Dogana di Mare (customhouse). In the evening it sets right in front, beyond the Baroque domes of La Salute and the Byzantine profile of the Basilica di San Marco.

Landing used to be on the **Molo**, the ancient waterfront built for this purpose just off the piazza San Marco. Even today the Molo is the best starting point for a tour of the area. The visitor is welcomed by two huge columns standing near the water. On top of the first is a statue of Saint Theodore, the ancient patron of the city who was dethroned by Saint Mark, while on the second is a puzzling animal with wings, a chimera, looted on some Eastern shore and still mysterious to scholars. (Etruscan? Persian? Chinese? The scholars who restored it in 1990 are still not sure. The prevalent feeling is that it was a Persian statue, looted in the East and later endowed with wings to make it look like Saint Mark's lion.) The two immense granite columns are booty of war as well (they were carried in by boat in 1170) and are just the first among countless precious objects shipped into the lagoon by the victorious fleet of the Republic—reminders that beyond the wealth, the power, and the beauty there lay war and conquest, cruel battles, and constant risk of life.

The area behind the Molo is called the **Piazzetta** (the small square). It seems magnificent enough, with the Palazzo Ducale on the right and the Renaissance building of the Libreria Marciana on the left, but as you walk through it, in the direction of the basilica with its gray-tiled domes, you see that the surprises are far from over. After the powerful shape of the campanile (bell tower), the view opens onto the piazza San Marco proper.

Piazza San Marco

Venetians often quote Napoléon as calling the piazza "the most elegant living room in Europe." He may indeed have said it, but the phrase is also attributed to Goethe, Byron, even Wagner, and is probably reinvented every year by dozens of tourists. It is pretty much impossible to say anything about Venice that hasn't been said by someone else; and the worst of it, as noted by Mary McCarthy in her book on Venice, is that nearly all these clichés are true.

But the piazza is indeed a living room. It may be less so during the tourist frenzy of the summer days, when the crowd is such that all perspectives get twisted, yet even in the summer it is enough to walk here after ten at night to find yourself in total agreement with Napoléon and company. This is, if anything, the prototype of stage settings, the Platonic Idea of them all.

A reference to Plato is not as arbitrary as it may seem. When the merchant fathers of the city decided that it was time to redesign the piazza as impressively as possible, they turned to the most acclaimed architects of their time. It was the height of the Italian Renaissance: The writings of Vitruvius had just been rediscovered and printed (in Venice, of course); Neoplatonic ideas had become fashionable among writers and figurative artists; the Venetian erudite Pietro Bembo had just written, in the quiet hills of Asolo, his treatise on love, inspired by Plato; Latin and Greek civilizations were the objects of endless study and painstaking philological attention. The general feeling was that a barbaric era was over and a new, refined civilization was just being born. The restructuring of the piazza became the subject of heated discussions in the parliament and the senate; we can say that no stone was laid without the patrician government studying it carefully from all angles.

The appointed architect was Jacopo Sansovino (1486–1570), a Tuscan who had worked in Rome with Michelangelo and Bramante. He was a great architect and a cunning self-promoter: For many decades until his death he was able to keep such rivals as Andrea Palladio out of the official commissions, so that Palladio had to limit himself to private villas on the mainland or, at most, ecclesiastical monuments in Venice (the church of San Giorgio Maggiore, for instance, which looks at Sansovino's piazzetta from across the Bacino di San Marco). Sansovino, Titian, and the Tuscan poet Pietro Aretino were a formidable trio in Venice at that time, close friends and undefeatable allies in obtaining or assigning every public project.

The piazza is probably at its best at night, when the ancient silence is not disturbed by too many tourists. Yet even in the middle of a summer day it remains an enchanted space. The wonder and admiration in the eyes of the colorful crowds; the relaxing, old-fashioned music played by three expert bands for the tourists sitting at the historic cafés; and, naturally, the total oblivion of the automotive world of the forsaken mainland, all contribute to a feeling of quiet ease. You almost forget that this space was designed to be the center of an efficient administration and the visible symbol of its wealth and power.

The Procuratie

The Procuratie are the two parallel buildings on the long sides of the piazza. They housed the government offices during the time of the Republic. (The *procuratori* were six magistrates high in the administration.) The building on the right (Procuratie Vecchie) was designed in 1500 by Mauro Codussi, one of the first architects to introduce the new Renaissance style in Gothic Venice; the one on the left (campanile side), Procuratie Nuove, is the work of Sansovino and his pupil Scamozzi (1586). The latter is definitely more imposing, in line with the grandiose ambitions of both architect and government. The side across from the basilica used to be closed by a small church, San Geminiano, until the French conquest. Napoléon's architects were invited to leave a visible mark of their presence, and they conceived the present structure, appropriately called Ala Napoleonica and today occupied by the **Museo Correr**, a collection of paintings and objects related to the history of Venice.

Three world-famous cafés open under the porticos of the Procuratie, each with tables outdoors and a small orchestra. The **Caffè Florian**, on the Procuratie Nuove, is the oldest café in town and is still decorated in the original 18th-century style. A pleasant surprise for visitors who don't particularly like "O Sole Mio" and "Love Is a Many-Splendored Thing": Inside Florian there is a small counter where you can sit, relax from too much walking, and enjoy refreshments at perfectly affordable prices (look for the counter, though; the prices jump dramatically if you sit in the lacquered rooms behind the windows).

Basilica di San Marco

"Nothing is sweeter to the human eye than the sight of gold," wrote Lorenzo Da Ponte, the Venetian-born author of three librettos for Mozart. The basilica is a triumphal monument to this precious metal. It shines on the mosaics of the façade, it reflects the sun from the four horses over the main door, it gleams mysteriously in the darkness of walls and domes inside. A strange atmosphere of mysticism and wealth receives visitors as they walk toward the central altar. It is a feeling totally different from that of any cathedral in the West.

Saint Mark, the apostle and evangelist, was said to have landed on the Venetian lagoon during his preaching years and to have converted the mainland communities, then under Roman domination. Venice had not been founded yet—its beginnings are set in the fifth century A.D. But when it later emerged as an international power, it needed a visible token of authority. The opportunity was offered in 828, when two Venetian sailors doing business in Egypt discovered that the saint's body was buried in Moslem Alexandria. They stole it, hiding the relic under a mass of salted pork (a taboo for the Arabs). On the right pillar next to the main altar, the scene is depicted vividly in mosaic: Against a huge sky of gold, the small vessel navigates with the precious body, while a caption reads, *"Kefir, kefir vociferantur"* ("Pork, pork they yell").

Over this relic the church grew in different stages. It was not the cathedral of Venice—that was San Pietro di Castello. It was at first only the private chapel of the doges, although it soon became the center of all important religious ceremonies. The present structure dates from the 12th century, and it is a strange mixture of different architectural styles, mostly Byzantine, Romanesque, and Gothic. The splendid floor, all in marble mosaics, was raised in the 12th century over the original level, to avoid submersion in case of flood. But nowadays that floor is again the lowest point in the whole city, and the first to be covered by high tides. This happens regularly many times a year, especially in November and December and again in February and March.

The basilica seems designed to embody, more than the Republic's religious feelings, its economic and military power. The four superb horses on the façade are booty of war, taken from Constantinople after the Fourth Crusade (they have recently been replaced with copies; the originals can be visited in a room off the basilica's main entrance). Most of the countless capitals, statues, bas-reliefs, and columns that adorn the basilica inside and out were carried over after victorious expeditions to the East—a rather strange way to pay homage to God. Among the large mosaics over the doors, only the central one represents a traditional religious scene (a 19th-century *Christ in Glory*), while the other four describe once again the legendary abduction of Saint Mark's body, the most interesting one being the first to the left (*Transportation of the Body,* 1260–1270), in which the basilica appears as it was at that time.

The floor plan has the shape of a Greek cross (all four arms equal in length), with one dome at the center and one in the middle of each arm. The interior mosaics, covering the top part of the church almost wall to wall, date from the 11th to the 16th century and anticipate the Venetian taste for rich, colorful decorations, while showing almost step by step the birth and development of a figurative style that originated in Byzantium and slowly acquired Romanesque, Gothic, and finally purely Venetian accents.

Some details of particular interest:

- Mosaics illustrating the Creation of Adam and Eve and other events from the book of Genesis in the entrance portico (13th century)
- Catwalks on inside galleries, which provide a closer look at the mosaics
- Iconostasis (separation between public space and altar), with 14th-century statues
- Pala d'Oro, an immense gold-plated altarpiece decorated on both sides, dating from the 10th to the 14th century
- Museo San Marco (same admission ticket as Pala d'Oro), in large part composed of precious objects carried over from Byzantium

For the visitor with extra time (a few hours or a few days), a close inspection of the mosaics with the help of a detailed description may turn out to be a memorable experience.

Palazzo Ducale

Next to the basilica, along the eastern side of the piazzetta with one wing facing the waterfront, the Palazzo Ducale is a miracle of Gothic engineering and one of the most famous buildings in the world. It typifies a feature of Venetian architecture: the predominance of open spaces on the fa-çades, especially in the low floors. This confers to Venetian palazzi their peculiar quality of lightness, emphasized in turn by the water environment and strongly contrasting with the stern, fortresslike aspect of so many buildings of the Florentine Renaissance.

The origin of this style lies not so much in an aesthetic

principle as in a set of circumstances. Only a rich Venetian, of course, could afford to build himself a palazzo, no matter how small; and every rich man in Venice owed his fortune to the sea trade. So the palazzi had to stand in front of a canal, possibly the Canal Grande, which was the largest of all; on the first floor the palazzo had to have space for the loading and unloading of merchandise from the owner's ships when they came in from their journeys. Hence the large first-floor porticoes, through which goods could be moved with relative ease. On the second floor, the residence of the owner and known as the *piano nobile,* a large balcony offered the double advantage of letting in floods of light and allowing constant surveillance of the operations.

A final element that made all this possible was the exceptional lack of family feuds within the Republic. While all other Italian cities were torn by civil wars between Guelphs and Ghibellines, the Venetian merchants were quietly counting their money; thanks to their much-admired constitution, nobody needed to fortify his residence against armed attacks by the neighbors.

Inside the Palazzo Ducale were the doge's apartments, the patrician parliament, and the government offices. It also included several prisons with different degrees of security, among them the famous *piombi* (the term refers to the lead-covered roof over the cells) from which Casanova escaped in 1756.

On the entrance next to the basilica, the **Porta della Carta** (1438–1443), once painted in blue and gold, is a masterwork of late Gothic architecture by Giovanni and Bartolomeo Bon, a father and son who adorned many palazzi and churches of Venice. The doge kneeling in front of the great lion is Francesco Foscari (1423–1457), one of the greatest rulers of Venice and the promoter of a new policy of expansion on the mainland. His predecessor, Tommaso Mocenigo, had warned the government against electing Francesco to succeed him. In a lucid and historically precious document he had listed the possessions of Venice, including ships, cash, and colonies, begging the patricians not to abandon the old ways in favor of involvement with European politics. But Foscari was elected, and some Venetians still believe that the roots of the Republic's decline are to be found in his leadership. In the courtyard, the façade facing the entrance is by Antonio Rizzo (1490).

The most impressive feature of this impressive building is the **Sala del Maggior Consiglio**, built in 1340 to be the largest hall in Europe without inside support, and redecorated after a fire in 1577. An entire wall is occupied by Jacopo Tintoretto's interpretation of Paradise, while one of the ovals on the ceiling contains the *Apotheosis of Venice,* one of Paolo Veronese's most acclaimed works. The standard tour of the palazzo includes a great number of halls, corridors, and stairs decorated with the most magnificent materials available and with paintings, mostly by Mannerists. The 1577 fire destroyed many works of art (remnants of Guariento's *Coronation of the Virgin,* which occupied the place of Tintoretto's *Paradise,* are conserved in the sala dell'Armamento), so that only a famous *Winged Lion of Saint Mark's* by Vittore Carpaccio and a *Pietà* by Giovanni Bellini are left from the preceding period (they are in two rooms off the sala del Maggior Consiglio). A ceiling by Veronese is in the sala del Consiglio dei Dieci.

The Merchant Patricians

The constitution of Venice was pretty much the backbone of the city's stability and success. It was studied and envied by political theorists (Machiavelli among them) for centuries, and it lasted unmodified until the fall of the Republic in 1797. (In the last 100 years before the fall, however, it was probably one of the main causes of the weakness that led to the end. The times had changed, but the patricians were unable to adjust.) The state was a democratic oligarchy, in the sense that within the ruling group democracy was jealously preserved, while the rest of the population was totally excluded from the political scene.

This ruling group, originally rather fluid, was defined precisely in 1297: All the families that were in it were allowed to stay, and no one else could join. They called themselves patricians (this was the only title of nobility allowed), and they formed the Maggior Consiglio (Greater Assembly), which met in the great hall at the Palazzo Ducale. The patricians formed 3 to 4 percent of the population; all the patrician males over 25 years of age sat in the Maggior Consiglio, for a total of 900 to 1,200 members. After the constitution of 1297, new families were allowed to enter the group only on rare occasions, mostly when a serious war was swallowing up the Republic's funds and new money was needed. The richest among the nonpatricians could then contribute to the war effort and be made patricians; this ensured a constant filling of the gap between ancient nobility and emerging bourgeoisie. The Maggior Consiglio elected from its own body the doge, the doge's counselors, including the later infamous Consiglio dei Dieci (Council of Ten), the senate, the judges, and all other magistrates.

To prevent consolidation of power in a few hands, all

periods of office were extremely short, ranging from six months to three years—only the doge was elected for life—and very few implied a salary. Civil service was considered a duty and an honor, and each family consigned at least one male member to a political career, supporting him with family funds (some posts, like the ambassadorships, required enormous expenditures).

Another 3 to 5 percent of the population enjoyed the title of *cittadini* (citizens). They had access to the bar and to the technical jobs in the administration and constituted a solid, expert, and faithful bureaucracy at the patricians' service.

The rest were the *popolani*. They had no political rights, but they were grouped in professional associations or corporations called *scuole* (schools), of which about 200 existed in town. As sponsors of buildings and paintings, the scuole were responsible for some of the greatest artworks in Venice; some of Carpaccio's and Tintoretto's best work was commissioned by them.

The government—that is, the patrician merchants themselves—used public funds to organize all important commercial expeditions and provide them with military protection. It was the Republic that built the ships in the huge Arsenale and rented them out to groups of patricians. The itineraries of the major yearly convoys were publicly established: They included Constantinople, Palestine, and Egypt to the east, and Gibraltar, France, and England to the west. Venice's organization was in effect an extremely smart corporation of merchants having at its disposal the resources of a whole state. When commercial success required the waging of wars, the state would provide funds and men; all aspects of the state's life, from education to justice to religion, were subordinate to the corporation's needs and especially to the final figures on its balance books—a real dream for some of our modern business conglomerates.

The Piazzetta

The area between the piazza San Marco and the lagoon goes by the name of the Piazzetta. Here the patricians—and only the patricians—could walk back and forth as they fixed alliances and discussed bills of law. They moved to the side that was in the sun or in the shade according to the time of year, and here the family members coming of age were officially introduced to the group, often with sumptuous ceremonies. It was Sansovino who redesigned all the architectural volumes, here as well as in the piazza. The side opposite the palazzo was rebuilt by Sansovino to host a precious collection of manuscripts bequeathed by Petrarch and later by Bessarion (1468); it still contains them and, as the **Biblioteca Marciana**, is today one of five national libraries in Italy. It is crowded with college students, while scholars from all over the world occupy the pleasant consultation rooms overlooking the back garden.

Today's Venice is a paradise for the historian and the art student. Besides the Marciana, they can work with great ease in the library of the Museo Correr, also in the piazza San Marco; in the **Palazzo Querini-Stampalia**, with its squeaking wood floors and large 17th-century canvases; amid Renaissance cloisters in the splendid art library of the **Fondazione Giorgio Cini** (see the section on the island of San Giorgio), aided by courteous assistants; in the music and opera library of the same foundation; in the theatrical studies library of the **Casa Goldoni**; in the uniquely rich **State Archives**; and in a number of smaller centers, including one for **Jewish studies** just off the campo del Ghetto.

Other Elements of the Piazza

The **Campanile** (bell tower) took its present shape in 1514. It collapsed in 1902 but was rebuilt exactly as it had been. The view from the top (open 9:30 A.M. to sunset, ascent by elevator) includes the whole city plus large stretches of the lagoon. The loggia at its base was built by Sansovino and includes four bronze statues and a terra-cotta group by him. The **Torre dell'Orologio** (clock tower) at one end of Procuratie Vecchie was designed by Mauro Codussi in 1496, and it is crowned by two large bronze Moors animated by a mechanism that makes them strike the hours on a bell (currently closed for restoration).

THE SESTIERI

Since time immemorial Venice has been divided into six districts called *sestieri,* three on each bank of the Canal Grande. The comb-shaped, six-tooth decoration on the front of all gondolas is supposed to refer to that division, while the lonely tooth on the comb's back stands for the separate island of Giudecca. The division into sestieri is still very much alive; all street numbers refer to the sestiere, starting with "1" in a more or less arbitrary location and winding through streets and squares to cover the whole sestiere. A house number in the thousands is therefore very common, and only the mail carrier knows where the corresponding door is to be found. The six sestieri are *San Marco, Castello,* and *Cannaregio* on the east bank of the Canal Grande and *San Polo, Santa Croce,* and *Dorsoduro* on the west bank.

Sestiere di San Marco

Strictly speaking, there is no separation between rich and poor neighborhoods in Venice. The patricians had their homes on the Canal Grande, which winds through the city, touching all neighborhoods. When that space was filled, other palazzi rose on important canals or along the major squares scattered throughout the city. Until recent times, the San Marco–Rialto bridge area was considered a very desirable place to live because it is central and monumental and because it contains the most offices and fancy shops. But today more and more Venetians prefer to live in other sestieri, away from the intense tourist traffic that often clogs the tiny streets in the center. Also, essential shops such as groceries and bakeries have tended to move out of San Marco because of the high rents, which only mask and souvenir shops now seem able to afford.

Mercerie. The main shopping alley is still called the **Mercerie**. It starts right under Codussi's Torre dell'Orologio in the piazza San Marco and winds lazily to meet the Canal Grande at the ponte di Rialto. Most of the houses in this part of town are 400 or 500 years old, and they have always been used as a display area by the Venice merchants. In the same little rooms where Oriental damasks and rare spices used to be sold, fancy modern windows today exhibit the best products of contemporary crafts, particularly in clothing: From Missoni to Armani to Krizia and Versace, all the great brand names are represented in Venice.

San Salvatore. Right off the end of the Mercerie, the splendid church of **San Salvatore**, its façade restored in 1990, is one of the first Renaissance buildings in Venice. It was planned and built in 1506 by architect Giorgio Spavento with a strictly mathematical scheme, based on a square of 15 by 15 feet, marked by a column on each corner and repeated vertically as well. It is a Neoplatonic attempt to achieve perfect proportions (Sansovino was to try the same effect on San Francesco della Vigna in Castello), and it remains a bit cold and distant, like most attempts to transpose metaphysics into objects (Brunelleschi did better in Florence).

Certainly not cold, on the other hand, is the *Annunciation* by Titian, behind the main altar. It is one of the last works by the great master (1566), and one in which he seemed to jump way ahead of his time in search of a technique that could be

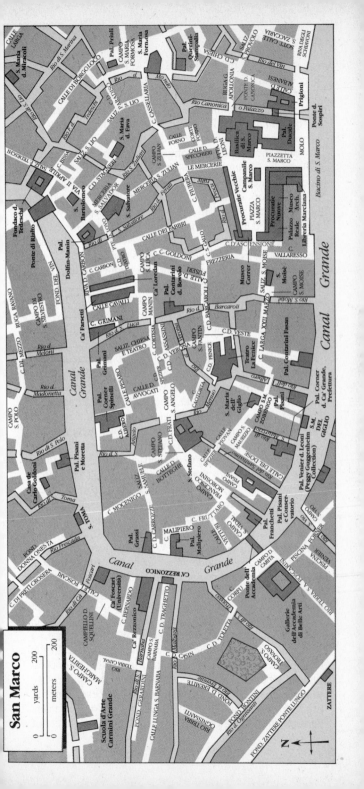

called impressionistic—or was he, as some historians suspect, too old to paint with his customary precision? "*Titianus fecit fecit*," he wrote on this painting, as though he intended to underline that what he had done, he had done intentionally.

Ponte di Rialto. The **ponte di Rialto**, which replaced a previous wooden drawbridge, was built in 1592 by Antonio da Ponte, the winner of a competition in which a project by Palladio had been rejected. Notice the sculpted Annunciation at each end of the bridge on the south side. The view from the top is magnificent. The whole area down the bridge on the San Polo side across from San Marco was reconstructed in the feverish second half of the 16th century, when the government of Venice was determined to dress up the city in the best Renaissance clothes available.

Santa Maria della Fava. Calle dei Stagneri, a tiny street parallel to the Mercerie and just before campo San Bartolomeo (a "campo" in Venice means a square), leads to a secluded church that hides two masterworks of 18th-century Venice. **Santa Maria della Fava** is the name of the church (in ancient times there was a pastry shop nearby where sweet beans, called *fave,* were sold), and the two paintings are *The Virgin with Saint Filippo Neri* by Giovanni Battista Piazzetta (1727) and *Saint Anne with the Virgin and Saint Joachim* by Tiepolo (1732). They both are among the best works by their creators, the young Tiepolo receiving Piazzetta's lessons and preparing to transform them into his own great visions. Organist Michele Fantini-Jesurum gives a concert of Baroque music here every Sunday to accompany the 10:30 A.M. mass.

San Moisè to Santo Stefano. From the piazza San Marco, the exit under the Ala Napoleonica leads to one of the busiest tourist circuits in town. Some of the best hotels of Venice are located in this neighborhood, close to the most monumental part of town. A street to the left, a few steps after the piazza's portico (calle Vallaresso), leads to **Harry's Bar**, on the Canal Grande across from the **Hotel Monaco**. Both places offer a welcome pause to the art viewer. Farther ahead, the modern façade of the Hotel Bauer Grünwald stands in embarrassed proximity to one of the weirdest products of the Venetian Baroque, the church of San Moisè.

San Moisè. As it was late in welcoming the Renaissance, so Venice only discovered the Baroque style when it had already triumphed in Rome and in quite a few other European capitals. The Venetians retained especially the impressive, spectacular aspects of the new style, purposely excluding the psychological unease so sharply present in the works of many Baroque artists elsewhere. The main Venetian architect of this period was Baldassarre Longhena (1598–1682; see his church of La Salute). In Venice, the architects of the Baroque churches often abandoned all pretense of mysticism (of which there was very little tradition anyway); they intended to create spectacular settings that often looked like theater props rather than religious monuments.

The church of **San Moisè** represents this trend at its climactic point. It was built in 1668 by Alessandro Tremignon, one of Longhena's rivals. Rather than religious symbols, this façade collects all kinds of decorative motifs; and rather than images of saints, it exhibits at its center the bust of the merchant/financier Vincenzo Fini, with those of two of his relatives over the side doors. This is a peculiarity of many Venetian churches, as is the habit of calling them by the names of Old Testament prophets.

Santa Maria del Giglio. Leaving San Moisè, cross two small bridges to reach the church of **Santa Maria del Giglio**, the façade of which was redone by Giuseppe Sardi (1683) and paid for with 30,000 ducats kindly offered by the Barbaro family. As a result, Captain Antonio Barbaro stands at the center, between the statues of Honor and Virtue, while four of his relatives look down at the passersby from huge niches at his sides. The plans of fortresses they had commanded are sculpted in bas-relief at the bottom of the façade. Walk west from the front of the church across the Rio di San Maurizio canal to the campo San Maurizio. After this campo, the next bridge offers a curious sight: Parallel to it, on the right-hand side, another bridge crosses the same canal. But it is not for pedestrians: It supports part of a gigantic church. Unwilling to limit the size of their ambitions just because of a canal, the friars of Santo Stefano simply ignored it and extended the church over it in the 15th century. Three large canvases by Tintoretto are preserved in the sacristy of the church.

Campo Santo Stefano. By this name Venetians know the campo Francesco Morosini—an official name that the population never picked up on. One of the largest in Venice, this campo is a busy but friendly crossroads. On the corner opposite the church's entrance, the **Caffè Paolin** is an important institution in town. Young and old Venetians meet here every evening before dinnertime and on Sunday mornings before lunch. They are grateful that, unlike the café across the square, Paolin has so far resisted the temptation to sell pizzas and salads at astronomical prices or to exhibit bright-colored umbrellas for shade. It is still a café for residents, and it serves delicious ice cream as well as (of course) "spritz"—white wine and seltzer with a touch of bitters and a lemon peel. Only after a few months of sharing spritzes does a Venetian's heart open up to friendship.

The Venice Conservatory. On the south end of campo Santo Stefano (the side toward the Canal Grande), a wide passageway opens onto campo Pisani. The large building dominating the campo is the conservatory of music in the **Palazzo Pisani**, built by Bartolomeo Manopola in the 17th century. In recent times it has been directed by well-known musicians such as Ermanno Wolf Ferrari and Francesco Malipiero. The musical traditions of Venice go back to the early Middle Ages, and the city soon achieved European fame, especially for the writing and performing of operas (a dozen opera theaters were active in the 18th century). The word "conservatory" actually originated in Naples, where it meant a place for the survival and education of abandoned children; these children were then prepared for musical careers. Venice had four such centers, called Ospitali, very famous in Europe for the quality of their musical performances. Among the great composers who worked in Venice were Adriaen Willaert, who moved here from his native Flanders and stayed until his death in 1562; Andrea and Giovanni Gabrieli (both Venetians, late 16th century); Claudio Monteverdi (from Cremona, but in Venice from 1613 to 1643); and Antonio Vivaldi (1675–1741). One of Italy's foremost contemporary composers, Luigi Nono, was a Venetian and lived near La Salute until his death in 1990.

Ponte dell'Accademia. Campo Santo Stefano is a crossroads because it is near the **ponte dell'Accademia**, one of three bridges on the Canal Grande. The wooden bridge was built in 1932 as a temporary structure to replace a hideous iron thing erected in 1854. But such is the feeling of awe for the city's appearance that no administration so far has dared approve of a replacement. When the bridge became unsafe in 1986 the administration decided just to reinforce it, leaving it as it was.

Palazzo Grassi. North of ponte dell'Accademia, in the area called San Samuele, Mr. Agnelli has played one of the most important cards in Fiat's image-building. He bought an impressive 18th-century palazzo on the Canal Grande, had it restored (one of the two architects was Tonci Foscari, descendant of Doge Francesco Foscari, and the other was Gae Aulenti, who also remodeled the Gare d'Orsay in Paris), and turned it into a center for cultural events. Immediately after its opening in 1985 with a show on Futurism, the **Palazzo Grassi** became a preferred rendezvous for visitors to Venice. Its exhibits, focused on art themes of general interest (Andy

Warhol, Leonardo da Vinci) or on broad archaeological themes (the Phoenicians, the Celts), attract over 2,000 people a day, more than any other museum in Venice.

The San Samuele Area. The area around the Palazzo Grassi is a very interesting hunting ground for shoppers in search of authentic Venetian artisans. Within a couple of hundred yards, from calle delle Botteghe (campo Santo Stefano, corner of Caffè Paolin) to the palazzo, there are some of the best wood-carvers in town (gilded frames, mirrors), an old-fashioned maker of marbled paper, and a wood sculptor who delights passersby with his works representing everyday objects with hyperrealistic precision and irresistible irony.

Campo Sant'Angelo. A calle along Santo Stefano's façade (calle dei Frati) leads to spacious, graceful **campo Sant'Angelo**. This offers a good opportunity to stop and muse about the freshwater supplies in ancient Venice.

Venice's urban structure is made up of small neighborhood units centered around large or small squares. In the middle of each campo or campiello one or more cisterns used to supply fresh water to the neighborhood. Since there is no fresh water available at reasonable depths, Venice's early inhabitants had to content themselves with rainwater. To that purpose, large cisterns 10 to 15 feet deep were dug in the middle of each campo and filled with river sand to act as a filter. A brick pipe at the center allowed water to be collected with buckets and pulleys. The visible part of the pipe (*vera da pozzo*) was often carved by the best craftsmen and was sometimes covered with bronze (as in the courtyard of the Palazzo Ducale). It is easy to recognize the square or rectangular shape of the cistern in every campo; it is marked by an inclination of the pavement that conveys the rainwater to special holes at the cistern's four corners (*gattoli*).

All patrician houses had their own private wells in the inner courtyards. The drinking water, however, rarely came from the wells. It was carried into the city by special boats and sold door-to-door. On the other hand, the wells could also serve other purposes: In 1716 one of those in campo Sant'Angelo yielded the body of a murdered woman.

La Fenice. Two narrow calli on the south side of campo Sant'Angelo lead to the nearby campo San Fantin, where the **Teatro La Fenice** has its main entrance. The sober Neoclassical façade of this theater, built in 1792, conceals one of the most elegant performing halls in the world. The Republic was enjoying its last years of independence when this ambitious project was realized by a group of patricians; the wealth and refinement of the decoration created an island of oblivion, a perfect place to savor the last pleasures offered by a dying century. The original interior was destroyed by fire in 1836 and immediately reconstructed—thus the theater lived up to its name (*fenice* means phoenix).

Scala del Bovolo. This is a curiosity much admired in this neighborhood (see the sign on campo Manin): an elegant staircase built in 1499 to permit external access to the top floors of the Palazzo Contarini del Bovolo (*bovolo* means snail, and the spiral shape of the staircase is clearly reminiscent of a snail shell and also of the Tower of Pisa).

Campo San Luca. Near La Fenice, campo San Luca is a meeting point for real-estate brokers, lawyers, and business consultants, all attracted by the delicious pastries and spritzes of **Rosa Salva Café.** The modern building on the campo— headquarters of a bank—bears a sign near the southeast corner reminding passersby that here were the printing presses of Aldo Manuzio, one of the first and greatest printers of all times. An unusually wide street (calle del Teatro) leads from this campo to the Rialto through the calle and ponte del Lovo. But first, turn west out of campo San Luca to a very tiny calle (calle del Carbon) that cuts through the buildings to the Canal Grande, one of the few points where it is possible to walk along its banks. Two handsome Byzantine palazzi adorn the canal at this level: Ca' Farsetti and Ca' Loredan, both of which now house city offices. (*Ca'* is an abbreviation for *casa,* and is most often followed by the name of the house's original owners.)

Ca' Farsetti and Ca' Loredan. Byzantine-style palazzi are among the most charming in Venice, and not only because they are the oldest. Even in their wealth they have a quality of simplicity and friendliness that is often absent from the architectural modes of the High Renaissance. The **Ca' Farsetti** and **Ca' Loredan** offer a good opportunity to identify the main features of this style: The arches are relatively narrow, characteristically elongated at the base, and set in long rows along the entire façade; between the arches are often inserted round decorations in carved stone representing stylized animals (*patere;* some splendid specimens are in the Basilica di San Marco, others on the façade of the Ca' da Mosto on the Canal Grande). A top floor has unfortunately been added to the Ca' Farsetti and Ca' Loredan, modifying their original elegance.

Byzantine-style buildings of minor size and importance are scattered throughout the whole town, and it is always a pleasant, endearing surprise to discover Byzantine details on a campo or a calle incorporated in later restoration or remodeling.

The Venetian Gothic. A look at the Canal Grande from the top of the ponte di Rialto is an unforgettable experience, both for visitors—who seem unable to get away from the bridge's rails—and for Venetians busily walking toward the vegetable and fish markets on the other side of the canal. The parade of façades on the canal's banks includes pretty much all the periods of Venice's history, with a slight predominance of Gothic elements (see the *vaporetto* tour of the canal, below).

The Gothic period—from the 13th to the 15th century—can well be called the first great building season in Venice. But the label of Gothic must be applied with particular care, since the Venetian version of that style has very little in common with the stern, often somber buildings that embodied the ideal of medieval mysticism. The first master builders to introduce the Gothic style in Venice arrived a long time after the great cathedrals had been conceived across the Alps, and by that time the style had evolved away from its original asceticism. The lagoon environment, the preexisting Byzantine look of the city, and the practical requirements imposed by the merchant patrons all further contributed to the creation of a very specific variety of Gothic in Venice. Even the two huge churches that most imposingly represent it here (Frari and Santi Giovanni e Paolo; see below) have kept nothing of the northern austerity.

Venetian Gothic immediately spread through the whole city, marking every corner of it with its unmistakable grace. The Byzantine principle of lightness of the façades was respected and at times carried to surprising extremes, while the pointed arch soon became a pretext for decoration, with effects approaching the look of embroidered stone. This process is documented in dozens of buildings along the Canal Grande.

The typical Gothic palazzo would have a waterfront with a portico for the usual loading purposes; on top of it there would be one or sometimes two floors for the owner's use. The large room just behind the Gothic balcony was normally a reception room, with doors leading to the offices and living quarters; very soon there also appeared an inner courtyard, often artistically planned to include a well and an open staircase.

Unaware, or rather, uninterested, in the building revolution brought forward by Renaissance architects in central Italy, the Venetians kept using their peculiar kind of Gothic until the end of the 15th century. Then the Renaissance exploded here too, in a conscious project of urban renovation (*renovatio urbis*, it was called) that was to serve as an exterior sign of the Republic's wealth and power—and found in Sansovino its greatest achiever.

Sestiere di Castello

This ancient and industrious sestiere has a totally different atmosphere from the San Marco–Rialto area to its west. The majority of the one-day tourists never walk its narrow streets, and very few of the national or international firms with offices in Venice choose this area—mostly because of its relative distance from the garages and the railway station.

Thus for the visitor Castello offers a new, unsuspected, and totally charming image of Venice. You can easily start from the piazza San Marco and walk east along riva degli Schiavoni toward the large public garden (Giardini Pubblici) that can be seen in the distance in the direction of the Lido. From May to September on even-numbered years, the garden turns into one of the most important art centers in the world when it hosts the **Biennale Internazionale d'Arte**—an exhibit of contemporary art in special pavilions built and decorated by the participating countries.

Ponte dei Sospiri and the Church of San Zaccaria. The first bridge after the Palazzo Ducale is the site of constant bottlenecks because of the view it offers of the famous **ponte dei Sospiri** (Bridge of Sighs), a passageway built in 1600 to join the Palazzo Ducale with the newly built prisons across the canal. After the next bridge, a portico leads to campo San Zaccaria. We are still in the monumental area of Venice; the church of **San Zaccaria**, built over a preexisting shrine at the end of the 15th century, is one of the most important religious buildings in town.

The creator of the façade was Mauro Codussi (1440–1504), an inspired architect who had moved to Venice from Bergamo, a city conquered by Venice in the 15th century. His work coincides with the abandonment of the old-fashioned Gothic style in favor of the new Renaissance principles inspired by Roman antiquity.

Codussi's typical façade was crowned by a central arch flanked by two half-arches corresponding to the inside naves. This principle, subsequently widely imitated in Venice, confers to Codussi's churches a grace that harmonizes with the Gothic environment (Venice is a city of curves, Florence of straight lines; or, as has been said so often, Venice is a feminine city, Florence a masculine one). The

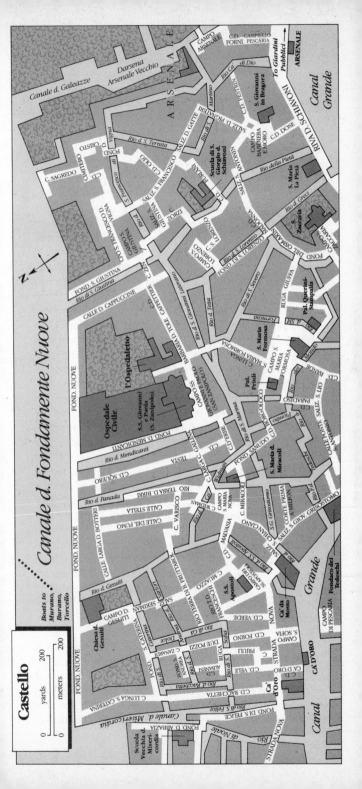

other great work by Codussi is the **Palazzo Vendramin Calergi** on the Canal Grande in Cannaregio; the last home of Richard Wagner, today it is the **Winter Casino** of Venice (in the summer, the Casino moves to the Lido).

Inside San Zaccaria a splendid painting by Giovanni Bellini—*Madonna with Child and Saints* (1505), on the second altar to the left—bears witness to the enormous ground covered by this Venetian master in abandoning previous Byzantine and Gothic techniques. A group of frescoes in the vault of the chapel of Saint Tarasius, attributed to Andrea del Castagno (1442), is thought to be one of the first examples of Renaissance art to arrive in Venice and to influence the Gothic- or Byzantine-oriented painters of that time. San Zaccaria was a crossroads of painting experiences: Paolo Uccello seems to have worked here next to del Castagno, while Antonio Vivarini was working at three old-fashioned polyptychs, also in the chapel of Saint Tarasius (1443).

Early Venetian Painting. In the fascinating years between 1450 and 1500 Venetian painters laid the foundations of an original school that was to climax with the great works of Titian, Veronese, and Tintoretto. Venice's **Gallerie dell' Accademia** contains in its first rooms a large collection of works by Byzantine- and Gothic-oriented masters, particularly Paolo and Lorenzo Veneziano, Michele Giambono, and Antonio Vivarini. These early masters seem to ignore not only the great lessons of Giotto, who painted in Padua in 1304–1306, but also those of Filippo Lippi, Donatello, and Paolo Uccello, who worked in Padua a century later. It was the Bellini family that opened Venetian painting to the Renaissance—first Jacopo Bellini, who kept close contacts with Padua (in 1433 his daughter married Andrea Mantegna), and then Jacopo's son Giovanni, one of the greatest painters in Venetian history.

With Giovanni Bellini (1430–1516) and his contemporary Cima da Conegliano (1459–1518), the Venetian School acquired the characteristics that were to distinguish it from the Florentine-Roman style: attention to color more than to line, to emotions more than to abstractions—little metaphysics and a lot of earthly interests, including the celebration of the families and deeds of Venetian history.

This attitude reflects the practical mind of the Venetians. It is also embodied in the parallel development of local architecture, which steered clear of pure abstractions and aimed at a balanced play between color, volume, and the lagoon environment. (Originally the exteriors of most of the rich palazzi were painted, sometimes by the best artists available;

Giorgione and Titian, for example, decorated the **Fondaco dei Tedeschi** near the Rialto.)

San Giovanni in Bragora. To see a fine work by Cima da Conegliano, it is necessary to take only a small detour. After walking back from the church of San Zaccaria to riva degli Schiavoni, take the street immediately after the church of La Pietà (see below) to enter campo San Giovanni in Bragora (also called campo Bandiera e Moro). On this very pleasant campo, where a charming Gothic building contains a small pensione (see the Accommodations section, below), the church of **San Giovanni in Bragora**—where Vivaldi was baptized—is decorated by one of the best paintings by Cima, the *Baptism of Christ* (1495), located over the main altar. For the first time in Venetian painting, Cima opened up the space behind the figures, letting more and more of his native landscape fill the background. (Other masterworks by Cima are at the Madonna dell'Orto and at Carmini.)

La Pietà. Back on the riva degli Schiavoni is the church of **La Pietà**—a fine specimen of 18th-century architecture. It was built to serve mainly as a concert hall for the famous orphaned girls of the nearby center for abandoned children—one of four similar institutions that taught music to the youth and were famous in Europe for the quality of their performances. Antonio Vivaldi composed and taught here, although he never saw the completed church, because he died—lonesome and poor in far-away Vienna—a few years before its consecration in 1760. Tiepolo painted the splendid ceiling (1755), and the whole church has an unusual oval plan, for acoustic reasons—another example of the Venetian primacy of spectacle over religion. The church was accurately restored in 1986.

The Arsenale and Minor Architecture in Castello. It may be time to leave the crowded streets of the tourist circuits and enter the labyrinths of the so-called minor Venice. From campo San Giovanni in Bragora it is not difficult—with the help of a map and by asking directions—to find your way through the back streets to the campo Arsenale, which is marked by a long crenellated wall and a triumphal door with two towers and four splendid stone lions.

The **Arsenale** was the large compound where Venice's ships were built—up to 16,000 persons could be employed at the same time, producing a ship a day in times of need. The Republic established the length of the working day, and it provided the workers with social assistance and housing (many of the homes in this area, some of which are four and five centuries old, were built for them).

The Arsenale's monumental entrance at the campo is the first Renaissance structure in Venice, built in 1460 and renovated after a great naval victory against the Turks (the Battle of Lepanto, 1571). The four lions were all taken from the East: The one standing alone at the left used to guard the entrance of Athens's Piraeus, and it carries a curious runic inscription dating from 1040 on its back (it had been given by an emperor to a group of Scandinavian sailors), while the one with the elongated body comes from Delos and goes back to the sixth century B.C.—a detail rather unimportant to the neighborhood children, who love to play on top of its comfortable back.

Today the Arsenale is semi-abandoned, although it is frequently the subject of heated discussion about its possible uses. Among the proposals have been a world's fair for the year 2000, a luxury marina, a university campus, and a new home for the Biennale.

From the campo Arsenale it is easy to find the wide **via Garibaldi**, planned by the French conquerors after 1797 according to a rather un-Venetian concept of what a boulevard should be. From via Garibaldi, a 15-minute walk through the depths of the sestiere leads to the church of **San Pietro di Castello**, one of the first churches in Venice and the city's cathedral until 1807 (see the inset on the Venice map). Most of the unpretentious homes in this neighborhood date back to the 14th, 15th, and 16th centuries; life here is quiet and pleasant, still centering around campi where everybody knows all his or her neighbors—down to the color of their bed sheets hanging out to dry as soon as a bit of sun appears in the sky.

On the way back from the former cathedral, a welcome rest can be enjoyed at informal cafés either in **campo di Ruga** (where there is also a restaurant, inexpensive and delightfully secluded) or in **campo Arsenale**, right in front of the monumental door. These are quiet places; at the Arsenale, too, you can choose between a café and a restaurant (**Da Paolo**; see the Dining section), both with outdoor tables.

You cannot leave this neighborhood without a visit to the Carpaccio works exhibited at the small **Scuola di San Giorgio degli Schiavoni**, five minutes west of the Arsenale.

Scuola di San Giorgio degli Schiavoni. The 15th century marks, as was said above, the entrance of Renaissance art onto the Venetian scene, and it also marks the beginning of a great tradition of social and civic paintings. In this community of merchants and diplomats, proud of their success and working hard to keep it going, the sense of the urban and social structure was as strong as the religious spirit in other places, often to the point of eclipsing it. Not only the state but more and more frequently the trade associations (*scuole*) began to commission buildings and paintings, and Carpaccio's work for the Scuola degli Schiavoni (1502–1508) is one of the first and more delightful cases of these new, more earthly interests (*Schiavoni* means Dalmatians, and Carpaccio was born in Dalmatia, although to a Venetian family). The subject of such paintings might well be religious, but the real intention was often transparently the glorification of the patrons.

Santa Maria Formosa. Another 15 minutes of labyrinthine wanderings will take you to the large and beautiful **campo Santa Maria Formosa**. (*Formosa* means shapely, and the word has a connotation of plumpness. Such was the image of the Virgin Mary that appeared to a bishop in the seventh century, ordering him to build a shrine here in her honor.) The church's façades (on the campo and on the canal) are embellished with the usual busts of the financing patricians. The remodeling of the interior was planned by Codussi. The buildings on the campo are a fruitful exercise field for the student of Venetian architecture: Down one of three parallel bridges behind the church is Ca' Malipiero (early 16th century, at number 5250), while on the campo, Palazzo Vitturi (number 5246) is a nice example of the passage between Byzantine and Gothic styles and Palazzo Priuli (number 5866) is full Renaissance (1580).

Calle del Paradiso. A few steps along the other canal bordering on the campo (Rio del Mondo) are the ponte del Paradiso and **calle del Paradiso**. This street is one of the best-preserved specimens of low-income housing from the 14th century. Gothic arches mark its entrance on both sides, and the purpose of those handsome wood beams over the ground floor (*barbacani*) was to enlarge the apartments without taking too much room from pedestrians while offering the shops that line both sides of the calle a bit of shelter from the rain. This may be a good opportunity to devote a few words to building techniques in this unique city.

The Building of a Lagoon City. It is often thought that Venice is built on piles stuck in the ground under the water, but that is not so. The reason many buildings rise straight up from the canals is that their façades were made to coincide with the borders of the preexisting islands on which they were standing. In some cases a passageway was left along the water; it was then reinforced and paved and took the name of *fondamenta* (as opposed to *calle,* which is a street *between* buildings). The sandy bottom of the islands was often not strong enough to support construction, especially in the case of churches or heavy palazzi. Therefore a special technique was required for laying and strengthening foundations in Venice.

1. The sandy bottom of the island was dug out to a depth of three to six feet.

2. Short, thick wooden poles were hammered in until they reached the next geological layer, which consists of clay mixed with sand. This layer is called *caranto* in Venice. It is stronger than the surface layer and here the Venetians were unexpectedly lucky: Rather than rotting the wood, it starts a process of mineralization that strengthens the poles forever.

3. On top of the poles a double raft of pine wood was laid, thus creating the first flat surface.

4. Over the pine raft were laid the large blocks of stone (imported from across the Adriatic and called *pietra d'Istria*) that would support the building's walls.

The number and disposition of wood poles varied with the nature of the ground and the weight of the building.

Sand and caranto are not as solid as rock—they move and adjust quite a lot—so the buildings had to remain elastic. This elasticity was achieved with the extensive use of wood in key places. Being experienced boatbuilders, the Venetian carpenters transferred to the land the skills they had acquired at sea, so that quite a few analogies can be found here between land buildings and ships, particularly in the roofs, which are often compared to upside-down hulls. Inside the brick walls the builders often inserted horizontal strips of wood, called *reme* (oars), that would alternate with layers of brick, permitting horizontal adjustment; wood lintels are still often seen over stone pillars, especially in shop entrances. This is the case with the ancient shops along both sides of calle del Paradiso.

The result of all this is that very rarely are straight lines or 90-degree angles seen in Venice. Inside homes, floors often lean heavily downward or upward, while walls and partitions have variously adjusted to the passage of the centuries. Most buildings shake heavily throughout if you take a little jump in a room; this is considered—and probably is—a good sign, since elasticity is a must to avoid collapse. The same principle, in a way, applied to the home and foreign policy of the Venetian state.

Campo Santi Giovanni e Paolo. From campo Santa Maria Formosa, on the side opposite the Paradiso, a small calle leads to another must in Castello, the glorious **campo Santi Giovanni e Paolo** (also called San Zanipolo; just follow the signs for the *ospedale*). Here are at least three landmarks worth visiting, so you might as well start with cappuccino and pastry at one of the oldest and least pretentious cafés in town, the *pasticceria* at number 6779, across from the side of the church. Its interior is exactly as it was a hundred or so years ago, and it seems that the owners have also remained the same: a mustachioed old man and his wife, the only ones in town to make a once-famous green pastry (*pastina al pistacchio*).

Thus encouraged, take a long look at the splendid monument in the middle of the canal-flanked square: The superb horse rider is Bartolomeo Colleoni, a mercenary captain who bequeathed a fortune in order to have a monument built in the piazza San Marco. The city fathers proceeded to pocket the money and place the statue in a less conspicuous setting, but they were considerate enough to entrust the commission to the great sculptor Verrocchio (1488), who created this masterwork, considered by many to be the best equestrian monument in the world.

The marbled façade bordering on the canal, now the entrance to the city hospital, is by Mauro Codussi, while the delicious trompe l'oeil in marble is by Tullio Lombardo. The building had been commissioned by one of the richest charitable associations in town, the Scuola Grande di San Marco, and was later united to a nearby monastery to form the city hospital. Entrance into the hospital is free, and it may be interesting to go and have a look at how medicine is practiced in this strange city: Two Renaissance cloisters are included in the compound, together with a couple of churches, a library and staircase by Longhena (1664), and countless other memorabilia; all this in the middle of noisy, sometimes frantic activity, not much cleanliness (dozens of cats wander around), and patients' relatives trying to find their difficult way in the labyrinth of alleys. Across a small body of water, the cypresses of the cemetery island of San Michele comment silently on the scene.

The gigantic edifice dominating the campo is the church of **Santi Giovanni e Paolo** (also called San Zanipolo), built by the Dominican friars in open competition with the Franciscans, who in the same years were planning the equally gigantic church of Frari in the sestiere of Santa Croce. Both churches date from the 14th century, and both are Gothic in style. But this is Gothic without the forest of pinnacles and gargoyles so frequent in the northern Gothic style (and abundantly present, for instance, in the Duomo of Milan). The façades and outside walls of both churches are made of uncovered brick, as though the builders wanted to emphasize their distaste for the great northern masters.

The interior contains an accumulation of priceless art treasures. You should see at least the funerary monument to Doge Pietro Mocenigo on the interior façade, to the right of the door (by Pietro Lombardo, 1476); an early polyptych by Giovanni Bellini on the second altar, right nave; the magnificent *Glory of Saint Dominic,* painted by Piazzetta in 1727 (San Domenico chapel, the last chapel on the right before the transept); Lorenzo Lotto's *Saint Antonino Pieruzzi* (right wing of the transept; this 1542 painting is one of the very few Lottos in Venice, where Titian unjustly eclipsed the glory of this rival); and the **Veronese paintings** in the ceiling of the Rosary Chapel off the left wing of the transept: *Annunciation, Nativity, Assumption.*

Santa Maria dei Miracoli. An additional walk of 300 yards from the bridge opposite the church's façade is well rewarded by a look at the fascinating little church of **Santa Maria dei Miracoli.** Inlaid with marble and flanking a canal on one side, this jewel of the Venetian Renaissance (technically in the sestiere of Cannaregio) was built in the 1480s and is a favorite wedding site for Venetians and foreigners alike. (On the opposite end of the wedding spectrum is the grandiose setting of La Salute.)

Getting married in Venice is not as hard as it may seem. Dozens of foreigners do it every year at Venice's city hall or in the Venetian churches. Among the pleasures involved is of course the gondola ride to the party after the ceremony. Gondoliers have special uniforms—and correspondingly special rates—for such occasions. Two gondoliers dressed in white and gold row on each gondola, amid the smiles and applause of the crowds standing on streets and bridges.

Sestiere di Cannaregio

Cannaregio is also a not-so-touristic sestiere, and it offers quite a few pleasant surprises to the visitor looking for a genuinely local atmosphere. It includes the entire northern part of Venice, on the left bank of the Canal Grande coming from the station, and is crossed lengthwise (parallel to the Canal Grande) by three long canals, each flanked by streets and lined with unpretentious homes. Very few tourists venture to walk along these canals, which are among the most handsome and romantic in town.

The Ca' d'Oro. A tour of Cannaregio may well start with this extraordinary palazzo, restored by the city administration and site of a pleasant museum called the **Galleria Franchetti** (public boat number 1, stop number 6, or a short walk from ponte di Rialto).

The **Ca' d'Oro** (c. 1450) is the most splendid achievement of the Venetian Gothic. Its elegant façade, almost an embroidery in stone, used to be covered in brilliant colors, with gold trimmings that gave the building its name (House of Gold). The best view of the façade is from the opposite bank of the canal, reachable by public gondola from the nearby campo Santa Sofia. The crossing costs 400 lire and is much used by Venetians going to shop at the fish and vegetable markets visible on the other bank. Both the crossing and an early morning browse in the colorful markets are highly recommended. In 1991, however, the Ca' d'Oro's façade was covered by scaffolding for restoration—it will probably stay covered and not visible through most of 1993.

The museum has been redecorated with great taste and remains open during the restoration. It would be worth a visit just for the view from the Gothic loggia at the *piano nobile,* but it also includes astonishing sculptures from the Veneto-Byzantine period, a delightful room devoted to early Tuscan painters, a famous *Saint Sebastian* by Mantegna, a Titian, a Van Dyck, and a collection of Renaissance bronzes and medals. The narrow calle along the Ca' d'Oro side leads to a street that is rather unusual for Venice. It is, extraordinarily, almost wide and almost straight, similar in this respect only to Castello's via Garibaldi. Called **strada Nova**, the street was opened in 1872 to serve as a quasi-direct link between the city's commercial center at Rialto and the then new railway station.

In 1846 the Austrian administration built (a first in Venice's history) a bridge on the lagoon, connecting the city to the mainland—a fact that changed the urban structure dramatically and that many Venetians still regret (more or less serious plans to destroy the bridge are introduced from time to time). This was followed by the construction of two extra bridges over the Canal Grande: ponte dell'Accademia in 1854 and Scalzi, near the new train station, in 1858. They were made of iron, like the future Eiffel Tower, and they cut across the canal with perfectly level spans (no arches but only a few steps at each end). Later administrations mercifully replaced them with less clashing structures; soon they became a vital part of the city, and they played a fundamental role in the new predominance of foot transportation over water transportation.

The strada Nova runs roughly parallel to the Canal Grande from the station to the Rialto area (acquiring various local names), and it has proved to be of capital importance in our own times to accommodate the streams of one-day tourists coming in from the mainland. It is certainly the quickest way

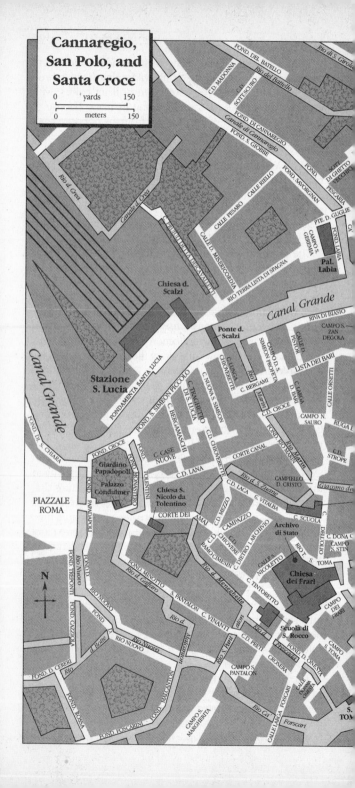

Cannaregio, San Polo, and Santa Croce

0   yards   150

0   meters   150

FOND. DEL BATELLO

Rio di S. Girola

Rio del Battello

FOND. DI CANNAREGIO

Canale di Cannaregio

FOND. S. GIOBBE

FOND.

SOTT.
DI GHETTO
VECCHIO

PESCARIA

C.D. MADONNA

SOTT. SCURO

CALLE RIELLO

FOND SAVORGNAN

CALLE PESARO

PTE. D. GUGLIE

FERMI DENTI DELLA FERROVIA

CALLE D. MISERICORDIA

RIO TERRA LISTA DI SPAGNA

CAMPO S.
GEREMIA

FOND. LABIA

CA

Pal.
Labia

Chiesa d.
Scalzi

Canal Grande

Rio d. Crea

Canale d. Crea

Ponte d.
Scalzi

RIVA DI BIASIO

CAMPO S. —
ZAN
DEGOLA

CALLE D.
PISTOR

Stazione
S. Lucia

FONDAMENTA SANTA LUCIA

FOND. S. SIMEON PICCOLO

C. LUNGA
CHIOVERETTE

C. TRAGHETTO
DI S. LUCIA

C. NUOVA S SIMEON

C. BERGAMI

RIO

CAMPO D. S.
SIMEON PROFETA

Canal Grande

FOND. DI S. CHIARA

FOND. CROCE

FOND.

C. CASE
NUOVE

C. BERGAMASCHI

C.D. CHIOVERETTE

MAFFI

LISTA DEI BARI

CALLE LARGA
D. BARI

C.D. CROCE

CALLE ORSETTI

CAMPO N.
SAURO

RUGA L

Giardino
Papadopoli

FOND.
PAPADOPOLI

FOND.
MONASTERIO

FOND.
TOLENTINI

Chiesa S.
Nicolo da
Tolentino

Palazzo
Condulmer

C.D. LANA

CORTE CANAL

Rio d. S. Zuane

FOND. RIO MARIN

Rio d. Marin

C.D.
STROPE

CAMPIELLO
D. CRISTO

Giacomo de

PIAZZALE
ROMA

FOND. PAPADOPOLI

RIO NUOVO

Rio Nuovo

FOND. D.

CORTE DEI
AMAI

C.D. MEZZO

C.D. LACA

CAMPAZZO

G. VITALBA

C. SCUOLA

C. DONA C

CAMPO
S. STIN

Rio d. Gaffaro

FOND. MINOTTO

S. PANTALON

C. VINANTI

C.D. CHIOVERE

RAMO CIMESIN

C. DIETRO L'ARCHIVIO

CALLE S.
NICOLETTO

RIO T. S. TOMA

Archivio
di Stato

DEL ROTO

C. DONA C

C. TINTORETTO

Chiesa
dei Frari

CAMPO
DEI
FRARI

N

FOND. TREPONTI

FOND. CAZZIOLA

Rio d. Tolletti

RIO NUOVO

Rio Nuovo

Rio d. Malcanton

Talon

RIO d. Manzuchetto

RIO d.

C. Talon

C.D. PRETI

CROSERA

Scuola di
S. Rocco

FOND. D ONESTA

CAMPO
S. TOMA

S.
TOM

FOND. D. CERERI

RIO d. Malcanton

FOND. MALCANTON

RIO Ca'

Rio Ca'

Forscari

CAMPO S.
PANTALON

CALLE LARGA FOSCARI

CALLE
SCUOLA
ONESTA

FOND. ROSSA

FOND. FOSCARINI

CAMPO S.
MARGHERITA

Forscari

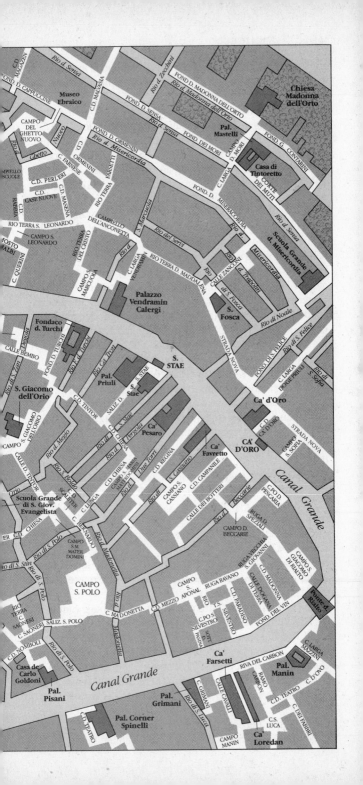

to reach the city's center, and it is not without its interesting, very Venetian stretches; but for less hurried and more knowledgeable visitors it is not the best itinerary.

Misericordia and Rio della Sensa. Cross through the busy strada and enter one of the calli on the other side of the Ca' d'Oro, and you will soon be in front of a huge brick building on the Canale della Misericordia. The **Scuola Grande della Misericordia** was planned by Sansovino to host one of the largest and most ambitious scuole in Venice; construction was never completed, and today the interesting interior is occupied by a basketball association, which has transformed it into a playing court. After following the side of the scuola to the first bridge, turn left to the delightfully quiet **rio della Sensa.** Following rio della Sensa, even at the cost of abandoning it for a few yards at corte dei Muti to find it immediately at your left, you will run into the quiet **campo dei Mori:** Four Eastern merchants, traditionally called the Moors, lived here in the 12th century, and their odd statues still decorate the campo's walls (only three are in the campo; the fourth is on the nearby *fondamenta* at number 3399 and next door to the house where Tintoretto used to live). The Moors—or their descendants—lived in Palazzo Mastelli on the canal on the other side of the campo (rio della Madonna dell'Orto), and they decorated the palazzo's façade with an amusing stone panel representing the source of their wealth: a camel well burdened with merchandise. Along this canal a great masterwork awaits the visitor: the church of **the Madonna dell'Orto.**

Madonna dell'Orto. The great Gothic façade, adorned with a double row of niches, was built in the 15th century. The church is very handsome in itself, but it also contains some extraordinary paintings. One of the best works of Cima da Conegliano is on an altar on the right side near the entrance (*Saint John the Baptist,* with a delightful landscape), and a *Madonna and Child* by Giovanni Bellini, one of the most intense and delicate painted by the master, is in the first chapel in the left nave.

The glories of this church, however, are the huge canvases by Tintoretto that adorn the main apse and one altar at its right. The latter is the *Presentation of the Virgin Mary;* on the left side of the apse, Tintoretto painted the *Adoration of the Golden Calf,* and on the side opposite, the *Last Judgment.*

Fondamenta degli Ormesini. There are two reasons to reach this *fondamenta* (second canal parallel to Madonna dell'Orto, on the south side) at sunset: One is the golden light that fills the street—with its small rowboats tied at the canal's banks—when the sky turns red, and the other is that there are two good restaurants along it. The first is an old wine shop, informal and inexpensive but genuine in quality (**All'Antica Mola**—see the name on the lantern outside); the other, far ahead after the iron bridge, is called **Il Bacco**. It offers a more refined cuisine, and the decor is the prototype for many Venetian imitations: wooden tables, no linen, but clean and efficient.

The Ghetto. Just down that iron bridge, the spacious **campo del Ghetto Nuovo** is the center of the tiny island (the contours are clearly visible) to which the Jewish community was relegated in 1516. This campo was called the Ghetto before their arrival, and it gave its name to all the ghettos in the world. Because they were obliged to stay within the confines of the island, the inhabitants could only build up, not out, and as a result the buildings here are among the tallest in Venice, reaching up to seven stories; their ceilings are unusually low. Of the five synagogues corresponding to the different nationalities and rites of the resident Jews, the most interesting ones are in the campiello delle Scuole (200 yards southwest of the main campo): the **Scuola Spagnola** (Spanish), rebuilt in 1635 probably by Longhena, and the **Scuola Levantina** (1538, with a later façade also by Longhena). Their interiors are splendidly decorated and definitely worth a visit. Also in the campo del Ghetto Nuovo are the other three synagogues and a **Jewish Museum** (Venetian Jewish art). The museum (Museo Ebraico) offers guided tours of the synagogues every hour.

In the centuries that followed the establishment of the Ghetto Nuovo, the Jewish residents of Venice were obliged to keep their three pawnshops open for the population in need of cash (which often included ruined members of noble families). The rate of interest was fixed by the city government (5 percent) and was totally insufficient to cover expenses. All of the Jewish communities of the mainland, and often those abroad as well, had to contribute financially to the operation—a condition for keeping the Jews in Venice—until the community was forced to declare bankruptcy in 1735. It then turned out that the Jews owed a great deal of money to the nobility of Venice. Contemporary historians agree that with the institution of these pawnshops the shrewd city fathers had found a way to make some money, exploiting the foreign community and letting the blame for moneylending fall entirely on someone else.

Fondamente Nuove. This long stretch of lagoon-side walk north of the hospital (see the Castello map) was built in the 16th century to define and strengthen the northern border of the city. The **fondamente Nuove** is very quiet, except for the small area where the public boats for Murano, Torcello, and other islands land and depart. It offers a wide view over the lagoon and the mainland, and on clear winter days the snow-capped mountains of the Veneto are perfectly visible. A walk on the fondamente can be a very romantic experience, particularly at sunset or at night, when the street is totally silent. The church of **Gesuiti**, easily identifiable because of its monumental Baroque façade, is famous for its marbled interior and contains a great Titian, *The Martyrdom of Saint Lawrence*.

The association of Cannaregio hotelkeepers has sponsored the publication of a small but detailed and intelligent guidebook to this sestiere; it is distributed free of charge by the concierges of Cannaregio hotels.

The Sestieri di San Polo
and Santa Croce

These two neighboring sestieri occupy the territory behind the right bank of the Canal Grande, from Piazzale Roma (parking lots) to the large curve before ponte dell'Accademia. They include some of the most charming canals and streets in Venice. A tour should start at ponte di Rialto with a walk through the vegetable market just down its steps. Farther along, the morning fish market is very active in this city where fish has always been the basic staple in any menu (closed Sundays and Mondays).

Unfortunately the lagoon is partly polluted, while the northern Adriatic has been heavily overfished and yields almost no catch anymore. Today, 80 percent of the fish marketed in Venice comes from other parts of Italy (mostly Sicily) or from abroad. Local species are limited to clams and mussels; a kind of bass called *cefalo;* very small quantities of *orate* (a delicious snapper) and *branzini* (sea bass) that sell at astronomical prices; and, in season, squid and cuttlefish. See the Dining section below for more details.

Campo San Polo. The usual maze of small *calli,* very busy with Venetians mostly shopping for food, takes you to the large and pleasant **campo San Polo**, a preferred playground for children and meeting place for their mothers at all times of the year. One of the possible ways to reach it is by walking northwest from the Rialto bridge to campo San Cassiano; you will see the colorful vegetable market around campo San Giacomo di Rialto and the fish market on campo della Pescaria. From San Cassiano walk west to the small and delightful campo Santa Maria Mater Domini, with its beautiful 13th- and 14th-century homes, both Byzantine and Gothic, then south through calle Bernardo to campo San Polo. This way you will have visited one of the most charming neighborhoods in Venice, very little known to the average tourist. A great and inexpensive place for lunch is the **Osteria Al Nono Risorto**, down the bridge from San Cassiano (see Dining). From campo San Polo it is only a short walk to the church of **Frari**.

Frari and 16th-Century Venetian Painting. The name *Frari* means friars, and this enormous church is the Franciscan response to the Dominican Santi Giovanni e Paolo. It was built in the 14th century over an existing shrine of more moderate size, which was kept functioning while the architects were surrounding it with the new structure. Like its rival church, the Frari is a world unto itself and would take days to explore, so it is necessary to be selective.

The greatest masterworks here are two paintings by Titian. Over the main altar his *Assumption* (1518) marks the first high point in a long and glorious career. Titian seems to have understood and magnified a concept of art that can be called typically Venetian: great emphasis on color; open exaltation of life as a positive, exciting adventure; and faith in the basic soundness of the social environment. The same elements can be found in the work of Paolo Veronese (1530–1588), although in his paintings we detect less of the sense of exciting discovery and more of a feeling of official, somehow artificial celebration.

On a left-side altar, before the transept, is another great work by Titian, the *Madonna Pesaro*. The two columns in the painting may be a perspective continuation of the church's columns as you approach the painting from the main door.

In May 1992, a great wooden crucifix was placed at the right side of the main altar. It had been abandoned in a sacristy until an art historian discovered that under the visible mediocre layer of 17th-century paint there lay a precious masterwork. Once restored, it turned out to be the work of a central Italian painter of the 13th century, and the oldest painting on wood existing in Venice.

Titian is buried in this church; the monument was sculpted in 1836 and is located on the right aisle next to the door. On the sacristy's altar (off the right wing of the transept) is a splendid *Madonna and Child* by Bellini (1488). Two small chapels away there is a wood *Baptist* by Donatello (1453). Finally, have a look at the monument to Antonio

Canova (left nave, toward the back), realized in 1827 by followers of the great Neoclassical sculptor from plans he had prepared for a monument to Titian.

Scuola di San Rocco and Tintoretto. A few steps away from the church's back, the members of the wealthy Scuola di San Rocco—one of many charitable associations—had a sumptuous Renaissance building, also known as the **Scuola di San Rocco**, erected for their meetings. They decided to commit the decoration of the interior to Jacopo Tintoretto (1518–1594), who painted some of his best canvases for this purpose. He created complex, intense, and often gigantic perspectives in which he played with light and surfaces with a strong foreboding of the new restlessness that was to characterize the European arts in the 17th century. Among the most successful canvases are the *Crucifixion, Christ before Pilate,* and *Christ Carrying the Cross.*

San Giovanni Evangelista and Rio Marin. A left turn down the bridge in front of the Frari façade will bring you to the nearby compound of the **Scuola Grande di San Giovanni Evangelista**. The very long building at the bridge's left contains the immense state archives, a wonderful mine of documents related to Venice's government and history. A few steps after the archives, the 1481 scuola deserves a look, at least from the outside, which was designed to impress the passersby.

The interior shines with a splendid staircase by Codussi; the paintings that once decorated the hall—a great cycle by Gentile Bellini and Carpaccio narrating the Miracles of the True Cross—are now in the Gallerie dell'Accademia. The scuola was believed to own a piece of wood from Christ's cross. The delightful canal near the scuola is called **rio Marin**. Here Henry James set the scene for *The Aspern Papers,* one of his many novels having to do with Venice. At the beginning of the rio, the **Caffè Orientale** is one of the best restaurants in Venice. It has a small terrace on the rio, and an early reservation may obtain you one of those coveted tables (see Dining, below).

San Giacomo dell'Orio. Across the rio Marin and down a calle or two, you reach a very old center of Venetian life, the church of **San Giacomo dell'Orio**. The area is still quiet and not well known to tourists. The church has at least three entrances because of modifications made during the 1,100 years of its existence. In the stunning interior, the play of wood beams that support the vault is one of many examples of shipbuilding carpentry transferred to ecclesiastical architecture. A particularly fascinating sight is the large painted crucifix by Paolo Veneziano (c. 1350), restored in 1988.

Campo San Zan Degolá. This name is the Venetian rendering of San Giovanni Decollato (Saint John the Beheaded). It is definitely worth taking the short walk north from San Giacomo dell'Orio to this quiet campo, with its 11th-century church (remodeled more than once) and its unpretentious old homes creating one of those enchanted environments so typical of Venice.

Sestiere di Dorsoduro

This is one of the largest sestieri and possibly the most charming. It occupies the southern and western part of town on the west bank of the Canal Grande, from Piazzale Roma all the way to La Salute, with a long stretch on the Canal Grande itself.

La Salute and Venetian Painting in the 17th Century. The extraordinary church of **La Salute**, a small distance across the water from the San Marco area, was designed by Baldassarre Longhena and built between 1632 and 1682. By that time architectural thinking had progressed to consider buildings not only for themselves, but in relation to the space they were destined to occupy. The Baroque feeling for scenographic setting plays an important role in the conception of this gigantic church, which marks the entrance to the Canal Grande across from San Marco. It was in this body of water that trading ships would stop and be moored, waiting for customs or for more commissions, as Canaletto's paintings abundantly confirm.

The church was built as a thanksgiving to the Virgin Mary after a terrible plague in 1630. That event is still celebrated by Venetians with astonishing devotion every November 21; they take advantage of a temporary bridge built over the Canal Grande at Santa Maria del Giglio. The November fogs, the lack of tourists at that time of the year, and the presence of children, candle vendors, and simple food stands—all these make the **Festa della Salute** the most intimate and cherished among Venetian traditions.

Inside La Salute, three altarpieces (the first three altars at the right of the main door) by Luca Giordano offer a good idea of Venetian painting in the 17th century.

The great masters of the Venetian Renaissance and Mannerism were not followed by personalities of comparable impact. Jacopo Palma il Giovane (1544–1628), for example, was a virtuoso of the brush but hardly an original painter. He was, however, greatly appreciated here, and he left canvases in just about every important building, including the Palazzo Ducale.

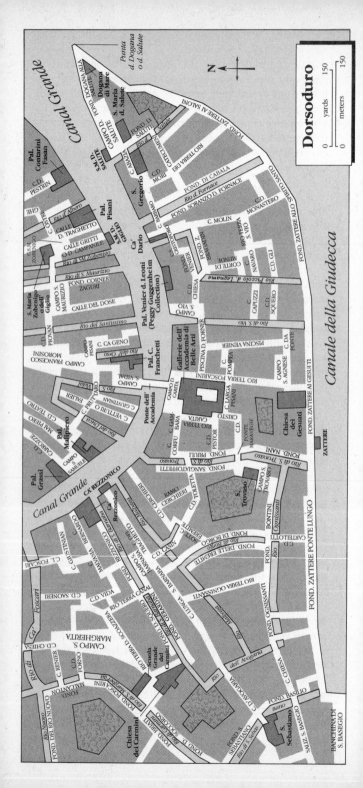

Dorsoduro

0 yards 150
0 meters 150

N

Canal Grande

Canale della Giudecca

Pal. Contarini Fasan
C.D. PESTRIN
GHE
C. OSTREGA
CALLE D. TRAGHETTO
CALLE GRITTI
O.D. CAMPANILE
S.M.D. GIGLIO
Pal. Pisani
Rio di S.M. Zobenigo
S.S.M. ZOBENIGO
Rio di S. Maurizio
S. Maria Zobenigo o Giglio
S. MAURIZIO
CAMPO S. MAURIZIO
FOND. CORNER ZAGURI
CALLE DEL DOSE
PIOVAN
Rio del Santissimo
CAMPO FRANCESCO MOROSINI
CAMPO PISANI
C. CA GENO
Rio dell'Orso
Pal. C. Franchetti
CAMPO S. VIDAL
Rio S. Vidal
C. VETTURI O C. GIUSTINIAN
C. FRU T.TO ?O
FALIER
C.D. TEATRO
MAL PIERO
Pal. Malipiero
C.D. CAROZZE
CAMPO S. SAMUELE
Pal. Grassi

Pal. Venier d. Leoni (Peggy Guggenheim Collection)
Ca' Dario
Gallerie dell' Accademia di Belle Arti
Ponte dell' Accademia
CAMPO CARITA
C. GAM BARA
FOND. PRIULI
C.D. TOLETTA
RIO TERRA FOSCARINI
PISCINA D. FORNER
C. CONTARINI CORFU
CAMPO S. AGNESE
PISCINA VENIER
C. DA PONTE
C.D. CERCHIERI
RAMO CERCHIERI

Fond. Dogana alla Salute
Punta d. Dogana o d. Salute
Dogana di Mare
S. Maria d. Salute
S.M.D. SALUTE
CAMPO D. SALUTE
FOND. D. SALUTE
Rio d.
FOND. ZATTERE AI SALONI
S. Gregorio
S. D. ABAZIA
RIO TERRA DEI CATECUMENI
C. BARBARO
S. MORI
FOND. DI CABALA
FOND. SORANZO D. FORNACE
Rio d. Fornace
C. MOLIN
RIO TERRA
C.D. NAVARO
FOND. VENIER
C. CRISTOFORO
CD. SQUERO
CORTE DI MENIGO
C.D. GLI
C.D. MONASTERO
C. CAPUZZI
Rio Piccolo d. Legname
FOND. ZATTERE ALLO SPIRITO SANTO
FOND. ZATTERE AI GESUITI
Chiesa dei Gesuati
FOND. ZATTERE PONTE LUNGO
C. LARGA PISANI
C. GESTO
C.D. PISTOR
PONTE MALPAGHE
NANI
FOND. NANI
ZATTERE
CAMPO S. TROVASO
S. Trovaso
Rio di S. Trovaso
FOND. S. TROVASO
FOND. SANGIATOFFETTI
FOND. DELLE EREMITE
C.D. EREMITE
FOND. DI BORGO
Rio di Borgo
FOND. OGNISSANTI
C. Ognissanti
RIO TERRA OGNISSANTI
FOND. DE OGNISSANTI
C. CASIN
BONTINI
CARTELLOTTI
C.D.
C.D. CHIESA

Ca' Rezzonico
CA' REZZONICO
Rio di S. Barnaba
BARNABA
FOND. REZZONICO
SALIZZADA
C.D. TRAGHETTO
C.L. NGA S. BARNABA
CAMPO S. BARNABA
RIO TERRA CANAL
C. LUNGA S. BARNABA
Fond. Foscari
Ca' Foscari
C.L. GIUSTINIAN
C. GIUSTINIAN
C.D. SAONER
C.D. VIDA
CAMPO S. MARGHERITA
C.D. CHIESA
C. RENIER
FOND. MOSCA
Rio Nuovo
FOND. DEL RIO NUOVO
FOND. DI S. MARGHERITA
RIO TERRA D. SCOAZZERA
Scuola Grande dei Carmini
C.D. FORNO
FOND. DE SOCCORSO
FOND. D. SOCCORSO
Chiesa dei Carmini
FOND. BRIATI
C.D. AVOGARIA
Rio dell'Avogaria
FOND. BASILIO
C. MOCENIGO
C.D. CHIESA
S. Sebastiano
FOND. S. SEBASTIANO
Rio di S. Sebas
SALIZ. S. BASEGIO
FOND. S. BASEGIO
BANCHINA DI S. BASEGIO

Most of the successful painters of the 17th century came to Venice from other centers. Today these painters do not attract more than a local interest, but their work should not be underestimated, as they introduced to Venice the great lessons of Caravaggio, Rubens, and other European masters. Their new concept of space, their Counter-Reformation solemnity, their compositions that sometimes are somber or even gloomy and sometimes shine with color, exercise a fascination of their own. And this period of research into color and perspective prepares the ground for the explosion of another golden period of Venetian painting in the 18th century.

The queen of the gigantic La Salute is a small image of the Virgin Mary carried over from Crete in 1672, a Greek-Byzantine icon identified by the population with the Virgin of Good Health (good health being the meaning of the word *salute*). The most interesting paintings are in the sacristy (left of the main altar): canvases and ceiling by Titian, and the *Marriage of Cana* by Tintoretto.

Punta della Dogana. Down the steps of the church and to the right, the extreme tip (*punta*) of Dorsoduro forms a triangle where the Republic used to have its customs offices (*dogana*). The promenade around the tip—a superb and crowded lovers' lane until very recent times (nowadays the young can take their friends home)—is part of Le Zattere, a long bank along the Canale della Giudecca, about which more will be said very soon. But for the moment, cross the bridge at the church's side and enter the enchanted atmosphere of the **San Gregorio** neighborhood.

San Gregorio. The area between La Salute and the Gallerie dell'Accademia has all the best characteristics of Venice: quiet, dotted with beautiful canals and frequent gardens, handsome and romantic. It is a preferred residential area for foreign expatriates, particularly Americans. Here used to be the American consulate, later closed in an attempt to cut government expenses and taken over by Wake Forest University of North Carolina for its Venice program, and here also was the home of American art patron Peggy Guggenheim, now a museum of contemporary art.

The palazzo housing the **Peggy Guggenheim Collection** has one side on the Canal Grande. It was begun in 1749 and never completed: Only the ground floor is now standing—a strange yet pleasing sight from the canal—surrounded by a large garden. The collection includes works by masters contemporary to Peggy Guggenheim and often intimate with her: René Magritte, Pablo Picasso, Max Ernst, Giorgio de Chirico, and Marcel Duchamp are represented, together with Jackson Pollock and a large selection from the Abstract Expressionist school.

Another, totally different art gallery awaits you a couple of hundred yards away, at the foot of ponte dell'Accademia. On your way you can sit for cappuccino at the outdoor tables of the café just down the bridge—the next gallery has no cafeteria—and prepare for a couple of hours of immersion in Venetian painting, from its beginnings to the 19th century.

Gallerie dell'Accademia. The grounds of the **Gallerie dell'Accademia** used to be occupied by a monastery and church—and of course by a scuola. Inside the monastery (now a school of painting) a cloister and staircase by Palladio can be visited with permission from the headmaster's office.

Among the countless masterworks included in the Gallerie dell'Accademia itself, even a rigorous selection would have to mention the early masters such as Paolo and Lorenzo Veneziano and, of course, Giovanni Bellini. Rooms 20 and 21 contain works painted for the scuole in the 15th century, among which are Carpaccio's *Cycle of Saint Ursula* (1475–1495) and a famous *Procession of the Corpus Domini* by Gentile Bellini, one of the first paintings in which the interest and pride in social aspects of life seem to overwhelm the religious inspiration.

Giorgione's *Tempest* and *Old Woman* are concrete evidence of the new humanistic world that the young master was introducing to a delighted audience. A *Portrait of a Young Man* by Lorenzo Lotto (1525; Room 7) is one of very few works to be seen in Venice by this Venetian genius who, eclipsed by Titian, had to look for recognition elsewhere.

The best Veronese in the gallery is the famous *Dinner at the House of Levy* (1573). It was supposed to be a Last Supper, and was to have adorned the dining room of the Dominican friars at Santi Giovanni e Paolo, but the picture's obvious delight in frivolous details provoked an intervention by the Inquisition. Veronese's brilliant solution to the problem was to change the title of the incriminating work. Tintoretto is abundantly and gigantically represented in Rooms 10 and 11; his work is delirious and stirring.

In Room 17 is the only Canaletto to be seen in Venice. This famous painter of cityscapes worked almost exclusively for foreign—particularly English—customers, and most of his works have remained abroad. A good selection of 18th-century works by Longhi and Guardi is shown in Room 17, together with seven pastel portraits by Rosalba Carriera, a painter who had become justly famous in 18th-century Europe for her mastery of this difficult medium. Over the door of the last room (24) there is a *Presentation of the Virgin* painted by Titian in 1538 to fit exactly in that spot.

Le Zattere. Such an intense exposure to art—without a lounge room or a cafeteria—deserves to be followed by a rest at a pleasant canal-side café. The **fondamenta delle Zattere**, just across the short width of Dorsoduro and along the Canale della Giudecca, offers exactly what the tired visitor needs. Le Zattere is a preferred walk for Venetians of all classes, sexes, and ages. In the warm spring days it is crowded during the first hours of the afternoon: Its southern exposure makes it sunny all day long. In summer, Venetians come here after sunset to meet friends and to eat relatively inexpensive pizza in one of three restaurants with tables on terraces over the canal.

La Giudecca. The **island of Giudecca**, right in front of Le Zattere, has both suffered and gained because of its separation from the rest of the city, to which it is connected during the day by vaporetti (lines 5 and 8) but at night only by an infrequent ferry, leaving Le Zattere in front of the Gesuati church. Its inhabitants may suffer some discomfort if they miss the ferry in the bitter winter nights (after midnight there is only one crossover every hour), but the island rewards them by remaining quiet and ancient, modest and charming. In 1984 Signor Cipriani, the owner of the Harry's Bar restaurant near San Marco, took over an abandoned storefront on the western tip of the island along the canal and turned it into the very successful **Harry's Dolci** (Giudecca 773), where he offers international cuisine at reasonable prices under elegant canopies. In his own time, Andrea Palladio also did his best to embellish the island; it was he who built the splendid church of the **Redentore** (like La Salute, built in thanksgiving after a plague), which is still the center of devoted pilgrimage—and fireworks—on the third Sunday of July every year.

Gesuati. Across at Le Zattere again, the large church at the corner of Le Zattere and rio terrà Foscarini (the wide, tree-lined alley that runs between the Gallerie dell'Accademia and Le Zattere) is properly named Santa Maria del Rosario, but it still goes under the name of **Gesuati**, a monastic order suppressed in 1688 and of course different from the more lasting Gesuiti (Jesuits). The church was built in 1743 by the architect Massari on commission from the Dominicans, who had taken over the grounds after the Gesuati's suppression. Its façade seems elegant to some, rather heavy to others, but it still basically represents a variation on Palladio.

It may be noted that here and elsewhere the canal bank is landscaped with steps built in proportion to the church;

access by boat was still the rule in the 18th century. Inside, the church contains a feast of paintings by another fashionable artist of those years and a frequent collaborator of Massari's, Giovanni Battista Tiepolo, who painted the ceiling and an altarpiece (first on the right), while Piazzetta contributed one of his best canvases, *Saint Vincent Ferraris*.

A Squero and the Rio di Borgo. On the way to the next museum—there are two more to come—take the first right turn after the church of the Gesuati, along the canal called rio di San Trovaso. A few steps farther, across the canal and near the church of San Trovaso, is the workshop of one of the oldest **gondola builders** in town, dating back to the 17th century (these workshops are called *squeri* in Venetian dialect); it is one of only two that have survived. The wood-topped houses behind the ramp are characteristic of the mountain area of the Cadore, where the wood for the gondolas used to come from. The whole workshop is a national landmark.

Behind the church of San Trovaso (17th century) is one of the most charming canals in Venice, the **rio di Borgo**, flanked by a street called fondamenta di Borgo but known as fondamenta delle Eremite. On this street is the entrance to **Montin**, one of the most popular restaurants in town, which features a pleasant garden (see Dining).

Ca' Rezzonico and 18th-Century Venice. Through calle Lunga and campo San Barnaba it is easy to reach the entrance of **Ca' Rezzonico**, a 17th-century palazzo with an impressive façade on the Canal Grande. The construction of this palazzo was begun in 1667 by Longhena (of La Salute) and completed in the 1750s by Massari (of Gesuati and La Pietà). Today it houses the **Museo del Settecento Veneziano**, a delightful experience and a good place to stop and muse about this extraordinary period in Venice's history. (See below for a discussion of the interior of Ca' Rezzonico.)

Venice's independence came to an end in the year 1797 under the blows of the very young Napoléon. It was an anticlimactic end, without even the appearance of a fight, and it poses a puzzling problem to historians: What were the causes of the decline and final collapse of this wealthy and civilized republic? All the superficial answers fail to withstand factual analysis. In the 18th century Venice was still the capital of a flourishing state where commerce, although deprived of its ancient splendor, was nonetheless active and profitable; in addition, the ruling class had been able to adapt to the new European reality, investing in land the large fortunes accumulated at sea and often increasing the profitability of their land possessions by applying the managerial spirit that was their tradition.

A fascinating theory suggests that the main cause of Venice's collapse was psychological. The new generations of patricians were managing a state and a wealth they had inherited, not created; they may not have had the energy and the motivation to run public life anymore. It may well be that when young Napoléon ignored the declared neutrality of Venice and invaded its territory in pursuit of the Austrian armies, and when he finally ordered—by messenger—the end of the glorious Republic, some of them felt relieved to lose their responsibilities. Without even considering resistance, the patrician government voted itself, the doge, and the whole administration out of office.

Whatever else may have been missing in Venice during the preceding 100 years, the desire to enjoy art and life was certainly still there. The process of beautification of the city had continued unimpaired: Some 49 new churches and convents were built, a large number of façades were redone in the fashionable modern style, and new bridges and streets were opened. Festivities and celebrations became more frequent and more elaborate; all year round, four musical centers were offering the best concerts to be heard in Europe (see church of La Pietà, above), while a good dozen theaters were active during the century—at least eight of them of first quality—and performing more new operas than anywhere else in Europe. It was in this environment that some of the best librettists learned their trade, which they exported abroad: Da Ponte, author of three libretti for Mozart; Mazzolà, an author preferred by Salieri; Bertati, author of Cimarosa's *Matrimonio Segreto*. In a way, Venice still lives off the memory of its glorious 18th century; the resurrection of the Carnival in the late 1970s is one of many signs of Venetians' attachment to this period—and their willingness to exploit it for the attraction of tourists.

In this artistically active environment a new golden age dawned for painting. The traditional Venetian values of light, color, and space found new expression in the works of Piazzetta and Tiepolo. Many churches and palazzi in Venice feature the latter's frescoes and canvases, rich in light and open spaces, spectacular and magical. Lovers of Tiepolo should see, besides the ones already mentioned, the churches of Santi Apostoli, San Stae, and Scalzi, and the frescoes in the sumptuous reception hall of Palazzo Labia in Cannaregio, the Scuola Grande dei Carmini, and Ca' Rezzonico.

Together with the Piazzetta and Tiepolo schools, another
manner of painting flourished in this period that was more
rational in a way, more attuned to the new scientific ideals of
the Enlightenment: the painting of *vedute,* or cityscapes. The
famous name in this field is Giovanni Canaletto.

Still another school is represented by the Longhi and
Guardi families, who painted mostly scenes of Venetian life,
very far from the triumphal views of Tiepolo or the impas-
sive, rational look of Canaletto: more intimate, enclosed
scenes in the Longhis, more airy scenes in the Guardis. The
latter propose a Venice still theatrical but somehow sentimental, perhaps already tinted with nostalgia. The shadows
of the 19th century seem to be lurking closer to these
painters' horizons.

The Interior of the Ca' Rezzonico. The furniture and
decorations of most of these rooms are not necessarily the
original ones, but they were transported here in order to
reconstruct as closely as possible the atmosphere of an 18th-
century palazzo. Among the artworks are ceilings by Tiepolo, some disquieting frescoes by his son Giandomenico,
pastels by Rosalba Carriera, astonishing furnishings by
Brustolon, a large collection of Longhi paintings, and in the
sala del Ridotto two of the best Guardi paintings (the *Nun's
Parlor* and the *Ridotto*).

Rio Terrà dei Pugni. From the rio di San Barnaba, the
canal flowing along the side of the Ca' Rezzonico, the third
street on the right is the spacious rio terrà Canal, better
known as dei Pugni, leading to the charming campo Santa
Margherita. On this *rio terrà* (a filled-up canal) is one of the
first and best mask shops in Venice, Il **Mondonovo**, where
Carnival masks are fashioned with imagination but also with
rare historical accuracy.

Campo Santa Margherita. This large and pleasant square is
a preferred rendezvous for Venetians, especially in warm
weather, when its three restaurants enlarge their outdoor
space as much as allowed by the city regulations—and possibly more. They serve pizza, of course, but other food as well.
They may not be the best in town, but they are reasonable in
price and the setting is so pleasant that no one cares about
gastronomic perfection. The **campo Santa Margherita** is a real
anthology of old building styles, and a closer look gives an
idea of the age of many other houses scattered over the city.
The two houses at numbers 2920–2935 were built in the 14th
century over preexisting structures. Notice the Gothic windows, the wood lintels over the shops' doors, and the arch
over the main portal (Byzantine, 12th or 13th century). The

two Gothic houses at numbers 2954–2962 belong to the 14th century. More recent are the small palazzi at numbers 3034–3035 and 3042–3043 (both from the 18th century, as are numbers 3429–3430 on the other side of the campo).

Scuola Grande dei Carmini. The **Scuola Grande dei Carmini** is near the church of the Carmini, off the west side of the campo. The scuola was built in 1663, and it is worth a visit because of the splendid ceiling in the main salon, decorated with nine canvases by Tiepolo (1744; they are considered among his best works). A smaller room also contains a *Judith and Holofernes* by Piazzetta.

Carmini. The 14th-century church of the **Carmini** has been redecorated several times, especially in the 17th century. It contains two exceptional masterworks: an *Adoration of the Shepherds* by Cima da Conegliano (c. 1500) and one of the few Lorenzo Lottos to be seen in Venice, *Saint Nicholas of Bari.*

San Sebastiano. Near the church of the Carmini and after the peaceful fondamenta del Soccorso, the fourth bridge at the right leads to a university building (door by Carlo Scarpa, a leader of 20th-century Venetian architects) and to the church of **San Sebastiano** (1505–1548), famous for its Veronese paintings. It was through his work here that the young painter from Verona claimed Venice's admiration, and it is here that he is buried. A visit should start with the ceiling of the sacristy and continue with that of the church and the friezes high up on the walls (best seen from the choir). Next come the main altarpiece, a grandiose *Virgin in Glory,* the organ's doors, and the main chapel with two large canvases representing scenes from the life of Saint Sebastian.

A VAPORETTO RIDE ALONG THE CANAL GRANDE

This princely waterway is the glory of Venice and one of the major glories of the world. No matter how many times you have seen parts of the Canal Grande reproduced in works of art or on postcards, it is hard to avoid a surge of genuine emotion when riding through it or looking at it from ponte dell'Accademia or ponte di Rialto. All of its palazzi can be reached on foot by back streets, and many have been discussed above in the appropriate sestiere; still, a view from the water is immensely rewarding and an absolute must.

This brief overview starts from the entrance at Piazzale

Roma (parking lots). It is a good idea to save this ride for the end of the day (sunset, as well as dawn, is a perfect time) after reaching the boat stop on foot through the sestieri.

The only way to have a leisurely view of the Canal Grande is by boarding a *vaporetto* (water bus) of line number 1 or 34. Unfortunately both are very busy lines, used by locals as well as tourists, and very often they are terribly crowded (in addition, only a very few places at the bow allow a good view). To avoid disappointment, it is important to choose the time and direction of your ride. In the morning, take it from the Lido and San Marco toward Piazzale Roma; in the evening, take it in the opposite direction. After 9:00 P.M. the boats run less frequently (every 20 minutes) but they are blessedly uncrowded, and at night the Canal Grande is unforgettably romantic, with the handsomest buildings illuminated and the water as smooth as a mirror.

Leaving from Piazzale Roma, the *vaporetto* stops at the railway station, after which the church of the **Scalzi** appears on the left, just before the bridge (1670, façade by Sardi; it contains three frescoes by Tiepolo).

Just after the San Marcuola boat stop, **Palazzo Vendramin Calergi**, a masterwork by Codussi and the first sizable Renaissance building to appear in Venice (early 16th century), appears on the left.

Almost directly across from it is the **Fondaco dei Turchi** (Turks' Warehouse), one of the oldest buildings on the canal, built by the Pesaro family and then assigned to the Turkish community for trading. Notice the Byzantine arches and the round *patere* between them.

Behind the San Stae landing, the church of **San Stae** (the façade dates from the early 18th century) includes paintings by Piazzetta and Tiepolo.

On the right, the second building after San Stae is the imposing **Ca' Pesaro** (Longhena, 17th century), which now houses a gallery of modern art as well as a museum of Oriental art.

On the opposite side, the **Ca' d'Oro** appears just before the landing of the same name (see the Cannaregio section).

Across from Ca' d'Oro is the portico of the fish market (*pescheria*), built in 1907 and featuring an odd combination of Gothic-style first floor and Renaissance-style roof.

At the curve of the canal, the **Ca' da Mosto** (left side), in need of restoration, is also one of the oldest Byzantine palazzi in Venice (13th century).

On the same side, just before ponte di Rialto, is the **Fondaco dei Tedeschi** (1505), a warehouse used by the German community. Its façade used to be adorned with frescoes by Giorgione and Titian, but these paintings are now lost except for a few fragments conserved in the Ca' d'Oro.

After ponte di Rialto, on the left side, is Palazzo Manin, built by Sansovino in 1538. Still on the left are the **Ca' Farsetti** and **Ca' Loredan**, both built in the 13th-century Byzantine style (see the San Marco section).

Palazzo Grimani, also on the left, was built in 1557 by Michele Sanmicheli to closely resemble Rome's Arch of Constantine. Again on the left, just before the Sant'Angelo landing, is another majestic Renaissance home: **Palazzo Corner-Spinelli** (1490), probably designed by Codussi.

On the right bank, before the San Tomà landing, is **Palazzo Pisani e Moretta**, with a particularly successful Gothic façade (15th century).

At the bend in the canal, on the right, is **Ca' Foscari** (15th century), today the administrative center of the University of Venice. Still on the right, just before the next landing, **Ca' Rezzonico**, with a façade by Longhena (1667), contains the Museo del Settecento Veneziano (see Dorsoduro).

Across the canal from Ca' Rezzonico, **Palazzo Grassi** (Massari, 18th century), lavishly restored by Fiat, hosts special exhibits.

On the left side, just after ponte dell'Accademia, is **Palazzo Franchetti**, built in the 15th century but somewhat spoiled by a 19th-century restoration. Still on the left, the huge Renaissance building is **Palazzo Corner** (Sansovino, 1545), the tallest on the canal. It is said that the immensely rich Corner family prevented the Venier family from completing the building across the canal, of which only the first floor was erected. The administration of the Venice Provincia (a *provincia* is a large district centering around a capital city, in this case Venice) has its offices in Palazzo Corner.

Right across, the unlucky Veniers planned an equally enormous home in 1749 (**Ca' Venier dei Leoni**). The unfinished building, full of a strange charm, was the house of Peggy Guggenheim and is now a museum, the **Peggy Guggenheim Collection** (see Dorsoduro). Still on the right side, the elegant, dangerously leaning palazzo on the canal after Ca' Venier is **Ca' Dario**, a delightful building dating to 1488 and recently acquired by the emerging Italian tycoon Raul Gardini, owner of an empire of chemical industries.

On the left side, just after the landing called Santa Maria del Giglio, is the 14th-century **Palazzo Gritti**, now a luxury hotel in the CIGA chain owned by the Aga Khan.

Two buildings after the Gritti, still on the left, is a smaller palazzo that is supposed to have been the house of Desdemona. Attached to Palazzo Contarini Fasan, it is easily recognizable by the elegant stone carvings on the balconies. In 1987 it was bought and restored by a private entrepreneur, who converted it into a luxury co-op.

On the right side, just before the Bacino di San Marco (the water basin in front of San Marco), the church of **La Salute** (see Dorsoduro) is followed by the ancient Dogana di Mare (customhouse, low building on the very tip), surmounted by a large gilded globe with a statue representing Fortune.

THE LAGOON ISLANDS
San Giorgio Maggiore

Like La Giudecca (see Dorsoduro), from which it is separated by a small canal, this island is effectively part of downtown Venice. It sits right in front of the San Marco area and marks the entrance to the Canal Grande with the handsome façade and campanile of the church of San Giorgio Maggiore.

A Benedictine center since the tenth century, this small island was landscaped and rebuilt in its entirety by Andrea Palladio, who could apply here the grandiose ideas he developed in his mainland villas. San Giorgio Maggiore is therefore a kind of *revanche* by this architect, whose plans for secular buildings in Venice had been systematically rejected as long as his rival Sansovino was alive and in charge of the building committees. Sansovino died in 1570, Palladio in 1580; after Palladio's death, other architects completed the realization of his project by 1610, possibly modifying a few details. Longhena added a sumptuous staircase to the first of two cloisters in the Benedictine monastery next to the church and built a handsome library there as well.

The church, still used for worship, represents one of Palladio's greatest achievements: Here the architect could apply his principles concerning the relationship between architecture and environment, conceiving the structure so as to inscribe it in the lagoon's space with a perfect sense of harmony. The façade, on the other hand, seems to embody Palladio's ideals of geometric perfection, painstakingly distilled from a lifelong study of Roman antiquity.

Two paintings by Tintoretto are the highlights of the interior: a *Last Supper* at the chancel's right wall and a *Deposition* in the so-called Deposition Chapel (1594; perhaps the last work by Tintoretto). Gregorian chants are sung by resident monks during mass every Sunday at 11:00 A.M.

In 1951 the wealthy Count Vittorio Cini restored the island and its structures and transformed the monastery into the home of the **Fondazione Giorgio Cini**, one of the most prominent cultural centers in Italy. High-level symposiums are constantly organized on its premises, and in 1982 the summit of the seven leading heads of state of the Western world was held here.

Palladio's two cloisters, now included in the foundation's grounds, can be visited by asking permission of the doorman (the entrance is clearly marked on the building at the right of the boat stop). The upstairs library is open to the public. With its beautiful windows, large collection of art-history books, and kind personnel, it is an invitation to abandon all other activity and turn to scholarship forever.

Murano

The public boat for Murano reaches the island in less than ten minutes from fondamente Nuove (Cannaregio). But Murano is also linked to Venice by the regular boat line number 5, the one that circles around the city and touches on its most important areas (station, garages, San Marco; a boat every 15 minutes).

Traditionally a center for the production of glass, Murano has greatly profited from the tourist boom, to the point of turning into a kind of bazaar. Serious, competent glass producers are side by side with improvised shops aiming at the exploitation of visitors. The rumor is that Murano prices are much higher than those in downtown Venice for the same items, so fruitful shopping in this island takes a bit of care and perhaps a lot of bargaining. A visit to the **Museo Vetrario** (Glass Museum; fondamenta Giustinian, not far from the first boat stop on Murano) may help you get your bearings; the most solid shops are **Barovier e Toso** (on the main shopping street just off the boat, number 28), **Venini** (at nearby number 50, but with a shop at San Marco in Venice), and **Nason e Moretti** (number 54 of the same street). But a visit to Murano is nevertheless pleasant if only for the lagoon ride and because of the beauty of the island itself. A real must is the church of **Santa Maria e Donato**, a 12th-century building with a splendid apse facing a canal and a mosaic floor dating back to 1140.

Burano

The boat to Burano leaves from fondamente Nuove approximately every hour; after Burano it continues to nearby Torcello, so that the two islands are best visited in the same day (the boat ride takes 45 minutes).

Burano is a friendly and pleasant island, famous for the

vivid colors on the walls of its homes. It is a traditional
center for the manufacture of lace. Unfortunately, the labori-
ous hand production generates astronomical prices, so that
most of the items sold today on the island are machine made
in the Far East. The **Scuola dei Merletti** (Lacemaking School)
on the piazza Galuppi (the main square), open to visitors,
keeps the tradition alive and has a shop where the real thing
is still sold. The largest assortment, however, is at the
Jesurum Workshop, not in Burano but in downtown Venice
(ponte della Canonica, behind the Basilica di San Marco).

Torcello

Before moving to the Rialto and San Marco area, the center
of the lagoon population was on this island, today almost
deserted and full of unforgettable charm. It boasts three
restaurants and the houses of a half-dozen families, but the
great surprise is the well-preserved religious center of the
old settlement: On a secluded, grassy little square along the
water there rise the **Baptistery**, **Cathedral**, and church of
Santa Fosca. A visit to these monuments, still surrounded as
they are by the friendly, almost untouched, lagoon, gives
the visitor an idea of life as it must have been at the
beginning of Venice's history. It is a place for silence,
meditation, and appreciation of ancient beauty.

The old cathedral (seventh century) was reconstructed in
the 11th and 12th centuries; as it stands now, it is reminiscent of the great Byzantine churches of Ravenna, both in the
basilica plan and in the rich mosaic decoration of the interior. It was a style particularly suited to the watery environment, inviting the sun's reflections in the large windows and
in the rich chromatic plays of the mosaic. It has been
compared to a great ship, a Noah's ark surviving a great
flood with its exquisite art products (Ruskin). Most remarkable are the mosaics with the blue-clad Mother of God on a
gold background in the main apse and the great mosaic of
the Last Judgment on the entrance wall (12th–13th century).
The oldest mosaics (seventh century) are in the right-hand
apse. Of great interest and beauty also are the Byzantine-
style bas-reliefs (10th and 11th centuries).

Of the three restaurants on this small island, the exclusive
and pricey **Locanda Cipriani** offers first-rate food and service
as well as a splendid view of the church of Santa Fosca
(reservations; Tel: 041-73-01-50; Fax: 041-73-54-33; closed on
Tuesdays and November through February; water-taxi service leaving every day at 12:20 from the riva degli Schiavoni,
in front of the Hotel Danieli). The Locanda also has four

rooms for overnight guests (weekend reservations required at least a month ahead). **Osteria al Ponte del Diavolo** is expensive and very pleasant (Tel: 041-73-04-01; Fax: 041-73-02-50; closed Thursdays and mid-November to March; open only for lunch, Saturdays also for dinner). The **Osteria Villa 600**, medium-priced, specializes in memorable risotto and fresh fish. (Tel: 041-73-09-99; closed on Wednesdays).

The Lido

See the beach section of the Veneto chapter for a description of this pleasant resort, comfortably located 15 minutes from the piazza San Marco, and of the close-by island of **Pellestrina**. In the Getting Around section, below, we discuss the pros and cons of establishing your headquarters on the Lido.

GETTING AROUND

When to Go
July and August tend to bring crowds of tourists and are sometimes hot and damp (and the south wind, the *scirocco,* can be a real nuisance). September usually offers splendid weather. It is also, unfortunately, the busiest month in the tourist season. The most crowded days are those between August 20 and September 10 (Film Festival, Historic Regatta—the latter held on the first Sunday of September). October is usually a very good month, with local life returning to normal after the tourist invasion and with the first thin fogs making the city especially romantic. In November and early December the temperature is mild and the city wonderfully intimate; the tide-related flooding called *acqua alta* is frequent. The Christmas weeks, lasting until January 6, are very busy in Venice, and so are the frantic but amusing Carnival weeks. Carnival climaxes on the seven days preceding Ash Wednesday; piazza San Marco is thick with people from all over Europe, often wearing costumes of astonishing sophistication and cost. Hotel reservations are necessary months in advance for this period. Spring is mild, and the skies over the lagoon are delightfully clear. May is probably the second best month after September so far as climate is concerned, and Venice is not at all crowded at this time. In June the first thick vanguards of tourists appear all over town.

Arriving
By Car. Arrival by car is to be avoided, unless it is a rental car, which you can drop off when arriving (Hertz, Avis,

Budget, and many other companies have offices at Piazzale Roma). Venice's car terminal, called **Piazzale Roma**, has only two garages, and they are almost totally filled by residents' cars; only in the off-off-season is there a chance to find available space. So the city administration built an artificial island nearby, called **Tronchetto**, devoted exclusively to parking space. At Tronchetto you can leave your car, but the price is 30,000 lire a day for outdoor as well as indoor parking. *Vaporetto* line number 34 departs every 20 minutes from Tronchetto for downtown Venice. The city administration has shamefully allowed Tronchetto to turn into a madhouse of people offering all kinds of dubious services to tourists, so it is a good policy to ignore all solicitors, no matter how official their caps and uniforms may look.

The city has built two other parking places on the mainland: **San Giuliano**, just before the lagoon bridge, for traffic coming from the east and the north, and **Fusina** for traffic coming from the west and south (both uncovered; closed in winter). They are rarely full, and they are very well connected to Venice by public boat service. Entrance into Venice actually *should* be by water: The short ride across the lagoon prepares the visitor for the new environment, and the view is much more exciting than at gloomy Piazzale Roma. From San Giuliano the boat goes to **fondamente Nuove**; from Fusina it stops at **Le Zattere** and **San Marco**; at both terminals it is easy to find porters and other boat lines. The parking lots are guarded day and night and are much less confusing than Tronchetto.

An interesting solution is also offered by the **Lido**, the very thin island that separates the lagoon from the open sea. It is open to car traffic, so that you can park right at your hotel door if you are staying here. The island affords a few miles of wide, sandy beaches and some of the best hotels in the world, plus a large number of less expensive places. (See Accommodations below, and see the beach section in the Veneto chapter for more information on the Lido.) There is very frequent public boat service from the Lido to the San Marco area; the splendid ride through the lagoon basin takes only ten minutes. To reach the Lido by car, just cross the lagoon bridge and look for signs for the Ferry-Boat (as it is called in Italian, too): It leaves from Tronchetto every hour and a half.

By Train. At the Venice station it is easy to find porters, currency exchange, and all the services offered by a modern terminal. Just outside the building is the beginning of the Canal Grande, with boat stops for all the main lines.

By Air. The Marco Polo Airport is connected with all Europe's capitals and most of its important cities by one or two flights a day (less frequently during the off-season) and even more frequently with other Italian cities (ten flights a day to Rome). A connection through Frankfurt, Germany, or Milan is used for most intercontinental flights; Alitalia now has direct service once a day from New York to Venice. Air France, British Airways, Lufthansa, Austrian Airlines, Crossair, and, of course, Alitalia have offices at the airport.

A bus meets every flight and connects the airport with Piazzale Roma (the car terminal in downtown Venice) in 25 minutes; tickets are 4,000 lire. Porters and boats are easily available at Piazzale Roma. A worthwhile luxury is the water taxi from the airport: It is rather expensive (60,000 lire plus a few extra for luggage), but it takes the exhausted traveller right to his or her hotel door, and again it enters the city the right way, from the water surrounding it and most likely through a stretch of the Canal Grande. Most Venetians, however, use the boat service run by Cooperativa San Marco, which is linked with most flights and lands right at the piazza San Marco after a stop at the Lido (one-hour ride, 15,000 lire per person; look for the counter in the arrival hall; the sign reads "Cooperativa S. Marco—Water bus"). Still another possibility is an automobile taxi to Piazzale Roma, which costs about 25,000 lire.

In Venice

Venice enjoys a double transportation system: the canals and the streets. In spite of appearances, every house and palazzo can be reached on foot, and this by far is what Venetians prefer to do. Private boats, although dramatically increasing in number with economic development, are exclusively for pleasure purposes. The city is far from immense, and very often the use of public transportation doesn't save any time, so people go on foot, except when they don't feel like walking or when they are carrying packages.

Vaporetti. The most used lines, served by relatively large boats called vaporetti, run through the Canal Grande. They are line number 1, a local line stopping every few hundred yards, usually at alternate sides of the canal, and line number 34, which covers the same route skipping a few stops (the express line, so to speak). Each runs every ten minutes, offering a service that is fabulous in wintertime and over-crowded in the tourist season. They both go all the way to the Lido, which is also independently served by a comfort-able shuttle service from the piazza San Marco (*motonave,* every 20 minutes).

Line number 2, a direct link between Piazzale Roma and San Marco and the Lido, is better left to Venetians: It runs through the wide Canale della Giudecca, not very interesting in terms of architecture, and it is so crowded in the summer that riders are totally unable to look around.

Traghetti. To avoid the detours necessary to reach one of the three bridges, a help to pedestrians is offered by public gondolas in strategic spots on the Canal Grande; for 500 lire the *traghetti* ferry people back and forth. This service runs only during the day and is particularly useful at the Rialto fish market (*pescheria*) as well as in San Tomà near the Frari church. These boats across the canal often make walking the quickest way between any two points in Venice.

The Gondolas. The other gondolas, finely polished and luxuriously cushioned, are used by Venetians only for marriages or rare ceremonies. Quite a few locals have never set foot in one of them: A 30-minute ride costs about 60,000 lire, and there is no reason to spend that when the public boats go much more quickly for much less. They are basically for the enjoyment of the tourists, and when so used they are worth the fee. A good idea, however, is to avoid taking them for just an aimless tour; gondolas are best used to go from one place to another, as, for instance, to ride back to the hotel after a day of visits, or to a nice restaurant for dinner.

Motorized Taxi Boats. They are numerous and quick, but again they are very expensive: A short ride within the city starts at 40,000 lire during the day (at night there is an extra charge). Venetians use them only in times of dire need, but they may be very useful to the visitor who doesn't want to bother with suitcases and searching out addresses.

Tourist Services

A very reliable agency for all kinds of sightseeing, including tours of the lagoon islands and nighttime gondola rides, is **American Express**, at San Marco 1471 (just behind piazza San Marco, near the church of San Moisé). **Venezia per Voi**, a high-class service managed by Contessa Lucia Zavagli, organizes any event one may desire to stage in Venice, from a marriage ceremony to dinner in a private palazzo, from a convention to participation in a Carnival ball (San Marco 3316, Tel: 522-60-88; Fax: 522-24-33).

ACCOMMODATIONS

The rates given below are projections for 1993; always check for up-to-date information before making reservations. Wide ranges may reflect the differences between low- and high-season rates. Unless otherwise indicated, the figures indicate the cost of a double room (per room, not per person). However, half-board (*mezza pensione*) rates, which include breakfast and one other meal per day, are per person. The service charge is included in the rate; inquire about the tax and breakfast.

The telephone and fax area code for Venice is 041. When telephoning from outside the country, omit the zero in the city code.

Preeminent among the luxury hotels of Venice are the Cipriani for its comfort and modernity and the Gritti for its atmosphere; they are both on a par with the best (and most expensive) hotels in the world. The **Hotel Cipriani** is quietly set on the island of La Giudecca, very close to San Giorgio Maggiore; its water taxis are always ready to take guests across the small body of water separating it from the San Marco area without fee. Among its amenities are an exceptionally good restaurant and a swimming pool (a real oddity for Venice). All of the room windows open onto the lagoon, mostly on the back side of La Giudecca, where the view can be almost achingly beautiful, with the quiet water dotted by small islands and often veiled by a thin layer of mist. Giudecca 10, 30133 Venezia. Tel: 520-77-44; Fax: 520-39-30. In U.S., Tel: (800) 223-6800 or (212) 838-3110; Fax: (212) 758-7367. In U.K., Tel: (0800) 18-11-23; Fax: (071) 353-1904. £430,000–£860,000.

The **Gritti Palace Hotel** occupies a 15th-century Gothic palazzo right on the Canal Grande and a short walk from San Marco. It is a preferred residence for successful intellectuals and artists; its halls are always quiet (no organized groups are accepted), and its terrace on the water, open for drinks and dining, is set in one of the most attractive stretches of the Canal Grande. For guests who really need a beach and/or a swimming pool, an hourly service connects the hotel to the great Excelsior on the Lido. (The Excelsior belongs to the same chain, CIGA, owned by the Aga Khan.) Campo Santa Maria del Giglio, San Marco 2467, 30124 Venezia. Tel: 79-46-11; Fax: 520-09-42. In U.S., Tel: (800) 221-2340 or (212) 935-9540; Fax: (212) 421-5929. In U.K., Tel: (0800) 28-92-34 or (01) 930-4147; Fax: (01) 839-1566. £450,000–£750,000.

The Monaco and Metropole are probably the best bets in the four-star category. **Hotel Monaco & Grand Canal** is also set on the Canal Grande, in a former patrician residence, and has kept a lot of its ancient flavor. Its ground-floor lounge and piano bar, with large windows on the canal, are wonderfully quiet and often visited by Venetians or by a few smart tourists looking for a rest between walks. (Unless, of course, they prefer to stop for the original Bellini cocktail at **Harry's Bar**, just across the narrow calle from the Monaco. The atmosphere is more colorful at Harry's, more intimate at the Monaco.) The Canal Grande terrace, open for drinks and dining, affords a splendid view. Calle Vallaresso, San Marco 1325, 30124 Venezia. Tel: 520-02-11; Fax: 520-05-01. In U.S., Tel: (800) 223-9832 or (212) 599-8280; Fax: (212) 599-1755. ₤200,000–₤362,500 April–October, December 21–January 6, and Carnival week; ₤200,000–₤450,000 the rest of the year.

The **Hotel Metropole**, on the riva degli Schiavoni near the piazza San Marco, is a modern and comfortable hotel with excellent professional service. Its front rooms open onto the Bacino di San Marco, with San Giorgio Maggiore and La Salute in full view; the southern exposure allows for enjoyment of sunrises on the Lido side and sunsets behind the domes of La Salute. All the rooms include a small safe for valuables, and most have at least one piece of antique furniture. Riva degli Schiavoni, Castello 4149, 30122 Venezia. Tel: 520-50-44; Fax: 522-36-79. ₤250,000–₤400,000 April–October, December 21–January 6, and Carnival week; ₤200,000–₤320,000 the rest of the year.

In a more affordable range, the relatively small **Pensione Accademia–Villa Maravegie** (27 rooms) offers all the comforts of a good hotel, plus a secluded canal-side garden for breakfast. The pensione is actually a small independent villa, surrounded by gardens on three sides and a canal on the fourth. The rooms are spacious and furnished with taste; the service is friendly and discreet. You have to reserve well in advance at this much-coveted place. Ponte Maravegie, Dorsoduro 1058, 30123 Venezia. Tel: 523-78-46; Fax: 523-91-52. ₤160,000–₤200,000.

A lesser-known hotel is the **San Cassiano–Ca' Favretto** on the Canal Grande near San Stae. The building goes back to the 14th century, with traces of earlier Byzantine construction, and in the 19th century it was the residence of the Venetian painter Giacomo Favretto. The setting, relatively far from the San Marco area, is very Venetian and pleasantly off the main tourist paths, near the colorful fish and vegetable markets; the hotel's layout favors conversation with other guests. San Cassiano, Santa Croce 2232, 30125 Venezia. Tel: 524-17-68; Fax: 72-10-33. ₤130,000–₤270,000.

On the beautiful campo Bandiera e Moro, a few minutes from San Marco, is the small pensione **La Residenza** (17 rooms). Like the hotels that follow on this list, it is affordable (110,000 lire for a double room with bath, breakfast included; when reserving, a private bath should be requested, since not all rooms have one). Its reception and breakfast hall is a nice example of Venetian Gothic, with a striking multiple window on the campo; rooms, doors, and walls have that old Venetian look—with its pros and cons (no use looking for a straight floor). La Residenza is perfect for people who prefer atmosphere over total comfort. Campo Bandiera e Moro, Castello 3608, 30122 Venezia. Tel: 528-53-15; Fax: 523-88-59. Closed November 10–December 7 and January 8–February 20. ₤140,000.

Restored to be more modern is the **Pensione La Calcina**, a former residence of John Ruskin, at Le Zattere, just behind the Gallerie dell'Accademia. For decades La Calcina has been the meeting point for those real lovers of Venice who cannot always afford the five-star hotels but who like a good degree of comfort in a friendly, almost family-like atmosphere. The pensione's location, on the sunny Zattere and just a short walk from all the major points of interest, could hardly be better. Zattere, Dorsoduro 780, 30123 Venezia. Tel: 520-64-66; Fax: 522-70-45. ₤90,000–₤140,000.

On the riva degli Schiavoni and near the Arsenale is the very interesting **Pensione Bucintoro**, run with friendly care and inhabited by a seemingly endless stream of French painters. The reason? The pensione occupies a corner building with a breathtaking view over the Bacino di San Marco, and all the rooms enjoy that view. Among its other advantages is its proximity to the Lido, the colorful via Garibaldi, and the Biennale grounds. Castello 2135/A, 30122 Venezia. Tel: 522-32-40; Fax: 523-52-24. ₤115,000–₤130,000.

Also on the riva degli Schiavoni, very close to the piazza San Marco and a few steps from the Bridge of Sighs, is the **Pensione Wildner**. A motherly, friendly lady runs it with love and pride. Two-thirds of the rooms have a splendid view over the Bacino di San Marco; weather permitting, breakfast and dining are out of doors, right on the riva. Castello 4161, 30122 Venezia. Tel: 522-74-63; Fax: 526-56-15. ₤60,000–₤170,000.

Very comfortable and superbly located between the Gallerie dell'Accademia and Le Zattere is the medium-priced **Albergo Agli Alboretti**. Renovated and refurnished in 1986, it also has a private garden for breakfast. In 1989 an independently run restaurant was added to this friendly, very civilized establishment. Rio Terrà Foscarini, Dorsoduro 882-4, 30123 Venezia. Tel: 523-00-58. ₤130,000–₤170,000.

Finally, a great bargain entailing a tiny bit of sacrifice: **Locanda Montin** near the Gallerie dell'Accademia has seven charming rooms for what is probably the cheapest price in Venice. The location is along a canal famous for its romantic ambience, and the **Restaurant Montin** is one of the best in town (American presidents have dined here, and the dining garden has been in quite a few movies). The drawback is the lack of private bathrooms (there are four bathrooms for the seven rooms). But the furniture is very pleasant and the Montin family runs the premises with a kindness and professionalism born of generations of experience in the restaurant business. Fondamenta delle Eremite, Dorsoduro 1147, 30123 Venezia. Tel: 522-71-51. ₤60,000–₤75,000.

Other Accommodations in Venice

The following accommodations, though somewhat less charming than the above, are also among the best in Venice.

Pensione Seguso. Zattere ai Gesuati, Dorsoduro 779, 30123 Venezia. Tel: 522-23-40; Fax: same. Comfortable, centrally located at Le Zattere. ₤70,000–₤90,000.

Hotel Al Sole. Santa Croce 136, 30125 Venezia. Tel: 523-21-44; Fax: 71-90-61. Near the Piazzale Roma, recently renovated, moderately priced. ₤50,000.

Alla Salute Da Cici. Dorsoduro 222, 30123 Venezia. Tel: 523-54-04. Very pleasantly located near La Salute. ₤50,000–₤85,000.

Accommodations on the Lido

Hotel Des Bains, of the CIGA chain, is a magnificent building dating from 1901, in the best hotel tradition of those years. All decorations are Art Deco originals, and the famous movie by Visconti, *Death in Venice,* was shot here. The hotel has a large garden, a swimming pool, and cabins on the beach. Lungomare Marconi 17, 30126 Lido (Venezia). Tel: 526-59-21; Fax: 526-01-13. In U.S., Tel: (800) 221-2340 or (212) 935-9540; Fax: (212) 421-5929. In U.K., Tel: (0800) 28-92-34 or (071) 930-4147; Fax: (071) 839-1566. Closed in winter. ₤231,250–₤450,000.

About one mile down the beach, the astonishing **Hotel Excelsior** (also a CIGA hotel) was built with Moorish touches in the same period. It is a rendezvous for the international movie crowd during the yearly film festival in September. Besides the beach, it has a swimming pool and is next door to **Casino of Venice**, one of four gambling houses allowed to operate in Italy. Lungomare Marconi 41, 30126 Lido (Venezia). Tel: 526-02-01; Fax: 526-72-76. In U.S., Tel: (800) 221-2340 or (212) 935-9540; Fax: (212) 421-5929. In U.K., Tel: (0800) 28-92-34 or (071) 930-4147; Fax: (071) 839-1566. Closed in winter. ₤430,000–₤550,000.

The Lido also hosts a large number of more affordable hotels and pensioni. Totally amusing is the tiled façade of **Hotel Hungaria**, right on the Gran Viale and a five-minute walk both from the seaside beach and from the lagoonside boat to San Marco. Gran Viale 28, 30126 Lido (Venezia). Tel: 526-12-12; Fax: 526-76-19. Closed in winter. Ł130,000–Ł210,000.

DINING

In 1987 a team of researchers in Venice's Marciana library unearthed 1,718 different books related to cooking, dating from 1469 on. This great gourmet tradition, however, succumbed first to French predominance, then to the tourist trade in more recent times. Today the Venetian dishes still in use can be counted, as the saying goes, on the fingers of one hand.

There is also a problem with the availability of things to cook. Venice's cuisine is based on fish, but the lagoon is partly polluted, and the Adriatic Sea doesn't yield much fish anymore. The best species are only rarely caught, and they go at astronomical prices, so that only a few restaurants can afford to serve them. In fact, 80 percent of the fish traded in the busy Venice market is imported from Sicily or abroad. The best and most expensive local species are *branzino* (a kind of sea bass, known as *spigola* in other parts of Italy and as *loup de mer* in France) and *orata* (a snapper). Both are also farmed on the lagoon. A few sole are also caught by the Chioggia fishermen. This fish should be ordered only in the best restaurants to be sure it is really fresh.

Some less rare species are still caught in abundance, and it is to those that a money-wise visitor should turn. Actually, Venice's restaurants have developed great expertise in cooking the available seafood; the only problem is the lack of variety. Clams and mussels are tasty and wonderful with spaghetti (they are supposed to be served with the shells, to guarantee freshness); cuttlefish (*seppie*) is a gourmet dish when cooked the Venetian way and accompanied by polenta; a local kind of crayfish, called *canoce,* is served as an appetizer or again as a base for spaghetti sauce; eel is always fresh, and is either grilled or stewed with tomatoes (*anguilla in umido*); a local crab, *granceola,* is one of the best appetizers to be found anywhere in the world. Even the homely sardine has become the base of an excellent and curious dish, called *sardine in saor,* an inheritance from the glorious heyday of the Venetian navy, which discovered that most proteins are well conserved in a bath of fried onions and vinegar.

Meat dishes are for the most part not regional, which doesn't mean that they are not prepared properly. At least two among the few meat restaurants in town seem to us particularly worthy of praise: Da Arturo and Da Ivo (see below).

See also the description of Torcello, above, for restaurants there.

Sestiere di San Marco—Rialto

Excellent fish is served at the first-class **Do Forni**, a landmark of cuisine in Venice, as is the world-famous Harry's Bar. At Do Forni, a couple of hundred yards from piazza San Marco on the Mercerie (San Marco 457; Tel: 523-21-48; Fax: 528-81-32), it is common to see the political and commercial leaders of Venice, in an atmosphere full of local color (closed Thursdays except in summer). **Harry's Bar** (calle Vallaresso 1323; Tel: 528-57-77; Fax: 520-88-22; closed Mondays and January 6–13) has become a must for all important visitors, whether American movie stars or world-famous writers. The restaurant's service is among the best in the world, and its second-floor windows looking onto La Salute are a splendid extra treat—which you'll pay for dearly.

The bar has now opened an extension called **Harry's Dolci** on the island of Giudecca; it is more moderate in price and has very quickly become a favorite with Venetian society. Tel: 522-48-44; Fax: 522-23-22; closed November 7–March 7; otherwise open daily.

On the campo San Fantin, right along the façade of La Fenice, **Al Teatro** has a blessed policy of staying open till late at night. This is where Venetians go for a meal after the Fenice performances. In the summer the restaurant takes over the handsome campo with its tables, and although a lot of its customers are tourists, many are also Venetians. The food is consistently good, the service very professional, and the prices in the upper-middle range. Tel: 522-10-52; closed Mondays.

Informal and very much liked by young Venetian professionals is **Vino Vino** on calle delle Veste, about 100 yards southeast of La Fenice. This modern, fancy version of the old wine shops offers a choice of 350 wines, a large number of snacks, and a complete restaurant menu at more than reasonable prices. Tel: 522-41-21 or 523-70-27; closed Tuesdays.

Down a narrow street from La Fenice, **Da Arturo** on calle degli Assassini (Tel: 528-69-74) is one of the best meat restaurants in town. It has only seven tables, which allows for total attention from the owner (whose name is, unexpectedly, Ernesto). Ernesto serves excellent meats, imaginative salads, and very good wines (his Amarone is memorable). This is also one of the few restaurants where customers are welcome to order just a pasta and a salad without feeling pressed for an entrée—a detail that makes it, paradoxically, the best vegetarian restaurant in town (Ernesto has a knack for interesting vegetable dishes). The prices are rather on the upper end of the range. Closed Sundays and three weeks in August.

In the same neighborhood, at calle dei Fuseri 1809 (from the theater turn left after calle dei Barcaroli), is the small but very refined **Da Ivo**. The owner is a Tuscan who seems to live for his culinary art. He supervises every dish personally and treats his customers with old-fashioned, delightful courtesy. His fish dishes are exceptional, and he is about the only one in town who can offer a real *bistecca alla fiorentina* (a large T-bone steak worthy of comparison with the best to be had in the United States). Either formal or informal dress, and not inexpensive, but worth every lira. Reservations recommended; Tel: 528-50-04. Closed Sundays and January.

Although technically in Cannaregio, the two restaurants that follow are mentioned in this section because of their proximity to the monument area. The **Fiaschetteria Toscana**, at San Giovanni Crisostomo 5719 (near the main post office at Rialto), has a large and faithful clientele of lawyers, architects, and gourmets from the rest of the professional world. In spite of its name, it is one of the leading centers of Venetian cuisine, and it has a special reputation for wines. In the summer it takes over a small area in the front square; it fills up very quickly, so reservations are a must. Tel: 528-52-81; closed Tuesdays and three weeks in July.

A few steps from the Fiaschetteria, the popular restaurant **Osteria Il Milion** (corte Prima al Milion 5841) is always crowded with young and not-so-young Venetians who are out for a good meal at affordable prices. The menu is handwritten, in Italian of course, on a pad that the owner will lend for a few minutes; the setting is totally unpretentious and gives a good idea of what in Italy is considered a pleasant family restaurant. The wines are good, and so is the service. Tel: 522-93-02; closed Wednesdays.

Sestiere di Castello

A number of tourist restaurants line the beautiful riva degli Schiavoni east of San Marco. Among them is **Il Gabbiano**, one bridge after the church of La Pietà (riva Schiavoni 4122). Gabbiano is one of those few restaurants here that truly care about food quality. The service is very professional and the setting is splendid. Tel: 522-39-88; closed Mondays.

In a tiny street between the Arsenale and campo Bandiera e Moro is **Corte Sconta**, one of the best fish restaurants in town. In the summer the tables are set on a delightful inner courtyard, with an informal but refined style that puts everybody at ease. Here the tradition is to lay aside the menu and let the two waitresses (the wife and sister-in-law of Claudio, the owner) run the whole show. They serve a long series of antipasti, with perfect timing and in increasing order of interest; then they introduce the three pasta dishes of the day, a taste of each, and for the few people who may feel up to it they offer a whole array of entrées. The house wine is perfectly fine: Prosecco or Marzemino from the Veneto hills. (Marzemino is the wine that Don Giovanni drinks in the last act of Mozart's opera. No wonder, since the librettist was from a village near Venice.) Calle del Pestrin 3886; Tel: 522-70-24; closed Sunday evenings, Mondays, and three weeks in August.

Rapidly emerging as one of the best restaurants in town is **Al Covo**, located a few steps from Riva degli Schiavoni. Opened in 1986, Al Covo is run by a young woman from Austin, Texas, and her Venetian husband—ideal for English-speaking guests. Try the *coda al covo* (baked monkfish with baby artichokes) or the *spaghetti al ragù di canoce* (spaghetti with mantis shrimp sauce). The service is highly professional and the atmosphere pleasantly relaxed although not too informal. Reserve early for an outdoor table (campiello Pescaria 3968, Tel: 522-38-12, closed Wednesdays, Thursdays, January, and August; expensive).

A real surprise in the heart of popular, colorful Castello is the **Hostaria Da Franz** (fondamenta di San Giuseppe 754). An elegant canopy announcing the sophistication of the establishment covers the outdoor dining area, and candle-light dining along the canal is an experience to be savored. The food and service are excellent, and prices, predictably, in the upper range. A walk back to San Marco along the riva degli Schiavoni will crown a memorable evening. Tel: 522-08-61 or 522-75-05; closed Tuesdays.

Another real find—this one on the unpretentious side—is a restaurant right on the campo dell'Arsenale at number 2389, with tables outdoors in front of the great lions that guard the Arsenale's monumental entrance. It has no name, but it is known as "**Da Paolo**," the name of the owner. His young wife and charming daughter—a student of architecture—try their best as waitresses. The setting is extremely pleasant, and the whole neighborhood sits here for pizza or spaghetti on the warm summer nights. They all seem to be friends and relatives of each other, and not very shy in calling for service. The prices are very affordable and the pasta is cooked to order; try spaghetti with clams or with *seppie*, or ask for the pasta of the day. Tel: 521-06-60; closed Mondays.

Inexpensive, friendly, and pleasantly populated by Venetians of all social classes is **Al Mascaron**, near campo Santa

Maria Formosa. Choose your meal from the display at the counter, or ask your waiter for the dishes of the day. Calle Lunga Santa Maria Formosa 5225; Tel: 522-59-95; closed Sundays and most of August.

Sestieri di San Polo–Santa Croce

In San Polo, not far from the Frari church, on charming rio Marin, is the **Caffè Orientale**. Sandro and Mario, the two brothers who own it, are Venetian to the core and have resurrected the name of their restaurant from a 19th-century establishment. Here the local fish reigns supreme: Sandro buys it directly from the fishermen every morning. The caffè has a tiny terrace over a canal, and you must call in advance to reserve a table on it: It makes for a quiet, intimate evening. Also, many people ask Sandro to call for a gondola at the end of their meals. The gondola will pick them up right at the terrace—no better way to end a day of Venetian relaxation. Ponte de la Late 2426, Tel: 71-98-04; closed Mondays.

A few steps from the Rialto bridge, **Trattoria Alla Madonna** is an extremely busy place in the tradition of Italian *trattorie:* informal, moderately priced, it offers the best in regional recipes and in fresh fish. If you want to try the best *branzino* or *orata* without going bankrupt, this is the place. Calle della Madonna 954; Tel: 522-38-24; closed Wednesdays.

L'Antico Dolo is a former *osteria* (wine bar) that is slowly turning into a restaurant. All dishes are cooked and served as they would be in an Italian home—informal, inexpensive, and delicious. Ruga Vecchia San Giovanni 778 (near the Rialto bridge); closed Sundays.

On a narrow street between campo San Polo and campo San Tomà is **Da Ignazio**, very busy with local customers who like Ignazio's fish dishes and his pleasant garden. The atmosphere is friendly, the service professional. Calle Saoneri 2749; Tel: 523-48-52; closed Saturdays.

The restaurant **San Tomà**, also in San Polo, is set on the quiet and charming campo of the same name (outdoor tables). It serves pizza, too, but it is very good with antipasti, pasta, and fish entrées. Campo San Tomà 2864-A; Tel: 523-88-19; closed Tuesdays except in summer.

In Santa Croce, the **Osteria Al Nono Risorto** is across the bridge off campo San Cassiano. It is a friendly and informal place, rather inexpensive, where the preparation of the food and quality of the service exhibit the touch of the experienced hand. Dining indoors or in the courtyard under a remarkable wisteria tree. Sottoportego de Siora Bettina; Tel: 524-11-69; closed Wednesdays.

A wonderful place for an inexpensive meal outdoors is

Trattoria Alle Colonnette, set in the campo San Giacomo dell'Orio, under the medieval bell tower and along a canal. Venetians go here for pizza as well as pasta; between 8:30 and 10:00 P.M. there could be a waiting line. Campo San Giacomo dell'Orio (no phone).

Pizzeria Alle Oche rates among the three or four best pizza places in town. One should go early (between 7:00 and 7:30 P.M.) to have a chance to sit at one of the few outdoor tables. Calle del Tintor 1552-B (right off campo San Giacomo dell'Orio); Tel: 524-11-61; closed Mondays.

Specializing in pasta and in vegetables, **Ristorante Alla Zucca** is patronized by intellectuals and nonconformist types. The prices are moderate and the wine is excellent. Ponte del Megio 1762 (right off campo San Giacomo dell'Orio); Tel: 524-15-70; closed Sundays.

Sestiere di Cannaregio

We mentioned Cannaregio's **Fiaschetteria Toscana** and **Osteria Il Milion** in the San Marco–Rialto section. After a visit to the Ghetto or to Madonna dell'Orto, two other restaurants in this neighborhood are to be recommended.

All'Antica Mola, on fondamenta degli Ormesini, is totally unpretentious, with family-style cooking and service. The *naïf* views of Venice on the walls bear witness to the simple yet somehow uncorrupted taste of the old owners (and take a look at the fresco in the back courtyard, though mosquitoes make it better to eat inside). Tel: 71-74-92; closed Saturdays.

Osteria Al Bacco, at fondamenta degli Ormesini down the iron bridge off the campo del Ghetto, is one of the best places for Venetian food in an informal yet pleasant setting. It was an old wine shop and has been remodeled with a reverence for tradition. One of the side pleasures is the walk back along the fondamenta degli Ormesini and fondamenta della Misericordia. Tel: 71-74-93; closed Tuesdays.

Sestiere di Dorsoduro

Montin, in the fondamenta delle Eremite near Le Zattere, is a real institution in town; its walls are crowded with the works of painters who patronize it, and there is a charming garden in the back. Many Venetians have held their marriage banquets here, and the atmosphere has a constant ring of festivity; it is not rare at all for otherwise stern university professors and business managers to show up with guitars and get lost in reminiscence with songs of the 1950s and 1960s. Giuliano Montin and his wife have known all these people since childhood, and this sort of thing is the real beauty of being a Venetian. Tourists, especially Americans, discovered this place years ago. In the summer they fill up the large garden rather quickly, so you should reserve. Fondamenta delle Eremite (also called di Borgo) 1147; Tel: 522-33-07; closed Tuesday evenings and Wednesdays.

Although it has no tables outdoors, restaurant **Donna Onesta**, at the foot of the bridge of the same name, is very well liked by Venetians for the excellent quality of the food and the affordable prices. Totally remodeled in 1990, it is still run in a friendly and competent manner by Gino, the original owner. Fish appetizers and pasta are the best choices; the wines are excellent. Ponte di Donna Onesta 3922; Tel: 522-95-86; closed Sundays.

Three sisters and their husbands run the **Ristorante Ai Cugnai** ("At the Brothers-in-Law"), near the Accademia bridge. Very informal, it offers no frills but tasty food and honest prices—no wonder it's always hard to find a table. Piscina del Forner 857; Tel: 528-92-38; closed Mondays.

In the summer evenings Venetians stream to romantic Le Zattere and stop for pizza or for a relatively inexpensive meal in one of two restaurants that have wood terraces along the water of the Canale della Giudecca (**Da Gianni**, near the boat stop for Giudecca, or **Alle Zattere**, a few yards away toward La Salute). The quality of the food, while not haute cuisine, is definitely acceptable, and the setting is magnificent. Customers sit out in the open, catching every breeze, seeing old friends, and watching the huge container ships that cruise past on their way to or from the Venice harbor.

Still on fondamenta delle Zattere (number 1473), but farther west in the direction of San Basilio, is one of the best finds in town: **Snack Bar Riviera**. In reality a full restaurant, it has tables along the canal and serves exceptionally good food at relatively moderate prices. Venetians fill it up very quickly, so reservations are a must; Tel: 522-76-21. Closed Sunday evenings and Mondays.

For a good pizza in a pleasant outdoor setting, the people of Dorsoduro go to **Al Sole di Napoli**, in the handsome campo Santa Margherita. There is a small ocean of outdoor tables, but they fill up quickly every night. Campo Santa Margherita 3023; Tel: 528-56-86; closed Thursdays.

The Lido

The boulevard connecting the boat stops to the beaches (Gran Viale Santa Maria Elisabetta) is lined with restaurants and *pizzerie*. They offer mediocre food but the surroundings are pleasant. A very good establishment at the Lido is **Ristorante Belvedere**, right across from the vaporetto number 1 stop, piazzale S. M. Elisabetta 4. Pleasantly crowded, it specializes in fish and risotto. Tel: 526-01-15; closed Mondays.

NIGHTLIFE

There are no nightclubs or discotheques in Venice. Most luxury hotels have a piano bar open to nonguests till one in the morning. Very pleasant are the ones at the **Hotel Monaco** (see Accommodations) and at the **Hotel Danieli** (on riva degli Schiavoni; the bar affords a view of the Gothic reception hall, the best feature of this otherwise overrated establishment). There is also a piano bar open until 3:00 A.M. at the **Antico Martini** restaurant (campo San Fantin, near La Fenice theater; closed Tuesdays).

Venice is one of four cities in Italy allowed to operate a gambling casino: April to September at the Lido (frequent boat service, the "Casino Express," from Piazzale Roma and San Marco); October to March at Palazzo Vendramin Calergi in Cannaregio (boat stop San Marcuola). The entrance fee is 15,000 lire; roulette, chemin de fer, blackjack, and occasionally craps; slot machines were installed in 1992.

SHOPS AND SHOPPING

Clothes, jewelry, shoes, Murano glass, Burano lace, Carnival masks—Venice is really a shopper's paradise. The narrow passageway between San Marco and Rialto, appropriately called the Mercerie (Merchandise Street), has been lined with all kinds of stores since the 14th century; today all the great brand names are abundantly represented, from Missoni to Armani to Krizia and Versace. Even Cartier has a luxurious extension on the Mercerie. The other busy shopping area— also near San Marco—is Frezzeria, running from Harry's Bar to the La Fenice theater. Only the constant stream of visitors could keep so many shops alive in this city of a mere 75,000; thus foreign languages, especially English, are spoken everywhere, to the point where it becomes difficult to practice your painfully learned Italian.

The prices, however, are another story: so high that most visitors wonder if Venetians use secret tricks for their own shopping. But there are no secrets. From shirts to shoes and from bread to tomatoes, Venetians have to pay the same inflated prices as visitors, unless they are willing to wait for the end-of-season sales or to ride all the way to the shopping centers on the mainland.

Murano Glass

You don't have to ride to Murano to find the best products of that island, or to find better prices. Actually, word has it that in most cases the Venice shops and glassmakers' furnaces are cheaper than those in Murano. For classic, traditional glass go to **Cenedese**, which occupies a whole palazzo on the Canal Grande near La Salute in Dorsoduro; quite a few antique pieces can be seen here, giving you a good idea of the history and evolution of the glass industry (there is also a furnace for demonstrations). For contemporary design, the most famous and praised among the large firms are **Venini**, with a shop on piazza San Marco, across from the left wall of the basilica, and **Barovier & Toso**, at campo San Moisè near San Marco. A very large assortment of works by the best glass masters is to be found at **Pauly's**, on the side of piazza San Marco all the way across from the basilica. Pauly's salespeople are true and serious professionals, and they ship reliably all over the world.

Burano Lace
The best lace production of Burano can be seen in the large **Jesurum** store in Venice, near ponte della Canonica behind the Basilica di San Marco and a few yards from the Bridge of Sighs (ponte dei Sospiri).

Carnival Masks
Ever since the Venetian Carnival was resurrected by the city's tourist office in 1979, shops of Carnival masks have been mushrooming in every neighborhood. The best are the ones in which advanced craftsmanship is coupled with a serious study of the old traditions; such is **Mondonovo**, a small and crowded shop run with great expertise by Guerrino Lovato and Giorgio Spiller at number 3063 rio Terrà Canal (dei Pugni), just off campo Santa Margherita, in sestiere Dorsoduro. Lovato is very popular among Venetians for his knowledge of art history and for his contributions to frequent spectacles requiring the use of masks; it is not unusual to find him involved in heated discussions about the Commedia dell'Arte with actors and directors amid the surrealistic decor of his often disquieting creations. He shows his stage sets, and sells them to the general public across the street from the mask shop.

Jewelry
It is well known that the large majority of the jewelry exported from Italy is manufactured in Vicenza, a town on the Venetian mainland. Therefore the local stores are very numerous and always up-to-date in terms of style. Quite a few are on the Mercerie, while some of the oldest and most reliable have their premises right on the piazza San Marco.

Among the latter, Venetians seem to prefer **Missiaglia** (piazza San Marco 125), which has been at their service for many generations. Another good shop is **Codognato** (San Marco, calle Ascensione 1295). Excellent jewelry, very courteous service, and, above all, really fair prices are to be found at **Gioielleria Elena**, which also specializes in wristwatches by Audemars Piguet, Buccellati, Chanel, and others (213–216 Mercerie dell'Orologio, a few steps from piazza San Marco).

Venetian Craftsmanship

Besides glass and lace, Venetian artisans used to excel in wood carving, textile printing, bookbinding, bronze casting, and many other fields. Some of these specialties have now been resurrected after a long period of neglect. More and more people are looking for handmade objects in spite of the necessarily high prices, and the offerings are increasing with the demand. A good area to explore for this purpose is the neighborhood of Santo Stefano–Palazzo Grassi. The stores that follow are concentrated there.

Marbled Paper. **Legatoria Piazzesi**, near campo San Maurizio (San Marco 2511), is an old institution in Venice. Formally a bookbindery, it has enlarged its scope to include a large variety of related items, from notebooks to calendars to picture frames. **Il Papiro**, a large modern shop on the calle Piovan between San Maurizio and campo Santo Stefano, boasts the greatest variety of high-quality paper items, most of it handmade in Venice and Florence. **Alberto Valese**, at salizzada San Samuele 3135 near Palazzo Grassi, prepares the paper on the small premises, and he doesn't mind if visitors watch him or his wife while they do it.

Wood-Carvers. Variously called *indoradori* or *marangoni da soase,* these artisans still flourish in Venice. They offer gilded frames, lamps, and wood statues, mostly in 18th-century styles. A good one, with no known name, is on salizzada San Samuele at number 3337; another, called **Cavalier**, is on nearby campo Santo Stefano, on the side closest to the ponte dell'Accademia, at number 2863/A.

Lino de Marchi, a few steps from Palazzo Grassi in sestiere San Marco, at salizzada San Samuele 3157/A, is halfway between an artisan and a sculptor. He produces delicately crafted wood sculptures that bear an astonishing resemblance to everyday objects. **Venice Design**, a gallery of contemporary design on the same street, specializes in glass and metal objects by known designers. Besides the items in the windows, it keeps some astonishing surprises in its safe.

Hats. A real marvel of Venice's craftsmanship is the store of

Signora Giuliana Longo. In her upstairs laboratory, Signora Longo creates hats of all styles and periods. The Carnival made her famous for her tricorn hats, and stage directors frequently go to her for reliable advice. As she opens the boxes containing her wonderful creations, her small store turns into a paradise of feathers, pearls, and cloth flowers of all kinds. On San Marco, calle del Lovo 4813 (between the Rialto bridge and campo San Luca). Tel: 522-64-54.

Textile Printing

A tradition of textile printing was established in Venice by the painter and inventor Mariano Fortuny (1871–1949). His work-shop is still producing textiles on Giudecca, and samples can be seen at **Trois,** in the campo San Maurizio near San Marco.

Marvelous velvets are still hand-printed in Venice using Fortuny's methods. A good assortment can be seen at **Arianna da Venezia**, the astonishing shop opened in 1989 by a high-society grande dame on the ground floor of a Canal Grande palazzo (in Dorsoduro, across from the vaporetto stop at Ca' Rezzonico, 2793). She hand-prints her velvets and cottons personally and uses them imaginatively for clothes, curtains, bedspreads, and to cover small objects such as notebooks, lamps, and Carnival masks. Tel: 522-15-35.

Books

While most good bookstores carry English-language publica-tions on Venice, the largest choice is to be found at the **Libreria Sangiorgio**, in the via XXII Marzo near the piazza San Marco. There is also an English bookstore called **Il Libraio a San Barnaba** (in Dorsoduro, number 2835/A, near Santa Margherita), a preferred rendezvous for the many English majors at the nearby university. In these places you will be sure to find such classics as Jan Morris's *Venice* and Mary McCarthy's *Venice Observed,* together with Toby Cole's collec-tion, *Venice, A Portable Reader,* and M. Battilana's *English Writers and Venice,* and of course a few English-language copies of Giulio Lorenzetti's *Venice,* the unsurpassed guide-book, constantly updated since its first publication in 1926.

Specializing exclusively in the astonishingly abundant liter-ary production about Venice is the **Libreria Filippi** in the Sottoportego della Bissa, near the Rialto in sestiere San Marco. To the visitor who can read Italian this bookstore offers a wide range of works, from the most specialized academic contributions to superbly illustrated volumes on Venetian architecture. Particularly interesting are the cata-logues, in many languages, of exhibits held in the city's museums.

THE VENETO

By Paolo Lanapoppi

Life is particularly sweet to the inhabitants of this privileged part of Italy. Within a two-hour drive they can move from some of the most impressive peaks in the Alps to a hundred miles of Mediterranean beaches; between those two areas gentle hills create a landscape known to the world through the paintings of Giorgione and Cima da Conegliano, in a countryside that is also home to some of the best wines—as well as some of the best cooking—in Italy. From the Romans to the Ostrogoths to the Renaissance and up to today, 20 centuries of civilization have left their artistic traces in every urban center, and in the past 40 years the local economy, previously depressed, has unexpectedly boomed, spreading prosperity and security through every level of society.

The Veneti take full advantage of this situation. They are hard workers, great managers, and proud professionals, but they love to enjoy their free time and would think nothing of driving an hour to try a new trattoria with a good reputation. They would then discuss the quality of its food and wines with astonishing energy. Because the Veneti are attached to family values and to the traditions of their land, they raise their children in old-fashioned ways, speak the local dialects in spite of the leveling effects of the centralized media, and know every corner of their region. Ever since they started to flock to vacations in Kenya, the Seychelles, and Thailand—like every good European—they have been comparing destinations, and they may not be wrong when they conclude that there are few—if any—corners of the world as worth visiting as the Veneto.

For visitors, the Veneto can be divided into three sections: the Plains, the southern area outside Venice that includes Treviso, Padua, Vicenza, and Verona; the Hill Belt, which includes the eastern shores of Lago di Garda, the thermal-water centers, Asolo, and the birthplaces of Giorgione and Cima da Conegliano; and the Mountain Belt, at the north of the Veneto, including Cortina d'Ampezzo and the Cadore.

MAJOR INTEREST

The Plains
Country villas, many by Andrea Palladio
Regional cooking
Old cities of Verona, Vicenza, Padua, and Treviso
Brenta canal, lined with villas
Bibione and other coastal resorts

Hill Belt
Fine cuisine and wines
Lago di Garda
Abano and Recoaro thermal baths
Castelfranco
Asolo's scenic beauty

Mountain Belt
Skiing, hiking, scenery
Cortina d'Ampezzo and other resorts
The Cadore

THE PLAINS

The spaces between the major cities on the plains of the Veneto have now become a continuum of farms, dwellings, and small firms, so the whole area can be considered a huge—although untypical—urban settlement. Here the houses are scattered throughout the land and join in clusters only in correspondence with preexisting (often medieval) towns and villages. All of the four major cities on the Veneto plains are rich in history past and present; almost all are built on a river of some sort and have large sections of green, making life in each more pleasant through constant contact with nature.

Verona

On the western side of the Plains, Verona is the natural link between Venice and Milan, as well as between the rest of

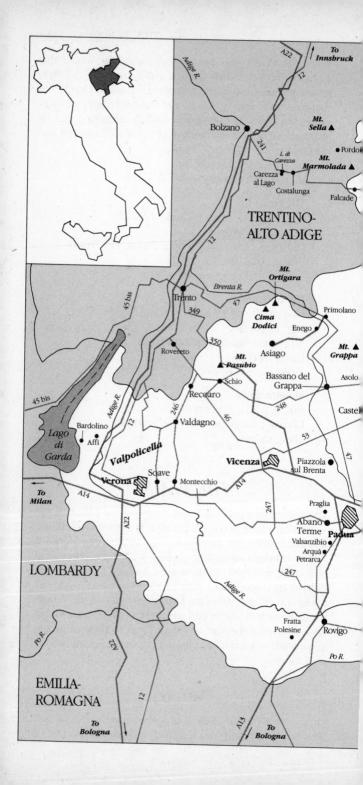

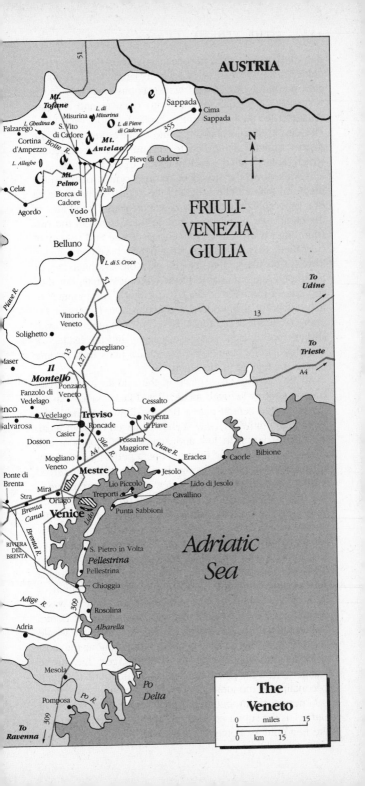

Italy and many other European countries. Its district includes the eastern shore of Lago di Garda, which is dotted with medieval citadels and world-famous vineyards and is very popular in the summer with German and Austrian tourists. (See the Lake Country chapter for more on Garda.) The city itself is probably the most interesting among the district capitals of the Veneto because of its architecture, which ranges from the ancient Roman to the Baroque.

A walk down the streets of Verona's center, between the medieval **piazza delle Erbe** and the Roman arena in piazza Bra, especially on a weekday morning, gives a good idea of the composite population living in the city and in the surrounding towns. A large percentage of café and restaurant customers are unmistakably farmers who have come downtown for business. They may still wear old-fashioned hats or be slightly uncomfortable in their business suits, but they run one of the most advanced agricultural communities in Italy; they are the modern and sophisticated heirs of the poor *contadini* of old times. Here in Verona they mix with lawyers, accountants, service managers, and the leaders of countless family businesses. The annual per capita income here is the highest in the Veneto.

All this activity takes place in the middle of an urban landscape crowded with medieval and Renaissance masterworks. In the central piazza Bra, the **Roman Arena** is the ancient amphitheater, only slightly damaged through its almost 2,000 years. In July and August 20,000 persons still crowd it every evening to watch opera performances. Lombardic and Gothic kings made Verona their preferred residence—and of course left a few signs of their passage—but the most impressive buildings are probably the medieval ones: The church of **San Zeno Maggiore** is Romanesque architecture at its purest (and includes a famous triptych by Mantegna); the piazza dei Signori was the former center of government, with its Palazzo della Ragione (1193), Palazzo del Governo (end of the 13th century), and beautiful Loggia del Consiglio (end of the 15th century). The great family of Della Scala—rulers of Verona between the time it was a republic and the conquest by Venice, protectors of Dante, and at a certain point serious candidates to rule the whole north of Italy—left a monument here that is among the most moving and seductive of the Middle Ages: the **Arche Scaligere**, near the piazza dei Signori, a compound designed to contain the monumental tombs of the family members.

A mere curiosity, but one that still attracts large crowds of tourists, is the supposed **tomb of Juliet** (she lived in Verona, like her unlucky Romeo). Whether historically accurate or

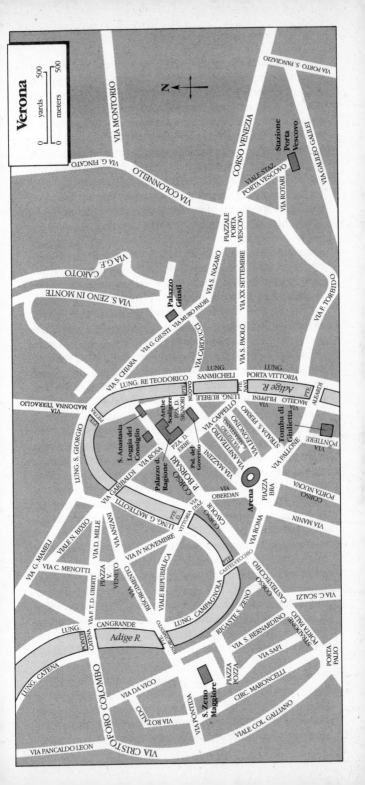

Verona

yards 500
meters 500

N

VIA PORTO S. PANCRAZIO
VIA MONTORIO
VIA G. FINATO
VIA COLONNELLO
CORSO VENEZIA
Stazione Porta Vescovo
VIA GALILEO GALILEI
VIALE STAZ. PORTA VESCOVO
VIA ROTARI
VIA G.F. CAROTO
VIA S. ZENO IN MONTE
Palazzo Giusti
VIA S. ZENO
VIA G. GIUSTI
VIA MURO PADRI
VIA S. NAZARO
VIA CARDUCCI
VIA XX SETTEMBRE
PIAZZALE PORTA VESCOVO
VIA F. TORBIDO
VIA S. PAOLO
VIA S. CHIARA
LUNG. SANMICHELI
LUNG. PORTA VITTORIA
Adige R.
VIA MACELLO FILIPPINI
ALEARDI
VIA MADONNA TERRAGLIO
LUNG. RE TEODORICO
NUOVO
PTE
LUNG. RUBELE
VIA CAPPELLO
Tomba di Giulietta
VIA PONTIERE
LUNG. S. GIORGIO
VILLA
PIETRA
Arche Scaligere
PZA. D. SIGNORI
PZA. D. ERBE
VIA CAMPESTRINO
VIA LEONCINO
STRADA S. FERMO
VIA PALLONE
S. Anastasia
Loggia del Consiglio
VIA ROSA
Pal. del Governo
VIA ANFITEATRO
VIA MAZZINI
PIAZZA NUOVA
CORSO
VIA GARIBALDI
Palazzo d. Ragione
CORSO D. BORSARI
Arena
PIAZZA BRA
LUNG. G. MATTEOTTI
PTE. VITTORIA
CORSO CAVOUR
VIA OBERDAN
VIA ROMA
CORSO PORTA NUOVA
VIA MANIN
VIALE N. BIXIO
VIA ANZANI
VIA D. MILLE
VIA IV NOVEMBRE
VIA C. SCALZI
VIA G. MAMELI
VIA C. MENOTTI
PIAZZA V. VENETO
VIA F. T. D' UBERTI
RISORGIMENTO
VIALE REPUBBLICA
Castelvecchio
CORSO CASTELVECCHIO
LUNG. CANGRANDE
Adige R.
PONTE CATENA
LUNG. CATENA
VIA CRISTOFORO COLOMBO
VIA DA VICO
VIA ROT. ALDO
VIA PONTIDA
LUNG. CAMPAGNOLA
RIGASTE S. ZENO
S. Zeno Maggiore
PIAZZA POZZA
VIA S. BERNARDINO
VIA SAFI
STRADONE PORTA PALIO
PORTA PALIO
VIA PANCALDO LEON
VIA COL. GALLIANO
CIRC. MARONCELLI

not, the legend is a good pretext to visit a romantic medieval corner ornamented with prints and paintings inspired by one of our greatest love stories (near the ponte Aleardi, just walking distance from piazza Bra). At via Cappello 27, near the piazza delle Erbe, fans of Juliet can also admire what are supposed to have been her house and balcony.

You can enjoy a panoramic view of this charming town from the huge terraced garden of the **Palazzo Giusti**. The palazzo was built in 1580; the garden, landscaped in the 18th century and very carefully preserved, is one of the most successful specimens of the Italian school of gardening.

Lunching and dining in Verona could pose a problem, because so many restaurants both in town and in the surrounding countryside are of a high level and reputation—and correspondingly expensive. Reservations can be made in English, however, and are strongly recommended—a telephone call a few hours in advance is usually sufficient (area code 045). The very famous **Dodici Apostoli** (Tel: 59-69-99; closed Sunday evenings, Mondays, and June 15–30), near the piazza delle Erbe at corticella San Marco 3, is a classic both in decor and in local cuisine. Rapidly becoming one of the best restaurants in the nation is **Il Desco** (on via Dietro San Sebastiano, near Juliet's house; Tel: 59-53-58; closed Sundays and June 15–30), where in a medieval setting the traditional food of the area—fish from Lago di Garda, venison, mushrooms—is served with daring and often memorable innovations. Verona also has two restaurants specializing in fish: **Il Nuovo Marconi** (sea bass or pike from Lago di Garda, on via Fogge, around the corner from Il Desco; Tel: 59-19-10; closed Sundays and July 1–15); and **Arche** (near the Arche Scaligere), the place for *branzino al cartoccio,* a delicious concoction of sea bass wrapped with mollusks (Tel: 800-74-15; closed Sundays and Monday lunch).

The best among the many hotels in town is the luxury-class **Due Torri Baglioni**—very central, endowed with a good restaurant, and noteworthy for the quality of its furnishings. The **Accademia**, also very central and also with a good restaurant, is more affordable. A pleasant and relatively inexpensive place is the **Antica Porta Leona**, between the arena and the river Adige; this renovated hotel has two 17th-century fireplaces in its salon.

Vicenza

Like Verona, Vicenza, in the center of the Veneto, has recently emerged from a history of relatively poor agricultural economy to become one of the most affluent centers on the peninsula. The *modello Veneto,* a much-studied pattern of economic transformation, has achieved some of its most striking successes here. (For more on this, see the Hill Belt section that follows.) Very important among the protagonists of this transformation are the countless goldsmiths, who fashion all kinds of jewelry for the international markets. Three times a year (January, July, and September) these patient, imaginative heirs of Benvenuto Cellini hold their international fair, a dazzling event: 15,000 professional buyers from all over the world come to Vicenza to buy from 1,000 exhibitors. On one afternoon per session the fair is open to the general public; no direct buying is allowed, though—only watching, admiring, and possibly writing down a few addresses for later visits.

Although a pleasant city in itself, with large green areas and three small, idyllic rivers, Vicenza owes its celebrity especially to Andrea Palladio, who moved to this city in early childhood from his native Padua and built some of his best palazzi here, as well as many villas in the surrounding countryside. These are the prototypes of hundreds of mansions and churches scattered throughout Europe (particularly England); Palladio was seen as having interpreted Roman antiquity in the best Italian Renaissance tradition. His masterworks are all within walking distance—or, at worst, within a short taxi ride.

A real must is the **Teatro Olimpico**, the last work by Palladio (1580, the year of his death; construction was completed by Vincenzo Scamozzi, who built important structures in Venice). With the Olimpico, the great architect, following his familiar Vitruvius, tried to re-create a Roman classical space but, of course, modernized it to meet the architectural and theatrical standards of his times, adding 95 statues and a famous trompe l'oeil scene representing the five streets of Thebes.

Not far from the theater is the **piazza dei Signori**, where Palladio rebuilt, or rather covered up with his façades, the old Palazzo della Ragione, calling it the Basilica, and added the powerful Loggia Bernarda. This is a fine starting point for a half-hour walk to cover some of the best Palladian palazzi in town. Across the nearby main street of Vicenza, appropriately called corso Andrea Palladio, is the famous **contrà Porti** (*contrà* is one of the local names for street). A few steps up the contrà, at number 11, is Palazzo Porto Barbaran, remodeled by Palladio in 1570 over an existing structure. At number 12 across the way a modern bank has taken over Palazzo Thiene (the eastern façade is by Palladio, 1558). At number 21, Palladio's Palazzo Iseppo Da Porto, unfinished, was deemed "unsurpassable" by Vasari. Many Gothic buildings line this beautiful and busy street. Along Palazzo Porto Bar-baran is the contrà Reale, leading to corso A. Fogazzaro, where Palladio built Palazzo Valmarana Braga (number 16). Back on corso Palladio (closed to traffic on Sundays), you can walk 500 yards to Palazzo Chiericati, near the Teatro Olimpico and now the Museo Civico. (Palladio built it in the 1550s.)

It was not exclusively out of love for his adoptive city that Palladio spent so much energy here. The truth is that in the capital city of Venice, his rival Sansovino—in alliance with Titian and with the poet Pietro Aretino—enjoyed a monopoly over all civic art. In Venice Palladio had to limit himself to religious buildings, and, moreover, he saw quite a few of his projects rejected by the city fathers.

A somewhat longer walk along the banks of the river Retrone leads to Palazzo Civena Trissino, one of the first works by Palladio and the one that made his reputation. The Trissinos were the discoverers of Palladio's talent when he was a young stonecutter in Padua; this 1540 building, now a private hospital, shows a clear kinship with the great Roman architecture of the time, particularly that of Raffaello and Bramante.

Because of this Palladian feast, little attention is usually given to structures in and around Vicenza that otherwise would merit much more than a passing glance. Such is the medieval compound of piazza dei Signori, piazza delle Biade, and piazza delle Erbe, with the daringly slim Torre di Piazza and the nearby house of the navigator Antonio Pigafetta (a companion and lieutenant of Ferdinand Magellan), an astonishing mixture of Gothic, Renaissance, and Spanish elements at via Pigafetta 5. Of great archaeological interest is the early medieval church of **Santi Felice e Fortunato**, with remnants of a fourth-century church, a kilometer (half a mile) west of Porta Castello.

Fifteen minutes by car from the medieval center, on top of a carefully landscaped hill, is the **Basilica of Monte Berico**, rebuilt in Baroque style at the end of the 17th century. (You can also go on foot, through the 192 steps of the strada delle Scalette departing from Porta Monte, and then under the 150 arches of an amazing 18th-century portico. The portico is also visible from the car.) The basilica offers a splendid view of town and countryside, and it hosts a grandiose canvas by Veronese: the *Supper of Saint Gregory the Great* (painted in 1572). At 25 by 15 feet, the painting is one of the largest of its kind, and it is considered to be among Veronese's master-works. Its purpose was to adorn the dining hall of the Berico friars, and for many centuries it must have brightened up their disciplined meals (just like the controversial *Last Supper* Veronese painted in 1573 for the Dominicans of Venice, a work whose interest in frivolous detail cost him a trial and a partial retraction).

On the slopes of Monte Berico, on the way from Vicenza to the basilica, is the 18th-century **Villa Valmarana**, called "Dei Nani" because of the dwarfs sculpted on the garden walls. (To get there by car from the train station, cross the Retrone at Porta Lupia and drive up viale 10 Giugno to the panoramic Spianata del Cristo; a small road on the left leads to the villa after half a mile.) To the surprise and delight of the casual visitor, this villa contains one of the most fascinating cycles of frescoes in the entire Veneto, done by Giovanni Battista Tiepolo and his son, Giandomenico. The father painted the Palazzina; the son, the nearby Foresteria (guest house). The Venetian 18th century is represented here at its zenith: luminous, optimistic, and festive from Giovanni Battista; and touched by a feeling of imminent catastrophe from the intense, disquieting Giandomenico (open March 15 to September 30, Monday through Friday, 3:00 to 6:00 P.M., and 10:00 A.M. to noon on Wednesday, Thursday, Saturday, and Sunday; October 1 to November 15, Monday through Friday 2:00 to 5:00 P.M.; closed November 16 to March 14).

A short walk from Villa Valmarana is another villa, perhaps the most celebrated among Palladio's masterworks: Villa Capra, known throughout the world by the name of **La Rotonda**. Only the outside of the building is open to visitors, and that only on Tuesdays, Wednesdays, and Thursdays, 3:00 to 6:00 P.M., from March 15 to October 15. Permission to visit the interior must be obtained from the counts Valmarana at their Venice address: San Marco 3903, Tel: (041) 522-29-44 (there are Dorigny and Maganza frescoes, of limited interest, inside). But no lover of Palladio is likely to want to miss this jewel of Renaissance architecture. Here the artist seems to have succeeded in his attempt—highly original for his times—to have the building merge with the landscape in a totally harmonious way. (He was able to achieve a similar result in the water and sky environment of Venice with the two churches of San Giorgio Maggiore and Redentore.) In accordance with its creator's aims, La Rotonda seems to represent physically the philosophical ideals of the late Renaissance: order and balance, elegance and harmony, even at the expense of other, perhaps equally positive, human characteristics, such as the tensions and emotional upheavals that were to resurface in the Baroque age.

Vicenza is abundantly served by good restaurants, although they are less princely than in nearby Verona. Here, too, the regional cuisine is the most popular: only fish at **Cinzia e Valerio** on the piazzetta Porta Padova near the old city walls (closed Sunday evenings, Mondays, July, and August; Tel: 0444-50-52-13); poultry and venison (and also the famous *baccalà alla Vicentina*) at the **Tre Visi** near the piazza dei Signori at contrà Corti 6 (closed Sunday evenings, Mondays, and July 15–30; Tel: 0444-32-48-68); and a remodeled rustic setting, with the possibility of outdoor dining, at **Da Remo**, a little over a kilometer (half a mile) outside the city walls at via Caimpenta 14 (exit through corso Padova, driving east toward Padua; closed Sunday dinner and Mondays; Tel: 0444-91-10-07). The first two are expensive.

The **Campo Marzio** is a small, pleasant four-star hotel in Vicenza, a few steps from Corso Andrea Palladio.

Padua

Very rich in medieval and Renaissance art, Padua (Padova in Italian) has grown dramatically and somehow frantically in the past 40 years. As of 1990, most of the historic center has been closed to traffic, making it easier for visitors to enjoy the many masterworks spread within the city limits.

In medieval and early Renaissance times, Padua was the most active patron city of the arts in the whole Veneto. Giotto worked here in the early 14th century, leaving a series of extraordinary frescoes in the **Cappella degli Scrovegni** (Scrovegni Chapel). More than a century later, Paolo Uccello, Filippo Lippi, and Donatello were called to Padua (nothing has remained here of the works of the first two), influencing Squarcione and Mantegna, who in turn introduced the Venetian painters (such as Giovanni Bellini, who was Mantegna's brother-in-law) to the new approach that was to form the core of so much Venetian art.

Besides the Scrovegni Chapel (off corso Garibaldi, a short walk from the train station), a landmark in the history of European painting, you should see (on piazza Eremitani, 200 yards from the Scrovegni Chapel) the **Eremitani** church, where Mantegna painted frescoes for one chapel in the 1450s. Unfortunately, World War II bombing destroyed a large part of the frescoes, leaving only two of them untouched (some of the others have been painstakingly restored).

Not far from the Eremitani is the ancient center of the **University of Padua**, which was founded in 1222 and is the second oldest in Italy after Bologna. Thousands of students still make the 20-minute walk daily from the station through corso Garibaldi, piazza Garibaldi, and piazza Cavour to the university. The ancient portals of the university building, known in Padua as Il Bo (The Ox), open on via 8 Febbraio, a hundred yards beyond the Caffè Pedrocchi. Here Dante, Petrarch, and Tasso studied, and for many years Galileo taught. The courtyards and stairs are decorated with the coats of arms of Italian and foreign families who sent their offspring here, and the atmosphere remains surprisingly close to that of a medieval university. A university it still is, crowded with students, professors, and administrators. Following an old Italian tradition, the grounds *and* classes are open to the general public. Enrollment is required (upon payment of a very moderate administrative fee) only to pass examinations and to receive credits. The entire university system in Italy is supported by the state, and—to complete this paradise of educational democracy—enrollment is open to any candidate who possesses a high-school diploma. Professors, in turn, are treated extremely well. Tenure is pretty much automatic; the teaching load includes only three hours of classes a week; courses start late in November and end at the beginning of May (with long recesses at Christmas and Easter, of course).

A visit to the basilica of **Il Santo** (the saint is Anthony, protector of Padua) offers a good opportunity to see one of Donatello's masterworks, the equestrian monument to condottiere Gattamelata (1447) on the square in front of the church (a 20-minute walk from Il Bo, down via San Francesco and via del Santo). There are other works by Donatello inside, including a marble bas-relief of Christ's Deposition that is familiar to every student of art history. In 1991 the precious reliquary containing relics of Saint Anthony was stolen in broad daylight, during Mass, by armed robbers. Fortunately it was recovered, and was returned to its place in a great public ceremony.

A short and pleasant walk protected from the city traffic is offered by the stretch between Il Bo and the two medieval squares **piazza della Frutta** and **piazza delle Erbe**, where the modern city has managed to use ancient structures for their original purposes. The fruit and vegetable market in this area is as active and colorful today as it was in the 13th and 14th centuries (open weekday mornings).

The same area, usually crowded with students as well as professionals and businesspeople meeting in the historic **Caffè Pedrocchi** (Neoclassical; 1831), also includes some of the best restaurants in a city justly famous for its cuisine: **Dotto** (via Squarcione 25), a preferred rendezvous for university professors and successful entrepreneurs, is equally crowded for Italian-style business lunches—a good couple of hours—as well as for more leisurely dinners. Fish and pasta entrées such as *pappardelle all'ortolana* (wide taglia-telle with the vegetables in season) are the specialties here. Tel: (049) 250-55, closed Sunday evenings and Mondays. **El Toulà** (via Belle Parti 11) is the most exclusive restaurant in town. Housed in a 15th-century palazzo, it serves regional dishes such as *risi e bisi* (rice and peas—unexpectedly delicious), roast goose, and fish. Reservations recommended; Tel: (049) 875-18-22. Closed Monday lunch, Sundays, and August.

A bit out of the way—a short taxi ride from the center—there is the informal and moderate **Da Giovanni** (at piazzale Stanga, via Maroncelli 22; reservations expected but not required; Tel: 049-77-26-20; closed Saturday lunch and Sundays), with an eclectic clientele that includes all social classes and a widespread reputation for boiled and roasted meats. At **Padovanelle**, a hotel and restaurant at Ponte di Brenta, only 6 km (4 miles) from the center of the city, well-to-do Paduans enjoy haute cuisine next door to an elegant horse-racing track in pleasant countryside surroundings. Padovanelle is known for its antipasti table, a buffet with 30 or more appetizers; for its risotti; and for giving a ceramic dish as a souvenir to customers who order certain entrées. The accommodations consist of pleasant chalets built around a garden. The grounds also boast a swimming pool and tennis courts. Tel: (049) 62-56-22; restaurant closed Sunday evenings, Mondays, and August.

Padua, like all the urban centers in the Veneto, is surrounded by an economically healthy and very active countryside outside its ring of modern development; and here, too, the good and great restaurants have steadily grown in number. Many people when visiting Padua prefer to stop for a good meal in the countryside, especially in the summer. Particularly beautiful is the Riviera del Brenta, a road connecting Padua to Venice along the Brenta canal and a preferred vacation spot for the Venetian nobility since the 16th century. Some of the best patrician villas are situated here, and along with them are some of the best fish restaurants in the Veneto (see The Patrician Villas, below).

Treviso

This delightful city a few miles north of Venice has managed to retain its idyllic atmosphere in spite of the extraordinary vitality of its economy. In fact, Treviso claims to have been the inventor of the economic *modello Veneto* (discussed in the Hill Belt section, below).

Huge economic and social changes lie behind the success

of the *modello Veneto*. Such transformations could not have taken place without long preparation, however. The people of Treviso are convinced that their present happy welfare has deep historical roots; this has always been a land where agriculture was mixed with commerce and manufacturing. Even more so than the other cities of the Veneto, Treviso has been since Roman (actually pre-Roman) times a crossroads between north and south and east and west. It was from here, for example, that the founders of Venice moved to the lagoon islands in the fifth century. Or, to take an example from our own times, the textile boom represented by such firms as Benetton and Stefanel (both from Treviso) is more than likely the consequence of the raising of silkworms and the weaving and selling of textiles for centuries—a typical combination of agriculture and industry.

The idyllic nature of Treviso is due largely to its quiet, romantic river (the Sile) and the canals branching off from it, their banks lined with poplar trees and weeping willows. Many homes have small or large gardens planted with flowers, especially roses. Naturally there is no lack of remarkable artistic monuments: The **Palazzo dei Trecento** and the **Palazzo del Podestà**, in the beautiful and very active piazza dei Signori, are Romanesque buildings of the early 13th century. The nearby **Duomo** is an interesting mixture of early Renaissance and 18th-century additions; the church of **San Nicolò**, a kilometer (half a mile) southwest of the Duomo, is an original architectural solution of the tensions between the Romanesque and Gothic. But the beauty of Treviso is best enjoyed by a stroll through its **Città Vecchia** (Old City), especially on the market days of Tuesday and Saturday. Make sure to allow some time for a meal in one of the many good restaurants; there is a wide choice of them in this sophisticated little town. **El Toulà** (also known as Da Alfredo), via Collalto 26, is the most elegant and exclusive. Tel: (0422) 54-02-75. Closed Sunday evenings, Mondays, and August. **Al Bersagliere**, via Barberia 21, in a 13th-century building with an ancient fresco and brick walls, has a quiet, relaxed atmosphere and is known for its *gnocchetti alla bersagliere* (gnocchi sautéed with vegetables) and *baccalà alla bersagliere* (a delicate version of this regional specialty). Medium-priced, it is closed Saturdays for lunch, Sundays, and the first two weeks of August. Reservations recommended; Tel: (0422) 54-19-88. **Le Beccherie**, piazza Ancillotto 10, offers an opportunity to try the real *baccalà alla vicentina con polenta* as well as a wealth of local and national dishes. Reservations; Tel: (0422) 54-08-71. Closed Thursday evenings, Fridays, and July 14–31.

As with the other cities in the Veneto, a surprising number of very good restaurants are also scattered about the prosperous Treviso countryside. Moderately priced, they range from fish restaurants such as **Tajer d'Oro**, at Fossalta Maggiore (Tel: 0422-74-63-92; closed Tuesdays and most of August), to places specializing in local venison (**Al Cacciatore**, at Roncade; Tel: 0422-70-70-65; closed Monday dinner and Tuesdays), to friendly, informal trattorie (a famous one is **Alle Guaiane**, at Noventa di Piave; Tel: 0421-650-02; closed Mondays, Tuesday evenings, August, and January 1–20). An extraordinary place, for both the cooking standards and the old farmhouse setting, is **Osteria Pasina** at Dosson near Casier, 6 km (3½ miles) southeast of Treviso, where the owner/chef and the customers seem to be equally knowledgeable about the traditional cuisine of the Veneto (Tel: 0422-38-21-12; closed Saturday lunch, Monday evenings, Tuesdays, and August). Finding these places is the easiest thing in the world: Everybody can give directions—often accompanied by a congratulatory smile—for miles around the lucky villages where they are located.

A delightful place to stay in the area is the **Villa Condulmer** at Mogliano Veneto, between Treviso and Venice. A former patrician villa, it has a large park, its own golf course, and tennis and horseback-riding facilities. The downstairs lounges still seem as if they are inhabited by 18th-century patricians. The restaurant, indoors or in the garden, is also excellent. Closer to Treviso, at Ponzano Veneto (11 km/7 miles to the northwest), is the **Relais El Toulà**, a quiet countryside retreat with only ten rooms, a swimming pool, and an excellent restaurant, mostly patronized by important clients of Treviso businesses.

The Patrician Villas

After the Venetian Republic conquered mainland territories in the 15th century, it became fashionable among its patricians to spend parts of the year, usually a month in the spring and one or two in the fall, at their country houses. Their homes (*villa* in Italian means "country residence") became more and more luxurious, competing with one another and even with the mansions of Venice. In many cases, it was the farmland and its revenues that made up for the decline of power overseas, so that the Venetian nobility transformed themselves from merchants to landholders (losing the entrepreneurial skills inherited from their fathers in the process). By the 18th century many a villa had become the real center of a family's wealth. The masters no longer went there to enjoy only a few months away from the city but more and more to supervise the production of crops. The long porticoed wings on both sides of the main façades, therefore, had a precise practical function—as storage and processing centers, exactly as the ground floors of the Venice palazzi had been merchandise warehouses during the great trading years.

There are some 3,000 of these homes scattered in the Veneto, and at least 700 of them are of artistic interest. A large number of the latter are in serious decay and can often be found for sale at prices that seem very low—until the contractors give their astronomical restoration and maintenance estimates. The periods and styles vary from Gothic to Renaissance to Baroque to Neoclassical, but the most celebrated villas are those built by Palladio in the 16th century. Palladio was able to express his enthusiastic understanding of Roman antiquity, but not without a more or less conscious process of modernization that went right to the heart of the patrician taste: splendor without vulgar display of means, harmony of volumes in a solemn yet friendly context. A careful study of a building's impact on the surrounding landscape was another of Palladio's concerns, one that was to win for him the admiration of so many English architects.

We mentioned La Rotonda in the Vicenza section; other Palladian masterworks are the **Villa Barbaro** at Maser, northwest of Treviso; the **Villa Emo Capodilista** at Fanzolo di Vedelago, west of Treviso near Castelfranco; the **Villa Foscari** (called "La Malcontenta"), halfway between Venice and Padua, at Mira; and the **Villa Badoer**, near Fratta Polesine in the Po delta southwest of Venice (16 km/10 miles west of Rovigo).

Villa Barbaro (with frescoes by Veronese) can be visited on Tuesdays, Saturdays, and Sundays, 2:00 to 5:00 P.M.; Villa Emo Capodilista (be careful; there are other villas with the name "Emo" in the Veneto) on Saturdays, Sundays, and holidays, 3:00 to 6:00 P.M. or 2:00 to 5:00 P.M. in winter; La Malcontenta on Tuesdays, Saturdays, and the first Sunday of the month, May 1 to October 30, 9:00 A.M. to noon. Villa Badoer has yet another schedule: In the summer it is open on Sundays, 10:00 A.M. to noon, Tuesdays and Thursdays, 9:00 A.M. to noon, and every day from 3:30 to 7:00 P.M. (in winter every day, 2:00 to 5:00 P.M.).

The city of Vicenza lists 56 villas of primary importance in its district, and Treviso and Padua can certainly boast at least as many. The best itinerary for a visit is probably by **boat ride along the Brenta canal**, a tranquil, lazy stream that flows from Padua to Venice. (There is a road along its banks, but it is rather crowded with traffic these days.) Many patricians had their villas situated near the Brenta, and the historic boat service up and down the river, called *Il Burchiello* (from the name of the large boats that were used for many centuries), has now been resurrected for sightseeing. Originally pulled by horses from the riverbanks, the boat is today motorized, but it advances slowly and romantically in a landscape that is striking for its mixture of nature and great architecture (that is, once it sails past the industrial area of Porto Marghera). The Brenta banks were, after all, the Beverly Hills of the Venetian nobility: Foscaris, Contarinis, Veniers, Valmaranas, and many others had their villas built here. The memorable voyage lasts a whole day, with return by bus, and it includes stops with guided tours at La Malcontenta, Villa Querini, and Villa Pisani in Stra, plus lunch at a riverside restaurant. The service is offered from March 23 to October 27. Departures from piazza San Marco in Venice are on Tuesdays, Thursdays, and Saturdays at 9:00 A.M., arrival in Padua at 7:45 P.M.; departures from Padua are on Wednesdays, Fridays, and Sundays at 8:00 A.M., return at 7:15 P.M. Tickets include guided visits and cost 85,000 lire per person; lunch is optional at 38,000 lire. In Venice call American Express at (041) 520-08-44, or buy your tickets at the American Express counter at San Moisé, near piazza San Marco; in Padua call Siamic at (049) 66-09-44, or go to its office on via Trieste 42. Most travel agents in both towns can also make reservations.

Although far from exhausting the architectural range of villas in the Veneto, this particular area will give you a good idea of their variety and beauty. All of them, of course, are also accessible by car. The most magnificent is definitely the 18th-century **Villa Pisani** at Stra, halfway between Padua and Venice, now a national museum. It includes a famous labyrinth-shaped garden and, more importantly, a series of splendid frescoes by Tiepolo (open 9:00 A.M. to 6:00 P.M., closed Mondays; from October 1 to May 31, open 9:00 A.M. to 4:00 P.M., closed Mondays; Tel: 049-98-00-590).

A few miles north of Padua is another jewel, 17th-century **Villa Contarini** at Piazzola sul Brenta (open 9:00 A.M. to 12:30 P.M. and 3:00 to 6:30 P.M.; closed Mondays).

The ride along the Brenta is a preferred excursion of Venetians and Paduans on warm spring days as well as in September and October, and this has encouraged the establishment of remarkably good restaurants, many of which specialize in fish from nearby Chioggia on the Adriatic: **Da Bepi el Ciosoto** at Malcontenta, near Villa Foscari, is large and comfortable and has a great display of fish and vegetables (Tel: 041-69-89-97; closed Sunday evenings and Monday lunch); **Il Burchiello**, at Oriago, near Mestre, is informal and easy to find (closed Sunday evening and Mondays; Tel: 041-

47-22-44); and **Margherita** is magnificently located on a bend of the Brenta at Mira (Tel: 041-42-08-79; closed Tuesday evenings, Wednesdays, and January 1–20). All three are in the expensive category.

Real connoisseurs in search of an exceptional gastronomic treat drive all the way to Mestre (just across the lagoon from Venice) and stop near the train station at a crossroads called La Giustizia to enjoy a meal at busy, colorful **Dall'Amelia**, one of the best restaurants in Italy, run with great competence by Dino Boscarato, the president of the International Association of Sommeliers. This restaurant keeps the great tradition of Italian trattorie alive: busy but very comfortable, it has none of the self-importance of some superior eating establishments, yet its chefs are among the best in the nation, the service is impeccable, and the wine list a collection of the best labels and vintages. Miraculously, all of this comes at less-than-sky-high prices. Tel: (041) 91-39-51; closed Wednesdays only in winter.

The Beaches

The beaches of the Veneto—there are almost 100 miles of them—were beautiful until the tourist trade transformed most of them into playgrounds for two-week vacationers from central and northern Europe. Only off-season or in a few secluded stretches is the old atmosphere conserved: a flat, gently curving coastline with mountains and hills on the far horizon, sand dunes dotted with wild bushes, frequent river mouths and lagoons.

In addition, a sad warning is, unfortunately, necessary about the quality of the water. In the summer of 1989 the northern Adriatic beaches were invaded by an abnormal growth of algae caused by phosphates and other chemicals. This resulted in a layer of a whitish jelly-like substance being washed ashore by currents and winds. Although the phenomenon particularly plagued the beaches farther south (Emilia-Romagna), it affected those in the Veneto as well. (Similar algal blooms appeared off the coast of Yugoslavia and, as a message to all Europeans, the German and Dutch coasts of the North Sea.) In 1990 and 1991 the algae returned, particularly in the hottest August days, but they were almost totally absent in 1992, and there is a good chance that they won't reappear in the next few years.

Among the developed centers, **Bibione**, at the far eastern end, has kept a large wood of umbrella pines right on the sea and can still offer some rest; **Caorle**, grown around a medieval center with an 11th-century cathedral and bell tower, has lined its beaches with modern hotels and pensioni, deck chairs and umbrellas; **Eraclea Mare** has three miles of beach also occupied by hotels and campgrounds; and finally **Jesolo**, the capital and pride of this kind of summer resort, is infested with portable radios and pizza parlors, souvenir shops, and immense campgrounds (some of them hold as many as 7,000 people).

Behind Jesolo, however, small local roads penetrate deeply into the islands of Venice's lagoon, which are deserted even in summer and still inhabited by fishermen and farmers. Jesolo is worth a visit just for a ride on the road that abandons the coast at Cavallino to enter the lagoon territory and its villages of **Treporti** and **Lio Piccolo**. The latter was acquired in 1989—school, church, and all—by an Austrian businessman who stated that he had no plans to exploit it touristically. It may well be so, but many Venetians are rushing to have another look at Lio Piccolo, in fear that it won't stay untouched for long.

An extra advantage of the Jesolo beaches is their proximity to Venice. From the tip of Punta Sabbioni—endowed with many parking facilities—public boats run back and forth all day to a landing at piazza San Marco. It is a pleasant half hour on the lagoon and a triumphal entry into Venice, much more exciting than the usual arrival by car from Mestre (see the Venice chapter).

The best beach in the Veneto is probably the **Lido** of Venice. Here the hotels are sparse and discreet, and at least two of them range among the best in the country (see the Venice chapter). The part of the beach that is closer to the Lido's major street (Gran Viale) is curiously occupied by thousands of small cabins in neat rows that often leave only a few yards of space near the water. Some hotels, but mostly the city administration itself, own these cabins and rent them out by the day or by the month. The whole area is fenced, with occasional gate openings. There is no admission charge, but city guards patrol the area to make sure nobody undresses on the beach or sits on the sand next to a bundle of clothes. A suggestion to the visitor who wants to take a swim: Go to an area called Zona A, next door to the Hotel Des Bains. It is run by the city, and a small cabin can be rented for the day at an almost affordable price. Or read further, and go to Murazzi or Alberoni for a free swim in much cleaner water.

A walk of half a mile in a southerly direction from the Gran Viale will take you to the last—and perhaps most impressive—of the beach hotels, the Hotel Excelsior. Now run by Aga Khan's CIGA, it was built at the turn of the century in an amusingly Oriental style with correspondingly voluptuous comfort. It stands a few steps from the summer Casino and the Palazzo del Cinema. During the International Film Festival in September, stars and important guests stay at the Excelsior and swim off its luxuriously serviced beach.

Just after the Excelsior, a long stretch of the seaside is formed by huge blocks of stone (*murazzi*) carefully laid to hold back the winter storms and prevent erosion. Venetians, especially the younger crowd, bathe at the **Murazzi** in total relaxation; the area is never crowded. Farther ahead, after the village of Malamocco, the Lido ends with an area called **Alberoni** (ten minutes by bus from the Excelsior, 15 from downtown). This area is still undeveloped and is a preferred destination for young families and topless women (topless is accepted on all beaches, however).

The coast then continues with the long, thin island of **Pellestrina** (frequent ferry service from Alberoni). It, too, is undeveloped and striking, with its two villages of San Pietro in Volta and Pellestrina (each graced by a renowned, informal fish restaurant) and the Adriatic visible on one side, the lagoon on the other. Swimming is possible, although in most places it is not very comfortable because of the boulders reinforcing the shoreline (there is a small sand beach right in the village of Pellestrina).

The lagoon's southern boundary is occupied by the ancient fishing center of **Chioggia**. The village itself has managed to retain much of its old atmosphere: It is really like a miniature Venice, without the grandiose architecture of the capital city. Most inhabitants are still fishermen (for sardines) and clammers, or they are involved in related activities; and the town is busy with old-fashioned occupations: Nets are fixed at people's doors, card games are played at cafés and restaurants, and the day's catch is sorted out and unloaded at the harbor.

The long beach of Chioggia—around a settlement called Sottomarina—has also been developed for tourists. Unfortunately, it will make you feel nostalgic for Jesolo, which probably was the model for Chioggia's local entrepreneurs.

South of Sottomarina, the coast breaks into small islands and marshes, most of them inaccessible by car but fascinating for their wild vegetation and fauna.

The Po Delta

Here, for a change, is an area that has been almost untouched by the recent economic boom in Veneto and has, therefore, kept its special character as a nature sanctuary.

This area stretches between two rivers, the Adige and the Po, down to the border with Emilia-Romagna, where both rivers divide into numerous branches before flowing into the Adriatic. The main feature of this silent, fascinating landscape is the water, slowly moving among very low strips of land inhabited by all sorts of rare birds; if it weren't for the occasional faint roar of a faraway motor, you would have the feeling of having travelled back in time. There is undoubtedly a subtly melancholic character to this vast expanse of water and land; the air is often misty and silence reigns, interrupted only by the calls of seagulls and wild ducks.

Yet here, too, among wood huts still used by fishermen and hunters, among canals and embankments built during centuries of fights against floods, you have the unexpected and almost dreamlike vision of buildings of ancient beauty. Such is the **Benedictine Abbey of Pomposa**, with its early medieval church and bell tower, rising in the middle of nowhere (50 km/30 miles south of Chioggia on route 309 and 10 km/6 miles past Mesola; Pomposa is technically in Emilia-Romagna).

This area, centering around the towns of **Adria** (east of Rovigo, the district capital) and **Rosolina**, on the Adriatic, has recently become very involved with a new Italian passion, so-called ecological tourism. Old-fashioned boats take awe-struck city dwellers through lagoons, canals, and marshes, while the guides point out the scattered remnants of ancient fishing and hunting cultures. **Albarella**, a beautiful island off the coast south of Rosolina, has recently been developed into an exclusive resort and become a paradise for wealthy lovers of boating, fishing (including deep-sea tuna fishing in the Adriatic), and bird watching, surrounded as it is by dozens of small islands untouched by humans. The island also offers shopping opportunities, a small harbor, and two elegant hotels: the **Golf Hotel**, open year-round, with its own 18-hole golf course, covered pool, gym, tennis courts, and beach; and the **Hotel Capo Nord**, open April to October, with a private beach and outdoor swimming pool. Summer rentals are also available by the week. All buildings are new on this recently developed island.

THE HILL BELT

Directly south of the high mountains, a series of gentle hills descends gradually into the southern plains of the Veneto. This belt runs from Lago di Garda in the west to the eastern boundary with Friuli, and it includes some of the best vineyards in Italy as well as a series of small urban areas with very long histories and, at the moment, promising futures. Starting from the eastern shore of Lago di Garda, you will encounter names such as **Valpolicella**, **Bardolino**, and **Soave**—all hill towns east of the lake and north of Verona made famous by the local wines. In the hills to the north of the road between Verona and Vicenza are also **Valdagno**, center of the Marzotto clothing factories, and the Liberty-style (as the Italians call Art Nouveau) town of **Recoaro**, a busy and elegant resort that owes its fortune to the abundant presence of thermal waters. This area is clustered, as well, with old villages turned productive agricultural and manufac-turing centers, more often than not without renouncing their ties to nature and tradition. Most roads are winding and narrow and would reward only a visitor willing to spend a day or two on a detour. For those so inclined, route 46 from Vicenza north to Schio, then west to Recoaro, and south again on route 246 through Valdagno and Montecchio (80 km/50 miles in all) is a scenic and relatively uncompli-cated option. Or you can take the road from Affi to Rovereto, over the mountain range between the Adige River and Lake Garda (with some sections as high as 4,000 feet above sea level).

The province of Padova, down to the south, boasts another important thermal resort, **Abano Terme**. It is set in the hills called Colli Euganei, southwest of Padua, and is visited every year by thousands of Italians for one or two weeks of cure in its warm waters (they emerge from underground at 190° F, and they *do* work—for rheumatism and arthritis as well as respiratory and urinary diseases). Many hotels in Abano now include their own swimming pool fed by the thermal waters. The Colli Euganei are by themselves a small universe, with old monasteries (such as the one at Praglia), ceramic facto-ries, and many patrician villas: A rare Baroque specimen is the **Villa Barbarigo** at Valsanzibio (the interior is not open to the public, but the park and exterior can be visited March 15 to October 31, 10:00 A.M. to noon and 2:00 to 7:00 P.M. Closed on Monday mornings, Sundays, and the rest of the year). Litera-ture and landscape lovers should not miss delicious **Arquà Petrarca**, where the father of the Italian love lyric spent the last years of his life in totally idyllic surroundings. The interior of the house, supposedly untouched since Petrarch's death in 1374, is open to visitors; and there is a wonderful restaurant nearby, **La Montanella**, surrounded by a large garden. La Montanella is a perfect initiation to the cuisine of Padova: homemade pasta, duck, quail, venison, and extremely good wines produced by the owners, all at moderate prices. Closed Tuesday evening, Wednesdays, and January 2–February 15; Tel: (0429) 71-82-00.

Grappa and Piave

Next in a northeasterly direction from Recoaro are the Grappa and the Piave, a mountain and a river equally dear to the Italian historic memory because of the fierce fights here against Austrian troops in World War I. (The Veneto has always been the gateway to Italy for populations invading or trying to invade from the east, from the barbarians who hastened the end of the Roman Empire to the Holy Roman Emperors during the Middle Ages. It took domination by a strong Venice to put an end to these invasions, which were immediately resumed after Venice's fall in 1797.) After a major Italian defeat in the first phase of World War I (the episode is described in Hemingway's *A Farewell to Arms*), Grappa and Piave became the absolute last line of defense; beyond them, the Veneto plains and the rest of Italy lay flat and open to the foreign troops. This time, however, the defenses *did* hold; the Austrians were pushed back, at a tremendous price in human lives on both sides. The bodies of 25,000 soldiers, almost all unidentified, are buried in a huge cemetery at the top of Monte Grappa. The Veneti come often to visit this vast memorial and bring their children with them. Not many places in Italy can teach such a solemn lesson on the futility of war, and it may well be that the memories of this and of World War II play an important role in the Veneto approach to life.

The Veneto has given Italy some of its best writers of the past 30 years, from Dino Buzzati and Giuseppe Berto to Luigi Meneghello and the poet Andrea Zanzotto, and it is probably the area where the Italian love for life and beauty blends most harmoniously with a wisdom that sometimes manifests itself as a melancholy awareness of human frailty.

To this section of the Hill Belt, roughly north and northwest of Treviso, belong the landscapes that appear in the works of the first great Venetian painters, from Cima (born north of Treviso in the town of Conegliano, from which he took his name), to Giorgione, born in Castelfranco, west of Treviso. (Another great painter, Titian, was born in Pieve di Cadore in the Mountain Belt.) Some of the works of these painters have remained in their hometowns and can be seen there. The Treviso section of the hills is one of the most interesting parts of the Veneto due to its fine climate (the hill roads are jammed on summer weekends, when everybody drives up from the plains in search of coolness), fabulous wines (this is the realm of the Prosecco), and countless specimens of minor architecture dating from as early as the 13th century.

It is here that the Venetian Republic assigned a territory to Caterina Cornaro at the end of the 15th century, after she inherited the kingdom of Cyprus from her husband. Because the island was of enormous strategic importance to Venice, it was decided that the new queen would graciously (although not necessarily with great enthusiasm) hand it over to her mother country in exchange for a dominion on the mainland. The chosen town was **Asolo**, where Caterina held a princely court until her death in 1510. Asolo, to the west-northwest of Treviso, is now a preferred goal for sophisticated tourists. The whole town has kept its Renaissance atmosphere, with narrow streets and handsome façades overlooking a splendid landscape. Among other things, it is famous for having been the residence of celebrities such as Robert Browning and Eleonora Duse, and in our own times for the splendid hotel **Villa Cipriani**, one of the best hotels in the Veneto. Included in the Relais & Châteaux Association, the villa is a sophisticated Renaissance country residence surrounded by a marvelous garden. In the small cemetery of San Vito di Altivole, 8 km (5 miles) south of Asolo, a handsome surprise awaits lovers of contemporary architecture: the **Mausoleo Brioni**, a compound built in 1968 by Carlo Scarpa (1906–1978) to house the tombs of a local family.

The hill area is also justly famous for its restaurants. At least a dozen of them are well worth the trip from Venice, Treviso, and even Milan, as is proven by the variety of the dialects spoken at the tables. Ranging in price from moderate to moderately expensive, these restaurants grew together with the now-flourishing local economy and are one of the rewards that this area offers to its successful entrepreneurs. Tables are usually for four or more, often for groups of more than ten; the head of the family or the boss of the small firm sits proudly at one end and unblinkingly pays the half-million-lire bill that a ten-person treat would probably cost.

The secret of the economic boom in this area, as in the nearby plains, is the smallness and specialization of the firms and their great ability for marketing and organization. More than 50 percent of the Veneto products go to foreign buyers, from the European Community to the U.S. to the Middle and Far East, and they are as varied in nature as eyeglass frames (in the Cadore), shoes and clothes, toys, and sporting goods. A special feature of the *modello Veneto* is that these firms do not concentrate in one single area but are, for the most part, evenly scattered throughout the territory so that they are all but unnoticed. Modern production has found a way here to coexist with the old agricultural traditions: The fields are still plowed and the crops are still grown, and most factory workers also moonlight as farmers.

In this context, it is not surprising that the local cuisine, based on very old traditions, has risen to formidable heights; so a visit to picturesque **Conegliano**, fortressed **Castelfranco**, or **Bassano del Grappa** (the seat of scores of ceramic factories) can easily become a pretext for a very memorable meal. Mushrooms, radicchio, home-raised poultry, venison, local vegetables, and great wines are the basic staples of the menus, while the settings can vary from elegant city dining, as in **Al Salisà** at via XX Settembre 2 in downtown Conegliano, with antique furniture and elegant service (Tel: 0438-242-88; closed Sunday and Tuesday evenings, Wednesdays, and August; English spoken), to a countryside patrician villa like **Tre Panoce**, on top of a hill near Conegliano, with a large landscaped garden (via Vecchia Trevigiana 50; Tel: 0438-600-71; closed Sunday evenings, Mondays, and August). **Da Lino**, at Solighetto in the Montello area northwest of Conegliano, boasts unusually fine cuisine in a very large and often crowded restaurant, the decor of which alone is worth the trip (Tel: 0438-821-50; closed Mondays and July). Da Lino also has a few comfortable rooms available at reasonable rates. The unpretentious yet impeccable **Barbesin** in Salvarosa, 3 km (2 miles) from Castelfranco, serves radicchio, truffles, and all kinds of meats; try the venison with apples and mushrooms. (Tel: 0423-49-04-46; closed Wednesday evenings, Thursdays, and August.) All of these choices are moderately priced.

A sumptuous and elegant setting for Hill Belt visitors staying the night is also offered by the four-star hotel **Villa Corner della Regina** at Vedelago, near Castelfranco. The hotel occupies a 16th-century villa, impeccably restored by its present owner, Count Dona' Dalle Rose, who is descended from ancient Venetian nobility. The villa is surrounded by a huge garden, and it vies with Asolo's Villa Cipriani for primacy among the Hill Belt accommodations.

THE MOUNTAIN BELT

This is a long rectangle that runs from the Austrian border in northeast Veneto to the northeastern shores of Lago di Garda in the southwest. The most scenic part is definitely in the north, where a lucky series of geological circumstances created the mountains known as the Dolomites, and human ingenuity created the town known as Cortina d'Ampezzo. One of the striking things about the Dolomites (originally underwater coral reefs) is the abruptness with which they rise to their more than 10,000 feet; another is the rare gray-pink color of their rocks.

The main Dolomite road—coming east from Bolzano in the Alto Adige through the hairpin bends of the Costalunga, Pordoi, and Falzarego passes to Cortina—gives a foretaste of the pleasures awaiting mountain lovers. (Driving is not very easy on these mountain roads, which are, however, perfectly well serviced in summer and winter.) Alpine lakes such as Carezza and Misurina; snow-covered peaks such as Sella, Marmolada, and Tofane; deep gorges followed by high panoramic terraces—all these are features of this landscape, which is dotted with typical Alpine buildings (stone or brick base, wood top and roof). Then the view opens onto the high Cortina valley (3,600 feet) and its glaciers—the site of one of the most exclusive mountain resorts in the world.

Cortina d'Ampezzo

Cortina has a very long touristic tradition, and it even hosted the Winter Olympics in 1956, but it has never yielded to the temptation of "land development." Because of super-strict zoning regulations, only the richest can afford to buy a few square meters of land here, and only the well-off can afford even a weekend of skiing or summer sightseeing. So Cortina has remained a small village, but one that nonetheless offers all the luxuries its demanding guests are used to: miles of ski runs at all levels of difficulty, funicular service to the peaks of Tofane (10,000 feet) and Faloria (7,000 feet), and exclusive hotels such as **Miramonti Majestic** (just outside of town, with garden, golf course, indoor swimming pool, tennis courts) and **Cristallo** (garden, heated pool, tennis courts; only full board guests accepted). Moderately priced—by the standards of expensive Cortina—is the **Parc Hotel Victoria**, an elegantly rustic hotel set in a beautiful garden. The few inexpensive accommodations in Cortina include such establishments as **Villa Nevada** and centrally located **Panda**. For longer stays, the Cortina tourist office provides accommodations with local families and apartments by the week: contact A.P.T. Cortina, piazzetta San Francesco 8, Cortina d'Ampezzo, Belluno; Tel: (0436) 32-31; Fax: (0436) 32-35. In addition, there are at least a half dozen high-quality restaurants in town, from **El Toulà**, the parent of what has become a small chain known for haute cuisine served in a carefully simple decor (via Ronco 123; Tel: 0436-33-39; open December 20 to April 15 and July 15 to September 15; closed Mondays), to the more affordable **Al Lago Ghedina**, specializing in local venison, poultry, and of course mushrooms, all served on a terrace overlooking a lake. The restaurant, in front of little Lago Ghedina, also has a very small hotel (six rooms in all), not terribly expensive for Cortina and certainly one of the most coveted by those regulars who prefer to be only a quarter of an hour away from the center of town and perfectly comfortable and pampered in the silence of the mountains. Closed Tuesdays, June, and November; Tel: (0436) 86-08-76.

The Cadore

This name refers to a large mountain area east and south of Cortina, basically the basin of the river Piave. We will also discuss the region to the southwest (technically Valle Zoldana and Valle Agordina), which is very similar to the Cadore in landscape and geology.

The mountain peaks of these areas, all made of dolomite, are among the most impressive in the Alps. The valleys, covered with intensely green grass alternating with pine forests, shine with dew on summer mornings and are white with snow in winter, making them almost too postcard-perfect. At the top of the green slopes, where the rock emerges from the base of the mountains and juts into the sky, comfortable wooden huts receive the courageous trekkers. The huts are called *malghe* or *baite*—summer residences of farmers who take their cattle to graze the cleanest fields. Robust women sell cheese, butter, and milk; sleeping accommodations are often available (local trekking maps give all the details).

Yet the most fascinating finds in the Cadore are probably the villages. Most of their present sites have been inhabited since pre-Roman times, and the whole Cadore bears the signs of millennia of human presence, causing a curious feeling in visitors used to the wilderness of other mountain ranges. Even in these days of affluence—and winter tourism is booming—most villages maintain their ancient charm: They include the square with church and bell tower, the grade school, the post office, many steep little alleys, and a spontaneous architecture born of simple taste and long experience.

The usual itinerary for a basic acquaintance with Cadore is a drive of about 30 km (20 miles) from Cortina down the valley of the Boite (a mountain stream) to Pieve di Cadore. The first sizable village is **San Vito di Cadore** (altitude 3,000 feet), with a 16th-century church (Madonna della Difesa), a pleasant little lake with a restaurant, and too many modern tourist facilities. The road then winds downhill, between the immense slopes of Monte Pelmo on the right and Monte Antelao on the left, to nearby **Borca di Cadore**, in a beautiful valley—a starting point for all kinds of mountain walks. An easy and rewarding one is to **Rifugio Venezia**, a mountain hotel with 60 beds at 6,000 feet, which you can reach in three hours.

Down through Vodo, Venas, and Valle (the latter with a well-preserved historic center and archaeological evidence of Roman settlements), the road leads to the large village of **Pieve di Cadore**, the birthplace of Titian. The main square—piazza Tiziano, of course—has a 16th-century palazzo and a 15th-century tower. The not-so-documented birth house of Titian hosts a museum of memorabilia related to the great artist (no paintings, although a fresco on the façade of a nearby house is attributed to the boy Titian).

From Pieve di Cadore you can easily head toward Venice using beautiful route 51. Mountain lovers, however, should not miss the memorable Valle Zoldana and Valle Agordina, which run parallel to the Boite valley (called Valle Ampezzana) to the southwest and are serviced by well-maintained although winding roads. In many places these valleys, slightly out of reach for hurried city skiers, have kept more of their original purity than the Ampezzo area.

Route 51 rides along the banks of the River Piave to **Belluno**, the capital city of the Mountain Belt (altitude 1,200 feet). Also a pre-Roman settlement, Belluno is now emerging from a long period of economic distress, and life is very active in the central piazza dei Martiri. The best architecture, though, is to be found in the nearby piazza del Duomo. The Duomo was built in the 16th century, the bell tower in the 18th. The Palazzo dei Rettori, at number 38, is an early Renaissance masterwork flanked by the 12th-century Civic Tower.

From Belluno, a 30-km (20-mile) stretch of route 51 leads to the autostrada at Vittorio Veneto, running along the large and beautiful Lago di Santa Croce, on the shores of which numerous cafés and restaurants offer healthy mountain food and panoramic terraces at very affordable prices.

The cuisine of the Cadore district is an attraction almost as celebrated as its landscapes, and the locals are even more demanding than the many visitors. So it is not surprising that the area includes restaurants famous throughout the Veneto and beyond, from the pure, family cooking of the inexpensive **Alle Alpi** in Cima Sappada, at the extreme northeastern corner of Veneto, near Austria (Tel: 0435-46-91-02; open December to Easter and July to September 20; closed Mondays), to the sophisticated yet affordable meals served by Signora De Dea in her **Val Biois**, in Celat, between Agordo and Falcade at the foot of the Marmolada and not far from beautiful Lago Alleghe southwest of Cortina—a good reason to visit the Valle Agordina. (Tel: 0437-59-12-33; closed Sunday evenings and Mondays.) There is also a small and delightful hotel attached to the restaurant (see the Accommodations Reference).

Altopiano di Asiago

Another mountain area, farther south and west of the Dolomites and due north of Vicenza, is the Altopiano di Asiago, a large tableland at about 3,000 feet that is rich in gentle green slopes. Ideal for pastureland (the well-known Asiago cheese is produced here), the Altopiano is also a growing tourist center. In the winter it is crowded with skiers from Verona, Vicenza, and Treviso, and in the summer it is one of the preferred rendezvous for outdoor eating, away from the heat of the plains. During World War I this area, together with the neighboring territory to the east, was the object of fierce battles between Italians and Austrians, and it is still scattered with trenches and other mementos; the names of mountains such as Pasubio, Ortigara, and Cima Dodici have entered Italian folklore through songs and novels, and the battle sites are frequently visited by Italian families. Particularly panoramic is the road from Asiago northeast to Enego and Primolano: Large woods of pine trees give way to apple groves and vineyards as the road descends in hairpin curves toward the Brenta valley.

GETTING AROUND

In the Veneto, as in the rest of Italy, public transportation is omnipresent, and most of the time it is comfortable and cheap. Trains go almost everywhere, and bus services connect the stations to the downtown areas. However, while the use of trains is easy and highly recommended, a good knowledge of Italian and quite a bit of patience are prerequisites for a bus trip. So the best way to visit the main cities in the Veneto is by making your headquarters in one of them—Venice, for instance—and taking one-day trips by train, using taxis when required. Almost all the places mentioned in this book are connected to Venice by frequent train service.

Cars are a hindrance in cities such as Padua, Vicenza, Verona, and Treviso; their interesting neighborhoods are in the historic centers, never beyond the reach of reasonable walks. Padua is particularly difficult to tour by car due to the intense traffic and one-way streets; it is definitely better to drop your car someplace (the train station is perfect) and continue on foot. Padua is, in addition, connected to Venice (piazzale Roma) by a very comfortable commuter bus leaving every half hour (a 45-minute ride to downtown Padua).

On the other hand, such areas as the Hill Belt and particularly the Mountain Belt should be seen by car, especially in view of the fine restaurants and hotels scattered throughout the countryside. The roads are comfortable, and visitors will be surprised how tame Veneto drivers have become compared to their old reputation for hair-raising irresponsibility. Car-rental agencies have outlets in all major centers, and the usual credit cards are accepted everywhere. Most companies have special convenient weekend rates.

Cars are also necessary to visit the beaches, except for the Lido. Most of the seaside resorts are not served by railroad at all; an interested visitor should instead rent a car in Venice (a very good superhighway runs parallel to the coast). For the Lido, see the Arriving section in the Venice chapter. The Po delta also requires a car, which can be rented in Venice, Padua, Rovigo, Ferrara, or Ravenna. All beaches are connected to Venice by bus, but trips are often long due to local detours, and service is infrequent.

A regular boat service connects Venice to Chioggia at the southern end of the lagoon, southeast of Padua, eliminating the long and unpleasant detour by road. The island of Pellestrina is also serviced by comfortable public transportation from Venice. Jesolo and the surrounding beaches can be reached from Venice by public boat with a bus connection from Punta Sabbioni. The Treporti–Lio Piccolo detour requires a car.

Horseback Riding in the Veneto

The Italian National Association of Horseback Riding (ANTE) has established agreements with more than a dozen stables and hotels in the Veneto to offer packages of a week or a weekend of room and board plus horse service (and instructors). The Veneto lends itself beautifully to this kind of vacation, and there are centers in the Mountain, Hill, and Plains belts. The prices vary. For information, write Conte Massimiliano di Benevello, via dell'Artigianato 13, 37135 Verona; Tel: (045) 50-02-64.

ACCOMMODATIONS REFERENCE

The rates given below are projections for 1993; always check for up-to-date information before making reservations. Wide ranges may reflect the differences between low- and high-season rates. Unless otherwise indicated, the figures indicate the cost of a double room (per room, not per person). However, half-board (mezza pensione) rates, which include breakfast and one other meal per day, are per person. The service charge is included in the rate; inquire about the tax and breakfast.

▶ **Due Torri Hotel Baglioni.** Piazza Sant'Anastasia 4, 37121 **Verona.** Tel: (045) 59-50-44; Fax: (045) 800-41-30. In U.S., Tel: (800) 223-6800 or (212) 838-3110; Fax: (212) 758-7367. In U.K., Tel: (0800) 18-11-23; Fax: (071) 353-1904. £370,000–£450,000; full board £330,000–£650,000.

▶ **Golf Hotel.** Isola di Albarella, 45010 **Rosolina.** Tel: (0426) 33-03-73; Fax: (0426) 33-06-28. Open April–October. £220,000–£280,000.

▶ **Hotel Accademia.** Via Scala 12, 37121 **Verona.** Tel: (045) 59-62-22; Fax: same. £195,000–£270,000.

▶ **Hotel Antica Porta Leona.** Corticella Leoni 3, 37121 **Verona.** Tel: (045) 59-54-99. Closed January. £130,000–£150,000.

▶ **Hotel Campo Marzio.** Viale Roma 21, 36100 **Vicenza.** Tel: (0444) 54-57-00; Fax: (0444) 32-04-95. £150,000–£240,000; half board £150,000.

▶ **Hotel Capo Nord.** Isola di Albarella, 45010 **Rosolina.** Tel: (0426) 33-01-39; Fax: (0426) 33-00-09. £160,000–£240,000.

▶ **Hotel Cristallo.** Via Menardi 42, 32043 **Cortina d'Ampezzo.** Tel: (0436) 42-81; Fax: (0436) 86-80-58. Open December 19–April 6 and July 4–September 6. £300,000–£600,000; half board £320,000–£370,000.

▶ **Hotel Miramonti Majestic.** Località Pezziè 103, 32043 **Cortina d'Ampezzo.** Tel: (0436) 42-01; Fax: (0436) 86-70-19. In U.S., Tel: (800) 223-9832 or (212) 599-8280; Fax: (212) 599-1755. Open December 20–March 29, July, and August. £250,000–£500,000; half board £220,000–£340,000.

▶ **Hotel Val Biois.** Vallada Agordina-Frazione Celat, 32020 **Belluno.** Tel: (0437) 59-12-33. Closed October and November. £60,000–£80,000.

▶ **Hotel Villa Cipriani.** Via Canova 298, 31011 **Asolo.** Tel: (0423) 554-44; Fax: (0423) 520-95. In U.S., Tel: (800) 221-2340 or (212) 935-9540; Fax: (212) 421-5929. In U.K., Tel: (0800) 28-92-34 or (071) 930-4147; Fax: (071) 839-1566. £350,000–£400,000; half board £280,000–£315,000.

► **Locanda da Lino.** Via Brandolini 1, 31050 **Solighetto.** Tel: (0438) 821-50. Ł95,000–Ł110,000.

► **Le Padovanelle.** 35020 **Ponte di Brenta.** Tel: (049) 62-56-22; Fax: (049) 62-53-20. Ł210,000.

► **Panda.** Via Roma 64, 32043 **Cortina d'Ampezzo.** Tel: (0436) 86-03-44. Closed November and May 5–June 20. Ł100,000–Ł165,000.

► **Parc Hotel Victoria.** Corso Italia 1, 32043 **Cortina d'Ampezzo.** Tel: (0436) 32-46; Fax: (0436) 47-34. Open December 21–April 7 and July 10–September 15. Ł200,000–Ł400,000; half board Ł125,000–Ł280,000.

► **Relais El Toulà.** Via Postumia 63, 31050 **Ponzano Veneto.** Tel: (0422) 96-91-91; Fax: (0422) 96-99-94. Ł320,000–Ł600,000; half board Ł260,000–Ł400,000.

► **Rifugio Venezia.** San Vito di Cadore, 32046 **Belluno.** Tel: (0436) 96-84. Open July 15 to September 15. Rates unavailable, but inexpensive.

► **Ristorante Al Lago Ghedina.** Lago Ghedina, 32043 **Cortina d'Ampezzo.** Tel: (0436) 86-08-76. Open June–October and December–April. Ł250,000.

► **Villa Condulmer.** Località Zerman, 31020 **Mogliano Veneto.** Tel: (041) 45-71-00; Fax: (041) 45-71-34. Closed January 8–February 10. Ł180,000–Ł300,000.

► **Villa Corner della Regina.** Località Cavasagra, 31050 **Vedelago.** Tel: (0423) 48-14-81; Fax: (0423) 45-11-00. Ł220,000–Ł440,000.

► **Villa Nevada.** Via Ronco 64, 32043 **Cortina d'Ampezzo.** Tel: (0436) 47-78. Open December 1–April 15 and June 15–September. Ł100,000–Ł130,000.

FRIULI– VENEZIA GIULIA

By Paolo Lanapoppi

Friuli is an ancient name, derived from *Forum Iulii* (Iulii refers to Julius Caesar). It applies to the area east of the Veneto, extending from the Grado lagoon at the south to the Austrian border at the north; Pordenone and Udine are its main cities. Venezia Giulia (Julius Caesar again), on the other hand, is a modern and rather awkward name, minted in 1863 in order to emphasize the links between Venice (and Italy) and the eastern area around the cities of Gorizia and Trieste. Venezia Giulia, although Italian by language, became a part of the Hapsburg empire in the 14th century, but it was considered Italian by the leaders of the reunification movement in the 19th century. It was finally annexed to Italy only in 1921 (Gorizia) and 1948 (Trieste). Friuli was a part of the Republic of Venice from 1420 until the Napoleonic conquest in 1797, when it passed under Austrian domination. It became part of the Italian kingdom in 1866.

A breed of stubborn, intelligent, and tireless workers inhabits this geographically varied area. Ethnically they derive from the Celts, whose language is still much alive in the local dialects; then there were additions of Roman and Slavic blood. All the barbarian invasions passed through here, and one of the invading populations, the Longobards, established a long-lasting kingdom centered in Cividale, where it left its rough but powerful monuments. Nothing could be further from the cliché of the noisy, gesticulating, singing Italian than the average *Friulano*. This population still finds its appropriate symbol in Primo Carnera, the *gigante buono* (good-hearted giant) who in the 1920s was the first Italian ever to achieve the world championship in boxing. With his powerful size, enormous energy, and disarmingly honest eyes, and his background of hard labor on poor mountain farms, he symbolized Friuli's recent past and illustrated the reasons for its present prosperity.

When a terrible earthquake shattered the entire area in 1976, the Friulani amazed all of Italy with the energy, competence, and uncorrupted probity they displayed in managing the reconstruction funds. While victims of previous earthquakes in Sicily and Campania were (and in large part still are) living in tents or prefabricated emergency lodgings, the people of the Friuli reconstructed their homes, schools, and hospitals with little fuss and great success. Some of these reborn villages are well worth visiting because after heated discussions, it was decided to reconstruct them exactly as they had been, renouncing an opportunity for technological improvement in favor of maintaining continuity with history and tradition. This was a great lesson to the developers (and destroyers) of so many other parts of Italy.

MAJOR INTEREST

Mountain roads in the Carnia
Longobard remnants at Cividale
The reconstructed towns of Venzone and Gemona
Wine-producing hills of the Collio
Osterie: inexpensive, colorful restaurants
Aquileia's Roman ruins
Grado's medieval town and its beaches
Medieval center of Pordenone
Trieste: the old city and the 19th-century city

Friuli–Venezia Giulia includes a vast flatland at the south, extending from the Adriatic beaches of Lignano and Grado north and northwest to the cities of Pordenone, Spilimbergo, and Cividale. North of this area, hills covered with farms and vineyards lead gradually north toward the Alps. Farther north and west, the high mountains of the Carnia mark the border with Austria, while other mountains at the east separate Venezia Giulia from Slovenia (formerly Yugoslavia).

We cover Friuli–Venezia Giulia starting at the northwest, in the Alpine area of the Carnia, then move down to the hill region around Cividale and Udine. From there we go to the plains and beaches bordering on the Adriatic (Gulf of Venice), working east toward Trieste on the little coastal strip of

Italy that stretches between Slovenia and the sea down to the Croatian peninsula of Istria.

Its location at Italy's eastern border contributes to Friuli's varied and fascinating history. Settlements centered around fortified villages called *castellieri,* hundreds of which have been located by scholars, were established here as early as 1500 B.C. In the second and first centuries B.C. the area was gradually conquered by the Romans, who established a capital at Aquileia; it soon became the fourth largest city in Italy (today it is reduced to a village of 3,000 inhabitants). In medieval times the bishops ruling Aquileia (and enjoying the appellation of "patriarchs") dealt with the barbarian invasions and later took active part in the wars, so deprecated by Dante, between the pope-oriented Guelfs and the emperor-oriented Ghibellines. In this period castles were built, roads improved, and churches erected, the remnants of which are a source of delight for visitors today.

This strife-torn era came to an end when Venice conquered Friuli in 1420 and Austria conquered Gorizia in 1500. The years that followed were substantially years of peace and welfare, until the Napoleonic storm and the Congress of Vienna (1815), when both Friuli and the future Venezia Giulia were assigned to Austria.

THE CARNIA

The Carnia is the Alpine region at the northwest of Friuli, bordered by the Dolomites at the west and Austria at the north. Friuli's main river, the Tagliamento, originates in this area and flows down to the hills and plains (its entire course, about 100 miles, runs inside Friuli territory). Although very near the busy highway connecting Italy and Austria at the Tarvisio pass, the Carnia has remained almost undiscovered by national and international tourism. The mountains may be less majestic than those in more renowned parts of the Alps, but here the traveller can find those qualities of silence and majesty that have been lost elsewere. (Its prices, too, have maintained a pleasant aura of past times.)

The mountain villages have remained unaffected by contemporary growth and display a taste for simplicity and a love of tradition, as well as a sense of order and cleanliness: The way firewood is piled in the back of homes (the most impeccable piles, and not a grain of dust around), the patterns made by geraniums of different colors on the windowsills, the immaculate bathrooms in bars and restaurants, all point to a neat, industrious population.

A tour of the Carnia should start by leaving the autostrada (A 23) at Tolmezzo, an ancient fortress on the road that crosses the Alps (not much has remained of its medieval walls and buildings). Heading west on route 52 to Ampezzo, along the Tagliamento river, will give you the first glimpses of a peculiarity of the Carnia: the frequent appearance of **chiese votive**—tiny, charming churches on the mountaintops and slopes. The best route from Ampezzo heads northwest to Sauris and continues through Sella di Razzo to Lorenzago di Cadore. Unfortunately, in the spring of 1992 a large landslide blocked the road just east of Sella di Razzo, and repairs are likely to take quite a while. This means that at Sauris you have to retrace your steps to Ampezzo. The Ampezzo–Sauris road (25 km/16 miles) runs through a narrow valley that widens occasionally, in a landscape typical of the Carnia: steep, rocky mountains covered by woods, with very rare pastures. One unexpected feature is the frequent tunnels on the road: Minimally paved, with the bare rock forming the walls and ceilings, they're more like rather frightening grottoes than like modern tunnels. The entire Ampezzo–Sauris stretch takes less than an hour to drive each way.

The village of Sauris, 3,000 feet above sea level, lies surrounded by green pastures in a vast, majestic mountain landscape. Stop in for a snack at the café in the **Hotel Morgenleit**; it's impeccably clean and has a terrace with a panoramic view. Nearby, the small Gothic church of **San Lorenzo** sits handsome and quiet in the stillness of a hilltop.

Because of the road interruption at Sella di Razzo, the only way to tour the Carnia mountains at present is to return to Ampezzo and head west on route 52, which will lead you quickly to Passo di Mauria, Lorenzago di Cadore, and Santo Stefano di Cadore. From Santo Stefano, continue on route 355 through Sappada, Forni Avoltri, and Comeglians, and return to Tolmezzo through Villa Santina (the full circle is about 107 km/66 miles). Technically a large part of this itinerary is in the Veneto. The most interesting section is the stretch around Santo Stefano di Cadore and Sappada, where the landscape is quite different than at Sauris. Although it is well above sea level (3,600 feet at Sappada), there is an abundance of green pastures on these more gradual slopes and wider valleys. It is an ideal setting for skiing and all kinds of winter sports, which have boomed in this area during the past two decades. Hotels and restaurants abound along route 355. At Sappada, **Hotel Corona Ferrea** and **Hotel Belvedere** offer modern comforts and expansive mountain views, and the hilltop town of Cima Sappada hosts one of the best restaurants in the area, the moderately expensive **Alle Alpi** (Tel: 0435-46-91-02; closed Mondays and September 20 to December 20), specializing in prosciutto, mushrooms, and venison.

In Roman and medieval times the road across the Alps passed through Monte Croce Carnico, now linked to Tolmezzo by route 52 *bis*. On that road, 15 km (9 miles) north of Tolmezzo, is the village of **Zuglio**, built by the Romans and capital city of this area during the Middle Ages (the Roman Forum here has been excavated and can be visited). About 3 km (2 miles) north of Zuglio, on the road to Fielis, you'll come to the church of **San Pietro di Carnia**, one of the oldest in this region. Built in the seventh century, it was remodeled around 1300. The church overlooks a large valley that hasn't changed much since the times when Zuglio was an important city and San Pietro was the cathedral seat of its bishops.

THE HILLS

Vineyards, corn and grain fields, villages and towns built around or near medieval castles, great wines, and excellent food are the features that characterize this northeastern corner of Italy. The gentle hills, descending in wide circles toward the flatlands along the coast, lend themselves to the growth of vineyards and to animal farming. A burgeoning tourist trade also helps the local economy, as do a number of small manufacturing firms, often with no more than half a dozen employees, that constitute one of the secrets of Friuli's newfound prosperity.

Cividale

Today Udine and Gorizia are the largest cities and the administrative centers of this area. Historically, however, the capital city was Cividale, which remains the most interesting town to visit in Friuli–Venezia Giulia, except for Trieste. Founded by the Romans in the first century B.C., it became important especially with the arrival of the Germanic Longobards, or so-called Lombards (A.D. 568–774). During that period some of the Longobard dukes acquired the title of king of Italy, in a series of events brilliantly described by Paulus Diaconus, one of the greatest medieval historians and a Cividalese by birth. After the fall of the Longobards and during the following centuries up to the Venetian conquest (1420), Cividale remained a very active cultural and political center. Its charm today lies in the survival of a great many remnants of the deep Middle Ages and particularly of the culture of the Longobards.

From the town's center (piazza del Duomo), a short walk downhill leads to the **Tempietto Longobardo**, a chapel built or rebuilt by the Longobards in the eighth century and later used by the Benedictine nuns of an adjacent monastery. The walk from the piazza del Duomo leads you into the medieval center of the Cividale, and the entrance to the Tempietto is beautifully situated on the bank of the Natisone river. Inside the Tempietto, the well-restored stuccoes on the back wall date from the eighth century, while the frescoes on the side walls and ceiling range from the ninth to the 16th century; the nuns' carved wood seats belong to the 15th century. There is an intensely medieval atmosphere in this little temple, which was most probably used by the Longobard dukes as a private chapel.

The handsomest square in Cividale is the medieval **piazza Paolo Diacono**, a well-proportioned, peaceful space (no automobile traffic is allowed) where the Cividalese still meet and chat, and where they sit in summer at the outdoor tables of the **Caffè Longobardo** while listening to the café's small orchestra.

Cividale's **Duomo**, rebuilt early in the 16th century, is attributed to the Venetian masters Pietro and Tullio Lombardo. Next to it is Cividale's splendid **archaeological museum**, in the Palazzo dei Provveditori Veneti, a building attributed to Palladio and beautifully restored after earthquake damage. (Open June 1 to September 14 from 9:00 A.M. to 6:00 P.M., Mondays until 1:30 P.M.; September 15 to May 31, every day from 9:00 A.M. to 1:30 P.M.) On the first floor there is an extensive collection of Roman and Longobard statues and bas-reliefs, which present a unique opportunity to view the gradual effects of romanization on "barbaric" culture. Unfortunately there are no labels on the pieces, and no booklet is available at the desk. Improved displays are planned and will probably be ready in 1993; the new exhibits have already been completed on the second floor, with excellent results (except for the fact that only Italian is used). The most precious items on the second floor are the sarcophagus of Duke Gisulfo (A.D. 568), the veil of Beatrice Boiani (an extraordinary embroidery, fourteen by six feet, under restoration in 1992), and a collection of ancient manuscripts that includes one of the oldest books in existence, a gospel according to Saint Mark copied in the fifth or sixth century.

Stay at the **Locanda Al Castello**, a very well run hotel in

what was once a Jesuit monastery, a couple of miles outside
of Cividale. The handsome ivy-covered building has beautiful views and is surrounded by a garden. Its restaurant is
also among the best in town.

VENZONE, GEMONA, AND
SAN DANIELE

Forty-eight kilometers (30 miles) northwest of Cividale are
two medieval towns that were at the epicenter of the 1976
earthquake and have been completely reconstructed. Whenever possible, the ancient stones were used in exactly the
same places: Mostly windowsills and a few cornerstones,
they are easy to recognize in the otherwise new façades.

Venzone is the smaller and more charming of the two
towns. It was famous before the earthquake because of its
intact medieval walls, now almost entirely reconstructed.
For the visitor, the contrast between the medieval architecture of this tiny town (2,600 inhabitants) and the shining
newness of the buildings creates a strange effect. (To get a
dramatic picture of the earthquake's destructive power, walk
to the church of **San Giovanni**, purposely left unrestored.)
The beautiful **Palazzo Comunale** (about 1400) was the only
building that somehow survived the devastation, thanks to
reinforcing that had been added in the 1950s. The powerful
Duomo is still being reconstructed.

The other town is **Gemona**, larger than Venzone (population 11,000) and a bit less charming, if it weren't for its
unusually beautiful **Duomo**, spared by the earthquake except for the right nave, now reconstructed. This is a small,
unpretentious duomo, built in 1290, with an asymmetrical
façade, a marvelous rose window, and, over the portal, nine
statues representing the Virgin Mary, the Angel of the Annunciation, and the Magi. A huge, outsize statue of Saint Christopher occupies the entire right side of the façade. Located in
a quiet corner of town, overlooking a green landscape, this
duomo, with its perfectly human proportions and the simple
beauty of its statues, is one of the most eloquent echoes of
the religious spirit of the Middle Ages.

Halfway between Gemona and Udine (about 24 km/15
miles southwest of Gemona on route 463), the town of **San
Daniele del Friuli** is associated in the minds of all Italians
with the production of prosciutto, the uncooked ham that is
rapidly becoming as famous a symbol of culinary Italy as
spaghetti, pizza, and Parmesan cheese. The tradition of pig

farming in the San Daniele area goes back to the Middle Ages, and the economic boom of modern Italy has contributed to the diffusion of this rather expensive delicacy, which needs no cooking and no preparation and lends itself admirably to all kinds of uses, from appetizer to snack to main dish. Everybody is a prosciutto expert in San Daniele, and in most cafés as well as restaurants prosciutto dishes are served in a variety of ways. The ideal time to arrive in San Daniele is lunch time, when you can try one of the many *prosciutteria* in town, such as the **Bar Gelateria Toran** (also known as the Bar Centrale), at via Umberto Primo 10, a few yards down the street in front of the duomo. Prosciutto and melon is an ideal lunch in the summertime, while in winter you can try a combination of different salamis or *stinco di maiale al forno* (baked pork shin), also a specialty of Friuli.

San Daniele has other graces to offer, too. On its main square, piazza Vittorio Emanuele, the **palazzo del Municipio** (to the right of the duomo) is typically late medieval in design, with its portico and its Gothic windows. The **duomo** itself has an 18th-century façade, as does the **palazzo** on its right (palazzo del Monte di Pietà), which used to house the public pawn shop.

There's a delightful little church on nearby via Garibaldi: **Sant'Antonio Abate**, rebuilt in the 15th century. Its simple façade, with a Gothic portal and a rose window, is a small miracle of architectural purity and balance, while the frescoes in the interior, painted by Pellegrino da San Daniele early in the 16th century, are considered by art historians to be the most important cycle of frescoes in the entire Friuli.

The Wines and Restaurants of the Collio

One of the best wine-producing areas in Italy is found in the hills south and east of Cividale: the **Colli Orientali** (Oriental, or Eastern, Hills) close to Cividale, and the **Collio**, closer to Gorizia. The Collio area is considered by wine connoisseurs to be slightly superior; its center is the village of Cormons, 14½ km (9 miles) west of Gorizia. Tocai, Sauvignon, Pinot Grigio (Gray Pinot), and Pinot Chardonnay are the best-known white wines produced here, together with the celebrated (and very expensive) Picolit, a thick sweet wine with an extremely rich perfume (there's also a dry variety). Among the red wines, the most famous are Cabernet, Merlot, and Refosco.

The landscape in both areas is gentle and pleasant, punctuated by frequent signs and arrows (generally on a yellow background) marking the *aziende agricole* (farms) where wine and other products can be bought from the producers. The largest and best organized of these concerns is 1½ km (1 mile) southwest of **Cormons**, on the road toward Mariano, where the **Cantina Produttori Cormons**, an association of farmers for the production, bottling, and marketing of their wines, has a large retail shop, run by two young women with typical Friuli courtesy.

One of the most interesting features of the Friuli hills is the *osterie*—popular, informal restaurants where genuine country food can be enjoyed at moderate prices. Prosciutto and Collio wines are naturally kings in these establishments, together with mushrooms and venison. Among the most memorable is certainly the **Mulin Vecio** at Gradisca d'Isonzo, 13 km (8 miles) west of Gorizia, where the large dining room is decorated with copper pans, flowers, and ancient wooden tables, and the counter is covered with a large assortment of prosciutto of all kinds. The price is very moderate and the customers are a merry, colorful bunch that includes all cuts of the local society (closed Wednesdays and Thursdays; no reservations). Or you could go to Prepotto, 13 km (8 miles) south of Cividale, and try **Da Mario**, near the village church: prosciutto again, with all kinds of salami, pasta, and risotto (closed Mondays; reservations suggested; Tel: 0432-71-30-04). These *osterie* are much more fun, and much more representative of the local cuisine, than the standard restaurants in the area.

Gorizia and Udine

The administrative capitals of the hill area are Gorizia in Venezia Giulia and Udine in Friuli. **Gorizia** has not retained much of its medieval past; nowadays it is essentially a commercial center with a pleasant main square (piazza della Vittoria) dominated by the Baroque church of **Sant'Ignazio Loyola**. The most interesting part of Gorizia is its **Castello**, which is on a hill above the town and overlooks surrounding hills.

Udine is an orderly city, active without being frantic, and, compared with Gorizia, rich in historic monuments as well as in good restaurants. Its size (100,000 inhabitants) is large enough to allow for a good number of museums, hotels, and cultural centers. Automobile traffic is well conveyed in a belt of streets around the center, and the historic area can easily be covered on foot. All of these features make it an extremely pleasant city, a model for many middle-size Italian cities in their efforts to combine modern technology with quality of life.

Udine's most attractive area is the old town core—rebuilt in the 15th and 16th centuries under Venetian domination—concentrated around the duomo. A visit might start with the wide piazza della Libertà: The building on its southwest side is the **Palazzo del Comune,** in Venetian Gothic style (15th century), and the elegant portico across the square from it, the **Porticato di San Giovanni,** was built in 1533. The clocktower behind it, also constructed in 1533, is reminiscent of the one in Venice's piazza San Marco (the two copper Moors on top were added in 1850). The arch at the left of the Porticato, the **Arco Bollani,** was designed by Palladio in 1556. It leads to a street that climbs to the nearby **Castello,** an early medieval building reconstructed in the 16th century. Inside the Castello, the **Galleria d'Arte Antica,** currently under reconstruction, includes a large collection of works by Friuli painters (Bellunello, Girolamo da Udine, Amalteo, Pellegrino da San Daniele, Pordenone, Bison) as well as some by better-known artists, among which are an exceptionally beautiful *Christ and His Blood* painted by Carpaccio in 1496 and a *Council in the Arena* by Tiepolo.

A few steps from piazza della Libertà, the **Duomo** is a 13th-century construction, remodeled in the 18th century. Along the right nave are three paintings by Tiepolo: a *Trinity* (first altar), *Saints Ermagora and Fortunato* (second altar), and a small *Christ's Resurrection* (fourth altar). The chapel consecrated to San Nicolò dei Fabbri (Saint Nicolas, protector of blacksmiths), left of the main altar, contains a cycle of 14th-century frescoes by Vitale da Bologna.

More paintings by Tiepolo are found in a small building near the duomo (on the right-hand side, across from the side entrance), the **Oratorio della Purità** (ask the duomo's custodian to let you in): a *Madonna* on the main altar and a remarkable *Assumption* on the ceiling. The other, monochrome frescoes in the chapel are by Tiepolo's son Giandomenico.

A stroll through downtown Udine should include **via Daniele Manin** (starting from piazza della Libertà), with its handsome 15th-century buildings, down to the small **piazza Patriarcato** and the church of **San Antonio** (façade by Massari, 18th century) and the **Palazzo Arcivescovile,** with frescoes by Tiepolo (open 8:00 A.M. to 12 noon; closed Sundays and holidays).

Udine and the surrounding countryside abound in the

osterie described above. They are definitely worth a stop—or many stops—because of the quality of the food and wine, the genuinely popular atmosphere, and the very moderate prices. Very close to the duomo you'll find **Ai Provinciali** (via Vittorio Veneto 14), with a wood-paneled dining room and such truly traditional cooking as *minestra d'orzo e fagioli* (barley and bean soup), cheese risotto, and herb omelets (no reservations necessary; closed Sundays and September). Five minutes from the piazza della Libertà, **Al Lepre** is slightly more formal (via Poscolle 17, closed Sundays and August, reservations suggested; Tel: 0432-29-57-98). The service is more professional and the choice of dishes is larger, including Friuli's famous *stinco di maiale con polenta* (pork shin with polenta), a winter dish, and pasta with mushrooms.

Among the hotels in Udine, the **Hotel Là di Moret** is quiet and has a garden, an outdoor swimming pool, and a tennis court. A few steps from the duomo, **Hotel Astoria Italia**, remodeled in the 1970s, is modern and efficient and a preferred spot for small conventions.

THE BEACHES AND PLAINS

In summer the Friuli–Venezia Giulia plains abutting the sea are bathed in torrid heat; the cornfields remain motionless for hours, with the crickets singing their insistent song while in town everyone is enjoying a siesta in well-curtained rooms. Late in the afternoon, a gentle sea breeze starts to blow and life resumes some kind of rhythm.

In fall and winter, mists and fogs are common along the coast, making travel difficult but adding a romantic touch to the deserted beaches and to the medieval towers of the old villages.

The long stretch of coastline between Jesolo (in the Veneto) and Trieste is totally flat and almost entirely blessed with a wide strip of pale sand. Behind the beaches, large lagoons have been created by the action of rivers, exactly as happened in the Venice area. The largest and most famous of these lagoons is the **Laguna di Marano**, where Grado is the main town. Long before the existence of Venice, the Laguna di Marano was the seat of an advanced and affluent civilization. Its capital city was Aquileia, founded by the Romans in 181 B.C. and quickly expanded to the status of fourth-largest city in Roman Italy. The Grado–Aquileia area remains the most interesting one to visit on the plains today.

Aquileia

Aquileia is nowadays a small village of 3,000 inhabitants, economically centered around tourist interest in the Roman ruins. It was from Aquileia and Grado that the first sizable (and wealthy) groups of fugitives found refuge in the Venice lagoon during the fifth and sixth centuries A.D., abandoning their dwellings to the barbarian invaders and establishing in their place the new city of Venice. Venice soon eclipsed and then gradually conquered the ancient motherland.

Aquileia's archaeological area includes a large set of Roman ruins and a compound of medieval monuments of rare beauty. A visit starts with the **basilica** (open every day, 8:00 A.M. to 7:30 P.M.): This early Christian church was reconstructed by the local community after its destruction by Attila, king of the Huns, in A.D. 452. The basilica we see today is the result of yet another reconstruction, which took place in the 11th century. The floor plan is the same as in the great Byzantine churches of Ravenna (Latin cross with three naves), but the **mosaic** on the floor, one of the most stunning pieces of art bequeathed to us from Roman times, dates from the fourth century A.D. It is richly decorated with symbolic animals, flowers, and geometric figures; its most beautiful section is in the area in front of the main altar, with scenes describing the story of Jonah (this population of fishermen and seamen must have been especially sensitive to scenes of marine life).

Outside the basilica, and connected to it by a medieval portico, is the former Church of the Pagans, now used as a small souvenir shop. Behind the basilica a large archaeological area has been excavated, showing the foundations and outlines of the Roman forum; a map displayed at the entrance visually reconstructs this neighborhood of the Roman city. A long walk flanked by cypresses leads from the basilica to the ruins of the Roman *porto fluviale* (river harbor). Not much remains to be seen, except for the outline of the docks (an impressive 350 yards of them) and the foundations of a few buildings.

Aquileia's **archaeological museum** is a five-minute walk from the basilica (open 9:00 A.M. to 6:30 P.M., Mondays 9:00 A.M. to 2:00 P.M.; closed on holidays between 1:00 and 2:00 P.M.). The hundreds of stone receptacles piled up in its garden are cinerary urns excavated from tombs. Thousands of other funerary objects in stone, glass, gold, and clay are elegantly displayed in the museum's rooms. The statues on the first floor are as complete a collection of Roman sculpture as you could hope to see anywhere other than Rome itself. A special treasure is the large collection of rings and seals, amazing for the precision of their minute carving and for the beauty of the scenes represented; they are made of jasper, cornelian, and amber, all materials for which Aquileia was famous in Roman times. On the third floor, a set of drawings reconstructs the features of the city as it appeared before the barbarian devastation.

Eleven kilometers (7 miles) outside Aquileia, on route 352 toward Grado, the trattoria **Al Morar** is a pleasant place for an inexpensive rustic lunch or dinner. Outdoors under a wooden roof, young local girls serve the passersby with a simple but substantial menu based on grilled meats (especially pork chops), prosciutto, of course, and spaghetti, salads, and french fries.

Grado and Lignano

Grado, 11 km (7 miles) south of Aquileia, has an attractive medieval core surrounding the old basilica of **Sant'Eufemia**, consecrated in 579. Inside the basilica, which was built in large part with stones taken from pagan temples, you'll see the original floor **mosaic**, laid in the sixth century. The pulpit is a rare piece of medieval art, technically called an *ambo,* decorated with figures of the four evangelists that were carved in the 11th century.

Since the 1960s the town of Grado has become an increasingly important beach resort, patronized particularly by Austrian and German tourists. It has specialized in campgrounds and low-cost hotels, allowing its beautiful coastline to be crowded with unappealing high-rise construction. However, it is still recommended for visitors who want to fight the summer heat with a swim in the Adriatic. Some relatively quiet stretches of sand can still be found at the end of the *pineta* (pine woods) along the beach, and the town itself has accommodated the invasion of tourists with remarkable grace.

The other important beach resort is **Lignano**, at the opposite (western) tip of the Laguna di Marano. This area was totally deserted as recently as 1903, when the first small hotel was built at the tip of a long peninsula covered by pines—it must have been an exciting place to visit. Today that tip, rebaptized Lignano Sabbiadoro (Golden Sand), has become a large and efficiently run beach resort, with the sand covered with orderly lines of umbrellas and beach chairs. In 1953 a new area called Lignano Pineta was developed, and in 1965 Lignano Riviera was added to that. Almost 300,000 people visit these three beaches during the peak season from July 1 to August 20. In June and in late September, when the prices go down and the hotels are quiet, Lignano can be an excellent choice for a few days on the beach, especially if you are equipped with camping gear.

Pordenone

Ancient Pordenone is the principal town in the Friuli plains. Its appearance reflects the phases of its urban development: Around a medieval core, the city grew suddenly in the 1920s and 1930s, developing a belt of dwellings and public monuments in the "Imperial Italy" style pushed by Mussolini; then, after World War II, one of the local factories (the Zanussi factory, maker of home appliances) grew to international size and importance, which favored yet another urban expansion. The modern sections boast a number of gardens, and there are a few quiet corners, especially near the Noncello river—but a stroll in the old town is certainly more rewarding.

The street to visit is **via Vittorio Emanuele**, a prototype of many other "main streets" in the towns of Friuli. It is almost completely closed to traffic and gives a good idea of the splendid balance that many Italian towns have been able to achieve between historic past and modern life. Both sides of the street are flanked by porticoes—precious in case of rain or snow and a very good defense against the summer sun. Under these well-restored vaults, often more than 500 years old, modern life goes on undisturbed: Emporio Armani, Benetton, and other upscale chain stores seem perfectly at ease here. The people of Pordenone do their shopping and talking, often pushing their bicycles, under these porticoes and pause for cappuccino in the many cafés.

At the end of the via Vittorio Emanuele, the **Palazzo Comunale** (early 14th century) used to be the seat of the town government. Small and extremely graceful, it seems to epitomize a time when governments were local and most citizens knew each other by name. They probably would sit, as their descendants do today, at the tables of the Caffè Municipio right in front, to discuss the events of the day.

At the **Vecia Osteria del Moro**, on via Vittorio Emanuele about 100 yards from the palazzo, customers are received in a deliberately old-fashioned ambience, with bare wooden tables and antique furniture. The prices are moderate, and the patrons feel free to stop at each other's tables for a chat. The owner, Angelo Fedrigo, offers a *minestra di radicchio e fagioli* (radicchio and bean soup), or in winter a typical Friulan *soppressa all'aceto* (*soppressa* is a kind of salami; here it is sautéed with a touch of vinegar and topped with a meat sauce). Most meals are accompanied by polenta, the cornmeal dish that used to be the daily staple of the Friuli farmers.

Palmanova, Redipuglia, and Miramare

There are three other places of interest along the coast between Lignano and Trieste.

Palmanova, less than 32 km (20 miles) north of Grado, is a fortress city that was planned and built by the Venetians in a few decades starting in 1593. Its purpose was to provide a defense for the eastern borders of the Venetian territory (it was only besieged once, in 1848). The architects of the time considered this a unique opportunity to plan an ideal city according to Renaissance standards. And since no buildings have been added either inside or outside the original walls, it offers us a good opportunity to visit a Renaissance town as it was conceived at the time. However, Palmanova is a bit disappointing because of the modest quality of the architecture; this was obviously planned as a military center, with not much room or money for extra frills. The most interesting things to see are the star-shaped, formidable, very well preserved walls and the layout of the town's streets, departing radially from the circular center.

Redipuglia is 24 km (15 miles) east of Palmanova on the road to Monfalcone and Trieste. During World War I this was the theater of repeated alternating assaults by the Italian and Austrian armies, with enormous casualties on both sides. In 1938 the Italian government created a grandiose memorial by landscaping two entire hills facing each other (the most interesting to visit is the one on the north side of the road). The **Sacrario di Redipuglia** is an impressive homage to those soldiers who gave their lives in battle: One hundred thousand men are buried here, under three enormous crosses at the top of one hill and along 22 gigantic steps, flanked by cypresses, that climb the hill's slope.

On the pleasant coast road between Monfalcone and Trieste, 8 km (5 miles) north of Trieste, the castle of **Miramare** (Sea View) was built between 1856 and 1860 as a residence for Austria's archduke Maximilian of Hapsburg. The unlucky archduke did not have a chance to see the work finished, as in those very years he led an expedition to Mexico, where he was taken prisoner and executed by Benito Juárez in 1867. In line with the architectural fashion of that time (especially in Trieste), the castle was built and decorated in a mixture of styles, from Gothic to Renaissance to Baroque and Neoclassical (open 9:00 A.M. to 1:30 P.M., Sundays to 12:30 P.M.; closed Mondays). The view from the castle lives up to its name; the interior has been kept as Maximilian had planned it, with bedrooms, studies, and living rooms varying in style from French to Dutch and Oriental, and decorated with exquisite, truly princely furniture. Outside the castle a panoramic walk is flanked by rare trees and Neoclassical statues (open every day, 9:00 A.M. to sunset).

TRIESTE

Part of the Austrian Empire until World War II, strongly influenced by the Slavic population across the border, Italian by language and Venetian by dialect, Trieste is the most atypical of all Italian cities, architecturally as well as sociologically. Yet something in it makes it unmistakably Italian and extremely *simpatica*. Its population is active, witty, and optimistic; in the cafés the waiters are impeccably dressed and naturally pleasant; in the streets and in the *trattorie* there's an atmosphere that can only be defined as highly cultured, with just a touch of irony to soften the hardships of life. Most of all, Trieste is a harbor and a seafaring city. It is one of very few cities where passenger ships are still docked right in front of the main squares and streets. In a way it is a Mediterranean town made gigantic by its fortunes in history but built like so many fishing villages, with life concentrating on the waterfront, where the tiny private boats of the inhabitants are moored next to immense cruising and merchant ships. Very few families in Trieste don't own a sailboat or a motorboat for swimming and small-time fishing. And many Triestini still indulge in the old habit of taking a summer evening walk along the waterfront to catch the sea breeze, to look at the huge passenger ships, and possibly to stop for a drink at the Caffè degli Specchi.

Trieste's complex culture has made abundant contributions to Italian literature. Italo Svevo, one of the greatest Italian novelists of the 20th century, was born and lived here (he ran a factory that produced marine paints), and so did his contemporary Umberto Saba, one of the most highly regarded Italian poets. Trieste was also (perhaps because of its cultural ties with Austria) the first center to accept and disseminate the theories of Sigmund Freud, during the same years when James Joyce, still unknown and a teacher of English, lived in town.

The city's physical structure developed through distinct historic periods. The center, behind piazza dell'Unità d'Italia and up to the church of San Giusto, is medieval; most additions were begun in the second half of the 18th century under Maria Theresia of Austria, and continued under her son and grandson. A new industrial and harbor area was added after World War II.

Medieval Trieste has been in part overshadowed by the great building booms of the 18th and 19th centuries, but some neighborhoods have maintained their character, and these are definitely the most charming ones to visit. (Other, more recent, sections are also striking, but in a totally different way.) To catch the best parts of the old city, go to the small **piazza Cavana**, a few steps behind the grandiose piazza Unità d'Italia, and climb via Felice Veneziano and via Cattedrale toward the cathedral church of **San Giusto**. In contrast with the well-planned imperial waterfront, the old city is made up of tiny streets with frequent Romanesque and Gothic buildings, and is still inhabited by artisans and shopkeepers, as it has been for many centuries. Not far from piazza Cavana, at the end of via del Teatro Romano, you'll see the well-preserved ruins of a **Roman theater** (first century A.D.). The walk up via della Cattedrale takes about 15 minutes and is a bit steep, but the reward is a splendid compound of buildings at the top.

San Giusto Cathedral and the Castle

San Giusto is the symbol of the city, and for all Italians a symbol of Trieste's fight for reunion with the rest of the country. Like Trieste itself, it is atypical; the church sits flat and asymmetrical next to a squat bell tower on top of the hill. Actually two existing churches were combined in the 14th century to form the present cathedral, and the impressive rose window was added at that time. Inside, the two left-hand naves belong to one of the original churches (Santa Maria Assunta, 11th century) and the two right-hand naves to the other (San Giusto); the central nave was added in the 14th century to create the new cathedral.

Just behind San Giusto, a very short walk leads to the **Castello** (open from 9:00 A.M. to 1:00 P.M.; closed Mondays). It was built in separate phases between the 15th and 17th centuries, and a walk along its high walls affords a really splendid panoramic view over the city and the sea—particularly late in the afternoon, when the sun sets right into the water. (The grounds are open from 8:00 A.M. to 7:00 P.M.)

Piazza Unità d'Italia

Trieste assumed its present form primarily in the second half of the 19th century. The only sea harbor available to the Austro-Hungarian Empire, it was well protected by the rulers in Vienna and benefited from special legislation to invite commerce. Trieste quickly became one of the wealthiest and most active Mediterranean harbors. Its citizens built companies that grew to international importance in the import-export business (almost all coffee consumed in Europe used to pass through Trieste) and in related activities, such as marine insurance (Assicurazioni Generali, the largest insurance company in Italy, originated and still has its headquarters here) and passenger lines (Lloyd Triestino and Compagnia Adriatica di Navigazione, among others).

Such wealth required a visual counterpart, and this led to the construction of the impressive **piazza Unità d'Italia**, right at the center of the waterfront. The piazza is splendid and horrific at the same time. Its large, harmonious palazzi surround a well-planned central space, with the south side open toward the sea. The effect is that of a capital city, important and aware of its importance. Yet the palazzi, viewed singly, reveal a lack of architectural imagination. They all imitate Renaissance features, with some new touches, but they remain copies, not works of creative genius. Looking at the piazza from the waterfront side, the first palazzo on the right is the headquarters of the Lloyd Triestino (built in 1883, Renaissance style; the two fountains on the façade represent salt water and fresh water); the next on the same side is the French-inspired Palazzo Vanoli, now home of the luxurious **Grand Hotel Duchi d'Aosta**, owned by Assicurazioni Generali. Still on the same side, the next building is Palazzo Pitteri, elegantly Neoclassical (built in 1785). The gigantic building on the side opposite the sea is the Palazzo Comunale, built in 1875 in a weird mixture of styles. On the other side, the first building from the waterfront is the Palazzo del Governo (1904–1905), decorated with mosaics. Then comes the Casa Stratti, where the most famous of the Trieste cafés, **Caffé degli Specchi**, has been operating since 1840; it was an important meeting spot for merchants, intellectuals, and politicians in pre-television times. In the summer a small orchestra in the café plays mellow old-fashioned tunes for tourists and neighborhood people (prices are moderate).

On the street between the Casa Stratti and the Palazzo Comunale, a few yards from the square, you'll find the very comfortable **Hotel Al Teatro**. This hotel is inexpensive yet

very well located at the town's center and, not unimportant
for light sleepers, in an area closed to automobile traffic. It
has elevators, and the rooms, certainly with no frills, are
spacious and totally satisfactory. Parking is difficult but not
impossible to find outside the no-traffic area, about 50 yards
from the hotel.

The Museum of the Sea

Trieste has a Museum of Art and History, a Museum of
Natural History, a small Museum of Contemporary Art, and
other minor cultural centers. But the one institution that
cannot be found elsewhere is the **Museo del Mare** (Museum
of the Sea). It concentrates mostly on local items, but it is
worth a visit for people interested in the history of navigation and in the boats and fishing methods used in the upper
Adriatic Sea. Naïve dioramas, created many decades ago,
reconstruct the Adriatic vessels and fishing grounds. Many
Triestini hope that the models of now-forgotten boats will be
used one day to create a floating marine museum. (Open
9:00 A.M. to 1:00 P.M.)

Dining in Trieste

A few hundred yards away from the center, the **Antica
Trattoria Suban** is one of the best and best-known restaurants in town, specializing in fish and serving (moderately
priced) dinner in a garden (via Comici 2; Tel: 040-543-68;
closed in August).

Close to the waterfront and within walking distance from
piazza Unità d'Italia, the moderately expensive **Al Bragozzo**
also specializes in fish and has a marine atmosphere (via
Nazario Sauro 22; Tel: 040-30-30-01; closed Sundays, Mondays, and three weeks during June and July).

In Trieste, as well as in the entire Friuli–Venezia Giulia,
you should not miss at least one visit to an *osteria,* the
popular, inexpensive, and colorful restaurants that offer
family-style food and the best local atmosphere. Near piazza
Cavana, the **Antica Giacceretta** (Old Icebox) is one such
place. The customers here speak the local dialect around the
simple tables covered with white-and-red-checked tablecloths; the wine is automatically the house wine; and
mamma takes the orders while the son and daughter-in-law
do the cooking. You won't find a better risotto with clams
anywhere, nor probably a better dish of fried calamari (via
dei Fornelli 2; Tel: 040-30-56-14; reservations recommended;
closed Sundays and three weeks during July and August).

Also near piazza Unità d'Italia, the *osteria* **Re di Coppe** (King of Cups) is a bit more elaborately decorated, with oil paintings hanging on the walls, and is run by a husband and wife. They make great *gnocchi* and a special *brodetto di seppie* (cuttle-fish casserole), and offer a large selection of wines (via Geppa 11; Tel: 040-37-03-30; closed Saturday evenings, Sundays, and the first half of August).

GETTING AROUND

The international airport closest to Friuli–Venezia Giulia is the Marco Polo airport in Venice, from which most of the region's centers can be reached by car in less than three hours (Pordenone is one hour away; Trieste two hours).

You'll want a car to tour the Carnia mountains and the hill areas (rentals at the Venice airport or at the Trieste train station). There is good train service between Venice and Trieste (the ride takes two hours); secondary lines depart along the way to reach Udine and Gorizia. Some local buses connect Venice with the beach areas of Grado and Lignano, but the service is infrequent and the ride is disproportionately long.

In all cities and towns, including Trieste, it's best to park your car near a hotel or in the main square, and then explore on foot. Most towns and villages have tourist offices near the main squares (they are variously called A.P.T. for Azienda di Promozione Turistica, Pro Loco, or Ufficio del Turismo), where maps and brochures are abundantly available. The tourist offices are usually marked by a square sign with an "i" (for "information") in the center.

ACCOMMODATIONS REFERENCE

The rates given below are projections for 1993; always check for up-to-date information before making reservations. Wide ranges may reflect the differences between low- and high-season rates. Unless otherwise indicated, the figures indicate the cost of a double room (per room, not per person). However, half-board (mezza pensione) rates, which include breakfast and one other meal per day, are per person. The service is included in the rate; inquire about tax and breakfast.

▶ **Grand Hotel Duchi d'Aosta.** Piazza Unità d'Italia 2, 34100 **Trieste.** Tel: (040) 73-51; Fax: (040) 36-60-92. ₤250,000–₤300,000.

▶ **Hotel Al Teatro.** Capo di Piazza 1, 34100 **Trieste.** Tel: (040) 36-62-20. ₤90,000–₤110,000.

▶ **Hotel Astoria Italia.** Piazza XX Settembre 24, 33100 **Udine.** Tel: (0432) 50-50-91; Fax: same. ₤170,000–₤200,000.

▶ **Hotel Belvedere**. Località Cima Sappada, 32047 **Sappada** (Belluno). Tel: (0435) 46-91-12. Open December–March and June–September. ₤90,000–₤100,000.

▶ **Hotel Corona Ferrea**. Via Kratten 17, 32047 **Sappada** (Belluno). Tel: (0435) 46-91-03. ₤90,000–₤100,000.

▶ **Hotel Là di Moret**. Viale Tricesimo 276, 33100 **Udine**. Tel: (0432) 469-79 or 47-12-50; Fax: (0432) 48-07-25. ₤110,000–₤120,000.

▶ **Hotel Morgenleit**. Piazzale Morgenleit, 33020 **Sauris** (Udine). Tel: (0433) 861-66; Fax: (0433) 861-67. ₤70,000–₤90,000.

▶ **Locanda Al Castello**. Via del Castello 20, 33042 **Cividale del Friuli** (Udine). Tel: (0432) 73-32-42. ₤80,000–₤90,000.

TRENTINO–ALTO ADIGE

By Paolo Lanapoppi

The great attractions of this Alpine region are its landscapes and its climate. To the west the area includes the eastern part of the Alps, from the watershed down, and to the east, a large section of the Dolomites, a mountain range different in origin and structure from the Alps. While the Alps, a much older chain, have been somewhat rounded by glaciers and atmospheric erosion, the Dolomites emerged from the ocean relatively recently—they are really gigantic coral reefs—and because of this they often rise vertically from their green slopes.

The area has been inhabited since prehistoric times and is rich in monuments dating from the Middle Ages, particularly castles and walled citadels. An important tourist trade, established in the 18th century, has been much developed in the past 45 years, during which winter tourism tied to skiing has come to surpass the area's traditional summer activity.

MAJOR INTEREST

Trentino
Madonna di Campiglio and the Dolomites of Brenta
Mountain lakes and streams

Alto Adige
Alpine and Dolomitic valleys
Merano
Bolzano
Medieval castles
Tirolese cooking

503

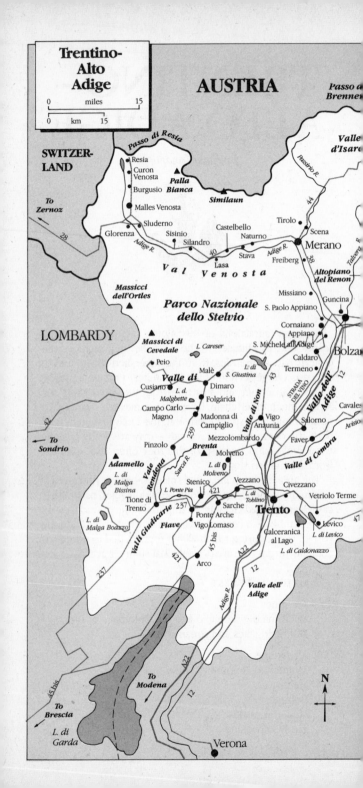

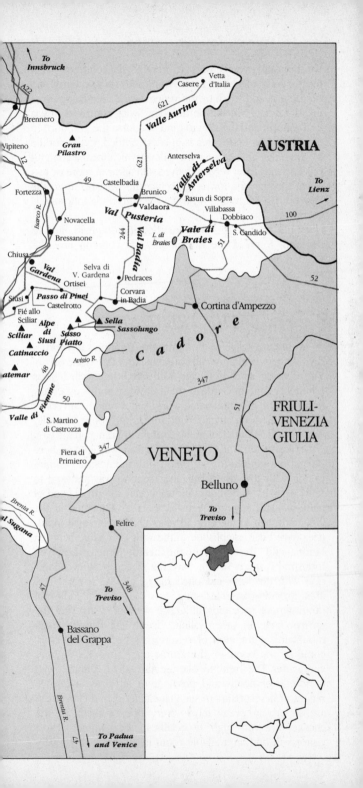

We start our coverage with the Trentino, the southern half of the area—bordered on the west and south by Lombardy and on the east and south by the Veneto—and then move up to the Alto Adige, which is bordered by Switzerland and Austria to the north and the Veneto (and of course the Trentino) to the south. The entire area is in effect divided up the middle by the Adige and Isarco river valleys, which form a continuous corridor from Verona in the south and run more or less north through the towns of Trento and Bolzano up to the Passo di Brennero and Austria. (The autostrada follows this corridor.)

To the west of this corridor the Alps dominate, and to the east, south of the Bressanone–San Candido line, the Dolomites.

THE TRENTINO

As in the Alto Adige to the north, the Trentino's territory is divided between mountains of Alpine and Dolomitic origin. The division runs along the Valli Giudicarie, which runs parallel to Lago di Garda to the northwest, and is especially dramatic and beautiful at the world-famous mountain resort of Madonna di Campiglio, with the Alpine Monte Adamello on the west and the Dolomitic Gruppo di Brenta on the east.

Unlike in the Alto Adige, only Italian was spoken here during the long history of union with the Austrian empire (along with the Alto Adige, the Trentino was annexed to Italy in 1918). Agriculture and especially the production of wine are still among the main sources of income in the area, although in the past 30 years clusters of small industries have been established in the Valle dell'Adige between Verona and Trento. As in the nearby Veneto, however, industrial workers usually have not given up their connection with the land and often moonlight as farmers. This area provides an interesting example of semi-industrial development spreading affluence without disfiguring the environment. In other valleys, deeply cut between high mountains, a tradition of poverty has been rapidly overcome by the boom of the tourist trade, in both summer and winter. The Trentino, like the Alto Adige, is dotted with hundreds of hotels and pensioni of all sizes and price ranges. It is surprising to see that efficiency and cleanliness are superb in pretty much every one of them, so the chances are very high, especially in the summer, that a visitor will find an available room in a pleasant hotel very close to any major attraction. (Not so in winter, and especially not over the Christmas period.)

Trento

The main historic event in the life of this quiet, industrious urban center, a crossroads of the German and Italian worlds, was the Council of Trent, a meeting of Catholic bishops held between 1545 and 1563 to formulate a Catholic answer to the Reformation movement. Important and lasting changes were introduced in Catholic doctrine and discipline during the 18 years of passionate discussion here. The location had been recommended by a great scholar and humanist from Trento, Bishop Bernardo Clesio.

A fine panoramic view of the city can be enjoyed from the area called Verruca or Doss Trento, a short ride from the railway station west across the river Adige.

The city's life revolves around the **piazza del Duomo** and the **via Belenzani**, a handsome street lined with 15th- and 16th-century buildings where many of the Catholic prelates lived during the long council years. The Duomo has a 14th-century façade; other interesting buildings on the square are the Torre Civica (11th century), the Castelletto dei Vescovi (13th century, at the right of the apse), and the Palazzo Pretorio (13th century, next to the tower). Inside this palazzo, the **Museo Diocesano** displays precious wood sculptures and Renaissance tapestries (open 9:30 A.M. to 12:30 P.M. and 2:30 to 6:00 P.M.; closed Sundays and November 16 to February 14).

A short walk from via Belenzani, through via Manci and via San Marco, is the **Castello del Buonconsiglio**, for many centuries the residence of the bishops of Trento. The Palazzo Magno, one of the buildings included within its walls, was greatly embellished by Bishop Clesio in an attempt to keep up with the great palaces that the noble cardinals were building for themselves all over Italy. The second floor includes an interesting **Archaeological Museum**, with artifacts from the prehistoric sites discovered in the Trentino; this material has invaded the bedroom, study, library, and wardrobe formerly used by the bishop. Other rooms are occupied by the **Museo del Risorgimento**, with documents related to the struggle of the people of Trentino against Austrian domination and in favor of annexation by Italy.

Very close to the castello, on a small street off via San Marco, the restaurant at the **Hotel Accademia** (vicolo Colico 6; Tel: 0461-98-15-80) is justly honored by the most demanding gourmets in town. The restaurant is attached to a very nice hotel of the same name, conveniently located in an ancient palace near the Duomo; it was recently renovated and is smoothly run by the two friendly women who own it. A reputation for regional cooking is also enjoyed by the famous restaurant **Chiesa**, via San Marco 64, which is a bit more expensive than Accademia and perhaps too crowded to keep the standards at a consistently high level; but you cannot go wrong by ordering such Trento specialties as the frog soup, the *strangolapreti* (a kind of pasta that is supposed to be so good as to have caused a few gluttonous priests to choke), or the cheese strudel (Tel: 0461-23-87-66; closed Sunday evenings and Mondays). Other good restaurants, all rather reasonable in price, abound in this refined city: Try the **Orso Grigio**, via degli Orti 19 (Tel: 0461-98-44-00; closed Sundays), or the **Roma**, via San Simonino 6 (Tel: 0461-98-41-50; closed Sundays and August). Or if you have a car, it's worth driving a couple of miles to the **Osteria Alla Baracca** in the suburb of Villazzano. Inexpensive, popular, and very colorful, it offers the best in regional food (via Galassa 4; Tel: 0461-92-00-49).

Comfortably located near the train station, the four-star **Hotel Buonconsiglio** was wholly renovated in 1989. The **Grand Hotel Trento** is another comfortable hotel with an excellent restaurant, **Al Caminetto**. A nice, quiet hotel is **Villa Madruzzo**, 3 km (2 miles) from downtown and surrounded by a beautiful garden.

For people driving on the autostrada as well as for those staying in Trento, a worthwhile detour is the village of Civezzano, 5 km (3 miles) east of Trento, for the **Maso Cantanghel**. In a marvelous countryside setting, this moderately priced restaurant is one of the best in the Trentino, although it is hard to find. Ask for directions at Civezzano, or call the restaurant at (0461) 85-87-14 (closed weekends and August).

The Food and Wine of the Trentino

The famous Alto Adige *knödel* (dumpling) appears in the Trentino with slightly different ingredients, as well as with the Italianized name of *canederli*. Among the pastas, a local specialty is ravioli, usually filled with meat. Beef, hare, and venison are the main meat staples; other great local recipes call for trout (*trote alla trentina,* accompanied by mint, lemon, and raisins) and eel (roasted and then cooked in wine—a real delicacy).

In fact, this region, with its dozens of small and large lakes and countless mountain streams, is the best place in Italy for freshwater fishing. Four small mountain lakes (each less than a square mile in surface) that are excellent for fishing are Lago di Malga Bissina, Lago di Malga Boazzo, Lago Careser, and Lago delle Malghette. Information and fishing permits can be obtained at Provincia di Trento, Servizio Foreste, Caccia e Pesca, Torri di Gardolo (Trento). (Torri di Gardolo is on the outskirts of Trento.)

Dozens of DOC (Denominazione di Origine Controllata) wines are produced in the hills of the Trentino. Cabernet and Merlot are the best-known red wines, while among the area's whites are Pinot, Riesling, and Traminer, nowadays sold all over Italy.

West of Trento:
The Dolomites of Brenta

The mountains of the Trentino are so consistently beautiful that ranking them on the basis of aesthetic appeal alone isn't feasible. However, an exploration of the area west and north of Trento will give you a good idea of the majesty of these landscapes. From Trento on route 45 *bis* it is easy to reach Toblino after a 20-km (12-mile) drive that passes through Vezzano. Little **Lago di Toblino** is delightful and romantic, with a medieval castle that is one of the most charming in the Trentino, and now the home of a wonderful restaurant, **Castel Toblino**, specializing in regional food such as mushrooms, venison, and trout (open March to November; closed Tuesdays; Tel: 0461-86-40-36). At **Sarche**, route 237 leads west to Ponte Arche and Tione di Trento along the river Sarca and the long artificial Lago Ponte Pia. A good restaurant farther south of Sarche, at Arco, just before Lago di Garda, is the inexpensive **Alla Lega**, located in a 16th-century palazzo (Tel: 0464-51-62-05; closed Wednesdays and November).

From Ponte Arche, a panoramic 16-km (10-mile) road runs south through the pleasant village of **Vigo Lomaso**, with its handsome medieval church (San Lorenzo; 11th and 13th centuries), to the **Fiavè plateau**, with its Torbiera, a site where prehistoric settlements have been discovered and studied. Corn growing and animal husbandry are the main activities of these small villages, which usually are built in tight, picturesque clusters, with narrow streets and medieval porticoes.

From Ponte Arche heading north, route 421 runs through the village of **Stenico**, with one of the most ancient and best-preserved castles in the Trentino. Within the castle walls are Romanesque and Gothic buildings, many with interesting 16th-century frescoes (ask the custodian for permission to visit). The quiet, pleasant, and reasonably priced **Hotel Flora**

is a nice place to stay here. About 20 km (12 miles) after
Stenico, a wide plateau opens up, with beautiful **Lago di
Molveno** at its center. Among the many hotels in the resort
town of Molveno, the **Hotel Ischia** offers a handsome garden
and a fine view of the surrounding mountains (Cima Brenta
is 9,500 feet high).

Farther west, at Tione, route 239 runs north through the
Val Rendena (river Sarca). A particularly green valley with
small villages, the Val Rendena cuts deeply between two
mountain giants: the **Gruppo dell'Adamello** in the west and
the **Gruppo di Brenta** in the east. A large part of this area is
now a national park, with an abundance of rivers and lakes
and inhabited by many species of deer, a few bears and
eagles, and the more common ermines and foxes. In the
village of **Pinzolo**, it is customary to stop at the church of **San
Vigilio** to look at the outside frescoes representing the
danza macabra, a memento mori painted in 1539. Knowledgeable Italians also prefer to stay here rather than in the
more famous Madonna di Campiglio; they say that Pinzolo is
a *real* town, with full-time residents of its own and a life
independent of tourism. They also object to the flashy aspects of Madonna di Campiglio, which has been accused of
having become a playground for the nouveau riche of Lombardy. Pinzolo and its immediate surroundings offer a large
choice of accommodations at very moderate prices. The
Hotel Centro Pineta is quiet and pleasant, while the local
tourist office has a long list of rooms and apartments available in private homes. Contact A.P.T. Pinzolo, 38086 Pinzolo,
Trento, for further information; Tel: (0465) 510-07. Pinzolo
also has one of the best restaurants in the Trentino, **Prima o
Poi**, on the road to Campiglio in the town of Le Pozze. It is a
small restaurant run by lovers of food, and it offers the most
refined versions of the local cuisine (Tel: 0465-571-75;
closed Wednesdays and July).

Madonna di Campiglio, to the north of Pinzolo, is justly
famous for its winter sports as well as its summer residences. The first hotel in this privileged valley was built in
the year 1872; soon afterward Madonna di Campiglio became a fashionable resort for the European aristocracy and
the bourgeoisie. Since the 1930s ski facilities have been
added and expanded, and today more than 40 miles of ski
slopes of all levels of difficulty surround the area. Hotels and
lodgings now abound in town, from the modern **Hotel
Cristallo** (excellent service, fine view from the rooms), to
the more affordable **Hotel Touring** (also with a garden and
nice view), to the quiet first-class **Golf Hotel** in nearby
Campo Carlo Magno. Located a mile and a half from down-

town, the latter has kept its turn-of-the-century charm, and its subdued sophistication shines through as old-fashioned class. Tyrolese charm is also the chief attraction of the affordable **Hotel Saint Hubertus**, with an outdoor swimming pool and an elegant restaurant. Among the restaurants in Madonna di Campiglio, the one at the hotel **Genzianella** is probably the best; try its *gnoccone di verdura*—a vegetable and dumpling concoction—and the roasted meats (Tel: 0465-412-31; closed Tuesdays).

Toward the **Valle di Sole**, through Folgárida and Dimaro—also well equipped for skiing—the road joins route 42 and continues toward **Malè**. The valley widens as it descends toward Lago di Santa Giustina, and the pine forests gradually give way to fruit orchards, which, together with tourism, are the main source of local income. **Ristorante Cusiano**, at Cusiano Valle di Sole, west of Dimaro, is a delightful adventure in genuine food at reasonable prices (Tel: 0463-712-10; closed Mondays). At Malè a good inexpensive restaurant is **La Segosta** (Tel: 0463-90-13-90; closed Tuesdays and September), while visitors with enough time for a detour to the Parco Nazionale dello Stelvio (leaving route 42 northbound at Cusiano) will find excellent food at **Il Mulino**, near the town of Peio, in an old water mill remodeled to offer a most pleasant setting (Tel: 0463-742-44; dinner only except in summer).

Following route 42 east of Malè through the Valle di Sole, you will come to **Lago di Santa Giustina**, the largest among the dozens of artificial lakes that produce abundant electricity for the Trentino as well as the nearby Veneto. Oblong in shape, it is very pleasantly situated in the green landscape of this gentle valley. From Lago di Santa Giustina route 43 leads back to Trento through the Valle di Non. About 11 km (7 miles) south of the lake it is well worth your time to take a short detour to the east to **Vigo Anaunia** and its hilltop *castello,* Thun, built in the 13th century and rebuilt in the 16th. This is really an entire walled compound of buildings and is one of the most striking castles in the Trentino, affording a splendid view over the Valle di Non (ask the custodian for a tour). At Mezzolombardo, just north of Trento, **Ristorante Al Sole**, via Rotaliana 5, specializes in meats and regional dishes at affordable prices (Tel: 0461-60-11-03).

East of Trento: Valle di Cembra and Valle di Fiemme

The river Avisio flows through a canyonlike gorge inside the Valle di Cembra, which runs northeast from the Valle dell'Adige between Trento and Mezzolombardo. At the gorge's edge, about 600 feet above the riverbed, is a green plateau dotted with villages and fruit orchards. At Faver, in the middle of the Valle di Cembra, is an old *maso* that has been transformed into **All'Olivo** (Tel: 0461-68-31-21), an excellent restaurant with genuine, simple regional cooking. (For an explanation of *maso,* see the Alto Adige section below.)

The town of **Cavalese**, northeast of Faver and technically in the Valle di Fiemme, is a preferred resort for Venetians and other city dwellers of the Veneto. It is well serviced with ski slopes and summer trails winding gently through the surrounding pastures. The **Hotel Panorama** here is true to its name; moderately priced, it offers good views of the surrounding mountains. The moderately priced **Il Cantuccio**, at via Unterberger 14, is a sophisticated restaurant featuring haute cuisine with an emphasis on regional dishes; it's justly famous well beyond the valley (Tel: 0462-301-40). The road (route 48 to 50) then continues eastward from Cavalese and down toward Feltre in the Veneto, with superbly scenic mountain passes leading into the towns of San Martino di Castrozza and Fiera di Primiero along the way.

Route 48 leads north from Cavalese through one of the most scenic areas of the Dolomites. From Predazzo to Moena and Canazei, all important ski resorts, it leads through the high mountain passes of Pordoi (7,000 feet) and Falzarego (7,500 feet) to Cortina d'Ampezzo (in the Veneto). The road is kept in excellent condition in both summer and winter (chains are often required in winter, however), and it rewards the patient driver with breathtaking views, warm and friendly stopovers, and genuine regional cuisine. See the Veneto chapter for more on this part of the Dolomites.

East of Trento: The Val Sugana

Running east from Trento, this rather narrow valley leads to the Veneto's Bassano del Grappa and to Venice. It also has the best road connection between Trento and the Treviso-Venice area (route 47), so traffic can be a nuisance in spite of the many attempts that have been made to widen the road. The main attractions of the valley are the beautiful **Lago di**

Caldonazzo and **Lago di Levico**, much loved by Venetians looking for a few days of rest and clean air. Still, the valley, although dotted with old castles and small villages, and particularly pleasant around the above-mentioned lakes, cannot compare in terms of scenic beauty with the Dolomitic valleys just described. It is best, instead, to keep it in mind as a convenient link between Trento and Venice or Treviso, or as the object of a comfortable excursion from the pleasant town of Bassano del Grappa (see the Veneto chapter).

At Calceranica, along the Lago di Caldonazzo, the **Ristorante Concorde** has a very pleasant garden and terrace overlooking the lake and takes special pride in its age-old recipes, but just its modern *gnocchetti verdi* (small green gnocchi, called spaetzel in the Alto Adige) would be sufficient to recommend it. The **Hotel Italia Grand Chalet** at Vetriolo Terme is very quiet and reasonably priced, with good views and excellent service.

THE ALTO ADIGE

The name Alto Adige refers to the very large basin of the river Adige, which originates in the northwest corner of the region, flows down through its main settlements (Merano and Bolzano), and continues its southbound course through Trento and Verona before emptying into the Adriatic Sea just south of Venice. At 255 miles, the Adige is the second-longest river in Italy (the longest is the Po). Of course, only the valleys in this very mountainous area are settled; they are often different from one another in aspect, vegetation, and local customs, and some have even kept a language of their own, called Ladino, which is an independent offspring of ancient Latin.

Until the end of World War I, the Alto Adige, like the Trentino, was part of the Austrian empire. When Italy turned out to be on the winning side of that war, it was agreed she would annex both areas, thus making the political boundaries coincide with those of the Alpine watershed. (The "liberation" of Trentino–Alto Adige was one of the main reasons Italy entered the war against Austria.) While the annexation did not create serious problems in the Trentino to the south (traditionally Italian speaking), it did in the Alto Adige, where the population was decidedly Austrian in language, traditions, and loyalty.

The area had been part of the greater Tirol, centering on Innsbruck, and its proper historical name was—and still is—Südtirol. The nationalistic government of Mussolini worsened the situation considerably by injecting large groups of Italian-speaking newcomers in an effort to submerge the German-speaking locals. Italian settlement, however, took place mostly in the cities, leaving the mountains and valleys untouched. In 1921 a mere 10 percent of the inhabitants spoke Italian as their first language, against 76 percent German.

Bolzano, the capital city, had only 10,000 inhabitants then. Today it has more than 100,000, a large majority of whom are Italian-speaking descendants of the "colonizers." After World War II the Italian government conferred a large degree of autonomy on Trentino–Alto Adige, but in spite of this the tension between the Italian- and German-speaking communities is still quite strong. Today the Italian-speaking population is about 35 percent of the total Alto Adige population of 500,000.

There are three main points of entry to the Alto Adige from the north, corresponding with deep cuts in the Alpine range. They are **Resia** to the west (Val Venosta), **Brennero** (Brenner Pass) in the center (Valle d'Isarco, also called Val d'Isarco), and **Dobbiaco** (Val Pusteria) at the far eastern end of the region. Each has a long Alpine valley running south of it, along which most of the Alto Adige settlements are to be found.

Together with tourism, farming is the principal source of income in this vibrant and economically comfortable region. Farmers here usually live in homes separated from the villages and surrounded by their own land (whereas in southern Italy they tend to live in the villages, walking, or today driving, to the fields). Their neat, well-kept homes are usually built of brick or stone and plastered and painted white, with a characteristic wood roof.

Inside, these homes invariably contain a *stube,* the ground-floor kitchen and living room, paneled in wood and endowed with a majestic ceramic stove that is the center of the family life. Together, the home and the land constitute a *maso* (in German, *Hof*), averaging about 60 acres. As it has been for centuries, this is still the amount of land considered sufficient to support a family. Under Italian law only one of a family's sons or daughters inherits the *maso,* and he or she is obliged to compensate the others; this tradition has contributed greatly to the survival of a prosperous farming community in this part of Italy.

The Food and Wine of the Alto Adige

The gastronomic traditions of this region have kept a personality of their own and are distinctly different from those of the rest of Italy, as well as from those of nearby Trentino. Clearly belonging to Austria and the mountains, the cooking is centered around hearty, substantial dishes necessary to sustain a population of mountaineers. A staple, served in countless variations, is knödel, basically balls of bread to which pretty much anything can be added: flour, milk, and butter (Semmel Knödel); bacon and salami (Tirol Knödel); liver (Leber Knödel); even apricots (Marillen Knödel).

Among the meat dishes, a delicious specialty is *Speck,* smoked pork prepared with different spices according to recipes that vary from village to village and often from family to family. *Speck* is served as an appetizer or as an entrée, often accompanied by smoked sausages (*Kaminwurzen*) and horseradish. Pork, smoked or boiled, is also the base of *Bauernschmaus,* an entrée usually served with sauerkraut. A specialty of Val Pusteria is *Tirtlen,* large fried ravioli, while Merano contributes a snail soup, *Meraner Schneckensuppe,* and the Val Venosta a soup of rye bread, *Bauernbrotsuppe.*

Sauerkraut, red cabbage, potatoes, and mushrooms are the main vegetables. A real must to try here is the *Pfinfferle,* a local mushroom fried with garlic and onion. Among the desserts, the king is the apple strudel, but there is also a delicious nut strudel and even a poppy strudel (*Mohnstrudel*); another favored dessert is *Schmarrn,* an omelet filled with prunes, cherries, or apples—or with all of them.

The Alto Adige is also an important producer of wines, many of which are well known in Italy and abroad and almost all of which are protected by the official DOC (Denominazione di Origine Controllata) system. Eighty percent of the production here is of red wines. Cabernet and Merlot, slightly lighter than Burgundies, are usually served with meats and are loved by the population of the nearby Veneto; Malvasia is great with *Speck,* while the Pinot Nero or Blauburgunder goes with venison. Among the white wines, the Pinot Grigio (Ruelander) has become a preferred aperitif all over Italy, while Sauvignon is a dry, slightly fruity wine ideal for trout. Gewürztraminer, full and round, goes equally well with fish and desserts.

Val Venosta

From 4,500 feet above sea level at the **Passo di Resia,** this valley, drained by the river Adige, stretches first south and then east to the handsome town of Merano. Most of the Alto Adige valleys cut deeply through the mountains, so their modest height above sea level doesn't give you a good idea of the height of the surrounding peaks. At the southern end of the Val Venosta are the *massicci* (massifs) **Ortles** and **Cevedale**, about 12,000 feet above sea level, while at its northern end the **Palla Bianca** and **Similaun** are more than 11,000 feet above sea level.

The Val Venosta is remarkably wide and green, with a dozen small centers in which you'll frequently encounter medieval churches and castles (we follow the valley down and east to Merano). Every village offers a choice of hotels and guest houses, most of which are consistently reliable in terms of quality and price. At Curon Venosta, near the northern end of the valley, restaurant **Stocker** is a fine example of the cuisine and courtesy of the Alto Adige; moderately priced, it offers a good selection of regional dishes and specializes in venison. Five kilometers (3 miles) out of Malles Venosta, near the village of Burgusio, is the 12th-century **abbey of Monte Maria**, an imposing compound that was the highest above sea level of any Benedictine abbey in Europe. Although largely rebuilt in the 15th century, the abbey retains some of the original features, among which is a fresco from 1180. Both the monastery and its chapel are open to visitors. A good restaurant in Malles is **Al Moro** (Tel: 0473-812-22; closed Tuesdays and November), informal and inexpensive and next door to the very pleasant **Hotel Plavina**, which also has a garden and an indoor swimming pool. Just below Malles is the village of **Glorenza**, still surrounded by its medieval walls (rebuilt in the 16th century).

Up above the town of Sluderno the **Castello di Coira**, built in the 13th century, is the most interesting among the Val Venosta castles because of its excellent state of conservation as well as the variety of precious objects it contains (open March to October, 10:00 A.M. to noon and 2:00 to 4:30 P.M.; closed on Mondays)—see the armor room in particular. The church of San Sisinio in the village of Sisinio also dates from the 13th century; the Coldrano castle near Silandro dates from the 16th century.

About 16 km (10 miles) farther along route 40, the **Schloss Kastelbell** at Castelbello has been accurately restored to its 13th-century appearance. The interior is closed for restoration, but is scheduled to reopen in the spring (call 0473-62-41-93 for details). A good hotel in Naturno is the **Sunnwies**, and just 2 km (1 mile) outside of Naturno, on the road to Passo Resia, you'll find the **Wiedenplatzer Keller**, an excellent, moderately priced restaurant rich in Alto Adige specialties (Tel: 0473-874-31; closed Tuesdays).

In this valley perhaps more than in others, the contrast between the luscious greens of the lower slopes and the snow-covered peaks above is particularly striking. In the spring this region offers a totally magical spectacle of flowering trees, since it is an area given mostly to the growing of pears, apricots, and especially apples—of which the Alto Adige is the largest regional producer in Europe.

Merano

As you approach Merano from the west, the valley widens and a quantity of vineyards start to appear next to the fruit orchards. The gentle landscape and climate of Merano have attracted tourists and vacationers since the 18th century—first the Austrian nobility, then the Viennese and European bourgeoisie. An important feature of its climate is the lack of humidity and the mildness of its temperatures (it is the northernmost part of Europe where palm trees can grow). To its luxurious 19th-century hotels Merano has added a great number of newer accommodations, and it is now booming with winter as well as summer tourism because of the splendid skiing facilities installed on the slopes of the surrounding mountains.

The medieval town, on the right bank of the river Passirio, is centered around the Gothic via dei Portici. Nearby are the **Castello Principesco**, a castle built in 1470 and furnished mostly with authentic antiques (open 9:00 A.M. to noon and 2:30 to 4:30 P.M.; closed on Sundays), and the **Duomo**, a Gothic building from the 15th century with a curiously crenellated façade. Along the river Passirio there are two pleasant walks, called Passeggiata d'Inverno and Passeggiata d'Estate (Winter Walk and Summer Walk); the first faces south, the second north.

The restaurant tradition in Merano pivots around internationally famous chef Andreas Hellrigl. Unfortunately Mr. Hellrigl decided to retire in 1990, and his restaurant and hotel **Villa Mozart** is now open only as a high-level cooking school, offering one-week courses to students and food lovers from all over the world (Tel: 0473-306-30; Fax: 0473-21-13-55). Exceptionally good restaurants are the expensive **Andrea** (via Galilei 44, Tel: 0473-374-00; closed Mondays and most of February) and **Flora** (via dei Portici 75, Tel: 0473-314-84; dinner only; closed Sundays and February). The former is perfect in decor and service, while the latter is a bit less formal but also slightly more affordable, serving salmon, trout, venison, and great pasta (a specialty in season is the ravioli filled with *Pfinfferle* mushrooms).

In addition to restaurants, some of the region's best lodgings are to be found in and around Merano. Among the truly remarkable first-class hotels are the **Palace**, on the via Cavour, with a large garden and swimming pool, and the **Castel Labers**, a couple of miles outside of town on the road to Scena (with a swimming pool and a striking garden). Another outlying hotel is the **Castel Freiberg**, a converted 14th-century castle 8 km (5 miles) south of Merano in the town of Freiberg. The medieval atmosphere is still strong here, in spite of the modern conveniences, and the views are incredible. Good walks are to be had in the surrounding hills.

About 3 km (2 miles) north of Merano and a short distance from the village of **Tirolo** is the **Castel Tirolo**, built in the 12th century by the counts of Venosta, who later became the rulers of the entire region. It was in 1363 that their last descendant handed their possessions over to the Hapsburgs of Austria, who were to rule until 1918 (in 1420 the capital was moved from Merano to Innsbruck). Although still inhabited, the castle can be visited from March 1 to October 31, 9:30 A.M. to noon and 2:00 to 5:00 P.M. (closed Mondays); guided tours are available every hour. The most interesting things here are the Romanesque chapel, with its 14th-century frescoes; the main entrance door, with 12th-century sculptures; and the sala del Trono (throne room), which also affords a magnificent view.

The main road, route 38, leads southeast out of Merano directly down to Bolzano.

Bolzano

This city lies in a deep but very wide valley at only 600 feet above sea level. Bolzano is located in the heart of the Alto Adige south of Merano on the north–south Isarco–Adige river corridor, which stretches from the Passo di Brennero down through Trento to Verona. Since the early Middle Ages it has been an important crossroads for commerce between Italy and Germany and famous for its trade fairs. Originally ruled by the bishops of Trento, it was conquered in the 13th century by the Merano-based counts of Tirol, thus passing to the German-speaking side of the Alps. (It seems that originally the local language had been Italian—a rather academic point that is often made nowadays in the disputes between the Italian and German communities.) It remained under

Hapsburg rule (with the usual Napoleonic exception) until 1918, when it was annexed to Italy. The Fascist government then tried to modify the ethnic balance in favor of the Italian element by encouraging immigration from other parts of the country. This fact created a rather tense atmosphere that is still felt today by a large part of the population.

The city lies at the confluence of the Talvera and Isarco rivers, just a couple of miles before they join the Adige. The presence of these rivers and the green slopes of the surrounding mountains give Bolzano a particularly friendly aspect; in a successful encounter between man and nature, Bolzano has become a city where the balance between human activity and a healthy environment is never lost sight of.

The charming medieval center of Bolzano is situated at the fork between the two rivers. It is striking, when walking along the old, well-preserved, basically Gothic **via dei Portici**, to compare it with the Gothic centers of other Italian cities, such as in Umbria or Tuscany; the feeling here is totally different—and clearly Nordic, with its pointed roofs, characteristic balconies, and the way people dress and act. At the center of the Old Town is the **Duomo**, Gothic and accompanied by a handsome bell tower from the 13th century; a few steps away is the **Convento dei Domenicani**, a monastery that has a chapel with 14th-century frescoes influenced by Giotto and a very pleasant 15th-century cloister.

Even more graceful and intimate is the cloister of the **Chiesa dei Francescani**, across via dei Portici, a church worth a visit because of its impressive **altarpiece of the Cappella della Vergine** (c. 1500)—one of the best examples of Flamboyant Gothic to be found in the Alto Adige.

At the Franciscan church, the via di Castel Roncolo leads half a mile to **Castel Roncolo**, originally built in the 13th century and reconstructed in the 16th. It contains a unique series of nonreligious frescoes (14th and 15th centuries) representing knights and dames in scenes from popular romances of chivalry, such as the story of Tristan and Isolde. The style is Gothic and the overall effect is quite moving due to the mixture of stylized elegance and delicious naiveté. A visit to this well-preserved castle gives a good idea of life at a Tirolese court in the late Middle Ages (open 10:00 A.M. to noon and 3:00 to 7:00 P.M.; closed Sundays and Mondays).

The best restaurant in Bolzano is probably **Da Abramo**, piazza Gries 16, with very elegant Viennese decor (outdoor dining in the summer) and a varied menu oriented toward the cuisine of the nearby Veneto (reservations advised; Tel: 0471-28-01-41; closed Sundays and June). Another pleasant experience is offered by the restaurant at **Castel Mareccio**, very close to the city center and surrounded by vineyards. The restaurant is rather informal and popular with both the Italian and German communities, perhaps because of its wide-ranging menu, which includes international dishes as well as local specialties (via Claudia de' Medici 12; Tel: 0471-97-94-39; closed Sundays). The **Fossa dei Leoni**, at piazza Dogana 3, is a busy, colorful, informal restaurant. In business since 1543, it serves the best in regional cooking (Tel: 0471-97-07-49).

This center of commerce and tourism is not lacking in good and very good hotels; you can also visit Bolzano while staying in one of the many secluded, idyllic hotels in the surrounding region. In town, the luxurious and centrally located **Park Hotel Laurin** has a splendid garden. The **Hotel Scala Stiegl** is also close to the center of town, as well as to the cable car to the Altopiano del Renon; it boasts a garden, too, where guests can dine in good weather. Both hotels are open year-round.

The **Castel Guncina-Reichrieglerhof** is just 3 km (2 miles) outside of Bolzano in the village of Guncina, but it is very rural and very quiet and has a nice garden with a swimming pool and a view of the city. Its 18 rooms, all with private baths, are reasonably priced. On the strada del Vino (see below) about 10 km (6 miles) outside of town is the **Schloss Korb**, a medieval castle that has been perfectly restored. In the middle of vineyards and orchards, it has great views, a large garden, two swimming pools (one indoor and one outdoor), and several tennis courts; open Easter through October.

The **Altopiano del Renon**, at 3,600 feet above sea level, is a green plateau overlooking Bolzano to the northeast. It offers a splendid view of the surrounding Dolomites, notably the peaks of Latemar, Catinaccio, and Sciliar, and can be reached either by car—24 km (15 miles) starting from via Rencio at the eastern edge of the city—or by a comfortable cable car departing from via Renon, a 20-minute walk from the Duomo.

The Strada del Vino (Wine Route)

This pretty route follows a wide and gentle valley running south from Bolzano and slightly to the west of the parallel Valle dell'Adige, which leads to Trento. For unhurried visitors it is a worthwhile alternative to the autostrada between Bolzano and Trento, running as it does through **Appiano** and **Caldaro** (ancient villages with Renaissance buildings; there's a wine museum at Caldaro) before reaching the river Adige again at Salorno. The landscape is one of gentle hills covered with uninterrupted vineyards and dotted with small villages that are famous in Italy for the wines that bear their names.

Wine shops and restaurants are, of course, abundant. Before Appiano, at **Cornaiano**, is the **Bellavista Marklhof**, via Belvedere 7, a former Benedictine monastery specializing in venison and serving its own wines (Tel: 0471-524-07; closed Mondays); at **Termeno** (Tramin in German, and the home of the well-known Traminer wine), the inexpensive **Traminerhof**, strada del Vino 33, offers the basic staples of any Alto Adige menu: smoked pork, sauerkraut, goulash, and knödel (Tel: 0471-86-03-84; closed Tuesdays); and at San Michele all'Adige, **Da Silvio**, via Brennero 2, offers a fixed-price menu (*menù degustazione*) that includes appetizers, first and second courses, and dessert. The dishes at Da Silvio vary from purely Alto Adige cuisine (San Michele is technically in Trentino) and include homemade ravioli, risotto, and freshwater fish (Tel: 0461-65-03-24; closed Sunday evening and Mondays).

Valle d'Isarco and Val Gardena

This long north–south valley is the traditional route between Germany and Italy, via Innsbruck and the **Passo di Brennero**. An autostrada now runs the 89 km (55 miles) between the pass and Bolzano. The best way to enjoy the scenic terrain, however, is probably to leave Bolzano on route 12, driving northeast through Siusi and then Castelrotto to the Passo di Pinei (on the other side of which are Ortisei and the Val Gardena). On the way to Siusi, the imposing mass of Mount Sciliar dominates the landscape on the right side. The town of **Siusi** is a famous ski resort, with slopes of all levels of difficulty at nearby Alpe di Siusi, 6,000 feet above sea level. But Alpe di Siusi is a marvelous place to visit in the summer, too, when the plateau is covered with grass and wildflowers dot the pinewoods. After Siusi, the road leads to Castelrotto and then winds through Passo di Pinei, where the splendid **Val Gardena** opens up on the right-hand side.

In Val Gardena you are in Dolomitic territory, as is apparent from the vertical peaks of Mounts Sella, Sassolungo, and Sasso Piatto, all over 10,000 feet high. Ortisei and Selva are the main centers of this valley, a real skier's paradise and one of the most crowded resort areas in the Alto Adige.

Back through the Passo di Pinei and into the Valle d'Isarco

heading northeast, you reach Chiusa and the impressive plateau on which is situated the town of **Bressanone**, a very old and tranquil urban center where the Tirol bishops had their residence. The **Duomo** (13th century, but remodeled in the 18th) and its handsome 14th-century cloister, together with the nearby **Palazzo dei Principi Vescovi** (early 17th century), are the main monuments to visit, but the town itself is very pleasant and one of the most attractive centers in the Alto Adige. Be sure to see via dei Portici Maggiori near the Duomo. Near Bressanone is the Augustinian abbey of **Novacella**, which was continuously enlarged and embellished from the 15th to the 18th centuries (guided visits every day, 10:00 to 11:00 A.M. and 2:00 to 3:00 P.M.).

Bressanone also enjoys an excellent reputation for cuisine, and one of its restaurants, at the **Hotel Elefante**, is among the best and most elegant in the Alto Adige—and quite expensive (reservations recommended; Tel: 0472-327-50; closed Mondays). The rooms in this 16th-century building, furnished with antiques, are also lovely. More informal but definitely very good are **Fink**, via dei Portici Minori 4, where the soups are a must (Tel: 0472-348-83; closed Wednesdays), and **Oste Scuro**, vicolo del Duomo 3, specializing in venison and mushrooms (Tel: 0472-323-44; closed Sunday evenings and Mondays).

The road heading northwest up the valley to the Passo di Brennero runs through Fortezza to **Vipiteno**, less than 16 km (10 miles) from the Austrian border, and also an important ski resort as well as a good spot for short walks on the valley's slopes. The **Hotel Krone** in the Old Town, formerly a monastery, has a handsome garden and an excellent restaurant, serving all the Tirolese specialties and more.

Thirty-two kilometers (20 miles) east of Bressanone a road enters the splendid **Val Badia**, which is connected to Val Gardena at Corvara, another 32 km (20 miles) to the south. This narrow valley, surrounded by imposing Dolomitic peaks and one of the preferred ski resorts of the Alto Adige, opens up at Pedraces.

Val Pusteria

Val Pusteria, in the northeast corner of the Alto Adige, is one of the few Alto Adige valleys that run east to west rather than north to south; it connects Bressanone with the Alpine pass of **Dobbiaco** and, beyond, Lienz in Austria. The northern side of this handsome valley is of course exposed to the south and so lends itself beautifully to fruit farming and wine making. It is also dotted with small villages and isolated *masi,* where visitors are often welcome to buy the local produce and sometimes to spend the night for a small fee (see Staying in Alto Adige, below).

This valley is, or rather was, one of the contact points between the European and African continents (it seems that, geologically speaking, all of peninsular Italy belongs to the African side). The African mass is still pushing northward, penetrating below the Alpine crust (hence the frequent earthquakes in Friuli as well as in southern Italy). The visual counterpart of this state of things is the obvious contrast between the rounded mountains north of this valley and the jagged Dolomites, composed largely of primeval corals, on its southern side.

Brunico, northeast of Bolzano and nearer Bressanone, is the main center of the Val Pusteria. It has a 13th-century castle still surrounded by walls (no admission), and is at the center of pleasant walks on the gentle slopes that surround it. One of its restaurants, **Andreas Hofer**, is well known for its affordable Tirolese specialties (via Campo Tures 1; Tel: 0474-854-69; closed Saturdays).

The long **Valle Aurina** runs north and east toward Vetta d'Italia, the northernmost point in Italy. As the road (route 621 out of Brunico) has no exit, the top part of the valley has remained a bit isolated and is one of the most picturesque parts of the Alto Adige.

Heading east along the Val Pusteria from Brunico toward Dobbiaco, at **Valdaora** a road to the left leads to the **Valle di Anterselva**. There is a refined restaurant with 15th-century decor at Rasun di Sopra in this valley: **Ansitz Heufler**, offering the best of Tirolese cooking to its affluent clientele (reservations recommended; Tel: 0474-462-88; closed Wednesdays). Another 8 km (5 miles) ahead on the road from Brunico to Dobbiaco, the **Val di Braies** opens up on the right; it is well worth driving the 12 km or so (7 or 8 miles) of this easy road to the famous **Lago di Braies**. Totally enchanting in the middle of thick pinewoods, it mirrors in its limpid water the high mountains that surround it (the lake is three-quarters of a mile by one-quarter, and it is possible to walk around it). Back on the main Val Pusteria road, at Villabassa, a superb Tirolese restaurant awaits visitors: **Friedlerhof**, via Dante 40, where the goulash is the best you will ever have and the prices are happily moderate (Tel: 0474-750-03; closed Tuesdays and June).

Five kilometers (3 miles) east of Dobbiaco is the village of **San Candido**, with the 13th-century La Collegiata, the best-preserved Romanesque church in the Alto Adige. San Candido is also a well-developed ski resort. A good and affordable restaurant nearby is the **Vecchia Segheria**, 3 km (2 miles) from San Candido on route 52. From San Candido it is easy to reach Lienz in Austria, while from Dobbiaco an easy scenic road leads south for 30 km (20 miles) to **Cortina d'Ampezzo**, the capital of the Cadore (see the Veneto chapter).

Staying in Alto Adige

Two centuries of touristic tradition have endowed the Alto Adige with a number of sumptuous hotels. The remodeling of castles and monasteries has recently added more guest facilities, often striking for their architecture and views (it seems that the ancient monks were very good at siting their retreats). The recent boom of the ski trade has added countless facilities in the middle and low price ranges, all of which are characterized by a love for order and cleanliness that often makes for quite a contrast with certain pensioni of peninsular Italy.

The Alto Adige Gasthof. Earlier we discussed the farming units called *masi* (*Höfe* in German). Many of them have recently converted part of their space to tourist use, which in some cases has become their main source of income. A publication by the Ufficio Provinciale per il Turismo (piazza Parrocchia 11–12, Bolzano) called "Agriturismo nel Sudtirolo" lists more than 400 of these *masi,* with a photograph of each and detailed information about location and services offered. All of the *masi* listed are very neat and well kept, and the prices for 1992 varied from just under 25,000 to 45,000 lire per person per night, breakfast included. For stays of only one to three nights the price is slightly higher. A week or so on a *maso* is a wonderful way to get to know the Alto Adige landscape and its people.

GETTING AROUND

Trentino–Alto Adige can be entered by train from the north (Austrian border) on the Munich–Innsbruck–Bolzano–Trento line, which continues through Verona to Milan and Venice and is one of the most important international lines in Italy. There are no other railroad lines from the north, and there aren't any from the west. To the east, a railroad connects Lienz in Austria to Bolzano and Trento via Dobbiaco and the Val Pusteria (Brunico, Bressanone).

From the south, in addition to the Verona–Trento–Bolzano line, there is an important train service from Venice to Trento via Bassano del Grappa (in the Veneto) and the Val Sugana (in the Trentino). There are also two local railroad lines: from Bolzano northwest to Merano, and from Trento northwest via Mezzolombardo and Lago di Santa Giustina ending at Malè (Valle di Sole).

The rest of this mountainous region is served by public buses, with the main terminals in Trento and Bolzano. From each of those centers it is possible to reach all the main villages located in the surrounding valleys by bus. Bolzano and Trento are also connected by bus to Milan and Venice, and buses connect most smaller railway stations to the villages in the region. Many of those local buses, however, run only once a day in each direction.

The best way to enjoy both the landscape and the tourist facilities is by car. The roads are safe, well maintained, and as comfortable as the mountainous nature of the region allows; the local drivers are much more disciplined than those in more southerly regions of Italy. The major car rental firms (Hertz, Avis, and others) have offices only in Bolzano, not in Trento, and offer the usual option of dropping the car elsewhere in Italy (or elsewhere in Europe) for an extra fee.

ACCOMMODATIONS REFERENCE

The rates given below are projections for 1993; always check for up-to-date information before making reservations. Wide ranges may reflect the differences between low- and high-season rates. Unless otherwise indicated, the figures indicate the cost of a double room (per room, not per person). However, half-board (mezza pensione) rates, which include breakfast and one other meal per day, are per person. The service charge is included in the rate; inquire about tax and breakfast.

Trentino

▶ **Golf Hotel**. Campo Carlo Magno 38084 **Madonna di Campiglio** (Trento). Tel: (0465) 410-03; Fax: (0465) 402-94. Open December through March and July through August. ₤270,000–₤350,000.

▶ **Grand Hotel Trento**. Via Alfieri 3, 38100 **Trento**. Tel: (0461) 98-10-10. ₤190,000–₤220,000 with breakfast.

▶ **Hotel Accademia**. Vicolo Colico 4, 38100 **Trento**. Tel: (0461) 23-36-00; Fax: (0461) 23-01-74. ₤200,000–₤240,000.

▶ **Hotel Buonconsiglio**. Via Romagnosi 18, 38100 **Trento**. Tel: (0461) 98-00-89; Fax: (0461) 98-00-38. Closed August 15–30. ₤190,000.

▶ **Hotel Centro Pineta**. 38086 **Pinzolo** (Trento). Tel: (0465) 527-58; Fax: (0465) 514-01. Open December–April and June–September. ₤150,000.

▶ **Hotel Cristallo**. 38084 **Madonna di Campiglio** (Trento).

Tel: (0465) 411-32; Fax: 406-87. Open December to April 20 and June 22–September 10. ₤150,000–₤280,000.

▶ **Hotel Flora**. 38070 **Terme di Comano-Stenico** (Trento). Tel: (0465) 715-49. Open all year. ₤70,000–₤85,000.

▶ **Hotel Ischia Alle Dolomiti di Brenta**. 38018 **Molveno** (Trento). Tel: (0461) 58-60-57; Fax: (0461) 58-69-85. Open Christmas–March and June–September. ₤85,000–₤130,000.

▶ **Hotel Italia Grand Chalet**. Vetriolo Terme 38056 **Levico Terme**. Tel: (0461) 70-64-14. Open Christmas through April and July through September 20. ₤65,000–₤110,000.

▶ **Hotel Panorama**. 38033 **Cavalese**. Tel: (0462) 316-36. Open June 20–September 20 and December–May. ₤65,000–₤90,000.

▶ **Hotel Saint Hubertus**. 38084 **Madonna di Campiglio** (Trento). Tel: (0465) 411-44; Fax: (0465) 400-56. Open December–Easter and July–September. ₤190,000–₤215,000.

▶ **Hotel Touring**. Via Belvedere, 38084 **Madonna di Campiglio** (Trento). Tel: (0465) 410-51; Fax: (0465) 407-60. Open December–Easter and July–September. ₤130,000–₤150,000.

▶ **Hotel Villa Madruzzo**. 38050 **Cognola di Trento**. Tel: (0461) 98-62-20. ₤100,000–₤140,000.

Alto Adige
(When writing to the hotels below, write "Bolzano" after all town names other than Bolzano itself.)

▶ **Castel Freiberg**. **Freiberg** 39012 **Merano**. Tel: (0473) 24-41-96; Fax: (0473) 24-44-88. Open April 22–November 4. ₤180,000–₤300,000.

▶ **Castel Guncina-Reichrieglerhof**. Via Miramonte 9, 39100 **Bolzano**. Tel: (0471) 28-57-42; Fax: (0471) 463-45. Closed January. ₤170,000.

▶ **Castel Labers**. Via Labers 25, 39012 **Merano**. Tel: (0473) 344-84; Fax: (0473) 341-46. Open April 10–November. ₤100,000–₤190,000.

▶ **Hotel Elefante**. Via Rio Bianco 4, 39042 **Bressanone**. Tel: (0472) 327-50; Fax: (0472) 365-79. Open Christmas and March–November. ₤100,000–₤200,000.

▶ **Hotel Plavina**. Burgeis 157, Burgusio 39024 **Malles Venosta**. Tel: (0473) 812-23. Closed May 1–16 and November–Christmas. ₤45,000–₤60,000.

▶ **Hotel Scala Stiegl**. Via Brennero 11, 39100 **Bolzano**. Tel: (0471) 97-62-22; Fax: (0471) 97-62-22. ₤110,000–₤130,000.

▶ **Hotel Sunnwies**. 39025 **Naturno**. Tel: (0473) 871-57; Fax: (0473) 879-41. Open March–November. ₤90,000–₤170,000; half board ₤70,000–₤115,000.

▶ **Palace Hotel**. Via Cavour 2, 39012 **Merano**. Tel: (0473)

21-13-00; Fax: (0473) 341-81. Open Christmas and April–November. ₤210,000–₤360,000.

▶ **Park Hotel Laurin**. Via Laurino 4, 39100 **Bolzano**. Tel: (0471) 98-05-00; Fax: (0471) 97-09-53. ₤180,000–₤290,000.

▶ **Schloss Korb**. Strada Castel d'Appiano 5, Missiano 39050 **San Paolo Appiano** (about 10 km/6 miles west of Bolzano). Tel: (0471) 63-60-00; Fax: (0471) 63-60-33. Open April–November. ₤115,000–₤200,000.

MILAN
AND
LOMBARDY

By David Tabbat

David Tabbat lives in Milan, where he works as an Italian-language advertising copywriter. He is the author of various articles and translations dealing with the history of Italian art.

For many visitors, Lombardy (*Lombardia*) means Milan. But the truth is that the region as a whole affords the traveller an astonishing variety of landscapes and experiences. Head east from the great, modern Milanese metropolis, and you'll soon find yourself in Bergamo, one of Italy's most beautiful hill towns. Go north, across the gently rolling landscape of the Brianza, and in less than an hour you'll be contemplating the legendary beauties of Lake Como. Head south, and you'll reach the handsome medieval city of Pavia, set in a flat countryside of vineyards and rice paddies. Alps, lakes, fertile plains, cities filled with art, modern industry: The only thing missing is the sea. Unusual for an Italian region, Lombardy is landlocked. Nonetheless, its completeness sometimes makes it seem less a region than a country or a world.

The Lombards themselves like to speak of their region as "the locomotive of Italy." It's a loaded image, fraught with grievance. Many people here believe that the area, one of the most advanced and productive in the country, generally finds itself in the position of dragging along behind it a host of more backward and benighted provinces. Although a host of homegrown political scandals in 1992 challenged many

Lombards' traditional belief that all would be well if they weren't stuck in a united Italy, the people of Lombardy do have grounds for pride. They are the national leaders in the financial, services, and industrial sectors. Furthermore, the local economy is a genuinely complete one, including an enormous agricultural capacity. The area produces an abundance of everything from rice to dairy products to silk.

The agricultural prosperity of the region dates from what should have been a disaster: the destruction of Milan by the German emperor Barbarossa in the 12th century. Not only did the citizens rebuild their capital, but they also drained the marshes of the surrounding countryside, created canals for transportation, and set up an irrigation system to water their crops (of which rice was soon to become the most important). It is difficult for us, entangled in a maze of modern roads, to imagine that more aquatic Lombardy, when sails could be seen drifting by the poplar trees, when Prospero's ship could arrive at the port of Milan, and when Beatrice d'Este could disembark with her ladies-in-waiting from a gilded barge at Pavia when she arrived from Ferrara for her wedding with Ludovico Sforza. Later, Leonardo invented locks that made the river Po navigable, and the Po remains one of the rivers that help define Lombardy's borders (in this case, the southern). The Ticino, which issues from Lago Maggiore and the glaciers of the north, forms part of the frontier with Piedmont, while to the east the Mincio drifts lazily down from the Lago di Garda, edging by the Veneto before reaching Mantua. Every now and then you can catch a view of ilex and crumbling farms reflected in the water and be reminded of the Lombardy that was: where Virgil was born; where Manzoni was inspired to write his novel devoted to this land, *I Promessi Sposi*. Lombardy was even to inspire a later, American, writer; one of Edith Wharton's first successes was *The Valley of Decision,* set here.

The name Lombardy harks back to the rough-going Nordic tribe of the Longobards, who swept down in the sixth century. They had been preceded in Milan by the Romans of the late Empire, who made it their capital for almost a hundred years before moving on to Ravenna. The region was to prosper under communal government in the Middle Ages and continued to prosper even after it fell to the Viscontis in 1277 and to the Sforzas during the Renaissance. These two families commissioned most of the art and architecture that you will want to see here, and it was they who created Milan's Golden Age.

Nothing but scorn has been poured onto the occupying forces of the centuries that followed, but the fact remains

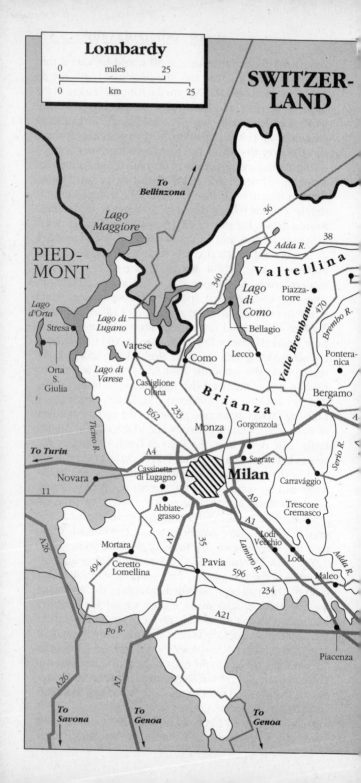

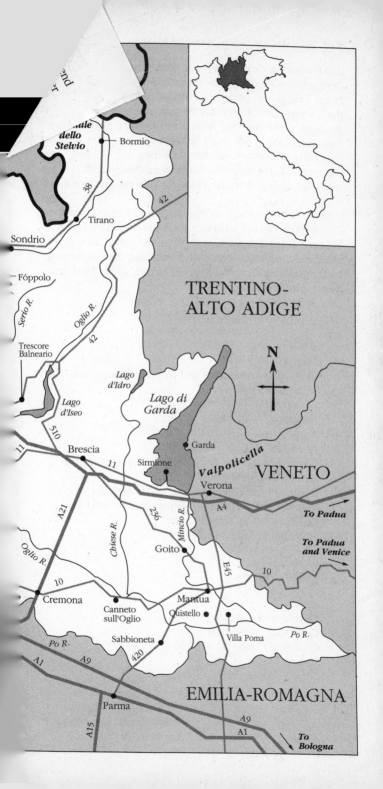

that the Lombard farmer was by no means on the losing
during those times of foreign rule. The Spanish, by she
force, brought an end to the days when the warlords and
their *condottieri* systematically ravaged the crops of the
peasants, while later the Austrians introduced new tax laws
that greatly aided the small landowners. The French under
Napoléon tore down the customhouses and did away with
the economic frontiers that had slowed down commerce for
centuries, laying the foundation for the prosperity we see
today.

Of course, this same economic boom has left its mark on
the countryside, but whatever their outskirts have ceded to
industry, Pavia, Bergamo, and other old towns have practically been preserved in amber; others, like Mantua, seem to
have stayed adrift in their splendid past, quite apart from
any current stream.

MAJOR INTEREST

Milan
Duomo
Leonardo's *Last Supper* and church of Santa Maria
    delle Grazie
Pinacoteca di Brera
Pinacoteca Ambrosiana
Poldi-Pezzoli museum
Teatro alla Scala
Castello Sforzesco (Pinacoteca and other museums)
Church of Sant'Ambrogio
Church of San Lorenzo Maggiore (Byzantine chapel)
Church of Sant'Eustorgio (Renaissance chapel)
Galleria Vittorio Emanuele II
Via Montenapoleone shopping

Monza
Duomo treasury

Pavia
Castello and museum
Church of San Michele
Church of San Pietro in Cielo d'Oro
Duomo
Certosa (5 miles north of town)

Cremona
Duomo and museums
Church of San Sigismondo

Bergamo
The Upper Town (piazza Vecchia)
Cappella Colleoni
Accademia Carrara
Lorenzo Lotto tour

Brescia
Piazza della Loggia area
Rotonda Romanesque church
Pinacoteca Tosio-Martinengo
Roman museum (Tempio Capitolino)

Mantua
Palazzo Ducale (Mantegna, private apartments of
    Isabella d'Este)
Palazzo del Te
Alberti's church of Sant'Andrea
The palaces at Sabbioneta

Castiglione Olona
Collegiata church
Baptistry

Food and Wine of Lombardy

The quality of the local agricultural products makes the excellence of Lombard cuisine a fairly sure thing, once those products have fallen into the hands of Milanese chefs, whose specialties have long dominated the province (apart from the once-Venetian enclaves of Garda, Brescia, and Bergamo). Again, the hated foreign rulers have left behind a few souvenirs, though in most cases "interchange" would be the preferred word. The Viscontis introduced rice, but the Spanish brought saffron. The pastures of Lombardy produced butter, but surely Gallic neighbors showed the Lombards how to use it with a light touch, and Lombardy remains one of the few Italian regions where, as in France, butter is frequently used instead of olive oil in cooking. Some specialties, including scaloppine *alla milanese,* were snapped up by the Austrians (in its case by their General Radetzky, and the Austrian result, by no means identical, was *Wiener Schnitzel*).

Many of the dishes produced here are so widely known that we forget their origin is Milanese. *Ossobuco* is one such: shank of veal with bone and marrow, simmered long enough to remind you that the Milanese, like their Germanic neighbors, prefer meat that is cooked through (a far cry from the Florentine passion for raw slabs of steak cast over charcoal). *Costoletta alla milanese,* veal cutlet on the bone, dipped in egg and bread crumbs before being fried in butter, has become an international favorite, as have scaloppine of veal cooked with capers and chopped onion, or with lemon or sage. A third meat dish encountered frequently is the *bollito misto*—again, a matter of long cooking, with a basis of boiled beef, capon, or chicken. The Modenese *zampone* (stuffed pig's foot) is thrown in later, and the dish is served with a *salsa verde*.

Bollito is very much a winter dish, and so, for many, is *minestrone,* the hearty vegetable soup served with rice in Milan; the vegetables vary with the season: carrots, squash, zucchini, beans, or cabbage. For most visitors the preferred first course is risotto, and though *alla milanese* can vary in its preparation, the basic ingredients remain the same: stock, chopped and browned onion, the cheese called *grana*—a young relation of Parmesan—saffron, and the patience to bring the rice to its final rich consistency. Because rice is Lombardy's staple food, it is natural to see it turn up in many other guises: with lentils, with mushrooms, with chopped leeks or celery, or *alla primavera,* using whatever spring vegetables the market might offer. It can be cooked with shrimp and saffron, or scooped out in the center and filled with diced veal kidneys (*rognoncini trifolati*). Other traditional risottos include those made with *luganega,* a kind of sausage, or with the tiny frogs known as *ranocchie.* These dishes are usually served as separate first courses, not as an accompaniment; except, at times, risotto *alla milanese* is presented alongside ossobuco.

The favorite side dish of the region has always been *polenta,* which might look familiar to travellers from the southern United States, as it is a form of cornmeal mush—with many variants. Once boiled it can be served still retaining a semiliquid texture, or it can be sliced into squares and be presented with anything from codfish to liver and onions. (Should you happen to read Alessandro Manzoni's celebrated novel *I Promessi Sposi* [*The Betrothed*], which gives a fine picture of life in 17th-century Lombardy, keep an eye out for the numerous references to polenta; it may seem to you that one character or another is forever putting some on the fire, stirring it, taking it off the fire, eating it, or offering it to a visitor!) As you head east to the former Venetian territories, headwaiters will urge polenta on you along with *uccelli,* small songbirds looking fairly unhappy, wrapped in bacon, and lying in state on a bier of polenta. Many Italians crave this delicacy, but if you don't, beware; it is often touted for its price, and there can also be a mind-bending scene like the one in the film *Gigi,* where the poor girl is taught how to eat *ortolans*. On the other hand, a dish definitely to search out is polenta *pasticciata,* a delicious combination of cheese, butter, and layers of polenta put into the oven until a crust forms on top. *Gnocchi,* found throughout Lombardy, can be treated in this same way.

Milan's gift to every Italian Christmas table, from Buenos Aires to Boston, is *panettone,* a light cake made of eggs, flour, and sugar and studded with sultanas and the candied peels of citrus fruit. Invented very quietly in the 15th century in a denser, less fluffy version than the one we know today, it has gone very public thanks to Motta and Alemagna, who export it all over the world. Less exportable is the fresh soft cream cheese called *mascarpone,* which can be eaten as a dessert on its own but which is best when it turns up in the heady combination known as *tiramisù,* where it is combined with soft sponge cake, chocolate, and alcohol.

Lombardy produces cheese in abundance, although few of the local varieties rank among the world's most interesting. *Grana padana* is an ever-so-slightly poorer relation of the Emilian *parmigiano reggiano,* which it closely resembles. Like its more prestigious cousin, it can be eaten by itself or grated over pasta and soups. *Quartirolo* is similar in appearance and texture to the Greek *feta* (although, unlike the latter, it is made exclusively from cow's milk.) *Crescenza* is creamy textured and buttery tasting, and goes well with salads. Similar, but a bit more tangy, is *taleggio,* which comes from the mountain valleys north of Bergamo. It's what the peasants call a *stracchino,* a "weary cheese," because it's made from the milk of cows tired out by the long trek down from their high Alpine summer pastures, and this is said to be perceptible in its flavor. A good *robiola* is the opposite of complex, conquering you by its utter freshness and purity; it's a sort of moister, Platonic ideal of cream cheese, putting the eater in mind of new-fallen snow. Two local cheeses have made good in the outside world. One is Bel Paese, a reliable (if not particularly interesting) industrial affair whose packaging is at least as familiar in New York or Buenos Aires as it is in Milan. The other cheese, however, is another matter entirely, the one great Lombard contribution to the repertory. Named for a village just north of the metropolis, the veined and creamy Gorgonzola (known familiarly as *zola* to the locals) comes in two basic types: *piccante* (sharp) and *dolce* (mild); the latter contains an admixture of *mascarpone*. Highly enjoyable by itself, *zola* is also used by the Lombards as a pizza topping and as a sauce for the dumplings known as *gnocchi.*

The wines of Lombardy have never rivaled those of

Piedmont to the west or the Veneto and Trentino to the east, and now, with modern transport available to rush in the Barberas, Barolos, Soaves, and Valpolicellas from outside, the astute growers of the plain of the Po have turned many vineyards into rice fields. There are, however, a few exceptions. Where the river Adda descends from the Alps and passes through Sondrio on its way to empty into Lago di Como, its banks are terraced to produce three fine Valtellina reds: Sassella, Grumello, and Inferno. From the southern shores of Lago di Garda comes a dry white Lugana, made with Trebbiano grapes, and excellent with trout and other freshwater fish. There are pleasant wines, too, from the area south of Milan called the Oltrepò Pavese: Pinot Grigio among the whites, Bonarda and a slightly sparkling Barbera among the reds.

Renaissance Heritage in Lombardy

The history of art in Lombardy starts in prehistoric times with the Valcamonica rock carvings, executed thousands of years before Christ. The region has been producing art ever since, and the story is far too long and complex to be recounted here. But for many travellers in Italy, Italian art means the Renaissance.

Milan has plenty of works by non-Lombard Renaissance artists: Raphael and Piero della Francesca in the Brera Museum, Botticelli and Pollaiuolo at the Poldi-Pezzoli, Michelangelo at the Castello Sforzesco, the great Venetians practically everywhere. And elsewhere in Lombardy, famous works by artists from outside the area abound: at Mantua, which still owes much of its character to the Paduan Mantegna and to Giulio Romano, the Roman disciple of Raphael; and at Castiglione Olona, which has important fresco cycles by the Tuscan Masolino.

But don't overlook the Lombard masters, who are adequately represented only in their home region. You won't generally find, in Lombard art, the poised and idealized classical rhetoric of the Florentine and Roman Renaissance or much virtuoso brushwork. What you *will* find is a peculiar attention to surfaces played on by light and shade, a sincere regard for the thousand nuances of small, everyday realities. There runs through the Lombard tradition an obstinate refusal to cancel the irregularities of the observed world in order to create a better one. And side by side with this antirhetorical strain, there runs another: an intensely dramatic, nearly romantic expressivity, relatively undiluted by the discipline of the ideal.

Lombard art reflects Lombardy's position as a crossroads which geography, trade, warfare, and politics laid open to influences from all over Europe: from Florence, passionate classicism, heroic figure drawing, and rational spatial construction; from Flanders and the Netherlands, meticulous attention to naturalistic detail; from the courts of Burgundy and France, an elaborateness of surface betokening luxury; and after the late but brilliant flowering of the Renaissance in Venice, a host of elements.

The characteristically ambivalent reaction of the Lombard artists to such a Babel of influences is already apparent in the work of **Vincenzo Foppa**, one of the two most important 15th-century painters the region produced. Recognizing the need to demonstrate his modernity, he incorporates into his paintings architectural settings whose lines spell out the perspective grid with nearly Florentine rigor. But his heart isn't in it; he's basically loyal to the older, "courtly" tradition of surface elaboration. He has a variety of clever strategies for resolving the conflict, for example by picking out in brilliant gold the very elements which, on the strength of the drawing, ought to define the recession into depth. Optically speaking, the gold lies right up on the surface of the picture, denying the three-dimensional space the drawing establishes. And so Foppa manages to have his cake and eat it too.

Ambrogio Bergognone, the region's other great Quattrocento master, was younger by a generation. His space is less mathematical than that of the Florentines; he shares with the schools of Flanders and the Netherlands an affectionate attention to the play of light on attentively described surfaces.

In the ambiguous artistic atmosphere of late-15th-century Lombardy, with its partial and half-hearted absorption of other areas' innovations, the arrival of two advanced Central Italian artists had a resonating effect. Leonardo da Vinci generated a host of followers who more or less attractively imitated his ideal figure type and *sfumato*—the shadowy blending of plane into plane. Donato Bramante worked in Milan en route to a great career as an architect in Rome, where he was to create—among other things—the first plan for what eventually became the St. Peter's we know today. The noble scope and grandeur of his classicizing art is readily apparent in his architectural contribution to the Milanese church of Santa Maria delle Grazie. But he was also active as a painter. His series of frescoes of men in armor, executed for a private house and now in the Brera, achieves a robust heroism. A local talent, Bartolomeo Suardi, who has gone down in history as Bramantino (little Bramante), created intensely imagined religious fantasies that are something of an acquired taste, for they make no concessions to conventional prettiness. A more soothing personality is Bernardo Luini, who fuses the traditional Lombard bucolic gentleness with '"modern" elements gleaned from Leonardo and Bramante.

Outside Milan, numerous local schools are worthy of mention. In the first half of the sixteenth century, Brescia produced a trio of great painters. Girolamo Salvodo was interested in Northern European art, where night scenes, "candlelight" illumination, and so forth were becoming familiar. His slightly younger contemporary, Romanino, is a more extroverted type, with a generally brighter palette and a fluid and dashing manner. The third master, Alessandro Bonvicino, called Moretto da Brescia, came to maturity in the period of the Catholic Counter-Reformation, and his religious work expresses an orthodox piety that may not be to everyone's taste. But his delicate sentiment and the elegant modulation of his silvery flesh tones make him a true heir to the work of Foppa and Bergognone, with their extraordinary refinement of surface and of lighting.

Nearby Bergamo was also a center of achievement. It's true that the greatest artist working there in the early 16th century was a "foreigner," Lorenzo Lotto from Venice. His stylistic traits are discussed in the section devoted to Bergamo. And it's easy to underrate Giambattista Moroni, whose portraits are sympathetic but honest, without a trace of the rhetoric that generates *chic* at the expense of penetration in society portraits by so many great painters, from Titian himself right down to John Singer Sargent.

While portraiture was moving in the direction of a scrupulous attention to the individual in Bergamo, the artists of nearby Cremona were reaching in their religious paintings for a supercharged expressionism that owed much to the influence of the Germans. At their best, the 16th-century Cremonese Mannerists still retain an almost hallucinatory power to reach out and transfix you in practically Blake-like fashion.

Many of the tendencies mentioned above in connection with one or another artist—an emphasis on the play of light, an intense psychological involvement, an empirical spatial construction, a warts-and-all honesty about how people actually look, a loving attention to the surfaces of the natural world—are prominent elements in the artistic makeup of the most celebrated Lombard painter of them all. Michelangelo Merisi, known as **Caravaggio**, after the town south of Bergamo, where his family originated, spent his formative years in Milan and in the Po Valley plain, but later went to

Rome, never to return. Save for a couple of things in Milan, you will find no work by him in Lombardy today.

There are a few real Lombard masterpieces of sculpture from the Renaissance, mostly in the realm of tomb sculpture: Solari's effigies of Ludovico Sforza and Beatrice d'Este at the Certosa, Bambaja's exquisite Gaston de Foix at the Castello Sforzesco in Milan. The most important Lombard Renaissance sculptors of all, however—Pietro Lombardo and his sons Tullio and Antonio—emigrated early to the Veneto region.

MILAN

Any guidebook will tell you that Milan is Italy's economic capital and the country's second city in population, and that its citizens are organized, industrious, and punctual almost to the point of being Teutonic—in distinct contrast to their southern neighbors. Of more immediate interest to the general visitor is the fact that Milan (Milano) is the most expensive city in Italy. This means that unless you are on an expense account or have unlimited funds at your disposal, a visit to the city's many sights should be carefully planned so you waste as little time as possible (i.e., try not to be there on a Monday, when much of what you want to see is closed). Most of Milan's art and history is to be seen in a galaxy of museums and several churches; sift through a list of their contents beforehand, select, and set off. You will find that the area of interest to you is nowhere near as extensive as you would expect from a city of this size; many sights of interest are within walking distance of the Duomo.

Walking in Milan these days is made easier by the air-pollution laws that keep the heaviest traffic away from the business area. Milan is a modern city in design partly because it suffered greatly from World War II bombs and has been largely rebuilt. Fortunately, some of its history has been preserved.

Earliest Milan

Milan became important when it was made capital of the Western Empire in 305, and it remained so for a century. It was here in 313 that Constantine adopted Christianity as the Empire's official religion, and it was here that the early Church fathers were to shape doctrines for a creed that was to become far more rigorous than many early converts had suspected. Saint Ambrose, who became bishop of Milan in

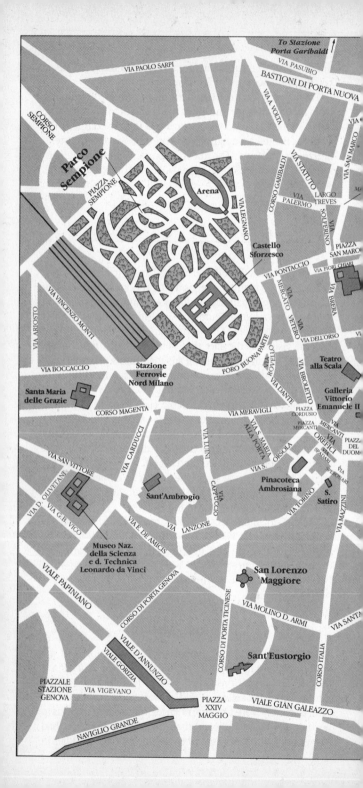

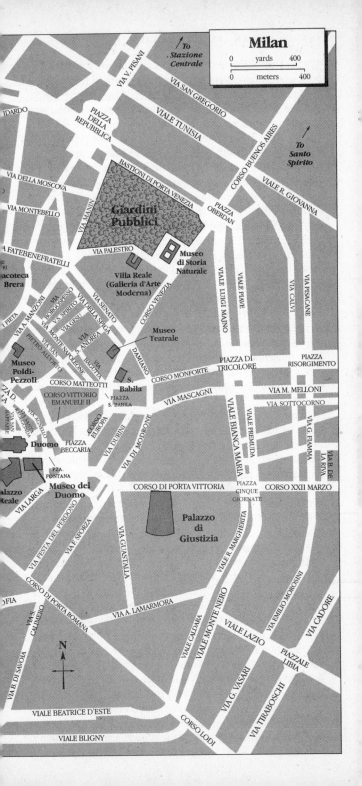

375, had the pagan temples closed, and the worship of pagan gods was outlawed. He governed Church affairs for decades, buried four Roman emperors, introduced hymns into church services, and founded a basilica (Sant'Ambrogio). In it he was to baptize Saint Augustine, who resided in Milan for four years with his mother, Saint Monica. The church of **Sant'Ambrogio** is still here, west of the Duomo, and is well worth a visit, with its handsome 11th-century atrium, its portico by Bramante along the side, and its gold Carolingian altar (the last is a reminder that later the Franks were to arrive and their king, Charlemagne, was to be crowned in Milan with the Iron Crown of the Lombard kings). The church took a direct hit during World War II, and the result was the near-total loss of a chapel with frescoes by Giambattista Tiepolo. (The war was particularly unkind to this greatest of 18th-century Italian artists; a fresco cycle by him in a Milanese palazzo and his great ceiling at the Scalzi church in Venice were also destroyed.) The piazza and complex of Sant'Ambrogio form an island of tranquillity near the town's center; its Romanesque and Byzantine treasures spill over into a little museum above the Bramante rectory (piazza Sant'Ambrogio 15; open 10:00 A.M. to 12:00 and 3:00 to 5:00 P.M.; open afternoons only on weekends and holidays; closed Tuesdays).

In the same neighborhood there are more remains of the Milan of Saint Augustine—amazing for a city that has been both extensively bombed and extensively modernized. The Milanese, whose French-influenced dialect is unfathomable to outsiders, pronounce Sant'Ambrogio "Sant'Ambroeus." (In its pure form, the local dialect has in fact become something of a rarity, having yielded to the homogenizing pressures of national unification, the mass media, and immigration from elsewhere in Italy. The Milanese draw on it nowadays primarily to provide a touch of color or, more maliciously, to set themselves apart from the *terroni,* the unpopular new arrivals from the South, who of course do not speak it.) **Sant'Ambroeus** is also the name of the most famous tearoom in Milan, renowned for its sculptures in ice cream, on the corso Matteotti at number 7 (Tel: 76-00-05-40), just off the main shopping street, the via Montenapoleone.

The church of **San Lorenzo Maggiore**, reached from Sant'Ambrogio along via Edmondo de Amicis, is reminiscent in its Syrian design of San Vitale in Ravenna, and its Cappella di San Aquilino is adorned with mosaics and sculpture akin to those of early Christian Rome. San Lorenzo is fronted by 16 impressive columns from a Roman temple. A subterranean canal surfaces alongside the church, a small remaining testimony of a city that still had a Venetian air in the early 19th century. Farther along the corso di Porta Ticinese is Milan's other great medieval church, **Sant'Eustorgio**, a treasury of late Gothic and early Renaissance art. The church's outstanding feature is the Portinari chapel, entered through a door to the left of the high altar. In Milan as in Flanders, the Portinari family were branch managers of the Medici bank. Their chapel accordingly speaks the architectural language of Quattrocento Florence. Perhaps more interesting than the harmonious but secondhand architecture is the fresco cycle showing scenes from the life of Saint Peter Martyr, a Dominican inquisitor who was assassinated along the Como road, not far from Milan. It's the work of Lombard artist Vincenzo Foppa.

The Duomo

The Visconti family came to power in the 13th century as archbishops of Milan, but they were a far cry from Saint Ambrose. Even for their time they were, with few exceptions, a vile breed of rulers—but at the same time they were great builders and scholars. They were to lay the foundations both of the Duomo and of the present Castello Sforzesco, which still stand near each other in the very center of Milan. By 1386, when Galeazzo Visconti III commissioned the Duomo as a votive offering toward having a male heir, the Viscontis had indeed come up in the world: Galeazzo's sister had married the duke of Clarence, son of the king of England, while his brutish uncle Bernabò had been able to force two abbots delivering an unwelcome letter from the pope to eat it. Decades later, Galeazzo's grandeur brought disaster to Italy. Because his first wife was a Valois, the French were given a claim to Milan's dukedom when their daughter married into the House of Orléans, and they were to pursue it with a vengeance. As for the cathedral, Galeazzo's prayer was answered. His church, dedicated to the Virgin, became one of the largest in Christendom. His granddaughter Bianca was to marry Francesco Sforza, who was one of the most popular and decent of the condottieri and was acclaimed duke when he entered Milan in 1450.

The Duomo of Milan was the last great Gothic cathedral to be built in Europe. Compared to the great French and German examples, with their powerful vertical impulse and harmoniously articulated elevation, it is a peculiar structure: a hypertrophic ground-floor arcade supports a mere dwarf of a clerestory, while the intermediate triforium level has vanished altogether, along with that sense of weightlessness, of the wall as curtain, that had been among the most significant traits of High Gothic architecture. In short, the building is completely *sui generis*. For better or worse, it must be taken as it is. Nonetheless, the atmosphere within the cathedral is one of such immense calm that its origins and oddities are soon forgotten amid the forest of columns and the reflections of stained glass. Saint Carlo Borromeo, born to one of Milan's noble families and destined to become the town's patron saint, cleared away much of the bric-a-brac in the Duomo's interior in the 16th century, and so you will encounter an overall feeling of vast space. There are still treasures to track down, however, from a huge French Gothic candelabrum to the tomb of Gian Giacomo Medici, in the right transept, the work of Leone Leoni. Among the more striking curiosities is the highly realistic statue of the flayed Saint Bartholomew, also in the right transept. The undoubtedly competent artist, from the nearby town of Agrate, has taken the trouble to tell us, in a Latin inscription, that "not Praxiteles, but Marco d'Agrate, made this." Modesty cannot have been among Marco's defining characteristics.

Borromeo is buried in the crypt, in a tomb donated by Philip II of Spain. His detractors say that he destroyed far too much of medieval Milan, but one of his main claims to fame was his valor in fighting the plague, and there might have been an element of sanitation in his alterations. The Duomo took so many centuries to build that the Milanese have an expression recalling the fact. When they call some process or other *la fabbrica del Duomo* (the construction of the Duomo), they mean that it takes forever. To get an idea of the armies of artists who worked on the Duomo, go to the roof and see the old town and the distant mountains through the legions of statues and pinnacles left behind by sculptors who came from all over Europe. Look up: At the very pinnacle of the tallest spire, you'll see a gold statue of the Virgin. Known affectionately as the *Madonnina* (Little Madonna), she is universally regarded as the symbol of the city, and the most famous of old Milanese songs is an apostrophe to her. This rooftop promenade was of course a "natural" for 19th-century visitors, particularly after Alfred, Lord Tennyson, penned his impressions of first seeing the Alps from it.

Castello Sforzesco

When you visit the Castello Sforzesco, which is directly up the via Dante from the Duomo, the Viscontis and the Sforzas move over from the Duomo with you, since the castle, built by the Viscontis and then destroyed by a populace who loathed them, was promptly reconstructed by Francesco Sforza when he came to power. The Castello was an arsenal of military might used to dominate Milan and its surroundings. It was used not only by the dukes but later, too, by the Spanish, who turned it into an impregnable fortress during the 200 years after Charles V took the city; and it was to the Castello that the Austrians retreated in the 19th century during the five days of heroic revolt on the part of the Milanese (all over Lombardy you find squares and streets called *Cinque Giornate*). The building as you see it today is in large measure a reconstruction from about the turn of the century, splendidly romantic though the ivy-covered ruined bits may seem to us now. The entrance tower is the work of the famous 15th-century architect and theorist who went by the name of Filarete, Greek for "lover of excellence." (Such conceits were typical of Renaissance erudition; you have only to think of the great Paduan architect Palladio, whose pseudonym is derived from the name of Pallas Athena.)

The castle hardly brought good luck to the Sforzas. Francesco's son Galeazzo Maria had inherited the best qualities of his Visconti mother and his Sforza father and began a brilliant reign that showed signs of rivaling that of Lorenzo de Medici in Florence. Then, after ten years of rule, he was murdered by three idiotic students who thought that they were reenacting the assassination of Caesar. This murder did for Italy about as much good as the shooting at Sarajevo was later to do for Europe. Galeazzo's heir, still a child, was raised by his uncle, Ludovico Il Moro, who became duke after the mysterious death of his ward. It was Ludovico who called in the French—and thereby signed the death warrant of the Renaissance in Italy.

But before that there had been a Golden Age, however brief, and this castle has many a reminder of it, in the frescoes of Bramante and in the bowered room supposedly designed by Leonardo. Both of them worked for Ludovico Il Moro and his delightful young wife, Beatrice d'Este, and like all court artists they were expected to design costumes and decorations for the endless masques and balls that echoed through the castello's chambers. Milan had never been so rich; when Beatrice's sister, Isabella, came up from Mantua she was amazed by the carriages of the wealthy and by the paved streets. Centuries later the cleanliness of Milan was still to be a matter of wonder—to Stendhal, for one, whose pre-Haussmann Paris was often little better than an open sewer. Isabella d'Este visited the castello during the happy days before her sister's tragic death at the age of 22, a loss from which Il Moro was never to recover. His luck was to decrease from then on, and at the end of his life he spent years in a wretched dungeon in the castle of Loches on the Loire, after having been deposed by the French king Louis XII.

Apart from the refurbished rooms where this couple once lived and played, the Castello is divided into several museums: The **Pinacoteca** (picture gallery) includes works by Bellini and Mantegna, as well as a fascinatingly ugly lunette painted by the youthful Filippo Lippi in a strenuous effort to match the style of Masaccio. Naturally there are numerous pictures by such important local artists as Bergognone, Bramantino, and Morazzone, who are less familiar to visitors than the great Tuscans and Venetians, but well deserving of attention nonetheless. Most noteworthy of all, perhaps, is the splendid room of portraits: It contains, along with much else, work by Correggio and Lotto (whose painting of an adolescent boy is a masterpiece of psychological penetration), as well as a good selection of work by the excellent Lombard portraitists of the 17th and 18th centuries. There's also a Van Dyck; this Flemish master lived for several years in Genoa, and his work is well represented in Italian collections.

The sculpture collection will come as a surprise to many, since its masterpieces include the last, unfinished work of Michelangelo—the very moving Rondanini *Pietà*—and also a head, said to be of the Empress Theodora, that is one of the finest Byzantine portraits extant. You should also be sure to see the recumbent statue of Gaston de Foix, a young French nobleman killed at the battle of Ravenna in 1512. The work of the Lombard master known as Bambaia, it is a funerary sculpture of astonishing refinement and beauty, the main element of a tomb whose other elements are scattered far and wide. There are sections devoted to reconstructed frescoes from outlying castles, and others to furniture and ceramics of the Renaissance, as well as tapestries, among them the series by Bramantino devoted to the months of the year. One of Europe's largest collections of ancient musical instruments is also here. It includes, along with such local artifacts as stringed instruments by the Milanese Testore family of builders, a harpsichord used by Mozart when he visited Milan in his youth; the keyboard, with elaborate inlays showing the names of the notes, is amusing. The *musei* of the Castello were Italy's first venture into "modern museum design": paintings without frames, lots of plate glass, and abrupt functional stairways. Some like it, some do not, but there is an emphasis on light—and the collections are not to be missed. One crucial practical note: incredibly, there are no rest rooms available in the Castello, so come prepared! (Open 9:30 A.M. to 5:30 P.M.; closed last Tuesday of the month.)

Also of Interest in Milan

The creative activity during the reign of Ludovico Il Moro was so frenzied that it was as if the artists—Leonardo and Bramante in particular—sensed that a deluge was due. Near the Castello is the church of **Santa Maria delle Grazie**. The nave is standard Lombard Gothic, but the crossing and apse are something else entirely. This is the famous "tribune" by Bramante, commissioned by Ludovico to receive the tombs of the Sforzas in a setting with which Milan could enter the new times—the Renaissance—and forget, if only for a while, its huge anachronism of a Gothic cathedral. Despite the persistence of a certain North Italian fussiness in details of decoration, the space achieves an air of severe and solemn *gravitas,* bringing vividly alive the Renaissance's aspiration to rival and surpass the architectural creations of ancient Rome.

Leonardo, who had scant time between creating designs for pageants and designs for war, managed somehow to paint his **Last Supper** in the refectory of the Carthusian monastery of Santa Maria. Trouble with maintenance of the fresco began within the artist's lifetime, for it was painted on a wall particularly subject to infiltrations of humidity. The most recent restoration removed all traces of the numerous repaintings to which the work had been subjected over the centuries; unfortunately, what's left today is a threadbare and ghostly wreck, though obviously worth seeing just the same.

Nearby is an old-fashioned tearoom, the **Pasticceria Marchesi** at via Santa Maria alla Porta 13, with its tall candy jars full of colored snowflakes of sugar and Parma violets. Not far from the church is the **Museo Nazionale della Scienza e della Tecnica Leonardo da Vinci** (via San Vittore 21; open 9:30 A.M. to 4:50 P.M.; closed Mondays), where, on the second floor, Leonardo's sketches for airplanes, submarines, and machine guns have been brought to life in reconstruction (his letter of introduction to Ludovico described him as an "engineer"). Not reconstructed, unfortunately, was his only masterpiece of sculpture: an uncast clay equestrian statue—larger than life—of Francesco Sforza that was once in the Castello and later was used for target practice by bored French soldiers. Yet the king of France, François I, was to be Leonardo's final host, at Amboise on the Loire, and Leonardo's most noted paintings reside in the Louvre.

Bramante managed another jewel of a church, **San Satiro**. And in this case, "managed" is the appropriate term. The challenge here was an unmovable street where the choir and apse should have been. Bramante resolved the problem with an ingenious bit of *trompe-l'oeil:* On the flat wall behind the high altar, he created a very shallow sculptural relief showing the vast architectural spaces he wished he'd been allowed to create. This exercise in early-Renaissance perspective fails to convince fully, because the artist was not in a position to control the exact vantage point from which his work was to be viewed. On the other hand, the odd blend of sophistication and ingenuousness embodied in this endearing device rarely fails to enchant the visitor; San Satiro is among Milan's more delicious surprises. The church is easy to visit because it is so near what is for many Milan's most enticing gallery of paintings: the **Pinacoteca Ambrosiana**. This gallery, housed in the same building as the famous library at piazza Pio XI 2, was founded by Cardinal Borromeo in 1609. Its collections are replete with souvenirs of the Sforza Renaissance: the De Predis profile of a girl now thought to be a daughter of Ludovico, and Leonardo's musing head of a musician. (His *Codice Atlantico,* which comprises most of his scientific sketches, is in the adjoining Biblioteca.) The miracle of the Ambrosiana is the full-scale Raphael working cartoon for his *School of Athens* in the Vatican. The master drawing is dramatically shown in its own room, giving no hint that it was once rolled up and hauled off to Paris by Napoléon (and later—astonishingly—returned). The Pinacoteca also has a perfect Caravaggio still life, a Titian *Adoration* commissioned by Henri II and Diane de Poitiers, and Cardinal Borromeo's collection of Jan Breughel. Naturally there are several fine examples of such local masters as Foppa and Bramantino, along with representative works by the great Venetians. It is a museum of an ideal size, too. Unfortunately, it is closed for restoration until 1994.

The **Biblioteca Ambrosiana** adds a few romantic notes: Petrarch's copy of Virgil, with his own annotations on Laura in the margin, and the letters exchanged between Lucrezia Borgia and the poet Cardinal Pietro Bembo. Byron read these here (they have been translated into English and published); he also stole a strand of Lucrezia's golden hair, a lock of which is now shown in a glass case upstairs.

Near the Ambrosiana is the **piazza Mercanti**, the only medieval square of the city to have survived. The old Broletto (town hall), from 1233, makes a striking contrast with the late-Renaissance elegancies of the Palazzo dei Giureconsulti, built 231 years later.

A stone's throw away is the piazza del Duomo and the splendid steel-and-glass **Galleria Vittorio Emanuele II**, with its many cafés—**Zucca's** (popularly called the Camparino), with its 1900 decor, being the most pleasant—where you can have an aperitif and watch the crowds.

The second of Milan's small but memorable museums of painting is the **Museo Poldi-Pezzoli**, at number 12 on the via Manzoni, which is one of the busiest thoroughfares in town (open 9:30 A.M. to 12:30 P.M. and 2:30 to 6:00 P.M., Saturdays until 7:30 P.M.; closed Mondays, and Sunday afternoons April through September). Founded by a wealthy collector, Gian Giacomo Poldi-Pezzoli, it echoes his personal taste with results reminiscent of the Frick Collection in New York, although rather less elegant. The paintings are set off with antique furniture, brocaded walls, and Renaissance bronzes, and the pictures include a Pollaiuolo profile of a girl that is so often reproduced that you may feel you know her, as well as superior Botticellis and Bellinis and a moody Guardi of a gondola drifting on a gray lagoon. Although the collection has good examples of many Italian and foreign schools, the Venetians are particularly well represented. You'll find works by Palma Vecchia (a sexy portrait of a courtesan), Cima da Conegliano (an enchanting group of little mythological scenes), Lotto, Tiepolo, and others. Be sure to see the room of society portraits by the 18th-century Bergamasque monk known as Fra Galgario; he's a Lombardy celebrity, by virtue of the high finish, dash, and evocativeness of his work. His portrayal here of a pallid, sunken-chested, neurasthetically supercilious gentleman is unforgettable. Like La Scala, practically across the street, the museum was so severely damaged in World War II that it required extensive reconstruction. But you'd never know it today; the somewhat musty and overstuffed atmosphere perfectly evokes the tastes of a bygone era.

The museum is just around the corner from the shopping center of Milan, the **via Montenapoleone** and its tributary streets such as via della Spiga and via Sant'Andrea. Milan is one of the most elegant shopping venues in the world, with the tradition of Bond Street, the chic of the Faubourg St-Honoré, the glitz of Beverly Hills, and the spending power of Düsseldorf all rolled into one. Milan is Italy's New York: No fashion designer, stylist, interior decorator, architect, artist, or writer has made it until he or she has made it to Milan, and it shows. Apart from the Guccis of international fashion, the little streets leading off the via Montenapoleone harbor a wealth of expensive boutiques on the first floors and in the courtyards of Baroque town houses. Milan is a window-shopper's paradise, each store vying with the next to see whose wares are displayed with the most pizzazz. (See "Shops and Shopping," below, for specifics.)

Those who like Italian painting of our century (and the preceding one) can find a good deal of it in the grandiose setting of the **Galleria d'Arte Moderna,** housed in the Villa Reale, which is on the via Palestro facing the Giardini Pubblici at the northern end of the via Manzoni (via Palestro 16, open 9:15 A.M. to 12:15 P.M. and 2:15 to 5:15 P.M.; closed Tuesdays). De Chirico, Morandi, and Marini—all represented here—have long been favorites with the international public. (Tommaso Marinetti of Milan, by the way, was the author of the highly influential Futurist manifesto of 1909.) But now the earlier age of Boldini, De Nittis, and Fattori is coming into its own, and, as so often happens in Italy because of a misunderstanding of designation, those who think they are going to be confronted by a mass of Jackson Pollocks in a museum of *arte moderna* find themselves instead in a 19th-century world copied time and again by Luchino Visconti in his films. More and more, visitors do *not* complain. As for the **Villa Reale** itself, it is well worth seeing for its own sake; built in 1790 for the counts of Belgioioso, it was the residence in Milan of Napoléon and his stepson, the viceroy Eugène de Beauharnais. Eugène was Josephine's son by her first marriage; Napoléon was devoted to him. He was an excellent administrator, and many of the reforms put through during his rule were to become, 50 years later, part and parcel of the New Italy. The French also brought into being a whole new class, hitherto unknown in Italy, of civil servants, educated and intelligent. They were to be sorely missed later, after the return of Austrian rule.

If you turn left when you come out of the Villa and then right in via Manin, in a minute or two you'll reach the **Palazzo Dugnani**. Now used for municipal offices, it contains a great ballroom-cum-banqueting hall with a fresco by Tiepolo, the only one of his in Milan that can be visited easily. (Of the other two he executed in the city, one is in private hands and rarely open, while the other was destroyed in the war; the *disjecta membra* of the latter are now in the Castello Sforzesco.) The magnificent scenes are drawn from ancient Roman history; chief among them is the Continence of Scipio, a typical *exemplum* of moral virtue, of the sort beloved by centuries of aristocrats who, of course, didn't always practice what they preached. This handsome hall is rarely visited, even by Italians. Although no one seems to know that it's here, it's easily accessible on weekdays, just so long as you avoid coming during the bureaucrats' lunch break.

At the other end of the via Manzoni is the piazza once occupied by a church dedicated by Bernabò Visconti's Veronese wife, Regina della Scala. In the second half of the 18th century, the church was pulled down to make way for a theater devoted to opera. The theater adopted her name, made Milan the musical capital of the country, and kept the city's upper classes busy from then on—thanks to boxes with facilities for eating, drinking, and playing cards (not permissible during arias). For foreigners, **La Scala** was a social haven for seeing who was in town, while for the natives it was a convenient escape route from more formal domestic entertaining. Various salons were reserved for "members"—just as they are today at New York's Metropolitan Opera—and the whole place naturally became a hotbed of intrigue, gossip, and amorous stratagems. One of the most enthusiastic foreign visitors to Milan, Henri Beyle (Stendhal), was quick to learn the local rules for marriage, for courtship, for love affairs. And none too soon, as he was to embark on a decade of passion for the enchanting *allumeuse* Gina Pietragrua, who was already surrounded by other suitors and was later to be a model for the Sanseverina. He also managed to be insulted by Lord Byron, who didn't know who Stendhal was and who was to live to regret it.

The theater was faithfully reconstructed after a bomb hit in World War II, and today looks much as it did in the immediate prewar period. The prevailing red plush and gold decor, however, conveys a somewhat misleading idea of what La Scala must have been like in its heyday; for, from the time of its inauguration down to the arrival of the Fascist regime, each box-holding family decorated its precincts inside the house according to whim, generally in its own heraldic colors. Although a shade musty today, it may still be the **Museo del Teatro**, which is entered from the piazza, that best gives the visitor an idea of La Scala's past. (Open 9:00 to 11:30 A.M. and 2:00 to 5:30 P.M., Sundays 9:30 to 11:30 A.M. and 2:30 to 5:30 P.M.; closed Sundays November through April.) Arranged with a judicious dose of nostalgia are souvenirs of singers, from Maria Malibran to Claudia Muzio and La Pasta. The composers are represented, too: Bellini, Donizetti, and above all Verdi, who is given two rooms of priceless documentation. There are rare portraits of both his wives, Margherita Barezzi and Giuseppina Strepponi. There is also a portrait of a more recent era's heir to the temperament of a diva, Maria Callas (a postcard of her costs more, and sells more, than any other at the exit counter). Her fans should go next door and have an aperitif at **Biffi Scala**, where she was wont to retire with her coterie after the opera.

The greatest and largest gallery of painting in Milan is the **Pinacoteca di Brera**, on the via Brera at number 28, within easy walking distance of La Scala. Among the most celebrated of the great works on display are Mantegna's *Dead Christ,* Raphael's *Marriage of the Virgin,* and Piero della Francesca's *Montefeltro Altarpiece.* The Mantegna is famous above all for the showy foreshortening of the Savior's body; it's optically inaccurate but aesthetically effective. The Raphael is an early work. The architectural setting shown in the picture is interesting: The pavement visualizes, as explicitly as possible, the perspective grid (a 15th-century Florentine invention), while the building in the background is a fine example of the perfectly symmetrical, centrally planned church—a type of structure that all Renaissance artists aspired to build because its geometrical regularity was held to symbolize the perfection of the godhead, but which the ecclesiastical authorities consistently discouraged because it was considered liturgically impractical. The Piero della Francesca features one of the best-known faces of the Renaissance: that of the *condottiere* Federico da Montefeltro, Duke of Urbino, who had lost an eye and part of his nose in a tournament. The place opposite him ought to have been occupied by his wife, Battista Sforza, but she had died shortly before, and the distribution of the figures makes us sense the poignance of her absence.

Another major piece, a huge Egypto-Venetian scene by the Bellini brothers, has long been the traditional trademark of the gallery. Alas, you won't be able to see it any time soon. The Brera, more than any other museum in Italy, has been plagued with administrative and labor problems, and the rearrangement of the rooms containing important large-scale works by Venetian and Lombard artists has been dragging on for years, with no immediate reopening in sight. Should you need a pause in your exploration of this fascinating museum, there's a snack bar on the balcony overlooking the courtyard, where you'll be able to get a sandwich or a salad. (Museum open 9:00 A.M. to 5:30 P.M. Tuesday through Saturday; 9:00 A.M. to 12:30 P.M. Sundays.)

We think of Milan as an industrial city with gleaming sky-scrapers, and yet apart from its art treasures and supremely elegant lifestyle, and the splendid Art Nouveau mansions in the residential areas such as the corso Venezia, Milan has many lesser-known charms—for example the area along the **Navigli**, or canals. The Navigli, southwest of the Duomo, ten minutes from the center, were once Milan's main link with the rest of the world, and they still are navigable today. A *brellin* (public open-air laundry) is preserved on the bank of the Naviglio Grande, but on the whole the medieval character of the area has given way to bistros, art galleries, boutiques, and discos, with the same mixture of charm and squalor as Greenwich Village in New York. A haunt of the younger, "alternative" Milanese, the Navigli are traditionally the place to spend a summer evening, away from the stifling city heat. The last Sunday of each month, except July and August, a flea market is held here, at the Naviglio Grande.

GETTING AROUND

Although the area of Milan of greatest interest to visitors is fairly compact and walkable, there are bits that are relatively far-flung. And with so much to see, it doesn't make sense to use up time and energy trudging about the heavily urbanized streets. Fortunately, the city boasts excellent public transportation of all kinds.

Taxis. They're plentiful and reasonably priced. You don't flag them down in the street; they wait for you (or vice versa) at the stands marked with a blue-and-white TAXI sign. The fare appears on the meter, but there are extra charges for baggage and for night service. You are not necessarily expected to tip. In an emergency, you can summon a cab by calling 85-85 or 67-67; in that case, you will, of course, also have to pay charges accrued while it was on its way to pick you up. Avoid touts offering a gypsy "taxi" (for example, in front of the railway station). Queue up if you must, and wait for a legal yellow one.

Metro and bus lines. Milan has an excellent, comprehensive bus and subway network. The three Metro lines intersect at various points, and each station features blessedly clear maps. You can buy a map of Milan showing bus and subway routes (*mezzi pubblici*) at newsstands or at the Duomo Metro station. All bus stops display a listing of all stops along the route, with an arrow showing which direction the bus is headed in. Depending on the route, bus and Metro service generally ends shortly after midnight.

The same ticket is good both above ground and below; in fact, a single ticket (*biglietto*) is good for 75 minutes from the time you stamp it, including any number of transfers, the only limit being that you can ride the underground only once. Hang on to your ticket—you can be fined if there's an inspection and you haven't got it.

Tickets cannot be obtained on board buses. You can buy them in Metro stations, or from cafés or newsstands displaying the yellow *Vendita Biglietti* sticker. They are sold singly or in a *carnet* of eleven tickets for the price of ten. More than one person can use the *carnet,* but to be valid, the tickets must always be kept together with the *matrice,* the last ticket in the booklet. In some of the principal Metro stations (Duomo, Stazione Centrale) you can buy a reasonably priced one-day or two-day *biglietto giornaliero* that gives you the right to unlimited use of bus and subway lines within the city limits.

Transportation to and from the airports. Linate, the principal terminus for European and domestic flights, is very close to Milan, in the neighboring municipality of Segrate. It is easily reached by taxi from the center; coming back into town, you can take either a yellow Milan cab or one of the white ones from Segrate. Fares are moderate, although there is an airport surcharge. There is also excellent city bus service every 20 minutes, shuttling between the airport and piazza San Babila downtown; it's the number 73 line (remember to buy a city bus ticket before boarding); the trip takes no more than half an hour.

La Malpensa, the international airport, is, alas, much farther away, up near Varese. There's a regular bus service from piazza Luigi di Savoia, around the side of Milan's Stazione Centrale. Before boarding, buy a ticket at the "Bus-Air Terminal" booth tucked into the side of the building. There's a departure at least once an hour all day, and every half-hour during the busiest times of day. You should aim to depart from Milan at least an hour before you need to be at the airport. For further information, call (02) 66-98-45-09.

The Milan yellow cabs will also take you to and from La Malpensa. The fare usually runs between 70,000 and 80,000 lire.

ACCOMMODATIONS

There are lots of hotels in the Lombard capital, but that doesn't necessarily mean it's always easy to find a satisfactory place to stay at a reasonable price. After all, Milan is the most expensive city in one of Europe's most expensive countries, and hotel rates reflect this situation. A double room at one of the top hotels can run you well over 500,000 lire a night. Although most Milan accommodations are not as frighteningly costly as that, it's safe to say that hotel prices constitute an extra inducement to make efficient use of your time in the city.

You may be able to negotiate a better deal by booking

ahead. And that's not the only reason for reserving your room. Milan is home to one of Europe's major trade fair centers, and when there's an important event on—the fashion shows, for instance—it can seem as if every desirable hotel in the city is full. (Of course you'll never, ever have this problem in August, when almost all Italians seem to be away in Sardinia, Greece, New York, or the South Pacific.)

The **Excelsior Hotel Gallia** is the city's traditional flagship business hotel. After some years of slow decline, it's back on form following a thoroughgoing restoration. The location, right next door to the Stazione Centrale, makes it convenient for excursions and for transportation to the airport at La Malpensa. The piazza out front is uninteresting, and even something of a mecca for winos and drug addicts (who are, however, unlikely to bother you). Piazza Duca D'Aosta 9, 20124. Tel: 67-85; Fax: 66-71-32-39. Ł605,000.

A more moderately priced hotel in the same immediate area is the **Mini Hotel Aosta**, not really as mini as all that, but offering clean modern rooms and even a few touches of designer elegance. Piazza Duca D'Aosta 16, 20124. Tel: 669-19-51; Fax: 669-62-15. Ł185,000.

A little nearer the historic part of town is the newish, comfortable, and not outrageously priced **Ibis**. Via Zarotto 8, 20124. Tel: 63-15; Fax: 659-80-26. Ł175,000.

Situated in the same general vicinity, on the enormous but rather empty piazza della Repubblica, halfway between the Stazione Centrale and the heart of old Milan, the **Principe di Savoia** is a large, luxurious place with Belle Epoque overtones. It's part of the CIGA chain, a synonym in Italy for top-quality (and top-dollar) lodgings. Piazza della Repubblica 17, 20124. Tel: 62-30; Fax: 659-58-38. Ł660,000. In U.S., Tel: (800) 221-2340 or (212) 935-9540; Fax: (212) 421-5929. In U.K., Tel: (0800) 28-92-34 or (071) 930-4147; Fax: (071) 839-1566.

The more modern **Palace**, directly across the piazza from the Principe di Savoia, is also part of the CIGA chain. Piazza della Repubblica 19, 20124. Tel: 63-36; Fax: 65-44-85. Ł630,000. (Same U.S. and U.K. numbers.) Many expense account travellers, and others on a generous budget, are partial to these two, not least because of the excellent service they offer.

To get from any of the above hotels to the part of Milan of most interest to travellers, you'll need to take a cab or use the Metro.

Still in the luxury category, the **Pierre Milano** is a bit off the beaten track; it is located in the discreetly bourgeois neighborhood near the Catholic University and the basilica of Sant'Ambrogio. Set in a restructured townhouse, it's blessedly quiet and has relatively few rooms, each one decorated differently. You'll probably want to take a taxi to get to the Duomo-Scala-Brera area from here. Altogether, though, it's a good place to stay for those whose means have kept pace with their taste. Via de Amicis 32, 20123. Tel: 72-00-05-81. Fax: 805-21-57. ₤660,000. Still near Sant'Ambrogio, but more economical and rather closer to the center, is the **King**. An older, mid-range hotel, it's not the last word in luxurious comfort. But it's been freshened up recently, and its slight residue of dowdiness may strike some travellers as more human than the sterile standardization of newer establishments. It's not far from the Castello Sforzesco, and an extra bonus is the view of the showy Baroque Palazzo Litta when you step out the front door. Corso Magenta 19, 20123. Tel: 87-44-32; Fax: 89-01-07-98. ₤154,000.

Another comfortable place in the same part of town is the **Ariosto**, near Santa Maria delle Grazie. *Mirabile dictu,* it has its own garden. Via Ariosto 22, 20145. Tel: 481-78-44; Fax: 498-05-16. ₤154,000.

In the corso Sempione neighborhood beyond the Castello is the sunny, comfortable, and (by Milanese standards) reasonably priced **Lancaster**. You'll need to ride the trams or use taxis to get into the center. Via Abbondio Sangiorgio 16, 20145. Tel: 31-56-02; Fax: 34-46-49. Closed in August. ₤200,000. Another just slightly out of the way, but generally satisfactory, solution is the modern **Lloyd**. Corso di Porta Romana 48, 20122. Tel: 58-30-33-32; Fax: 58-30-33-65. ₤295,000.

If you're sensibly determined to stay right in the center, you'd be well advised to reserve far in advance at the **Antica Locanda Solferino**, a really charming place with its own excellent restaurant, a stone's throw from the chic intellectual enticements and narrow old lanes of the Brera district. The comfortable rooms are actually quite cheap. The hitch is that there are only 11 of them. As the Gershwins said, it's nice work if you can get it. Via Castelfidaro 2, 20121. Tel: 657-01-29; Fax: 29-00-52-31. ₤140,000.

Another quiet and intimate place, a shade more luxurious than the Solferino, is the **Manzoni**, in the heart of the expensive and elegant via Montenapoleone–via della Spiga quarter. It's a fine, snug retreat from the hurly-burly of modern tourism. Unfortunately its old-fashioned charm extends to a resolute refusal to accept credit cards. Via Santo Spirito 20, 20121. Tel: 76-00-57-00; Fax: 78-42-12. ₤165,000.

Tucked away in a side street right next to the Duomo is the little **Casa Svizzera**. The rooms, while clean, are really minuscule for the price, but the location is a dream: a very few minutes (or seconds) on foot will get you to the Galleria, La Scala, the Poldi-Pezzoli, the Brera, and the expensive temptations of "Montenapo." Via San Raffaele 3, 20121 Milan. Tel: 869-22-46; Fax: 349-81-90. Closed in August. Ł155,000. Almost equally strategic, if a little less glamorously located, is the aptly named and quite serviceable **Centro**. Via Broletto 46, 20121. Tel: 87-52-32; Fax: 87-55-78. Ł139,500.

Near the Fiera Campionaria, the great trade fair center, is the tiny **Campion**. It's not as inconvenient to the downtown area as you might think, because it's just opposite the Amendola Metro stop. Old-fashioned, not without charm, it's also inexpensive. Via Berengario 3, 20149. Tel: 46-23-63; Fax: 498-54-18. Ł142,500.

Not far from the Castello Sforzesco, the via Rovello contains a number of modest hotels that may prove to be a blessing to the pocketbook; among them are the **Giulio Cesare** and the **London**. Giulio Cesare: Via Rovello 10, 20121. Tel: 72-00-39-15. Ł64,000. London: Via Rovello 3, 20121. Tel: 72-02-01-66; Fax: 805-70-37. Closed in August. Ł110,000.

A word should be reserved for the **Villa Malpensa**. As the name suggests, it's not in Milan, but up near the city's inconveniently far-off international airport. Not exactly your typical anonymous airport hotel, this attractive place is set in spacious grounds, has a pool and a nice restaurant, and can provide a stress-free evening before your early-morning flight home. Via Don Andrea Sacconago 1, 21010 Vizzola Ticino. Tel: (0331) 23-09-44; Fax: (0331) 23-09-50. Ł185,000.

DINING

Most of the food you'll find in Milanese restaurants today has little to do with the older local tradition, which relied heavily (and that really is the *mot juste*) on animal fats, and which pretty much excluded pasta in favor of rice and, above all, of *polenta*. You can still find a few traditional Milanese restaurants here and there, but they're the exception rather than the rule, and the locals go to them almost as they would to an exotic eatery. Only in such places will you commonly find old Milanese dishes such as the incredible meat-and-vegetable stew called *cassoeula,* which includes odd hog parts like ears and trotters, sausage, cabbage, carrots, and lots more besides. What you do find on the menu in most places today is a mixture of various Italian traditions, modern inventions, and assorted foreign influences.

As befits a highly self-aware capital of fashion and finance, Milan is a city where one can eat very well indeed. But let's face it: in a country where eating out is generally costly, the

Lombard capital is the most expensive city of them all. That's why, in the name of financial realism, we've also listed a number of practical alternatives to the high-style gastronomy for which the city is noted.

Inexpensive

Anywhere you go in the city, you'll find lots of cafés (called bars in Italy) offering a variety of sandwiches. If the words *tavola fredda* appear in the window, you'll also find a selection of cold dishes: cold cuts, cheeses, and the like. If you see the phrase *tavola calda,* there will generally be some not-very-good hot dishes as well: warmed-up pasta, meat drenched in recycled oil, and so forth. It's often a better bet to go to a bakery (*panetteria*) and buy a slice of pizza or *foccaccia,* topped with potatoes, olives, herbs, or what you will.

If you're really in a hurry, there are a number of American-style fast-food hamburger chains in town, with strategically located branches all over the central neighborhoods. Then there are the numerous Chinese restaurants, many of which offer an ample if undistinguished fixed-price meal at lunchtime for about 12,000 lire. You'll find a good number of them in and around via Fabio Filzi, near the Stazione Centrale; another dense concentration is in the via Paolo Sarpi area, which is about as close to a Chinatown as you'll find in Milan.

Don't despair just yet, though. A few more inspiring solutions to the problem of eating economically in Milan do exist. We've arranged them here roughly in order of ascending costliness. You'll be able to get out of the first places listed for under 10,000 lire; none should run you much more than 20,000 lire.

Just behind the Rinascente department store, near the Duomo and the Galleria in the heart of town, **Luini** is a Milan institution. Its specialty, though, is the *panzerotto,* an invention that comes from Puglia, in the South. You fight your way to the counter and are awarded with a little pouch of pizza crust filled with melted cheese and tomato. It's as filling as it is tasty. Closed Sundays and Mondays. Via Santa Radegonda 16; Tel: 80-69-18. Duomo Metro stop.

Just off the Galleria in the heart of town, **Il Cantinone** also features an acceptable restaurant; but what interests us here is the part where you stand at the counter and eat a satisfying bean soup or the traditional Milanese meatballs called *mondeghili,* washing everything down with excellent wines by the glass. Closed Saturday lunch and Sundays. Via Agnello 19; Tel: 80-05-91. Duomo metro stop.

Brek is a chain of self-service places where you take your tray and wander about from counter to counter, assembling a meal of freshly prepared pasta and meat dishes, cold salads, cheeses, or anything else that strikes your fancy. Clean, pleasant surroundings; quite reasonable food. Two of the more useful locations are in piazza Giordano Bruno in the center, and on via Lepetit near the Stazione Centrale. Closed Sundays. Also with several locations, **Ciao** is similar to Brek, but pride of place here goes to the roast meats: veal, roast beef, turkey, chicken. It's a toss-up as to which of the two chains is better. Locations in the center of town include piazza del Duomo and corso Europa. Closed Sundays.

Just off corso Europa in the center, the **Trattoria da Bruno** offers an exceptional bargain. The fixed-price meal costs less than a single course in most other restaurants. You begin with a simple but well-made first course of pasta or a filling soup. There follows a selection of chicken, meat, or seafood, along with a salad or other vegetable dish, lots of bread, and wine or beer to wash it all down. The atmosphere is friendly and unpretentious. Closed Sundays. Via Felice Cavalotti 15; Tel: 76-02-06-02. San Babila Metro stop.

Although the neighborhood, tucked away between the Brera and the Castello Sforzesco, has been growing nattier by the minute, the rustic, functional decor at the **Pizzeria Sibilla** hasn't changed in decades. More important, the place still serves some of the best pizza in Milan, along with a variety of other dishes. It's all very good, and dirt cheap by today's standards. Closed Mondays. Via Mercato 14; Tel: 86-46-45-67. Lanza metro stop. Not far from the chic Brera district, with its great museum, **Grand'Italia** offers main-course salads, pizza, spaghetti, and more; there's an ample choice of beers and wines. The crowd is young, the atmosphere informal. Via Palermo 5; Tel: 87-77-59. Moscova metro stop. A small family-run place, **Keren** specializes in Ethiopian food of a sort you don't often find in North America. The spicy, stewed meat and vegetables are eaten along, so to speak, with the plate, which is a great round of flat, rather spongy bread, served hot and used to shovel everything into your mouth. Closed Sundays. Via Malpighi 7; Tel: 22-14-52. Porta Venezia metro stop. **Metrò 2** is open only at lunch, Monday through Friday, and is generally bustling with thrift-minded advertising people. This sit-down restaurant near the great Romanesque church of Sant'Ambrogio serves a variety of abundant meat dishes as well as various other things. It's all very simple, but of more than acceptable quality. Via Terraggio 20; Tel: 86-73-68. Sant'Ambrogio metro stop.

One way of keeping costs down is to eat **pizza**. Not the warmed-over sort they serve in bars—heaven forfend!—but the kind that's been made a minute before. Serious pizza in Italy is divided into two basic types, regardless of topping. The natives distinguish between *quella alta* (the thick kind) and *quella bassa* (the thin kind). The former is usually served in places that advertise *pizza al trancio* (by the slice); depending on how hungry you are, you order your portion *abbondante* or *normale*. The thin kind is usually served by places that also do a more or less full-fledged restaurant service; rather than part of a pizza made for the masses, you get your own individual affair, made to order. A pizza rarely costs more than 8,000 or 10,000 lire, plus a moderate cover charge; it's the extras like beer and dessert that will tend to run your bill up if you aren't careful. *Pizzerie* are so thick in Milan (although the dish is Neapolitan, not Lombard, in origin) that there isn't much point in listing many of them here. Just pick a likely looking place in the neighborhood in which you happen to find yourself. One important pointer, though: It's vital that you choose a pizzeria with a *forno a legna* (wood-burning oven). You'll get a much better pizza than you ever could from an electric oven.

Moderate

Moderate is what you make of it, of course; prices very much depend on what you choose once you're at the restaurant. That said, here's a by-no-means-exhaustive listing of places that rarely fail to give satisfaction. A meal consisting of a pasta dish, a meat dish, and a vegetable or salad (ordered separately), with wine and coffee, will generally cost between 35,000 and 45,000 life. Such extras as an antipasto, a dessert, or a liquer will tend to send your bill skyrocketing.

A word about fish. It generally costs significantly more than meat or fowl. The more expensive kinds, such as *branzino* or *orata,* are usually sold by weight; the price you see on the menu is the price per *etto* (just under four ounces); you'll have to multiply it a few times over to arrive at the cost of your portion. If you absolutely need to know ahead of time how much you're going to spend, you may want to stick to swordfish (*pesce spada*) or cuttlefish (*seppie*), which are priced like meat dishes and sold at a fixed price per portion.

Il Gazebo is a small, elegantly informal place. It's run by a young couple who often include in the ever-changing menu traditional dishes from their native Mantua, along with splendid inventions of their own. The emphasis here is on real cooking: none of that throw-it-on-the-grill-and-away-we go stuff that's all too common in Milan these days. Despite its sophistication, the cuisine stays light, in keeping with the tastes of our health-conscious times. Homemade desserts (most restaurants, even many good ones, buy them ready-made), and exceptional attention to the quality of the reasonably priced wines. Not near any metro line, it's just a short cab ride from the center. Closed Saturdays and Sunday lunch. Via Cadore 2; Tel: 59-90-00-29.

The pasta dishes at **da Renzo** are lackluster, but never mind. You come here for the *tagliata,* which is what London broil would be like if it were (a) bathed in olive oil, fresh rosemary, pepper, etc., and (b) divine. You'll want to share a platter with your companions (order it for however many people are in the group), and you'll probably wind up fighting politely over the last slice. Via Paracelso 5; Tel: 20-11-51. Between Loreto and Lima metro stops.

Bright lights, lots of energy, the seats a bit too close together, fast turnover: At **Replay,** just off the very central corso Vittorio Emanuele, you may almost feel as though you're in New York. But it's handy and reasonably priced, the food is fine, and the staff is pleasant (maybe you *aren't* in New York, after all!). Anything you like, from a huge and varied antipasto to pizza, from traditional pasta dishes to satisfying and affordable single-course meals (a dish where you get everything you need on a single plate is called a *piatto unico,* and it's the exception in Italy). Closed Tuesdays. Via Pattari 2; Tel: 805-94-09. Duomo or San Babila metro stop. Like Replay, which is run by the same management, **Charleston** is very centrally located and always busy. Pizza, homemade pasta, well-prepared meat and fish. Service is a bit frenetic at times, but the prices are quite reasonable: they'll vary greatly according to what you eat. Closed Mondays. Piazza Liberty 8; Tel: 79-86-31. Duomo or San Babila metro stop.

Antica Trattoria della Pesa is the traditional place for an all-Milanese meal, from risotto with saffron to *ossobuco.* And then, of course, there's the highly characteristic stew called *cassoeula.* The least one can say about this dish is that it's not kosher. If you're feeling less adventurous, there's always a veal cutlet or the braised beef (*brasato*). That's very Milanese, too, especially when eaten with *polenta* to soak up the sauce. In a town in which most restaurant decor goes for austerely modern chic, this place looks like an inn from the turn of the century. On an off-night, the service can give you a feeling of weary routine; but the Pesa is an institution, and it's unique. Closed Sundays. Via Pasubio 10; Tel: 655-57-41. Stazione Garibaldi metro stop.

Perhaps the nicest thing about **da Berti** is the opportunity to eat outdoors, in a pleasant garden of near-bucolic calm, a stone's throw from the heavily urban atmosphere of the Stazione Centrale, the Gallia and Hilton hotels, the Pirelli skyscraper, and other adjacent monuments to Milan's status as a major modern city. The well-made food is eclectic with a Tuscan bias; the antipasto buffet is outstanding. At lunchtime, the place is popular with businesspeople and bureaucrats in dark suits. Closed Sundays. Via Algarotti 20; Tel: 60-81-69. Gioia metro stop.

The absurd name may lead you to expect barbecued spareribs at **Ranch Roberta**; but nostalgic Neapolitans swear that the food here is a welcomely authentic taste of home, from the steamed mussels to the spaghetti in red clam sauce and the excellent mozzarella. The decor is nothing fancy, and neither is the choice of dishes; it's a fine neighborhood place, the neighborhood in question being the *zona fiera,* the area adjacent to the trade fair center. Closed Mondays and Saturday lunchtime. Via Masaccio 18; Tel: 469-61-16. Lotto metro stop.

A bit far north of the center, but easily reached by cab or metro, **Mykonos** offers by far the best Greek food in town, served in a dazzling white decor that will make you feel as though you'll find the "wine-dark sea" at your feet when you step back outside. You won't, though—just a picturesquely run-down bit of the Naviglio della Martesana, one of the few survivors from the network of waterways that used to criss-cross this part of Lombardy. Warning: reservations are essential (and not always easy to get). Closed Tuesdays. Via Tofane 5; Tel: 261-02-09. Gorla metro stop.

Music haunts the neighborhood around **La Ranarita**, a six- or seven-minute stroll from La Scala. Across the street is the fine Gothic church of San Marco where Verdi's *Requiem* received its first performance; Mozart stayed in the adjacent conventual buildings when he came to Milan as an adolescent. La Ranarita serves good pizza, pasta, and meat and fish dishes at reasonable prices, in a bright, pleasant environment. Closed Sundays. Via Fatebenefratelli 2; Tel: 805-58-72. Montenapoleone metro stop. There's nothing Turkish about **Topkapi**, which offers huge salads, a fine antipasto table, pizza, pasta, grilled meat, and fish. Just opposite the fine piazza del Carmine at the edge of the once-Bohemian, now-trendy Brera district, it's also convenient to the Castello Sforzesco. The place is crowded, cheerful, and relatively inexpensive. Closed Wednesdays. Via Ponte Vetero 21; Tel: 80-82-82. Lanza metro stop. Not far from the Brera area, **Rigolo** provides fish and meat dishes and grilled vegetables, most of them with a Tuscan inflection. There are homemade desserts and good wines. Closed Mondays and Tuesday lunch. Largo Treves; Tel: 80-597-68. Moscova metro stop.

There's nothing much to say about **Paper Moon**, a well-known pizzeria-cum-trattoria, except that it's a convenient and not-very-demanding solution to the question of where to go for a bite after a shopping outing in via Monte-napoleone, just around the corner. The brusque service can border on rudeness. Closed Sundays. Via Bagutta 1; Tel: 76-02-22-97. San Babila metro stop. The food is good without being outstanding, but visitors always enjoy coming to **Al Mercante,** and they have every reason to. Where else in Milan can you eat outdoors in a fine medieval and Renaissance piazza, closed to motor traffic, just a stone's throw from the Duomo? (Nowhere else.) Closed Sundays. Piazza Mercanti 17; Tel: 805-21-98. Duomo and Cordusio metro stops. **Olivia** is primarily a vegetarian restaurant; and as such, it's proof that an all-vegetable meal needn't have that austerely penitential, granola-flavored air that we all know (and that few of us love). Interesting soups, beautifully grilled and seasoned vegetables, and much else besides. For the heretics in the party, there are some good meat and fish dishes, too. Not on the metro; take the number 60 bus or the number 12 tram and get off at piazza Cinque Giornate. Closed Saturday lunch and Sundays. Via Sottocorno 5/a; Tel: 76-00-35-71.

You can eat good pasta, fish, or meat dishes at **Le Specialità,** but it merits a place here above all for its pizzas. They're among the finest—perhaps *the* finest—in the city (although occasionally the toppings and seasonings are a bit *recherchés* for the tastes of some traditionalists). They will, accordingly, cost you rather more than a perfectly decent pizza somewhere else; but the gain in deliciousness justifies the difference. The room is big, with tables on the ground floor and on the balcony; the rustic decor features wagon wheels and agricultural implements. Closed Sundays and Monday lunch. Via Pietro Calvi 29; Tel: 738-82-35.

Never mind the Venetian-looking emblem on the sign—the **Trattoria Masuelli San Marco** specializes in simple, traditional Milanese food of the sort one rarely encounters any more: chick-pea soup with pork ribs, the local meatballs called *mondeghili.* There's also a smattering of Piemontese recipes: beef prepared in Barolo wine, and the highly characteristic dish called *bagna cauda,* a dialect term meaning, more or less, "hot bath"—you dip the raw vegetables into hot olive oil heavily laced with garlic. The physical evidence of the latter will stay with you for quite a while, but the pleasant memory will linger even longer. The restaurant may seem a bit out of the way, but it's just a short taxi ride from the center. When you get there, you'll find simple decor and friendly service. Closed Sundays and Monday lunch. Viale Umbria 80; Tel: 55-18-41-38.

The name is dialect for "iron bridge," and **Al Pont de Ferr** does in fact face a footbridge in the picturesque zone at the southern edge of the city where the canals have never been paved over. It's a good area for a wander, especially late on a fine evening, when it's crawling with crowds of the youthful and would-be youthful. The old-fashioned inn has a very limited selection of traditional Milanese cooked dishes, of which the most unusual is the stewed ass. But that's not really the point of this highly unusual place. Let the oddly beautiful Russian-Italian proprietess arrange for you a meal of cold cuts and/or of cheeses; and above all, follow to the letter her instructions on the order in which they are to be eaten. The result will be a slow crescendo, progressing from subtle delicacy to robust intensity. The right wine is also an essential part of the experience: Once again, follow the advice you're given and you won't be disappointed. Reservations recommended; the place is very small. Open evenings only, closed Sundays. Ripa di Porta Ticinese 55; Tel: 839-02-77. Port Genova metro stop.

As the reference to Bologna suggests, **Mauro il Bolognese** specializes in good cooking from the Emilian region. The homemade pasta dishes are outstanding, and there are good meat and fowl dishes as well, including various sorts of game in season. The wine list pays special attention to the sparkling wines of Emilia; don't snub them out of a general prejudice against anything fizzy! When the weather's nice, you can eat outdoors here. The restaurant is a bit out of the way but easily reached by cab. Closed Mondays. Via Lombardini 14; Tel: 837-28-66.

The **Osteria di via Pré** is named after a famous street of ill repute in Genoa, and cooking from Liguria (the region of which Genoa is the capital) is what it's all about. Here you'll find *trofie al pesto* and other pasta specialties, fresh fish, and the celebrated Ligurian white wines, all served in a decor designed to showcase the nonculinary work of the owner, who is an able photographer as well as an excellent cook. Service, alas, can be irritatingly slow. The restaurant is in the Navigli district, where people strolling along the picturesque canals lend animation after dark. Closed Mondays and Tuesdays. Via Casale 4; Tel: 837-38-69. Porta Genova metro stop.

Il Verdi is a five-minute walk from the Brera museum. The emphasis here is on main-course salads and on *piatti unici:*

full meals on a single plate. Although the restaurant has been here for ages, it doesn't feel old-fashioned. *Al contrario*—it's all quick, light, trendy, and relatively economical. Closed Saturday lunch and Sundays. Piazza Mirabello 5; Tel: 659-07-97.

Just down the street from the Romanesque church of Sant'Ambrogio, this bustling, cheerful place is not utterly out of striking distance from Leonardo's *Last Supper* fresco and the rest of the monumental complex of Santa Maria delle Grazie. **Ai Tre Fratelli** calls itself a *trattoria toscana,* but the extensive menu features both Tuscan and non-Tuscan dishes. It's all quite good, and affordably priced. Via Terraggio 11; Tel: 87-32-81. Sant'Ambrogio metro stop.

Although it tends toward the high end of our price range, **La Pantera** is by no means too expensive—by Milanese standards, of course—for what it gives you. Excellent pasta, rice, fish, and meat dishes; good drink; a room of elegant modernity; and attentive service. The restaurant does wonders with truffles and mushrooms. Near the Università Statale, a five-minute walk from the Duomo. Closed Tuesdays. Via Festa del Perdono 12; Tel: 58-30-74-08. Duomo metro stop. The area around the Stazione Centrale is short on charm, but you may find yourself there before or after an excursion. If so, you'd be well advised to head for the small family-run trattoria called **Davio**. Everything is good; the seafood dishes are particularly well prepared, including such treats as freshly made ravioli stuffed with fish. Closed Saturday lunch and Sundays. Via Tarra 6; Tel: 60-36-89. Stazione Centrale metro stop.

Expensive

You can eat very well in many a moderately priced establishment, but there's no denying that some occasions do seem to call for that really memorable, festive meal. Here are a few suggestions, along with one or two cautionary notes to prevent disappointment. Prices will vary, depending on the place and on what you order, but it's a safe bet that you'll spend at least 60,000 lire, and in several of these restaurants it's easy to spend 90,000 lire or more.

An institution with the chic Milanese upper classes, **Don Lisander** is tucked away off the very central via Manzoni, close to the Scala and to the Poldi-Pezzoli museum. (A visit to the collection followed by a meal at this restaurant makes for an epicurean day indeed.) The rooms are magnificent, but there's also a charming little outdoor garden; reserve specifically if you hope to eat outdoors. A mixture of Lombard, Tuscan, and other Italian dishes are on the menu; whether you choose fish or fowl, game or the *bistecca fiorentina,* you're unlikely to go away disappointed. Closed Saturday evening and Sundays. Via Manzoni 12/a; Tel: 76-02-01-30.

When the weather is fine, you can eat outdoors at **Boeucc** in a handsome courtyard. When it's not, the elegance of the rooms will easily console you. The imaginative and varied menu provides outstanding seafood as well as lovingly re-created recipes from the Lombard tradition. A special mention for the desserts: The chestnut ice-cream with *zabaione,* for example, is one you won't find in too many other places. The restaurant (whose very Milanese name is pronounced somewhere between "butch" and "betch") is convenient to the Galleria and La Scala. Manzoni, the writer to whose memory Verdi dedicated his celebrated *Requiem,* lived in the piazza where Boeucc is located. Step around the corner and have a look at the remarkable sculptured façade of the aptly named Palazzo Omenoni (Palace of the Huge Men), in the street of the same name. Closed Saturdays, Sunday lunch, and August. Piazza Belgioioso 2; Tel: 76-02-02-24.

Alfredo Gran San Bernardo is a bit out of the way, but that's nothing a short taxi ride won't take care of. The room is expensively contemporary, but the fidelity to the popular traditions of a bygone Lombardy is unchanged. Here you'll find all the classic dishes of the Milanese repertoire, prepared with devotion and without a hint of cheap nostalgia. Closed Sundays and August. Via Borgese 14; Tel: 331-90-00.

The **Osteria del Binari,** in a neighborhood rapidly undergoing gentrification, is surrounded by *case di ringhiere,* the traditional Milanese tenements with long balconies that serve as outdoor corridors. It's perhaps best visited in the warmer part of the year, when you can eat in the large and shady garden. The menu is suspiciously long and varied, ranging from Lombard and Piedmontese specialties to seafood, vegetarian dishes, and even the usually discouraging "international cuisine." Have no fear: it's all quite good. If your mood is more convivial than confidential, this bustling, cheery place can be confidently recommended. Open for dinner only, closed Sundays. Via Tortona 1; Tel: 89-40-94-28.

If you're looking for a small, elegant fish restaurant, **L'Ami Berton** should suit you very well. It offers an extraordinarily imaginative variety of beautifully executed seafood dishes, along with excellent desserts and a fine selection of wines and after-dinner drinks. There's plenty to keep the non-ictheologically minded happy, too. Reservations are a must. Located in a quiet residential neighborhood, the restaurant is easily reached by taxi. As is generally the case where fish is involved, prices tend toward the high end of our range. Closed Saturday lunch, Sundays, and August. Via Francesco Nullo 14; Tel: 71-36-69.

Many visitors have heard about **Bagutta** even before they've consulted a guidebook. That's partly a consequence of its central location, just off via Montenapoleone with its famous shops, and even more the result of its unforgettable decor. Hung with numerous pictures by prominent Italian artists of the past half-century, the rooms have an amusing air of Bohemian chic. Would that the food were as good as the setting! Unfortunately, it's generally no more than adequate. To be fair, the prices are not unduly inflated, especially considering the expensiveness of the neighborhood. Closed Sundays and August. Via Bagutta 14; Tel: 76-00-09-02. The decor and atmosphere at **Il Cestino** will put you in mind of an intimate, rather old-fashioned Parisian bistro; and so, perhaps, will the cuisine. Not that the dishes appearing on the rather limited menu are French, precisely. This place serves, among other things, one of the handsomest *costelette alla milanese* in the city. But should you want a change from pasta, you'll be able to start with a fine onion soup, or with the delicious soup made from artichokes. This nice little restaurant, located in the heart of the trendy Brera area, is closed Sundays and Monday lunch. Via Madonnina 27; Tel: 805-84-68.

The name **Boccondivino** contains a pun: it means "a divine bit of food," but also suggests "a sip of wine." And that pretty much sums up the philosophy of this unusual establishment, where the emphasis is less on cooking as such than on offering the very best hams, salami, cheeses, and so forth in combination with an appropriate sampler of fine wines. It can make an especially pleasant late-evening solution on a day when lunch has been an adventure in more elaborate *haute cuisine*. A few minutes' walk from the Castello Sforzesco and the Cadorna railway station, Boccondivino is not as expensive as some other places in this section. Dinner only; closed Sundays and August. Via Carducci 17; Tel: 86-60-40. If you think that fish is always best when it's left absolutely simple, a meal at **Calajunco** may lead you to think again. The inventiveness of the kitchen here finds new and unexpected potential in even the most familiar Mediterranean seafood, but it's all done with a light hand, and you're unlikely to find yourself wondering whether the search for originality hasn't gotten the better of the chef's judgment. Closed Saturday lunch, Sundays and August. Via Stoppani 5; Tel: 204-60-03.

Very Expensive

When all is said and done, **Savini** remains just what it has always been: Milan's flagship restaurant, the local symbol of traditional dining elegance. The decor is redolent of *haut-bourgeois* wealth and taste as they were in an earlier, more luxurious epoch; the rather conservative menu features all the Milanese classics (including an outstanding variety of risottos), along with a sprinkling of "international" recipes. You may not rave about the cooking, but you'll find nothing to complain of, either. The location is as choice as could be: right in the Galleria. Closed Sundays. Galleria Vittorio Emanuele II; Tel: 72-00-34-33.

Gualtiero Marchesi is Italy's most famous chef. His cooking, served in the restaurant bearing his name, has sometimes been thought of as the country's answer to *nouvelle cuisine;* although there may be an element of oversimplification in that definition, there's something in it. Recipes are generally light and portions on the small side, but nobody leaves here feeling deprived: The imaginative dishes are flawlessly executed, and the restaurant is often regarded as the best in the city, despite its being at that delicate age when it's no longer the latest thing but hasn't yet become a full-fledged classic. Closed Sundays, Monday lunch, July, and August. Gualtiero Marchesi is tucked away in a quiet residential street, a short cab ride from the center. Via Bonvesin de la Riva 9; Tel: 74-12-46.

After several mediocre years, **Biffi Scala** is under new management, and the quality of the cooking has improved significantly, although you may still see no reason to pay these prices for dishes from the popular repertoire such as *minestrone, baccalà* (dried cod), or *ossobuco*. In any event, in bad years as in good, the place has always been a musical and society institution. Tucked away right next to La Scala and built by the same architect—Piermarini—it's where singers, conductors, and theatrical folk come for a late supper after particularly important performances: a sort of operatic Sardi's, but operating on a higher plane of elegance than that New York temple ever did. Closed Sundays. Via Filodrammatici 2; Tel: 86-66-51.

Every Milanese knows that **Peck**, located near the Biblioteca Ambrosiana in the heart of the city, is one of the world's most elegant (and expensive) delicatessens and food specialty shops. There's also a fine restaurant, with an extensive and ever-changing menu. Closed Sundays and July 2–23. Via Victor Hugo 4; Tel: 87-67-74. The eponymous **Aimo e Nadia** run one of the best restaurants in Milan. Their menu is more inventive than traditional, and the selection of dishes is unusually varied. Suffice it to say that everything works, from the chestnut flakes in rabbit sauce to the pigeon sauteed with porcini mushrooms. The ample assortment of rare and excellent cheeses deserves a special mention. Closed Saturday lunch, Sundays, and August. Via Montecuccoli 6; Tel: 41-68-86.

If you hear what's offered at **La Scaletta**, you may wonder at first why such apparently humble dishes should call for such an elegant restaurant: lasagne, snails with polenta, risotto with saffron and kidneys, *baccalà* (dried cod). It may sound like the menu of a working-class trattoria from 50 years ago, but everything is light, in keeping with modern requirements, and it's all delicious. Don't be misled into thinking the place is near La Scala: it's in the Navigli district at the city's southern edge, where the canals remain picturesquely uncovered. Closed Sundays, Mondays and August. Piazza Stazione Genova 3; Tel: 58-10-02-90.

The cooking at **Soti's** is eclectic, in the sense that the menu offers several dishes with a strong French accent (and even some showing a Swiss touch), along with those of unmistakably Italianate character. Whatever you choose, it's hard to go wrong. The restaurant is small, with room for only about 30 guests; the beautifully deployed antique furniture lends a warmth and charm often absent from the generally hard-edged Milanese chic. In the summer, you can eat in the flowery little garden. The restaurant is in the same residential neighborhood as Gaultiero Marchesi (although it probably wouldn't do to take two such meals back-to-back; stomachs and pocketbooks do have their limits). Closed Saturday lunch and Sundays. Via Pietro Calvi 2; Tel: 79-68-38.

Located near the town of Abbiategrasso at **Cassinetta di Lugagnano**, 22 km (14 miles) west of Milan, the **Antica Osteria del Ponte** is not on any of the sightseeing itineraries in this chapter, but for many it will merit an excursion on its own; it is widely considered the best restaurant in Lombardy. With its stretch of canal, the setting for this tiny, elegant place is an almost surreally perfect bit of a Po Valley landscape that scarcely exists any more, save in the Platonic musings of nostalgic Lombardophiles. The splendidly eclectic and inventive cooking, however, is open to numerous nonlocal influences, French above all; the ever-changing menu defeats efforts to characterize it in one or two representative dishes. You can order à la carte or take whatever is on the thoughtfully constructed *menù degustazione*. Closed Sundays, Mondays, and August. Piazza G. Negri 9; Tel: (02) 942-00-34.

SHOPS AND SHOPPING

In such a moneyed and display-conscious city as Milan, the opportunities for spending are nearly endless. The following listing can thus be nothing more than very partial signposts, in a matter where everything depends on individual tastes and financial resources. A practical note: Most shops close over the lunch hour (although some, mostly in the center, do remain open), and they generally remain closed on Monday mornings.

Department Stores

Beyond any question, **La Rinascente**, on piazza Duomo, is Milan's leading department store. It owes its rather romantic name, which means "the reborn one," to the great poet, novelist, and political adventurer Gabriele D'Annunzio; the reference is to the store's resurrection after a fire. Inside you will find all the usual department-store offerings, from stylish ready-to-wear clothing and accessories to designer housewares, practical and impractical alike. The top floor, offering a close-up view of the spires of the Duomo just across the street, is devoted to food and drink (to be consumed on the premises rather than packed up and taken away). There's everything from a coffee bar to a somewhat English pub to a new restaurant run by the culinary superstar Gualtiero Marchesi.

The "other" department store is **Coin**, on piazza Cinque Giornate, just outside the center and easily reached by public transportation. The name has nothing to do with penny-pinching; it's an Italian variant of the surname Cohen. Prices here are often rather lower than at La Rinascente, and the selection of goods, while somewhat less rich and varied, is adequate.

Clothing

Milan is the fashion capital of Italy—and, with Paris and New York, of the world. In the 1980s, while Paris's runways still glittered with wear-it-once creations, Milan was developing styles for contemporary active women to wear to work. Georgio Armani and others made terms such as "off the rack" and "ready to wear" respectable, and soon "Made in Italy" was *the* most coveted label. Many of the major designers have their boutiques in the area between **via Montenapoleone** and **via della Spiga**. They include established names like **Versace**, **Valentino**, **Krizia**, **Ferragamo**, **Missoni**, and **Max Mara**, as well as newer talents like **Jean-Paul Gaultier**. Each has afficionados; do a little window-shopping and see what strikes your fancy. Several of the designers also offer more popularly priced lines, sold in separate shops in the immediate vicinity. Try **Emporio Armani** (via Durini 24) or, for highly wearable women's wear only, Max Mara's **Max & Co.** (corso Vittorio Emanuele at via San Pietro all'Orto). A bit pricier and less straightforward, but charmingly lacy and hyperfeminine, are the things at **Mariella Burani** (via Montenapoleone 3).

You'll find a noteworthy collection of upper-middle-range designer boutiques with a youthful emphasis in the mini-mall known as **Galleria Caffè Moda** (via Durini 14). To reach it in a jiffy from via Montenapoleone, you cross piazza San Babila, with its horrendous Fascist-period architecture, and turn right past the Burghy fast-food restaurant.

Of course, even Milan has excellent clothing that doesn't necessarily bear a designer label. Good shops abound; there's room here for only a few suggestions. **M. Bardelli** (corso Magenta 13) is rightly a standby with the Milan bourgeoisie of both sexes. For classic menswear, **Larusmiani** (via Montenapoleone 7 and via Manzoni 43 are among the locations) and **Boggi** (piazza San Babila 3) are good bets. If you're looking for something a bit cheaper, trendier, and even, on occasion, funkier, try the numerous little shops in **via Solferino**, not far from the Brera, or in **via Paolo Sarpi**. Or wander down **corso Buenos Aires**. Long, straight, and relentlessly modern, it's short on Old World charm. But there's almost no limit to what you can buy here, generally at a reasonable price.

Another way around the high price of dressing is to try your luck at the shops offering fashionable labels at bargain basement prices: surplus production, last year's remnants, or items worn just once by a model, for a fashion show or a photo session. Places you might check out include **Salvagente** (via Fratelli Bronzetti 16) and **Blue Shop** (via Morgantini 28).

Accessories

If you can stand the prices, Milan is a fine place for accessorizing yourself from head to toe. Let's start with the head—in this case, primarily the male head. **Borsalino**, a hole in the wall in the Galleria Vittorio Emanuele, is probably the most celebrated hat shop in continental Europe. Even the most classic models have a slightly raffish and dashing air that sets them apart. Women do come in for more evenhanded (or even-headed) treatment at Borsalino's other locations (corso Vittorio Emanuele 5 and corso Europa 19).

And now for the toes. Shoes, of course, have long been an

Italian specialty. **Fratelli Rossetti** (via Montenapoleone at the corner of corso Matteotti) offers *dernier cri* fashion in moderately priced men's and women's footwear. **Tanino Crisci** (via Montenapoleone 3) specializes in a more classic elegance. For women only, **Alfonso Garlando** offers shoes in a spectacular range of colors and in all sizes. His shop (via Madonnina 2) is in an attractive street in the Brera district. **Spelta** (via Solferino at via Pontaccio) is a good bet for casual women's shoes at less-than-astronomical prices. **Pollini** (corso Vittorio Emanuele 30) is a good classic shop for men and women alike. A word of warning: Italian shoes stores generally offer only a single width per size, and especially if you have a narrow foot, it can require a certain amount of hunting about to find something that really fits.

As for other leather accessories, there are small shops all over the city purveying elegantly crafted handbags, wallets, and the like. A famous, classically elegant purveyor is **I Santi** (corso Vittorio Emanuele at Galleria Pattari and several other locations).

A wag once suggested that with all the rings Milanese women wear, they must have better marriages than other people. Without going so far as to subscribe to this theory, we can certainly confirm that nobody around here is shy about wearing lots of jewelry. Of course they don't always buy it at such expensive establishments as **Bulgari** (via della Spiga 6). Among more moderately priced sources of supply, the aptly named **Anaconda** (via Bergamini 7) specializes in items made of silver; its things have a clean, handsomely modern look. If you like your modern design with an admixture of flamboyant colors and patterns, you may find what you're looking for at **James Rivière** (beginning of via Brera, just behind La Scala), where platinum, enamels, and semiprecious stones are among the standard ingredients. At a more affordable price level, **Il Faggio** (via San Giovanni sul Muro 7) often has amusingly nostalgic costume jewelry and other *bibelots*. Once again, a hunt along corso Buenos Aires often yields just the thing you were looking for (or, more likely, the thing you didn't know you were looking for until you saw it).

For the House

No doubt about it, Italians are house-proud. It may have something to do with the fact that 70 percent of them own their own homes and on the whole, move far less frequently than Americans. At any rate, they're usually willing to spend lots of time, money, and energy getting their houses just right. And the rich, fashion-conscious Milanese are among the national champions in this regard.

As a visitor, you won't want to take home a designer kitchen or a life-size garden statue for your bathroom, but there are lots of less bulky items worth looking at. We've already mentioned the emporium in La Rinascente's basement, where you can find everything from fine porcelains to the latest Guzzini plastic salad bowls. For top-of-the-line dishes and utensils, another standby is **Picowa** (piazza San Babila 4/D). It's the classic place for new brides to register. A couple of blocks away, the Florentine firm **Richard-Ginori** (corso Matteotti 1) is a centuries-old producer of high-quality porcelain. Fabrics have also been an Italian specialty since time immemorial, and **Frette** (via Manzoni 11) has long been the city's favorite supplier of fine linens, towels, and the like. Another dealer in fine fabrics and laces, with a specifically Venetian slant, is **Jesurum** (via Verri). If you're looking for real Murano lace, you'll find it here—but don't say you weren't warned about the prices. *A propos* of Venice, three of the Lagoon's most celebrated blown-glass-makers have outlets in via Montenapoleone: **Barovier & Toso** at number 1, **Venini** at number 9, and **Salviati** at number 22.

If it's top-quality kitchen equipment you're after, there's no better place than **Alessi** (corso Matteotti 9), whose stainless steel pots, pans, and utensils are to be found backstage in celebrated restaurants throughout Europe. Should you desire something particularly esoteric—say a truffle slicer or a sea urchin opener—**G. Lorenzi** (via Montenapoleone 9) is ready to supply it. This famous store will also help you attend to your personal grooming, with shaving gear and nail clippers of peculiar refinement.

Art

You're unlikely to find any bargains in Milan's art galleries. Prices are comparable to those charged by dealers in other capitals, although the city has been kept off the major circuit by rigid regulations governing the exportation of important works. It's certainly possible to find a real Canaletto or whatever; but, other considerations aside, you're unlikely to have budgeted such an expenditure into your trip. Nonetheless, there is one field in which the Milan market offers such an abundance of choice that you may well feel like having a look around: it's the market for **old prints** (which are also easy to get home). Good examples of etchings and engravings by such masters as Tiepolo *père et fils,* Grechetto, Jacques Callot, and others are fairly easily come by, although they aren't cheap; by comparison, late impressions of the 17th-century master Stefano della Bella can be picked up for a song. Among the more reliable dealers are **Salamon** (via San Damiano 2), which also sells paintings, and **Valeria Bella** (via Santa Cecilia 2), who specializes in prints.

Of course, art isn't only prints. If auctions interest you, **Finarte** (piazzetta Bossi 4 and via Manzoni 38) is the principal house. Should you find yourself smitten with the unspectacular charms of the flat Po Valley countryside, with its rows of poplars and tranquil canals, one of Marco Corrieri's handsome landscape paintings will make an evocative souvenir; he sells them at his own gallery, **Il Quadrangolo** (via Lanzone 24, not far from the church of Sant'Ambrogio). Modern art, mostly in innocuous varieties of trendiness, is all over the place. You might try strolling along via Brera and its side streets and see what turns up.

Books

Good, centrally located sources of English-language reading matter include **Le Messaggerie Musicali** (corso Vittorio Emanuele at Galleria del Corso), and the **American Bookstore** (in largo Cairoli, right in front of the Castello Sforzesco). You'll find a particularly well-nourished guidebooks section at **Rizzoli** in the Galleria Vittorio Emanuele. Two excellent suppliers of art books, often including out-of-print rarities, are **Libreria Bocca** (in the Galleria) and **Hoepli** (via Hoepli 5); all things considered, the latter is probably Milan's best bookstore, and not only for publications on art. The charmingly musty and Old-World **Gallini** (via Gorani 8) specializes in old books on music and in hard-to-find scores. Less exotic musical items can, of course, be found at **Ricordi** (via San Raffaele, just around the corner from La Rinascente and the Galleria). The firm is mentioned here mostly for its great past as Verdi's publisher; today it offers something for everyone, from the lover of Frescobaldi to the heavy-metal fiend.

For Kids Who Have Everything

There's bound to be something the kids *haven't* already got at **Fate i Capricci** (via Lanzone 7, not far from Sant' Ambrogio). After all, the toys on display here also happen to be antiques—with prices to match. Among the many alternative, less rarefied solutions to the problem of finding something for the children are **Noé** (via Manzoni 4), a good, all-purpose toy store, and **Città del Sole** (via Dante 13, between the Duomo and the Castello Sforzesco), where you'll find "intelligent" playthings with an emphasis on natural materials. A word should be reserved for **Naj-Oleari** (via Brera 5), a famous shop specializing in cheery cotton prints. Upper-middle-class Milanese children get their outfits here, everything from coats to knapsacks—and so, often enough, do their moms.

Food

It's worth having a look at the showy foodstuffs in certain Milan shop windows, quite independently of any intention to buy. You won't believe the marzipans at the Sicilian sweetshop **Fratelli Freni** (corso Vittorio Emanuele); they're shaped and colored to resemble everything from ripe figs to salami sandwiches. **Il Salumaio di Montenapoleone**, at number 12 in that street, displays more wordly concoctions of aspic, quail, salmon, and everything nice, teased into sculptural forms worthy to grace some of the richest and most snobbish tables in the world. **Peck**, the traditional flagship of the city's luxury food trade, has already been mentioned. It has a number of shops, differentiated by specialization and all concentrated in the area near the Biblioteca Ambrosiana, not far from the Duomo. Among them are the **Casa del Formaggio**, the cheese store at via Speronari 3, and the delicatessen at via Spadari 9. These street names are themselves marvelously evocative, recalling the days when this corner of Milan produced some of the finest armor in Europe: *speronari* made spurs and *spadari* made swords. Still in Peck land, although in a less strikingly named street, is **La Bottega del Maiale** (Hog Shop), at via Victor Hugo 3, offering every conceivable (or inconceivable) sort of sausage.

LOMBARDY OUTSIDE MILAN

The most obvious retreats to offer beauty and quiet near Milan are the lakes—Como and Garda in particular—and they can quite easily be the base for excursions to some of Lombardy's historic towns. (Sirmione on Garda is less than 50 km/30 miles from Mantua, for example.) There are, however, a welter of old towns in every direction from Milan, each of special interest and all with facilities for lunching (on a day trip) or for spending the night.

Monza

The least expected attraction happens to be the nearest to Milan (north-northeast on the way to Bergamo): Monza, known to most for its auto races, is actually a city that can take you back to the sixth century, when the Longobards were devastating the countryside. Their leader, Authuri, took time out to go to Bavaria and court a flaxen-haired princess of whose beauty he had heard. Theodolinda became his queen and calmed him down for the one remaining year of his life. As an early widow she was asked to choose another man to help her rule, and with unseemly alacrity she elected the best-looking warrior around (Agelulf, from Piedmont). Together they ruled for 20 years.

Pope Gregory was grateful to the northern princess on several counts, and among the gifts he sent her, we see in the **cathedral** of Monza the most famous of all: the Iron Crown of Lombardy. Marvelously constructed around what is said to be a nail from the true cross, it was later used in the coronations of Italy's kings and rulers—44 emperors in all, from Barbarossa to Napoléon. The latter had the crown brought in an elaborate procession from Monza to the cathedral in Milan when he became king of Italy in 1805; he even had the façade of the Duomo completed (finally) for the event. Monza's treasury harbors much more, however, that is interesting: crosses and reliquaries in ivory and gold; other Byzantine articles; and Theodolinda's gilded set of chickens at play. The Chapel of Theodolinda, where the crown is displayed, is one of the most extensive and best-preserved examples of the late medieval International Gothic style of decoration that was so popular with the Lombard aristocracy. The walls are covered with elaborate frescoes and work in *pastiglia,* a kind of patterned three-dimensional plasterwork. It was all created around 1444 by the Zavattari brothers, who were the leading purveyors of such things to the Visconti and their circle. The rather late date is important: Taste here was still closer to the "courtly" concerns of Burgundy and France than to the classicizing Florentine manner. Monza's Duomo, designed by Matteo da Campione, has a handsome striated façade that presides over a quiet square and seems far indeed from Milan.

From the Duomo, it's just a few steps to piazza Roma, with its 13th-century **Arengario** (town hall). The building is cast in a form common throughout much of northern Italy; you'll find similar examples at Bergamo and in Milan, in the piazza dei Mercanti. Upstairs there's a great room for meetings, while the ground floor is left open on all sides in order to house a street market.

Monza's history by no means ended with the Middle Ages; its **Villa Reale** served as country residence to Eugène de Beauharnais, and it was he who landscaped the vast park in the romantic manner called *à l'anglaise* (if it looks familiar, it is because it was used extensively in the film *The Garden of the Finzi-Continis*). Another less fortunate resident of the villa was King Umberto I, who in 1900 was shot in Monza by an anarchist. Now the Reale is a museum of Neoclassical paintings and furnishings. Villa Reale is currently undergoing restoration, but the promised reopening has yet to materialize. Until then, it is possible to take group tours of the gardens by calling (039) 38-41-13. The *orangerie* in the garden is used for temporary art exhibitions.

Castiglione Olona and Varese

Castiglione Olona, 50 km (30 miles) northwest of Milan, is one of the oddest places in Lombardy. Even today, this pretty little hill town gives you a sense of almost otherworldly sleepiness. But in the early 15th-century, a powerful churchman who had been born here decided to import the latest Florentine artistic and intellectual ferment into his isolated native town. And so he called on the Tuscan Masolino da Panicale, who worked here on and off from 1428 until 1435. This artist's basic style tended to late-Gothic decorative prettiness of an unusually high order. But when he came to Castiglione, he was fresh from his shattering collaboration, at the Brancacci chapel in Florence and in San Clemente in Rome, with the younger artist Masaccio, whose antique austerity, moral intensity, and rigorously rational pictorial space were unmatched among Early Renaissance painters. Masolino's resulting stylistic disorientation may be read in his frescoes in the **Collegiata** church and in the adjacent **Baptistry**. Enchantingly doll-like figures attempt an enactment of real-life dramas in a landscape in which painted porticoes, meant to define a recession into measurable distance, get drunk on their own purely decorative rhythms. There is no better illustration of what happens when a gifted artist, reared in an older taste, tries and fails to come to grips with "the shock of the new." Masolino had a number of collaborators at Castiglione, of whom the best known today is the Sienese master Vecchietta.

The same ecclesiastical patron, Cardinal Branda Castiglioni, paid for the construction of the nearby **Chiesa di Villa**, a church in an approximation of those geometric, Brunelleschian forms that were then creating a sensation in Florence. You can visit the Cardinal's family home, the 14th- and 15th-century **Palazzo Branda Castiglioni**, containing what may be some of the earliest frescoes of pure landscape since the days of the Roman Empire. (Open 2:30 to 5:00 P.M.;

Saturdays and holidays, 10:00 A.M. to 12:30 P.M. as well; closed Mondays.)

You may want to take advantage of your presence at Castiglione Olona to travel the 8 km (5 miles) or so that will bring you to **Varese**, a wealthy, bustling provincial capital, where you can make the acquaintance of the peculiar artistic-religious institution known as the **Sacro Monte** (Holy Mount). The first and most important such mount was founded in the 16th century at Varallo in nearby Piedmont, and aimed to give locals a chance to duplicate the pilgrimage to the shrines of the Holy Land without having to go on a long journey and risk capture by the Turks. Varallo set the pattern for a number of similar foundations in Piedmont and northern Lombardy: a series of freestanding chapels dot the hillside, and in each one you find a series of unnervingly realistic, life-size, polychrome sculptures enacting biblical or other religious scenes against the background of a painted diorama. The Sacri Monti were centers of popular devotion for centuries; today they still make for an agreeable and interesting outing when the weather is fine. The one at Varese dates from the 17th century and offers 14 chapels; be sure to see number 7, with its fine fresco background by the important Lombard master Morazzone.

If all this hiking about the hillside has given you an appetite, and if you're feeling gastronomically ambitious, you may want to head for the Varese restaurant called **Lago Maggiore**, where you'll find often unorthodox but always well-made meat and fish dishes served in a setting of tranquil, old-fashioned rustic elegance. (Via Carrobbio 19; Tel: (0332) 23-11-83; closed Sundays and Monday lunch.) Be prepared to spend about Ł70,000 per person. If you're looking for something simpler, perhaps to fortify you at the outset, you'll find a couple of serviceable places right at the entrance to the Sacro Monte.

Pavia

Pavia, 38 km (22 miles) south of Milan, was a Longobard capital that once rivaled the now much more important city. Its Castello served as a secondary residence both to the Visconti and to the Sforza, and its university, once considered second to none, was attended by a variety of students including Petrarch, Columbus, and the Venetian playwright Goldoni. Its physics department was to light up the world by graduating Volta—whose electrical experiments we can still see here. The Visconti had much to do with enlarging the university in the 14th century, and Stendhal was delighted to find that its main benefactor had been the same Galeazzo II, evidently a real charmer, who had experiments made to enable his victims to be tortured for 41 days before they died. Those who weren't destined for this end apparently had the right to a good education, and soon the schools and courts of Pavia were rising on every side. Its **Duomo**—both Bramante and Leonardo were among its architects—is one of the best examples of Lombard Renaissance; its dome, the third largest in Italy, dominates the town's center. You will no longer see the Torre Civica, which recently collapsed (as did the campanile of San Marco in Venice at the beginning of this century). Also to be seen in Pavia is the Romanesque church of **San Michele** (south of the center, near the river, off corso Garibaldi), with a remarkable façade, and **San Pietro in Ciel d'Oro** (north of the center near the Castello), with its main altar and the extraordinary *arca* of Saint Augustine. The *arca* is the tomb of the saint, whose remains took centuries to travel from Hippo to Sardinia and then here.

One of the wonders of Pavia is the Old Town itself and the care with which it has been preserved. In the area around San Michele, completely cut off from traffic of any sort, there are courtyards and streets, green with plants and grass, that resemble the Italian scenes painted by Hubert Robert in the 18th century.

Pavia's **Castello** is a museum, and a good one, for paintings, sculpture, and the elaborate arcaded courtyard where Ludovico Il Moro and Beatrice d'Este were to spend some of their happiest years. Many say that if he had married her hard-willed sister, already the marchioness of Mantua, the French armies never would have flooded down. But he didn't and they did, and the Castello library, accumulated by the Viscontis, is now part of the Bibliothèque Nationale in Paris, while several of the towers were destroyed by the maréchal de Lautrec. In 1525, François I was taken prisoner at the Battle of Pavia by Charles V, and the French adventure gave way to centuries of Spanish occupation.

Too many visitors to Pavia skip the town and rush to the Certosa, the famous monastery that the Viscontis founded on its northern outskirts in 1396, to see the Pantheon of the Visconti and the Sforza. This by no means indicates that the Certosa is an easy visit. It closes in the morning at 11:30, which means that visitors inside are given warning signs by 11:00. The traffic from almost any direction is formidable, thanks to Milan's proximity, so unless you are willing to arise very early, an afternoon visit between 2:30 and 6:30 (4:30 in winter; closed Mondays) is more convenient—particularly since there happens to be a lucky choice of restaurants in the vicinity. One, the **Chalet della Certosa**, is right outside the gates of the monastery. A specialty for the unprejudiced is the polenta with frogs. (Closed Monday and January; Tel: 0382-92-56-15.) Another, **Al Cassinino**, considered one of Lombardy's best, is a couple of miles before the Certosa on the Milan–Genoa road. (Closed Wednesdays and December 20 to January 10; Tel: 0382-42-20-97.)

The **Certosa** remains, along with Milan's Duomo, a testament to the building mania of the Viscontis. Its façade, like a huge intaglio of colored marbles, is enlivened by large circular medallions based on Roman coins and resembles the architecture in the backgrounds of Mantegna's paintings. The interior is a veritable museum of frescoes (many dedicated to the religious gestures of the founding family); of paintings, from Perugino to Luini; and above all of sculpture, most of it adorning tombs. The finest is on those of Gian Galeazzo Visconti and Ludovico Il Moro and his Beatrice. The latter tomb was formerly in Milan's Dominican church of Santa Maria delle Grazie, which Il Moro had conceived as a Sforza mausoleum. The monks there took it upon themselves to sell the tomb, and the Certosa bought it. (It was these same Dominicans who were so reluctant to pay Leonardo for his *Last Supper*. If they could have dislodged it, they probably would have sold that, too, since money seems to have been high on their list of priorities.)

About 40 km (25 miles) west of Pavia near Mortara, in the heart of the rice fields, is Ceretto Lomellina and the restaurant **Cascina Bovile**. The Lomellina area is famous for its geese—not so long ago a girl in these parts would not find a husband without a goose-feather duvet as her dowry. Geese and other barnyard fowl figure largely on the menu—including foie gras, which Luigi Perotti, the restaurant owner, maintains was invented by the Romans and bequeathed only later to the French. Closed Mondays. Tel: (0384) 999-04.

Cremona and Lodi

Like Pavia, Cremona is on the river Po (farther east), and it shares with Pavia the honor of being one of Lombardy's most monumental architectural cities—its **piazza del Comune** being, along with that of Siena, one of the finest in Italy. The piazza is faced on one side by a Gothic arcaded Palazzo Comunale and on another by an octagonal Romanesque baptistery; it is fronted by the magnificent façade of the **Duomo**, which is Romanesque, with a gigantic rose window. Alongside is Italy's tallest campanile, the **Torrazzo**, built in the 13th century but with later additions, such as its enormous clock. The cathedral's interior is literally covered with late Renaissance frescoes, and very good ones, in particular those by Boccaccino, Romanino, and—above all—the astonishing scenes of Christ's crucifixion, entombment, and resurrection by Pordenone, a 16th-century artist from the Friuli. Try to go in the morning, when the light is good.

For that matter, with its lively markets, Cremona is a morning town anyway. Until recently the **Pinacoteca** in the Museo Civico had no electric light at all, so that to see its Cremonese masters, its Magnascos, and a superb Veronese *Deposition,* you had to come equipped with your own source of illumination. It was a good lesson in what Goethe and other travellers on the Grand Tour must have gone through to perceive the masterpieces about which they wrote so well. The museum is currently undergoing a thorough renovation, although it remains open to the public. The first new section, unveiled in May 1992, is a disappointment: the tricky lighting and glass cases tend to create glare, and besides, pictures can look oddly unhappy when they're hung on screens in the middle of a room. Still, it's best to suspend judgment until the project has been completed. (Open 9:30 A.M. to 12:30 P.M. and 3:00 to 6:00 P.M.; closed Sunday afternoon and Mondays.)

The painters of 16th-century Cremona are today recognized as being among the most important formative influences on Caravaggio (whose name comes from a nearby town). Their extremes of expressive intensity and dramatic *chiaroscuro* lighting could not fail to impress that rebellious young artist. But such Cremonese Mannerist painters as Antonio and Giulio Campi and Bernardino and Gervasio Gatti—the two clans were related through marriage—amply merit attention in their own right. You can—and, if at all possible, should—see them at work, in an ambitious campaign of frescoes and altarpieces at the church of **San Sigismondo**, located 2 km (1½ miles) outside the center, along the Casalmaggiore road. The church itself was commissioned in 1463 by Francesco Sforza and Bianca Maria Visconti, to replace the older structure on the same site where they had been married (a momentous event in Lombard history, for it paved the way for the Sforza succession to the Visconti dynasty).

The very name of Cremona brings to most minds another art: music. Two famous composers were born here centuries apart: Claudio Monteverdi, who did much to launch opera as a form (in Mantua), and Amilcare Ponchielli, who later livened it up with *La Gioconda*. But it was the manufacture of one type of musical instrument that made the town famous. Around 1530 Andrea Amati created the violin, and a new sensitivity was to enter musical composition. Amati also founded a school for making the instruments, and later such great craftsmen as Guarneri and Stradivari were to perfect his invention. Stradivari made about 16 violins a year, but since he lived to be 93, they added up. About 600 are extant— turning up, often in surprising ways, and selling for a lot more than the already hefty price that Stradivari charged. A couple can be seen on show in the **Palazzo Comunale**, but most of the documentation of value, along with more violins, is in the **Museo Stradivariano**, in the same Museo Civico that houses the Pinacoteca (via Dati 4).

You can lunch well (and expensively) in Cremona near the cathedral at the **Ceresole**—which is so exceptionally good that it is best to reserve. Closed Sunday evening, Mondays, and August. Via Ceresole 4; Tel: (0372) 233-22. Also good, and slightly less costly, is the **Aquila Nera** in the cathedral square itself (via Sicardo 3). Closed Sunday evening, Mondays, and August. Tel: (0372) 256-46.

A country restaurant between Milan and Cremona well worth the detour is the **Trattoria del Fulmine** (Lightning Inn) at Trescore Cremasco, with a flower-filled garden where guests can eat in summer. Here the polenta is served toasted with homemade foie gras, and Clemy, the chef and the owner's wife, is famous for her duck with cabbage. Closed Sunday evening, Mondays, and August. Tel: (0373) 27-31-03.

One of the most pleasant stopping places between Milan and Cremona is the **Albergo del Sole** at Maleo, which has been run by the same family since 1893—but that's only part of the story, for this old-fashioned roadside inn has been here since 1464. It still retains the same welcoming atmosphere as always, and there are even a few rooms upstairs for diners who wish to sleep over—a sensible precaution during the fogbound Lombard winters. In warmer seasons, you will enjoy eating in the splendid courtyard, shaded by a romantic pergola. It's moderately expensive. Closed Sunday evening and Mondays. Tel: (0377) 581-42; Fax: (0377) 45-80-58.

You may choose to combine your trip to Cremona with a stop at the tranquil little town of Lodi, located about halfway between Milano and Cremona. In the picturesque, arcaded main piazza stands the Duomo; it's in a mixture of styles, all rendered rather chilly by overenthusiastic restoration. The great treasure of the town, though, is the church of the **Incoronata**, located just a few yards away in a side street.

This deliciously ornate jewel of the Lombard Renaissance was built at the end of the 15th century and has an octagonal interior with a cupola and an elegant loggia. The paintings on the altars are interesting. Most are by members of the local Piazza dynasty; but at the sides of the second altar on the right you will find four exceptionally beautiful panels by Ambrogio Bergognone, perhaps the greatest Lombard master of the earlier Renaissance. With their loving attention to the play of light and shade over small things, their precise annotations of the quotidian, they will put you in mind of early Netherlandish painting.

Nearby Lodi Vecchio, 5 km (3 miles) away, is a separate, tiny hamlet worth dropping in on for the 14th-century church of **San Bastiano**, with a ceiling featuring an early-14th-century fresco of a secular subject: four agricultural carts being pulled by pairs of oxen. Far from distinguished as a work of art, the scene has an oddly moving capacity to bring us closer, however fleetingly, to the daily lives and concerns of the people who lived and worked in Lombardy long ago.

Bergamo

Northeast and east of Milan, Bergamo and Brescia are two Lombard towns that share a Venetian past, as they were both ruled by La Serenissima from 1428 until Napoléon's advent. But, diet apart, that is about all they share, since in character they are different indeed. Neither should be missed by visitors to Lombardy.

When we think of Bergamo we usually mean the *Città Alta,* the **Upper Old Town**, girded by green and jutting out on its Venetian bastions from the hills of the Valtelline, which rise sharply from the plain below. So bucolic in spirit that you would scarcely guess it is only 50 km (30 miles) east of Milan, Bergamo is a blessing to the inhabitants of that larger city; when they can, they drive up the steeply winding road, passing beneath hanging gardens and pergolas, to reach the cool, ancient city. Exhaust fumes are left behind at the gates, and inside is a chessboard of piazzas and fountains, cafés, palaces, and restaurants. This Upper Town is studded with monuments bearing traces of centuries of Venetian rule, centered around the **piazza Vecchia**, with its fountain of stone lions and its arcaded Palazzo della Ragione. It is easy to believe that the composer Gaetano Donizetti was born here, as one vista gives onto another with the rapidity of scenes in an opera. A step through the arches of the Palazzo della

Ragione, and you are faced with the resplendent façades of the church of **Santa Maria Maggiore**, its baptistery, and the **Cappella Colleoni**. Colleoni was the same successful condottiere seen by so many in Venice, thanks to Verrocchio's equestrian bronze. In gratitude for the soldier's services, the Venetians gave him the Bergamasque region to govern. Here he sits astride a gilded horse of wood, and in his elaborate mausoleum he lies near his favorite daughter, Medea, beneath a ceiling frescoed by Tiepolo.

The interior of Santa Maria Maggiore was heavily refurbished in the late Renaissance, hung with tapestries and its choir encased in wooden intarsia designed by Lorenzo Lotto, a Venetian who lived in Bergamo for a decade and whose work here is discussed below in greater detail. The intarsia are always displayed during Lent; the rest of the year, your chances of seeing them are a matter of luck.

Not far from Santa Maria is the **Museo Donizettiano** (via Arena 9), dedicated to that composer and exhibiting his pianos, manuscripts, and various souvenirs. His birthplace— far from grand (he always said he was born in a cellar)—is in the borgo Canale. Bergamo also gave birth to the commedia dell'arte, which influenced much opera of the 18th century. Gian Carlo Menotti considered having his music festival here before he fell upon Spoleto; considering the nearness of Milan and the enthusiasm of its public, it wouldn't have been a bad idea.

The charm of Bergamo's Upper Town should not tempt you to skip the **Accademia Carrara**, one of Italy's finest painting museums, whose quality announces itself right away with Pisanello's portrait of Lionello d'Este; Botticelli's of Giuliano de Medici; and one of a sulky, dark head—said to be Cesare Borgia—against a Giorgionesque background. This gallery, at the far east side of the Upper Town, can actually be reached on foot, descending via the church of Sant'Agostino; its Bellinis, Guardis, Titians, Mantegnas, and Tiepolos are worth that short walk.

A particular specialty of the Accademia is Lombard portraiture. At the end of the left-hand wing on the top floor, you'll find a whole room of pictures of local notables by the Bergamasque Giambattista Moroni, whose unrhetorical and sensitive work, deprecated by Berenson, has come into its own. In the same wing, you'll find an enigmatic, romantically fascinating portrait of a man by the insufficiently known Cremonese master Altobello Melloni. The stormy sky and the blasted tree in the background suggest that the sitter has been through a crisis; but the tree is putting forth a small green shoot, and one can only hope that the man has,

analogously, found new hope. There's further arcane symbol-
ism, but of a different sort, in Lotto's nearby portrait of
Lucina Brembati. The Italian word for moon is *luna,* and if
you look carefully at the moon painted in the upper left-
hand corner, you'll read the letters *ci.* What does it all mean?
Lu-ci-na, the sitter's name, of course: *ci* inscribed in *luna.* In
the other wing there are more portraits: representative work
by the 18th-century monk Fra Galgario, and above all, an
enchanting portrayal of a red-headed girl, the work of the
fascinating Brescian Giacomo Ceruti, called Il Pitocchetto.
The girl looks out at us shyly but with unblinking gravity:
stiff, ill at ease, *farouche,* not conventionally pretty but
instantly lovable nonetheless. However powerful the lure of
the excellent Bellinis, Raphaels, and so forth elsewhere in
the Accademia, do not leave without having made her acquaintance.

If the paintings shown are of a rare excellence, it is no
accident. The Accademia was founded by Count Carrara,
and on the brochure's list of later donors there appears a
raft of names. The one that should be noted is that of a
Senator Morelli, who was one of the first Italian collectors
to devote himself to the correct attribution and classifica-
tion of Italian paintings. It was thanks to the reputation of
the senator that a young, penniless, and very serious student, Bernard Berenson, would come here at the start of
his career, to make sure that "every Lotto is a Lotto," and
from then on change the face of connoisseurship on two
continents. Ironically, these classifications had been started
by the French under Napoléon—whose soldiers, out of
ennui, had destroyed so much (when a Bolognese aristo-
crat complained to Stendhal about a family canvas slashed
to ribbons by French bayonets, he was cooled down with
"If it hadn't been for us, you never would have heard of
Montesquieu!"). The fact remains that the monks and
priests of Italy had little idea of who had produced the
masterpieces that they guarded, and when hundreds of
their churches and monasteries were deconsecrated, Bonaparte called in an army of experts to clean, classify, and—
all too often—take away. Even the dates of the founding of
most Italian museums make a case; that of the Carrara
(1795) is typical. (Open 9:30 A.M. to 12:30 P.M. and 2:30 to
5:30 P.M.; closed Tuesdays.)

Berenson once wrote that had he become an artist, he
would have painted like Lorenzo Lotto (1480–1556). But
these days, Lotto no longer needs the Berensonian seal of
approval to make him a figure of immense interest. A slightly
older contemporary of Titian, he had a hypersensitive visual

and emotional makeup that made him an outsider in his
native Venice. Uninterested in celebrating the social rank of
his sitters or the corporate triumphs of the state, he painted
psychological portraits of unsurpassed penetration. Incapa-
ble of heroic public rhetoric, he was an intimist; even his
large altarpieces are inhabited by ethereal creatures of flame
and shadow. Solitary, anxious, tormented by the religious
crisis of his time, Lotto had difficulty finding his niche in the
ebullient mercantile atmosphere that surrounded him at
home, and so spent most of his career in "the provinces."
During the 1520s, his base was in Bergamo, where he left a
large number of pictures.

Lotto's work for Santa Maria Maggiore has already been
mentioned. As you make your way down via Porta Dipinta
on your way to the Accademia Carrara, you come to the little
church of **San Michele in Pozzo Bianco**. Inside, the entrance
arch and lunettes in the left transept chapel have frescoes by
Lotto of the life of the Virgin. Naturally there are several
good things in the Accademia itself. After (unless it's time for
the early afternoon church closing), continue up via San
Tomaso to via Pignolo, where there are no fewer than three
churches with his work: **Sant'Alessandro** (in the sacristy),
San Bernardino (a great *Sacra Conservazione* on the high
altar), and **Santo Spirito** (fourth chapel on the right). There's
more of Lotto elsewhere in town. But if you have a car and
are interested in continuing your Lotto tour, you may prefer
to head for Ponteranica, a village 7 km (4 miles) to the north,
where the church has a fine Lotto polyptych. Like Titian
himself when the latter worked for a patron at Brescia, Lotto
had to accept this by-then archaic form because the "out-of-
town" audience (far from the Venetian metropolis) still felt
most comfortable with it. Or you may choose Trescore
Balneario, equally nearby but situated to the east, at the
beginning of the Val Cavallina road. There you'll find the
Villa Suardi, where the gatekeeper will generally be happy
to let you visit the large chapel frescoed by Lotto. Tel: (035)
94-00-10.

Bergamo is on the edge of Brianza, which produces some
of the region's best cheese and meat, and at the foot of the
Valtelline, with their vineyards, so the cuisine here is of a high
order. There are very good (and rather expensive) restaurants in the Lower Town: **Dell' Angelo** (borgo Santa Caterina
55) is near the Carrara. Closed Mondays and for three weeks
in August; Tel: (035) 23-71-03. And **Lio Pellegrini** is right
across from the museum, at via San Tommaso 47. Closed
Mondays, Tuesday lunch, and the first week of January. Tel:
(035) 24-78-13. But the appeal of dining on the piazzas and in

the courtyards of the Upper Town is difficult to resist. A view both of the *Città Alta* and the Valtelline hills can be accompanied by imaginative cooking at the **Gourmet**, which also has ten quiet and comfortable rooms. Closed Tuesdays. Via San Vigilio 1; Tel: (035) 25-61-10. In the evening you can opt for the extreme sophistication (but reasonable prices) of **Alla Nicchia** in piazza Mercato del Fieno (Tel: 035-22-01-14; closed Sunday dinner, Tuesdays, and August) or for more rustic spots such as the **Trattoria del Teatro**, on the piazza Mascheroni, where the younger generation goes (Tel: 035/23-88-62; no credit cards; closed Mondays and July 15–30). The **Agnello d'Oro** has the double qualification of good food and of being the best hotel in the Upper Town (20 rooms only, so reserve ahead; Tel: 035-24-98-83; closed Sunday evening, Mondays, and January).

Brescia

Brescia, east of Bergamo on the way to Verona, is Lombardy's other "Venetian city," and from a distance the natural reaction to its belt of industry is to step on the accelerator or stay on the train. The manufacture of arms was already making Brescia one of the richest cities during the Renaissance. Once you pass through the suburbs, however, you emerge into a town of fountains, palaces, medieval churches, and Roman temples. The **via dei Musei** harbors the ruins of the former forum, and the **Tempio Capitolino** has been turned into a Museo Romano, a museum for ancient finds, which include the oft-reproduced bronze *Victory of Brescia*. The **Museo dell'Arte Cristiana** (via Pianarta 4) deals with the Byzantine and is adjacent to the Romanesque church of San Salvatore. Later art is well shown in the **Pinacoteca Tosio Martinengo**, at via Martinengo da Barca 1, a high-caliber collection of the School of Brescia—Moretto, Savoldo, Romanini, and Foppa—as well as Raphael, Lotto, and even Clouet. Closed for rehanging, it is scheduled to reopen in January 1993. Tel: (030) 29-55-27.

If you have a particular interest in Venetian painting, you will want to make time as well for the church of **Santi Nazaro e Celso**, in corso Matteotti near the railway station. Over the high altar is an oddity that is also a sort of flawed masterpiece: Titian's *Averoldi* altarpiece. The Brescian bishop who commissioned the work constrained the very "advanced" artist to accept the no-longer-viable polyptych form. Titian didn't completely rise to the unfamiliar challenge of creating unity in such a situation, but he did achieve some gorgeously romantic lighting effects and—with the help of a quotation from the recently unearthed Hellenistic statuary group of Laocoön in Rome—created some notably heroic poses and figure types.

This town is not divided, like Bergamo, into upper and lower sections, nor does it particularly cater to tourists, being very well off on its own. But the crowded central section is remarkable for its array of medieval buildings; the **piazza della Loggia**; the Romanesque **Rotonda**; and the medieval *Broletto* (town hall). They are all within easy call of one another, and if they were in France would be considered something to rival the palaces of Avignon. As it is, travellers dash by in a rush to get to Venice, while instead they could lunch here in a palace, the Martinengo delle Palle. **La Sosta**, while not an outstanding gastronomic landmark, is something of an institution in Brescia and is fairly expensive. Closed Mondays and August. Via San Martino della Battaglia 20; Tel: (030) 29-56-03.

Mantua

It is by a hair's breadth that Mantua (Mantova) is part of Lombardy at all, thanks to a technical boundary and the meanderings of two rivers. Mantua lies within a triangle formed by three cities, Parma, Verona, and Padua (Padova)—none of them Lombard towns, though it can be visited easily from each. The city's history has been very much its own; this celebrated capital of the Gonzagas was for centuries an independent dukedom known to every court in Europe, with a palace second in size only to the Vatican.

In the arts its list of celebrities begins with a native son: the poet Virgil, who was born just outside but considered Mantua his town, to which his fame was to add luster. Its broad, reflective river, the Mincio, flows through his *Bucolics*. As Gilbert Highet notes in *Poets in a Landscape,* there is a certain sadness in Virgil's every description of this country. Centuries later this despondency was echoed by Aldous Huxley in *Along the Road:* "I have seen great cities dead or in decay—but over none, it seemed to me, did there brood so profound a melancholy as over Mantua."

That was written in the 1930s, before the Palazzo Ducale had been restored and when it was still a shadow of its former self: "For wherever the Gonzagas lived, they left behind them the same pathetic emptiness, the same pregnant desolation, the same echoes, the same ghosts of splendor." This about the family that nonetheless brought to Mantua the painter Andrea Mantegna, the architect Leon Battista Alberti, and the court composer Claudio Monteverdi.

Nor, thanks to their marriages with the great houses of their day—the Sforza, the Montefeltro, and the Medici among them—were the Gonzagas isolated. The marriage in 1490 of Isabella d'Este to Francesco Gonzaga brought one of the most brilliant women of her time to Mantua, and she was to be followed by much that was best in the humanist Italy of her day: poets, philosophers, and writers such as Castiglione. By way of these shrewd marriages and clever politics the Gonzagas made a miraculous leap from their peasant origins, starting in the year 1328, when they took Mantua from its ruling family, the Bonacolsi. That battle was the beginning of their success, but the truth is that it was their benevolent and stable government—the dead opposite of the rule of the aristocratic Visconti in Milan—that kept them in power. The Gonzagas never had the money of the Medici, but by their contacts they were able to hire the best artists of their day and to receive such luminaries as Emperor Charles V (who made them dukes in 1530), Henri III of France, and Pope Pius II. The arrival of the Hapsburgs and the Spanish was by no means a tragedy for the Gonzagas; they made more marriages that consolidated their position in international politics—all of this despite their often unfortunate looks and the recurrent back ailment that the family inherited from the Malatestas, a clan of powerful overlords with whom they intermarried.

It is not, however, for the Gonzagas' politics that you go to Mantua. It is to see their *reggia* (ducal palace) and its satellite palaces both in Mantua and in the nearby village of Sabbioneta. The entrance to the **Palazzo Ducale**, Gothic and crenellated, is on the rectangular piazza Sordello (near the water at the northeastern end of the city) and gives small hint of the splendors within: the Baroque halls; the wide, winding stairways; the elaborate quarters for the court dwarfs; and the later additions, Empire and Rococo, made when the Austrians came. (The palazzo is closed Sunday afternoons and Mondays.) It is the medieval part of the Castello, however, that contains the most of interest. Designed by the same architect who built the castle at Ferrara, it is mirrored in the lagoons formed by the Mincio.

When an inventory of the Gonzaga holdings was made in 1627, it was found that there were 2,000 paintings in the Castello alone, the villas and pavilions apart. Most of these were later sold or looted, but not the most priceless of all—because it was painted on the walls of a room and could not be moved. Andrea Mantegna took nine years to paint the **Camera degli Sposi** for Ludovico Gonzaga, initially to celebrate the fact that one of Ludovico's sons had been made a cardinal. By the time the fresco was finished it included new figures, such as the King of Denmark and Emperor Frederick III, who had visited Mantua during Mantegna's meticulous travail. It remains our finest view of a Renaissance court at work, crowned by a circular trompe l'oeil from which spectators stare down at the viewer. Mantegna painted three series of frescoes in his lifetime: one in the Belvedere of the Vatican that is completely lost; the second—a work of ten years of his youth—in the Ovetari chapel of Padua's church of the Eremitani, which was leveled by a direct hit by an Allied bomb in World War II. This leaves the Camera as the sole survivor of the master's fresco work.

The Gonzagas had gone to great trouble to lure Mantegna to Mantua. He already had commissions elsewhere, and his marriage to Giovanni Bellini's sister gave him connections aplenty. But come he did, and he settled here for the rest of his life, which was fortunate for him and for us. Creations for court masques apart, he could devote his time to one occupation: painting. Vasari depicts him as the gentlest and most affable of men, but Vasari was often wrong, and others make it clear just how disagreeable Mantegna was: litigious, tight-fisted, and constantly engaged in feuds. Born the son of a carpenter and adopted by a certain Paduan painter, promoter, and antiques dealer called Squarcione (with whom he had his first feud), Mantegna soon developed the love of Classical art that he was to retain throughout his career.

Some of his most famous paintings were done for the *studiolo,* or little study, of the most celebrated occupant of that part of the palace known as the Castello. Hardly had Isabella d'Este arrived in Mantua when she started to plan the decoration of this room, and for it Mantegna painted his famous *Parnassus.* This and his other works that adorned it, as well as its Perugino and Correggios, are in the Louvre—and the Mantuans want them back. In later life Isabella moved her private apartments downstairs, where we see them still, marquetry, marble doors, and ceilings intact. This series of salons was the magnet for cultivated visitors to the Castello during her lifetime, which was a fairly long one. She arrived in 1490 at the age of 16 and died in 1539, which gave her 50 years to devote to her collections of antiquities and paintings, dealing with everyone from Leonardo to Michelangelo. She was a difficult patron, demanding the best artists and dictatorial in her orders. Nor, in spite of her own income, did she have all that much money; one reason that she so disliked her sister-in-law, Lucrezia Borgia, was the fact that the latter was very rich. She had little in common with her husband, who was a warrior, but she was devoted to her son Federico, who turned out to be one of the most avid collectors in Italy: a friend to Titian and capable of buying 120 Flemish landscapes as a lot.

When he was young, Federico had been held prisoner in Rome—on a very grand scale—by Pope Julius II and had met all the artists of note there. Among them was Raphael's pupil, Giulio Romano, who was finally induced to come to Mantua, where at great expense he redesigned much of the town, the Palazzo Ducale, the Duomo, his own house, and Federico's **Palazzo del Te**, which you can reach by following the via Roma (it changes its name several times) south through the city from the piazza delle Erbe. This palazzo, a former stable, was rushed to completion to receive Charles V. It was never intended to serve as a residence, but rather as a suburban retreat on hot summer days and a place where pageantry could be staged, unconstrained by the medieval space limitations of Mantua's center. The place is one of the wittiest and most sophisticated buildings in Europe, meant to amuse jaded courtiers with its subtle transgressions against the established rules of Classical architecture, which by this stage of the Renaissance had become thrice-familiar to the cultivated classes. Note, for example, the keystone in the monumental archway in the courtyard; it appears to have slipped from its proper place, dangling dangerously low and destabilizing (optically at least) the whole structure. Inside, Giulio Romano's great frescoes celebrate all of the Gonzagas' favorite things: horses, astrology, mythology, and sex. (Where this last topic is concerned, the Gonzagas had certainly come to the right man: Giulio had previously gotten into terrible trouble in Rome over a series of pornographic engravings, the *Modi*, which caused a scandal even in that most licentious and dissolute of cities.) The main attraction, however, has nothing to do with Eros. The *Sala dei Giganti* (Room of the Giants) shows the fall of the Titans, overthrown by the gods. Architecture and painting collaborate to give us the uncomfortably convincing sense that the place is falling about our ears: the right-angle intersections between ceiling and wall, and between wall and wall, have been rounded out, practically canceled, in an effort to disorient the viewer.

Many of Federico's paintings were in the Te, too, and when, by 1627, the Gonzaga debts had become as large as their collections, Duke Vicenzo decided that something had to be done. It was known that Charles I of England was an enthusiastic buyer of pictures; with the mediation of a fellow art lover, Lady Arundel, it was arranged to sell the best part of the Gonzaga paintings to the English king. The sum asked was enormous: 5 percent of the exchequer. The Stuart ruler, having dissolved Parliament, already had financial problems. By the time the paintings arrived—and it took a decade—the purchase seemed to the English a folly just as the sale had seemed to the Italians a scandal. When the English Civil War broke out, the Puritans gave short shrift to art of any sort, and this incomparable collection, which would have made London the equal to Paris and Madrid in masterpieces, was put up for auction by Cromwell. Now many of the paintings can be seen in the Prado and the Louvre (the royal families of France and Spain were quick to send agents). Some have lauded Cromwell for holding back the Mantegna series of the *Triumphs of Caesar,* which have now been cleaned and can be seen in Hampton Court Palace. He probably liked them for their military subject matter.

Near the gates of the Te, which is on the inland edge of Mantua beyond the Porta Pusteria, is the house of Mantegna, which, with its oval courtyard, he himself designed. Across the way is the small church of San Sebastiano, created by the architect Leon Battista Alberti. This was by no means his only church in Mantua, as it was to his designs that the largest in town, **Sant'Andrea**, was built.

For many of today's architects Alberti was among the most interesting practitioners in the Renaissance. The miraculous lightness and simplicity of his work has taken centuries to come back into its own. Many would trade just one of his arches, seemingly floating in space, for the whole ornate façade of the Certosa in Pavia. And Sant'Andrea here in Mantua remains perhaps his purest creation. It is worth sitting in the café on the piazza Sant'Andrea across from the church to appreciate an approach to architecture that has had such influence—influence always acknowledged, as by Philip Johnson. (Those who can't visit Mantua immediately might go to Madison Avenue and 55th Street in New York City to see, on the AT&T building, how far the façade of Sant'Andrea has come.)

The piazza delle Erbe, with its market stalls, is near Alberti's church, but by the time you get here you will have trekked through miles of palace corridors, and a restaurant is the first thing that you will want to see. One of the most beautiful in Italy is **Il Cigno**, occupying yet another palace—this one on the piazza d'Arco—and serving the finest food around: pigeon cooked in black grapes; duck in liver and orange sauce. The menu might have appealed to the Gonzagas. The interior, with its patios, paintings, and charmingly arranged fruit and flowers, certainly would. Closed Mondays and Tuesday lunch; Tel: (0376) 37-21-01. Humbler—but still in a remarkable setting—is the **Aquila Nigra**, set in a former 14th-century convent, its frescoes and arched rooms intact. Closed Sunday evenings, Mondays, and August. Vicolo Bonacolsi 4; Tel: (0376) 35-06-51. There are trattorias aplenty near the Palazzo Ducale, but it just might be that you want to get away from tourist mobs, and both of these havens will guarantee coolness and calm.

Staying over in Mantua is not a bad idea; there are lots of walks to take, and when evening falls almost all the other visitors go away. Those who want to spend the night have the hotel **San Lorenzo**, just off the piazza delle Erbe—a traditional old hotel furnished with antiques and reproductions (no restaurant)—and the more modest **Dante** to choose from.

Those with the energy for more palaces will drive on to **Sabbioneta**, on the Parma road: a whole little town of them, created by Vespasiano Gonzaga. It has come a long way since Huxley and his Bloomsbury friends found Sabbioneta an abandoned wreck. Now the Palazzo Ducale on the piazza has been repaired, and so has the festive garden palace, alive with mirrors and frescoes. Concerts are held once more in the Teatro Olimpico (which was a cinema when visited by Vita Sackville-West), and antiques shops line the piazza Castello.

Two restaurants near Mantua that should be worked into your itinerary are the **Ristorante al Bersagliere** at Goito, 16 km (10 miles) from Mantua on the way to Brescia (via Statale 258; Tel: 0376-600-07; closed Mondays, Tuesday lunch, and August), and **Dal Pescatore** at Canneto sull'Oglio, halfway between Mantua and Cremona. (Both are in the expensive category.) At the family-run Ristorante al Bersagliere, many of the recipes are those of Maestro Stefani, chef at the court of the dukes of Gonzaga. Dal Pescatore has been in the same family for three generations, and today the whole family still works in the restaurant: Father bakes the bread and cooks fish from the nearby river Oglio, mother Bruna prepares the pasta, while son and daughter-in-law divide the rest of the chores. Closed Mondays, Tuesdays, January 1–17, and August; Tel: (0376) 703-04.

Near the southeast corner of Lombardy, two extraordinary restaurants have been created that draw food fanciers from around the world. At Quistello, **L'Ambasciata** seems at first glance a simple country trattoria. But the menu—sturgeon from the local river, Scotch salmon, caviar, pheasant, guinea hen—is not *cucina tipica*. It is expensive, however. Via Martiri di Belfiore 33; Tel: (0376) 61-82-55; closed Wednesdays, Thursday lunch, January 1–16, and August. The other restaurant, in the town of Villa Poma, is called **Concorde**. Its expensive menu is based on local ingredients and changes four times a year with the seasons. The pasta is hand-rolled and the tablecloths are damask. Piazza Oamano-Mazzali 8; Tel: (0386) 56-66-82; closed Sunday evening, Mondays, and August. Dinner only, except Sundays.

A Trip to the Mountains

Even in the flat plains of the Po Valley, in Lombardy you're always conscious that there are mountains nearby. For one thing, they're unhappily responsible for much of the damp, foggy weather that characterizes Milan and other North Italian towns during most of the winter: the humidity coming in from the Mediterranean condenses when it hits the Alpine barrier and then just sits there. There are, however, many occasions on which your awareness of the Alps takes a happier turn. Driving east from Milan toward Bergamo, for instance, you're accompanied all the way by a chain of snow-capped mountains to your left. They look so close that you'd think you could reach them in half an hour, although, alas, that's not exactly the case. Sometimes, on a clear day, you look down a street in busy Milan and there, at the end of it, is an Alp. It's like a mirage, stirring getaway longings. And the Milanese do indeed get away. Many are ardent skiers, who couldn't live without their annual *settimana bianca* (white week), a winter vacation devoted to the pleasures of snow. But of course the mountains are there all year long, and should they call you, you may want to respond.

The most famous peaks in Italy—Monte Bianco and Monte Rosa, for example—are in the Valle d'Aosta and in Piedmont, not in Lombardy. One Lombard mountain nearly everyone in Italy *has* heard of is the Resegone, near Lecco on Lake Como. Its celebrity is abetted by its unmistakable form (the name, meaning something like 'Sawblade Mountain," captures it exactly), but it owes its fame to a literary source: It's a constant presence in *I Promessi Sposi,* Manzoni's beloved novel of 17th-century Lombardy.

With so many mountain and valley retreats to choose from, everyone in Lombardy has a favorite. Still, the region's Alpine valley *par excellence* is certainly the **Valtellina**, which runs northeast from the top of Lake Como all the way to the Stelvio and Bernina passes, which take you into Switzerland.

Many of the natives still speak a highly exotic dialect in preference to standard Italian, and the area has its own cuisine too. Among the most famous specialties are *bresaola, pizzoccheri,* and *polenta taragna. Bresaola* is beef, dried and cured: just the thing to get a mountaineer through the winter. Before you imagine the worst, be reassured: the stuff does *not* taste like beef jerky. It's sliced thin, and is at its best when consumed with a touch of olive oil, a squeeze of lemon, and lots of pepper. *Pizzoccheri* are coarse, flat ribbons of buckwheat pasta. The authentic preparation calls for the addition of lots of local cheese, potatoes, cabbage, melted butter, and sage. The same mountain cheese also figures prominently in the preparation of *polenta taragna,* which differs from regular *polenta* in that it's made from a darker variety of cornmeal. The cheese is melted over the top just before serving. Normally eaten as a meal in itself, *poltena taragna* was traditionally accompanied, on festive occasions, by the sausage called *luganega.* Naturally not every wine can stand up to these hearty peasant dishes, but Inferno and Grumello, the famous full-bodied Valtellina reds, are more than up to the challenge.

At the far end of the Valtellina is the vast **Parco Nazionale dello Stelvio**, with the magnificent peaks and glaciers of the Ortles-Cevedale chain. There's wildlife, too: everything from hawks to chamois. The Visitors' Center to the park is at **Bormio,** a town 4,018 feet above sea level: a perch less lofty than some other mountain resort towns, but still high enough. The medieval center is deliciously intact, and many of the old houses and public buildings have portals and frescoed façades going back to the town's heyday as a much-frequented gateway to the Alpine passes from the 14th through the 16th centuries. There are some attractive and not overly demanding walks you can take in the immediate vicinity of the village; for something a bit more ambitious, you may want to avail yourself of the services of the skilled local guides. There are lots of ski lifts, too; but even in winter, you never get the feeling that skiing is all there is to the place. The leading hotel is the **Palace**. Other options are numerous. They include the **Posta,** an elderly *doyenne* that has been happily rejuvenated. For food, try the **Cendré** or the simple but authentic **Kuerc,** named after the nearby open loggia where, in the old days, the local authorities used to dispense justice.

Obviously the trip to the Valtellina is best not done as a day trip from Milan. Bormio is 192 km (120 miles) from Milan, and the roads, while good, do not allow for anything resembling autostrada speeds. It's nice to have a car in the mountains, but it's not absolutely essential; you can take the train as far as Sondrio, the Valtellina's capital, and go on to Bormio and other destinations in the area by bus.

A little less than halfway between Sondrio and the higher

reaches of the Valtellina, and reachable from Sondrio by a local train line, is **Tirano**. You may want to stop here briefly for a look at the valley's finest artistic monument, the handsome **Santuario della Madonna**. This surprisingly refined Renaissance church reveals close stylistic affinities with the Duomo down in Como, and the ornate interior, with its elegant Cinquecento stuccoes and Baroque organ loft, seems to inhabit a different world from the simple, rustic one outside. We can but guess at its impact on the local folk, back in the days before modern transportation gave everyone access to everywhere.

The Valtellina isn't your only choice if you're in the mood for mountains. Among the more easily accessible alternatives, especially if you have a car, is the **Val Brembana**, one of several long valleys reached by heading north from Bergamo. A possible stopping place is **Piazzatorre**, a hillside hamlet that is the base for a number of attractive excursions. Or you may choose to push on to **Fòppolo**, an even tinier place farther up the valley, and at 4,946 feet, a little nearer to the sky. There's skiing in the winter; in the summer you can enjoy the meadows and evergreen woodlands while admiring the snow-capped Orobie mountain chain that dominates the scene. Although neither village boasts absolutely first-rate accommodations, the **Hôtel des Alpes** at Fòppolo offers quite decent bed and board.

Two important practical hints: If you can help it, never drive into the mountains on a Friday evening or Saturday morning, or out of them on a Sunday evening. Many Italians spend their weekends here, and the traffic can be heavy at those times. Also, some hotels in the mountains close for weeks at a time when business is slow, so always call ahead and check things out. For advice and assistance, call the local tourist boards (called variously A.P.T., E.P.T., or Pro Loco).

GETTING AROUND

Like the rest of Italy, Lombardy has an excellent and comprehensive railroad system. There are three important stations in Milan: Centrale, Lambrate, and Garibaldi. Most, but not all, trains leave from or arrive at the Stazione Centrale. (There's also a separate railway, the Ferrovia Nord, which leaves from the Stazione Nord at piazza Cadorna. It serves mostly commuters from the northern suburbs, and is of interest to Milan visitors only as the best way to reach the waterfront in Como. It comes out right in front of the pier, where you can get a boat for a lake cruise.) For information on schedules, you can call the state railway information (Tel: 675-00), ask at a travel agency, or check the timetable. A railroad timetable (*orario ferroviario*) is, in fact, a useful item to carry with you throughout your stay in Italy; it's not very bulky, costs only a few thousand lire, and is available at most newsstands.

Practically every corner of Lombardy is served by bus lines, most of which leave from largo Cairoli in front of the Castello Sforzesco in Milan. However, the routes are divided up between numerous companies and there's no centralized information service, so that schedules can be hard to come by. You're probably better off with the train or driving.

Auto rentals. Using a car in Milan is more trouble than it's worth, because the city center is closed off to unauthorized motor traffic for most of each working day, and because parking can be an expensive proposition. Nevertheless, a rented car may prove useful for visiting the rest of the region. All the major companies have several locations downtown, at the airports, and at or near the Stazione Centrale. It makes no difference in the rates whether you rent in town or at the airport.

ACCOMMODATIONS REFERENCE

The rates given below are projections for 1993; always check for up-to-date information before making reservations. Wide ranges may reflect the differences between low- and high-season rates. Unless otherwise indicated, the figures indicate the cost of a double room (per room, not per person). However, half-board (mezza pensione) rates, which include breakfast and one other meal per day, are per person. The service charge is included in the rate; inquire about tax and breakfast.

For hotels in Milan, see the Milan Accommodations section, above in this chapter.

▶ **Agnello d'Oro**. Via Gombito 22, 24100 **Bergamo**. Tel: (035) 24-98-83; Fax: (035) 23-55-12. ₤80,000.

▶ **Albergo del Sole**. Via Trabattoni 22, 20036 **Maleo**. Tel: (0377) 581-42; Fax: (0377) 45-80-58. ₤290,000.

▶ **Dante**. Via Corrado 54, 46100 **Mantova**. Tel: (0376) 32-64-25; Fax: (0376) 22-11-41. ₤105,000.

▶ **Gourmet**. Via San Vigilio 1, 24100 **Bergamo**. Tel: (035) 25-61-10. ₤84,000.

▶ **Hôtel des Alpes**. Via Cortivo 9, 24010 **Foppolo**. Tel: (0345) 740-37; Fax: same. Open December 8–April 20, July, and August. ₤85,000.

▶ **Palace**. Via Milano 52, 23032 **Bormio**. Tel: (0342) 90-31-31; Fax: (0342) 90-33-66. Closed in November. ₤140,000–₤210,000.

▶ **Posta**. Via Roma 66. 23032 **Bormio**. Tel: (0342) 90-47-53; Fax: (0342) 90-44-84. Closed May, June, September, and October. Ł180,000–Ł212,000 with breakfast.

▶ **San Lorenzo**. Piazza Concordia 14, 46100 **Mantova**. Tel: (0376) 22-05-00; Fax: (0376) 32-71-94. Ł180,000–Ł250,000.

LAKE COUNTRY

By Simon Finazzi-Williams and Joanne Hahn

Simon Finazzi-Williams, a writer and poet, lives on the shores of Lake Como and works as a translator and author for the Reader's Digest *in Milan.*

The lakes of northern Italy are so varied in character that it is tempting to say that all they have in common are the backdrop of the Alps and a certain similarity in luxuriant flora. They are crisscrossed by borders—not only of provinces but also of countries—and each has its own enthusiastic partisans, including the many writers who have visited them in the past. Before the days of air travel, the lakes were often the first part of Italy that many travellers would see; the ardor that they engendered in those arriving from the fog and rain of northern climes was often kindled as much by the sun-drenched wonder of being in Italy at all as by the lakes' unique beauty.

MAJOR INTEREST

Scenic beauty

Lago d'Orta
Island and church of San Giulio
Baroque chapels at Sacro Monte

Lago Maggiore
Gardens and villa of Isola Bella
Gardens of Villa Taranto in Pallanza

Lago di Como
Como's Duomo and Gothic town hall

Basilica of Sant'Abbondio
Villa Brunate Olmo
Villa d'Este hotel in Cernobbio
Villa Carlotta in Tremezzo
Villa Melzi in Bellagio
Boat ride from Cadenabbia to Bellagio

Lago d'Iseo
Monte Isola

Lago di Garda
Roman villa and grottoes of Catullus on scenic point
Castle of the Scaligeri
Villa Vittoriale, D'Annunzio's home
The scenic drive from Salò to Riva along the
    Gardone Riviera

The Food of the Lake District

Meat and game dishes and, of course, lake fish dominate the local cuisine. Fresh trout and perch are popular fish here; they find their way into the varied *ravioli ripieni di pesce del lago* or are served grilled. Other delicacies are *agoni,* a local type of shad; *tinca,* a delicate, sweet whitefish; and the bite-size *alborelle.*

Polenta, a derivative of the Roman dish *puls,* which during the days of the Empire was made with a variety of grains, is today made with cornmeal. It is served in many ways, most typically either creamy or in a slab, baked or pan fried.

Agrodolce, a sweet-and-sour sauce, is found on many menus and is served in a number of dishes, such as *stracotto con cipolline,* tender braised beef and small onions that have been marinated in the sauce.

In the area of Lago d'Orta, in the province of Piemonte, the food reflects the region's French history with such tempting dishes as *fonduta,* a local fondue made with Fontina and eggs, and often laced with grated truffles, and *bagna cauda,* an ambrosial hot sauce of butter, olive oil, anchovies, and cream for raw vegetables.

Near Lago di Varese, just west of Como, the popular Lombardy dish risotto takes on an exotic accent when eels cooked in a spicy sauce are added. Northeast, in the area of Sondrio in the beautiful Valtellina valley, you find *pizzoccheri,* hearty buckwheat noodles that are usually combined with potatoes, leeks, and cabbage, and *polenta taragna,* a buckwheat and cornmeal combination served in slabs with butter and grated cheese. The area also produces rich sausages and salamis, such as the *mortadella di fegato,* a velvety

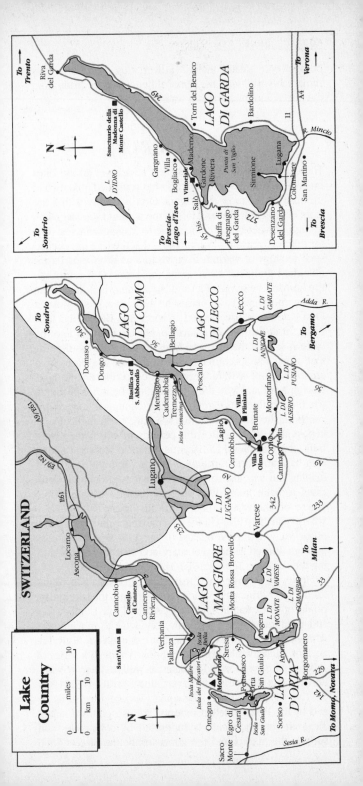

Lake Country

Left Map

SWITZERLAND

To Sondrio

To Trento (top of right map)

LAGO MAGGIORE

LAGO DI COMO

LAGO DI LECCO

LAGO DI LUGANO

L. DI LUGANO

L. D'ORTA

Locarno
Ascona
Cannobio
Castello di Cannero
Cannero Riviera
Sant'Anna
Verbania
Pallanza
Isola Madre
Isola Bella
Isola dei Pescatori
Motterone
Omegna
Stresa
Baveno
Isola
San Giulio
Ego di Cesara
Soriso
Arona
Angera
Sacro Monte
Borgomanero
To Momo, Novara
Sesia R.
142
229
33
Motta Rossa Brovello
L. DI VARESE
L. DI MONATE
L. DI COMABBIO
Varese
342
233
To Milan
Lugano
E9/N2
E61
198
A8/N26
340
Domaso
Dongo
Basilica of S. Abbondio
Menaggio
Cadenabbia
Tremezzo
Isola Comacina
Laglio
Cernobbio
Villa Olmo
Como
Brunate
Villa Pliniana
Montorfano
Cammagna volta
Bellagio
Pescallo
36
L. DI ANNONE
L. DI ALSERIO
L. DI PUSIANO
Lecco
L. DI GARLATE
36
Adda R.
To Bergamo
49
233
To Sondrio

N

miles 0 — 10
km 0 — 10

Right Map

To Trento

LAGO DI GARDA

Riva del Garda
249
Sanctuario della Madonna di Monte Castello
Gargnano
Villa Bogliaco
Maderno
Il Vittoriale
Salò
45 bis
To Brescia-Lago d'Iseo
L. D'IDRO
Gardone Riviera
Torri del Benaco
Punta di San Vigilio
Bardolino
Sirmione
Lugana
San Martino
Colombare
Raffa di Puegnago del Garda
572
Desenzano del Garda
To Brescia
R. Mincio
A4
11
To Verona

N

bologna-type salami including liver; this mortadella goes remarkably well with the regional beers that are made from the purest mountain-stream waters.

LAGO D'ORTA

There are some who elect as their favorite of all the lakes one that not only is small but also has remained unknown to the majority of today's voyagers. Orta is wholly within the frontiers of Piedmont and just to the west of Lago Maggiore, though nowhere near comparable to Maggiore in size. It is for this very reason—its intimacy—that the lake has elicited such feelings of warmth from visitors as diverse as Balzac ("Studied grandeur is far away; the proportion returns to the human," he wrote of it) and Nietzsche, who found it one of the most evocative places he had ever seen. Most of Orta's devotees have stayed in **Orta San Giulio**, the little town set at the end of a small peninsula that juts into the eastern side of the lake and faces an island across the way that, along with its church of **San Giulio** and its palace of the archbishops of Novara, seems to be floating on the lake. During April and May, the city could not be more beautiful, when lights flood its gardens during the annual flower festival. Both the island and the town have been meticulously kept within the styles of the periods in which they were built, from medieval to Baroque. Boats to **Isola San Giulio** spin back and forth throughout the day, and it is well worth making the trip just to see the Romanesque church dedicated to Saint Julius, who slew the island's dragon. While you're on the island, dine at the **Ristorante San Giulio**— where you have the choice of enjoying either the picturesque views from the terrace or the 17th-century frescoes indoors (closed January, February, and Mondays except during the summer; Tel: 0322-902-34; moderately priced).

However, the tree-lined main square of Orta San Giulio itself, piazza Principale, which looks out onto the lake and its points of embarkation, is so well provided with shaded cafés and restaurants that it is hardly conducive to moving anywhere at all. And June offers the allure of a ten-day festival of ancient music, while September hooks you with a series of classical music concerts. For dates, as well as other information, contact the tourist office, via Olina 9-11, Tel: (0322) 903-54; Fax: (0322) 90-56-78. The square is dominated at its far end by the **Palazzo della Comunità**, a frescoed town hall of the 16th century, which is supported by colonnades and surveys the market and the goings-on below. Streets lined with palaces sporting beautiful loggias radiate from the square, some of them leading to the churches and sanctuaries atop the surrounding hills.

The most famous of these sanctuaries is the **Sacro Monte**, reached by a narrow path of beech and pine trees. Along the way you can visit 20 Baroque chapels harboring 376 painted terra-cotta figures that depict scenes from the life of Saint Francis of Assisi, with murals in the style of Neapolitan *presepi* as background. Another place of pilgrimage on the Sacro Monte is of quite a different sort: The **Ristorante Sacro Monte**, installed in a 17th-century villa surrounded by lush greenery, is the best around, serving among its specialties prosciutto from Val Vigezzo, curried chicken with risotto, *tagliolini al pesto,* many truffle dishes, and a large selection of local wines (the more usual of which around here are of course those of Piedmont: Barolo and Barbera for red, Gavi for white). Reservations suggested; moderately priced; Tel: (0322) 902-20; closed Tuesdays and January 7–30.

The road to Orta from Novara and the south is paved with good restaurants. For example, at Momo the **Macallè**, via Boniperti 2, a rustic haven with a few Art Deco touches, serves splendid rabbit, guinea hen, and other dishes that go surprisingly well with the wines of the area, such as Sizzano and Ghemme (reservations needed; Tel: 0321-92-60-64; closed Wednesdays, January 8 to 15, and August 1 to 15). The prices here are in the medium-high range. The pricier **Pinocchio**, at Borgomanero (via Matteotti 147), has warm wood paneling and a lovely garden and serves up such tasty (and costly) temptations as pigeon with balsamic vinegar, risotto with frog legs, and a prize-winning *agnolotti* (reservations needed; Tel: 0322-822-73; Fax: 0322-83-50-75; closed Mondays, Tuesday lunch, July 20–August 12, and December 24–30). **Al Sorriso**, at Soriso (about 5 km/3 miles southwest of the lake), is elegant but cozy in decor. Angelo and Luisa Valazza create highly personal dishes, like shrimp with zucchini flowers, as well as more traditional fare (reservations suggested; Tel: 0322-98-32-28; Fax: 0322-98-33-28; closed Mondays, Tuesday lunch, August 7–21, and January 10–31). They even have eight quaint rooms, if you wish to spend the night—they cost less than the rather expensive meal. (When you settle in at Orta it is preferable to avoid any sort of pension arrangement that might tie you down.)

The hotels in Orta are by no means grandiose; Stresa is right over the hills, and its hotels are more than capable of catering to opulent tastes. Here at Orta, the **Orta**, a charming white villa, is right on the main piazza, with its restaurant on a terrace overlooking the lake, while the **San Rocco**, perhaps the lake's most luxurious hotel, is located in a remodeled 17th-century convent astride the lake, with all the modern conveniences, including tennis courts and swimming pool. The terrace restaurant, hovering over the lake, affords sweeping views, tranquillity, and excellent lake fish such as *bronzino*. San Rocco is small and slightly out of town, so reserve well in advance. More modest quarters can be found a few miles north of Orta San Giulio, at Pettenasco, where the pleasant and moderately priced hotel **Giardinetto** is located. Family-run, it sits right on the lake and has a swimming pool, private beach, and fine restaurant.

Horseback riders can take an excursion into the wooded hillsides, starting in the morning at Egro di Cesara and reaching almost a mile (1,400 meters) above the lake, where they can halt for polenta and cheese at the **Alpe Sacci Ristorante**, and then return by a gentle descent through birch and larch woods. Contact Azienda Agricola "Il Bosco," via Piano Egro, Cesara. Tel: (0323) 82-71-70. For those who prefer waterborne sports, waterskiing is available at Gozzano (Sci Nautico Sporting Club, Tel: 0322-93-667) and at Omegna (Sci Nautico Cusio, Tel: 0323-86-26-01).

Of all the drives in the Lake District the most spectacular must be the one from Orta to Lago Maggiore, over the narrow ridge of mountains called the Mottarone. From the summit of the ridge you can see both lakes, the Alps, and the Po Valley. In the winter there is skiing on the Mottarone, and all year round there are rustic lodges where travellers can break their journey.

STRESA AND LAGO MAGGIORE

There is nothing rustic about Stresa, the touristic capital of Lago Maggiore, which has been famous for its villas and gardens since the days of Imperial Rome. It is on the main Paris–Milan rail line, and so convenient a stop that it attracts multitudes who descend from trains that have barely just passed the Swiss border. Its most renowned hotel, **Des Iles Borromées**, along the lake, with an ornate, regal façade, has been taken over by the CIGA chain, which has wisely kept the hotel within its original Belle Epoque period. Its spacious rooms overlook well-tended gardens. The hotel offers everything—including a fine restaurant, swimming pool, tennis courts, gym, and health spa—to create a fairy-tale vacation. You may recall that Frederick Henry used it as a refuge in Hemingway's *A Farewell to Arms*. Open year-round. Its neighbor, the **Regina Palace**, keeps it good company, with tennis courts and genteel rooms overlooking beautiful gardens. A perfectly delightful vantage point from which to view this opulent setting is at the waterside square, piazza Maròni. The renowned September music festivals (from late August to late September) are held in Stresa, with concerts taking advantage of every possible site.

In the town itself there is a choice of lodgings around the piazza Imbarcadero that run to more reasonable rates; of these, the **Milan e Speranza au Lac**, with spacious rooms (some with balconies) and a pleasant restaurant, is most inviting. Two other good bets are the **Albergo Italia e Svizzera**, simple but comfortable, with some lakeside rooms, and the **Hotel Moderno**, on via Cavour in the heart of the shopping section, just two blocks from the lake. Agreeably modern, with a few flourishes like decorated tile floors, it offers garden dining in the rear and balconies on its front rooms. If you don't mind staying out of town, the **Villaminta** is superb, less than a mile away on the state road, via Sempione. In addition to attractive rooms and the most spectacular view of the islands, the hotel has a pool, tennis courts, a small beach, and a fine restaurant specializing in lake fish and dishes from other regions of Italy. In town is the best restaurant around, **L'Emiliano**, at corso Italia 50 right on the waterfront, where fish is favored and fêted in highly imaginative ways—with pasta, in summer salads, and in risottos. The shrimp with eggplant, in a sweet/sour sauce, is a highlight. Reservations imperative; medium-high prices; Tel: (0323) 313-96; Fax: (0323) 334-74; closed Tuesdays and Wednesday lunch, and January 15 to February 28. Another good bet (at somewhat lower prices) is the **Ristorante Piemontese**, via Mazzini 25, with warm wood paneling and delicate wall sconces that cast a honey glow. The service can be a bit crisp, but the food redeems all. Its specialty is linguine with mussels and squid sauce, and the house ravioli, bathed in a creamy porcini mushroom sauce, is superb. Fresh fruit and the sharp runny *stracchino* cheese top off a meal nicely. (Tel: 0323-302-35; closed Mondays, January, and February). If you just want a simple, inexpensive meal in a pleasant garden setting, try **Il Triangolo**, via Roma 61. (Tel: 0323-327-36; closed January 15–30 and November 15–30, and Tuesdays from October to May.) The new management at **Le Chandelle**, via Sempione 23, offers the unusual starter of prawns in fruit sauce, followed by the even more exotic marinated sturgeon, all served in a gracious setting at medium prices. (Tel: 0323-300-97; closed Mondays).

You can combine beautiful lake views with a round of golf at the **Del Iles Borromées Golf Club** in the small village of

Motta Rossa Brovello, just 7 km (4 miles) from Stresa. (Tel: 0323-302-43 or 292-85; closed Mondays except during July and August). And for aquatic sports—from chugging about in a motorboat to more strenuous activities under sail, plus Windsurfing and waterskiing, the **Club Nautico Stresa**, via Sempione Sud 17, offers lessons for beginners and rentals for the experienced (Tel: 0323-280-49).

Far and away the best means of seeing Maggiore is by boat, which allows perfect views of the walled villas on the lake that are difficult to see from the road. Boats leave frequently from the Imbarcadero, and excursions to well-known gardens can often be combined with scenic dining. One exception is the well-named **Isola Bella**, one of the Borromean islands, which is best visited during off-hours, after the crowds have dispersed.

The island is the best-known sight on the lake and was already so in the 18th century when the French scholar Charles de Brosses said that it looked as if it had been dropped from the Hesperides. It looks much more so now, for the centuries since Count Carlo Borromeo started it in 1630 have added a riot of verdure to the originally rather bare series of terraces and parterres designed by the Crivellis. No money or time was to be spared on Isola Bella, named after the count's wife, Isabella; its gardens took 40 years in their construction. For Englishmen on the Grand Tour, Isola Bella was *de rigueur.* The villa at the far end can be visited and has some very fine Baroque paintings, murals, furniture, and a substructure of grottoes, encrusted with shells, that are worthy of Arcimboldo. Don't miss the lavish bedroom where Napoléon and Josephine slept in August 1797. Or the Borromean family puppet theater, which houses exquisitely carved puppets.

The second island, **Isola dei Pescatori**, sometimes called Isola Superiore, is a typical fishing village, unadorned, with weathered homes, narrow twisting lanes, and fishing nets everywhere. There's a good little hotel here, the russet-colored **Verbano**, with just 12 rooms, great views, and an excellent restaurant where homemade pasta is a specialty (closed Wednesdays and January 8 to February 28).

The third island, **Isola Madre**, rivals the beauty of Isola Bella, with its gardens ablaze with camellias in April and azaleas in May. The island is occupied by a single villa that has some interesting family memorabilia; its garden and villa are open to the public.

An ideal excursion from Stresa combining sights and a good table would be a boat trip to the gardens of the **Villa Taranto** at Pallanza, just outside of Verbania and clearly visible from Stresa's shore. The terraces beneath the 18th-century villa abound in exotic and rare tropical plants, and the gardens combine formal French parterres with thickly forested walks and mossy steps springing with violets. The Victorian greenhouses, with their gargantuan water-lily and lotus specimens, are particularly striking. If you feel like lingering at Pallanza-Verbania, the pricey **Hotel Majestic** on the lake will cosset you with gardens, tennis courts, a pool, and an exceptionally fine restaurant, **La Beola**. There are two other superior restaurants here: **Il Torchio**, via Manzoni 20, a charming place with a limited but delicious menu, including *pennette* with pesto or creamy tomato and Parmesan sauce (medium-high prices; reservations suggested; Tel: 0323-50-33-52; closed Mondays and June 20 to July 20); and the slightly less expensive **Milano**, housed in a dignified old villa at corso Zannitello 2 with lakeside terrace dining and some of the best fish, homemade pasta, and antipasti in the area (reservations required; Tel: 0323-55-68-16; Fax: 0323-55-66-13; closed Tuesdays and January 10 to February 10).

Just outside Verbania, you can take guided horseback rides on the wooded slopes, with spectacular views of the lake. Contact Maneggio Forte, via Tiro a Segno 56, Trobaso (Tel: 0323-55-34-09).

Another major attraction of Stresa is the gardens at the **Villa Pallavicino** (the villa is not open to the public), where splendid palms and semitropical shrubs share space with pert parrots, peacocks, and other exotic birds that roam freely throughout this small zoological garden. Open March to October.

The northern shores of Maggiore shelter the medieval towns of Cannobio and Cannero on the Stresa side, but a step too far and you are in Switzerland near the resort town of Ascona. **Cannobio** is a small, unspoiled village of ancient origin, lying at the foot of the Val Cannobina. From here you can hire a boat for a visit to the impressive **Orrido di Sant'Anna**, a deep, rocky gorge chiseled by the waters of the Cannobina stream. A good choice for lodging is the petite **Del Lago**, just ten rooms in the locality of Carmine Inferiore, just south. The rooms are simple but tasteful, but it's the hotel's restaurant that draws the crowds and gives the place its true identity. On a lovely garden terrace overlooking the lake you can dine on savory lake fish and lobster bathed in the most elegant and subtle sauces. The menu is pricey, and the restaurant is closed Tuesdays and Wednesday lunch. From **Cannero** a ten-minute boat ride will take you to the **Castello di Cannero**, a rocky island with the ruins of two medieval castles.

The eastern shore of the lake, though not as luxurious as the western, shelters one of the finest restaurants of the area, **Del Sole**, located in the hamlet of Ranco, just above Angera. Subtly charming, this old country inn overlooking the lake has been run by the Brovellis for years. Their masterful creations, such as the lake fish cannelloni, will astonish you, as will their high prices. Rooms are also available. (Reservations needed; Tel: 0331-97-65-07; Fax: 0331-97-66-20. Closed Monday dinner, Tuesdays, and January 2 to February 15.)

Just around the headland, it is impossible to miss the castle of **Rocca di Angera**. Perched high on a crag of pale rock, the castle served as a fortress for Milan's Visconti family until the 15th century, when it became the property of the Borromeos, who made their home here. Apart from the beautiful frescoes in the Hall of Justice, there is also a pretty **doll museum** (opened in 1988) with more than 200 exhibits from the collection of Princess Bona Borromeo.

LAGO DI COMO

Of all the lakes, Como comes to us as the most heavily romantic. From the earliest days of the Roman Empire the Plinys wrote about its incomparable lush beauty. Even its structure—three different basins, each seeming a lake in itself—lends itself to an emotional turn of mind. Its steep hills cascade to a finale of villas and gardens reflected in azure water, and the sentinel Alps hover close behind. The very names of its tiny ports evoke nostalgia in those who have known them even for brief periods: Cadenabbia, Bellagio, Menaggio. Castles and convents were built on its shores in the Middle Ages, and villas in the Renaissance; but when the Romantics of the 19th century arrived it was love at first sight, a magnificent love that was to make the lake famous all over the world. Franz Liszt was so enraptured by the lake that when his daughter was born here he named her Cosma; later, as Cosima, she married Richard Wagner. Lord Byron stayed at the Villa Pliniana, where Rossini wrote one of the first passionate operas of the 19th century, *Tancredi;* later, at the Villa Margherita, Verdi composed most of *La Traviata*. Poets by the dozen lauded the lake, but it was a writer of prose who set it before us most vividly: Stendhal chose Como for many of the opening episodes of his novel *The Charterhouse of Parma* and depicted the younger days of his hero, Fabrizio, on its shores.

The Napoleonic years were glorious ones for building

on Como, as we shall see, and the emperor and his stepson, Eugène de Beauharnais, were constant visitors. It was
not until the middle of the century, however, that hotels
opened and were filled with Russian grand dukes and the
wealthy from all over Europe. Their comings and goings
were well described in a novel of our own time, written
anonymously, entitled *Madame Solario*. (The work has
since been republished under the author's name—Gladys
Huntington.) The eponymous heroine, with her friends of
rank and fashion, would glide back and forth by boat for
luncheons and parties in very much the same places that
we still visit. In the town of Como there is a disused ramp
descending from the Stazione Nord to an embarkation
dock. There, surely, in the days when an English milady
might travel with 20 trunks, such visitors arrived and were
wafted by boat to their hotels.

Como the Town

The town of Como is situated at the lake's southern end and
is all too often bypassed or rushed through on the way to the
more natural settings to be found on farther shores. This is a
shame, as Como is an active, charming city full of things to
see, and with restaurants and hotels of every sort. It has the
advantage of two railroad stations: San Giovanni, with its fast,
comfortable international trains leaving every hour for the
35-minute trip to Milan's imposing Stazione Centrale; and
the two-track Nord, whose trains take an hour to arrive at the
Stazione Nord in Milan, almost adjacent to the Castello
Sforzesco. This means that for those who wish to see Milan
without paying the steep prices of its ever-packed hotels,
and who don't mind returning in the evening to a quieter
place where there is fresh air, Como can be a convenient
alternative. Of its hotels the most appealing is the four-star
Metropole Suisse, with its tastefully furnished rooms, facing
the lake on the main square, the piazza Cavour. The
Imbarcadero restaurant (owned separately) within is formal
but warm, with fine architectural detail and quite good food
at medium-high prices. In warm weather you can sit on the
lakeside terrace, which is ringed with shrubbery (Tel: 031-
27-73-41; closed January 1–15). Also in the piazza, but set
back, is the **Hotel Barchetta Excelsior**. Recently renovated, it
has rather a business traveller's appeal, with pleasant modern rooms overlooking the lake. And in the town of
Montorfano, 6.5 km (4 miles) southeast on route 342 at via
Como 19, is the small and genteel **Santandrea Golf Hotel**, a
remodeled ancient farmhouse set amid thick woods and

lush greenery—ideal for unwinding. Facilities include a nearby golf course, a small private beach, and a superior restaurant where you can dine alfresco.

Como, first Roman, then a Longobard capital, is very old indeed. From its early medieval period comes the impressive Romanesque basilica of **Sant'Abbondio**, with its frescoed interior, on the outskirts of town. The main street, via Vittorio Emanuele II, cuts through the center of this old quarter and passes the rear of the basilica of San Fedele. Through a tiny door with unusual medieval carvings, you enter the dimly lighted Romanesque church, still filled with the atmosphere of early Christian worship. On the far side you emerge on piazza San Fedele, with its wood-beamed 16th-century houses. Here, tucked away in the narrow medieval streets, far from the intrusion of traffic, you may sit in the pretty cobbled square and enjoy delicious ice creams, or in cooler weather a *latte macchiato,* hot milk laced with coffee.

The pride of Como is its **Duomo**, also along via Vittorio Emanuele II, built over centuries but always by the "Maestri Comancini," Italy's premier sculptors and masons, who also contributed to the magnificent stonework of Milan's Duomo. Its highly original polychrome marble façade is divided by four marble pilasters, filled with statues that include two of those senior citizens of Roman Como, the Plinys. Perhaps they deserve their position as honorary Christians, for it was Pliny the Younger who wrote to Emperor Trajan asking him to spare the industrious Christians and assuring him that their mysterious fad would soon die out. The interior is a veritable museum of tapestries, sculpture, and paintings, including several by Luini. The dome was designed by the same Juvarra who helped build 18th-century Turin, and the church is considered Italy's finest example of hybrid Gothic/Renaissance. Alongside the cathedral is the striped façade of the **Broletto**, the municipal palace, which is set above the square on arcades. At the rear of the stately Duomo, just across the tracks of the Nord, the ultimate in contrasts presents itself: the "rationalist" **Casa del Fascio**, built by another of Italy's great architects, Giuseppe Terragni, in 1936. The square itself is lined with inviting cafés. The small streets of the old town are dotted with trattorias, some of them very good. The best known is **del Gesumin**, situated in a 14th-century stable at via 5 Giornate 44 (Tel: 031-26-60-30; closed Sundays and August 10–20), which does wonderful handmade pasta with truffles and asparagus. **Da Angela**, housed in a former monastery at via Foscolo 16, takes many

Piedmontese dishes to new heights (reservations suggested; Tel: 031-26-34-60; closed Mondays and July or August). It specializes in agnolotti with truffles, and at lunchtime it offers a low-priced macrobiotic menu. (Del Gesumin is moderately priced at dinner; Da Angela slightly higher.)

As a capital of silk-making, a tradition maintained since the 16th century, Como has outlets for silk fabrics and ties and scarves. **Centro della Seta** has two outlets in Como at via Volta 64 and via Bellinzona 3. Along the principal shopping street, via Vittorio, **Emanuele A. Picci** (among others) sells scarves and such; on nearby via Ballarini, **Rainoldi** sells silk fabrics. And for designer silk scarves, as well as fabrics at a considerable discount, you can't beat **Ratti**, via Cernobbio 19.

A short drive from the historic center at via Filippo Turati 3 is the **Sant'Anna** restaurant, housed in a faceless building but serving incredibly fine food in an elegant setting (expensive; reservations suggested; Tel: 031-50-52-66. Closed Fridays, Saturday lunch, and July 25 to August 25). Try the spaghetti with Sardinian caviar and the terrific sea bass. Two miles east, on via Pannilani in the town of Camnago Volta, is the popular restaurant **Navedano** (Tel: 031-26-10-80; closed Tuesdays and August 1–15). Set amid lush hills with surrounding gardens, this attractive haunt features gnocchi with porcini and wonderful lake fish (also expensive) that can be enjoyed on a summer terrace.

The best aperitivo in town can be had at the **Pub Hemingway**, a short stroll from the piazza Cavour (via Juvara 16; Tel: 031-27-63-51). The genial barman, Lino, who speaks excellent English, presides over a lively coktail bar and restaurant, always crowded with locals and visitors. To explore the lake itself, take the hydrofoil or one of the slower excursion boats; they leave regularly from the terminal opposite piazza Cavour.

Before heading off to some of the more serene resorts on the lake, it is worthwhile to take the funicular up to **Brunate**, a village perched high on a rocky plateau affording spectacular views of town and lake. Hidden in a narrow lane is the tiny house where the man who gave us electricity, Alessandro Volta, was born. A short walk up an ancient mule track takes you to the **Faro Volta** monument for great views across the Swiss Alps and the lakeside mountains. And if hiking is your pleasure, you will see further splendid panoramas unfold along the mountainous lakeside track. A string of attractive off-the-beaten-track *rifugi* can be found here, offering unpretentious bed and board and such mouth-watering local specialties as polenta and wild boar. (**Rifugio CAO**, Tel:

031-22-02-64, is open weekends and all of July and August. **Baita Carla**, Tel: 031-22-01-86, is open year-round except Tuesdays.)

The Shores of Como

Within walking distance of the town of Como is the first of the large villas on the western shore of the lake: the **Villa Olmo**, now a communal cultural center and open to all. Begun by the Odescalchi family in the 17th century, the villa changed styles toward the end of the 18th; its present Neoclassic façade was ready in 1797 to witness the arrival of Napoléon and Joséphine as guests. Its terraces, with a striking view of the town, are used for concerts during the autumn music festival.

Not so accessible is the **Villa d'Este** at Cernobbio, a bit up the coast; you will have to show identification (passport) at the gates of what has been one of Europe's most luxurious hotels since 1873. The hotel has two restaurants, one in the grand style as part of the main building, the other a well-designed modern grill near the sporting facilities. The lobbies are dripping with the villa's past treasures, and the aura of affluence continues right into the hotel's fancy jewelry and antiques shops. The amenities are overwhelming: three swimming pools (one indoor, one outdoor, and one for children), eight tennis courts, squash courts, putting green, discotheque, spa, and seven 18-hole golf courses in easy reach—a world unto itself! The villa was begun by the hugely rich Cardinal Tolomeo Gallio in the 16th century and refurbished in the late 18th by the Marchesa Calderera, who cleverly married one of Napoléon's ministers. The most famous occupant, Caroline of Brunswick, retired here after the scandalous trial for adultery and sedition brought on by her husband, George IV of England. While continuing her riotous way of life, she decided that she was obscurely related to the Este family and changed the villa's name to suit her whim. Later in the 19th century, another resident, the Russian Empress Maria Fedorovna, was to bring to it a final social fling—before its doors opened to a wider public.

If you find yourself reeling from the opulence, head ten minutes north to Laglio, site of the discreetly charming **San Marino** restaurant at via Regina Nuova 64. The Ruggeri brothers regale their guests with superb food—specializing in a variety of appetizers and lake fish—and service equal to the marvelous scenery. But it's remarkably reasonable, and you can spend the night (Tel: 031-40-03-83; closed Wednesdays). After a hearty lunch, take a short drive from Cernobbio up the pleasant tree-lined road to **Mount Bisbino**, where you can leave your car and follow the not-too-steep Monte Bisbino path. The summit overlooks Lake Como in Italy and Lake Lugano in Switzerland, offering spectacular views of snowcapped Alps.

About 30 km (19 miles) north, at Tremezzo, looms the **Villa Carlotta**, probably the most famous villa on the entire lake, due largely to its remarkable gardens. The building itself has remained faithful to the period of Bonaparte, with a collection of Neoclassic paintings, sculpture (including a copy of Canova's lovely *Cupid and Psyche*), and Thorvaldsen's frieze of Alexander entering Babylon, which Napoléon commissioned, all well set off by the Pompeiian ceilings and the Empire furniture. The villa was built largely by Giovanni Sommariva, who made a fortune supplying the emperor's armies; the "C" over the door stands for his Clerici wife. The "Carlotta" was to come later with the arrival of a new owner, Carlotta of Nassau, sister to the kaiser and married to a Saxe-Meiningen, from whom the Italian government confiscated the villa on the outbreak of World War I. It was the German owners, however, who transformed the gardens, making them larger and less formal, adding the paths that in the spring blaze with azaleas and rhododendrons, and creating the sudden operatic vistas of fern forest and jungle. Como is hardly on the same latitude as Palermo, yet there seems to be something in its climate that fosters a flora worthy of the Amazon.

The **boat ride** from Cadenabbia, just north of the Carlotta, to Bellagio, which is right across the lake, is breathtaking. In the 19th century this one-and-a-half-mile span was admired almost as if it were the Grand Canal in Venice, and hotels sprang up on both sides. On the Carlotta side a good one is still the **Grand Hotel Tremezzo Palace** (surprisingly reasonable), where palm trees and other tropical vegetation spill onto the grounds, though a room with a lake view (all have balconies) is probably preferable. There is swimming in the pool and in the lake, tennis and golf are available, and there's a fine restaurant. Right next to the villa is a very nice café called **Timon**.

But if you want to enjoy a bracing yet tranquil rural setting with sterling lake views, head about 1½ km (1 mile) up the hills to **Al Veluu** restaurant in Rogaro, where lake fish and mountain kid are prepared with equal skill. Tel: (0344) 405-10; open April to October, closed Tuesdays. Or for something really offbeat, escape to the deserted island of **Comacina**, just south of Tremezzo, an Arcadian wilderness of Roman ruins and home to the 50-year-old restaurant

Locanda dell'Isola. Reached by a little gondola, called a *lucia,* from Ossuccio or Sala Comacina, the restaurant serves a single (expensive) *menu-degustazione* of the most tempting delights, including mixed antipasti, trout, roast pressed chicken, fruit, and dessert. You will enjoy hours of splendid eating on the tree-shaded grounds, with a ringside seat for viewing the villa-strewn shores of the lake as a bonus. Reservations suggested (Tel: 0344-550-83. Open March to October; closed Tuesdays except mid-June through September).

The road continues along the lake to the area where the Como and Lecco "legs" meet to form what locals call *l'om,* "the old man of the lake." The water in this upper basin is crystal clear, and it is a center for water sports. At the head of the lake is Domaso, which commands superb views of still largely untouched nature. You can arrange for Windsurfing or water-skiing at the Hotel Camping (Tel: 0344-960-44).

The best wine-tasting on the lake is found in the center of Domaso at the **Enoteca del Porto**, via Regina 53 (Tel: 0344-961-71), where you can sample vintage wines from all over northern Italy in a rustic setting and with good country fare.

Bellagio, "pearl of the lake," sits high on the headland just where the lake forks, on the actual tip of the triangle of land, called La Punta Spartivento ("the point that divides the wind"), enjoying one of the most privileged positions on the lake. This dignified old village flows gently over quaint cobbled streets onto a long plaza lined with shops and cafés. On misty days the lake becomes moody, and it is pleasant to sit on the grassy embankment at the **San Remo** café and watch the rainbow-colored homes across the lake creep up the tree-studded mountains and into oblivion or to browse near the café at **Silvia Albertini**'s shop, which offers a lovely selection of knitted and crocheted items.

Also along the arcaded piazza Mazzini and lungo Lario Manzoni are lovely, though modest, hotels. One, the **Hotel du Lac,** a comfortable family-run place essentially modern in decor, with a roof garden that is perfect for sunbathing, also has a restaurant on the balcony. Or you may wish to eat out on the tree-domed lakeside terrace at the **Hotel Florence** a few doors down.

The **Grand Hotel Villa Serbelloni** is the town's showpiece. Gardens brimming with bright flowers kept strictly in line surround the lavish palace, whose rooms are richly frescoed. The amenities include tennis, pool, and lovely sheltered terraces.

The 50-acre garden at the **Villa Serbelloni** (not the hotel), on the site of a villa owned by Pliny the Younger, covers much of Bellagio's point, and although the villa is not open to the public (it now belongs to the Rockefeller Foundation), there is an excellent tour of the grounds, which include grand terraced gardens. Open twice daily, at 11:00 A.M. and 4:00 P.M., from Easter to mid-October. To the south along the road they join the gardens of the **Villa Melzi**, which was constructed by Francesco Melzi d'Eryl, vice president of Bonaparte's Northern Italian Republic and a personal friend of the consul. Its manicured lawns, with exquisite Japanese maples, sphinxes, and fountains, will remind you of Malmaison—except that here the urns are original Etruscan ones. It is perhaps this same luxuriant beauty that attracted Liszt and his mistress, Countess Marie D'Agoult, who bore one of their daughters, Cosima, here. There is a perfect Neoclassical chapel, a pavilion with mementos of Napoléon, and a fine collection of Egyptian sculpture. The villa itself, however, is closed to the public, as it still belongs to the Gallarati Scotti, a Lombard family of diplomats and writers who graciously allow visitors onto their grounds.

Restaurants in Bellagio are of a modest stripe. One that is very popular is the inexpensive **La Pergola**, located in Pescallo, less than a mile southeast of Bellagio. This hotel-restaurant, with just 13 rooms, is loaded with rustic charm and family coziness, with mama tending the kitchen and the other family members the hotel. It's best to go with the daily specials of fresh lake fish. (Tel: 031-95-02-63; restaurant closed Tuesdays and November to February).

LAGO D'ISEO

Iseo has neither the sumptuous trappings of lakes Garda and Como nor the crowds. Roughly halfway between Milan and Lago di Garda, Iseo is surrounded by quaint villages, olive trees, and rugged mountains. Its waters brim with eel and trout, and flocks of wild ducks swoop over the lake, enjoying the extremely gentle climate, which some say is milder than Como's.

The lake can be approached from Lovere, where, apart from the attractive Basilica di Santa Maria in Valcunda, you will want to visit the **Palazzo Tadini**, which houses one of the most important art collections in Lombardy. Among the fine porcelains and sculptures are masterpieces by Bellini, Parmigiano, and Tiepolo (open daily from May to October).

Steamers run frequently between Sarnico and Lovere, and local service connects the smaller towns on the banks of the lake. The river Oglio, the main source of the lake, flows through the bosom of the Val Camonica, a spectacular Alpine valley that shelters impressive prehistoric sights. **Capo di Ponte**, the center of the best finds, is located north of Breno in the **Parco Nazionale della Incisioni Rupestri Preistoriche** (open daily until one hour before sunset). The Naquane rock, in the park, has been carved with more than 900 figures spanning 8,000 years from the Neolithic to the Roman era. Hikers will find the village of **Marone**, midway between Pisogne and Iseo, an excellent base from which to ascend the lush and scenic Monte Guglielmo. Excellent paths lead from the town to Zone, where the eerie *piramidi di erosione* (erosion pyramids) loom like huge stalagmites in the forest.

From the towns of Iseo and Sulzano, boats leave daily to **Monte Isola** (called Montisola by the locals), a small, lush island in the center of the lake, covered with olive and chestnut trees, dotted with rustic villages, and—delightfully—free of cars. The ferry lands there at Peschiera Maraglio; nearby along the quay is the flower-bedecked **Trattoria del Pesce Archetti**, a simple, comfortable place set in an old manor bustling with local patrons (Tel: 030-988-61-37). Its exceptional (and inexpensive) seafood dishes include *antipasto del lago*—a medley of little *lavarello* fish served with a sweet-and-sour sauce and home-cured lake sardines—and *pesce in carpione*, small fish fillets marinated in a spicy sauce. Closed Tuesdays except August, and November 1–21.

A delightful path encircles the island with roads leading up to hilltops crowned with small villages and historic sights, such as **Rocca Martinengo** and the **Santuario della Madonna della Ceriola**. Minibuses linking all the hamlets make frequent runs around the island; bicycle rentals are available at Peschiera Maraglio.

If you have time to spare or are waiting for a boat to Monte Isola, you may enjoy lunching at **Il Volto**, via Mirolte 33, in Iseo. A simple, tiny tavern with superb food, thanks to the creative passions of friends who combined their talents, the restaurant favors local ingredients and has quite a decent wine list, including excellent local Franciacorta wines such as Cadelbosco and Bellavista. In fact, so inspired were these virtuosos by Il Volto's success that they formed another restaurant, **Le Maschere**, vicolo della Pergola 7, where the dishes and decor are a bit more sophisticated and quite wonderful. Le Maschere offers a dual menu: one medium-, one high-priced. Il Volto is closed Wednesdays, Thursday lunch, and July (Tel: 030-98-14-62). Le Maschere is closed August 21 to September 7, January, Sunday evening, and Mondays (Tel: 030-98-21-542).

In the town of **Borgonato**, just 20 km (15 miles) southeast of Iseo in the wine-producing region of Franciacorta, the Fratelli Berlucchi, principal winegrowers of the area, offer a splendid tour of their wine cellars, housed in an elegant 16th-century villa set on lush grounds. Visitors are welcome to taste their fine sparkling wines.

The lake also offers a variety of water sports, from canoeing to water-skiing, at **Camping del Sole**, just on the outskirts of Iseo (Tel: 030-98-02-88; closed October to April). And for golfers there is the **Franciacorta Golf Club and Hotel** complex. Just 6 km (4 miles) from the lake, the course was designed by two famous specialists, Pete Dye and Marco Croze. The club offers an expert "golf clinic" for beginners and experienced golfers.

LAGO DI GARDA

The colors of Garda, on the eastern side of Lombardy, are the colors of the Adriatic: turquoise and opaline. The **peninsula of Sirmione**, a splinter of land jutting up from the south, is the lake's most popular resort. Once you get beyond the throng of day-trippers that clogs every inch of the road leading to the village, you are greeted by the magnificent 13th-century crenellated castle of the Scaligeri, lords of Verona. It hovers above the narrow stone bridge that provides access to the historic center, where only the cars of hotel guests are permitted. To enter, you must confirm your reservation at the information center (just before the bridge) and obtain a car pass. (Anyone may visit on foot, however.) If you don't have a reservation you can arrange it there. The village is a botanical extravaganza rich in olive groves and flowering cacti and rigid with soaring cypress and cedars that guard the ancient Roman ruins and opulent hotel and villas. Sirmione has been attracting visitors since the days of the Roman poet Catullus, whose father often hosted Julius Caesar when the future emperor was still proconsul of Gaul. The ruins of the family villa, dating from the first century B.C., are set amid olive groves and can be visited from 9:00 A.M. until dusk, except Mondays. Near the villa is the Romanesque church of San Pietro in Mavino with its interesting early frescoes.

Of hotels in Sirmione there are plenty. The **Grand Hotel Terme** is perhaps the most convenient, since it is right by the castle and has excellent food, a large swimming pool, and facilities for those who wish to take the cure. And it is surprisingly reasonable. Pride of place, however, belongs to the **Villa Cortine Palace Hotel**, a romantic hideaway set in

sumptuous gardens that occupy over a third of the peninsula. The 19th-century villa has been updated, but the frescoed ceilings and regal atmosphere have been preserved. It
offers swimming, tennis, a private beach, and alfresco
dining—and it's very expensive. For scaled-down pleasures,
you cannot beat the **Hotel Sirmione**, which sits atop gardens
running down to the lake and has attractive sitting rooms, a
thermal spa, and lovely lakeside dining. And for really good
value, try the **Hotel Broglia**, via G. Piana 36, conveniently
located across from the spa facilities, with a lake view,
shaded terrace, and every modern convenience, including a
heated pool. Similarly affordable is the **Hotel Ideal**, located
in a quiet corner of Sirmione overlooking the lake and
facing the Archaeological Park, with its own private beach.

Many travellers, however, stop at Sirmione just to have
lunch while en route from Milan to Venice. The menus are
laced with hints of Venetian cuisine: cod à la Gardiana is
served with polenta, and *tiramisù,* the richest of all chocolate-
and-cream desserts, begins to make an appearance. Bardolino, the best of the local reds, comes from its own town on
the eastern shore of the lake, while the most refreshing of the
whites, Lugana, is produced just south of Sirmione. One of the
most attractive restaurants in Sirmione is **Grifone–da Luciano,** at via delle Bisse 5. A minute by foot from the center, it
seems much farther when you are ensconced on its terrace
with a sweeping view of the lake. (Reservations suggested;
Tel: 030-91-60-97; open March 10 to October; closed Wednesdays except from July to September.) Or try **Ristorante La
Griglia**, via IV Novembre 14 in Colombare, the hamlet at the
base of the peninsula. Warm and inviting, with a range of
tantalizing antipasti and grilled meats and fish that reflect the
seasons' bounty, the restaurant is moderately priced and open
until midnight. Tel: (030) 91-92-23; closed Tuesdays and January. Just beyond the road leading to Sirmione a bit east of
Colombare, in the hamlet of Lugana (where the white wine is
produced), lies **Vecchia Lugana**, an 18th-century inn with
rustic elegance and medium-high prices. Meats are roasted
on a spit in the ancient fireplace, and during the summer
months there is dining on a terrace overlooking the lake. The
menu changes seasonally and includes a tempting mosaic of
antipasti, an asparagus *pasticcio,* and *filetto di tinca alla salsa
di rucola.* The wine list is extensive. (Via Lugana Vecchia; Tel:
030-91-90-12; Fax: 030-990-40-45; closed January, Monday dinner, and Tuesdays.)

It is particularly important at Sirmione to have a few
refuges of your own. Germans tourists predominate here,
and you may want to find more Italianate havens—or start

reading the *Frankfurter Allgemeine*. Sirmione is, in any case, an ideal base for visiting Mantua, Verona, and, of course, the rest of the lake.

Leaving Sirmione for the scenic drive along the magnificent road, La Gardesana, that encircles the lake and heading west, travellers first pass through the small port of Desenzano Del Garda, where a stop at the highly regarded restaurant **Cavallino**, at via Gherla 22, is recommended (Tel: 030-912-02-17; closed Mondays and Tuesday lunch). On a pretty outdoor patio you can feast on carp ravioli in a creamy truffle sauce, among other fine dishes. Simple fare such as delicious *crespelle* (crepes) and steak in juniper sauce can be had at **Taverna Tre Corone**, a nice little taverna at via Stretta Castello 16, in the delightful old section of town (Tel: 030-914-19-62; closed December, and Tuesdays from October to June). Sightseeing may be the last thing on your mind after eating at either of these two restaurants, but do visit the church of Santa Maria Maddalena for a look at Tiepolo's *Last Supper*. Or if secular thoughts prevail, visit the famous fourth-century Roman mosaic floors in a recently excavated Roman villa on via Crocifisso.

And if you want to work off the meal, you can rent a bicycle in Desenzano at Girelli Luciano, via Annunciata 10 (Tel: 030-991-22-00), and cycle up into the Morenic hills, with their unique landscape of plains and undulating slopes. The itinerary starts in San Martino and takes in charming villages such as Pozzolengo, Castellaro, and Solferino, as well as ancient abbeys and *cascine,* the classic Italian farms. Alternatively, you can tour the hills in traditional style in a horse and trap by calling Centro Equestra La Giorgiana, Soiano del Lago (Tel: 0365-67-46-21).

Between Desenzano and Salò, pull in at **Venturelli's** in the little village of Raffa di Puegnago del Garda. Here you can stock up on the finest local olive oils, exquisite pastas made with chiles, soybeans, or wheat germ, and ready-made savory sauces. You can also taste the best regional DOC wines here, such as Colle San Pietro Cru, Lugana, and Groppello (via Nazionale 68, Tel: 0365-65-42-81).

Salò, where a handsome cluster of old buildings rims the lakeside promenade, is perhaps the loveliest spot on Lago di Garda. Its Gothic Duomo contains fine paintings by Romanino and Paolo Veneziano. A splendid place to spend the night here, though not on the lake, is the **Hotel Laurin**. Dressed in dainty Art Nouveau style (called Liberty in Italy) with all the comforts of a modern hotel—including a pool, golf, and tennis—the villa has a felicitous dining room with sumptuous frescoes and chandeliers crowning its marble floors. A few miles up the road is **Gardone Riviera**, and at Gardone di Sopra (on the hill) is Garda's foremost villa to visit. It is by no means out of a distant past; **Il Vittoriale** was the home of the poet Gabriele D'Annunzio, who lived here from 1921 until his death in 1938. D'Annunzio was a man of action as well as a writer, and there are mementoes of his political past on the grounds of the villa: the patrol boat that he used in World War I and the tomb of the companions who joined him in his dashing and successful rally to retake Fiume. There are also souvenirs of his other past—as the Don Juan of his age. Though small in stature and unprepossessing in looks, he had a magnetic hold over women, an attraction that was certainly enhanced by the sensuality of his poetry and the glamour of his warrior's life. His conquests read like Leporello's catalogue in *Don Giovanni,* with one important difference: There were no Zerlinas or chambermaids, just women of talent or of high birth—among them his wife, the duchess de Gallise. The affair most featured in the villa was with the celebrated actress Eleanora Duse, to whom D'Annunzio gave quite a few years of almost guaranteed unhappiness. It is odd, though, to see so many art reproductions instead of originals in the home of a man who had so many artist friends (including a particularly devoted one, the American painter Romaine Brooks). For Italians, D'Annunzio's spirit is kept alive through his plays, which are performed in the outdoor theater at the Vittoriale; the most famous, thanks largely to Duse, is *La Città Morta.*

If D'Annunzio's villa is a bastion of eccentricity, then the **Grand Hotel** is a bastion of luxury. Dramatically situated on the lake, it is one of Europe's largest hotels, with 180 rooms and grand salons that flow one into the other. Churchill retreated here (the bar is called Winnie's) after a political setback in 1948, no doubt to enjoy the lush garden terraces, pool, private beach, and excellent dining. Surprisingly affordable. For superb value, you cannot beat the intimate **Montefiore** hotel with its garden, swimming pool, and lovely decor. Where villas abound, why not eat in one of the truly exceptional ones—the **Villa Fiordaliso**, a dainty turn-of-the-century restaurant rich in marble and inlaid woodworks, serving classic Garda and Lombard dishes with a creative flair. The villa also has seven rooms to let, one of which sheltered Mussolini and his mistress, Clara Petacci. But only double rooms are available, and you must take the half-board plan, which includes breakfast and dinner—and which turns out to be pretty reasonable. Anyone with an interest in horticulture must visit the **Giardino Botanico Hruska**, located on via Roma, which leads northward from corso Zanardelli (you'll see the sign across from the Grand Hotel). Built in 1903 by the Swiss Arturo Hruska, a dashing dentist with a desire for the good life, it is laced with artificial streams and studded with imported tufa rocks, mini tropical forests, and more than 2,000 species of plants and flowers, some of which he acquired on his frequent traipses through far-off and mysterious lands (all the while tending to the dental care of Pope Pius XII and Czar Nicholas II).

One hotel that really deserves its name is the **Grand Hotel Fasano**, in Fasano, a suburb of Gardone Riviera, about a mile north. (The name Fasano comes from *Fasan,* German for pheasant.) Built in the mid-1800s as a Hapsburg hunting lodge, it is *anything* but rustic and sits in a glorious park on the lake, with rooms designed to receive the royal family at any moment. Considering its opulence and extensive facilities, it's a bargain.

As you make your way to Gargnano, a particularly pretty stretch of road encompasses Bogliaco, Villa, and finally Gargnano. At **Bogliaco**, you'll see the magnificent lakefront villa of the Bettoni family, who still live here. The house is not open to the public, but if you write to Count Bettoni in advance, he'll gladly arrange a visit (Villa Bettoni, 25080 Bogliaco). **Villa,** just beyond Bogliaco, makes a perfect stop, if only to lunch or dine at one of the loveliest places on the lake, the **Baia d'Oro,** which offers views and food in perfect equation (Tel: 0365-711-71; medium-high prices). The restaurant also has 11 stylish rooms, should you wish to spend the night. The most attractive ones have lakeside terraces. **Gargnano** is the last home of the leader to whom the poet gave his early support: Benito Mussolini. After the victory at Fiume, Mussolini was quite happy to pursue an independent course and leave D'Annunzio comfortably on Garda—far from Rome and far from possible embarrassment to Fascist policies.

Il Duce's final years on the lakes ended badly. The capital of his Fascist republic (1943–1945) was on Garda, at Salò, as was his residence, the Villa Feltrinelli at Gargnano. When Mussolini tried to escape to Switzerland, Dongo, on the north shore of Lake Como, was his Varennes. He and his mistress were recognized by partisans and met a quick and grisly death.

It's easier to ponder these intrigues over a plate of pasta or some such, which you can do at **La Tortuga,** an intimate little restaurant with excellent food, just a few meters from the harbor. Run by Danilo Filippini and his wife, the restaurant changes its menu daily and laces many a dish with the local lemons, which were first introduced into the area by

Franciscan monks from Tuscany and Umbria. (Reservations suggested. Tel: 0365-712-51; closed Tuesdays, Mondays from October to January, and January 1 to March 15.) There's also a pleasing pensione here, the **Giulia**, which although a bargain is rich in attributes: gracious dining rooms, stylish bedrooms, garden, lakeside terrace, pool—and Old World charm.

The north shore of Garda brings one magnificent view after another; from the heights of the Sanctuario della Madonna di Monte Castello, a church in Gardola built on the ruins of a Scaliger castle, to the cool promenades and fjord-like beauty of Riva del Garda, at its northern end in the Alto Adige, and on the way to Trento and then Bolzano. Along the lakeshore, delightfully terraced lemon and lime groves are made more brilliant by the surrounding mountains—with a hint of Switzerland to the north. The east coast, described in the chapter on the Veneto, is less majestic than the west coast but has its own allure and two fine attractions: **Torri del Benaco**, which can be reached by boat from Maderno, on the west coast, is a lovely town, perfect for strolling. There is a good little restaurant at the **Hotel Gardesana**, overlooking the charming piazza that resembles a Venetian *campo*. And the delightful **Punta di San Vigilio**, the verdant peninsula above Garda, is home to the enchanting and expensive **Locanda San Vigilio** hotel. Long the stylish refuge of some notable English patrons, including Winston Churchill, Vivien Leigh, and Laurence Olivier, the hotel, owned and run with peerless taste by Count Guarienti, has seven double bedrooms and the atmosphere of an elegant country home—which it is—plus a superb restaurant (Tel: 045-725-66-88). The restaurant is very pricey, and is closed on Tuesdays except from June to August.

GETTING AROUND
The major cities on each lake—Como, Stresa, Desenzano, and Orta San Giulio—are accessible by train directly from Milan. The towns along the lakes are linked by regular bus service, and ferries and hydrofoils ply the lakes, connecting the mainland to the islands and one town to the other.

ACCOMMODATIONS REFERENCE
The rates given below are projections for 1993; always check for up-to-date information before making reservations. Wide ranges may reflect the differences between low- and high-season rates. Unless otherwise indicated, the figures indicate the cost of a double room (per room, not per person). However, half-board (mezza pensione) rates, which

include breakfast and one other meal per day, are per person. The service charge is included in the rate; inquire about tax and breakfast.

Lago di Como

▶ **Hotel Barchetta Excelsior.** Piazza Cavour 1, 22100 **Como.** Tel: (031) 32-21; Fax: (031) 30-26-22. ₤225,000; half board ₤218,000.

▶ **Hotel du Lac.** Piazza Mazzini, 22021 **Bellagio.** Tel: (031) 95-03-20; Fax: (031) 95-16-24. Open Easter–October 15. ₤92,000; half board ₤89,000.

▶ **Grand Hotel Tremezzo Palace.** Via Regina 8, 22019 **Tremezzo.** Tel: (0344) 404-46; Fax: (0344) 402-01. ₤240,000; half board ₤145,000–₤170,000.

▶ **Grand Hotel Villa Serbelloni.** 22021 **Bellagio.** Tel: (031) 95-02-16; Fax: (031) 95-15-29. Open April 15–October 20. ₤360,000; half board ₤240,000–₤310,000.

▶ **Metropole Suisse.** Piazza Cavour 19, 22100 **Como.** Tel: (031) 26-94-44; Fax: (031) 30-08-08. Closed December 18–January 14. ₤160,000.

▶ **La Pergola.** 22021 **Pescallo.** Tel: (031) 95-02-63. Closed November–February. ₤51,000.

▶ **San Marino.** Via Regina Nuova 64, 22010 **Laglio.** Tel: (031) 40-03-83. ₤56,000.

▶ **Santandrea Golf Hotel.** Via Como 19, 22030 **Montorfano.** Tel: (031) 20-02-20. Closed January 10–February 10. ₤175,000; half board ₤170,000.

▶ **Villa d'Este.** Via Regina 40, 22012 **Cernobbio.** Tel: (031) 51-14-71; Fax: (031) 51-20-27. In U.S., Tel: (800) 223-6800 or (212) 838-3110; Fax: (212) 758-7367. In U.K., Tel: (0800) 18-11-23; Fax: (071) 353-1904. Open March–November. ₤480,000–₤640,000.

Lago di Garda

▶ **Baia d'Oro.** Villa, 25084 **Gargnano.** Tel: (0365) 711-71; Fax: (0365) 725-68. ₤84,000; half board ₤110,000.

▶ **Hotel Broglia.** Via G. Piana 36, 25019 **Sirmione.** Tel: (030) 91-61-72; Fax: (030) 91-65-86. Open March 28–November 8. ₤200,000; half board ₤150,000.

▶ **Pensione Giulia.** 25084 **Gargnano.** Tel: (0365) 710-22; Fax: (0365) 727-74. Open April–October. ₤130,000; half board ₤110,000.

▶ **Grand Hotel.** Via Zanardelli 72, 25083 **Gardone Riviera.** Tel: (0365) 202-61; Fax: (0365) 226-95. ₤300,000; half board ₤200,000.

▶ **Grand Hotel Fasano.** 25080 **Fasano/Gardone Riviera.**

Tel: (0365) 210-51; Fax: (0365) 210-54. Open May–October. ₤269,000; half board ₤147,000.

▶ **Grand Hotel Terme**. Viale Marconi 7, 25019 **Sirmione**. Tel: (030) 91-62-61; Fax: (030) 91-65-68. In U.S., (800) 223-9832 or Tel: (212) 599-8280; Fax: (212) 559-1755. Open April 16–October 25. ₤370,000; half board ₤280,000.

▶ **Hotel Ideal**. Via Catullo 31, 25019 **Sirmione**. Tel: (030) 990-42-43. ₤120,000; half board ₤115,000.

▶ **Hotel Laurin**. Viale Landi 9, 25087 **Salò**. Tel: (0365) 220-22; Fax: (0365) 223-82. Closed December 20–January 20. ₤210,000; half board ₤165,000.

▶ **Locanda San Vigilio**. 37016 **Punta di San Vigilio** (Garda). Tel: (045) 725-66-88. Open mid-March–November. ₤300,000 with breakfast.

▶ **Montefiore**. 25083 **Gardone Riviera**. Tel: (0365) 211-18; Fax: (0365) 214-88. Closed November. ₤130,000; half board ₤95,000.

▶ **Hotel Sirmione**. Piazza Castello, 25019 **Sirmione**. Tel: (030) 91-63-31; Fax: (030) 91-65-58. In U.S., (800) 223-9832 or Tel: (212) 599-8280; Fax: (212) 559-1755. Open April–October. ₤156,000; half board ₤140,000.

▶ **Villa Cortine Palace Hotel**. Via Grotte 12, 25019 **Sirmione**. Tel: (030) 91-60-21; Fax: (030) 91-63-90. Open March 25–October 25. ₤400,000; apartments ₤800,000.

▶ **Villa Fiordaliso**. Corso Zanardelli 132, 25083 **Gardone Riviera**. Tel: (0365) 201-58; Fax: (0365) 29-00-11. Closed January 7–February 10. Double rooms and half board only: ₤350,000 for two.

Lago Maggiore

▶ **Albergo Italia e Svizzera**. Piazza Imbarcadero, 28049 **Stresa**. Tel: (0323) 305-40; Fax: (0323) 326-21. ₤102,000.

▶ **Del Lago**. Località Carmine Inferiore S, 28052 **Cannobio**. Tel: (0323) 705-95; Fax: same. Closed January 20–March 1 and November 11–December 7. ₤70,000.

▶ **Del Sole**. 21020 **Ranco**. Tel: (0331) 97-65-07; Fax: (0331) 97-66-20. ₤240,000; half board ₤190,000.

▶ **Grand Hotel Des Iles Borromées**. Lungolago Umberto I 67, 28049 **Stresa**. Tel: (0323) 304-31; Fax: (0323) 324-05. ₤381,000; half board ₤363,000.

▶ **Hotel Majestic**. Via Vittorio Veneto 32, 28048 **Pallanza-Verbania**. Tel: (0323) 50-43-05; Fax: (0323) 50-63-79. Open Easter–October. ₤220,000; half board ₤150,000.

▶ **Milan e Speranza au Lac**. Piazza Imbarcadero, 28049 **Stresa**. Tel: (0323) 311-90; Fax: (0323) 327-29. Open April–October 28. ₤150,000; half board ₤110,000.

▶ **Hotel Moderno**. Via Cavour 33, 28049 **Stresa**. Tel: (0323)

304-68; Fax: (0323) 315-37. Open March–October. ₤90,000; half board ₤80,000.

► **Regina Palace**. Lungolago Umberto I 27, 28049 **Stresa**. Tel: (0323) 301-71; Fax: (0323) 301-76. In U.S., Tel: (800) 223-5695 or (914) 833-3303. Closed January. ₤240,000; half board ₤210,000.

► **Hotel Verbano**. 28049 **Isola dei Pescatori**. Tel: (0323) 304-08; Fax: (0323) 331-29. Closed January and February. ₤125,000; half board ₤110,000.

► **Villaminta**. Strada Statale del Sempione 123, 28049 **Stresa**. Tel: (0323) 324-44; Fax: (0323) 324-47. Open April 7–November 15. ₤200,000; half board ₤170,000.

Lago d'Orta

► **Giardinetto**. 28028 **Pettenasco**. Tel: (0323) 892-19; Fax: same. Open April–October. ₤115,000; half board ₤100,000.

► **Orta**. 28016 **Orta San Giulio**. Tel: (0322) 902-53; Fax: (0322) 90-56-46. Open April–October. ₤100,000; half board ₤90,000.

► **San Rocco**. Via Gippini da Verona 11, 28016 **Orta San Giulio**. Tel: (0322) 90-56-32; Fax: (0322) 90-56-35. In U.S., Tel: (800) 631-7373 or (908) 273-7373. ₤320,000; half board ₤260,000.

► **Al Sorriso**. 28018 **Soriso**. Tel: (0322) 98-32-28; Fax: (0322) 98-33-28. ₤130,000–₤190,000; half board ₤190,000.

PIEDMONT

By Bill Marsano

Bill Marsano travels regularly to Italy. The author of two books, he is the recipient of a Lowell Thomas Travel Writing Award for his mazagine article on the Columbus landfall controversy, which he wrote as a contributing editor of Condé Nast Traveler *magazine.*

Piedmont (Piemonte), high in Italy's northwest, derives its name quite simply from *ai piedi del monte* (at the feet of the mountains). From almost every vantage point in Piedmont you can see the snow-peaked barrier of the Alps. The vivid green of Piedmont's fields and orchards makes a starker contrast with the snows beyond than you would find in, say, Switzerland because the region basks in a southern sun. It was this verdant prospect that whetted the appetites of the barbarian hordes who laid waste to Imperial Rome, and it lured the armies of the north that were later to descend in the Middle Ages and the Renaissance.

The rolling hills of the Langhe and Monferrato regions on the eastern side of the region are still studded with castles and abbeys, but they now also produce some of the best wines in Italy. The once fearsome mountains have long since opened up to well-known ski resorts—in Sestriere, west of Turin near the French border, and a dozen other places—and for nature lovers they hold the flora and fauna of the Parco Nazionale del Gran Paradiso in the Valle d'Aosta.

Piedmont is a province rich in every way, and its beauties include the sheltered tranquillity of its lakes, which range from the intimate beauty of Orta to the splendid expanse of Lago Maggiore (both covered in the Lake Country chapter). But the province is especially rich for lovers of Baroque architecture, fine paintings, and good food. Available in varying degrees throughout the province, they come together in splendid abundance at Turin, its capital.

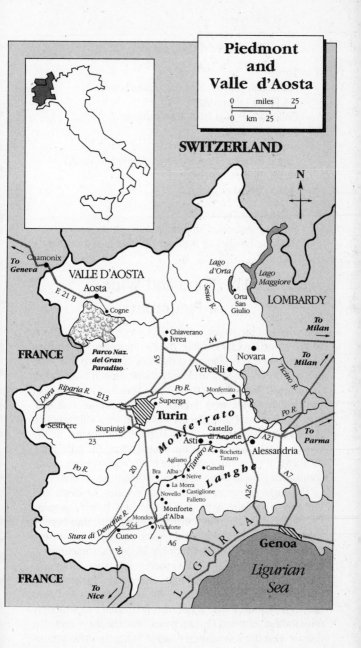

Piedmont
and
Valle d'Aosta

0 miles 25
0 km 25

SWITZERLAND

N

To Geneva
Chamonix

VALLE D'AOSTA
E 21 B
Aosta
Cogne

Lago d'Orta
Sesia R.
Orta San Giulio
Lago Maggiore

LOMBARDY

To Milan

Chiaverano
Ivrea
A4

Novara

To Milan

FRANCE

Parco Naz. del Gran Paradiso

A5

Vercelli

Ticino R.

Dora Riparia R. E13

Po R.
Monferrato
Superga

Turin

Monferrato

To Parma

Sestriere
Stupinigi

23

Asti

Castello di Annone
A21
Alessandria

Rochetta Tanaro

Po R.

Agliano
Canelli

20

Bra
Alba
Neive

Tanaro R.

Langhe

A26

Po R.

La Morra
Novello
Castiglione
Falletto

Monforte d'Alba

A7

Stura di Demonte R.
Mondovì
564
Vicoforte

Cuneo

A6

20

LIGURIA

Genoa

FRANCE

To Nice

Ligurian Sea

MAJOR INTEREST

Food and wine
Sestriere ski resort
Parco Nazionale del Gran Paradiso

Turin
Piazza San Carlo (cafés, Baroque churches)
Via Roma (shopping)
Galleria Sabauda (major art museum)
Museo Egizio
Museo Civico d'Arte Antica
Cappella della Sacra Sindone (Shroud of Turin)
Museo dell'Automobile
Museo del Risorgimento

Environs of Turin
Baroque palace of Stupinigi
Baroque Basilica di Superga (Pantheon of the Savoys)

The Food and Wine
of Piedmont

The wines of Piedmont, particularly the reds, are excellent, and the food isn't far behind. The Piedmontese are less than pleased when it is suggested that this excellence might be the result of their to a proximity to the French border, but there might be a hint of truth in the assumption. François I was drinking wine from French vineyards in the 16th century, and the Nebbiolo grapes, which farther south produce Barolo and Barbaresco, begin right at the frontier in the French-speaking enclave of the Valle d'Aosta. The hills of the southeast also produce the white truffles and porcini mushrooms that play so large a part in Piedmontese cuisine.

The most common of the region's wines, Dolcetto and Barbera, are relatively modest in price and hearty company for much of the country cuisine. Red wine is king here—robust, deep in color, and nearly endless in variety. Barbaresco and Barolo lord it over all others, sometimes at considerable expense, and there are also Ghemme, Gattinara, Carema, and Nebbiolo, among many others. If you decide to splurge on a bottle of noble lineage you will want one by a producer who is not merely reliable but genuinely outstanding. Ratti and Ceretto wines head the list of reds that deliver what the wine expert Sharron McCarthy calls "visions of heaven."

Simon & Schuster's Guide to Italian Wines by Burton

Anderson comes into its own in a place like Piedmont as a helpful pointer to the region's best. But in fact you can choose almost blindly, for here, as in Tuscany, getting a bad wine isn't easy. That makes it a pleasure to experiment and trust to luck. Many towns have small enotecas selling the wines of local vintners, sometimes those of a single vintner. (In that case the wine you taste before buying is likely to be sold to you by the man who made it, or at least a member of his family. Shopping in an ordinary liquor store at home will never be the same.)

From the vineyards around Asti come the best of the whites. For decades Italians all over the world have been celebrating special occasions with bubbling Asti Spumante, but—though the town remains a wine capital—tastes have changed. For younger generations drier whites are in favor, and the growers here have produced one, Gavi, that is pale, dry, and delicious when served chilled. It appears in most restaurants and is a name to remember. In time, it may develop to the point where it ranks among the best of Italy's wines. Another very promising white is the delightful and relatively new Arneis, which Ceretto has developed with great success from a grape variety formerly used only for blending. Also, the sparkling white Moscato d'Asti is worth trying. Like Asti Spumante it is a festive wine, low in alcohol (as little as 5 percent), and sweet but not sticky and cloying. When served in the traditional *coppa,* a wide-mouthed goblet, it releases generous wafts of the richly perfumed Moscato (Muscat) grape.

The cooking of Piedmont—both the dishes inherited from France and those offered by local Italian tradition—goes well with its wines. In the first category are the varieties of fondue—here called *fonduta*—made with the local Fontina cheese and often served with a grating of white truffles. There is also *sivé,* derived from the French civet of rabbit or game. From the Piedmontese countryside come minestrones of fresh vegetables; polenta, which is served with many main courses; and the region's favorite pasta, *agnolotti*—a form of large ravioli. Gnocchi are another favorite; so is the *bollito misto* of boiled meats and chicken served all over northern Italy, with *salsa verde* and other condiments.

Wine is often used in the cooking: red, for example, with braised veal, and white in the savory risottos. The desserts are often laced with the nuts of the mountains, whether in tarts or *amaretti,* and often contain apples and pears from the local orchards. Many of the cakes and pastries are examples of the Austrian and Swiss bitter-chocolate tradition.

Torrone, the soft honey and almond mixture often found in American and British specialty stores, is a Piedmont confection. After dinner a frothy *zabaglione* of egg yolks, sugar, and Marsala honors its founder, San Giovanni Bayon, patron saint of pastry chefs.

Dining in Piedmont

There is no reason to wait for this fine fare until you reach Turin; on every road leading to the capital there are restaurants that would merit a detour if they weren't already in the path. Coming from Chamonix you pass through the ancient Roman town of **Aosta**, encircled by dramatic mountain peaks. In its center is the superb **Cavallo Bianco**, at via Aubert 15, where the wines are Valdostana and the cuisine is an excellent introduction to what lies ahead. A random choice might include *agnolotti* stuffed with foie gras and wild mushrooms, or tournedos cooked in red *pinot,* served with gnocchi made of polenta. (Tel: 0165-36-22-14; closed Sunday evening, Mondays, October, and November.)

For those driving up from Nice on route S 20, the particularly charming arcaded town of **Cuneo** near the border offers two fine possibilities. One is the thoroughly Italian **Tre Citroni**—with *fondutas,* risottos, and fresh salmon—at via Bonelli 2 (Tel: 0171-620-48; closed Wednesdays and two weeks in June and September). The other is the more Provençal **Le Plat d'Etain**, at corso Giolitti 18 (Tel: 0171-68-19-18; closed Sundays).

If you enter from Parma and the east, you will come through **Asti**, a medieval town famed not only for its wines but also for its poet, Vittorio Alfieri. Asti will welcome you at the **Gener Neuv**, lungo Tanaro 4, with an (expensive) avalanche of antipasto, fresh trout, and rabbit brewed in Barbaresco (Tel: 0141-572-70; closed Sunday evening, Mondays, and August). The **Falcon Vecchio**, at via San Secondo 8 (Tel: 0141-531-06) is another good, less expensive choice (closed Sunday evening, Mondays, and August). The entrances from the northeast pass the lakes, which have a world of restaurants all their own (covered in the Lake Country chapter).

In the countryside around Asti you can experience Piemontese cooking while staying at a country inn, **Il Cascinale Nuovo**, where tradition and modern taste are honored in decor and dining. There are only 13 rooms and 7 suites, so reserve well in advance. From there you can visit **La Fioraia**, in Castello di Annone, about 7 miles away (via Mondo 26, Tel: 0141-40-11-06; closed Mondays and July 18 to August 7), for perhaps a fresh asparagus risotto and a roast with a pastry crust. At **Il Martinetto** in Rocchetta Tanaro (via N. Sardi 4, Tel: 0141-140-30), you can enjoy meals created from their own farm's products. Nearby farms, called *aziende,* welcome visitors who want to enjoy a snack (*merenda*) or to buy their products: **Azienda Agricola Milin**, Frazione San Marzanotto (reserve; Tel: 0141-349-16); **Azienda Scarampi**, via Crena 2, Agliano (Tel: 0141-95-45-56); and **Azienda Cornero**, Località Regione Aie, Canelli (reserve; Tel: 0141-83-16-43).

Several hotels of unusual charm dot the hills near Asti. The converted convent, **Locanda del Sant'Uffizio**, has secularized outrageously, adding a swimming pool, tennis courts, and good food. Nearby, to the northeast at Monferrato, the stylish 11-room **Castello di San Giorgio**, of tenth-century vintage, is imposingly pink amid green parkland, and serves truffles with abandon.

Piedmont's largest truffle market is held in **Alba**, southwest of Asti, on Saturdays during October, November, and December.

Pastry in Alba is not hard to find. Some of the finest is at **Pettiti**, via Vittoria Emanuele 25, and **Io . . . tu . . . e i dolci** (You and I and the Desserts), piazza Savona 12, where chocolate-covered hazelnut truffles are the sweet of record.

Near Alba in Neive, spend a night at the delightful **La Contea**, where Tonino Verro and his wife, Claudia (who is also the chef), have created an inn-restaurant that makes guests decide to return as soon as they arrive (assuming a healthy credit line). Menus may include a vegetable flan with fonduta cheese, agnolotti with braised beef, and several other courses if you opt for the *menu degustazione*. The terra-cotta floors and tiles and the woodburning fireplaces— accompanied by homemade grappa after dinner— are not a bad setting for after-dinner musings. (Most rooms face the street, and so noise can be a problem, but additional rooms are being prepared in another house nearby.)

TURIN

Turin (Torino) shares with Genoa, in Liguria to the south, a distinctive paradox: Both are large, much-visited cities that are nevertheless little known to travellers in general and Americans in particular. The paradox dissolves when it is realized that most visitors—vast shoals of them every year— come bearing briefcases, not guidebooks. They are business-people and these are business cities. The happy result is that both cities retain a thoroughly Italian atmosphere, while

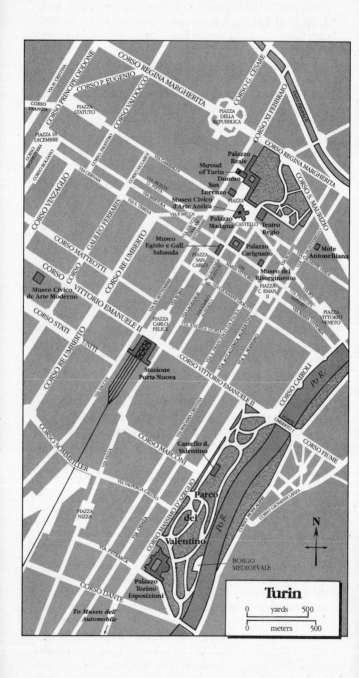

Turin

| 0 | yards | 500 |
| 0 | meters | 500 |

Rome, for example, has become an international center and Florence an international art school.

Turin means not only business but manufacturing as well. That, too, has led some visitors to dismiss it, as if it were a factory town. The factories are there all right, Fiat and Pirelli among them, but far enough from the center of town to leave undisturbed one of the most sumptuous Baroque cities to be found anywhere. The heart of the old town has not changed much since the 18th century, when Charles de Brosses called it the "most beautiful city in Italy—if not in Europe—thanks to the planning of its streets and the proportion of its buildings."

Planning and proportion are what strike you when arriving at Porta Nuova, a train station with an air of sober confectionary, like all great 19th-century rail terminals. Emerging from the station, you see the effects of this planning immediately in the gracious **piazza Carlo Felice**, with its contoured *giardino* of greensward, trees, and flowers embraced by arcades of shops, restaurants, and cafés. This "garden" is strewn with benches; it is a place to sit and marvel at the day, to take repose. It affords a fine view down the via Roma, through the gray colonnades of the Mussolini years to the arcaded expanse of **piazza San Carlo** beyond, with its end-to-end café tables, some with upholstered chairs outside. Most piazzas elsewhere were principally places of assembly, gritty public spaces where the citizenry, on its feet, confronted the prospect of new taxes, sieges, or plagues; many retain that air today. Turin's civilized piazzas are open-air living rooms whose calm survives even the din of traffic.

There is proportion of structure as well. Turin is a low-built city, in human scale, and as Mark Twain noted, a spacious one: "In the matter of roominess it transcends anything that was ever dreamed of before, I fancy. It sits in the middle of a vast dead-level, and one is obliged to imagine that land may be had for the asking." This much is the legacy of its ducal past; add the prosperity of modern commerce and the smart shops and smart dressing that follow, and the result is a pleasing atmosphere of eager serenity, of quiet vivacity in the soft, slightly misty air of spring and fall—the seasons that show Turin to its best advantage. (Winter brings iron winds down from the mountains; in summer the mistiness from the nearby River Po is all heat and clinging humidity.)

The Torinese become irritated with the tired accusation that their town is the "most Italian city of France," but in fact Turin was once the capital of the ducal House of Savoy, and the Savoy territories included much of present-day France—

not just Savoy, but Nice and the Côte d'Azur as well. Much of Turin was built during the long reign of Louis XIV (whose Continental dominance in matters of taste was bound to have a heavy effect upon the city's appearance). As with the building of St. Petersburg, leading architects were called in from outside. The Baroque was a very viable regal style, used from Naples to Stockholm, so it is natural that in the border state of Piedmont we should find echoes of Fischer von Erlach in Vienna; the brothers Assam in Munich; and Mansart in France. One of the pleasures of Turin is the quest that takes place within your own memory for the places of which it is reminiscent.

During the 17th and 18th centuries Turin was fortunate to engage the services of three very imaginative architects. The most Francophile of the three was the count of Castellamonte, to whom we owe the royal palace, the **Castello del Valentino** (which would be at home in the Ile de France), and the design of the piazza San Carlo. The Castello del Valentino is located in the extraordinarily beautiful Parco del Valentino on the banks of the Po south of the Duomo. Another attraction in the park is the **Borgo Medioevale**, with authentic reconstructions of medieval Piedmont buildings. Within the Castello keep, the restaurant **San Giorgio**'s riverside terrace is all candlelight and flowers at night (viale E. Millo 6; closed Tuesdays and August; Tel: 011-669-21-31).

During his long life (1550–1640) the count had much to do with the planning of the capital (which involved the destruction of most of medieval Turin), and its streets are as rectilinear and clear-cut as those of the *bastides* of Périgord or of Richelieu in the Val de Loire. The scale of construction became even grander after the arrival of the Sicilian Filippo Juvarra, an architect of the Rococo who had been assistant to Carlos Fontana in Rome. He was called to Turin in 1714, barely a year after the ruling house had graduated from ducal to royal. Juvarra, who earlier in his career had devoted much time to theatrical design, knew just how to celebrate this augmentation: with the Palazzo Madama, which cleverly masks one side of the medieval **Castello** on the enormous piazza Castello (the other sides are a shock of all brutal military masonry, accentuated with the bronze statuary of war memorials); with the **Basilica di Superga**, just above Turin, the so-called Pantheon of the House of Savoy; with the churches on the piazza San Carlo; and best of all, at **Stupinigi**. Here, on the outskirts of Turin, he was called upon to design a royal hunting lodge, and the resulting palace reminds us that Versailles was born the same way. The *palazzina* at Stupinigi is one of the most dynamic concepts in Baroque art: a domed, centrifugal pavilion with the wings jutting out like the arms of a windmill.

The most original of the three architects was a monk from Modena, Guarino Guarini, who arrived in 1666. In a class with Bramante and Bernini, he has been hailed as the most adventurous architect of his period. His extraordinary church cupolas distinctively mark the silhouette of the center of town, while the wavelike contours and geometrically patterned courts of his **Palazzo Carignano** make it far and away the most remarkable of Turin's royal residences. (The palace now houses the Museo del Risorgimento; see below.)

Turin on Foot

The architectural district of Turin can easily be explored on foot, and it is with delight that the walker discovers how very well the concepts of its original planners have worked out. No wonder Turin was Napoléon's favorite Italian city. His love of law and order in civic planning was shown clearly enough by what he did to the piazza San Marco in Venice, but here that order is tempered to serve the convenience and leisure of the citizens. In cool weather the cafés on the piazza San Carlo offer relaxing interiors typical of the time of Stendhal; in warm weather the cafés spill out onto the square. Many of the streets are pedestrians-only; the graceful arches that enclose the old quarter frame views of the hills and mountains beyond while giving a perspective within that is worthy of De Chirico. The main streets for elegant shopping, such as the **via Roma**, are arcaded or colonnaded, so you can stroll in shaded leisure and linger in front of the windows that feature Gucci, Armani, Ferragamo, and the usual lot. This neighborhood offers two things in convenient tandem for most visitors: museums and restaurants.

Of the former, two of the most notable are contained in the huge 17th-century Palazzo dell'Accademia delle Scienze on the piazza San Carlo. The **Galleria Sabauda** (via Accademia delle Scienze 6) is one of the finest art galleries in Italy, its collections having been built around those of the House of Savoy—from which it gets its name—and later much expanded. Its Italian Renaissance paintings are of high quality—from Fra Angelico to Botticelli. But so are its Flemish paintings: Memling, van der Weyden, a gem of a Van Eyck of Saint Francis, Rubens, and the well-known series of Van Dyck portraits of the family of England's Charles I. (Open 9:00 A.M. to 2:00 P.M. Tuesday, Thursday, and weekends; 2:30 to 7:00 P.M. Wednesday and Friday; closed Mondays.)

Downstairs from the Sabauda is the **Museo Egizio** (Egyptian Museum), second only to that in Cairo. It is here thanks to a series of circumstances that began with the fervid collecting that followed Napoléon's Egyptian campaigns. The collection includes tombs, small temples, papyruses, murals, and wooden sculptures that are a miracle of preservation.

Painting is by no means confined to the Sabauda. The picture that is perhaps the most precious of all—a small portrait of a man in red by Antonello da Messina—is in the **Museo Civico d'Arte Antica**, along with a fine gathering of Tuscan and Piedmontese primitives. The Civico is installed in Turin's former medieval Castello on the piazza Castello. It is currently closed for restoration.

When Christine of France retired to the castello as a widow it became known as the **Palazzo Madama**. To enter it you pass through Juvarra's façade (assuming, with a great deal of optimism, that the restorations have been completed on time) and beneath his magnificent staircase. The museum's interior remains that of the castello, however, and the result is somewhere between the Cluny Museum in Paris and the Isabella Stewart Gardner Museum in Boston: medieval furnishings, sculpture, and woodwork, much of it collected by the prominent Torinese Azeglio family.

More paintings are to be found in the **Palazzo Reale** on the same square. A guided visit is required for the royal palace, which contains a huge collection of armor and some splendid 18th-century chinoiserie rooms.

Almost part of the Palazzo Reale is the **Duomo**, the cathedral of Turin. Most of the structure is Renaissance, the dry work of severe Tuscan architects, but to its original dome Guarini added his own, the fantastic **Cappella della Sacra Sindone**, a chapel built to house the **Shroud of Turin**, the treasured cloth said to have enfolded Christ when he was taken from the cross and believed to bear his image. (The relic's authenticity, however, has recently been denied by the Catholic Church.) The altar shelters the shroud beneath a blaze of Baroque gold statuary; the chapel itself, lined in black marble, is surmounted by Guarini's splendid cupola. Built on receding rings of lithe, segmental arches, each of which springs lightly from the keystone of the arch below it, it has sinuous lines that seem to anticipate the forms of Antonio Gaudí in Barcelona centuries later. Another Guarini cupola, this one vigorous and muscular, can be found around the corner at **San Lorenzo**—probably his most perfect church.

Turin's most unusual building—and some say its ugliest—
is the **Mole Antonelliana**, an eclectic 19th-century horror
show near the Po on via Montebello. The building was begun
as a synagogue more than a century ago, and taken over by the
city in mid-construction. Its design is a grab bag of Classical
elements, cast-iron bravado, and whatnots. From its base, a
pyramid with arched sides, to the star at its tip, the tall needle
of a spire resembles an upended ice-cream cone interrupted
by balconies and a couple of double-decker Greek temples.
The view from the spire's lookout is superb, at least in part
because it is one of the few in which this grotesquerie does
not offend the horizon.

Dining in Turin

Luckily for your feet, this monumental section of Turin is
replete with cafés and restaurants. The opera house—**Il
Teatro Regio**—demands them. Near the Regio, at piazza
Castello 29, is the most famous of Turin's vintage cafés,
Baratti & Milano (Tel: 011-54-59-92), with a side entrance
under a glass-covered galleria that could have been sent
down from 1900 Vienna. The pastries served with its
cappuccinos could have been sent from Vienna, too, and the
café's interior, sparkling with mirrors, painted glass, and
chandeliers, has been carefully kept within its period. Turin
produces most of Italy's aperitifs: the vermouths—Martini
and Cinzano—and Carpano. But as elsewhere in the north
there are many who prefer a cold glass of sparkling white
wine, a *frizzante*.

The cheeses of the region are superb; ask for *formaggio
locale* (locally made cheeses) at **Toja**, via Torino 48.

With regard to their restaurants, the Torinese show all the
enthusiasm—and fickleness—of their French neighbors. The
best places are by no means the most expensive, while
some of the staid and starred have become slack in service
and negligent in cuisine and have been replaced by newer
favorites. One of the liveliest of these is the **Montecarlo**, via
San Francesco da Paola 37, within a stone's throw of the via
Carlo Alberto and the Sabauda. At lunchtime its bright arcaded interior is thronged with a clientele partaking of Piedmontese cuisine treated with a light touch: *risotto alla
parmigiana;* civet with polenta; *fonduta;* or brains *al burro
fuso (au beurre noir)*. To start, have a delectable spinach
mousse, and for dessert, a coffee *zabayon*. For wine you
might consider a chilled white Gavi San Pietro. (Tel: 011-83-
08-15; closed Saturday lunch and Sundays.)

Some of Turin's more venerable restaurants *have* kept

their standards, and, cuisine apart, their interiors are a treat. Situated in a town that has done wonders to retain its turn-of-the-century heritage, they offer the same elegance that patrons of that period expected. One, the charming and rather expensive **Due Lampioni** (Tel: 011-839-74-09), is right on the via Carlo Alberto, at number 45 (closed Sundays). Opposite, at **Balbo** (via Andrea Doria 11; Tel: 011-812-75-42; closed Mondays) the food outdoes the decor; but another seat of old elegance, the **Vecchia Lanterna**, is at corso Re Umberto 21, not far from the main train station (Tel: 011-53-70-47; closed Saturday lunch and Sundays). At all three a full dinner for one will seriously damage a $100 bill—before wine.

Very convenient and different in decor are the trattorias. Not that they are rowdy or rustic by any means; their largely young clientele is stylishly dressed, the service is efficient, and the pasta and house wines are dependable. One of the best is the **Vittoria** (via Carlo Alberto 34; Tel: 011-54-19-23; closed Sundays and Monday lunch). These places are not only near the museums, they are also in the district of the Stazione Porta Nuova. Perhaps the best trattoria, a favorite of the Torinese *buongustaio* and wine consultant Francesco Battuello, is **Dai Saletti** (via Belfiore 37, near the church of Santa Cuore; Tel: 011-68-78-67), while the most *caratteristico,* in blue-collar terms, may be **Ristorante da Carla e Marcella** (via Conte verde 4, no phone). It's plain; homely but homey. Wine buffs may be tempted by the Rosatello, seldom seen. But don't succumb—take the reliable Dolcetto instead; it's made by the waiter's uncle. Italians do wonders with produce, so **Il Punto Verde** (via Belfiore 15; Tel: 011-650-45-14) will serve vegetarians well and perhaps even win converts to the cause.

Staying in Turin

Some of the most luxurious hotels, usually filled with European executives, also are located near the station—among them the traditional **Turin Palace** and two hotels of the Jolly chain, the luxurious **Principi di Piemonte** and the modern **Ligure**. The newly redecorated **Victoria**, small and stylish, is nearby.

Less expensive is the **Bramante**, near the auto museum. A good choice in the moderate range might be any of the five Best Westerns: The **Stazione e Genova** and the **Genio** flank the station; the **Gran Mogol**, **Piemontese**, and **Boston** are nearby. There's even a sixth—the **Crimea**—across the Po (see below).

Shopping in Turin

In many cities the neighborhoods surrounding central railroad stations are polluted and shabby, if not dangerous. In Turin, although the station is hardly a garden spot, it is less depressing than most. But don't let its fine 1868 façade, or the charming view of the *giardino* and piazza Carlo Felice, distract you from protecting your wallet.

As the via Roma runs from the Porta Nuova to the Palazzo Reale it passes through a gamut of styles. The bazaar of cafés and street vendors of Carlo Felice is soon exchanged for the cool elegance of some of the most expensive shops to be found anywhere, and for the first few blocks of the avenue they are ensconced under Mussolini's monolithic columns. The columns terminate in the small piazza C.L.N., which almost functions as an anteroom to the piazza San Carlo.

For the Merino wool items now in demand, go to **FACIT**, via Monte di Pietà and via Viotti.

Turin's many annual fairs, including the widely attended auto show, are to be avoided at all costs because of their effect on hotel space, but a permanent museum like the **Museo dell'Automobile**—which to lovers of art and history might sound like a festival of boredom—displays the degree of originality that the Italians had long before Nervi. A family such as the Bugatti included artists in many areas. The museum, which is just south of the Parco del Valentino at corso Unità d'Italia 40, even got its hands on the Isotta Fraschini used by Gloria Swanson in the film *Sunset Boulevard*. Open 9:00 A.M. to 12:30 P.M. and 3:00 to 7:00 P.M.; closed Mondays.

Museo del Risorgimento

Of all the museums in Turin, the one that surprises the visitor most with its excellence is the Museo del Risorgimento, fittingly located in Guarini's Palazzo Carignano (via Accademia delle Scienze 5), which saw the birth both of Italy's first king from the House of Savoy, Vittorio Emanuele II, and of its first parliament. From its name you would gather that the museum deals with the movement that led to the unification of Italy, but in reality it goes far beyond that and emerges as a matchless résumé, in documents, letters, reconstructed rooms, and paintings (some of them very well known), of the country's history from 1709 on. The year 1709 was the date of the Battle of Torino, when Eugène de Savoie Carignan defeated the French troops of Louis XIV in the War of the Spanish Succession—the beginning of the end of foreign rule on the peninsula.

The victorious Eugène's House of Savoy remained in power until 1946, when by plebiscite the royal family was voted into exile (whether or not the ballot boxes were stuffed by the ever-energetic Communist Party depends on which Italian you are talking to, and where).

The museum is open from 9:00 A.M. to 6:30 P.M., Sundays 9:00 A.M. to 12:30 P.M.; closed Mondays and holidays.

AROUND TURIN
Restaurants and Enotecas

The **Villa Sassi–El Toulà**, about a mile east of Turin, is the place to stay if you prefer the country. A 17th-century villa with its original fireplaces and marble floors, Villa Sassi also houses a restaurant that is part of the famous El Toulà group, with a wine cellar of 90,000 bottles in case you're thirsty.

The town of **Bra**, about 40 km (25 miles) southeast of Turin, has its own version of special effects: At the church of Santa Chiara you can look through a skylight to a paradise of angels. The **Arcangelo** restaurant, on a hill above the town, is housed in a splendid 19th-century villa whose terrace hovers over the Langhe hills. The cooking is down to earth, however, both robust and refined, with white truffles the prize (Strada San Michele 28; Tel: 0172-42-21-63; closed Wednesdays).

A scenically tortuous road from Bra leads to the restaurant **Belvedere** in La Morra. An aerie above the valley, it is redolent with scents of game, herbs, pâtés, and polenta, with grappa an appropriate ending to the feast—and very reasonably priced (piazza Castello 5; Tel: 0173-501-90; closed Sunday evening, Mondays, January and February).

Many Langhe district wineries and enotecas are open for visits. For a complete listing, contact the regional wine centers at Barolo, Tel: (0173) 56-277; Grinzane Cavour, Tel: (0173) 62-159; and Barbaresco, Tel: (0713) 635-251. The best bets are the enotecas: Welcoming the public is their business, so you can be sure of not presuming on anyone's hospitality. Enotecas come in all sizes. Typical is **La Morra's**, a few yards from the excellent Ristorante Belvedere. This one represents numerous local producers (pick up the brochure that shows walking paths through the vineyards, then take a short hike with a picnic lunch). A few steps away is the **Vinbar**, a corner center for wine, gossip, and espresso, favored by the Ratti clan and other winemakers.

Less typical but entirely charming is the enoteca of **Sergio**

Giudice at piazza Umberto I 15 in **Serralunga d'Alba**, an exemplar of the concentric defensive design of medieval hill towns. Sergio represents only his own wines: He doesn't export; he is not a national, let alone an international, force. But he is a lifelong professional winemaker whose Barolo and Nebbiolo del Piemonte are fine, honest wines at good prices. A visit with such a craftsman—your few words of Italian complementing his few of English—helps explain why wine buffs say "the bottle is just the beginning."

At **Monforte d'Alba**, about 60 km (38 miles) south of Turin, the **Giardino da Felicin** is a small country inn that provides superb meals (Tel: 0173-782-25; closed Sunday evening, Mondays, and January). Eight km (5 miles) south of **Alba**, near Bra, is the **Enoteca Regionale di Grinzane Cavour**, the principal wine-tasting enoteca of Piedmont (Tel: 0173-26-21-59); Camillo di Cavour, Italy's first prime minister, lived in this 13th-century castle. Its trattoria features regional specialties, adding the scent of hare and truffles to the wine-rich air.

See "The Hill Towns of Piedmont" (below) for more on this area south of Turin.

Outdoor Activities

The **Parco Nazionale del Gran Paradiso**, once the preserve of the Savoys, stretches from near Ivrea, 50 km (32 miles) north of Turin, across the regional border into **Valle d'Aosta** and west into France. Chamois and ibex occasionally sprint past the hiker in the brilliant Alpine scenery, and a choice array of flowers brightens the meadows. While enjoying the park stay at the **Bellevue** hotel in **Cogne**, where garden, sauna, and pub all conspire to soothe city nerves. It's open mainly in the summer. The **Petit Hotel** is less expensive and has a garden, tennis courts, and amiable staff; it's open all year.

Sestriere, west of Turin on the French border, is part of a skiing network that encompasses hundreds of slopes. Snow machines ensure a white terrain, and an assortment of cable cars and ski lifts provide ascent and wonderful views. Hotels range from the scenic **Grand Hotel Sestriere** and the **Principi di Piemonte**, each in its own park, to less extravagant rooms with views at the **Sud-Ovest**. To soothe the wind-burned palette, the **Last Tango Grill**, via La Glesia 5 (Tel: 0122-763-37; closed Tuesdays and November), skewers snails in Cognac, whirls taglione in lemon sauce, and roasts lamb. An Alpine cheese and herb pie is the thing for a lighter snack. Sestriere is probably the liveliest of the resorts, by night as well as by day. All levels of almost all sports, winter and summer, are to be enjoyed here.

The Hill Towns of Piedmont

South of Turin lie the sweeping landscapes of **Le Langhe** (La Langa, in dialect), the great font of the region's red wines, and **Roero**, a center of whites.

The capital of wine and white truffles in Le Langhe is **Alba**, a compact and handsome old valley town (about 45 km/28 miles from Turin) with a good hotel, the **Savona**, and too many good restaurants to mention—simply stroll along the via Vittorio Emanuele (known to locals as via Maestra) and pick one at random, or if you're willing to break the bank, stop at one of the stores selling the precious white truffles, which are far richer than the black truffles of Umbria (and more expensive: $70 an ounce and up). The best way to take these treasures home is packed in a jar filled with rice, which will absorb the powerful aroma and make a splendid risotto.

Stay in Alba or travel a few miles farther south to the hill town of **Novello**, which affords magnificent panoramas and has two attractive hotels, either of which would serve as a base for further explorations. The **Barbaduc** is a small but very modern hotel of only nine smallish but comfortable rooms built into an old house on the town's main street. (It also has a good restaurant and friendly staff.) A few yards away is Novello's crown—visible for miles around—**Al Castello da Diego**. This colossal pile is the result of a previous owner's restoration of a ruin on the site. As the ruin consisted solely of one ancient wall, the restorers had a free hand and they set to work with a will, if not the same degree of taste. What they produced is a towered and turreted masonry Victorian horror that looks like a red-brick fright wig (you can easily imagine Lucille Ball wearing something like this) or a castle from Charles Addams's Italian period. The rooms are spacious and filled with period furniture, in light and airy contrast to the Addamsian gloom of the "grand" main floor. You might want to pass on the restaurant: No matter how good it may be, it seats a thousand, and in this little-trafficked neck of the woods you'll probably be either totally alone or lost in a sea of 999 wedding guests.

From here launch a drive among the hill towns, which are plentiful and appealing. **Serralunga d'Alba; Monforte d'Alba; Roddi**, home of a "university" for truffle hounds (its graduates are so valuable that some have been dognapped); and many others, including **Castiglione Falletto**, home of the wine-making Cerettos and two very good restaurants, **Le Torri**, at piazza Vittorio Veneto 1 (Tel: 0173-629-55) and the **Gran Duca** (piazza del Centro 4, Tel: 0173-628-29). At the latter you must reserve (they buy only enough food for the guests they expect), and at both you'll dine well, with excellent wines.

Farther on, in the "deep south" of Piedmont, are other finds. **Mondoví** is a thriving small city in two parts. The lower section, called simply Breo, is merely modern, but the upper, older section, called Mondoví Piazza, has the great central piazza Maggiore, which still retains some of the sleepy, calm atmosphere of Italy in the early fifties. There are handsome churches that are worth seeing, as is the horizon-wide view from the **Giardino del Belvedere**.

Nearby is **Vicoforte**, which contains an enormous and impressive 16th- to 18th-century sanctuary church that towers over all around it. Its great oval dome and its interior are sumptuously decorated. A few miles away is **Bastia Mondoví**, where an attempt to see the small 11th- to 15th-century church of San Fiorenzo provides another taste of 1950s Italy. You'll find that few in the town have heard of San Fiorenzo, but if you go to the rear of the town's modern church, you'll be in piazza Monsignor Forzano. Ring the bell at number 2 and (with luck) someone will come down and simply hand you the key. San Fiorenzo is visible from the piazza, a tiny white thing about 3 km (2 miles) off. Simply follow the road out of the piazza, take the second fork to the right—and you're there. Almost. First you'll have to unlock the place (wind the key about six turns clockwise); then you'll have to grope for the light switches. You'll find them on the left wall of the side chapel to the left of the altar. A barely legible sign pleads with you not to turn all the switches on at once—if you do, you'll probably blow every fuse for miles around.

This little adventure alone is worth the detour; what you get when the lights are on is pure gravy: a stunning series of 51 frescoes, many in very good condition, in Late Gothic Provençal style. They cover both main walls and reach almost from floor to ceiling.

From here you can return north by meandering roads through innumerable other towns, or—if you're heading south to Liguria—take the road west to Cuneo and the thrilling crossing of the Alpine barrier.

GETTING AROUND

Alitalia's Volobus Torino connects Turin with Milan's Malpensa International Airport from spring to fall. It takes two hours each way and is very efficient: Train service from

Milan is good, but the necessary bus ride into Milan (up to an hour from Malpensa) and the possibility of not making perfect connections can double the travel time. From Milan and Rome, train connections are frequent to Turin and from Turin to Asti. From these two cities, bus service is good to smaller towns in the region. Turin is also linked by air to Rome and Milan and to other Italian airports, as well as directly to many principal European cities, including London, Paris, and Frankfurt. Airlines serving Turin include Alitalia, Air France, British Airways, Sabena, Alisarda, Lufthansa, and Swiss Air.

ACCOMMODATIONS REFERENCE

The rates given below are projections for 1993; always check for up-to-date information before making reservations. Wide ranges may reflect the differences between low- and high-season rates. Unless otherwise indicated, the figures indicate the cost of a double room (per room, not per person). However, half-board (mezza pensione) rates, which include breakfast and one other meal per day, are per person. The service charge is included in the rate; inquire about the tax and breakfast.

▶ **Bellevue.** Gran Paradiso 20, 11012 **Cogne.** Tel: (0165) 748-25; Fax: (0165) 74-91-92. Open December 21–April 21 and June–October 10. Ł190,000; half board, Ł155,000.

▶ **Boston.** Via Massena 70, 10128 **Torino.** Tel: (011) 50-03-59; Fax: (011) 59-93-58. Ł115,000–Ł165,000.

▶ **Bramante.** Via Genova 2, 10126 **Torino.** Tel: (011) 67-76-39; Fax: (011) 63-45-92. Ł80,000–Ł165,000.

▶ **Al Castello da Diego.** Piazza G. Marconi 4, 12060 **Novello.** Tel: (0173) 73-11-44; Fax: (0173) 73-12-50. Ł75,000.

▶ **Castello di San Giorgio.** Via Cavalli d'Olivola 3, 15020 **San Giorgio Monferrato.** Tel: (0142) 80-62-03. Fax: same. Closed January 1–10 and August 1–20. Ł160,000.

▶ **La Contea.** Piazza Cocito 8, 12057 **Neive.** Tel: (0173) 671-26; Fax: (0173) 673-67. Ł180,000.

▶ **Crimea.** Via Mentana 3, 10133 **Torino.** Tel: (011) 660-47-00; Fax: (011) 660-49-12. Ł115,000–Ł160,000.

▶ **Genio.** Corso Vittorio Emanuele II 47, 10125 **Torino.** Tel: (011) 650-57-71; Fax: (011) 650-82-64. Ł200,000.

▶ **Stazione e Genova.** Via Sacchi 14b, 10128 **Torino.** Tel: (011) 54-53-23; Fax: (011) 51-98-96. Ł185,000.

▶ **Giardino da Felicin.** Via Vallada 18, Monforte d'Alba, 12065 **Cuneo.** Tel: (0173) 782-25. Closed January and July 1–15. Ł54,000–Ł80,000; half board Ł90,000

▶ **Grand Hotel Sestriere.** Via Assietta 1, 10058 **Sestriere.** Tel: (0122) 764-76; Fax: (0122) 767-00. Open December 21– April 23 and June 7–August. Ł242,000; half board Ł170,000.

▶ **Gran Mogol.** Via Guarini 2, 10123 **Torino.** Tel: (011) 561-21-20; Fax: (011) 562-31-60. Ł200,000.

▶ **Hotel Barbaduc.** Via Giordano 35, 12060 **Novello.** Tel: (0173) 73-12-98. Ł90,000.

▶ **Hotel Savona.** Piazza Savona 2, 12051 **Alba.** Tel: (0173) 44-04-40; Fax: (0173) 36-43-12. Ł90,000.

▶ **Jolly Hotel Ligure.** Piazza Carlo Felice 85, 10123 **Torino.** Tel: (011) 556-41; Fax: (011) 53-54-38; in U.S., Tel: (212) 213-1468 or (800) 221-2626; Fax: (212) 213-2369; in U.K., Tel: (923) 89-62-72 or (0800) 28-27-29; Fax: (923) 89-60-71. Ł298,000; half board Ł275,000.

▶ **Jolly Principi di Piemonte.** Via Gobetti 15, 10123 **Torino.** Tel: (011) 562-96-93; Fax: (011) 562-02-70; in U.S., Tel: (212) 213-1468 or (800) 221-2626; Fax: (212) 213-2369; in U.K., Tel: (923) 89-62-72 or (0800) 28-27-29; Fax: (923) 89-60-71. Ł340,000; half board Ł340,000.

▶ **Locanda del Sant'Uffizio.** Cioccaro di Penango, 14030 **Asti.** Tel: (0141) 912-71; Fax: (0141) 91-60-68. Closed January 3–25. Ł200,000–Ł220,000; half board Ł220,000.

▶ **Petit Hotel.** 11012 **Cogne.** Tel: (0165) 740-10; Fax: (0165) 74-91-31. Closed January 15–February 15 and March 20–June 20. Ł40,000–Ł80,000; half board Ł55,000–Ł80,000.

▶ **Piemontese.** Via Berthollet 21, 10125 **Torino.** Tel: (011) 669-81-01; Fax: (011) 669-05-71. Ł95,000–Ł120,000.

▶ **Principi di Piemonte.** Via Sauze, 10058 **Sestriere.** Tel: (0122) 79-41; Fax: (0122) 702-70. Open December–April. Ł360,000; half board Ł220,000.

▶ **Il Cascinale Nuovo.** Statale Asti-Alba, 14057 **Isola d'Asti.** Tel: (0141) 95-81-66; Fax: (0141) 95-88-28. Closed early January and August. Ł115,000–Ł145,000.

▶ **Sud-Ovest.** Via Monterotta 17, 10058 **Sestriere.** Tel: (0122) 773-93; Fax: (0122) 75-51-66. Closed May and October. Ł100.000; half board Ł85,000.

▶ **Turin Palace Hotel.** Via Sacchi 8, 10128 **Torino.** Tel: (011) 562-55-11; Fax: (011) 561-21-87. Ł320,000; half board Ł340,000.

▶ **Victoria.** Via Nino Costa 4, 10123 **Torino.** Tel: (011) 561-19-09; Fax: (011) 561-18-06. Ł120,000.

▶ **Villa Sassi–El Toulà.** Strada al Traforo del Pino 47, 10132 **Torino.** Tel: (011) 89-05-56; Fax: (011) 89-00-95. Closed in August. Ł340,000; half board Ł240,000.

LIGURIA
THE ITALIAN RIVIERA

By Bill Marsano and Barbara Coeyman Hults

L iguria is an arc of mountainous land along the northwest coast of Italy, beginning in the southeast at the Tuscan border and sweeping up the knee of the boot north and west to France's Côte d'Azur. One of the smallest regions of the country, it is also one of the oldest; the Ligurians were among the earliest primitive inhabitants of Italy.

Shielded from northern winds by the Alps and then the Apennines, Liguria has one of the mildest climates in Europe. Its Apennines absorb the brunt of winter, providing the coastal strip with an eternal spring where bright blossoms and bushes flower all year round. In the 19th century, sufferers from the *mal sottile* would come to winter along the Riviera.

Liguria has *two* Rivieras, the **Riviera di Ponente** at the west, between the French border and Genoa, and the more spectacular **Riviera di Levante** continuing eastward, where we find Genoa itself, Portofino, the Cinque Terre, Lerici and Tellaro, and Ameglia. Although the Riviera di Ponente is a popular haunt for tourists in summer, the Riviera di Levante takes most of the prizes and is the more likely venue for visitors descending on Liguria.

The coast can easily be travelled without a car. Trains and buses link the entire resort area, and in summer boats maintain regular service—providing the best views as well.

MAJOR INTEREST

Genoa
Columbus quincentennial museums
Via Garibaldi
Art museums at Palazzos Bianco, Rosso, and Spinola

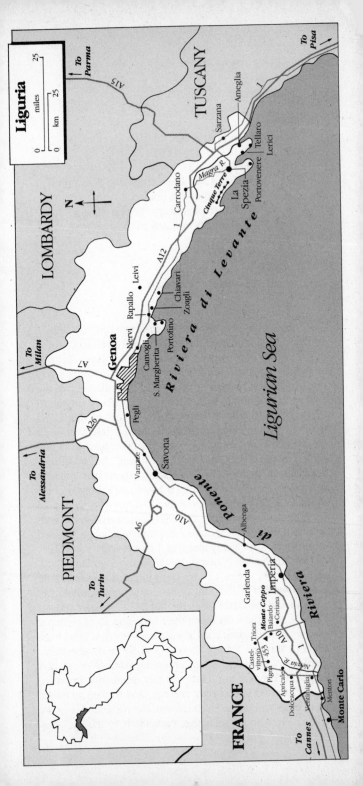

Piazza San Matteo
Medieval city
Street markets

Riviera di Ponente
Ventimiglia and hill towns

Riviera di Levante
Coast drive from Chiavari to Zoagli and Portofino
Coast by sea, by excursion boat
Camogli and other picturesque fishing villages
Ca' Peo restaurant above Chiavari
The Cinque Terre
Lerici, especially at night
Tellaro
Locanda dell'Angelo in Ameglia

Since time immemorial, life for the Ligurians has been a struggle. Dependent on the sea for their livelihood, these peace-loving people were a constant prey to pirates. To grow grapes and olives and basic crops, the Ligurians literally had to carry the soil by boat or on their backs and stick it to the rock face, creating a style of terrace agriculture unique in Europe and found elsewhere only in parts of China and Peru. Everything Ligurians have achieved has been with blood, sweat, and tears, and Ligurians prize hard work and thrift above all other virtues. (Among other Italians, Ligurians in general and Genoese in particular retain a reputation for intensely shrewd business dealings and for thrift unto stinginess.) Even today, it seems as if work is in progress on every inch of the landscape, littered as it is with ladders and tools, as though these tireless laborers planned to return to work at any moment. Unfortunately, particularly on the Riviera di Ponente, much of the Ligurians' hard-earned money seems to have been invested in *villette,* little bungalows that no amount of cascading bougainvillaea can redeem. On the other hand, the hill towns wedged into the mountains in the west retain their brooding air of medieval mystery, and the coast road along the Riviera di Levante from Chiavari through Zoagli, Rapallo, and Santa Margherita toward Portofino is one of Italy's more memorable drives, past languidly elegant turn-of-the-century villas and imposing hotels swathed in luxuriant creepers and flanked by lolling palm trees and pines. From the sea, the enchantment of the coast is even more seductive, particularly in the late afternoon.

GENOA

The keystone of Liguria's long and narrow arc, Genoa, like Turin, has remained predominantly Italian in atmosphere. The great flow of annual visitors has had little effect on it because the vast majority are business travellers, not tourists. Tee-shirts and gewgaws are not for sale everywhere; every shopkeeper does not speak English; and relatively few restaurants offer the tired old *menu turistico*.

Genoa is still Italy's greatest port, and is still awash with the splendor and squalor of great ports around the world. Genoa was for centuries a powerful independent republic— a blood rival of Venice and a financial center of international power. Columbus was born here; Genoese patriots fired the Risorgimento and Garibaldi gathered his Thousand here for the invasion of Sicily, which led to the unification of Italy in the mid-19th century.

Genoa's greatest days were as a republic, when her empire covered all of Liguria and included many outposts reaping the riches of the Eastern spice trade. It was frequently at war, fending off Saracen pirates and defeating such commercial rivals as Pisa (also a maritime power before its port silted up) and Amalfi. Genoese fleets took part in the Crusades (but, with hardheaded business sense, only at a price), and there were frequent clashes with Venice. The Genoese usually lost those battles, but by accident they won the war: When Columbus discovered the New World, the entire focus of Old World trade turned west, leaving Venice to slowly shrivel in the east.

Genoa crowds the shore with its grimy port and climbs into the greenery of natural amphitheaters in the Ligurian Apeninnes. It is not a city to be summed up with quick impressions. Via Garibaldi, a regal stretch of brilliant palazzi, is one of Europe's finest streets. A few blocks away, the city plunges in an urban landslide down dark, almost vertical lanes to the medieval city below and the port beyond. Above the city, a semicircle of lush greenery provides a backdrop for its amphitheater form. Genoa's center is shot with façades of black and white stripes of marble, precise forms that typify an industrious citizenry. The typical building is ponderous but touched with gaiety; façades are enlivened with monumental sculptural forms, gods lounging about doorways or monster faces with windows for mouths.

Genoa has gone its way without outside interference, and with little interest in—or from—tourists. In Grand Tour days and afterward, a raft of literary travellers stopped

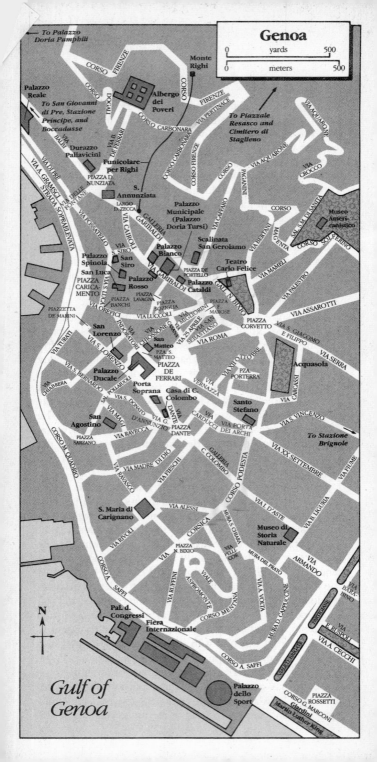

here and later published their impressions: Thomas Gray, Leigh Hunt, Charles Dickens, and Thomas Hardy among the English; Washington Irving, Herman Melville, and Mark Twain among the Americans; and Henry James representing both groups. Yet crowds did not follow, perhaps because Genoa, as Tobias Smollett wrote in 1766, "has the face of business." Even in the ocean-liner era, when transatlantic giants like the *Rex* and the *Conte di Savoia* were based here, most passengers simply grabbed their bags and ran for Florence.

Not that the Genoese much cared, for since the days of their glorious empire, they have been somewhat insular, somewhat inward-looking. Most Italians take pride in their history, but the Genoese are intensely proud of it, and many still speak Genoese, which they assert is not merely a dialect. And if the difference between a dialect and a language is that a dialect is a degraded form whereas a langauge is a distinct form with a written grammar, they are right. Indeed, a parallel publishing industry thrives by issuing books in Genoese, including expensively produced translations of such Italian classics as Dante's *Divine Comedy.*

Yet 1992 changed some of that. For the Columbus quincentennial, some of the thick commercial grime was scrubbed off; palaces were renovated; frescoed walls were renewed. Genoa built a modern complex of maritime museums in the port and (finally) rebuilt its historic opera house on piazza de Ferrari, the Carlo Felice, which was destroyed in World War II. The opportunity to reap the riches of tourism came at a time when Genoa's port, like the shipping industry all over the world, is in decline. And so the business-oriented Genoese decided to venture some capital on the tourist trade. Ever cautious, however, the Genoese got a late start; ever reserved, they publicized their city fitfully. The result? The quincentennial events were only moderately successful. That disappointed the booster-club crowd, to be sure, but it left the city undamaged by any touristic tsunami.

The tiny, totally restored house thought to be **Columbus's childhood home** is located just off piazza Dante, near the merloned towers of **Porta Soprana.** Columbus's father was, we're told, gatekeeper here when Cristoforo was young. (He was born in 1451, according to several documents, but exactly *which* gate his father kept is the subject of scholarly dispute—as is almost everything else about Columbus.) The cloisters still stand gracefully alongside his house; they are all that remain of the church of **Sant'Agostino,** largely destroyed by World War II bombs.

Columbus was not the only noted navigator to pass the city's portals. The English explorer John Cabot (Giovanni Caboto) was born here, and Marco Polo dictated his book of travels while in a Genoese prison. (The Genoese flung into jail every Venetian they could lay their hands on.)

If you continue along via Dante to piazza de Ferrari, the hub of the city, you can turn into via XX Settembre and walk a couple of blocks to see, on your left and above street level, the 11th-century church of **Santo Stefano**, parish church for the Colombo family and the place where, according to church records, Cristoforo was baptized. This church, too, has been much restored after extensive wartime damage. Its black-and-white Gothic Romanesque style prevailed in Genoa well into the Quattrocento (1400s), while central Italy was basking in its Technicolor Renaissance.

On piazza Dante is a brick-and-marble building tall enough, for Genoa, to have earned the name *grattacielo* (skyscraper). At its rear, on via G. D'Annunzio, a bus information center sells a handy tourist ticket for 3,000 lire, good for a day and night (12 hours) of bus and trolley rides. The city's compactness is an important advantage for visitors. By bus, trolley, funicular, and especially on foot, Genoa is easily navigated.

Across the street from piazza de Ferrari and behind the Ducal Palace stands one of the charms of the city. At **piazza San Matteo** the Doria family, whose seagoing ways made Genoa a center of commerce, created an architectural delight in the simplicity of the family's narrow vertical houses. The church of **San Matteo** was founded in 1125 by Martino Doria, who gave it elegance by setting it on an elevated space above the piazza. The cloisters, newly renovated, are decorated with plaques commemorating important events in the family history. The great admiral Andrea Doria is buried in the church's crypt. The Doria houses loom over this tiny square; their portals are striped in black and white (a civic honor) and decorated with reliefs of Saint George (of dragon fame), one of Genoa's two patron saints.

A different kind of history is found in nearby piazza Soziglia. *Marrons glacés* were invented in Genoa, and the best *pasticceria*—or *confetteria,* as it styles itself—is the splendidly frescoed **Romanengo** at via Soziglia 74/R, unchanged since it was founded in 1790. In the piazza, **Kleinguti**, number 100/R, is a marvelous café (Risorgimento patriots met here to scheme and argue) and it also makes its own ice cream.

By following via Luccoli from here you'll reach **piazza Fontane Marose**, where via Garibaldi begins.

Via Garibaldi

This street of stage-set perfection was part of a 16th-century gentrification program designed to give Genoa some of the chic it otherwise lacked. Galeazzo Alessi was chosen for the job, and the result was praised throughout the continent. For visitors, part of the appeal is that most of the buildings are now in the hands of banks or the municipal government, and so can be visited, at least as far as their interior courts.

Stop at number 11, the **Palazzo Bianco**, the city's most acclaimed art gallery. Works by David and Rubens are among the finest of the collection. The **Palazzo Rosso**, opposite, displays the Veronese *Judith* and a Dürer *Portrait of a Youth* in lavish surroundings.

The Banco di Chiavari at number 2, and the Chamber of Commerce at number 4, have sumptuous interiors that are sometimes open to the public. Continuing to the right will lead you into via Cairoli, which curves down into largo della Zecca, where a **funicular** will take you high above the city, up hills so steep that houses are often entered from the roof. If you want a meal with your panorama while on Monte Righi, the **Ristorante Montallegro** will do nicely (via Mura delle Chiappe 30, Tel: 010-21-96-71; closed Monday dinner and Tuesdays).

For a panoramic half-day walk, turn left out of the restaurant and follow the road, which connects seven fortresses and fortified towers. Called collectively the Lords of Genoa, they fended off would-be invaders from the north as the hills themselves still ward off the arthritic winters of Piedmont and the Lombard plain. The forts themselves are not open to visitors, but the road follows the rim of the city's amphitheater; there are a few small cafés en route, and paths lead into the quiet groves of trees, where you can picnic, doze in the sun, or regard the vast panorama of the port and the Gulf of Genoa. The route finally winds down at the northern end of the port, below **La Lanterna**, the ancient lighthouse that is Genoa's civic symbol.

The Medieval City (Centro Storico)

Beyond via Garibaldi's palazzi, the city changes its stripes. From largo della Zecca, walk to piazza della Nunziata and turn left, down via delle Fontane, which leads to the port and another of the ancient gates, Porta dei Vacca. Now you enter the *centro storico* (historic center)—the original medieval heart of Genoa. Its dark and narrow *caruggi* (alleys) have a menacing air but are actually quite safe during the day and early evening, when most stores are open. Don't go in the dark of night, and don't flaunt jewelry or your wallet; be prudent but not fearful. And perhaps some heavenly protection is afforded: Above almost every corner a *Madonnetta,* a statue of the Madonna, looks down from atop flowers and tiny votive lights. More secular versions of these statuettes show ordinary 18th-century Genoese women, complete with aprons. They were erected by various artisan guilds or by sailors who left the port to sail around the world.

This is a twilight world of ancient churches (almost every one of which is worth looking into) and markets, prostitutes and families, wandering Africans selling plastic cigarette lighters, stores gleaming with real gold jewelry, and cheap blue jeans piled on the sidewalks; it is the most fascinating part of Genoa.

Turn left and go through the gateway along via del Campo (which will change names twice without warning, to Fossatello and San Luca). A little way along is **piazza Vacchero,** witness to the fact that Genoese internal rivalries were as violent as those of Florence. Behind a shabby wall supporting a ruined fountain is a *colonna d'infame* (column of infamy). Its Latin inscription denounces Giulius Caesaris Vacherij as a traitor "most damned" who was beheaded for his villainy. It adds that his family was expelled from the city, his house razed to the ground, and his goods distributed. The column curses his memory—and thus prolongs it—for eternity.

Beyond piazza Fossatello, turn left up Salita di San Siro to the church of **San Siro.** In its original form, San Siro dates to the fourth century, when it was the cathedral of Genoa, as its thoroughly rebuilt interior would indicate. Retrace your steps and walk on along this delightful mess of a street (now called San Luca) all the way to piazza Banchi, marked by a church under eternal restoration and the carts and stalls of vendors selling books, prints, and vegetables. (Follow via del Campo in the opposite direction as well if time permits. This street, under various names, is the *caruggio diretto*— through street—of Genoa. Long, narrow, and free of traffic, it leads to the Crusaders' church of San Giovanni di Pre, with its peculiar form—it has apses at both ends—and a handsome campanile with five spires. On the way to San Giovanni you'll pass one of Genoa's street markets at **piazza Sant'Elena.** The dry goods may come from Asia but the food is pure Genoa—*focaccia,* the thin, olive oil–dressed bread baked with onion and sage, and *farinata,* a chick-pea flatbread baked in wood-fired ovens.)

Via San Luca is flanked with palaces whose interiors belie their shabby façades. Marble doorways and reclining giants hint at the riches within. A palace you'll want to enter is the nearby **Palazzo Spinola**, or the Galleria Nazionale, whose treasures include a rare Antonello da Messina painting, *Ecce Homo* (if it's back from restoration). The statue of Justice (*La Giustizia*) by Giovanni Pisano is part of a monument to Margaret de Brabant.

Back on the via San Luca you'll see signs pointing to the church of **San Luca** off to the left. This church and piazza was created in 1138 by two of Genoa's prominent families, the Spinolas and the Grimaldis. Ahead on via San Luca stands the **Loggia dei Banchi**, which was the center of business here until it became an exhibition hall. On the via dei Orefici (Street of the Goldsmiths) ahead, gold shops are still much in evidence. Look for a lovely *Adoration of the Magi* inset above the door at number 47.

The flea market at piazza Lavagna can turn up fascinating oddities. Ahead in piazzetta Luccoli, the elaborate façade of the Palazzo Franzone hides a herbalist's shop inside the main doorway.

Nearby there are two inexpensive trattorias, **Ugo** at via Giustiani 86 and **Bruno's** at vico Casana 9, off piazza de Ferrari. Bruno's, upstairs, is reminiscent of a *pensione* dining room, friendly and spacious. Ugo's is very informal; you may share a table with local workmen. The food is fine and very inexpensive, but the WC is not for women—it offers only metal footrests, as seen surprisingly often in sophisticated Liguria. (The more sophisticated restaurants in Genoa are listed below.)

Further exploration of the *centro storico* is deserved, but only with a good map. (Good city maps, with detailed plans of this section, are available at any newsstand.) It is rewarding to wander for a day among the narrow *caruggi,* which immerse you in the past. Looking up between the crowding rooftops you may see jet vapor trails in the sliver of blue sky and realize that you are in two centuries at once. Despite its weight of history, the *centro storico* is not a mummified showplace but a vibrant quarter as alive today as it was in the time of Columbus.

From here it is but a few steps to the port proper and the new museum installations designed by Renzo Piano, Italy's foremost modern architect. (Although Piano was co-designer of the Place Pompidou in Paris, the prickly, frankly mechanical externals of that structure are not representative of the body of his work.) The design motif of the installations is nautical; the exhibit halls resemble enormous ships and parts of ships, and contain exhibits of Genoa's past as a port, republic, and maritime empire. There are also spaces for cultural displays and concert performances.

The Cathedral

Genoa's majestic cathedral of **San Lorenzo** was built on this site in about the ninth century, then enlarged in Romanesque style during the 12th century. The side portals are richly decorated with carvings of human and animal figures. Its Gothic features were created about a century later. The front is guarded by two very fine stone church lions (their frankly apprehensive appearance suggests to some that even the king of beasts fears the King of Kings).

One of the chapels is dedicated to John the Baptist, Genoa's *other* patron saint, whose ashes, it's thought, were brought here by the Crusaders. His chapel, the work of Domenico and Elia Gagini, contains sculpture by Matteo Cividali and Andrea Sansovino. The high, dimly lighted interior is plain, austere, even severe. In a corner at the right front is a reminder of how heavily bombed Genoa was during World War II: a heavy-caliber naval artillery shell. Fired from a British battleship, it crashed into the cathedral but landed—miraculously, perhaps—without exploding. The cathedral's Treasury is magnificent: rare jeweled chests and a first-century Roman glass basin which, according to tradition, was used at the Last Supper.

The Principe Station Area

Near this main railroad station of Genoa, several palaces have survived in shabby but fascinating condition. In back of the station on the port side, the **Palazzo Doria Pamphili** was magnificently situated facing the harbor—when the harbor view was magnificent. Today we need imagination. The palace, the proud creation of Andrea Doria, still shows signs of its noble past; Charles V and Giuseppe Verdi were on the guest list. The Gallery of Heroes, the Hall of Giants, and the Neptune fountain are of special interest.

In front of the station (nearby there is a statue of Columbus and a bus terminal), the regal via Balbi begins. It's flanked by palaces that have been turned over to the university or to the state. The unimpressive grayness at number 10 was the **Royal Palace** (Palazzo Reale). As usual, the interior is another story. It was completed in 1705 after Carlo Fontana worked on the then-lovely garden. Today the interior courtyard is surprisingly colorful, perhaps because it houses the

Fine Arts Academy. Upstairs, the *piano nobile* has been turned into an art gallery but needs much renovation. The Gallery of the Mirrors and the Veronese Salon are impressive, as are works by Guido and Van Dyck. The Durazzo family, who lived here, gave eight doges to the Republic, including Giralamo (1739–1809), the last doge of Genoa.

The university library occupies number 3, converted from a church. The **palazzo Durazzo Pallavicini**, at number 1, retains the charm and opulence of a patrician residence. It was built originally as a Jesuit college at the beginning of the 17th century, taking advantage of the hillside as it was laid out in courtyards, loggias, and gardens.

Ahead is the church of the **Santissima Annunziata**— magnificent within, almost a gallery of 17th-century Genoese artists.

An unusual landmark on the outskirts of town is the cemetery of **Staglieno**, definitely an acquired taste. Its tombs are adorned with outrageous 19th-century monuments in a conglomeration of styles. Here many veterans of Garibaldi's Sicilian campaign, and also the great political theorist Giuseppe Mazzini, lie buried. The image of death at Staglieno embraces a seductive form that grew from a bizarre preoccupation. Life-size figures stand at prayer or lie draped, naked, over a tomb in erotic grief. Visit the cemetery—a 15-minute bus ride from central Genoa—only during daylight, and not between noon and 3:00 P.M., when the custodians are at lunch. (It is sometimes inhabited by drug addicts.)

Staying and Dining in Genoa

The most famous of Genoa's great hotels is—was—the Columbia, but this majestic mammoth has spent years in decline followed by closure followed by reconstruction followed today by utter desuetude. The gap is more than filled by a hotel few know exists: The **Bristol Palace** *is* a palace, several centuries old, with a modest entrance on via XX Settembre. As is common in Genoa, the splendor lies within (thus did cagey Genoese conceal their wealth). The Bristol is airy and spacious, furnished with period and reproduction furniture, and serenely served by a pampering Old World staff as quiet as footpads. It has quiet class and no glitz; it walls out the noise of traffic by triple-glazing its huge windows; the only thing it lacks is a restaurant (there is an excellent breakfast room, however).

The new first-class **Star Hotel President** near Brignole Station has good modern accommodations, but prices are high. The modern four-star **Jolly Hotel Plaza** has a good location off piazza Corvetto, but the **Hotel City** (pronounced "chitty") has a better, even more central one on a tiny, silent piazza on via San Sebastiano. It was a gloomy ruin a few years ago, but its director, Gianfranco Castganetti, has since turned it into a smart, comfortable hotel with cozy modern rooms. The **Agnello d'Oro**, in the port area below Principe station, is recommended for the tighter budget. A perfectly adequate and centrally located little hotel is the inexpensive **Metropoli**. (See the section on Camogli, in the Portofino section below, for an alternative to staying in town.)

Although there are no outstanding restaurants in Genoa, the general standard is high, as the Genoese, serious in everything they do, take eating very seriously. Menus are often based on fresh fish from the Ligurian Sea: An unusual anti-pasto is *gianchetti*—tiny newborn fish steamed and served with the local olive oil and lemon. Besides pesto, typical fare includes the *torta pasqualina,* an Easter pie (eaten all year round) filled with beet greens or artichokes. As an alternative to fish there is *cima* (veal breast stuffed with vegetables and egg) and the traditional cake, called *pandussa*. This heavier (but not leaden) version of Milan's famous *panettone* is heartier and more rustic—like a fruitcake rather than a fruit bread.

Only the most chauvinistic of Ligurians would claim that the region makes great wine, but it does make some good ones, though they are seldom exported. Rossese di Dolceaqua is a simple, companionable red; the whites are Vermentino, Pigato, and Cinque Terre. This last once had a degree of deserved fame but then fell on evil times. Through the efforts of a hard-working wine cooperative, it has been granted DOC. status (that is, use of the name Cinque Terre is legally controlled in a manner similar to France's *appella-tion controlée* laws), and the quality has recovered signifi-cantly. To get the best you must request "Cinque Terre DOC." (pronounced "doc") and see the co-op's symbol, a stylized number 5 on a cluster of grapes, on the label. A rich, intensely sweet version called Sciacchetrà (shock-e-TRA), also DOC., is golden in color and luscious in taste.

The best restaurant in Genoa, **Le Fate**, is the most sophisti-cated venue in town (via E. Ruspoli 31, Tel: 010-54-64-02; closed Saturday lunch and Sundays). Their pesto is irresist-ible with gnocchi, and the fresh fish, exquisitely cooked with herbs, is served with a good international wine selection. The **Gran Gotto** (via Fiume 11/R, Tel: 010-56-43-44; closed Satur-day lunch and Sundays), near Stazione Brignole, is a very professionally run restaurant with a classic decor, inventive fish menus including delicious hot antipasti, and, like Le Fate, superb wines. **Da Giacomo**, at corso Italia 1/R (Tel: 010-36-96-47; closed Sundays), is an elegant, expensive restaurant like the other two; it's much favored by businesspeople—often the best judges of great food. Da Giacomo's wonderfully fresh antipasti still smelling of the sea, their fish risottos, and particularly a pasta dish called *pennette di Giacomo* are justly famous. **Aladino**, in the heart of Genoa's *centro storico* (via Vernazza 8/R, Tel: 010-56-67-88; closed weekends), is a very popular landmark, again featuring pesto in many guises, as well as the *torta pasqualina* and an unusual dish: capon with shellfish.

The best wines in Genoa can be savored by the glass at the moderately priced **Enoteca/Bar Sola** (via C. Barabino 120/R, Tel: 010-59-45-13) along with typical Genoese specialties (closed Sundays). Almost impossible to find is the delightful, inexpensive **Il Giardino dei Glicini** (Scalinata San Gerolamo), a period piece from the 1930s (Tel: 010-29-68-87; closed Sundays). **Osvaldo a Boccadasse** is another simple, down-to-earth trattoria, on via Dellacasa in an old picturesque Boccadasse, an old fishing village once east of the city but now absorbed by it. It serves typical local dishes in a very authentic atmosphere. Osvaldo has very few tables and, though not expensive, is not as cheap as you might expect (Tel: 010-377-18-81; closed Mondays). **Vittorio al Mare**, at Boccadasse's tiny port, is a popular midday rendezvous for seafood lovers (Tel: 010-31-28-72; closed Tuesdays). Boccadasse is well worth the short bus ride from central Genoa. Mind your wallet, local residents say.

Genoa is a very masculine city, the equivalent in urban terms of a sober pin-striped suit. It is therefore not surprising that, although the city also has a chic shopping street (the via XX Settembre) with all the usual designer names, the real shoppers' finds are for *men*. **Lucarda** at via Sottoripa 61 has everything for the sailor and his boat, including jeans—appropriately, as *blue jeans* comes from Genes (the city's early name), "blue of Genes" being the color originally worn by the dockworkers of Genoa. **Finollo**, a tiny store with an authentic turn-of-the-century aura, has the reputation of being the best shirt-maker in Italy, with famous names among its clientele; it specializes in English men's fashions of the Jeeves era. **Hobby Pipe** at via XII Ottobre 148 is an elegant tobacconist, while **Novielli** at via Santi Giacomo e Filippo 23 makes shoes to order. **Jost** at piazza Corvetto 9 is a little store with a large selection of watches. The **Libreria Antiquaria Dallai** in piazzetta De Marini sells antique maps, prints, and books for the den, although the main antiques stores are in via Cairoli and via Garibaldi. A present for a woman can be found at **Parodi**, the best jeweller in Genoa, at via Ceccardi 3, or at **Deco**, under the Portici dell'Accademia which carries all the best names in Italian prêt-à-porter.

To enjoy the city from the sea, take a harbor cruise from the **Stazione Marittima**, where boats leave for Ligurian resort towns as well. Marexpress, among others, travels east to Santa Margherita Ligure (near Portofino) and west along the coast, connecting at Alassio for Monte Carlo (Tel: 010-25-67-75). There's also a cruise-service cooperative (Tel: 010-26-57-12 for harbor tours, 0185-28-46-70 for the towns of the Portofino promontory). One-way and round trips are available. For sea connections it's best to check with the tourist office at via Roma 11. (If it's not there, it's still in its "temporary" quarters at via Porta dei Archi 10, second floor, and a little hard to find: Halfway along this short street is an unnamed, unsigned alley running off at a right angle; the entrance is 50 feet along on the left.)

One of the main reasons people come to Genoa is for the **Fiera**, a vast exhibition area on the sea that hosts a number of trade fairs, the most famous of which is the Salone Nautico, from October 22 through November 1 every year. Every four years there is the Euroflora, when the stands of the Fiera overflow with plants and flowers. In July there is an outdoor ballet festival in the **Parco di Nervi**, a complex of four palatial country villas just east of Genoa. Information can be obtained from the Teatro Comunale dell'Opera. Another beautiful villa is the **Pallavicini** at Pegli, west of Genoa and easily reached by train or bus, where for just ten days in spring the botanical gardens can be visited. They feature a collection of, among other things, carnivorous plants. Special out-of-season visits can be arranged for groups.

THE RIVIERA DI PONENTE

If your itinerary takes you from Genoa west to the Riviera di Ponente on your way to France, an ideal stopover is at **La Meridiana**, an enchanting hotel in the middle of an 18-hole golf course in Garlenda, between Imperia and Savona. The hotel, which also has a very good restaurant, **Il Rosmarino**, is quite pricey (closed for lunch from September to June).

The Riviera di Ponente, the western Riviera, is admittedly a less-than-alluring area, studded with faded resorts for the beach-and-casino crowd, but it is not entirely without appeal. **Ventimiglia**, 159 km (99 miles) west of Genoa, is an

other worthwhile stop going to or coming from Genoa. It's
part garden and part seedy, an unpretentious, likable place
with an old quarter focused on a handsome 11th- to 12th-
century cathedral and baptistery that should be seen. The
Sea Gull is a modest, quiet, and reasonable hotel, and **Il
Vesuvio**, a local hangout, offers reasonable meals in slightly
raffish surroundings on the port (via Trosarelli 14; Tel: 0184-
356-397).

Just west of Ventimiglia at Mórtola Inferiore is the
Giardino Hanbury, a botanical garden of great renown
founded in the 1860s by Sir Thomas Hanbury and his
brother Daniel. Here exotic Asian and African plants were
acclimatized and planted among local flora; the results are
botanically important but also restful and beautiful. The
grounds contain an exposed stretch of ancient Rome's via
Aurelia and a plaque listing some of the notables who
travelled it (Saint Catherine of Siena being one of the best,
the brute Napoléon one of the worst).

Ventimiglia is also the portral for a rewarding drive of one
or two days—the "Ring of Hill Towns." The maps given away
by the Sea Gull and other hotels are, surprisingly, perfect for
the purpose.

The Hill Towns of Liguria

"Hill towns" is a term so firmly attached to Tuscany that it
may appear astonishing that any other region has them. But
Liguria has them aplenty—and in some ways it has better.
Charming as they are, Tuscan hill towns like San Gimignano
are tame and pretty. Liguria's retain a brooding atmosphere
that suggests strongly why these nearly inaccessible outposts
were built in the first place: fear. Communications and trade
in the Roman empire were based on its great road system—
and so Roman towns were built on plains and in valleys.
Civilization went dark in the Middle Ages as Rome's rule—
and order—collapsed. And so fear built the hill towns. Fear
of brigands, of jealous neighbors, of Saracen pirates—fear
too of the expanding, imperial Genoese—drove the peasants inland to build high and fortify. The cold and silent
mountains, with their neck-craning heights of menace and
dizzying knife-slash valleys, underscore the point.

Start at the east end of Ventimiglia and strike inland,
following the road along the flood channel of the Nervia.
There are plenty of hotels and restaurants along the way
(this is a popular area for small-scale tourism). The roads are
excellent, if narrow and curvy in the heights: Don't rush.

Dolceacqua, astride the stream with a superb single-arch medieval bridge, is six miles along, portal to the hill towns. It's a good stop for an early snack, and opposite the church in the square on the far side of the river you can buy your Rosese di Dolceacqua from Mauro Zanno (Tel: 0184-20-61-62), the man who made it—and (in spring) just bottled and corked it in the back. (On a slow day he'll take you to visit the local woodworker's crafts shop; you may even decide to rent Zanno's handsome little efficiency flat in the hills.)

Now it's hill towns in earnest. **Apricale** lies strung along its steep ridge, quiet and half depopulated (as are many hill towns, which can't provide enough jobs while cities beckon); then comes **Pigna**, higher up yet overawed by towering **Castelvittorio** (sometimes written "Castel Vittorio"). There are two pleasing, reasonably priced restaurants here with balcony tables above a dizzyingly deep valley: **Osteria del Portico** via Umberto I 6, Tel: 0184-241-352) and **Ristorante Italia** (via Umberto I, Tel: 0184-241-089). Both serve local seasonal dishes.

Molini di Triora, a center for edible snails, crouches by a stream; it's **Triora** itself, on a superbly high but unusually spacious height, that brings the Middle Ages back into focus. From there, backtrack a little and climb Monte Ceppo, truly alone in a vast harsh landscape at 5,300 feet toward **Baiardo**, **Ceriana**, and **Bussana Vecchia**, a ghost town smashed by an earthquake in the 1860s and let lie abandoned until a small colony of bohemian artist types made it a permanent if precarious encampment a century later.

All of these lonely outposts have their charms or mysteries (Pigna's is a splendid church, Castelvittorio's a stream-fed fountain, Baiardo's a panorama from picturesque ruins, Triora's a witch), and the farther into the mountains you go the less likely it is that you will meet anyone who was not born where he stands. There are no magnificent restaurants in these places, no fabulous shops. They contain only the sights and sounds of small-town life undamaged by five decades of mass tourism. Village Italy, like village England, contains certain slants of light that will stay with you long after you spill down onto the highway and find yourself but 30 minutes from where you started.

THE RIVIERA DI LEVANTE
Portofino

It is along the Riviera di Levante that Liguria's coast begins to come into its own. In the west it is mostly housebroken; here it becomes wild and rugged, with mountains plunging into the Ligurian Sea and the Gulf of Tigullio, tiny, heart-breakingly pretty towns wedged into clefts and coves, and all in all an aspect of windswept drama and romance missing from the uninteresting littoral of Tuscany and Lazio to the south.

According to one story, the Greeks called the Ligurians dolphins because of their skill at the sea; Portofino means port of dolphins. The port was renowned throughout antiquity and today is famous as a haven for the conspicuously consuming rich, titled, and socially well-connected. Whereas nearby Santa Margherita and Rapallo have seen better days, Portofino still has the power of enchantment that captivated the first English tourists during the last century. Because Portofino's horseshoe-shaped inlet, a few miles east of Genoa, is so tiny, few boats can moor at its jetties. For that reason, and because the town's boutiques and bars are so exclusive and expensive, mass tourism has never been a major threat here.

Despite the unique setting, none of the restaurants on the seafront is particularly remarkable. It is best to scout out the cheapest with harborside tables, since a plate of pasta with pesto tastes much the same everywhere along the coast. The most common kinds of pasta are lasagna, but without the meat filling and cheese sauce, and *trenette*. The pasta will be cooked with potatoes if it is the Ligurian "real thing."

Il **Pitosoforo**, a classic restaurant upstairs at molo Umberto I 9 (Tel: 0185-26-90-20), has looked out on the port for more than three decades. During dinner the house lights are turned out for a few minutes so diners can enjoy the spectacle of the port at night. The management has changed, but the traditions continue. (Closed Tuesdays, Wednesday lunch, and mid-December to mid-February.)

The **Hotel Splendido** in Portofino is indeed splendid, especially since it has been bought and revamped by the same chain that relaunched the Orient Express. Stout colonnades support rampant vines that shade a vast terrace on a hill dominating the bay. Those who cannot afford the pampered luxury of a room here can at least enjoy a long-drawn-out drink with a view on the terrace.

Not all the hotels in Portofino require a Swiss bank account. The tiny **San Giorgio** has 19 rooms overlooking bright rooftops, and the **Nazionale** has reopened, with suites that overlook the port, where the right sort of yachts glide to the dock.

The local beaches, such as Paraggi, tend to be overcrowded in summer, but during the tourist season a regular public boat service can take you around the castle on the headland overlooking the port to swim in the little **Bay of San Fruttuoso**, with its ancient abbey and the tombs of the Dorias. Andrea Doria was the most glorious of Genoa's seafaring heroes, the *Re del Mare* (King of the Sea) who fought with the Spaniards against the pirate Barbarossa and under whose leadership 16th-century Genoa, like Britannia later, ruled the waves.

At the top of the Monte Portofino promontory (it's too stubby to be called a peninsula) is a handsome *parco naturale;* it and the whole of the promontory are laced with footpaths offering opportunities for vigorous walks followed by lazy picnics above romantic panoramas. One of the best walks is from the rear of Portofino up steep stairs and through the *parco* to a sweeping descent into San Fruttuoso.

Camogli

A refreshing spot to stop in while visiting Genoa and Portofino is the tiny picturesque fishing village of **Camogli**, where an extensive seaside promenade acts as a panoramic main street.

Camogli has preserved its integrity amazingly well, given its location (its fishing boats have actually seen fish). (Avoid July as usual, and August as always.) Because nightlife is not a Genoese attraction anyway, taking a room in Camogli makes good sense. It's only 40 minutes from Genoa by frequent train service and well connected with Portofino by bus (change in Santa Margherita Ligure). There is a popular beach along the promenade, or you can travel to San Fruttuoso by car or boat.

The town's most festive time is the second Sunday in May, when a gargantuan pan is set up for a community fish fry.

Inexpensive accommodations begin at simple hotels such as the **Camogliese**, whose proprietor, Bruno Rocchetti, takes pride in having the latest information about schedules and local events. Some rooms have sea views, and true lira-savers will relish the (optional) inexpensive pensione meals. The **Casmona**, nearby, also offers good value for the lira.

At the deluxe end of the hotel scale is the **Cenobio dei Dogi**, a luxurious villa complete with pool and tennis courts that stretches along its own promontory.

Small fish restaurants dot Camogli's promenade to the point where it ends in a sheltered fishing-boat harbor beneath the cathedral. Among them **La Camogliese** (the same family but different management from the pensione) is cantilevered over the sea, friendly, and moderately expensive (which is true of "moderate" Italian fish restaurants in general). Reservations recommended. Tel: (0185) 77-10-86. Closed Mondays.

Higher up in town, the **Ristorante Rosa** also has a seaward-looking terrace. Another family enterprise, Rosa began as Nonna Rosa's pensione in the postwar years. Ligurian seafood (again, fairly expensive) and pesto are served here, along with hand-rolled pasta (largo Casabona 11, Tel: 0185-77-10-88; closed Tuesdays, November 6 to December 6, January, and February).

After dinner, the place to go is **Revello's**, via Garibaldi (the promenade) 183, near the cathedral. At this take-out bakery, the rum cream puffs make an after-dinner drink superfluous.

A more adventurous place to stay, about 20 minutes east along the coast from Portofino, is **Ca' Peo** (Tel: 0185-31-90-90). This restaurant with rooms is perched on a hilltop above Chiavari, a seemingly endless drive heavenward to a tiny place called Leivi. Ca' Peo is short for Casa di Pietro (Peter's House); there have been Peos in the owner's family for generations, tending the olives that grow on the slopes below the restaurant. (Ligurian olive oil is much lighter and less dense, not green like Tuscan olive oil, but a transparent golden color; it is ideal for the typical local fish recipes.) Franco and Melly Solari, like true Ligurians, have worked hard to earn for their sunny French-style country restaurant the grandiloquent accolade of the "Girardet of Liguria" from France's *Le Figaro*. The food is indeed superb, from the opening terrine of *porcini* mushrooms, through the *tortelli* (pasta filled with eggplant and goat's cheese) and the Genoese *tomaxelle* (veal rolled around sweetbreads and home-grown herbs), to the flambéed chestnut ice cream. Franco is a connoisseur of the wines of Liguria, some of which, like the Pigato and Rossese, are practically unknown even in the rest of Italy.

In the rooms some of the taste in decoration is dubious, but the windows do look out on a sweeping vista of the Riviera, from the Cinque Terre to Portofino. Ca' Peo is expensive but worth every lira.

The Cinque Terre

The Cinque Terre (Five Lands) are five little hamlets set among the rocks and coves of the Ligurian Sea; from west to east they are **Monterosso al Mare**, the largest and most touristy, **Vernazza**, **Corniglia**, **Manarola**, and **Riomaggiore**. The train and roads along the coast here are excellent.

But here a word of warning: If you intend to approach the Cinque Terre by road (only some of the towns are accessible) or rail, you might as well passs them up entirely. For one thing, you'll enter via the back door, so to speak, which will do nothing to serve the towns' fragile, stage-set beauty—and you'll have to climb into the hills to see the towns well anyway.

The Cinque Terre are a romantic near-illusion; they require the gesture of approaching by **footpath** (once the only entry except by boat) to make the illusion real. Seen in the distance, appearing and disappearing behind the spurs of the mountains, the towns beckon as goals worthy of effort. Taken from behind after effortless arrival by vehicle, they may leave you asking what the fuss is all about.

Those who do walk should be warned as well: This is no stroll, although various aerobic fanatics like to knock off all five towns in a single day. In truth the crow-flight distance is only about three miles, but the paths run much longer as they wind among the vineyards, reach deep into clefts in the hills, and climb hundreds of feet above the sea.

To plan a walk, get a map (*carta dei sentieri delle Cinque Terre,* about 400 lire at newsstands) and examine the coastal routes (there are many high in the chestnut forests of *castagneti* as well). A real walker would start in the north at Levanto and go all the way to Portovenere, but beginners can easily start with one or two sections and a pair of sturdy shoes.

The stretches between Levanto, Monterosso al Mare, Vernazza, and Corniglia are very scenic sections; Corniglia to Manarola is dull except for the last stretch (each leg so far takes about three hours); Manarola to Riomaggiore along the via d'Amore is brief but boring despite the name. From there to Portovenere is the toughest and longest leg, about six hours, but the climb to the Madonna di Montenero (where now you can rent a riding horse and get lunch) is rewarding, and the long reach to Portovenere, along a precipitously steep moutainside that disappears dramatically toward the horizon, is eternally memorable.

Difficulty of access has kept this unique coastline safe from tourist buses, and the people of the Cinque Terre for the most part live their lives—oblivious of tourists—the way they have for centuries, fishing and tending their pocket-handkerchief–sized vineyards that stepladder down the hillsides to the sea.

Staying and Dining
in the Cinque Terre

At **Monterosso** (the "al Mare" drops away rather quickly) are
two good seafood restaurants, **Ciak** and **Moretto**, opposite
each other in the old quarter, a few yards in from the beach.
Fanny and Giovanni Moretto also have a very attractive
pensione upstairs with airy, well-equipped sea-view rooms
and reasonable prices. (Getting back to your hotel is easy
anywhere in the Cinque Terre; the towns are connected by
frequent local trains; rides are short.) **Vernazza** is a cluster of
pastel houses surrounding a sunwashed piazzetta facing a
tiny port. There's a breezy restaurant below the perfectly
cylindrical Genoese lookout tower above the town, and the
old church is severely beautiful within (do not enter in
shorts or other "disrespectful" garb). The port of **Manarola** is
large enough for only two or three boats at a time, so that
the others have to be hauled up with winches every evening
when the fishermen come in with their catch. In the old
days, anyone sailing past Manarola had to pay a toll, and
shirkers would be swiftly apprehended by sailboats darting
out of the tiny port in hot pursuit. All the Cinque Terre were
frequently raided by the Saracens; the Porta Rossa (Red
Gate) in Manarola commemorates the blood shed during
one of those attacks.

For centuries the local diet here has been governed by
the fact that olive oil was the only available kind of fat, since
keeping a cow was largely impracticable, and by the abundance of fish. Anchovies would be salted to eat in winter,
and meat was on the table only at Christmas and Easter. For
other essentials the inhabitants relied on weekly boatloads
of supplies from La Spezia. Today the Cinque Terre abound
in unpretentious trattorias such as **Aristide** at Manarola;
Aristide overwhelms you with antipasti and is known for
zuppa di datteri, or date-clam soup. Tel: (0187) 92-00-00.

The **Gambero Rosso** at Vernazza's port is partly a grotto
carved out of the cliffs. Here you can taste—besides *zuppa
marinara*—a local specialty, *tian Vernazza,* with tomatoes,
anchovies, and potatoes, to be complemented with the local
D.O.C. Cinque Terre wine. Dessert is a deep-fried custard
(piazza Marconi, Tel: 0187-81-22-65; closed Mondays, February, and November 1–20).

If you travel by train, leave your luggage at the *deposito
bagagli* in Monterosso and train-hop until you find the
perfect spot. The tourist office on the level below the train
station is helpful in finding the right place. Apartments for a

week or a month can be found at the *immobiliare,* or rental agent.

Manarola has two tiny establishments, one of which, the **Marina Piccola,** has a few rooms overlooking the sea and takes credit cards. It also has a restaurant next door. A little farther up the main—and almost only—drag is **Ca d'Andrean,** also a good choice. The best-equipped hotels are found in Monterosso. The **Porta Rocca** is one of the best here, with good sea views.

Lerici

The **Gulf of La Spezia** is also known as the Gulf of Poets because, besides D. H. Lawrence, both Shelley and Byron lived here, as have artists such as William Turner and Arnold Böcklin. This is, however, La Spezia's only claim to poetry; today it is a dusty and industrious seaside city.

Baroness Orczy wrote *The Scarlet Pimpernel* while staying in Lerici at the eastern end of the gulf, and Mary Shelley was inspired by the dark outline of Lerici Castle to write *Frankenstein.* There are more tourists in Lerici now than there were in Shelley's day, and his house at Santerenzio could no longer be described as "a lonely house close by the seaside surrounded by the soft and sublime scenery of the bay of Lerici." Shelley complained about the contrast between "the two Italies," the one exemplifying the magnificence of the landscape, the other the odious ways of contemporary Italians, some of whom, he wrote in disgust, actually ate "garlick"! Shelley drowned while returning to Lerici by boat from Livorno, in Tuscany, and was cremated by his friend Edward Trelawney on the beach. Byron, who was present, requested the skull as a memento, but Trelawney, remembering that Byron had formerly used a skull as a drinking cup, was "determined Shelley's should not be so profaned."

Lerici can still be magical at night, with the lights of the port shaking out snakes of light in the oily water and the castle looming menacingly on the headland. It is an enjoyable place to visit for a drink after dinner at one of the bars on the port, to gaze languidly at vociferous Italian families whose children seem never to go to bed, and to browse in the usual seaside boutiques.

Ristorante Vecchia Lerici has earned a Michelin star for its grilled fish dishes (piazza Mottino 10, Tel: 0187-96-75-97; closed Thursdays, Friday lunch, July 1 to 15, and November 1 to December 25). At the informal (moderately priced) **Trattoria La Conchiglia** you may want to follow the suggestions of Massimo Lonate, the proprietor, or choose your own sea creatures (piazza del Molo 3, Tel: 0187-96-73-34; closed Wednesdays and January).

During the season, excursion boats leave from Lerici for the Cinque Terre and **Portovenere**, a fishing village and resort town famous for its narrow rocky promontory that leads out to the sturdy Romanesque church of **San Pietro**, on a site originally occupied by a pagan temple.

A short drive, or bus ride, south from Lerici takes you to Tellaro.

Tellaro

"When I go to Tellaro to collect the post I expect every time to meet Jesus talking to his disciples, while I am walking along halfway up the hill, underneath the shining gray trees." The road D. H. Lawrence took is no longer the same, but Tellaro itself must be substantially unchanged. An unspoiled fishing village on two levels, Tellaro is very like its counterparts in Greece—blue vistas of the sea suddenly appear around windswept corners of low, old stone cottages in narrow alleyways meandering down to the tiny port and its diminutive church. Lawrence retells the legend of the octopus of Tellaro, which, during a Saracen raid, managed to pull the bell ropes with its tentacles to alert the sleeping populace. Despite the occasional boutique and a couple of bars, Tellaro lives its life impervious to tourists, who have not yet found their way en masse to this little fishing haven.

The **Ristorante Miranda**, once a small family-run restaurant, has totally renovated its villa, which is now a glamorous (and pricey) place to taste the innovative cooking of Angelo Cabani, whose theory is that the ingredients that complement meats will do the same for fish, if the right fish is selected. His use of red wine sauce with some fish courses may have you rethinking the wine charts. Giovanna Cabani enjoys explaining her husband's culinary idiosyncrasies, and the *degustazione* menu offers a lesson-in-a-meal in Angelo's cooking. From the upstairs rooms, now redone with antiques and brightly patterned fabrics, the sea is visible through the lush greenery in this upper level of the town. Closed Mondays and from mid-November until the end of February. Tel: (0187) 96-40-12.

Ameglia

A medieval hamlet perched above the Bocca di Magra not far from Lerici where the River Magra enters the sea, Ameglia was mentioned by Dante, who paused here on his way to Paris in order, he said, to find peace (*"Io vo cercando pace"*). Ameglia is most famous for the restaurant **La Locanda dell'Angelo**, on via XXV Aprile.

Angelo Paracucchi was among the first Italian chefs to be awarded Michelin stars. His beautiful restaurant was designed by Vico Magistretti, one of the most important designers in Italy today. A large personality and a showman, Paracucchi has since fallen into the trap that has attracted many famous chefs: He now spends more time travelling and promoting than cooking in his kitchen, to the detriment of the cuisine. If you happen by on a day when he is in Ameglia and in top form, however, this restaurant—with its *nouvelle* menu and fine selection of wines—is still worth the detour, although it will be an expensive one (reservations recommended; Tel: 0187-643-91; closed Mondays, early January, and July 15 to September 15). La Locanda also has 37 rooms for the perfect gastronomic weekend, with the scent of the many rosebushes wafting through the windows. To get there, exit from the Autostrada at Sarzana.

Just to the south of Ameglia lies Tuscany.

GETTING AROUND

Alitalia's daily Volobus Genoa connects Genoa with Milan's Malpensa Airport in two and a half hours, halving the time required, even with perfect connections, for the bus to Milan followed by the train to Genoa (a decidedly unscenic ride). Genoa is also on the main line of the French-Italian railroad route connecting it with Nice and other Riviera towns.

You can reach most of Genoa's outlying sights by public transportation: the Parco di Nervi by bus number 17 from the piazza de Ferrari; the Pallavicini at Pegli by bus number 2, 3, 4, or 5 from the piazza Caricamento or by train from Genoa's two train stations, Principe and Brignole; the cemetery at Staglieno by bus number 34 from the piazza Corvetto.

Coastal towns along the Riviera di Levante are easily reached from Genoa on autostrada A 12, from which there are exits for Portofino and other towns. However, no one visiting this part of the world should miss the opportunity to pick up the coast road at Chiavari and follow it to Zoagli—or vice versa. Trains, buses, and boats link coastal towns with welcome frequency.

ACCOMMODATIONS REFERENCE

The rates given below are projections for 1993; always check for up-to-date information before making reservations. Wide ranges may reflect the differences between low- and high-season rates. Unless otherwise indicated, the figures indicate the cost of a double room (per room, not per person). However, half-board (mezza pensione) rates, which include breakfast and one other meal per day, are per person. The service charge is included in the rate; inquire about the tax and breakfast.

▶ **Agnello d'Oro.** Vico delle Monachette 6, 16126 **Genoa.** Tel: (010) 26-20-84 or 26-23-27; Fax: (010) 56-11-24. £65,000–£90,000.

▶ **Ca d'Andrean.** Via Antonio Discovol. 19017 **Manarola.** Tel: 0187-92-00-40. £85,000.

▶ **Ca' Peo.** Strada Panoramica 77, 16040 **Leivi.** Tel: (0185) 31-96-96; Fax: (0185) 31-96-71. Closed November. £130,000.

▶ **La Camogliese.** Via Garibaldi 55, 16032 **Camogli.** Tel: 90185) 77-14-02. £50,000–£65,000.

▶ **Casmona.** Salita Pineto 13, 16032 **Camogli.** Tel: (0185) 77-00-15. £75,000–£130,000; half board £80,000–£105,000.

▶ **Cenobio dei Dogi.** Via N. Cuneo 34, 16032 **Camogli.** Tel: (0185) 77-00-41; Fax: (0185) 77-27-96. Closed January 7– March 10. £185,000–£390,000; half board £200,000– £250,000.

▶ **City Hotel.** Via San Sebastiano 6, 16123 **Genoa.** Tel: (010) 55-45; Fax: (010) 58-63-01. £170,000.

▶ **Hotel Bristol Palace.** Via XX Settembre 35, 16121 **Genoa.** Tel: (010) 59-25-41; Fax: (010) 56-17-56. £215,000–£308,000.

▶ **Hotel Ristorante Italia.** Via Umberto I, 18030 **Castel-vittorio;** Tel: (0184) 24-10-89. Rooms under construction and not priced at press time.

▶ **Jolly Hotel Plaza.** Via Martin Piaggio 11, 16122 **Genoa.** Tel: (010) 839-36-41; Fax: (010) 839-18-50; in U.S., Tel: (212) 213-1468 or (800) 221-2626; Fax: (212) 213-2369; in U.K., Tel: (923) 89-62-72 or (0800) 28-27-29; Fax: (923) 89-60-71. £210,000–£330,000; half board £210,000–£255,000.

▶ **La Locanda dell'Angelo.** Viale XXV Aprile, 19031 **Ameglia.** Tel: (0187) 643-91; Fax: (0187) 643-93. Closed January 7–28 and July 15–September 15. £78,000–£158,000; half board £180,000.

▶ **Marina Piccola.** Via Antonio Discovolo, 19010 **Manarola.** Tel: (0187) 92-01-03. Closed January. £60,000–£80,000; half board £70,000–£80,000.

▶ **La Meridiana.** Via ai Castelli 11, 17033 **Garlenda.** Tel: (0182) 58-02-71; Fax: (0182) 58-01-50. Closed January and February. £265,000–£350,000; half board £210,000– £250,000.

▶ **Hotel Metropoli.** Via Migliorini 8, 16123 **Genoa.** Tel: (010) 28-41-41; Fax: (010) 28-18-16. £100,000–£120,000.

▶ **Miranda.** Via Fiascherino 92, 19030 **Tellaro**. Tel: (0187) 96-40-12. Ł100,000; half board Ł110,000–Ł120,000.

▶ **Nazionale.** 16034 **Portofino**. Tel: (0185) 26-95-75; Fax: (0185) 26-95-78. Closed January 10–March 15. Ł80,000–Ł180,000.

▶ **Pensione Moretti.** Piazza Colombo 13, 19016 **Monterosso al Mare**. Tel: (0187) 81-74-83. Ł80,000.

▶ **Porta Rocca.** Località Corone 1, 19016 **Monterosso al Mare**. Tel: (0187) 81-75-02; Fax: (0187) 81-76-92. Ł160,000–Ł230,000.

▶ **San Giorgio.** 16034 **Portofino**. Tel: (0185) 26-92-61; Fax: (0185) 26-92-62. Closed January and February. Ł100,000–Ł150,000.

▶ **Sea Gull.** Via Marconi 13, 18039 **Ventimiglia**. Tel: (0184) 35-17-26. Ł55,000; half board Ł62,000–Ł70,000.

▶ **Hotel Splendido.** Viale Baratta 13, 16034 **Portofino**. Tel: (0185) 26-95-51; Fax: (0185) 26-96-14. Open April 7–October 22. Ł361,000–Ł617,000; half board Ł405,000–Ł453,000.

▶ **Star Hotel President.** Corte dei Lambruschini 4, 16147 **Genoa**. Tel: (010) 57-27-15; Fax: (010) 553-1820; in U.S., (800) 448-8385. Ł385,000; half board Ł285,000–Ł375,000.

CHRONOLOGY
OF THE HISTORY
OF ITALY

Prehistory

Italian prehistory extends at least as far back as 700,000 B.C., when the earliest known relics of humanoids were left in Molise in central Italy. On the rugged hillsides of Sardinia, Stone Age inhabitants built towers called *nuraghi,* and archaeologists in Apulia and Sicily have uncovered Paleolithic cave drawings. After 3000 B.C. the peninsula was settled by migrating Indo-Europeans.

From their base in Carthage, the sea-travelling Phoenicians established settlements in western Sicily and Sardinia during the eighth century B.C. Their influence eventually spread across the sea to the shores of Latium.

Between the eighth and fifth centuries B.C., Italy was colonized in the north and south by Etruscans and Greeks respectively. The Etruscans, an advanced people probably from Asia Minor, are believed to have absorbed the culture of Greece without relinquishing their own cultural identity. Little is known about their architecture, but wall paintings and decorated sarcophagi found at their burial grounds attest to a pronounced realism, a love for drama, and an attraction to the grotesque.

The Greeks

In the early eighth century B.C. Greeks from various centers founded more than 40 colonies on the coasts of Sicily and southern Italy, which in the aggregate were called Magna Graecia. A number of pre-Socratic philosophers, including Pythagoras and Parmenides, made important contributions here, and Plato himself lived in Magna Graecia for a time.

The Greek Doric temples in Sicily are more numerous and better preserved than those in Greece.

The Foundations of the Roman Empire

Some of the most lasting expressions of Roman artistic creativity are in the areas of architecture, engineering, and urban planning. Highly successful open spaces, such as the forum, continue to ensure the vitality of civic and commercial life today. As Jacob Burckhardt observed, the Romans set the seal of immortality on everything they did.

The major architectural contribution of Roman art was the refinement of vaulted construction (for the vast spatial advantages it allowed) and its use in the building of baths, amphitheaters, palaces, aqueducts, and triumphal arches. During the republican period (510–30 B.C.) portrait sculpture became more realistic, departing from the ideal.

- **753 B.C.:** According to legend, Rome is founded by Romulus on April 21.
- **800–500 B.C.:** Sardinia is occupied by Phoenicians from Carthage, who war with the Greeks and eventually take over large sections of Sicily.
- **600–501 B.C.:** Greeks bring olive trees to Italy.
- **700–500 B.C.:** Etruscan political and cultural power at its highest in Italy.
- **510 B.C.:** Rome is transformed from a kingdom into a republic.
- **500 B.C.:** The Greeks begin their intermittent war with the Carthaginians.
- **500–451 B.C.:** Viticulture begins.
- **494 B.C.:** Led by Rome, 30 Latium cities form the Latin League.
- **396 B.C.:** Rome captures the Etruscan city of Veii, which marks the decline of Etruscan rule.
- **390 B.C.:** Gauls invade Italy and occupy Rome.
- **348 B.C.:** League of Latin Cities dissolved.
- **312 B.C.:** Construction of Appian aqueduct and Appian Way begins.
- **264–241 B.C.:** First Punic War. Rome wars with Carthage and drives it out of Sicily.
- **220 B.C.:** Flaminian Way finished.
- **219–201 B.C.:** Second Punic War. Hannibal crosses Alps, invades Italy, and captures Turin; defeats Romans at Lake Trasimeno (217 B.C.). Romans, led by Scipio, carry war

back to Spain and Carthage; Hannibal is defeated by Scipio at Zama (203–202 B.C.).

- **209 B.C.:** Taranto, the last Greek city-state in Italy, is subjugated by Rome.
- **149–146 B.C.:** Third Punic War—Carthage destroyed.
- **133–17 B.C.:** Sicily becomes the "granary of Rome." Numerous slave revolts, including one led by Spartacus, result in protracted, bitter wars; reform movement of the Gracchi.
- **60 B.C.:** The first Triumvirate is created by Pompey, Crassus, and Julius Caesar.
- **58–51 B.C.:** Julius Caesar conquers Gaul.
- **49–45 B.C.:** Caesar defeats Pompey; in 45 B.C. he is elected dictator for life.
- **44 B.C.:** At the height of the internal wars in Rome, Julius Caesar is assassinated. His great-nephew and ward Octavius ushers in a new form of government, the *principate.*
- **43 B.C.:** The second Triumvirate is formed by Mark Antony, Lepidus, and Octavius, Caesar's great-nephew.

The Early Empire

In the early Roman Empire the equestrian statue is perfected, as evidenced by the bronze statue of Marcus Aurelius (A.D. 165) on the Capitoline Hill in Rome. Painting reaches its highest achievement in the Roman cities of Pompeii and Herculaneum.

- **31 B.C.:** Battle of Actium; Mark Antony and Cleopatra defeated by Octavius, and commit suicide; Egypt becomes a Roman province.
- **30 B.C.–A.D. 14:** Octavius, given the name Augustus by the Senate in A.D. 27, establishes the Roman Empire and presides over a cultural awakening (Virgil, Horace, Livy, Seneca, and Ovid are among the writers and thinkers of the time); Pantheon in Rome is begun.
- **A.D.14:** Tiberius assumes *principate,* followed by Caligula in A.D. 37.
- **54–68:** Reign of Nero; has his mother, Agrippina, and wife, Octavia, killed; commits suicide.
- **79:** Pompeii and Herculaneum are demolished by the eruption of Mount Vesuvius.
- **98–117:** Under the emperor Trajan, the Roman Empire reaches its pinnacle.
- **161–180:** Reign of philosophical emperor Marcus

Aurelius; writes his *Meditations;* beginning of barbarian attacks.

- **200:** Bishops of Rome gain predominant position.
- **212:** "Civis Romanus Sum"—every freeborn subject in Empire is granted Roman citizenship.
- **220:** Arabs, Germans, and Persians, among others, begin attacking the frontiers of the Roman Empire.
- **249–269:** Persecution of Christians increases.
- **284–305:** The Illyrian emperor Diocletian reforms government.

Constantine and the Later Empire

- **313:** Emperor Constantine (306–337) formally recognizes Christianity with the Edict of Milan. In 330 he moves the capital to Byzantium and renames the city Constantinople. Rome is in decline.
- **349–397:** Saint Ambrose becomes bishop of Milan (374); refuses surrender of church to Arians; converts and baptizes Saint Augustine of Hippo.
- **391:** Theodosius declares Christianity to be the state religion; becomes last ruler of a united Empire.
- **395:** The Roman Empire is divided into a western empire, with its capital at Ravenna, and an eastern empire (Constantinople).
- **410:** Alaric, king of the Visigoths, invades Rome; Saint Augustine writes *The City of God* (411).
- **425:** Valentinian III is western Roman emperor under guardianship of his mother, Galla Placidia. During fourth and fifth centuries, Latin begins to replace Greek as the formal language of the Church.
- **455:** The Vandals, led by Gaiseric, sack Rome.
- **476:** The German general Odoacer brings an end to the western Roman Empire, although a strip of coast around Ravenna remains under eastern Roman rule until 751.

The Founding of the Holy Roman Empire

From the fourth century, when Constantine moved the capital from Rome to Byzantium, until the 13th century, Byzantine art, mainly Christian in its themes, dominates the Italian peninsula. The most significant monuments of early Byzantine art are its catacombs and basilicas (Ravenna, Venice, and Rome).

- **480–543**: Saint Benedict of Nursia, patriarch of Western monasticism, devises his "rule."
- **493**: Odoacer is succeeded by Theodoric the Great.
- **500**: First plans for Vatican palace drawn up.
- **524**: Boethius, Roman scholar and adviser to Emperor Theodoric, is accused of treason; while imprisoned, he writes his *De consolatione philosophiae.*
- **532–552**: Ostrogoth kingdom of Italy occupied by Byzantine general Belisarius; Totila ends Byzantine rule in Italy and becomes king; begins ravaging Italy.
- **553**: The Byzantine emperor Justinian succeeds in reimposing the rule of Constantinople on Italy.
- **568–572**: The Lombard king Alboin drives the Byzantines out of northern Italy, Tuscany, and Umbria. Lombards establish strong principalities in these areas. The rule of the eastern empire extends to Ravenna, Rome, parts of the Adriatic coast, and sections of southern Italy.
- **590–604**: Papacy of Gregory the Great, architect of Medieval papacy.
- **751**: Ravenna falls to the Lombards.
- **754–756**: The Carolingian king Pepin defeats the Lombards and forces them to recognize Frankish sovereignty.
- **773–774**: Charlemagne unites the Lombard kingdom with the Frankish kingdom.
- **800**: Charlemagne is crowned emperor in Rome by Pope Leo III. Sicily and Sardinia are conquered by the Arabs as Islam expands in the Mediterranean.
- **Ninth century**: Rival states are established and anarchy reigns with the demise of the Carolingian Empire.
- **828**: Founding of St. Mark's, Venice.
- **846**: Arabs sack Rome and damage Vatican; destroy Venetian fleets.
- **879**: The pope and patriarch of Constantinople excommunicate each other.
- **962**: The German king Otto I is crowned emperor and founds the Holy Roman Empire of the German Nation. His attempts to conquer southern Italy fail.

The Papacy and the Empire

The Romanesque style developed from Early Christian architecture in the 11th century and embraced numerous regional variations. In architecture, the Romanesque style is characterized by round arches and by large, simple geometric masses. The Duomo at Pisa is one of the finest examples. The figurative sculpture and the painting that began to appear in the Romanesque churches of the 11th century showed considerable Byzantine influence.

- **1000–1200**: Independent city-states emerge. The sea republics of Genoa, Pisa, and Venice emerge.
- **1076–1122**: In the confrontation between the empire and the papacy, known as the Investiture Conflict, the pope distances himself from the emperor and focuses on the emerging states.
- **1077**: The excommunicated emperor Henry IV humbles himself before pope Gregory VII.
- **1095**: Pope Urban II declares the First Crusade.
- **1119**: Establishment of the first university in Europe at Bologna.
- **1152–1190**: Frederick Barbarossa of Hohenstaufen wars with Lombard cities and destroys Milan; Saint Francis of Assisi is born (1182); communes arise and northern and central cities in Italy experiment with self-government.
- **1198–1216**: Papacy of Innocent III, great church reformer; Fourth Crusade; Venice leads in fighting Constantinople; introduction of Arabic numerals in Europe.
- **1224–1250**: Inquisition under Dominicans commences; Pope Gregory IX excommunicates Frederick II; Frederick II's court establishes first school of Italian poetry; crusades and commerce enlarge intellectual boundaries of Italy, and Arab scholars translate the Greek classics; commercial and industrial boom in northern and central Italy.
- **1256**: Hundred Years War between Venice and Genoa begins.

The Renaissance and the Emergence of the City-States

From 1250 to 1600 a politically fragmented Italy saw its city-states grow in both cultural and economic importance. During this same period humanists (Dante, Petrarch, Boccaccio) rediscovered ancient (so-called Classical) literature.

The Gothic style, represented most notably in church architecture by pointed arches, was introduced into Italy by the mendicant orders. The earliest Gothic church in Italy was completed in Assisi in 1253. The Duomo in Milan maintains true northern Gothic style; large public buildings and palaces, among them the Palazzo Vecchio in Florence and the Doges' Palace in Venice, also exemplify its lofty principles. Gothic painting was advanced by Giotto (1266–1337), who, breaking away from Byzantine iconography, imbued biblical scenes with naturalism and humanism.

With the patronage of wealthy ruling princes, and a theologically less restrictive approach to architecture, painting, and sculpture, the Renaissance evolved. In 15th-century Florence it reached its zenith. The architects of the Quattrocento (1400s), as the early Renaissance is known, adopted a new style modeled on Classical architectural forms. The subject matter of sculpture, heavily influenced by Classical art, now included secular, mythological, and historical themes. Portrait sculpture emphasized greater realism.

- **Late 13th–early 14th century**: Thomas Aquinas (1225–1274) writes *Summa contra Gentiles* and *Summa theologica;* teaches at Orvieto; Cimabue begins to soften the Byzantine look in art; Marco Polo (1254–1324) journeys to China, and returns to Italy in 1295. Giotto (1266–1337) revolutionizes painting by cracking the Byzantine mold; frescoes painted in Assisi and Padua. Dante Alighieri (1265–1321) writes *La vita nuova* (1290) and the *Divina commedia* (1307). Pisano family of sculptors works in major cities. Boccaccio (1230–1313) writes the *Decameron.* Petrarch crowned poet on the Capitol (1304); Pisa University founded; plague devastates Italy and rest of Europe.

- **14th century**: Italian cities divide their allegiance between pope (Guelphs) and emperor (Ghibellines). The sea republic of Venice is at the height of its power. Florence establishes its reign over a large section of northern and central Italy. In Milan the House of Visconti emerges as sole ruler (later replaced by the Sforzas).

- **Late 14th–early 15th century**: Flourishing artistic period—works of Botticelli, Titian, Bramante, Piero della Francesca, Perugino. Ascent of Medici in Italy; become bankers to papacy. Great Schism (1378–1417) begins after Pope Gregory XI dies; two popes elected. Papal exile in Avignon (1309–1377); Saint Catherine of Siena (1347–1380) helps bring back popes from Avignon. Brunelleschi (1377–1446) discovers perspective.

- **1451**: Christopher Columbus (Cristoforo Colombo) is born.

- **1453**: Fall of Constantinople.

- **1466**: Probable year of birth of Andrea Doria, admiral and statesman, who governed the republic of Genoa and was instrumental in defeating Barbarossa.

- **1493**: Lodovico "Il Moro" Sforza is invested with the duchy of Milan.
- **1463–1498**: Giovanni Pico della Mirandola (1463–1494), humanist and wandering scholar, writes *Oration on the Dignity of Man*. Aldine Press in Venice publishes comedies of Aristophanes.

The High Renaissance

From the first half of the 16th century onward the High Renaissance spread to the great cities and courts of Europe. It was during this period that Donato Bramante (1444–1514) designed the new St. Peter's in Rome, and Michelangelo Buonarotti (1475–1564) executed the plan. Michelangelo's works in Florence included the famous statue of *David* and the mausoleum of the Medici in San Lorenzo. In Rome he painted the magnificent ceiling frescoes in the Sistine Chapel. Leonardo da Vinci (1452–1519), sculptor, architect, painter, scientist, and builder, worked in Florence, Rome, France, and at the Sforza court in Milan. Major scientific discoveries, particularly the Copernican revolution, shook the foundations of the religious community. The Neoclassical architecture of Andrea Palladio (1508–1580) evoked the splendor of ancient Rome in San Giorgio in Venice and the Venetian villas, and provided a model for all of Europe. Titian's (1477–1576) paintings presaged the development of the Baroque style.

- **1492**: Columbus sails from Spain on the flagship *Santa Maria* with a crew of 70; discovers Watlings Island (San Salvador), Cuba, and Haiti.
- **1493**: Columbus returns to Spain and then leaves for a second voyage, during which he discovers Dominica, Jamaica, and Puerto Rico. Travels for three years.
- **1494**: Italy is invaded by Charles VIII of France, who deposes Piero de Medici and then captures Rome.
- **1494–1498**: Leonardo da Vinci paints *The Last Supper* and develops his scientific studies.
- **1496**: Michelangelo's first stay in Rome; begins to paint Sistine Chapel (1508).
- **1502**: Columbus sails to Honduras and Panama, marking his fourth and last voyage. Returns in 1504 and dies in 1506.
- **1512**: Copernicus produces his *Commentariolus,* in which he asserts that the Earth and other planets revolve around the Sun.
- **16th century**: The Austrian House of Habsburg and the French kings begin their struggle for northern Italy, which

is divided into numerous small states as a result. Subsequently, almost all ruling houses of Italy are subjugated by either the Austrian or the Spanish line of the House of Habsburg. Palladio works on villas, theaters, and churches in the Veneto.

- **1521**: Machiavelli writes *Dell'arte della guerra,* and *Il Principe* in 1532.
- **1527**: Castiglione writes *Il libro del cortegiano;* Rome sacked by Charles V's troops.
- **1545**: Council of Trent meets to discuss Reformation and establish principles of Counter-Reformation.

The 16th Century to the Napoleonic Era

The art of the Counter-Reformation (mid-16th century to mid-17th century) became known as Mannerism because it emphasized the study of attitudes and expression. The Baroque style developed out of Mannerism in the 17th century and the early part of the 18th century. Painters of the Baroque style included Caravaggio (1573–1610), who delighted in the theatrical and emphasized the effects of lighting, movement, perspective, and trompe l'oeil.

No form of music is more Italian by nature than opera, and no country is more passionate about opera than Italy. Claudio Monteverdi (1567–1643) was the first composer to make opera available to a wider audience. The operatic music of Alessandro Scarlatti (1660–1725) and Giovanni Battista Pergolesi (1710–1736) set the stage for the flowering of Italian opera in the next century.

- **1570**: The Turks declare war on Venice.
- **1573**: Peace of Constantinople establishes peace between the Turks and Venice.
- **1578**: The catacombs of Rome are discovered.
- **1598–1680**: Life and works of Bernini, master spirit of the Baroque, in architecture and sculpture; splendid colonnade of St. Peter's.
- **1600**: First opera, Florence.
- **1601**: The University of Parma is founded.
- **1608**: Galileo constructs an astronomical telescope, which he uses in 1610 to observe the planets and discovers Jupiter's satellites.
- **1615**: Galileo faces the Inquisition for the first time. The following year he is prohibited from further scientific study.

- **1626**: The pope inherits the duchy of Urbino from the last of the Della Rovere family.
- **1633**: Galileo is forced by the Roman Inquisition to recant his acceptance of the Copernican view of the universe. Dies in 1642.
- **1648**: Aria and recitative become two distinct expressions in opera.
- **17th century**: The popes join the French in the battle against the Spanish-Austrian rulers. Savoy becomes the strongest state in northern Italy.
- **1706**: As a result of the victory of Prince Eugene near Turin, Austria controls all of Lombardy.
- **1713**: Following the Spanish War of Succession, Austria receives the kingdom of Naples and the island of Sardinia, making Austria the major power in Italy.
- **1713–1714**: With the Treaty of Utrecht, Austria receives large sections of central Italy, but in return must yield Naples and Sicily to the Spanish Bourbons. With the demise of the Medici in Florence, the Grand Duchy of Tuscany also becomes part of Austria.
- **1725**: Casanova, author and adventurer, is born. Dies in 1798.
- **1796**: Napoléon Bonaparte begins his Italian campaign.
- **1797**: The French defeat the Austrians at Marengo. With the Peace of Campoformio, Italy is ruled by France. Austria retains Venice and land south of the Adige. Eventually, Napoléon dissolves the papal states and incorporates them into Italy.
- **1805**: Napoléon crowns himself king of Italy.
- **1806**: Joseph Bonaparte, Napoléon's brother, becomes king of Naples.
- **1809**: The papal states are annexed to the French empire. Pope Pius VII is imprisoned in France in 1812.
- **1814**: The demise of the Napoleonic regime. Pope Pius VII returns to Rome.

The 19th-Century
Unification Movement

The ornate Baroque style of the 18th century gave way to the simpler lines of Classicism (or Neoclassicism), which was modeled after Greek and Roman art forms. The foremost Italian painter of the style was Antonio Canova (1757–1822). Verdi (1813–1901), whose works include *Rigoletto, l Trovatore, Aida,* and *Otello,* escalated opera to an extraordinarily popular music form. Puccini (1858–1924) continued the development of the operatic form with *La Bohème, Tosca, Madama Butterfly, Gianni Schicchi,* and *Turandot.*

- **1814–1815**: The Congress of Vienna reestablishes the former state structure. The supremacy of Austria in Italy is reaffirmed. Lombardy and the Veneto become Austrian provinces. Tuscany is placed under Austrian rule, and Naples and Sicily are invaded. The papal states are reinstated.
- **1831**: Bellini's operas *La Sonnambula* and *Norma* are performed in Milan.
- **1831**: Following several popular revolts against the Austrians, Giuseppe Mazzini founds the secret movement for independence, "Young Italy." The national resentment of the Italians against the Austrians (the *Risorgimento*) grows.
- **1848**: A general insurrection against Austria under the leadership of the king of Sardinia is crushed by the Austrians.
- **1849–1850**: Victor Emmanuel II of the House of Savoy becomes king of Sardinia. Cavour's government organizes the state of Piedmont.
- **1858**: Cavour and Napoléon III create an alliance at Plombières.
- **1859**: War is declared by Austria against France and Piedmont. Victor Emmanuel II places his army under the command of Garibaldi. Franco-Piedmont victories result in Piedmont obtaining Lombardy, and France obtaining Savoy and the county of Nice.
- **1860–1861**: Garibaldi frees the south from the Bourbons. The kingdom of Italy is proclaimed, with Turin as its capital. Victor Emmanuel II is crowned.
- **1866**: Italy declares war on Austria but is defeated. The Austrian admiral Tefgthoff sinks the entire Italian fleet. The Prussians join Italy and defeat the Austrians near Königgrätz, forcing them to retreat from Italy.
- **1870**: France withdraws its troops from the papal states and Rome becomes the capital of Italy. The Italian unification is complete. The pope retains sovereignty over Vatican City.
- **1882**: Italy makes peace with Austria. Under Umberto I, Italy forms the Triple Alliance with Germany and Austria-Hungary.

Italy in the 20th Century

- **1900**: King Umberto I is assassinated, and Victor Emmanuel III ascends to the throne.
- **1909**: Marconi receives the Nobel prize in physics.
- **1913–1934**: Works of Luigi Pirandello; receives the Nobel prize for literature (1934).
- **1915**: Although initially neutral, with territorial guarantees from Britain and France, Italy declares war on Germany and Austria, annexes Istria, Venezia-Giulia, and Trentino–Alto Adige.
- **1919**: With the peace treaty of St.-Germain-en-Laye, Italy receives South Tirol up to the Brenner Pass, Istria, and a number of Dalmatian Islands.
- **1922–1926**: After his march on Rome, Benito Mussolini is granted dictatorial powers by parliament and his Fascists take over the government.
- **1929**: The conflict between church and state is settled with the Lateran Pact. The Vatican is established.
- **1935–1936**: Italy invades and annexes Abyssinia in North Africa.
- **1936**: Germany and Italy enter into the "Rome-Berlin Axis." Italian troops fight for Franco in Spain.
- **1940**: Although at first remaining neutral, Italy eventually sides with Nazi Germany and declares war on France and Britain.
- **1941**: Italy loses Abyssinia.
- **1942**: Enrico Fermi splits the atom.
- **1943**: Allied troops land in southern Italy and conquer Sicily. Italian forces surrender; Mussolini is arrested and the Fascist government falls.
- **1945**: The German army surrenders. While fleeing, Mussolini is executed by partisans. The Christian Democratic Party forms a government led by de Gasperi.
- **1946**: King Victor Emmanuel III abdicates.
- **1947**: In the Treaty of Paris, Italy cedes Istria to Yugoslavia, and the Dodecanese to Greece. Italy renounces its colonies.
- **1953**: The Christian Democratic Party loses control; the frequent rise and fall of governments becomes the norm.
- **1954**: Trieste is divided between Yugoslavia and Italy.
- **1957**: The European Economic Community (EEC) is founded in Rome. The reconstruction of the country moves quickly.
- **1966**: Northern and central Italy are flooded; irreplaceable works of art in Florence and other cities are destroyed.

- **1970:** Following widespread strikes and unrest, the Statuto del Lavoratore (the Statute of the Worker) provides job security.
- **1976:** Earthquakes in Friuli and in the province of Udine cause severe damage.
- **1978:** Aldo Moro, chairman of the Christian Democratic Party, is kidnapped by the Red Brigade and found murdered 54 days later.
- **1980:** Severe earthquakes rock southern Italy.
- **1981:** Pope John Paul II is gravely injured in an attack.
- **1983:** Bettino Craxi is the first Social Democrat to become head of the Italian government.
- **1987:** Italy ranks fifth among Common Market countries as an economic power, nosing out Great Britain. Craxi's Socialist government ends. Mafia trial in Palermo convicts 338 people.
- **1988:** Bernardo Bertolucci wins nine Oscars for his film *The Last Emperor.*
- **1989:** Conductor Claudio Abbado assumes the directorship of the Berlin Philharmonic.
- **1990:** Former porn star and stripper Cicciolina is elected to Parliament.
- **1991:** The Italian Communist Party dissolves and is renamed the Democratic Party of the Left. Prime minister Giulio Andreotti resigns, ending the 49th postwar government.
- **1992:** Genoa hosts celebrations commemorating the historic voyage of native son Cristoforo Colombo to the New World 500 years ago.

Italy's worst political crisis since World War II leaves the scandal-ridden government in shambles, the lira devalued, and EC membership in question.

—Joanne Hahn

INDEX